W9-AZU-138

Introduction to Business Communication

Introduction to Business Communication

Second Edition

Zane K. Quible
Oklahoma State University

Margaret H. Johnson
University of Nebraska

Dennis L. Mott
Oklahoma State University

PRENTICE HALL, Englewood Cliffs, New Jersey 07632

Library of Congress Cataloging-in-Publication Data

QUIBLE, ZANE K., 1942–
Introduction to business communication / Zane Quible, Margaret H. Johnson, Dennis Mott.—2nd ed.
p. cm.
Includes index.
ISBN 0-13-479072-3
1. Business communication. 2. Business writing. I. Johnson, Margaret H. II. Mott, Dennis L. III. Title.
HF5718.Q53 1988
808'.066651—dc19 88-4035
CIP

Editorial/production supervision: Robert C. Walters
Interior design: Ann Lutz
Cover design: George Cornell
Manufacturing buyer: Ed O'Dougherty

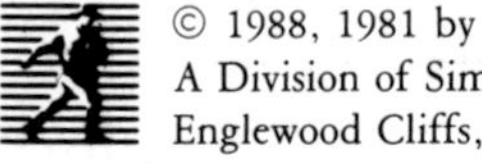

A Division of Simon & Schuster
Englewood Cliffs, New Jersey 07632

Printed in the United States of America

10 9 8 7 6 5 4 3 2 1

ISBN 0-13-479072-3

Prentice-Hall International (UK) Limited, *London*
Prentice-Hall of Australia Pty. Limited, *Sydney*
Prentice-Hall Canada Inc., *Toronto*
Prentice-Hall Hispanoamericana, S.A., *Mexico*
Prentice-Hall of India, Private Limited, *New Delhi*
Prentice-Hall of Japan, Inc., *Tokyo*
Prentice-Hall of Southeast Asia Pte. Ltd., *Singapore*
Editora Prentice-Hall do Brasil, Ltda, *Rio de Janeiro*

To: Patricia and Christopher
Carolyn and Greg
Karen, Nicole, and Bryan

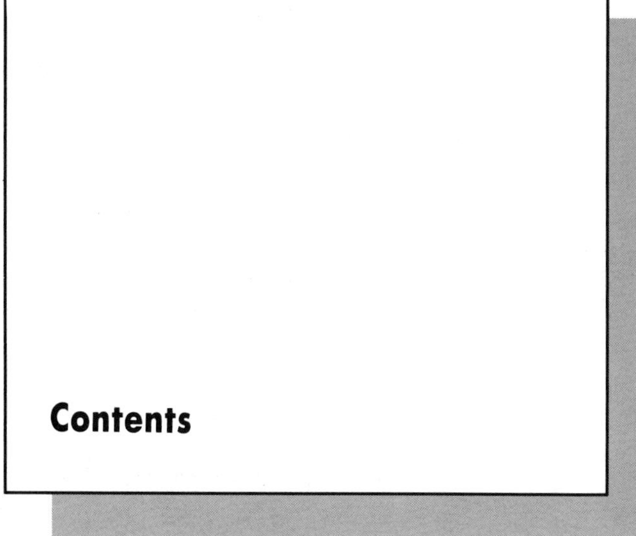

Contents

Preface

At no time during the last three or four decades have the communication skills of individuals in the business world come under closer scrutiny than today. And never before have those who work in the business world needed better, more effective communication skills.

The emerging technology appears to be increasing, rather than decreasing, the need for effective communication skills. As more individuals have ready access to desk-top equipment to process written communication, fewer support personnel will be readily available to provide editing assistance. Therefore, well-developed communication skills among originators are more important to success than ever before.

The second edition of this text, like the first edition, is suitable for several different audiences, including students in four-year colleges and universities, junior/community colleges, and private business schools. Although the educational goals of these various audiences may differ from one another, this text is suitable for each of these groups.

The scope of this edition has been expanded. A new chapter, entitled "Administration Communication: Proposals, Manuals, Instructions, Performance Evaluations, and Product Information," has been added in response to the growing written communication responsibilities of increasing numbers of individuals in the business world.

The organization of this edition closely parallels the first edition. The text begins with two chapters that provide an overview of communication in the modern organization. Following are two chapters that present the writing fundamentals of business communication. The next four chapters are devoted to the types of business letters: direct-request, good-news, disappointing news, and persuasive.

Three chapters cover the employment process, including the resume, employment letters, and interviewing. Three chapters on report writing are also included. Specialized written communication, such as administrative communication, professional writing, and pre- and post-meeting communication are also detailed in three chapters. Because the electronic office is beginning to impact significantly on written business communication—and will do so even more in the future—a chapter on this topic is included. The last chapter is devoted to oral communication.

Some of the special features found in this edition are:

1. Numerous examples of effective as well as ineffective writing in the letter-writing chapters. The authors have found that students studying written business communication can learn as much, if not more, from ineffective examples of written communication as they do from effective examples. An abundance of effective and ineffective sentences, paragraphs, and entire letters are included in these chapters.
2. Many new, varied application problems in the writing-oriented chapters. The number of problems has been increased. While the majority of problems require the writing of a letter or report, some are designed to give students an opportunity to develop the often overlooked skill of editing.
3. Many new application problems in the non-writing-oriented chapters. These problems typically require an intermediate step, such as interviewing someone or undertaking research, with the preparation of a written assignment as the final outcome.
4. New topics, such as nonverbal communication, sex-neutral language, various types of interviews, feasibility reports, audit reports, manuals, instructions, performance evaluations, product information, and electronic technology.

Successful features that have been retained from the first edition are:

1. A letter plan for each type of letter presented.
2. Sequential progression from less complicated types of letters and reports to more complicated ones.
3. A thorough discussion of each part or section of the various types of letters and reports presented in the text.

The teacher's manual that accompanies this text provides a number of suggestions that business communications instructors will find helpful. Especially useful are the suggestions for saving paper-grading time and masters for making overhead-projector transparencies. In addition, the manual contains multiple-choice and true-false test questions for each chapter, as well as answers to the end-of-chapter review questions.

We acknowledge the assistance of the following individuals: Robert Walters, production manager; Susan Jacob, acquisitions editor; and Connie King, who assisted with the typing.

Zane K. Quible
Margaret H. Johnson
Dennis L. Mott

Part I—The Essentials of Communication

Chapter 1

The Importance of Communication in the Modern Organization

LEARNING OBJECTIVES

After studying this chapter, you should be able to

1. Discuss the differences between organizational communication that is directed downward, upward, and laterally.
2. Identify the different types of media commonly found within each of the various directions of communication flow.
3. Discuss the differences between internal and external communication.
4. Identify and discuss the types of communication skills that individuals who work in the business world find helpful.
5. Discuss the ways in which effective communication benefits the entire organization.

In what types of communication activities do employees engage?

Communication is a basic process of the modern organization. The amount of time employees spend communicating ranges from an average of 50 to 75 percent of their waking hours. While listening and speaking activities consume more time than reading and writing activities, all four activities are equally important in most jobs.

In what way are communication skills beneficial?

Effective communication skills benefit not only employees, but also their employers. Those with effective communication skills often become more visible within the organization, which generally has a positive impact on their career progression. Ineffective communication skills among employees, on the other hand, can result in problems with motivation, coordination, attitudes, and leadership.

THE NATURE OF COMMUNICATION IN THE MODERN ORGANIZATION

Of all the elements comprising the modern organization, communication is among the most widely used as well as the most diverse. In fact, communication is used extensively in the managerial functions of planning, organizing, staffing, directing, and controlling. Virtually every task that a manager performs requires the use of communication in one form or another.

The nature of communication in the modern organization can be studied by examining the direction of communication flow and the destination of the communication. While communication in the modern organization flows downward, upward, and laterally, its destination can be either internal or external.

Communication Flow

What media are used in the communication process?

A variety of media are used in the communication process. Some of the media are used in all three directions of communication flow while others are exclusively used in only one direction. To illustrate, downward, upward, and lateral communication often use interoffice memos and reports. While bulletin boards are a common downward communication medium, rarely would they be used for upward or lateral communication. Suggestion systems and attitude surveys are common upward communication media, but they are not suitable for use in communicating in a downward direction.

Downward-directed communication

What is the primary downward function of communication?

The primary function of downward communication is to inform employees about things important to them, such as information about their jobs, organizational policies and procedures, feedback about their performance, and organizational and unit goals and objectives. The absence of information in any of these areas will negatively affect employees' productivity, their attitudes, and their job satisfaction.

What types of downward communication media are used?

Types of media used in downward communication are: interoffice memos, reports, bulletin boards, company newsletters and magazines, staff meetings, audio/visual programs, public address systems, manuals, pay envelope inserts, and conferences. While some of these media use written communication, others primarily involve oral communication.

The interoffice memo, the most commonly used written communication medium in the majority of organizations, is used extensively to communicate with others in the organization. Its informality tends to make it unsuitable for use in communicating outside the organization. Not only do memos lack some of the formal parts of a business letter (inside address, salutation, and complimentary close), but also they are often written in a more informal style than business letters.

Reports are used to transmit a variety of different types of downward-directed internal information to employees. The various types of informal reports discussed in Chapter 12 are appropriate for this application. Although the formal reports discussed in Chapters 13 and 14 can also be used internally, they are more likely to be used externally.

As a downward communication medium, bulletin boards can provide a valuable function, although they should be used with discretion. Because some employees rarely read the information contained on bulletin boards, another medium should be considered when communicating important information. The location of bulletin boards often determines whether their contents will be read. Important information is more likely to be read if it is always posted in the same location and identified as "important."

Company newsletters and magazines are often used by top management to keep employees at various lower levels informed about important events, activities, operations, and issues. Information typically contained in these publications that is of greatest interest to employees is news about themselves—promotions, retirements, transfers, marriages, and so forth. Company newsletters and magazines are also considered to be useful in helping persuade employees to accept management's decisions and to take the action desired by top management.

Staff meetings depend heavily on oral communication, although some written communication, such as agendas, minutes, and reports, is also likely to be used. While staff meetings can be used by management to inform employees about important matters, they can also be used effectively to persuade employees to do certain things and to help employees change their attitudes. The information presented to employees at staff meetings can also be presented in a written medium. Many managers opt for the staff meeting when they desire to convey a more personal concern for the way the information they are communicating influences their subordinates or when they wish to stress the importance of the information they are presenting. Staff meetings are also used effectively by organizations that use participative decision making.

Audio/visual programs are often used to inform employees about a new program, a new work unit, or changes in operating procedures. These programs are more useful as an information-presentation medium than as a medium designed to persuade individuals. In some instances, the information is presented using slides and tapes, while in other cases, video tapes are prepared. The primary advantage of using audio/visual programs is that information can be presented to large numbers of people in a relatively short time. However, in some cases, audio/visual programs fail to convey the importance of the information being presented.

Public address systems are typically used to make announcements or to transmit information of an emergency nature. Because most employees do listen to information transmitted on the public address system, this medium can provide an effective communication function.

Two general types of manuals are found in today's organizations: orientation manuals and functional manuals pertaining to specific areas of the organization, such as records management, procedures, policy, and operations. Much of the success of these manuals can be attributed to the skill and care given to each phase of their development. Especially critical is their ease of use and understandability.

Some organizations use pay-envelope inserts to transmit important messages to employees. The information contained on inserts should be kept fairly brief and have a high relative importance. Overuse of this medium will diminish the importance that employees attach to the information provided on the inserts.

Conferences are conversations between a supervisor and subordinate and are used by supervisors to mobilize support, communicate information to the subordinate, take disciplinary action against the subordinate, inform the subordinate of performance appraisal results, and so forth. Although most conferences are oral in nature, some written materials may also be used. The skill of the supervisor in conducting these conferences has a significant impact on whether the desired objectives are achieved. Telephone conversations are also included in this category.

Upward-directed communication

What is the purpose of upward communication?

While the purpose of downward-directed internal organizational communication is generally to inform employees, the purpose of upward-directed communication is to provide managers with the feedback they find useful in making important decisions. The better the quality of information they receive, the more useful and effective it will be in their decision-making efforts. A potential problem with some upward-directed communication is that certain employees are reluctant to transmit negative views to their superiors. These employees are likely to "filter out" negative information in messages that are transmitted upward.

What types of upward communication media are used?

Types of media used to direct information upward are reports, interoffice memos, suggestion systems, attitude surveys, supervisor-subordinate conferences, management-employee councils, and grievance procedures.

Reports are used to transmit information upward in much the same way that they are used to transmit information downward. In some instances, upward-bound reports are prepared on a regular basis, while in other instances they are prepared as the need arises. When reports are prepared on a regular basis, their preparation is typically part of their preparer's normal job duties. Employees in some organizations are commonly asked to prepare reports on an ad hoc basis. While most reports are solicited by an individual who has a higher rank than the preparer, other reports are written at the preparer's discretion and then transmitted upward.

The information contained in upward-directed interoffice memos is often used to provide managers with information they find helpful in making decisions. Upward-directed memos also provide important documentation or are used by the preparer to request permission to engage in a certain activity, such as to go on vacation.

Suggestion systems have provided many benefits for the organizations that have implemented such programs. Employees are invited to submit their suggestions for improving the efficiency of certain organizational operations. Because employees are generally considered to be more knowledgeable about the various activities that comprise their jobs, their input is often more valuable than the input provided by managers. The most effective suggestion systems are those that provide employees with material rewards, such as cash, the amount of which is often directly related to the value of the suggestion.

Attitude surveys are used by top management to determine areas in which employees feel managerial or operational effectiveness can be improved. These surveys often use a questionnaire as the input medium. In some instances, the nature of the topic being surveyed is quite general—fringe benefits, for example. In other instances, the topic is quite specialized—for example, a specific type of fringe benefit. After the employees have completed the questionnaires, the information is tabulated and subsequently used by managers in their decision making.

Conferences between employees and their superiors are a useful means of transmitting information upward. These sessions can be used in a variety of ways: to discuss problem situations with superiors, to provide superiors with input that will be helpful in their decision making, and to discuss ideas and suggestions that employees have for improving the efficiency of organizational operations. The effectiveness of these conferences is largely determined by the nature of the superior-subordinate relationship. Telephone conversations are also included in this category.

Manager-employee councils, although dependent on two-way communication, are primarily designed to serve the interests of employees rather than employers. For that reason, these councils are classified as an upward-communication medium. Those who serve on councils are usually elected by the employees in their respective work units and are generally considered by their peers to be most capable of effectively representing their constituents. The topics discussed at the council meetings cover a wide range, although in unionized organizations, union-management topics may be excluded from discussion.

While most unionized organizations have a formal grievance procedure, an increasing number of nonunionized organizations are also installing grievance programs. Grievances are filed by employees when they feel they have been treated unfairly by their supervisor or by someone else in the organization. In unionized organizations, the union steward plays a key role in the filing of the grievance; in nonunionized organizations, the employee has virtually no assistance in filing the grievance. The resolving of grievances involves the use of both written and oral communication media.

Lateral communication

What is the function of lateral communication?

The operating efficiency of the modern organization is greatly enhanced through lateral communication, the communication between individuals of equal hierarchical rank. Employees use lateral communication to exchange ideas and information when solving problems and performing job duties as well as to coordinate work on projects. Those communicating laterally may work in the same departments or in different units.

Most lateral communication is of an oral nature, involving a conference between the participants. When those who are communicating with one another work in different specialized units of the organization, their discussions can be enhanced by using language and terminology that each participant understands. In some instances, the conference is conducted by telephone.

Another common type of lateral communication is the grapevine, an informal communication medium that involves the informal or social interrelationships among employees. The grapevine is considered to be an informal medium because the communicators and the direction of communication pattern changes from situation to situation. To illustrate, Employee A may pass X information on to Employee B, but Y information on to Employee C. Information transmitted through the grapevine is often communicated much more rapidly than information transmitted through a formal medium, such as an interoffice memo or report.

Some individuals mistakenly believe that the grapevine is used only to pass along gossip or rumors and that grapevine information transmitted is amazingly inaccurate. While this is true in some instances, the grapevine has been found to be an excellent source of exceptionally accurate information. In most cases the information transmitted through a lateral grapevine will eventually become accessible to management. At that time, management will wisely assess its accuracy. If the information is inaccurate and pertains to an organizational matter, management may wish to correct the inaccuracy by transmitting the correct information to the appropriate individuals.

Grapevine information can also be transmitted upward and downward through individuals at different hierarchical levels. Managers may consider the upward-directed information as input into their decision-making processes. In some instances, managers wisely use downward-directed grapevine information as a barometer to assess employee acceptance of a certain action.

Communication Destination

What types of communication destinations are found?

The destination of communication is either internal or external. The ratio between internal and external communication varies from organization to organization. As the size of the organization increases, the amount of internal communication tends to increase at a faster rate than the amount of external communication.

Internal communication

What types of internal media are found?

Each of the communication mediums discussed earlier in the downward, upward, and lateral communication sections is also classified as an internal medium. Interoffice memos, reports, and conferences are the most commonly used internal mediums within the modern organization. Because the various internal mediums were discussed earlier, they will not be discussed again in this section.

External communication

What types of external media are found?

Because most modern organizations have close ties with various publics—in fact, they often depend on these publics for economic survival—external communication plays a significant role in their operations. Examples of publics that organizations communicate with are consumers, stockholders, contributors, governmental agencies, news media, suppliers, wholesalers, and retailers.

Types of media used to communicate externally are: letters, reports, stockholder reports, proposals, news releases, stockholder meetings, proposals, telephone conversations, and conferences.

When contrasted with interoffice memos, letters are considered to be a more formal communication medium. A variety of letters are used—inquiry letters, request letters, acknowledgment letters, order letters, claim letters, adjustment letters, sales letters, credit letters, and collection letters. Much of the success of these letters is attributed to the care and skill that goes into their preparation. Ineffective letters cost American organizations millions of dollars each year—a waste that could be greatly diminished if employees would improve their letter-writing skills.

While informal reports tend to be used commonly within the organization, formal reports are more commonly used externally, along with certain types of informal reports. The formality of the situation for which the report is being prepared will determine whether a formal or informal report should be used. Generally, formal reports are longer than informal reports. Employees in many organizations are now finding that their responsibility for report preparation is increasing.

Stockholder reports are designed to provide the organization's stockholders with important information. These reports are generally prepared annually, although less extensive reports may be prepared and transmitted quarterly to the stockholders. Topics included in stockholder reports are financial information and information about products, services, employees, plants, research and development, and community activities.

In some organizations, proposals are widely used. This is especially true of organizations extensively involved in contract-type research and development activities. To illustrate, let's assume Company A is interested in installing a management information system. Because of the complexity of the project, the company decides to use outside assistance in the design and installation of the new system. A request for proposal (RFP) that outlines the company's expectations with regard to the new system is prepared and distributed to the organizations that specialize in developing such systems. Each interested organization then prepares and submits a proposal to Company A. After reviewing each proposal, Company A is likely to contract with the organization that submitted the most effective proposal for the installation of the new system.

News releases are used to provide news media agencies—both broadcast and print—with information about the organization that is of interest to the public. Most organizations try to capitalize on favorable information by keeping the public well informed and up to date. News releases are also used by organizations to minimize the impact of negative situations.

Organizations that have stockholders hold annual stockholder meetings to conduct official business—such as electing individuals to the board of directors—as well as to present information of interest to the stockholders. These meetings, although comprised mostly of oral communication, also use some written communication.

An increasing amount of organizational business is conducted over the telephone. Although the use of the telephone should result in the effective use of time, many employees are now finding that the telephone has been a fairly significant time waster, especially when several calls have to be made before the callee is reached. Excessive amounts of small talk during phone conversations can also waste time. Especially wasteful of time, human resources, and monetary resources is the practice of providing a written document to confirm the substance of the phone conversation. When this happens, the primary reason for using the phone in the first place—to save time—actually takes more time because of the duplicate effort involved in making the phone call and then preparing the written documentation.

A certain number of employees in most organizations spend part of their time engaged in face-to-face conferences with individuals outside the organization. Included among these individuals are purchasing agents, sales representatives, upper-level managers, and department managers. Considerable good will can be lost easily—which may be very costly to the organization and to the outsider—unless both parties treat each other with courtesy and respect.

HOW EFFECTIVE COMMUNICATION SKILLS BENEFIT EMPLOYEES

What types of job-entry communication skills are needed?

Never before has the need for effective communication skills received so much attention. Evidence of the need for these skills is the increasing number of organizations that are listing "effective written and verbal communication skills" as a primary job qualification in their job vacancy notices. Figure 1–1 illustrates some examples.

Although the specific communication skills that a person is expected to have vary from job to job, the possession of certain job-entry communication skills will pay rich dividends throughout one's career. Not only do effective communication skills lead to a more satisfying initial-employment experience, but also to a more rapid series of promotions throughout one's working life.

The following list identifies a number of common job-entry communication and related skills that will immeasurably benefit new employees:

Conflict resolution
Decision making
Listening
Motivation
Persuasion
Problem solving
Public relations
Questioning
Relationship building
Speaking
Writing

Figure 1–1 Examples of Required Communication Skills Found Listed in Job Vacancy Notices

. . .excellent communication skills.
. . .effective communicator, both orally and in writing. . .
. . .well-developed oral and written communication skills.
. . .excellent communicator. . .
. . .excellent communication skills are especially important in making presentations.
. . .oral and written communication skills are crucial. . .
. . .skill in writing reports is essential. . .
. . .outstanding communication skills required.
. . .excellent communication skills essential.
. . .must have excellent communication skills.
. . .excellent verbal and written communication skills required.

Francis W. Weeks conducted a six-year study of job openings listed at the University of Illinois Coordinating Placement Office in which he identified a number of communication skills that employees are expected to possess. He found that 340 jobs in thirty fields required the ability to communicate well. Some of the specific requirements were the following:

What types of communication requirements are common?

1. Must be able to communicate effectively with all levels of management
2. Must have substantial experience and/or training in oral and written presentations and must demonstrate good writing skills
3. Must have ability to prepare special analyses, research reports, and proposals
4. Must have ability to compose effective correspondence
5. Must have ability to communicate and ''sell'' ideas
6. Must be able to cultivate and maintain good customer relationships
7. Must have skill in gathering, analyzing, and interpreting data and in writing analytical reports.[1]

During the initial stages of employment, individuals who possess well-developed communication skills are more often labeled as ''better performers'' than those whose communication skills are average or below. Consequently, employees with effective communication skills are likely to receive immediate recognition of their effective performance.

While effective communication skills are the most important requirement in some jobs, they are of secondary importance in other jobs. Types of jobs in the business world that require substantial communication skills are: management, marketing, accounting, public relations, sales, customer relations, labor relations, research, and training. Other fields, such as visual and print media, science, politics, medicine, teaching, and engineering also require effective communication skills. As a rule, as the amount of mental effort in a job increases, so does the need for the job holder to possess effective communication skills.

An increasing number of executives are finding that their promotability is largely dependent upon effective communication skills. While many executives have the technical ability to be promoted to higher-level positions, their inability to communicate effectively prevents steady career progression. As the amount of time that a person spends communicating on the job increases, so does the importance of communication to one's promotability.

HOW EFFECTIVE COMMUNICATION BENEFITS THE ORGANIZATION

Effective communication benefits the organization by providing a more positive image to outsiders, reducing costs, improving employee morale, and increasing employee productivity. In many instances, putting a little more effort into the communication process provides rich dividends for the organization.

1. Francis W. Weeks, ''Communication Competencies Listed in Job Descriptions,'' *The ABCA Bulletin,* September 1971, pp. 18–37, and December 1974, pp. 22–24.

Essential for Positive Image

What impact does communication have on an organization's image?

The image outsiders have of many organizations is negative because of ineffective communication by employees. In some cases, employees knowingly use ineffective communication, but in other cases, they do not realize that what they say or write produces damaging results. Employees, when using either a written or oral communication medium, have an almost infinite number of opportunities for tarnishing the organization's image. The damaging situations can range from failing to answer a question to the outsider's satisfaction to knowingly communicating totally incorrect information.

Effective communicators are concerned about the impact of what they say or write on the listener or reader. In many instances, the *implication* of what was said—rather than what was *actually* said—produces damaging results. An unfortunate situation arises when the listener or reader receives a totally incorrect perception of what the speaker/writer intended.

Essential for Cost Reduction

How does communication reduce costs?

Effective communication skills make a significant contribution to organizational cost reduction. To illustrate, consider the cost of preparing a typical business letter. The cost of preparing a business letter by the early 1990s will likely exceed $10. If an employee prepares a letter that is not effective—one that results in the need for additional correspondence—the organization's profitability is decreased.

Figure 1–2 provides another illustration of the annual cost to the employer when an employee wastes an hour a day. Employees with poorly developed communication skills are likely to incur at least one hour of wasted effort each day for the organization. Although the time that employees waste because of ineffective communication skills may be rather nebulous, many organizations do cite the weak communication skills possessed by many of their employees as a problem of major proportions.

Essential for Employee Morale

How does communication affect morale?

In many instances, managers unknowingly contribute to employee morale problems because they fail to communicate effectively with their subordinates.

Figure 1–2 Annual Costs of Wasting an Hour a Day*

Salary	Cost to Employer
$ 7,500	$ 935
10,000	1,250
12,000	1,500
14,000	1,750
16,000	2,000
18,000	2,250
20,000	2,500

*Assumes an eight-hour day, a three-week annual vacation, and nine holidays.

Managers frequently underestimate the amount of communication employees desire from them. As a result, information that employees would find useful simply does not get communicated. This lack, in turn, creates an impression among the employees that their managers are not concerned about them nor the positions they hold. When this impression is created, employee morale deteriorates.

Individual managers and supervisors need to determine the types and quantities of information their subordinates desire. Because this is likely to vary from work group to work group, prescribing a predetermined quota of what constitutes an adequate amount of communication for a given group is impossible. However, if employees desire more information than they are currently receiving from management, every effort should be given to make more information available.

Essential for Employee Productivity

How does communication affect productivity?

Many organizations are presently concerned about their inability to improve their productivity, a necessity for their economic well being. A variety of factors can be identified that negatively affect organizational productivity, including ineffective communication.

In some organizations, employees are not as productive as they might be because management fails to communicate its expectations to them. Some employees have difficulty improving their productivity when they have not been made aware of what management expects of them or when they have not been fully informed how certain job tasks are to be performed. Management's failure to communicate its goals and objectives to employees is another factor that may contribute to decrease productivity.

CHAPTER SUMMARY

In a business organization, information flows in three directions: downward, upward, and laterally. Examples of downward communication are interoffice memos, reports, and newsletters. Types of written information flowing upward are: memos, reports, suggestion system ideas, and attitude surveys. Lateral communication involves the exchange of information between two or more employees, conferences, and the grapevine.

Communication in an organization is characterized as being either internal or external. Internal communication is comprised of the downward, upward, and lateral mediums mentioned above. A variety of media are used in external communication, including letters, reports, proposals, news releases, and phone conversations.

Regardless of the jobs you eventually hold, you will find an effective communication ability helpful in your career progression. A number of communication skills are needed. Some are more important in certain jobs than others.

Effective communication also benefits the organization by enhancing the organization's image, improving cost effectiveness and employee morale, and increasing employee productivity.

REVIEW QUESTIONS

1. Which communicating activities consume the greatest amount of the typical business employee's work day?
2. What is the primary function of downward-directed communication?
3. What types of media are typically used in communicating downward?
4. What is the primary purpose of upward-directed communication?
5. What types of media are typically used to direct information upward?
6. What uses are made of attitude surveys?
7. What is lateral communication?
8. What types of media are used in communicating laterally?
9. What is the function of news releases?
10. What types of job-entry communication skills help new employees?
11. How does effective communication benefit the organization?

APPLICATION PROBLEMS

1. Examine as many of the following as you can: informal report, formal report, company newsletter, and attitude survey. Analyze each to determine the type of material that is included.

2. Examine a business letter and interoffice memorandum. Analyze and compare their formality.

3. Examine a stockholder report. What type of material is included in the report?

4. Assume you are a time management expert. Prepare a list of suggestions that will help business employees avoid wasting valuable time on the phone.

5. Examine the "Help Wanted" section of a large daily newspaper. What percentage of the ads mention effective communication skills as a job qualification? What types of jobs require effective communication skills?

6. Prepare a list of the communication skills mentioned as qualifications in the ads you examined for application problem 5.

7. Examine the list of common job-entry communication skills that are beneficial to new employees. Do a self-appraisal to determine how well each of your skills is developed.

8. Informally interview several individuals who work in the business world. Have each interviewee identify the ways in which effective communication skills are important for job success.

9. Scan several newspapers and magazines to find evidence that communication can affect the image of a company, that communication is essential for cost reduction, that communication is essential to employee morale, and that communication is essential for employee productivity.

Chapter 2

The Elements of Communication in the Modern Organization

LEARNING OBJECTIVES

After studying this chapter, you should be able to

1. Discuss how the functions of communication in the modern organization differ from one another.
2. Discuss the characteristics of the communication process.
3. Discuss the elements of the communication model that is presented in this chapter.
4. Identify the types of nonverbal communication that can affect the communication process.
5. Identify barriers to the communication process.

One of the most complex—and pervasive—elements of modern organizations is the communication that takes place within them. Communication is essential to virtually all employees as they perform their job duties. Varying in their complexity, communication activities range from a simple request for information sent by one employee to another to the negotiation of a new labor contract by management and union representatives.

The purpose of this chapter is to give you a better understanding of the major elements of the communication process. Included is a discussion of the functions of communication in the modern organization, characteristics of the communication process, types of communication, a model of the communication process, nonverbal communication, and barriers to effective communication.

THE FUNCTIONS OF COMMUNICATION IN THE MODERN ORGANIZATION

What functions does communication fulfill?

Communication in the modern organization fulfills the functions of informing, controlling, persuading, and coordinating. Each of these functions is now discussed.

The Informing Function

The modern organization, if its various components are to function properly, needs a vast amount of information. Managers, to make effective decisions, require accurate, timely, and well-organized information. Employees also need accurate, timely, and well-organized information to perform their jobs effectively.

In most organizations, the quality of the information available to employees as they carry out their jobs greatly affects the quality of their work performance. For this reason, most organizations attach considerable importance to the availability of accurate, timely, and well-organized information.

The communication that performs the informing function is transmitted by letters, memos, reports, manuals, staff meetings, conferences, and interviews.

The Controlling Function

Because certain activities do not always proceed according to plan, organizations must be able to determine how well anticipated and actual results match one another. The control function, therefore, provides the means by which corrective action can be taken.

What types of communication media are used in the controlling function?

Many of the activities of the controlling function are dependent on communication. Examples of communication media used in the controlling function are operations manuals, policies and procedures statements, instructions, etc. The more effective the communication in each medium, the less time consuming the controlling function is likely to be.

Communication often determines whether or not those being controlled fully respond to the authorization and power of the individual responsible for control. The more effective the communication skills of the person responsible for control, the more effectively those being controlled are likely to respond to the control process. The sender's communication skills will determine whether the receiver perceives the control process as being legitimate and whether the receiver perceives the sender to have credibility and the power to exert control over the receiver.

The Persuading Function

What communication medium is well suited for the persuading function?

Many managers believe that given the choice of either persuading or forcing subordinates to take a certain course of action, persuasion is the better alternative. The use of persuasion often results in voluntary compliance—which can produce greater commitment than forced compliance. The communication medium well suited to the persuading function is one-on-one communication.

The Coordinating Function

The purpose of the coordinating function is to give the organization the unity and cohesion it needs to operate smoothly. Activities commonly found in the coordinating function are defining goals and objectives, determining work schedules of individuals and departments, communicating task assignments, and providing feedback about job performance. The coordinating function has a secondary purpose in helping employees better identify with the organization. Ineffectiveness within the coordinating function is often reflected in decreased organizational productivity and dissatisfied employees.

Types of communication media used in the coordinating function are one-on-one and small-group conferences, written memos and reports, written performance evaluation summaries, job descriptions, and manuals.

CHARACTERISTICS OF THE COMMUNICATION PROCESS

Several characteristics of the communication process can be identified: It uses symbols, it is dynamic, it is understandable, and it involves two or more unique individuals. The absence of any one of these characteristics results in something other than communication.

Symbolic

In what way is communication symbolic?

Communication takes place through the use of symbols such as words (both spoken and written) and nonverbal cues (such as gestures, facial expressions, and tone of voice). These symbols have no meaning in themselves but rather transmit meaning as they are used by those communicating with one another. The communication process is effective when both the sender and receiver attach the same meaning to the words and nonverbal cues. On the other hand, if the receiver interprets a word differently than the sender intends, the communication process may break down. When individuals communicate, the use of symbols that mean the same thing to the sender and receiver is critical.

Dynamic

In what way is communication dynamic?

The communication process is dynamic in that it is continually changing. This characteristic is essential if we are to communicate effectively because it allows us to adapt our message to the individual with whom we are communicating. It also allows us to adapt our message to the circumstances of the situation about which we are communicating. One minute we may need to be persuasive while writing a sales letter, yet direct and blunt the next minute as we try to get a subordinate to change an unacceptable behavior pattern. Likewise, we may attach one meaning to a certain word when interacting with Person A but quite another meaning to the same word when interacting with Person B. Because both Persons A and B attach the same meaning to the word that we intended, we have communicated effectively even though the word was used in a different way with each person.

Understandable

When communication is effective, it is understood by the receiver. Ineffective communication, on the other hand, frequently results in a lack of understanding. One of the distinct advantages of oral communication, when contrasted with written communication, is the greater ease with which understanding can be brought about. When the receiver is unsure about the meaning intended by the sender, he/she can ask questions to increase the level of understanding.

In written communication, questions can also be asked about the intended meaning, but the clarification will not be immediate.

Unique

In what way is communication unique?

Communication is a process that involves two or more unique individuals. The more closely we gear our communication to those with whom we are communicating, the more likely our communication will be effective. Most communication is aimed at persuading the receiver to do something—to buy our product, to accept what we believe to be true, or to change unacceptable behavior. Therefore, our communication is not an end in itself, but rather a means to an end. The extent to which we are successful in getting the receiver to do what we desire is greatly dependent on how effectively we communicate with that individual. We must remember that our failure to take receivers into account as we communicate will likely result in unsuccessful communication.

TYPES OF COMMUNICATION IN THE MODERN ORGANIZATION

What types of communication are found in the modern organization?

A variety of different types of communication are found in the modern organization—oral communication, written communication, oral and written communication, visual communication, and nonverbal communication. Examples of the kinds of communication found in each of these categories are now presented.

Oral and written communication

Videotape presentations
Film presentations
Closed circuit television
Slide-tape presentations
Television presentations

Visual communication

Photographs
Illustrations
Signs
Drawings
Building design
Office design
Clothing

Nonverbal communication

Facial expressions
Gestures
Time
Body movement
Odors
Space utilization

Oral communication

Staff meetings
Conferences
Interviews
Orientation sessions
Training sessions
Sales presentations
Task assignments

Written communication

Letters
Memoranda
Reports
Advertisements
Manuals
Bulletins
Policy statements
Newsletters
Magazine and newspaper articles

The types of communication presented above are effective communication media because they are capable of conveying a message. Those communicating are responsible for using the media effectively. Our ability to write an effective message, to deliver an effective presentation, to prepare effective illustrations, or to use gestures that are consistent with the spoken message can impact significantly on our communicating effectiveness as well as our job effectiveness.

A MODEL OF THE COMMUNICATION PROCESS IN THE MODERN ORGANIZATION

What are the elements of the communication process?

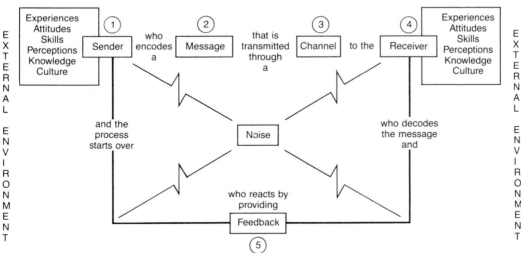

A model of the communication process is illustrated in Figure 2–1. An examination of the model will reveal the following pattern: The communication process, which is affected by the external environment in which communication takes place, begins when a sender creates a message that is transmitted through a channel to the receiver. The receiver subsequently interprets the message and reacts by providing feedback. At this point, the communication process starts again, with the receiver now the sender and the sender the receiver. Noise can infiltrate the process at any point. To illustrate how the elements of the communication process interact, external environment, sender, message, channel, receiver, feedback, and noise are discussed in detail.

External Environment

The environment in which individuals communicate affects the success of their interaction. Care needs to be exercised to assure that the environment enhances rather than impedes the process. Overall, the nature of the situation determines what constitutes an appropriate or inappropriate environment. An inappropriate environment can have a disastrous effect on the process, especially when it results in either communication breakdown or miscommunication.

Figure 2–1 Model of the Communication Process

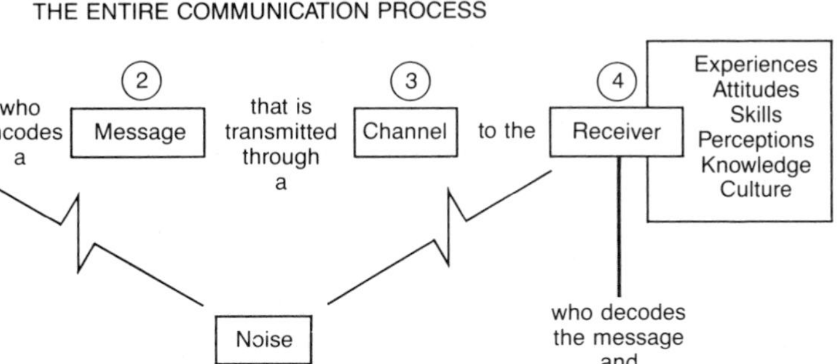

An appropriate environment assures that the communication takes place in a location that provides the needed amount of privacy, the level of formality required by the situation, and an appropriate distance between the sender and receiver. Inattention to any of these three elements of environment will increase the opportunity for miscommunication.

Certain types of communication situations found in modern organizations require privacy. For example, when a supervisor (sender) needs to reprimand a subordinate (receiver), the encounter should be conducted in a private setting. Privacy is also needed when conducting performance appraisal interviews. When a supervisor chooses a public location to discuss either of these situations, the subordinate will not only lose respect for the supervisor, but also he/she will not be receptive to the supervisor's comments.

Some communication situations in the modern organization call for an informal environment while others require a formal environment. Using an inappropriate level of formality or informality will reduce the effectiveness of the communication process. Generally, common sense and good taste help determine the appropriate level of environmental formality for the situation. To illustrate, the negotiation of a multi-million dollar contract in a neighborhood pub is not as appropriate as the use of a board or conference room.

The nature of the situation determines what constitutes an appropriate distance between the sender and receiver. The greater the distance between the sender and receiver, the less personal and private the situation will be. Increased distance can interfere with hearing as well as make more difficult observing the nonverbal cues used by the sender and receiver. When distance between the sender and receiver becomes too great, a mechanical device—such as a telephone—will have to be used. Face-to-face communication, which enables the sender and receiver to ''read'' each other's nonverbal communication, is generally considered more personal than a telephone conversation.

Sender

What factors affect the sender's encoding of the message?

The sender begins the communication process by encoding the message he/she wishes to transmit to the receiver. A variety of factors influence the sender's encoding of the message, including his/her experiences, attitudes, skills, perceptions, knowledge, and culture. The sender must select symbols—written words, spoken words, gestures, facial expressions, illustrations, etc.—that the receiver understands.

Not only must the sender select appropriate symbols and provide an appropriate environment for the situation, but also he/she must select a channel that is appropriate for the situation. To use an oral channel when a written medium would have been more appropriate will reduce the effectiveness of the communication process. Feedback, another element in the communication process, helps the sender determine how effectively he/she has communicated with the receiver.

Message

Individuals communicate because they have a message they wish to transmit to one or more other individuals. Thus, the desire to transmit a message is the sole reason for becoming involved in the communication process.

Two categories of messages are used in the modern organization: verbal and nonverbal. While the verbal symbols are comprised of both written and spoken words, the nonverbal symbols consist of facial expressions, gestures, body movement, drawings, and pictures.

What categories of messages are used in the communication process?

The sender must remember that the symbols he/she selects to convey the message do not themselves possess meaning. Symbols have no meaning until those involved in the communication process give them meaning. In the encoding process, the sender should strive to select symbols that mean the same thing to the receiver.

The sender has to make sure that the message contains the necessary content, that the content is communicated with clarity, and that it is accurate. A number of the chapters in this text are devoted to helping learners improve the effectiveness of various types of written messages.

Channel

The channel in the communication process is the medium that the sender uses to transmit the message to the receiver. Care needs to be exercised in selecting the most effective channel for each message. Even though both an oral and a written medium may be appropriate to transmit a particular message, one medium may be more effective than the other. To illustrate, let's assume that an individual desires an immediate reply to a question. Although the message could be in either an oral or a written form, the oral medium most likely will be more effective because of its characteristic of immediacy.

In selecting an appropriate channel, the sender must assess the following factors as they relate to the situation: need for immediate transmission of message, probable need for immediate feedback, need for permanent record of the message, degree of negotiation and persuasion required, the destination of the message, and the nature of the content of the message. In addition, the sender should take into consideration his/her skill in using each of the alternative channels, as well as the receiver's skill in using each of the channels.

What factors need to be considered in selecting an appropriate channel?

Receiver

The receiver, the individual to whom the sender transmits the message, gives the message meaning by decoding it, which is essentially an interpretation process. Just as the encoding process used by the sender is influenced by a number of factors, so is the receiver's decoding process. The receiver's experiences, attitudes, skills, perceptions, knowledge, and culture can affect his/her decoding of the message.

Critical to the success of the message at this point is the receiver's correct interpretation of its content. The sender, when encoding the message, wisely considers the receiver's background, knowledge of the subject, and attitudes as a means of gearing the message to the receiver. When the sender fails to take these factors into consideration, he/she may create a message that produces ineffective results. The greater the commonality of understanding between the sender and the receiver, the more effective the communication process is likely to be. And the greater the commonality of experiences the sender and receiver have, the easier it will be for them to communicate with one another.

Feedback

In the communication process, feedback is a key element, because in its absence, the sender cannot be sure that he/she has communicated effectively with the receiver. Feedback enables senders to become receivers and receivers to become senders. In addition, feedback is the element of the process that provides two-way communication. Its absence will result in one-way communication.

What corrective function does feedback perform?

Feedback plays an important corrective function in the communication process. When the sender realizes that he/she is not being understood by the receiver, additional information can be provided to create greater understanding. Feedback is also used to confirm agreement, to clarify viewpoints and positions, and to assess the receiver's level of understanding about a situation in order to determine if additional information is needed.

The various communication channels are not equally suited to obtaining feedback. When selecting an appropriate channel for the situation, the astute sender will take into consideration the amount of feedback that may be needed or that may be desirable. As the need for feedback increases, the use of an oral communication channel, as opposed to a written channel, becomes more attractive.

Just as the original message can be communicated in a variety of ways, so can feedback be communicated in a variety of ways. In addition to verbal and written feedback, other types include gestures, facial expressions, and body movement. Obviously, feedback need not be in the same form as the original message.

Feedback is provided intentionally and unintentionally. In fact, even if the receiver offers no reaction to the sender's message, feedback is being provided. Therefore, the absence of detectable feedback is one of many different types of feedback. By sitting motionless in a chair a receiver may provide just as much feedback to the sender as a verbal response does.

Noise

What is noise?

The presence of noise can result in fairly significant problems in the communication process. By definition, noise is the perception of anything that was not part of the original message the sender intended to transmit to the receiver.

Many types of noise can have a negative impact on the communication process, including physical noise that prevents the receiver from hearing and/or concentrating totally on the message transmitted by the sender, as well as a variety of inaudible signals. In the latter category are such things as typographical errors in a letter, poor quality illustrations in a report, a sender's speaking mannerisms that irritate the receiver, a sender's mode of dress that the receiver finds distasteful, and grammatical errors made by the sender. Other forms of noise are a receiver who is experiencing pain, which makes it impossible for him/her to concentrate fully on the sender's message, or a receiver who stares at the floor or ceiling when the sender is talking, which makes it impossible for him/her to read the sender's nonverbal communication cues.

Senders and receivers who want to maximize the effectiveness of the communication process will work toward minimizing distractions or noise. This can be done in several ways. The most effective way is to communicate in a noise-free environment. If uncontrollable noise does occur, then communicators need to minimize its impact by concentrating more intently on the message and less intently on the environment. Another way is to control, as much as possible, the environment in which the communication is taking place.

NONVERBAL COMMUNICATION

Another important element of the communication process is nonverbal communication. While most people tend to associate nonverbal communication with the verbal communication process, it can also accompany written communication as well. In the verbal communication process, the verbal and nonverbal messages need to be consistent with one another. When they contradict one another, the nonverbal message typically expresses true feelings more accurately than does the verbal element. In many cases, the overall impact of a message comes from the nonverbal message.

What are the nonverbal factors of the communication process?

The nonverbal element of the communication process is comprised of several factors including appearance, facial expressions, eye contact, gestures, touch, posture, voice, silence, space use, and time. While most of these factors more significantly affect verbal communication than written communication, some factors do have special significance for written messages.

Nowhere is nonverbal communication more important than in job interviews that are used in conjunction with such written documents as application letters and resumes. In fact, the interviewee's nonverbal communication may be the critical factor that determines whether or not he/she receives a job offer.

Appearance

In what way does appearance affect the communication process?

Appearance is one aspect of nonverbal communication that has important implications for both written and verbal communication. The appearance of one's written material has much to do with the impression it creates. Written material with noticeable error corrections, strikeovers, faint printing, grammatical errors, or illegible handwriting fails to create an effective impression. Material that contains any of these flaws tends to transmit a nonverbal message that discredits the originator.

In written material, the originator, when wishing to emphasize certain words or points, can underline or put in all caps the portions to be emphasized. Material highlighted in this manner carries a different nonverbal message than material that is not emphasized by either of these mechanical means.

In verbal communication, one's physical appearance also affects the message. Such elements as clothing, hair style, overall cleanliness, jewelry, cosmetics, body size, and body shape transmit messages. If any of these elements are outside the range considered acceptable, normal, or standard for the situation, the communication process may be affected negatively. In extreme cases, these elements may inject so much "noise" into the communication process that the clarity of the message is distorted. A person's physical appearance can affect the impression others receive of his/her credibility, honesty, trustworthiness, competence, judgment, or status.

The physical appearance of one's work area also sends nonverbal messages. The objects found on a person's walls, shelves, and desk transmit messages as does the overall cleanliness of the office area. Cluttered work areas tend to send nonverbal messages that the office holder is unorganized and may have inefficient work habits.

Facial Expressions

What nonverbal messages is the facial area capable of sending?

One's facial area (eyes, eye brows, forehead, mouth, and chin) is more capable of communicating nonverbally than any other part of the human body. The face sends messages about one's happiness, sadness, anger, frustration, disgust, fear, or surprise. In fact, we generally do not have to ask people if they are happy or sad—their faces reveal their present emotional state.

Because humans are capable of controlling their facial expressions quite well, they spontaneously use expressions that complement their verbal messages. If one is trying to communicate that he/she is happy, a happy facial expression is just as important to the communication process as the words he/she speaks that convey the same feeling. Individuals whose verbal message and nonverbal facial expressions contradict one another add confusion to the communication process. So do individuals whose facial expressions appear to the receiver not to be genuine.

Eye Contact

What nonverbal messages does eye contact signal?

While eyes play an important role in communicating emotions, eye contact is used in quite a different way in the communication process. Establishing and/or maintaining eye contact signals that a person desires to communicate—that the communication channel is open. Eye contact can also be used to signal a person's desire to be included in a conversation, as well as to make another person somewhat uncomfortable by putting him/her under stress.

Breaking eye contact also sends several signals. Among these are the telling of an untruthful statement, an uncomfortableness with the communication topic or situation, a desire for the communication encounter to end, or an acknowledgement of status differences between the sender and the receiver.

Gestures

What nonverbal messages are communicated by gestures?

The use of gestures in the verbal communication process can also add meaning to the message that the sender is transmitting. While some gestures (clenched fist, foot stomping) indicate anger, others can indicate nervousness (foot tapping, finger tapping). Head nodding indicates agreement while head shaking indicates disagreement. Head nodding also signals the receiver's desire for the sender to continue talking. Keeping one's arms closed tends to signal uncomfortableness while open arms tend to reveal openness and acceptance.

Gestures do not have universal meaning in all cultures. For example, an "A-OK" gesture (circle made with the thumb and forefinger) is considered by Latin Americans to be a sign of contempt. Individuals whose jobs require interaction with peoples of other cultures should do their utmost to learn which gestures are acceptable and unacceptable in those cultures in order to avoid offending those with whom they communicate.

Touching

During the communication process, touching can transmit important messages, such as decisiveness, solidarity, assurance, or reassurance. The amount and nature of touching considered appropriate for the situation varies from culture to culture. While an embrace between business associates in some cultures is quite appropriate, Americans consider such an embrace distasteful and inappropriate.

What nonverbal messages are transmitted by touching?

A handshake not only transmits greetings, but also transmits a feeling of solidarity and assurance. Many people assess the firmness of the handshake because of the belief that a firm handshake transmits a message of decisiveness and strength while a weak handshake conveys an impression of weakness and lack of vitality. Other forms of touching that communicate are grasping a person's right elbow during a handshake to convey solidarity and a pat on the back to convey assurance or reassurance.

Posture

The posture displayed by individuals in the communication process also transmits signals about a variety of things, including status, confidence, interest, and openness. Higher-status people often stand more erect and hold their heads higher than do lower-status people. In a sitting position, however, higher-status people are likely to have a more relaxed posture than lower-status people who tend to sit in a rather rigid, erect position.

What nonverbal messages are transmitted by posture?

Self-confident individuals usually stand more erect than those lacking confidence. Those interested in a conversation tend to lean forward toward those with whom they are communicating, while those lacking interest may slump down. Finally, the posture of several individuals talking with one another conveys a message about their willingness to allow another person into their group. Those turned inward toward one another convey the impression that they are not willing to accept others, while those turned outward are willing to accept others.

Voice

The manner in which individuals express themselves communicates a message that accompanies their verbalizations. In many cases, voice mannerisms—pitch, rhythm, range, rate, nonwords (such as "ah," "um," "uh"), and pauses—communicate more than the actual words.

What voice mannerisms transmit signals?

Voice mannerisms also communicate messages about the sender's emotional state. Excitement is communicated by a high-pitched voice and rapid rate of speaking. Messages communicated in anger are often accompanied by a loud speaking voice, while seriousness and sadness are communicated by a low-pitched voice. Pauses may indicate uncertainty on the part of the sender.

Silence

As a type of nonverbal communication, silence has implications for both written and verbal messages. A lack of immediate response to a letter stressing the urgency of the situation or to a letter that requests an immediate reply indicates that the receiver is either unwilling or unable to respond favorably. The old adage of "no news is good news" may not be appropriate in these situations as many letter writers tend to put off preparing an immediate response to a negative situation. When concerned about public relations, an individual who receives a letter requesting an immediate response will wisely do so if at all possible. If for some reason an immediate response cannot be provided, the recipient should consider acknowledging receipt of the letter and explain that a decision will be forthcoming.

In verbal encounters, silence on the part of the receiver can communicate several things. It can communicate that the receiver wishes the sender to continue talking. A receiver who outranks the sender in the organization might use silence to make the sender feel uncomfortable. A receiver's silence can also signal that he/she is contemplating a response before verbalizing it.

Space

How does space affect the communication process?

The space an employee is assigned in the organization and the way he/she uses that space communicates. After employees take possession of their space, they become uncomfortable when others invade their territory. For example, most individuals consider the area behind their desks to be off limits to others. Most employees prefer that others not invade this space, and they consider it inappropriate for others to do so, especially those of a lower hierarchical rank.

Many individuals believe that staying behind their desk during a conversation sends a message that they are occupying the most powerful area in the office. They believe they can use this space to their advantage when they need to assert their authority or enhance their competitiveness. In conversations in which the office occupant does not wish to maintain an authoritative or powerful position, he/she will wisely move to more neutral territory in the office, such as a conversational area or a conference room.

The amount of space an employee is given in an organization is typically determined by the hierarchical rank of the individual. Higher-ranking individuals are generally given a greater amount of space with more luxurious appointments than lower-ranking employees. And the higher-ranking employees are often able to control their space more effectively than lower-level employees. When employees are able to control their space, they can make it temporarily off limits to virtually every one of lesser rank.

Time

How does time affect the communication process?

The time of day that people communicate sends signals about the importance they attach to the message. The message in a telephone call received from one's supervisor at midnight is typically perceived as being more important than when the identical message is received by the employee while at work.

The way individuals use their time also communicates nonverbally. Arriving late for an appointment may diminish the importance that the visitor is perceived to attach to the appointment. Making someone wait for a scheduled appointment can also be interpreted to mean that the visitor is not very important to the person with whom he/she has the appointment.

Cultures vary widely in the way they interpret the meaning attached to the use of time. Americans believe in arriving on time for an appointment.

People of some other cultures are not offended by a visitor who arrives an hour late for an appointment.

BARRIERS TO EFFECTIVE COMMUNICATION

What barriers affect the communication process?

As the communication process is often impeded, sometimes quite seriously, by a variety of barriers, effective communicators work toward minimizing their effects. The most significant barriers are language, semantics, insufficient information, excessive information, perception, and defensiveness.

Language

Many people take the English language for granted, most likely because it is the first language they learned to speak. Failure to abide by rules of grammar, spell words correctly, or pronounce words correctly can present formidable communication barriers. The receiver who is aware of these errors committed by the sender may be distracted by them and momentarily lose his ability to concentrate on the message. If an important part of the message occurs during the concentration lapse, the communication process will be affected negatively.

Semantics

What is semantics?

Related to language is the concept of semantics—the meaning of words. Significant communication problems arise when the meaning that the sender attaches to a word is different from the receiver's. Communication problems caused by semantics can be reduced by using words as precisely as possible, using concrete rather than abstract words, defining words that may be misinterpreted by the receiver, and using the simplest possible word that the communication situation will allow.

Insufficient Information

Communication problems can also arise when a sender fails to provide sufficient information for the receiver. In some cases senders are purposely evasive. Most, however, miscalculate the amount of information needed by the receiver to achieve understanding. When the voids are sufficiently large, significant barriers can result. To overcome problems of this nature, the sender should make every attempt to determine what and how much information the receiver will find helpful—and then provide the desired amount of information. Depending on the nature of the relationship between those communicating, the receiver may be too intimidated by the sender to ask appropriate questions. When this situation occurs, very little can be done to salvage the communication process.

Excessive Information

In what way is excessive information a barrier?

Providing the receiver with too much information—either oral or written—can create communication problems. When receivers are given an excessive amount of written information to digest in a limited time, they may run out of time to read it completely or carefully. Either situation can result in the receiver's missing important information. In oral communication, excessive information can result either in the receiver's being unable to sort the important from the unimportant or forgetting important information.

Perception

Our perceptual skills can also create communication barriers. Perception refers to our awareness of a message. If we are unaware that a message was transmitted, we are unable to perceive it. Therefore, unperceived messages cannot be received.

How does perception affect the communication process?

The fact that so many messages bombard us each day—and often they do simultaneously—makes it difficult to perceive all of them. In some instances, so many come toward us at one time that we are not able to perceive more than one or two. In other instances, we may be able to perceive a message, but because of the number of messages that are being received at the same time, we are unable to perceive fully and accurately the whole message. For example, we may miss some of the subtleties of the nonverbal aspect of the message.

Because of the rate at which messages are received, we have to be selective, a phenomenon known as selective perception. Ineffective selection will impede our ability to make use of effective communication processes, which results in the creation of communication barriers.

Defensiveness

A defensive attitude on the part of the sender or the receiver can also create a communication barrier. Defensiveness is reflected by being closed minded, mentally forming a reply to the sender rather than concentrating on his/her message, and protecting one's ego rather than being receptive to suggestions or new ideas. A severe defensiveness creates a communication barrier by making it impossible for the receiver to concentrate on or to accept the sender's message.

CHAPTER SUMMARY

Communication in the modern organization performs the functions of: informing, controlling, persuading, and coordinating. Each function is critical to the success of the modern organization.

The communication found in the modern organization has several characteristics. Among these are its use of symbols, its dynamic nature, its need to be understandable, and its involvement of two or more unique individuals.

Several elements comprise the model of the communication process: external environment, sender, message, channel, receiver, feedback, and noise. Problems with any of the elements can have a serious impact on the effectiveness of the communication process.

Oral communication is often affected by nonverbal communication. Appearance, facial expressions, eye contact, gestures, touching, posture, voice, silence, space, and time are nonverbal elements that can affect the communication process.

The success of communication can be impeded by several barriers. Language itself can be a barrier, as can semantics. Others are insufficient information, excessive information, perception, and defensiveness.

REVIEW QUESTIONS

1. What functions does communication fulfill in the modern organization?
2. How is communication used in the controlling function of the modern organization?

3. What are the important characteristics of the communication process?
4. What is meant by the "dynamic" characteristic of the communication process?
5. What different categories of communication are found in the modern organization?
6. What factors affect the sender's ability to encode a message?
7. What is the channel in the communication process?
8. What role does feedback play in the communication process?
9. What are some examples of noise in the communication process?
10. What messages is the facial area capable of communicating?
11. What does posture communicate?
12. In what way can semantics be a barrier in the communication process?
13. In what way can perception be a barrier in the communication process?

APPLICATION PROBLEMS

1. Prepare a list of several situations you have experienced in which the absence of one or more of the communication characteristics resulted in communication breakdown.

2. Using the communication model presented in Figure 2–1, explain in writing how the preparation of a business letter will flow through the various steps of the model.

3. Prepare a list of several situations you have experienced in which a lack of feedback resulted in communication breakdown.

4. Observe two or more individuals conversing with one another. What types of feedback were used?

5. Prepare a list of several situations you have experienced in which the presence of noise in the communication process resulted in communication breakdown.

6. Observe two or more individuals conversing with one another. What types of nonverbal communication did you observe?

7. Observe two or more individuals conversing with one another. What messages did their facial expressions convey?

8. Prepare a list of several situations you have experienced in which language became a communication barrier.

9. Prepare a list of several situations you have experienced in which semantics became a communication barrier.

10. Prepare a list of several situations you have experienced in which your perceptions or the perceptions of those with whom you were communicating became a communication barrier.

Chapter 3

Elements of Effective Written Communication

LEARNING OBJECTIVES

After studying this chapter, you should be able to

1. Discuss the ways in which you can incorporate courtesy into the material you write.
2. Discuss how you can be sure of writing at a correct language level.
3. Discuss ways to make your writing more concise.
4. Discuss the ways to achieve unity, coherence, proper emphasis, and pace in the material you write.
5. Discuss ways to make your writing more concrete.
6. Discuss the need for completeness in the material you write.

Because written communication plays such a significant role in our economy and in the daily routines of the vast majority of organizations, an understanding of the essentials of written communication is critical. You must know *what* you want to say and *how* to say it! In addition, you must design your messages to portray exact meaning as well as create a favorable impression. Well-worded messages not only bring you and your reader closer together, but also make you appear more friendly, helpful, and interested.

In order to choose the right words and sentences for your letters, you need to be familiar with the elements of effective written communication.

What are the elements of effective written communication?

These elements are:

Courtesy—You use courtesy to enhance the relationship between you and the reader and to increase the reader's self-esteem. The consideration you show your reader in your correspondence also enhances your company's quality and prestige.

Correctness—Your correspondence is properly written and formatted, and it is free of errors in punctuation, word usage, spelling, and grammar. The documents you prepare are also neat and attractive in their appearance.

Conciseness—You use the fewest number of words in presenting the information.

Clarity—You tell the reader exactly what he/she wants and needs to know, using words and a format that make your communication totally understood with just one reading.

Concreteness—You provide the reader with information that is specific, definite, and presented in vivid terms.

Completeness—You tell the reader all that he/she wants and needs to know. All questions the reader asked (or may have) should be answered.

COURTESY

Review of actual business correspondence reveals that special attention should be devoted to assuring the courtesy of business communication. Effective writers visualize the reader before starting to write. You will want to consider your reader's desires, problems, circumstances, emotions, and probable reaction to your request. This step will enable you to develop your communication from the reader's point of view.

You-Attitude

(reader benefit)

What is you-attitude?

Writing with a you-attitude shows sincere concern for the reader. Emphasizing the reader's (you) viewpoint rather than the writer's (I) viewpoint demonstrates sincerity. Merely replacing a few *I's*, *we's*, *our's*, and *my's* with *you's* and *your's* throughout a letter, however, will not guarantee the presence of the you-attitude. To establish a you-attitude, you must create a positive state of mind through your suggestions and decisions.

A you-attitude is more than simple courtesy or politeness. It hinges on demonstrating a clear understanding of the reader's problem or question. If a reader feels that you are genuinely concerned about his/her problem or question, the overall impact of the message will be greatly enhanced.

Incorporating a you-attitude into your messages will help give them *reader benefit,* which shows the reader how he/she will benefit by complying with your request or announcement. Readers are more likely to comply if the benefits appear to be worth their time, effort, or cost. Even though the benefits of compliance may not be readily apparent to the reader, your message can be made much more effective by including reader-benefit material.

Reader-benefit material can be expressed by

How can reader benefit be expressed?

1. Assuring the reader that he/she made a wise purchase.
2. Assuring the reader that your company can accommodate his/her needs well.
3. Assuring the reader that you have something of value to offer, as in the case of a letter of application.
4. Assuring the reader that you are concerned about his/her needs.

The first of the following two sentences got very little response when it was used in a collection letter; however, when the sentence was revised to include reader-benefit material, the letter was much more successful.

Change: Please send your check for the amount you owe.
To: By sending your check for $298.87 today, you will be able to maintain your good credit reputation.

Merely inserting the second-person pronoun *you* into a sentence does not necessarily assure a you-attitude or reader benefit. The first version of the next example lacks reader benefit, although it does contain the word *you*. The revised version, by mentioning "shopping convenience," contains reader benefit.

Change: You will be glad to know that we are now open until 9 on Friday nights.
To: For your shopping convenience, we are now open until 9 on Friday nights.

Sentences that contain the first-person pronoun are not necessarily lacking in reader benefit. Consider the following examples.

Do sentences that contain "I" lack reader benefit?

I look forward to helping you with your appliance needs.

In this sentence, the writer is telling the reader that "I can be of benefit to you by being able to help you with your appliance needs." Another sentence containing reader benefit that uses the first-person pronoun *I* follows.

I believe my qualifications match the requirements for the "hard-working, energetic sales representative" for whom you advertised in today's *News-Press*.

In effect, the writer of this sentence is saying, "Because I have the qualifications you are looking for in a sales representative, I can be of benefit to you."

Many inexperienced writers mistakenly confuse the you-attitude for courtesy in the opening sentences of their letters. This results in their thanking the reader or expressing appreciation in the opening, as the first two sentences illustrate.

Change:	Thank you for your recent order for a new set of Continental luggage.
Change:	We appreciate your recent order for a new set of Continental luggage.
To:	Your Continental luggage was shipped today and should reach you early next week. The quality of this luggage will give you many years of excellent service.

Why should readers be given in the opening of the message the information of greatest interest?

Although each of the first two sentences is courteous and makes use of *you* rather than *I,* neither contains reader benefit. Because they fail to give the reader information he/she is most interested in—that the order has been processed or that the luggage is on its way—both are weak opening sentences. The revised version is much more effective because it immediately tells the reader what he/she wants to know, and it reassures the reader that he/she made a wise purchase. Appreciation for the order can be expressed later in the letter, perhaps in the closing.

One of the most effective ways to achieve reader benefit is to make the reader, the product, or the reader's employer the subject of your message. Although using *you* and *your* rather than *I* or *we* is moving in the right direction, substituting second-person pronouns for first-person pronouns will not always guarantee success, as you have already seen.

The first of the following two paragraphs is weak in reader benefit even though the word *you* is found a number of times. The revised version contains reader-benefit material because it clearly points out to the reader the benefits of becoming a coach.

Change:	You are encouraged to become involved this summer as a volunteer coach of a youth softball team. You can take pride in the fact that you made the summer a little more rewarding for these youngsters. If you can provide your services, please try to attend the orientation meeting at 7 next Monday evening in the Potter Park Center.
To:	Can you think of any activity more rewarding than helping a group of energetic, enthusiastic, and eager young softball players develop more proficient playing skills? Or any activity more rewarding than becoming involved with what promises to be the highlight of the summer for many of these youngsters? These rewards can be yours by becoming a coach of a youth softball team. Attending the orientation meeting at 7 next Monday evening in the Potter Park Center will enable you to learn more about our summer program.

Tone

How does tone affect the message?

Although a written communication may be grammatically correct and in proper form, tone may make the difference between the reader's accepting or rejecting the message. Improper tone is most likely to occur in negative messages. Because the reader wants to receive a ''yes'' response and you are having to say "no," the reader will react not only to what you say, but also to how you say it.

Although you may have little or no control over the content of the letters you prepare, you do have control over their tone. An improper tone is certain to create a more negative reaction to an already negative situation. Other factors over which you have no control that are also likely to perpetuate a negative reaction are:

1. The nature of the authority relationship between you and the reader.
2. The nature of the reader's frame of mind.
3. The nature of the reader's attitude toward you.
4. The nature of the circumstances surrounding the reader at the time he/she receives the message.
5. The nature of the reader's disposition at the time the message is received.

Our daily lives are filled with disappointing and exasperating situations. We have plenty of opportunities to be discourteous in the messages we write, especially when preparing collection, claim, and adjustment letters. The effective writer never gives way to anger or indulges in sharp insinuations that are bound to arouse resentment. Consider these sentences that contain a negative tone and their positive-tone counterparts.

Change:	It is absurd for you to think that you will be able to get away without paying your long-overdue account.
To:	We are certain you plan to pay your account so that you will be able to maintain your good credit reputation.
Change:	You failed to specify the color of coat you wanted.
To:	The coat you ordered is available in the following colors: rust, maize, and tan. So that you are assured of getting the color you want, please return the enclosed card to us after you have marked your color choice.
Change:	Why can't you pay us like our other customers do?
To:	The enclosed envelope will make it convenient for you to send us your check as payment on your account.

The negative examples are belittling, curt, and show insensitivity toward the reader. They are bound to create ill feelings. The rewritten versions treat the reader in a more courteous manner.

How does presenting excessive information affect the tone of the message?

Tone problems in written communication can also occur in ways other than the inclusion of negative words or phrases. For example, when writing to a superior, you will want to "put your best foot forward." Inexperienced writers often believe that the more important their readers are, the more facts and details they need to present in their message. Some believe that if they present an abundance of facts and details, they will show their superior how conscientious and hardworking they are. And some inexperienced writers also believe that they can be more convincing by presenting additional facts and details. Unfortunately, inexperienced writers too often forget that their superiors are extremely busy people and that they most likely will not have time to read a wordy message in its entirety.

In addition to negativism and the inclusion of unneeded facts and details, the effectiveness of written communication is also impeded by undue flattery, bragging, and preaching. Skilled writers avoid such negative writing when preparing written communication.

How does excessive flattery affect messages?

Messages that excessively flatter the reader are generally considered to be lacking in sincerity. Although the reader should be given credit where credit is due, the wording should not be too lavish. The first sentence in the following example illustrates the use of undue flattery that is likely to be offensive to the reader. The revision is sincere and genuine.

> Change: Your phenomenal contribution to our understanding of tax laws is remarkable.
> To: Thanks to you, we all have a better understanding of tax laws.

How does a bragging tone affect messages?

Some writers believe that a bragging tone can be effective in written communication when, in fact, it is often offensive to the reader. Skilled writers take special effort to avoid words that connote superiority. Bragging is often interpreted by the reader as a display of arrogance, and it can easily destroy any goodwill that may have existed. The following sentences illustrate how bragging material can be effectively revised.

> Change: It is difficult for us to understand how you could have been overcharged because we pay meticulous attention to detail.
> To: Your account balance has been corrected. We are sorry you were overcharged.
> Change: The numerous quality-control measures we have implemented make it difficult for us to understand how you could have received a garment as poorly sewn as you claim.
> To: Your satisfaction with our garments is important. Therefore, we are sending you another dress just like the one you purchased from us earlier. At your convenience, please return the first dress you purchased.

What does a preaching tone do to messages?

A preaching tone in written communication is also offensive to the reader. Commands, forceful suggestions, and claims that "you should" or "you must" are wisely avoided. An effective writer will not tell readers how to conduct or manage their affairs unless his/her advice is solicited. Notice the preaching tone in the following sentence and how it has been removed in the revised version.

> Change: If you expect to have an ample supply of Royal soil tillers on hand for the upcoming spring planting season, you must replenish your inventory right now.
> To: By replenishing your inventory of Royal soil tillers now, you can be sure of having an ample supply to meet your customers' needs during the upcoming spring planting season.

Another habit that affects negatively the tone of a message is thanking the reader prematurely. Thanking the reader before he/she does something for you conveys the impression that you are taking the reader for granted, which is an insinuation you will want to avoid. When you are asking someone to do something for you, show courtesy by expressing your appreciation. After the reader has complied with your request, extending thanks is appropriate.

Why should you avoid thanking readers in advance?

A Four-step Plan

Guidelines for a simple four-step plan that results in courteous writing are:

1. Exclude words and expressions that may anger, irritate, or demean.
2. Include meaningful apologies when appropriate.
3. Include words and phrases that show appreciation, thoughtfulness, and tact.
4. Respond in a reasonable time frame.

Exclude irritating expressions

Many words and phrases that are used effectively in oral and interpersonal communication are perceived as inappropriate in written communication. Figure 3–1 presents a list of words and phrases often considered discourteous because they tend to anger, irritate, or belittle the reader.

What words and phrases are irritating?

We react negatively to words and phrases which imply that we are lying or are dishonest. Yet, that is the implication you are likely to receive from phrases such as "You claim that . . . ," "You state that . . . ," "According to your letter . . . ." Writers can also belittle readers and make them feel stupid by stating: "As we have explained to you many times . . . ," "Why can't you understand our position?" Readers are likely to find the following opening sentence irritating: "I regret you are having problems with the S–20 lawn-mower you recently purchased from us." (After all, you are probably more interested in learning how the writer is going to help you with your lawn-mower dilemma than in the fact that he/she acknowledges your problem.)

As a writer, you need to be aware of these trouble spots and should avoid using words or phrases that might evoke a negative reaction.

Include meaningful apologies

Business correspondence often calls for sincere apologies or a willingness to grant the action that was requested. As you will discover in a later chapter, the "good news" should usually be presented first in the letter and followed by a sincere explanation or apology, if needed.

When you receive a discourteous letter that incorrectly accuses you, the wisest approach is to reply in a courteous manner. By using this approach, you may win a life-time customer. Another effective way to enhance goodwill is to apologize for a mistake or error even before the customer discovers it. For less serious mistakes or errors, a printed form may be suitable; but when the mistakes or errors are serious, a personalized letter is the only appropriate communication medium.

How soon should one apologize for making an error?

We deny your claim	complaint
We do not believe	confusion
We are not sure	contrary
We find it difficult to understand	contrivance
We expect	delinquent
We insist	deny
We are forced	disagreeable
We take issue	exasperate
We did not	failure
You neglected	ignorance
You failed to	impatience
You misunderstood	incompetent
You must	incredible
You should know	inexcusible
You do not have	inference
You are delinquent	insincere
You insist that	insinuate
You did not say	insulting
You forgot	intolerable
Your credit refusal	irresponsible
Your recent complaint	irritated
Your failure to	lack
Your misunderstanding	neglect
Your neglectful attitude	objection
Your disregard for	obnoxious
Your insinuation	offensive
Your lack of communication	unbelievable
Your delinquent account	uncooperative
Your ignoring	

Figure 3–1 Words and Phases That Anger, Irritate, or Belittle

Include courteous wording

Omitting discourteous wording does not necessarily guarantee courteous messages. Although some messages are void of discourteous words, they can be overly harsh or blunt. Notice how the blunt, harsh wording of the material on the left side of Figure 3–2 can be revised to be more pleasant as the material on the right side illustrates.

You will notice a difference between the begrudging tone in the first paragraph and the courteous tone in the second paragraph of the following illustration.

> Change: To change the closing date of your charge account will create a great deal of extra paperwork for us. However, as you requested, we will comply with your desire to have the closing date of your account changed from the 15th of each month to the 1st of the month.
>
> To: The closing date of your account has been changed from the 15th to the first of each month, as you asked. I can fully appreciate the reason for your wanting to have this change made.

Blunt, harsh wording	Tactful wording
1. You did not read my recent letter.	Please refer to my June 10 letter.
2. The Executive Board did not receive notification.	Several members of the Executive Board inquired about the time of our December meeting. Will you please send them a follow-up?
3. Your letter was not clear.	I would appreciate an outline of our marketing differences that you mentioned in your October 14 letter.
4. John, I suggest you read the Constitution and By-Laws to clarify our position.	John, our Constitution and By-Laws and Section IV on page 9 should answer our questions concerning silent members. Let me know if you feel we should discuss this matter before the meeting.

Figure 3–2 Comparisons Between Blunt, Harsh Wording, and Tactful Wording

The reader could probably care less about the extra paper work that will be involved in changing the closing date of his/her account. And notice how much more "gentle" the word *asked* is than the word *requested.*

Respond in a timely manner

Why should you respond to the sender as soon as possible?

Although one person's priority may be another person's timewaster, prompt attention to customer questions and needs is imperative. When we do not receive an answer to a letter within a reasonable time, we believe that our concerns are not important to the person to whom we wrote. Delaying a response can be severely damaging to the writer-reader relationship.

When the action requested by a customer cannot be completed in a reasonable time, he/she should be notified of the delay. Sending a short note like the following will distinguish you as a courteous person.

> We will examine your camera to determine the shutter-response problem and have it back to you within three weeks. If repairs are needed, I will call you on Friday, January 11, for approval to make the repairs.

Or, when the person to whom a business letter is addressed is out of town for an extended period, the following is a suitable response.

> Mr. Nettleton is out of the office until next Wednesday. I am sure he will be able to provide you with all of the information you requested when he returns.

Many companies have found that prompt answers to questions result in satisfied customers and help generate additional business. Courteous writing is more than words and sincerity. It is a total effort to demonstrate sincerity through positive writing and prompt attention to customer questions and inquiries.

Perception

Even though you select what you consider to be appropriate words, eliminate vague and abstract words, and write concisely, your messages may not accomplish what you intend because readers may perceive word meanings differently than you do. To illustrate, ask a friend to recommend a decent place to eat. You may regret heeding the advice because of a difference of opinion or perception. A decent place to eat might mean good food, fast service, or inexpensive prices to your friend, whereas you were interested in eating in an elegant restaurant offering leisurely dining, plenty of atmosphere, and a gourmet menu.

How is a word given meaning?

A word is a written symbol that is given meaning by its use in communication. Readers who apply emotions to words that affect their understanding may risk creating an inappropriate or unusual meaning.

Because of varying perceptions, the following words could cause a misunderstanding between a writer and a reader:

vivacious date	immature
liberal teacher	crooked
honest student	biased
great teacher	premature
family man	careless

What a writer thinks he/she is saying may not coincide with the reader's perceptions. Consequently, use words that convey exact meaning or that explain questions or purpose precisely.

Positive Wording

In written communication, the use of positive wording is essential for building goodwill. The elimination of words that have negative connotations will provide a pleasing and comfortable link with the reader. Examples of positive and negative wording are shown in Figure 3–3.

Negative writing can result from asking questions that are bound to produce negative responses. Careless wording often creates a negative attitude, even though negative wording is not used. Notice the differences between the first and second verisons of the following sentences.

Change:	Wouldn't you rather drive a Johnson cycle? (causes the reader to seriously consider all of his/her options)
To:	A Johnson cycle can be delivered to your home tomorrow morning.
Change:	Why not try our facial products? (encourages the reader to think of reasons why other facial products might be better)
To:	Smith facial products will add to your beauty and mystique.

Positive writing also requires a conscious effort to exclude words that readers normally consider to be negative. You cannot use such words as ''sorry'' or ''unfortunately'' without conveying to the reader that the situation is going to end with somewhat less than desired results. Some words cannot be used

Negative Wording	Positive Wording
1. You do not qualify for the free gift because you did not respond within ten days.	You probably did not notice that your order was mailed after our special gift offer had expired.
2. I expect you to send the order immediately.	Can you assist us in our special sale of your products by rushing the merchandise to us?
3. Naturally, you have not received your order because, as you should remember, we had to special-order the material from London.	Your special order of London fashions will be shipped as soon as it arrives at our Houston store.
4. Circumstances will not allow us to send final analysis of your samples at this time.	When our extensive analyses are completed, we will send you a copy of the results.
5. I cannot send you a certificate because you have an incomplete grade in Business Writing 3113.	Your record of performance at City College reveals that you have completed all requirements for a certificate except for an incomplete grade in Business Writing 3113.
6. We are very sorry that we cannot send you our Time Management booklets by December 15.	The production department has assured me that you will have the Time Management booklets by January 1.

Figure 3–3 Negative Versus Positive Wording

without causing the reader to react to the *word* rather than to the *intention* of the writer. Furthermore, you cannot use words such as *disappointment, inconvenience, delay, broken, lost, cannot, unable,* and *deny,* without conveying a negative tone.

Writing in a positive tone requires emphasizing what can be done (positive) rather than what cannot be done (negative). Nearly every situation contains both positive and negative features—your task is to isolate the positive features and give them emphasis.

What can you do to make the tone of your message more positive?

Sex-neutral Terminology

Your writing should be void of sexist language, which is offensive to at least half of the population. You can sometimes eliminate sexist language by using the word "person," rather than a third-person singular pronoun.

How can you make sexist terms nonsexist?

Change: Please share this report with your supervisor. He will find it interesting.
To: Please share this report with your supervisor, who will find it interesting.

You can also eliminate sexist language by using plurals and by using the words "you" and "your," as the following examples illustrate.

Change:	The attitude of an employee is important if he expects to be promoted.
To:	The attitudes of employees are important if they expect to be promoted.
Change:	An employee must be cooperative if he expects to be promoted.
To:	You must be cooperative if you expect to be promoted.

A number of terms common to the business world have sexist overtones. The following list suggests replacements for a number of these terms.

Businessman—replace with businessperson
Businessmen—replace with business employees
Chairman—replace with chairperson
Foremen—replace with supervisors
Salesman—replace with sales representative or sales person
Spokesman—replace with spokesperson
Stockboy—replace with stock clerk
Workman—replace with employee or worker

Although it is sometimes more cumbersome, you may appropriately use "him/her" or "he/she" when the material you are writing requires a singular pronoun of either sex. While these constructions are often more cumbersome to write, your creative ability will enable you to incorporate these singular pronouns effectively into your writing.

CORRECTNESS

How can you improve the correctness of the material you write?

In the broadest sense, the term correctness means that the writer should (1) write at a level that will be understood by the reader; (2) assure the accuracy of the words, information, and data; (3) apply principles of grammar and punctuation; and (4) spell words correctly.

Correct Level of Language

The reader's understanding of written communication determines whether your writing is effective. Therefore, the reader's understanding is often affected by the reading level of the material you compose.

What does the Fog Index determine?

Robert Gunning developed the Fog Index[1] to determine the readability level of written communication. The following steps are involved in using this index:

1. Count the number of words in a group of sentences. Then divide the total number of words by the number of sentences. This gives you the average sentence length of the passage.

1. Robert Gunning, *The Technique of Clear Writing*, rev. ed., 1968, (New York: McGraw-Hill Book Company). Copyright by Robert Gunning.

2. Count the number of hard words (those containing three or more syllables) in the passage. Do not count words that are (a) capitalized, (b) combinations of short words, such as "bookkeeper" and "butterfly," or (c) verb forms made into three syllables by adding "ed" or "es" (such as "created" or "trespasses"). Divide the number of hard words by the total number of words in the passage. Multiply this by 100 to determine the percentage of difficult words in the passage.
3. Add the average sentence length to the percentage of hard words. Multiple this total by 0.4. This answer corresponds to the number of years of education needed to understand the passage.

The following passage shows how the Fog Index is calculated.

Three types of application letters are used. An unsolicited letter is used when an individual applies to a company without knowing whether or not an opening exists. The blind-ad letter is sent to a post office box number without knowing the identity of the company in which the opening exists. The solicited letter is used when the person writing the letter knows of an opening in the company to which the letter is being sent.

Step 1: 81 words divided by 4 sentences = 20.25 words per sentence

Step 2: 8 hard words divided by 81 words multiplied by 100 = 9.87 percent

Step 3: 20.25 plus 9.87 multiplied by 0.4 = Fog Index (12.048)

Some examples of the Fog Index for different magazines and grade levels follow.

	Fog Index	*Reading Level By Grade*	*By Magazine*
	17	College graduate	
	16	College senior	
	15	College junior	No popular magazines
	14	College sophomore	
Danger line	13	College freshman	This is difficult
	12	High school senior	*Atlantic, Harper's*
	11	High school junior	*Newsweek, Time*
	10	High school sophomore	*Reader's Digest*
Easy-reading range	9	High school freshman	*Better Homes and Gardens*
	8	Eighth-grade level	*Ladies' Home Journal*
	7	Seventh-grade level	*People, TV Guide*
	6	Sixth-grade level	*Comic books*

Writing at a level appropriate for your reader is crucial. The words you use and the way you use them to form sentences affect comprehension and also convey an unwritten message. If you write in a stiff, formal way, you will give the impression of being formal, whether or not you intend to be. On the other hand, if you write as casually as you speak in conversation with your friends, you may create an impression of informality. Formal English, like formal dress and formal manners, is appropriate for formal reports, research papers, and addresses delivered on serious or solemn occasions.

Informal English is the language of business correspondence written for a general readership. The conventions of informal English are less rigid than those of formal English. Sentences may be long or short, and they tend to sound more conversational than formal English. For example,

Formal	*Informal*
Please inform me of the manner in which you intend to liquidate this balance.	Please let me know when you plan to pay the outstanding balance of your account.

The vocabulary of informal writing is less difficult. Compare the following lists, noting the differences between the formal and informal (or business) usage.

Formal	*Informal*	*Formal*	*Informal*
approximately	about	inquire	ask
ascertain	find out	obtain	receive
assist	help	participate	share
construct	build	purchase	buy
contribute	give	sufficient	enough
difficult	hard	utilize	use

Business associates judge you by your language usage. If you deviate from the conventions of standard English, they are likely to think more about how you are expressing yourself than what you are saying. Although how you write is the pattern of your expression, it is not the purpose of your communication.

In matters of usage (as well as in dress), note this advice of Lord Chesterfield:

> Take great care always to be dressed like reasonable people of your own age, in the place where you are; whose dress is never spoken one way or the other, as either too negligent or too much studied.

If your usage conforms to the conventions of standard English, your main concern will be in adapting your language to the situation about which you are writing. Keeping your reader in mind will help you accomplish this goal.

What is the crucial test in word usage?

The crucial test in word usage is: Will the wording be understood? If the communication is directed to the public, to a customer, or to a vendor, the wording should maintain goodwill as well as ensure that the average reader will understand the message.

As an effective writer, you should develop a vocabulary that enables you to exchange thoughts and feelings with people whose vocabulary may be at different levels. Carefully choosing your words will help the reader understand your message.

Word, Information, and Data Accuracy

Effective business communication requires the use of accurate words, information, and data. The goodwill that perhaps required years to develop can be destroyed with even a minor error. One error in a letter, a figure, or a digit can make a big difference. To ensure the accuracy of your facts, you should recheck before signing a document.

Because of the increasing rate of change in laws, technical developments, and other conditions that affect business, the effective business writer must keep abreast of current conditions and language usage. The writer should also be aware of troublesome words—those that are often confused in usage—and develop skill in correct usage. Below is a list of the words and phrases often confused. If you are unsure about the use of the various words and phrases in this list, make a special effort to become familiar with their correct use.

a lot/alot (no such word as ''alot'')
all right/alright (no such word as ''alright'')
cannot/can not (only in rare cases is ''can not'' used)
different from/different than
due to/because of
effect/affect
fewer/less
in/into
lie/lay
principal/principle
that/which
their/there/they're
wait for/wait on
who/whom

Correct Grammar and Punctuation

Many people in business organizations incorrectly apply principles of grammar and punctuation. The proper use of these two language fundamentals is crucial. Even if the content of the document is appropriate and contains the essential qualities of written communication, the presence of incorrect grammar and punctuation will have a negative impact on the message. Mistakes generally fall into the following categories:

What types of grammar errors are commonly made?

Grammar:

Lack of agreement between the subject and verb

Lack of agreement between a pronoun and the noun to which it refers

A modifier that dangles

A modifier that is misplaced

An illogical sequencing of ideas, resulting in an incoherent, illogically organized paragraph

Pronouns with unclear referents

Punctuation:

Misuse of commas

Misuse of apostrophes

Misuse of punctuation, resulting in fragmentary sentences or run-together sentences

Appendix A contains a condensed guide of correct grammar usage. Writers who feel a need for an extensive review of grammar rules and procedures could benefit from a grammar course or from studying one of the many excellent texts on business English and grammar. Appendix B contains a list of punctuation rules.

Correct Spelling

Administrative assistants provide a valuable service to supervisors, managers, and executives by ensuring the correct spelling of words. Some word processing software programs also have spelling subprograms that help identify incorrectly spelled words. While the first draft of a written message is the responsibility of the typist or word processing specialist, the final product is the responsibility of the person signing the document.

The best advice for making sure the words in documents are spelled correctly is to refer to a dictionary when uncertain about the correct spelling of any word.

CONCISENESS

What is concise writing?

Effective writing is concise—each word, sentence, and paragraph counts. Conciseness should not be interpreted to mean brevity, which may result in an incomplete message. To illustrate, a 150-word letter that could be written in 100 words without a loss in meaning is not concise. A two-page letter that cannot be shortened without a loss in meaning is concise.

Concise communication does the following:

1. Omits trite expressions
2. Avoids wordy expressions and unnecessary repetition
3. Includes only needed facts
4. Includes positive sentences

Trite Expressions

What is a trite expression?

Words and phrases, when overused, become trite. Such expressions are also referred to as hackneyed words, clichés, and stereotyped expressions.

Trite expressions, which lack excitement and zip, should be avoided. The following paragraph contains several trite expressions that have been removed in the revision.

Change:	Please be advised that it has come to my attention that you need your order for a trash compactor filled at the earliest possible time. Your position is relevant to our situation, and we will act in accordance with your request.
To:	Your R600 trash compactor will arrive by rush delivery on January 16.

The essential information appears in the revision, but the overused, wornout expressions found in the earlier version have been eliminated.

Some common trite expressions that you should avoid are:

acknowledge receipt of
as a matter of fact
as soon as possible
as the case may be
at an early age
at this time
at your earliest possible convenience
avail yourself of this opportunity
crack of dawn
don't hesitate
due to the fact that
enclosed herein
enclosed please find
feel free
hoping to hear from you
I wish to state
in terms of
in the near future
it has come to my attention
kindly advise
more than happy
please be advised
please be advised that
previous to
pursuant to your request
take the liberty to
thanking you in advance
this is to inform you
under separate cover
we regret to inform you
with kindest regards
with reference to

The list of trite expressions is almost endless. The point is that you need to guard against their use in your writing.

Wordy Expressions and Unnecessary Repetition

Using unneeded words increases the length of sentences and forces readers to carry excess words in their minds. In the first of the following two paragraphs, the writer was not careful in selecting words. Notice the conciseness of the revised paragraph.

Change:	We would like to ask you to return the form enclosed herein at your earliest possible convenience. In accordance with your request, we have a consensus of opinion that the washing machine that you purchased when you were in our store is at this time still under warranty.
To:	The warranty on your washing machine is still in effect. As soon as you return the enclosed form, we will send our repair technician to your home.

How does concise writing affect clarity?

Unless your message is clear to the reader, you have wasted the time you devoted to writing. Concise writing enhances clarity because the reader is relieved of the difficult task of separating important facts from unessential information.

Wordiness often results from using modifiers that simply repeat an idea or fact. Several examples of words, phrases, and unneeded modifiers follow. The correct usage appears in italics.

1. *Could be heard* by ear
2. *Light* in weight
3. *Join* together
4. *Round* circles
5. *Alone* by himself
6. *Each* and every *person*
7. Fair, *just,* and equitable
8. Silently *think* to yourself
9. *Merge* together
10. *Modern* up-to-date *equipment*

Although unnecessary words should be eliminated, you should not sacrifice meaning to obtain brevity. If the message is still clear after the revision, you have achieved conciseness.

Figure 3–4 illustrates wordy and concise writing.

Unneeded Facts

What should be done with facts that serve no purpose in a message?

Another way to achieve conciseness is to include only the facts that are needed to develop the purpose of your message. Facts that serve no purpose should be left out. To include an abundance of unneeded facts is confusing to the reader because the added words do not enhance the meaning of the message.

The following examples show how unneeded facts can be removed from sentences to make them concise.

Change:	This is to acknowledge receipt of your letter of January 10 in which you ordered sixteen cases of Jones Applesauce. I am answering your letter at this time to hereby let you know that your order has been packaged and sent according to the specified directions in your letter.
To:	Sixteen cases of Jones Applesauce have been shipped to your Dallas office via Nord Delivery Services.

Wordy	Concise
1. We would like to ask	please
2. For the month of August	for August
3. Pursuant to the end of this week	now
4. A long period of time	a long time
5. At this time	now
6. Is at this time	is
7. The weight was higher than I expected it to be	the weight was greater than expected
8. During the year of 1987	During 1987
9. For the development of	for developing
10. In the city of Dallas	in Dallas
11. The problem was that the car would not start	the car would not start
12. Square in shape	square
13. In accordance with your request	as you requested
14. Sign on the front of this form	sign this form
15. During the time that	while
16. Consensus of opinion	we agree
17. Remember the fact that	remember
18. Held a meeting	met
19. This is the situation at this time	now

Figure 3–4 Wordy Versus Concise Writing

Figure 3–5 presents a list of commonly used phrases that can be made concise by using the wording in the right-hand column.

Positive Sentences

Although positive wording was discussed in an earlier section of this chapter, you should be aware that conciseness can be achieved by making sentences positive.

Figure 3–5 Examples of Unneeded Facts

Unneeded Facts	Needed Facts
1. as soon as possible	by July 10
2. as you indicated in your letter	as you indicated
3. at all times	always
4. at this time	now
5. continue to utilize the old form until such time as the new form is available	start using the new form on February 1
6. despite the fact that	despite
7. for the month of April	for April
8. for the obvious reason that	because
9. I would ask that you	please
10. in conjunction with	with
11. in the more recent past	recently
12. in the unlikely event that	if
13. in the unlikely event that I am unable to be on time, please	if I am late, please delay the meeting
14. in view of the fact that	because
15. it will be greatly appreciated if you	please
16. our production of the new product will commence on July 1	production will begin on July 1
17. please be advised that we expect you to review the enclosed contract	please review the contract

Change:	If the error is not found by the time we are ready to process the data, we cannot continue.
To:	We can continue with the processing of the data after we find the error.
Change:	If employees are opposed to Phase II, we will not continue with Phase III.
To:	We will continue with Phase III if employees approve of Phase II.

Conciseness can also be achieved by changing sentences from passive to active voice and from the indicative to the imperative mood.

Change:	The paper was presented by John.
To:	John presented the paper.
Change:	Data are normally processed only after it is possible to assure their accuracy.
To:	Process data only after their accuracy can be assured.

Another effective way to tighten wordy writing is to use subordination.

Change:	John's paper was well typed and the graphic aids he included in the report were helpful.
To:	John's well-typed paper included helpful graphic aids.

CLARITY

How can you improve the clarity of the material you write?

Clarity—or clearness—in writing is achieved in several ways. Two of the ways have already been discussed—using words the reader is certain to understand and writing at a level appropriate for the reader.

Logical development, the use of effective sentences and paragraphs, and the pace with which you present your ideas can also affect clarity. Other ways to enhance clarity are maintaining a consistent point of view (first person or third person) and using clear transitions. Limiting the use of jargon, those words commonly used in your field that persons in other fields are not likely to understand, to situations when you are sure the language will be understood by your reader will also help you achieve clarity.

Logical Development

Unless you use logical development when originating written communication, you run the risk of confusing the reader. Methods used to develop logical written communication are:

Cause and effect: Used to present information about a problem and its solution. Good for presenting information about a problem.

Chronological: Used to present information that has an important time sequence. Good for presenting information about a problem.

Comparison: Used to present information about several alternatives and their comparative advantages and disadvantages. Good for presenting information about recommended action.

General to specific: Used to present information that ends with specific details. Good for certain types of reports.

Sequential: Used to present information that has an ordered, sequenced nature. Good for instructions.

Specific to general: Used to present information that begins with specific details. Good for certain types of reports.

Well-Written Sentences and Paragraphs

Well-written sentences and paragraphs are easy for the reader to understand. While the content of a sentence or paragraph may be beyond the reader's comprehension level, the way you express your ideas should enhance the comprehension process. When the expression of your ideas rather than the ideas themselves confuses the reader, you are not communicating effectively.

The first of the following two paragraphs illustrates how the expression of ideas (rather than the ideas themselves) can be confusing to the reader. The second paragraph illustrates how the same ideas can be expressed with greater clarity.

Change: When you have to purchase your next suit, please be aware that although an increase in labor costs is forcing all suit manufacturers to increase their prices, some stores did purchase their spring inventory before the price increases took effect and, therefore, they may be willing to sell their earlier-purchased stock for less than the current prices.

To: Rising labor costs within the clothing manufacturing industry have resulted in increased prices of men's suits. The stores which still have a supply of suits that were purchased before the price increases may be offering this stock at the original price.

Why should a long series of equal-length sentences be avoided?

A long series of sentences of approximately the same length is monotonous and increases the reading difficulty of written material. You should also avoid stringing together a series of short independent clauses. To improve the quality of your writing, you can either connect these clauses with subordinating connectives or make separate sentences out of some of the clauses that are related to one another. The following example illustrates the effect of stringing together a series of independent clauses.

Change: Marshall Corporation was founded forty years ago, and it now has branch offices in four states, and it employs nearly 400 individuals.

To: Marshall Corporation was founded forty years ago. With branch offices in four states, it now employs nearly 400 individuals.

Why should a series of short sentences be avoided?

While long sentences lack clarity, too many short sentences make writing sound choppy and immature. Sentence length averaging between 15 and 20 words is typically recommended. Paragraph length in letters should average around four to six lines, with ten lines being the absolute maximum. Paragraph length in reports can be extended to 14–16 lines as the absolute maximum. To enhance clarity and reading ease, shorter sentences and paragraphs can be used to present complex ideas.

Unity

What is unity?

To achieve unity, your sentences and paragraphs should contain only one main idea and closely related bits of information. Sentences and paragraphs containing unrelated information are difficult to comprehend. The first example shown below is a sentence that lacks unity, while the second example shows a paragraph that lacks unity.

a. We do have the VCR in stock that you inquired about, and we are planning to double the size of our electronics department in the near future.

b. No other computer manufacturer currently offers a warranty as favorable as the one offered by Electro Computer Corporation. We offer an unlimited warranty for one year after the date of purchase and a limited warranty for the next four years. Our company is growing by leaps and bounds. Much of our success has to be attributed to the creative advertising of our products.

Paragraph unity is achieved by expressing the main idea in a topic sentence and the supporting ideas in the other sentences. The topic sentence should be placed in an emphasis position, which is typically at the beginning of the paragraph. The sentences that follow provide the supporting information.

To break the monotony of always placing the topic sentence first, you can include it as the last sentence of a paragraph. In this case, it serves as a summary rather than an introduction. When having to state refusals in letters, such as those presented in Chapter 7, including the topic sentence as the last sentence of the paragraph may be psychologically advantageous. The supporting details leading up to the refusal are presented first.

The first of the following paragraphs lacks unity because the topic sentence does not clearly stand out. The second paragraph has unity.

Change: When compared with last year, our sales this year have increased approximately 20 percent. Coupling this with the fact that the achievements of our newly installed employee productivity program are exceeding expectations promise to make this one of Howerton's most profitable years in recent history. The full impact of the new employee training program, which has undoubtedly contributed to our success, is also just now being realized.

To: Howerton is currently experiencing its most profitable year in recent history. Several contributing factors can be identified: sales are 20 percent higher this year than last; and the success of two new programs, the employee productivity program and the employee training program, is being felt.

Coherence

To help improve the clarity of your writing, your sentences and paragraphs need to be coherent. Sentences and paragraphs lacking coherency do not hang together, and the ideas presented in the material appear to be disjointed. Coherency is achieved by making sure the relationships between parts of sentences and paragraphs are clear to the reader and by placing the modifiers in the correct location in each sentence.

What is coherence?

The following sentences illustrate how the positioning of modifiers can readily change the meaning of a sentence.

> Only I have one pencil. (means that of those in a group, you are the only person with one pencil)
>
> I have only one pencil. (means that you have one pencil—not two)
>
> The car is in the garage that he wrecked. (means that he wrecked the garage that housed a car)
>
> The car that he wrecked is in the garage. (means that he wrecked a car and it is in the garage)

The following list of suggestions will help you achieve coherence.

How can coherence be attained?

1. Use parallel construction when presenting a series of facts or ideas of equal emphasis or importance.
2. Use repeating construction to tie a series together. Example: The following identifies the things I most enjoy doing: attending concerts, attending ballet performances, traveling in foreign countries, and reading "good" works.
3. Use conjunctions (and, but, or, nor) and transitional phrases (in addition to, as well as) to achieve smoothness between phrases, clauses, and sentences.

Emphasis

The technique of emphasis is used when you want certain words, phrases, clauses, or sentences to stand out. Some of the emphasis techniques that you can employ are position, repetition, quantity, and mechanics. Overuse of any of these techniques tends to have a de-emphasizing effect on the information you want to emphasize.

Emphasis stands out in two positions: the beginning and the ending. The beginning is generally the preferred location, unless you are presenting negative information. When using the repetition technique, you simply repeat the words you want to emphasize. In addition, you can emphasize an idea by increasing the number of words devoted to its discussion. Emphasis can also be achieved by presenting a key idea in a short paragraph and then using the paragraphs that follow to present additional information. Finally, several mechanical means of emphasizing ideas are available, including underlining, putting information in all capitals, and using a different color ink.

What are the two positions of emphasis?

Skip

The first of the following two sentences illustrates how overuse of the repetition technique can have a negative impact.

Change:	I enjoy playing football, playing soccer, and playing baseball and watching the sports of basketball and rugby.
To:	I enjoy playing football, soccer, and baseball and watching basketball and rugby.

Effective paragraphs, like effective sentences, contain the identical essentials of unity, coherence, and emphasis. Paragraphs have unity when each sentence contributes to the development of the main or core idea. Coherence holds sentences to one point of view and to one tense. Coherence is also achieved by carefully choosing transitional words so ideas are tied together as they are developed.

Pace

What happens when you present material at too fast a pace?

The ideas you present must be appropriately paced for both the reader and the subject of the material you are writing. When you present ideas at too fast a pace, clarity can be negatively affected. The pace appropriate for your writing depends upon the level of knowledge the reader has about the subject as well as the technical orientation of the subject. When you are in doubt about the amount of knowledge the reader has about the subject, you will wisely slow down your writing pace.

The following paragraphs illustrate a fast-paced message and then a slower-paced revised version.

Change:	The microcomputer about which you inquired has an 8-bit processor, it has 256K of RAM that can be expanded to 640K of RAM, it comes equipped with both serial and parallel ports, it has a dual disk drive, it has five function keys that can be reprogrammed, and it has a numeric keypad.
To:	The microcomputer you inquired about uses an 8-bit processor and comes equipped with a dual disk drive. In addition, its 256K standard RAM is expandable to 640K. This microcomputer can be interfaced with most types of printers because it is equipped with both serial and parallel ports. Two other desirable features are the five reprogrammable function keys and the numeric keypad.

How can you slow down the pace of your writing?

To slow down the pace of your writing, you can use different types of sentence structure and incorporate transitional words and phrases. The following paragraphs illustrate how the pace can be improved by using transitional phrases and a different sentence structure.

Change:	The equipment had been malfunctioning for two days. We were not aware of it. It finally became inoperable on the third day.
To:	Although we were not aware of it, the equipment had been malfunctioning for two days. On the third day, the equipment became inoperable.

CONCRETENESS

What is concrete writing?

Business communication should be concrete rather than abstract. Concrete writing makes specific references to persons, places, objects, and actions while abstract writing makes general references to these items. Perhaps the best way to distinguish between the two is whether you give the reader "something to grab onto." If you don't you are likely to leave your reader in the precarious position of "dangling in thin air."

How can you make your writing more concrete?

To make your writing more concrete you should

1. Include as much specific information as possible.
2. Use active rather than passive verbs as much as possible.
3. Use words that provide exacting detail rather than fuzzy meaning.

Include As Much Specific Information As Possible

Unfortunately, what is concrete to us may not be concrete to our readers. An effective way to overcome this dilemma is to provide as much specific information as possible rather than general information. For example, knowing how "fast" "fast" is in the following sentence is impossible without presenting additional information.

Change: She is a fast typist.
To: She types at the fast rate of 85 words per minute.

Another example of a general statement and a more concrete revised version follows.

Change: She lives nearby.
To: She lives in Orange County, which is about 20 miles from here.

General words are often interpreted differently by the reader from what you intended. The following is a partial list of particularly troublesome words.

a great deal of time	bad
large	good
small	around
old	convenient
young	little
majority	large
minority	most
less	

You may wish, however, to use general words rather than specific words when you need to be diplomatic or when the situation does not require specificity.

Use Active Rather Than Passive Verbs

What is the difference between active and passive verbs?

A verb with a direct object is in active voice. Passive verbs, on the other hand, always require a verb phrase consisting of a form of the verb *be* (or sometimes get), followed by a past participle. The following two examples illustrate the difference between active and passive verbs.

active:	Bill terminated Neal's employment.
passive:	Neal's employment was terminated by Bill.

Using active voice focuses attention on the subject, is more forceful, and makes your writing more specific, concise, and emphatic. Using passive voice, on the other hand, focuses attention on the verb—what is being done to the subject. The use of passive voice is less forceful.

When is the use of passive verbs recommended?

The use of active verbs is more suitable for business communication than the use of passive verbs, except: (a) when you want to avoid being accusatory or blunt, or (b) when the situation makes it desirable for you to emphasize the object of the sentence rather than the subject. Both situations are illustrated in the following sentences.

a. Purchasing the materials on the following list is required by each student. (Example (a) is more diplomatic than: You must purchase the materials on the following list.)

b. It has been brought to our attention that your grades this semester are the best they have ever been. (Example (b) puts more emphasis on your grades, which is what the writer wished to emphasize rather than on "we," the subject which is emphasized in the following sentence: We have been made aware that your grades this semester are the best they have ever been.)

Choose Words That Provide Exact Meaning Rather Than Fuzzy Detail

Clarity in writing comes from using words that convey exact meaning. Unless care is exercised, fuzzy details rather than clarity will result. Examples of sentences containing fuzzy detail and revised versions containing more exacting detail are illustrated.

Change:	John is a good worker.
To:	John, who is a good worker, is conscientious about meeting deadlines, is a loyal employee, and can always be counted on to do his fair share of the work.
Change:	This report is weak.
To:	The following flaws weaken the quality of this report: the numerous grammatical errors, the inaccurate information that is presented, and the absence of feasible recommendations.

COMPLETENESS

In what ways are incomplete messages costly?

Incomplete messages quickly increase the organization's communication costs. Any time a message is prepared that requires the preparation of another message, the cost of communicating about this specific situation has doubled. Incomplete messages are costly in other ways as well because they can result in:

1. Loss of goodwill
2. Loss of valued customers
3. Loss of sales
4. Cost of returning merchandise because of an incomplete order
5. Waste of time trying to make sense out of an incomplete message.

Some inexperienced writers have learned the hard way about message completeness because they follow the adage of "when in doubt, leave it out." In business writing, a more appropriate strategy is to include information unless you are reasonably certain the reader is already familiar with it. Most readers are less offended by your telling them something they already know than they are when not properly informed. In too many instances, they get the impression that they are not very important to you when you fail to inform them adequately.

What test can you use to determine if your message is complete?

Perhaps the best way to determine if you have provided essential information is to subject your writing to the following questions: Who? What? When? Where? Why? How? If you have provided clear answers to these questions (assuming they were asked), your response is likely to be complete. If you cannot answer these questions, you probably should consider adding additional information.

CHAPTER SUMMARY

One of the most important elements of written communication is courtesy, which is conveyed by a you-attitude, an appropriate tone, positive wording, and sex-neutral language. In addition, courtesy can be affected by perception.

Written communication should also possess the element of correctness. This means that it has a correct level of language, that words are used correctly, and that data and information are correct. Other attributes of correctness are spelling, grammar, and punctuation.

Conciseness is another important element of written communication. To write concisely, you avoid trite expressions, wordy expressions, and unnecessary repetition. Unneeded facts are eliminated and sentences are written using positive language.

Clarity is achieved when the material is developed logically and sentences and paragraphs are well written with unity and coherence. Emphasis and pace are two other aspects of clarity.

Concrete material is specific, and it tends to be written with active verbs rather than passive verbs. In addition, the material contains words that provide exact meaning. The final element of effective written communication presented in this chapter is completeness.

REVIEW QUESTIONS

1. What is meant by reader benefit as a quality that should be included in business correspondence?
2. What are some of the ways that reader benefit can be incorporated into business correspondence?
3. In addition to using negative words or phrases, what are some of the other ways that tonal problems occur in business correspondence?
4. What impact does perception have on business correspondence?
5. How do you achieve correctness in the material you write?
6. How is conciseness achieved in the material you write?
7. What is a trite expression?
8. What alternatives are available for logically developing the material you write?
9. What is meant by unity?
10. What is meant by coherence?
11. How can you make your writing more coherent?
12. How can you make your writing more concrete?
13. In what ways is lack of message completeness expensive to business organizations?

APPLICATION PROBLEMS

1. Using the Fog Index, calculate the readability level of: material you have written; material in your local newspaper; and material in a weekly news magazine, such as *Time* or *Newsweek.*

2. For each of the sentences/paragraphs that follow, identify the major writing flaw and then rewrite the material eliminating the flaw. No sentence/paragraph contains more than one major flaw. All but three flaws found in the following list are found in the sentences/paragraphs:

1. Contains bragging material
2. Includes misspelled words
3. Lacks clarity
4. Contains negative wording
5. Uses faulty pace
6. Contains trite expressions
7. Lacks courteous wording
8. Contains irritating expressions
9. Lacks active voice
10. Lacks correct use of words
11. Lacks you-attitude
12. Contains flattering material
13. Contains faulty punctuation
14. Uses faulty emphasis
15. Lacks coherency
16. Contains imprecise wording
17. Contains wordy expressions
18. Lacks reader benefit
19. Thanks in advance
20. Lacks unity
21. Lacks parallel construction
22. Contains unneeded facts
23. Contains formal writing

a. Please be advised that on October 1, our business office will have a new telephone number. This is to inform you that the new number is 349–4980. Enclosed please find a sticker listing our new number that you can affix to your phone book. Our number is being changed due to the fact that we have installed a new phone system that allows individual phone numbers for various departments.

b. Your order of February 10 has been received and is in the process of being filled. It will be shipped according to the directions you specified on your order—which is shipment by freight. The order will be sent just as soon as it has been filled.

c. The following identifies the specifications you requested for the power converter: it is 4 inches wide, 6 inches long, and 5 inches deep; it can be used to operate any electrical appliance or motor that uses 300 watts or less; it requires no belts or pulleys; it produces 110 volts of AC electrical power; and it can be used as a battery charger.

d. Of the two, John is the better employee.

e. The affect of the decision can not be felt at this time. Perhaps the principle architect of the decision—which was John Grant—has a better feeling about its likely impact than I have. Alot of time and effort went into the deliberations before the committee was ready to lie its recommendation on the table.

f. I can assure you that our group took your best interests into consideration as we made a decision.

g. We tried to ascertain how difficult it would be for each committee chair to assist Mr. Jones for approximately 2 hours. We utilized our best judgment in constructing a feasible work schedule. A two-hour period of assistance should be sufficient.

h. We find that the motor is light in weight and that when it is running, the sound can hardly be heard by the ear. Each and every person who buys this motor is sure to be just as impressed as I am impressed. Silently think about the impact that modern up-to-date research has had on the development of this new engineering marvel.

i. I still cannot understand why you have not taken advantage of our offer. As you know, more than ever before, families need better financial protection. It is imperative that you return the attached form if you wish to take advantage of our offer to increase your insurance protection by 10 percent.

j. The need for active participation is well documented if we expect to be able to achieve our goals. Please remember that it takes a commitment from each member to achieve at the desired level. No one better understands this than the current members of the executive board.

k. A characteristic that is required for managerial success, dedication to the job, is a must for every job applicant.

l. Please inform us of your choice of fabric as soon as possible.

m. Our concern for our employees and our desire to make sure they are always treated fairly has finally paid off as they declined to approve a collective-bargaining recommendation. We always appreciate tangible evidence of our effective management practices.

n. Thanks for sending the brochures that we are requesting.

o. According to your letter, you feel that you have not been treated fairly. Obviously, we do not agree with you.

p. Please do not hesitate to contact me if you have other questions.

q. Our goal is to increase production by 10 percent over the next two years, and our employees are better trained now than ever before.

r. The meeting will be attended by both Mr. Jones and Ms. Brown.

s. We have plans for organizing the new department and plans to implement the decisions recently made by the executive committee.

t. Do you want us to replace the broken part on your camera? Our service technicians are well qualified.

3. Rewrite the following sentences to eliminate the negative tone.

a. I am sure you will see, once you examine the attached price list, that our prices are no higher than our competitors' prices.

b. I am sorry that I cannot amend Policy No. 34543 without your wife's signature.

c. Because one of our major suppliers is on strike, we will not be able to ship your order until we find another supplier.

d. We are informing you of this change in our operating procedure so that we will not have a misunderstanding later on.

e. We will delay shipping your order until we learn which color of coat you wish.

f. To avoid damaging your credit rating, please send your check for $129.54 immediately.

4. Rewrite the following sentences to improve the you-attitude.

a. We will honor your request.

b. To help us best accommodate our customer's needs, we ask that all our customers begin making appointments when they need their cars worked on.

c. We will give you a cash discount of 6 percent on purchases made before November 15.

d. We hope to have the pleasure of serving you in the near future.

e. We quit providing receipts two months ago because most customers said that they use their cancelled check as a receipt.

f. I wish to inform you about our mid-summer sale that begins next week.

5. Rewrite the following sentences to eliminate the weakness that each contains.

a. Allow me to take this opportunity to extend to you a cordial invitation to join us in our ten-year anniversary celebration.

b. Your letter of January 14 has arrived in which you requested that we give you a cash refund of the $13.98 purchase price of two LP records, which we are going to do.

c. A careful study has been made by the finance committee.

d. Your tape deck has been repaired and it is our hope that you will experience no further trouble with it.

e. Please be assured that we are doing everything in our power to accommodate your wishes even if it does not seem that we are.

f. For your information and enlightment, attached hereto is a carbon copy of the letter I received nearly three weeks ago on January 14 about the proposed changes and amendments to their operating policy.

6. Rewrite the following letter to eliminate the weaknesses.

> Dear Ms. Mathison:
>
> In accordance with your request recently transmitted to us that we send you a service manual to replace the one you did not receive when you purchased your new Sanger sewing machine, I am all to happy to do so.
>
> We are convinced that you certainly made a wise choice when you purchased your new machine. Believe it or not, sales of this machine are exceeding our expectations by a significant margin. Obviously, that is good news for us.
>
> I would like to thank you for your graciousness and understanding in this situation.

Chapter 4

Preparing to Write, Writing, and Dictating Business Communication

LEARNING OBJECTIVES

After studying this chapter, you should be able to

1. Discuss the steps found within each of the stages of writing.
2. Discuss ways to determine the content appropriate for the document you are writing.
3. Identify the differences between the direct and the indirect methods of organizing the material you write.
4. Identify the characteristics of effective sentences and paragraphs.
5. Suggest ways in which you can make your paragraph beginnings and endings more effective.
6. Identify several questions you will want to ask yourself during the editing process.
7. Identify methods that will help you proofread more accurately.
8. Discuss the steps involved in dictating a message.

Effective business writers prepare for writing. In fact, much of their writing success can be attributed to the quality of their preparation. Occasionally, preparing to write may be as time consuming as the actual writing.

Preparing to write is a multifaceted activity that includes the planning and organizing stages, which are followed by the drafting or dictating stage. Most inexperienced writers also find it necessary to edit their first draft—and in some cases several drafts—before they are satisfied with their message.

In this chapter, the topics of planning, organizing, drafting, editing, dictating, and proofreading are discussed. Dictation is included because an increasing number of business writers now choose dictation over drafting.

Several steps are found within each of the stages. The following outline identifies these steps.

What stages are included in the writing process?

Planning Stage

1. Determine your purpose and select the medium
2. Consider your reader
3. Determine the appropriate content for your message

Organizing Stage

1. Outline the topics you plan to include in your message
2. Determine the appropriate order of the topics

Drafting/Dictating Stage

1. Develop appropriate beginning paragraph
2. Compose the body
3. Develop appropriate ending paragraph

Editing Stage

1. Review and assess how well your message conforms with
   a. principles of effective communication
   b. appropriate content
   c. appropriate organizational structure
   d. sentence and paragraph construction
   e. grammar, punctuation, spelling, and word usage fundamentals
2. Make needed changes

Proofreading Stage

1. Check for accuracy of dates, figures, amounts, numbers, and so forth
2. Check for misspelled words
3. Check for typographical errors
4. Check for omissions and additions of material
5. Check for proper sequence of material
6. Check for proper format

PLANNING

What steps are included in the planning stage?

The more time you devote to planning your message, the more effective it will be because planning will help you determine what material to include given the nature of the situation and the reader. During the planning stage you determine your purpose, consider your reader, and determine the appropriate content for your message.

Determine Your Purpose

What is involved in determining message purpose?

The first step you undertake in planning a written message is to determine your purpose. Is the message to be sent to the reader as a response to a message you received from him/her? Does the message have to be persuasive? Is the nature of the situation positive or negative? The purpose of your message determines the content as well as the order in which you present the material.

You must determine your purpose before you begin the actual composing process. Becoming familiar with your purpose early will help you avoid wasting time because you know what you have to accomplish. Familiarity with the purpose will also help you focus more specifically on the reader's needs, which, in turn, will enable you to communicate more effectively with him/her.

What three levels of writing objectives are found?

Becoming familiar with your purpose will help you formulate your writing objectives. Typically, writing objectives are three fold: broad, specific, and desired outcome. The broad objective involves stating in general terms the problem you are attempting to solve or what you hope to achieve. The specific objective outlines the suggested action you are proposing in order to accomplish your broad objective. The desired outcome is what you perceive will be the results of your efforts.

These three levels of writing objectives are illustrated in the following example.

Broad	*Specific*	*Desired Outcome*
Increase employee motivation	Implement flextime plan	As a result of my report, a flextime program will be installed
Hire better qualified employees	Improve employee quality	As a result of my report, managers will have a better idea of how to identify the best qualified applicants

Having your purpose clearly in mind before you begin writing will enable you to write with obvious direction and will keep you from ''wandering.'' When your purpose is clear, you can more readily communicate with your reader.

Consider Your Reader

Effective writing is readily understood by your reader. Unless you are familiar with your reader and have considered his/her background, you may have difficulty focusing on his/her needs. The approach and content you use in writing for one reader may not be appropriate for another reader.

What determines how much you need to know about your reader?

The purpose of your message will determine how much you need to know about your reader. The amount of necessary background knowledge will vary from situation to situation. For example, when you are composing a reply to an invitation to speak at a convention, you will need to know less about your reader than when you are composing a sales letter designed to promote the computer supplies distributed by your company. In the first example, you will want to write in a concise, courteous, and straight-forward manner. In the second case, you will want to know the type of computer supplies the "typical" reader buys, in what quantity, for what popular brands of equipment, and so forth. Knowing this information will enable you to "pitch" your message to the reader.

To give full consideration to your reader, you will want to have answers to the following questions.

Why do you need to be aware of the technical background your reader has of the situation?

1. How much technical background does your reader have? The less technical background your reader has about the topic, the less technical your message will need to be. Presenting technical information to readers who do not have a sufficient background not only wastes their time—but also yours. The use of jargon should also be avoided when individuals are not familiar with it.

2. Are you preparing material for one reader or for multiple readers? Writing a message for one person is much easier than writing for several readers. Writing for multiple readers becomes especially complex when some are quite familiar with the topic and others are just as unfamiliar. You will have to master the art of simplifying your message for those whose background is lacking while simultaneously making your message interesting enough to entice the knowledgeable person to read the message.

3. Is your reader from within the organization or outside the organization? This factor will determine how much background information you have to provide. The assumption is generally made that employees tend to be more familiar with the circumstances of the situation and therefore will need less background information. Non-employees, on the other hand, are likely to need more background information. To present unneeded information is boring for the reader, while failing to provide the needed background information can impede the understandability of your message. The employee or non-employee status of your reader may also determine if he/she is likely to be interested in the topic of your message—or do you have to create interest?

What impact does the reader's occupation and income level have on the message?

4. What is your reader's occupation and income level? These are important to the success of some types of business communication—especially sales messages because they affect people's beliefs, value systems, interests, wants, attitudes, and needs. Professional individuals with high income levels have different needs and interests than their counterparts, for example. Persuasive messages based on incorrect background characteristics are generally less effective than messages based on appropriate background characteristics.

5. What is your reader's age? The age of your reader is an important consideration when you are writing certain types of letters, such as sales or promotion letters. What appeals to a reader in one age group may not appeal to a reader in another age group. Readers' values, beliefs, and interests tend to change with age.

Why do the reader's habits have to be considered?

6. What important habits of your reader should be considered? Different readers have different habits that will affect how they will react to your message. Busy executives have less time to read unimportant messages than individuals whose jobs are less demanding of their time. In addition, busy executives are likely to find that unnecessary letters and reports lack appeal. The habits of your reader often determine what you have to do to attract the reader's attention and keep it.

Why does the reader's educational level need to be considered?

7. What is the educational level of your reader? Generally the more education a reader has, the less likely you will have to ''write down'' as a means of assuring reader understanding. Some jobs are characteristically filled by college graduates. Therefore, if the individual to whom you are writing holds a job that is typically restricted to college graduates, you might assume that your reader also has a college degree. The educational status of your reader is useful in determining the types of information your reader is likely to understand and what background information may have to be provided.

8. What is your reader's geographical location? The geographical location of your reader may affect the suitability of your message's content. Because people living in different parts of the country have different needs, wants, interests, customs, habits, and so forth, you may need to become familiar with these specific characteristics, especially if they are likely to affect the reader's acceptance of your message. Failure to do so may readily alienate you from your reader.

9. Is your message likely to be read as part of your reader's routine? When you prepare messages that are not likely to be read by your reader as part of his/her daily routine, you will have to be more concerned about attracting and keeping his/her attention. To illustrate, think of the material you receive that is customarily classified as ''junk mail''—most of which you probably discard without opening. Those who write this material do not have immediate destruction of their work as the intended outcome.

10. What do you expect your reader to do with the information contained in your message? Knowing reader expectations will enable you to focus your message more readily on his/her needs. When you have a specific expectation of your reader, your message will differ from a message in which you have a general expectation. Whatever the reader expectation is, it should be readily apparent to him/her.

Once you are familiar with your reader, you then need to decide how to work effectively with that individual. On the basis of what you know, is your reader likely to be interested or disinterested in your message? Is the reader likely to react positively or negatively? Is the reader likely to trust or distrust you? Is the reader likely to comply with your wishes readily, reluctantly, or not at all?

Some situations you write about will not be well received by your reader. In these instances, you will need to make special effort to increase receptivity to your message. The more writing experience you have, the easier it will be to determine which techniques are likely to work best in various types of situations.

How can you increase the receptivity of your writing?

To increase receptivity of your writing, you can clearly relate your message to your reader's needs. This is what we called reader benefit in Chapter 3. Relating the message to the reader's knowledge level, value system, and specific interests is important.

Receptivity can also be enhanced by your ''putting your best foot forward.'' You should try to convey the impression that you are knowledgeable. All too often, inexperienced writers diminish their communication effectiveness because they do not express themselves clearly, they hedge, they make grammatical, punctuation, spelling, or word usage errors, and they disregard the basic elements of effective business communication.

Furthermore, receptivity can be enhanced by making the message as appropriate for your reader as possible. For example, the approach you use in preparing a report for a superior may be quite different from your approach in preparing a report for several of your subordinate supervisors. While your superior may prefer a fairly brief report, the unit supervisors for whom you are responsible will probably want considerably more detail. Not only will the depth of material vary from reader to reader, but also the actual content will vary from reader to reader. The material, for example, that a superior is interested in will differ from the material a subordinate is interested in. Communication effectiveness is readily hampered when inexperienced writers fail to use an appropriate approach.

Determine the Appropriate Content

The extent to which you effectively determine the content appropriate for your message will strongly affect its success. Failure to do so is bound to produce a communicating disaster. Determining the content appropriate for some situations is easier than for others. For example, determining the content for a letter in which you are responding to a request is easier than when you are initiating the communication relationship. When responding to a request, you simply answer the questions asked in the originating letter, adding any additional information that you feel would be helpful to your reader. But when the letter you are preparing is the first of a series, you have no prior correspondence to guide your decision about what material to include.

How can you determine the appropriate content of a message?

To determine appropriate content, you might find answering the following questions helpful.

1. What information is relevant for this situation, given the purpose of the message and the reader's needs?
2. What information should be included to make the message complete?
3. If I were the recipient of this message, what information would I find helpful?
4. What material needs to be included to make the message conform with the content customarily found in the type of message I'm preparing.

Once you have determined the broad topics to be included in the message, the planning stage is completed. The next stage, organizing the material, now begins:

ORGANIZING

The organizing stage builds on the steps you undertook in the planning stage. During this process, you will outline the topics you plan to include in your message and then determine the appropriate order of these topics.

Outline the Topics

Once the broad areas to be included in your message have been identified, your next step is to outline them. This step involves identifying the various subtopics to be discussed within each of the broad topics.

To illustrate, assume you are composing a letter to send to a client whose credit account has had a past-due balance for four months. One of the broad topics you decide to discuss is the need for the client to pay the amount of the past-due balance. The following partial outline summarizes the information you plan to include in the discussion of this broad area.

A. Need to have account paid in full by January 20
   1. The customer can protect his/her credit reputation by paying now.
   2. Receipt of payment now will help you avoid having to borrow short-term money, which will benefit the customer in the long run because you will not have to increase your prices.
   3. The customer can avoid paying additional finance or interest charges on his/her account.

In what way is careful outlining helpful?

Careful outlining is helpful for several reasons. In addition to helping you improve the clarity of your message, outlining also saves writing time later. You will find that making changes in an outline is much easier than in written material. Furthermore, careful outlining improves the chances of your fulfilling your communication objective.

Careful outlining also enables you to emphasize properly the various topics in your message. Although exceptions do occur, the topics that you decide to emphasize are the ones most likely to receive the greatest amount of discussion. Placing the most important points at the beginning or end of a paragraph is more emphatic than presenting them in the middle.

What three methods are used in developing your message?

Although several methods can be used in developing topics in written business communication, the most common are topical, direct, and indirect. By determining which of these methods to use before you actually begin the outlining process, the chances of your preparing a well-developed message are greatly enhanced.

Figure 4–1 illustrates a portion of an outline that uses the topical method of outlining.

After the outline has been prepared, it should be assessed in terms of completeness, logical order, emphasis of topics, and so on. The more outlining you do, the easier the process becomes.

When is the direct method preferred?

The *direct method* involves presenting a general statement first, followed by specific supporting statements. This method is generally preferred when presenting positive or good-news information because the reader is immediately given the information of greatest interest. The supporting information, which is of lesser interest, can be presented next. This method is consistent with the reader-benefit concept discussed in Chapter 3.

An example of the direct method is shown in the outline that follows. However, before you actually begin to write the letter, you should review your outline to make sure the topics are presented in an appropriate order. Determining the appropriate order of the topics, which is discussed in the next section, is the last step in the organizing stage.

I. Health Insurance

   A. Mutual of Lincoln
   B. HMO
   C. Federal plan
   D. Dependent coverage

II. Life Insurance

   A. Basic life insurance

      1. Option I
      2. Option II

   B. Federal plan

III. Long-Term Disability

   A. Mutual of Lincoln
   B. Federal plan

IV. Dental Insurance

   A. American Dental Plan
   B. Green Cross Plan
   C. Dependent coverage

V. Retirement

   A. Social Security
   B. State Retirement
   C. TIBB/GREF
   D. Civil Service

Figure 4–1 Topical Outline

A. Mention that replacement scanner is on its way
B. Discuss that examination of scanner revealed two defects
   1. Weak transistor
   2. Short circuit in one of the electronic components
C. Mention that quality control does not find all defects; incorporate resale material
D. Discuss warranty on new scanner
E. Express "satisfaction guaranteed" in courteous closing

Figure 4–2 illustrates the letter that was written on the basis of the direct outline shown above.

The *indirect method,* which is more appropriate for negative-news messages, presents the specific information first, followed by the conclusion. Therefore, by the time the reader has read the conclusion, the reasons for your being unable to accommodate him/her have already been presented. This approach gives you psychological control over your message.

Dear Mr. Jones:

A HD-40 Reliable Scanner was sent to you this morning to replace the scanner you recently sent us for repair.

An examination of your scanner revealed a weak transistor and a short circuit in one of the electronic components. Because your scanner was still under warranty, we prefer--and I am sure you will agree with our decision--to replace the scanner with a new one.

Our electronic equipment is subjected to rigid quality control tests during several stages of its manufacture. These tests find nearly 99 percent of the defective components--which is the best performance record in the industry. The reliability of our products is responsible for the feeling shared by many of our customers that "If you want reliability, buy Reliable."

The 120-day warranty on your replacement scanner will take effect upon its receipt. Please complete and return the warranty card enclosed with the scanner.

You are sure to have many hours of listening enjoyment provided by your scanner. Remember, your satisfaction is guaranteed.

Figure 4–2 Example of Direct-Method Letter

The following outline of a letter uses the indirect method.

A. Use a neutral opening that compliments the reader for having good credit references
B. Discuss the reasons that the credit account cannot be approved for $1,000
   1. Company requires minimum yearly income of $30,000 for this credit limit
   2. Is advantageous to applicant by helping him avoid assuming a potentially greater financial burden than can be effectively handled on this income level
C. Mention that the credit account can be opened for $750 but not for the $1000 that was requested
D. Suggest that the reader, if he desires, can have account reviewed after one year to determine if credit limit can be increased

The letter that resulted from the indirect outline is shown in Figure 4–3.

Determine the Appropriate Order of the Topics

Once you have prepared your outline, the next step involves reviewing the topics to make sure they are discussed in an appropriate order. You may occasionally find it wise to delay determining the appropriate order of the topics until after the outline has been completed. This is especially true when ideas are being generated at a fast rate. In fact, you probably will find that it is easier to determine the appropriate order of the topics once you are certain which ones you plan to include in your message. You can also add additional topics to your outline during this step.

```
Dear Mr. Quigley

Each of the individuals you listed as credit references on your charge account
application spoke favorably about your bill-paying habits.  You can be proud
of this record.

A minimum yearly income of $30,000 is required to open an account for the
$1,000 maximum that you requested.  Your present yearly income is listed as
$24,000.  We find that this limit actually benefits many of our customers
because it helps them avoid assuming a greater financial burden than they
might be able to handle on incomes of less than $30,000.

Your income level qualifies you for a charge account with a credit limit of
$750.  If you would like for us to open an account with this credit limit,
please sign and return the enclosed card, which we need as authorization to
open an account for you.

If you wish, we will review your account after one year to determine if the
maximum limit can be increased to $1,000.  All you need do is request the
review.

A Bailey's charge account can enhance the convenience of your shopping in our
store.
```

Figure 4–3 Example of Indirect-Method Letter

How can you determine the appropriate order of the topics for an outline?

When you are determining the order of the topics, you should review your outline, keeping the following questions in mind.

1. Are the ideas of equal importance presented in a parallel manner?
2. Is the sequence of the topics appropriate for the development method I'm using (topical, direct, indirect)?
3. Is the sequence of the topics likely to add clarity to my message?
4. Are related topics properly sequenced?
5. Are the topics presented in the sequence recommended for the type of message I'm preparing?

To illustrate how changing the order of topics in an outline can improve message clarity, consider the outline in Figure 4–1. The individual who prepared the outline, after reviewing the preliminary draft, decided to discuss employee and dependent coverage separately. By changing the order of the benefits, she discovered that all of the insurance benefits could be discussed before the noninsurance benefits. Furthermore, discussing dental insurance immediately after health insurance seemed logical because these two types of benefits are more closely related than retirement and dental insurance, their order on the preliminary outline. Changing the order of these topics should improve message clarity. A new outline is presented in Figure 4–4.

DRAFTING

Once you have completed the planning and organizing stages, you are ready to draft (or dictate) the message. Because drafting and dictating are quite different from one another—although the end result is the same—each is discussed in a separate section of this chapter. Because you are probably more

```
I.  Types of Employee Benefit Plans and Coverage

    A.  Health Insurance

        1.  Mutual of Lincoln
        2.  HMO
        3.  Federal plan

    B.  Dental Insurance

        1.  American Dental Plan
        2.  Green Cross Plan

    C.  Life Insurance

        1.  Basic life insurance

            a.  Option I
            b.  Option II

        2.  Federal plan

    D.  Long-Term Disability Insurance

    E.  Retirement

        1.  Social Security
        2.  State Retirement
        3.  TIBB/GREF
        4.  Civil Service

II. Dependent Coverage

    A.  Health Insurnace

        1.  Mutual of Lincoln
        2.  HMO
        3.  Federal plan

    B.  Dental Insurance

        1.  American Dental Plan
        2.  Green Cross Plan
```

Figure 4–4 Revised Topical Outline

familiar with the drafting process than with the dictating process, drafting is discussed first.

Topics in this section include a discussion of sentence construction, paragraph construction, beginning paragraph construction, ending paragraph construction, and body composition.

Sentence Construction

The sentence, which is the fundamental unit of thought, thoroughly and readily conveys one or more ideas. However, the effectiveness of many sentences is destroyed because of their faulty construction. For example, sentences in which the intended meaning is unclear are confusing to the reader. Taking a little extra time to assure the clarity of the sentences you compose is well worth your effort.

Characteristics of effective sentences are: unity, coherence, emphasis, variety, correct use of modifiers, brevity, parallelism, personalization, tone, voice, and avoidance of expletives.

What are the characteristics of effective sentences?

Sentence *unity* means that all ideas presented in the sentence belong and are relevant. Presenting irrelevant ideas in a sentence is confusing to the reader and will result in a loss of reader understanding. Furthermore, when sentences contain irrelevant ideas, the reader has more difficulty separating the important ideas from the less important ideas.

Notice how removal of the irrelevant ideas from the first version of the following sentences improves the revised version.

Change:	John Jones, who has a car like mine, was extremely helpful in solving the problem with the computer program.
To:	John Jones was extremely helpful in solving the problem with the computer program. (The clause, "who has a car like mine," is irrelevant to this sentence.)
Change:	Even though our company was not as profitable as we had forecast, the employees seem to enjoy working here.
To:	Our company was not as profitable as we had forecast.
Or:	The employees seem to enjoy working here. (Presenting the two unrelated ideas in the same sentence destroys its unity; you should use whichever idea is appropriate for the discussion and eliminate the other.)

Sentence *coherency* also affects the ability of the reader to understand your message. In a coherent sentence, the relationship between the ideas is obvious to the reader. Even when the relationship between the ideas is obvious to you, sentences will lack coherence if the reader is unable to grasp the nature of the relationship between the ideas.

What is the function of sentence coherency?

While the first sentence in each of the following sets lacks coherency, the second sentence in each set is an improved version.

Change:	Lack of unity destroys the effectiveness of sentences, and well-written paragraphs are critical to the success of your message.
To:	Sentence unity and well-written paragraphs are two of the critical elements that will affect the success of your message.
Change:	Our company has been a leader in this field since it was founded, and it is now in its 67th year.
To:	Our company, which was founded 67 years ago, has always been a leader in this field.

Emphasis in sentences enables you to stress important ideas by putting them in the most prominent places. The beginning of a sentence tends to be more prominent than its ending, while the middle is the least prominent.

What is the most emphatic position in a sentence?

Knowing which idea you want to emphasize in the sentence will enable you to place it in the most prominent location. In complex or compound-complex sentences (sentences with both independent and dependent clauses), you will wisely use the independent clauses for the ideas you want to emphasize and the dependent clauses for the less important ideas. In sentences that contain both positive and negative information, place the positive information in the emphasized position and the negative information in the de-emphasized position. If you wish to emphasize a person or thing, make the person or thing the subject of the sentence; if you wish to emphasize an action, make the action the subject of the sentence.

In each of the following sets, the first sentence has faulty emphasis; however, the main ideas are properly emphasized in the revised sentences.

Change:	Our new employee, Mary Johnson, is a specialist in labor relations.
To:	Mary Johnson, who is a new employee, is a specialist in labor relations. (That Mary Johnson is a new employee is relatively unimportant; therefore, that fact either can be omitted or included in the middle of the sentence.)
Change:	One of the essential characteristics of effective writing, which is clarity of expression, is often overlooked by many inexperienced writers.
To:	Clarity of expression, which is an essential characteristic of effective writing, is often overlooked by many inexperienced writers.

Why is sentence variety important?

Variety in the sentences you write is critical to message effectiveness. You can achieve variety by using different sentence types and sentence lengths and varying their structure. Consistent use of the same type of sentence throughout a message becomes monotonous and boring. Messages that contain consecutive sentences of equal length are as uninteresting as messages containing sentences that consistently use the same internal structure. To illustrate, using introductory prepositional clauses or phrases in several consecutive sentences is monotonous.

The types of sentences used in the English language are simple sentences, compound sentences, complex sentences, and compound-complex sentences. You can make your writing more exciting when you use a variety of sentence types.

The following examples identify the differences among the four types of sentences.

Simple sentence

What is a simple sentence?

A simple sentence contains only one independent clause and no dependent clauses.

After the meeting, he went home.
Please return the form as soon as possible.
Your order was mailed today.

Compound sentence

Compound sentences contain two or more independent clauses joined by one of the coordinating conjunctions (*and, but, or, nor, for,* or *yet*).

Our business offices are located in California, and our plant is located in New Jersey.

The business climate is deteriorating, and we have little hope that it will improve in the near future.

John will be out of the office next week, but he will be here the rest of this week.

Complex sentence

A complex sentence contains a principal (or independent) clause and one or more dependent (or subordinate) clauses. The main idea is expressed in the independent clause and is enlarged in the dependent clause.

What is a complex sentence?

If you would like to receive our illustrated catalog, just sign and return the enclosed card. (one dependent and one independent clause)

When you read Chapter 2, please pay particular attention to the section on punctuation. (one dependent and one independent clause)

Mr. Jones said that whenever possible, he gives the employee the benefit of the doubt. (one dependent and one independent clause.

Compound-complex sentence

This form of sentence contains two or more independent clauses (joined by *and, but, or, nor*) and one or more dependent clauses.

What is a compound-complex sentence?

If we have good weather, we will complete construction of the building by September 1; and landscaping crews can move in any time after that date.

I thought he told me that he was to leave tomorrow; but when I arrived at work this morning, I discovered he left yesterday.

John Jones, our last president, no longer works full time; but he still has considerable influence here.

To enliven your writing, you can also vary sentence length. A series of sentences of approximately equal length should be avoided. A message comprised of alternating short, medium-length, and long sentences is more interesting than messages comprised of equal-length sentences—whether they are predominately short, medium-length, or long sentences. Notice how much more exciting the variable length sentences make the revised example.

Change: The first thing you do in writing a letter is to determine your purpose. After this step, you consider the background and needs of your reader. Then you determine the appropriate content, given the nature of the purpose and reader background.

To: Several steps are undertaken in writing a letter. You begin by determining your purpose, which is followed by considering the reader's background and needs. Next, you determine the appropriate content for your message, given the nature of the purpose of your message and the reader's background.

When you use a variety of sentence types, you may be automatically varying sentence length. Although exceptions do exist, simple sentences generally tend to be the shortest type of sentence, while compound-complex sentences tend to be the longest. The length of compound and complex sentences often falls somewhere in between the length of simple and compound-complex sentences.

Why is variety in the internal structure of a sentence important?

Some writers tend to overuse a certain type of internal structure, which reduces the effectiveness of their writing. The first paragraph in the following example illustrates what happens when the writer began each sentence with an infinitive phrase. Notice how much more exciting the revision is to read.

Change:	To work hard is a quality I have always admired. To be on time, whether arriving at work or submitting a report, is another quality I have always admired. To continue to learn is another trait I appreciate among employees.
To:	The following outlines desirable employee characteristics I have always admired: (1) working hard; (2) arriving at work and submitting work on time; and (3) continuing to learn.

The following revised passage has been made more interesting by varying sentence structure.

Change:	John, who is the production manager, has worked here 17 years. Mary, who is the executive vice president, has worked here 13 years. Jim, who is the personnel manager, has worked here for 11 years.
To:	Several of our employees have worked here for more than ten years. For example, John, the production manager, has worked here 17 years, while Mary, who is currently the executive vice president, has been here 13 years. With 11 years of tenure is Jim, the personnel manager.

What results when modifiers are not used correctly?

You also need to be concerned about the *correct use of modifiers.* Incorrect use of modifiers destroys sentence clarity—and sometimes results in humorous writing—as the following example illustrates: ''Your desk should be cleared of all confidential materials before leaving work at the end of the day.'' Read literally, this sentence sounds as though the desk leaves work at the end of the day.

Among the troublesome modifiers are misplaced modifiers and dangling modifiers. A misplaced modifier results from placing the modifier too far from the word it modifies, causing an incorrect modification. The following examples illustrate how sentences containing misplaced modifiers can be corrected.

Change:	Competent in work measurement, the productivity of the company improved considerably after Mr. Jones implemented the PRO-IM Program. (This sentence reads as though productivity is competent in work measurement.)
To:	The productivity of the company improved considerably after Mr. Jones, who is competent in work measurement, implemented the PRO-IM Program.

Change: The interviewer discussed the opportunities with the applicants for promotion. (This sentence reads as though the interviewer is interviewing certain applicants, who are known as "applicants for promotion.")
To: The interviewer discussed the opportunities for promotion with the applicants.

Dangling modifiers are most apt to occur when a sentence begins with a participial phrase, an infinitive phrase, or a gerund phrase. To correct dangling modifiers, either (1) add the proper subject to the independent part, or (2) make the dependent part agree with the main clause and the main subject. The first sentence in each set·contains a dangling modifier, while the second sentence is a corrected version.

Where are dangling modifiers most likely to occur?

Change: Having read your report, a few questions come to mind.
To: Having read your report, I have a few questions. (Sentence corrected by adding the proper subject to the independent clause.)
Change: To produce quality work, good materials must be available.
To: To produce quality work, you must have good materials available. (Sentence corrected by adding the proper subject to the independent clause.)

Misinterpretation often results from misplacing the adverbs, *almost, hardly, merely, nearly, scarcely,* and *only*. Of these, *only* is the most troublesome because it is both an adverb and an adjective. Therefore, *only* can modify almost anything and will fit into a sentence at almost any point. Notice how each of the following sentences changes as the word *only* is relocated.

Only I urged him to try.
I only urged him to try.
I urged only him to try.
I urged him only to try.
I urged him to only try.
I urged him to try only.

Another characteristic of effective sentences is *brevity,* or conciseness, which is achieved by economizing on the words you include in your messages. Brevity can be attained by using enumerations, avoiding the statement of obvious ideas; shortening modifying phrases, and using compound adjectives.

How can you attain sentence brevity?

The following revised examples show how brevity is achieved by using enumerations.

Change: One of the important duties of this job is maintaining the departmental budget. The holder of this job is also responsible for preparing the year-end reports. Another important responsibility involves the supervision of other employees. In addition, the holder of this job is expected to prepare periodic employee performance appraisals.

To:	Among the important duties of this job are the following: 1. Maintaining the departmental budget 2. Preparing year-end reports 3. Supervising other employees 4. Preparing periodic employee performance appraisals

The brevity of many sentences is destroyed because the writer states what is clearly implied. If a later action implies an earlier action, the discussion of the earlier action can most likely be eliminated without destroying the clarity of the sentence.

Notice how the following sentences have been shortened by implying rather than stating the earlier action.

Change:	Mary rode the train and enjoyed her ride.
To:	Mary enjoyed her train ride. (Mary had to ride the train if she enjoyed riding it; therefore, let the "rode the train" be implied.)
Change:	She proofread the letter and found three typographical errors.
To:	She found three typographical errors in the letter. (Let the proofreading task be stated by implication.)
Change:	The builder examined the house and found three serious construction errors.
To:	The builder found three serious construction errors in the house. (Let "examined" be stated by implication.)

Sentence brevity can also be achieved by shortening modifying phrases. In many instances, modifying phrases can be shortened to one word, as the following examples illustrate.

Change:	He spoke in a hesitating manner.
To:	He spoke hesitatingly.
Change:	This is the machine that is malfunctioning.
To:	This is the malfunctioning machine.
Change:	Omit the material for which you have no use.
To:	Omit the useless material.

Using compound adjectives will also help you achieve sentence brevity. The modifying phrase is converted to a compound adjective and placed before the word it modifies. The following sentences illustrate this technique.

Change:	These imports that are duty free are selling well.
To:	These duty-free imports are selling well. (Notice that compound adjectives are hyphenated.)
Change:	This book that is up to date has been helpful.
To:	This up-to-date book has been helpful.

The use of *parallel construction* will also enable you to improve the clarity of your sentences. If you use a gerund (verb ending in *-ing* that is used as a noun) to express an idea in a sentence, other related ideas should also be expressed using a gerund. Or, if you use an infinitive phrase to express an idea, other related ideas should also be expressed in the infinitive form. The first sentence in each of the following sets violates the parallel-construction rule, while the second sentence in each set is a corrected version.

Change:	Selling subscriptions, buying supplies, and the collection of money are important activities.
To:	Selling subscriptions, buying supplies, and collecting money are important activities.
Change:	To order flowers, to greet new members, and helping plan the annual banquet are important functions of the hospitality committee.
To:	To order flowers, to greet new members, and to help plan the annual banquet are important functions of the hospitality committee.
Change:	That program was interesting and motivational.
To:	That program was interesting and motivating.

What is the impact of personalizing sentences?

You will find that *personalizing* your sentences with your reader's name will help attract his/her attention. For personalizing to be effective, the reader's name has to fit naturally in the sentence. When personalizing is distracting, either because it is unnatural or because it is used excessively, the effectiveness of your message will be diminished.

The following sentences illustrate the use of effective personalizing.

Mr. Jones, members of the Citizens Club enjoyed your excellent talk.
I look forward to meeting you next week, Ms. Brown.
Bill, could you please return the completed form as soon as possible?

An increasing number of individuals now omit the salutation of letters (Dear John) and personalize the first sentence of the letter; "John, will you please sign the enclosed card and return it by the end of next week?"

What are expletives?

Avoiding the use of *expletives* in your writing will improve its effectiveness. By definition, expletives are meaningless words. In business communication, expletives are commonly used in sentence beginnings. Some of the most common are "There is(are)" and "It is" beginnings. Rewriting sentences to avoid expletives, regardless of their location in the sentence, is well worth your effort.

Notice how removal of the expletives in the first sentence of each of the following sets improves the revised sentences.

Change:	There are three errors on page 23.
To:	Page 23 contains three errors.
Change:	It is most likely that he will not be here.
To:	He most likely will not be here.

The *tone* of the sentences you write influences the reader. With a little creativity, a negative idea can often be presented in a positive tone. Mentioning what you can do rather than what you cannot do is preferable. Tone can also be improved by using the subjunctive mood (see 2.1.3 in Appendix A) when expressing a negative idea. Another technique you may find useful when having to express a negative idea is to include a positive idea, if possible, in the same sentence.

In the revised sentences that follow, the negative idea found in each of the original sentences is made positive by mentioning what can be done rather than what cannot be done.

Change:	We cannot leave until 1:30 on Tuesday.
To:	We can leave at 1:30 on Tuesday.
Change:	We cannot begin on the Johnson project until after the Smith project has been completed.
To:	We can begin on the Johnson project after we complete the Smith project.

The subjunctive mood is a useful technique for improving the tone of negative information that cannot be made positive. Because the subjunctive mood enables you to express what you wish you could do rather than what you can do, its use will enable you to express yourself more diplomatically.

The use of the subjunctive mood is illustrated in each of the following revised sentences:

Change:	I cannot attend the budget committee meeting scheduled for Thursday morning.
To:	I would like to attend the budget committee meeting scheduled for Thursday morning, but I will be in Los Angeles.
Change:	We cannot accept your recommendation.
To:	I wish we could accept your recommendation.

If circumstances allow, you can improve the tone of a sentence by including a positive idea along with the negative idea. The positive idea helps offset the negative idea, as the revised sentences illustrate.

Change:	We cannot open a credit account with a $500 limit as you requested.
To:	Even though we are unable to open a credit account for you at this time, we thought you would be pleased to know that your references spoke highly about your bill-paying habits.
Change:	We regret that we have to increase your premium.
To:	While we regret that we have to increase your premium, you actually benefit because of the significant increase in your coverage.

The effectiveness of most sentences can be improved by using *active voice* rather than *passive voice*. Sentences written in active voice make the subject the doer of the action, while in passive-voice sentences, the subject is acted upon. Active voice is generally preferred because it makes sentences more exciting. However, passive voice has two effective uses:

1. It helps break up the monotony resulting from the consistent use of active voice.
2. It helps state negative information in a more courteous manner, as the following two sentences illustrate.

Active:	Mary turned in her assignment three days after it was due.
Passive:	Mary's assignment was turned in three days after it was due.

The first sentence in each of the following examples is written in passive voice and then rewritten in active voice. Notice how much more exciting the revised sentences are when the subject is the doer of the action.

Change:	The election was won by Mary. (passive)
To:	Mary won the election. (active)
Change:	The policy was written by the rules committee.
To:	The rules committee wrote the policy.

Paragraph Construction

Just as effective sentences possess certain qualities, so do effective paragraphs. The presence of grammatically correct sentences in a paragraph does not assure effective writing. Other essential qualities are: a topic sentence, variety, coherence, emphasis, and sequence.

What is a topic sentence?

The *topic sentence,* which expresses the main idea of the paragraph, should be obvious to the reader. The most common location of the topic sentence is at the beginning of the paragraph. Another acceptable location, although less common, is the last sentence of the paragraph. Although seldom found, the topic sentence can also be placed in the middle of the paragraph.

When the topic sentence is included as the first sentence of the paragraph, it tells the reader what the paragraph is about. Each sentence that follows the topic sentence provides supporting information. When included at the end of the paragraph, the topic sentence performs a concluding or summarizing function.

The following three paragraphs illustrate topic sentences located in the three possible positions.

Opening:	*The role of the personnel manager in improving the quality of an organization's work force is vital.* For example, the personnel manager is responsible for determining which recruitment techniques attract the best qualified applicants. Another important responsibility is the interview, which allows the manager to identify the most desirable applicants. The manager is also responsible for designing an effective testing program that helps identify those applicants who are best qualified for the positions for which they are being considered.
Closing:	The personnel manager is responsible for determining which recruitment techniques attract the best qualified applicants. Another important responsibility is the interview, which allows the manager to identify the most desirable applicants. The manager is also responsi-

ble for designing an effective testing program that helps identify those applicants who are best qualified for the positions for which they are being considered. *These responsibilities give the personnel manager a vital role in improving the quality of an organization's work force.*

Middle: The personnel manager is responsible for determining which recruitment techniques attract the best qualified applicants. Another important responsibility is the interview, which allows the manager to identify the most desirable applicants. *These responsibilities give the personnel manager a vital role in improving the quality of an organization's work force.* In addition to the responsibilities already mentioned, the personnel manager is also responsible for designing an effective testing program that helps identify those applicants who are best qualified for the positions for which they are applying.

Variety in paragraph construction is achieved by varying their length. Written material comprised of a series of equal-length paragraphs is less interesting than material with a number of variable-length paragraphs. Your material will be more inviting to read if you include some paragraphs that are shorter than average length and others that are longer. In letters, the average length is 6–8 lines, while in reports, 10–12 lines are standard. Enumerating a series of ideas creates variety, as does a variety of different types of sentences in each paragraph.

What is paragraph coherence?

Another quality of effective paragraphs is *coherence,* which means that each of the ideas presented in a paragraph is related to the paragraph topic. When the reader is unable to determine how various ideas in a paragraph are related to one another, the paragraph becomes incoherent. Coherency can be achieved by making sure that one idea leads to another throughout the entire paragraph.

How is paragraph coherence achieved?

In addition to content coherency, you should also be concerned about reading coherency, a quality that enhances the ease with which your material can be read. To achieve reading coherency, you can repeat key words and use transitional words, pointing words, explanatory statements, and enumeration (numbers or letters to indicate a series).

Repeating key terms: includes the repetition of key terms to facilitate the readability of the paragraph.

As children, we were taught to take responsibility for our actions. We were taught to respect the views of others. Our parents also taught us the virtues of hard work and the necessity for relaxation.

Transitional words: includes the use of such words or phrases as *therefore, for example, in addition, in contrast.*

The new president is interested in enhancing the firm's public image. In addition, she is interested in diversifying the product line. Therefore, I think you will see more emphasis placed on the public relations and marketing units than ever before.

Pointing words: includes the use of such words as *this, that, those, these, such, some, a few.*

> I will be in Philadelphia on May 18. Thus, I will be able to discuss with you your ideas for the marketing strategy you have been working on for our new paint line. These ideas, which many of us are looking forward to receiving, are critical to our financial future.

Explanatory statements: includes the use of explanatory statements to support an earlier-stated idea.

> John's performance the last few weeks has deteriorated. For example, he rarely submits reports on time now, nor does he seem to care about the direction of the marketing department. Furthermore, he regularly arrives late to work and leaves work early several times each week.

Enumerations: includes the use of either letters or numbers to identify the series of ideas that may be presented in either tabular form or paragraph form.

> The following outlines the reasons that I feel this way:
> 1. We cannot afford to purchase a new word processor at this time.
> 2. We cannot afford to hire more employees now.
> 3. We cannot afford to expand the size of the word processing center for at least another year.

Effective *emphasis* results from skillful use of position and proportion. The major idea in a paragraph reflects its importance when placed in a strategic position, usually the beginning or ending of a paragraph. You can use the middle of the paragraph to discuss ideas of secondary importance.

The proportion of space devoted to an idea also reflects its significance to the total communication. For example, if you write eight lines about active voice and three lines about passive voice, you are emphasizing active voice and de-emphasizing passive voice.

An idea of minor significance may be presented in a dependent clause whereas an idea of more importance may be given an entire sentence. An idea of great importance should perhaps be developed into a series of several sentences.

Emphasis can also be achieved by such mechanical means as printing words in italics, in capital letters, or in boldface, or by underlining key words, phrases, or sentences. Depending on the printing process used, the emphasized material can be printed in a different color from the remainder of the message.

The *sequence* of the material in the message affects its understandability. In some of the material you write, the ideas have to be presented in a certain sequence because of their relationship to time or to importance. A relationship between components occasionally determines the sequence. Presenting the material in a logical sequence that is apparent to the reader will enhance his/

her understanding and comprehension. Using transitional words and phrases, pointing words, and repeating key terms will also help the reader more clearly understand the logical sequence of the material.

For example, notice how the illogical sequence in the first of the following two paragraphs has been remedied in the second paragraph.

Change: Once the appraisal process has been completed, an appraisal interview should be conducted. However, before you conduct the appraisal interview, you should do a background check to make sure the applicant is suitable for the position for which he/she is being interviewed. Following the interview, the selection tests should be administered.

To: You should begin the applicant appraisal process by undertaking a background check that will help you determine if the applicant is suitable for the position for which he/she is being considered. If the background check reveals no significant weaknesses, an appraisal interview should be conducted. Following the interview, the selection tests should be administered.

Beginning and Ending Paragraphs

The beginning and ending paragraphs of your messages are critical to their effectiveness. Because they usually occupy positions of emphasis, they are likely to be carefully scrutinized by the reader.

Beginning paragraphs

The beginning paragraph may determine whether the reader reads your message in its entirety. As your goal is to entice the reader to read the entire message without putting it aside, the wording in the beginning paragraph is critical.

How can you improve the effectiveness of beginning paragraphs?

The following suggestions are offered to help you improve the effectiveness of your beginning paragraph.

1. Make sure the beginning is appropriate for the reader.
2. Make sure the beginning is appropriate for the situation. Normally, in good-news letters, begin with the good news; in neutral or direct-request letters, begin with the main idea or request; in disappointing-news letters, buffer the beginning with neutral information or information with which the reader will agree; and in persuasive messages, begin with information that will catch the reader's attention.
3. Avoid the inclusion of negative information or discourteous wording by emphasizing what can be done rather than what cannot be done.
4. Use a you-viewpoint (rather than an I-viewpoint) in the opening.
5. Use a fast-start beginning rather than a slow beginning in which you provide information that is obvious to the reader.
6. Keep the beginning paragraph fairly short.
7. Make sure the beginning paragraph possesses unity and coherence.

Notice how the first of the following two paragraphs fails to present good news in the beginning of a good-news letter. The reader's curiosity about the status of his/her order will be quickly satisfied with the material found in the revised paragraph.

Change: We appreciate your recent order for a variety of decorating accessories for your interior design studio. The items you ordered are sure to be popular among your clients. (This beginning paragraph fails to convey the good news first.)

To: Your order for a variety of decorating accessories was shipped by UPS this morning. The items you ordered are sure to be popular among your clients.

In a direct-request letter, the opening sentence can present the request. In the first of the following two paragraphs the reader will not know why he/she received a letter after reading the opening. In the revised paragraph, notice how much more quickly the reader will learn the purpose of the letter.

Change: I am a student at Iowa College and am currently enrolled in a business finance course. One of the projects in the class is to make an in-depth financial analysis of a *Fortune* 500 company. I have selected your company for this project. (The main idea—which was to request an annual report from the selected company—is not presented in the beginning paragraph.)

To: Would you please send me an annual report for use in making a financial analysis of your company. Making a thorough analysis of the financial condition of a *Fortune* 500 company is one of the requirements for a business finance course I am enrolled in at Iowa College.

To begin a disappointing-news letter with negative information complicates a negative situation even more, as the first of the following two paragraphs illustrates. Psychological advantages result from delaying the negative news until later in the letter. Notice the up-lifting nature of the revised version. Such a beginning paragraph will give the reader a greater emotional advantage when he/she reaches the disappointing material in the letter.

Change: We are sorry to have to inform you that we are unable to open a charge account at Kelsey's Department Store. Unfortunately, you have too many liabilities in relation to your assets to qualify for a charge account. (A beginning like this will surely irritate the reader.)

To: You will be pleased to learn that the credit references you listed on your credit application commented favorably on your bill-paying record. Several were also impressed with your promptness that has enabled you on numerous occasions to avoid interest charges. (Using a beginning such as this in a disappointing-news letter will help put the reader in a more positive frame of mind before reading the disappointing news.)

We are not always inclined to read unsolicited mail unless something in it attracts our attention. In persuasive messages, attention-getting beginnings are especially desirable. Notice how the first of the following two paragraphs, which does nothing out of the ordinary, fails to capture the reader's attention, while the revised paragraph creates a greater amount of initial interest.

Change:	We are soliciting volunteers to donate an hour or two of their time each month to work at the information desk in Portsmouth Art Museum. We hope you will consider volunteering. (A beginning like this in a persuasive message will do little to entice the reader to comply with your request.)
To:	What could be more exciting than helping direct visitors at the Portsmouth Art Museum to the location of the work of their favorite artist? You can share the excitement of our visitors by volunteering to work at the information desk in Portsmouth Art Museum an hour or two each month.

One of the most effective ways to get readers to read your messages is to focus on their needs, concerns, and questions. This suggestion is violated by extensive use of the pronoun "I." While the pronoun "you" does not necessarily guarantee the you-viewpoint, its use is a step in the right direction, as the second of the following two paragraphs illustrates.

Change:	I will appreciate your signing the enclosed card and returning it to me as soon as possible. Once I have the signed release, I can begin the process of modifying your insurance policy. (The excessive usage of the I pronoun in this paragraph focuses the attention on the writer rather than on the reader.)
To:	Will you please sign the enclosed card and return it to me as soon as possible. Doing so will enable me to make the requested changes in your insurance policy.

The use of slow-start beginnings should be avoided. A paragraph containing information that is obvious to the reader is an example of a slow-start beginning. Notice how much more effective the second of the following two paragraphs is because it tells the reader something he/she does not know rather than something he/she is already familiar with.

Change:	We have received your letter of October 15 in which you asked for the name of the Arnson lawnmower dealer located closest to you. Bill's Hardware in Eli is our closest dealer to you. (This is a slow-start beginning because it provides information that is obvious to the reader—that his/her letter of October 15 has been received. If the letter had not been received, you would not be responding.)
To:	Bill's Hardware in Eli is the Arnson lawnmower dealer located nearest to you. This dealer carries our complete line of Arnson lawnmowers.

Ending paragraphs

The ending paragraph of your messages is likely to determine if your reader complies with your wishes. In the ending, you have an opportunity to do two things: (1) to concentrate on the action you desire the reader to take (if appropriate); and (2) to show courtesy toward the reader.

Suggestions for improving the effectiveness of the ending paragraph of your messages are:

How can you improve the effectiveness of ending paragraphs?

1. State the desired action clearly and completely.
2. State who is to perform the desired action if the action is to be performed by someone other than the reader.
3. State how the action is to be performed.
4. Make the action easy to be performed.
5. State when the action is to be performed, if appropriate.
6. Include reader-benefit material, if appropriate.
7. Show appreciation to the reader, if appropriate. Remember, until the reader does something for you, thanking him/her is inappropriate.
8. Avoid the inclusion of negative information in the ending.
9. Offer to be of assistance, if appropriate.
10. Keep the ending paragraph as short as circumstances will allow.

Notice how the first of the following two paragraphs fails to specify clearly and completely the action desired by the reader. The revised version removes any doubts the reader may have about the desired action.

Change: Please let us hear from you.

To: Just as soon as you sign and return the enclosed authorization card to us, we will be able to make the requested modifications to your retirement plan. (This paragraph is effective because it tells when, who, what, how, and why, as well as contains reader-benefit material.)

In the first of the following two paragraphs, the writer failed to mention in the closing who is to take the desired action. The revised version clearly points out who is to do what.

Change: Upon receipt of the enclosed form, we will be able to add Mrs. Brown's name to your savings account.

To: Please have Mrs. Brown sign the line marked with a red "x" on the signature card. As soon as we receive the card, she will be entitled to use this savings account. (This paragraph identifies who, what, where, why, and when, in addition to containing reader-benefit material.)

Notice how the first of the following two paragraphs violates several of the suggestions for writing effective ending paragraphs. The violations are removed in the revised version.

Change: Let me know when you would like to come for an interview.
To: Please call at 654–2347 early next week to let me know a convenient time for you to come for an interview. (This paragraph identifies what, where, when, and why.)

The negative information found in the first of the following two paragraphs has been removed from the second version.

Change: We regret that we do not have the information you requested.
To: Best wishes for the successful completion of your project. Your effort to obtain actual material for inclusion in your project is commendable. (The refusal, which was stated earlier in the letter, should not be repeated in the closing paragraph.)

The premature statement of thanks found in the first of the following two paragraphs is revised in the second paragraph to include a statement of appreciation.

Change: Thank you for sending me the requested material.
To: I will appreciate your sending me the requested material that will enable me to include more helpful information in the feasibility study you commissioned me to undertake. (This paragraph shows appreciation as well as reader benefit.)

The first of the following two paragraphs lacks courtesy, in addition to some of the other elements of ineffective ending paragraphs, while the second paragraph is a much-improved version.

Change: Send your check to us today.
To: To maintain a good credit standing, please send us your check for $323.23 today. (This sentence contains reader-benefit material, is courteous, and tells the reader how much and when.)

An offer to be of assistance is appropriate in some closing paragraphs. In the first of the following two paragraphs, an offer, although appropriate, is missing. Notice how much more effective the revised paragraph is because of the offer to be of assistance.

Change: Enclosed you will find the two reports you requested. (The writer should have notified the reader in the opening that the requested material was being sent. If the writer mentioned earlier in the letter that the material was being sent, it need not be mentioned again in the closing.)
To: If you have any questions after reading the enclosed material, please contact me at (407) 377–2999.

Body composition

The body of the message should be composed after the beginning paragraph is prepared but before the ending paragraph is written, contrary to the order of the discussion of these three parts in this chapter.

In addition to the elements of effective sentence and paragraph construction, correct grammar, and the other elements of effective business communication, you also need to be concerned about the content of the message. The content may well determine if your message is effective or ineffective. In each of the following chapters that pertain to specific types of written communication, such as letters and reports, information is presented that will enable you to determine what material to include. Failure to include the suggested information may significantly reduce message effectiveness.

EDITING

After you have completed the initial draft of your message, ideally you should put it aside for several hours before you begin the editing process. However, a time limitation may not allow you to do so. As you gain more writing experience, you will find that the time lapse between initial drafting and editing becomes shorter. A time lapse becomes more critical as the complexity of the message increases or as the nature of the communication situation becomes more unpleasant.

What questions should you evaluate your work against in the editing process?

The editing process will be simplified if you evaluate your work, keeping in mind the following questions.

Evaluate for Compliance with Principles of Effective Communication

1. Have you accomplished your purpose for writing the message?
2. Have you shown courtesy for the reader regardless of the communication situation?
3. Is the information in your message correct?
4. Can you verify the accuracy of all facts and figures?
5. Is each word in your message necessary?
6. Is the information in your message clear?
7. Will your reader be able to understand your message?
8. Is the information in your message presented with as much specificity and concreteness as possible?
9. Is your message complete?
10. Have you answered all the questions asked by the reader?
11. Have you provided additional information which you feel the reader will appreciate having?

Evaluate for Appropriate Content

1. Have you followed the recommended plan for the type of message you are preparing?
2. Have you included all of the information appropriate for the type of message you are preparing?

3. Can the inclusion of each part of your message be justified?
4. Is the content appropriate for the reader?

Evaluate the Organizational Structure

1. Are your ideas presented in a logical sequence?
2. In disappointing-news messages, is the negative information delayed until after the beginning paragraph?
3. In good-news messages, is the good news presented in the beginning?
4. In direct-request messages, is the request presented in the beginning?
5. Is the ending paragraph appropriate for the message?
6. Are related ideas grouped together?
7. Is the material presented in a sequence appropriate for the type of message you are writing?

Evaluate the Effectiveness of the Sentences and Paragraphs

1. Is the construction of each sentence consistent with the principles of effective sentences?
2. Is the construction of each paragraph consistent with the principles of effective paragraphs?

Evaluate for Compliance with Grammar, Punctuation, Spelling, and Word Usage Fundamentals

1. Is the grammar in each sentence correct?
2. Is each sentence punctuated correctly?
3. Is each word spelled correctly?
4. Is each word used appropriately?

PROOFREADING

The failure of writers to find errors in their messages is costly not only in terms of dollars, but also in terms of image and respect. Many readers think less of writers whose work contains errors. Even though you may not type the final draft of a message, you—not the typist—are responsible for assuring its accuracy.

What should be checked during the proofreading process?

As you proofread you should check for

1. Accuracy of dates, figures, amounts, numbers, and so forth
2. Misspelled words
3. Typographical errors
4. Omissions and additions of material
5. Proper sequencing of material
6. Correct format

In checking the accuracy of numerical information, comparing the numbers against original numbers is wise. If messages are revised several times, errors can occur during one of the revisions. To check the accuracy of the numerical information of the final draft against the numbers in the next-to-last draft may be inviting trouble. If the message contains a considerable amount of numerical information, having someone read aloud the numbers in the final draft as you compare these numbers against the original numbers is suggested. When the message has mathematical calculations, recalculating the numbers to check their accuracy is recommended.

Verifying the correct spelling of words is especially critical (1) when you dictated your message, (2) when the typist is not a good speller, or (3) when you are not a good speller. Programs that electronically check the spellings of words are available for most word processing equipment and other devices capable of performing word processing functions. These programs, however, are unable to differentiate between words with similar pronunciations that are spelled differently, such as "principle" and "principal."

The presence of typographical errors in your written messages also detracts from their effectiveness. Typographical errors, which are misspelled words, occur in the typing/keyboarding process when the typist fails to correct errors made by depressing incorrect keys. For example, while "receivef" is a typographical error, "reciever" is more likely to be considered a misspelled word. The spelling programs are also helpful in locating typographical errors. When checking manually for typographical errors, you use the same process that you use for locating misspelled words.

Checking the context of material is also necessary because of the possibility that words are either omitted or added. An interruption in the typing/transcription process may result in the omission of words or the addition of words. To check the context, read the material word by word, comparing the last draft with the next-to-last draft.

You may decide to proofread a document twice—once to check for spelling and accuracy of numbers and another time to check for context. To try to accomplish both goals in one reading may result in your overlooking errors. Proofreading for accuracy is often best accomplished by examining the words or numbers character by character, while proofreading for context is done by reading the material word by word.

Interruptions in the typing/transcription process may also result in changing the order of the material in the document. Proofreading for context may or may not enable you to locate such errors. This proofreading task is also best accomplished by comparing the last version of the document against the next-to-last version.

Material typed/keyboarded on word processing equipment greatly simplifies the proofreading process. Because the unchanged material prepared on such equipment is not rekeyboarded during each revision, the unchanged material will continue to be printed in the same way during each revision. Therefore, the material that is correct in one version will continue to be correct in subsequent versions. When material is typed on conventional typewriters, each revised draft has to be proofread as carefully as the first draft.

Figure 4–5 presents standard proofreading marks that you should use in revising and/or proofreading your work.

These standard proofreader's marks are helpful when you are revising and proofreading.

℘	Delete, omit word.
⁀	Close up.
#	Leave space.
¶	New paragraph.
No ¶	No paragraph.
⤷ or ⤹	Run on. Connects words when space has been left out or you have crossed out several lines of text.
(more)	Rest of paragraph continues on next page.
] [	Center.
(t)(s)	Transpose letters or words.
(10)	Spell out; don't abbreviate.
Stet Let it stand	Let it stand (when copy appears to be deleted but you want it to remain).
lc or /	Lowercase capital letter.
c ≡	Capitalize lowercase letter.
∧,	Insert comma.
∨'	Insert apostrophe (or single quotation mark).
∨" ∨"	Insert quotation marks.
∨;	Insert semicolon.
∨:	Insert colon.
∨=	Insert hyphen.
⊙	Insert period.
organization (triple underlined)	Make all capitals.

Figure 4–5 Proofreading Marks

DICTATING

One of the most effective ways for increasing the amount of time available to devote to other duties is to use dictating/recording equipment rather than handwriting in the origination process. Executives with efficient dictating skills find that they can dictate much faster than they can originate material by handwriting.

While dictation systems vary, the dictation process is the same regardless of the type of system being used. In some systems, dictators input their dictation into the system by using their office telephones; in other systems, a special dictation microphone is used. In some systems, the dictation is recorded in a centralized dictation system located in the word processing center; in others, the magnetic medium on which the dictation is recorded is transported to the individual responsible for transcribing the material.

When a centralized dictation system is interconnected with the telephone system, executives are able to use the system 24 hours a day, provided they have access to a telephone. To access the system, they simply dial (or depress keys on the phone) a three-or four-digit number if they are calling from within the building. A seven-digit number is used to access the system when calling from a local number. The system can also be accessed by making a long distance call.

Once the system has been accessed, depressing a certain one-digit number on the phone keypad will activate the recorder. Other one-digit numbers control other recorder functions, such as reviewing dictation, making changes in dictation, giving special instructions to the transcriber, and ending the dictation.

To help increase the efficiency of the dictation process, you will be asked to follow a set of instructions that all other dictators in the organization are also expected to follow. The uniformity resulting from these instructions is helpful to the individuals responsible for transcribing the material. An example of such instructions, which are presented in the form of a checklist, is illustrated in Figure 4–6.

What is the purpose of marginal notes?

If you are dictating a response to a letter you received, you may find the use of marginal notes helpful, as illustrated in Figure 4–7. These notes are used to "jog" your memory about points or information you want to include in the response. The use of notes is also helpful in the dictation of originating correspondence. Figure 4–8 is an illustration of notes used by an individual when dictating a letter of inquiry.

Some of the errors found on the first transcribed draft of a dictated message result from carelessness in the dictation process. Figure 4–9a is an illustration of what the dictator had intended; but carelessness resulted in the letter shown in Figure 4–9b.

A major portion of dictated material is comprised of letters, memos, and tables. You may find the following instructions for each of these three categories helpful.

How to Dictate a Standard Letter

1. This is (your name) of (office/division/department).
2. This letter is to be typed on letterhead, and (number) copies are required.
3. It is addressed to (spell proper names and give full addresses).
   For example:
   Mr. John Winchell (W–I–N–C–H–E–L–L)
   The Brownlee (B–R–O–W–N–L–E–E) Corporation
   2457 (two–four–five–seven) Enterprise (E–N–T–E–R–P–R–I–S–E)
   Avenue, Omaha, Nebraska 68540 (six–eight–five–four–zero)
4. Dear John.
5. Dictate the body of the letter, including paragraphs and punctuation, when possible.

```
This is a checklist of instructions to be given before, during, and after your
dictation:

Before

   1. Identify yourself--name, position, and department.
   2. State type of document dictation:
      _____ Letter
      _____ Memo
      _____ Report
      _____ Proposal
      _____ Contract
      _____ Form number
   3. State number of copies.
   4. State type of transcription:
      _____ Rough draft
      _____ Revision
      _____ Final draft
   5. State type of stationery to be used (letterhead, plain, etc.).
   6. State special instructions--format, spacing, etc.
   7. State name and address of recipient--spell out.
   8. State any mailing instructions.

During

   1. Spell:
      _____ All names and addresses
      _____ Technical/unusual words
      _____ Words commonly confused
   2. Describe special punctuation and format, such as:
      _____ Underscoring
      _____ Capitals
      _____ Tabulations
      _____ Indentations
      _____ Paragraphing
   3. Dictate closing, only if differing from Item 1, "Before" section.

After

   1. Dictate names and addresses of persons receiving copies.
   2. List enclosures.
   3. Provide instructions for retention of magnetic medium.
```

Figure 4–6 Dictator's Checklist. This is a checklist of instructions to be given before, during, and after your dictation.

6. Dictate the complimentary closing and your name and title.
7. (Number) enclosures will be included.
8. Please send a copy of the letter to (name, title, and address).

How to Dictate a Memorandum

1. This is (your name) in (office/division/department).
2. This is a memorandum and I will need (number) copies.
3. It is to be addresed to (name/title/department).
4. It is from (your name and title).
5. Dictate the subject and message, indicating paragraphs and punctuation when possible.

Dear Ms. Leland:

Are you interested in speaking on the topic of your choice at the 45th Annual Convention of the Business Communication Association to be held in St. Louis on May 25? Your name was suggested to me by several individuals who have heard you make excellent presentations at other meetings.

The following session times are available: 10:30, 1:30, and 3:30. If you will be able to speak, please select whichever time best fits into your schedule, as well as choose the topic of your presentation.

Our convention speakers are given a $200 honorarium, in addition to the reimbursement of travel expenses. Complimentary tickets are also given to speakers who are available to attend the various meal functions during the convention.

I hope your busy schedule will allow you to speak at our convention. Please let me know your decision as soon as possible.

Yes, schedule Clear

1:30 Nonverbal Communication

Won't be able to stay for meal functions

Figure 4–7 Marginal Notations

Wood-Tone Computer Desk
- how much assembly required?
- adjustable height for keyboard?
- freight charges from St. Louis to Chicago?
- wood finishes?

answers needed within 3 weeks

Figure 4–8 Dictation Notes

6. This memo will be accompanied by (number of) enclosures (or attachments).
7. Address an envelope to (name(s) and addresses(es) of recipient(s)).

How to Dictate a Table

1. This is (your name) in (office/division/department).
2. This is a table.
3. The title of the table is (title of table).
4. This table contains (number of) column headings. They are (name of column headings).
5. The longest line in each column contains spaces (number of) respectively.

Dictated:

Ms. M. R. Pierre
7510 Hale
St. Louis, Missouri 67890

Dear Melissa:

I heartily share your belief that effective communication is one of the biggest problems of business today.

I am convinced that a great deal of effectiveness is lost in the simple mechanics of dictation. Perhaps a good communications training program would have some value in your organization.

Mr. Pitt, of the X-L Company, has developed an excellent dictation training course. If you will contact him at 444-8018, he will be happy to give you some suggestions.

I am looking forward to seeing how you approach this problem in your company.

Sincerely,

Jack Fieden

Jack Fieden

Transcribed:

Ms. M. R. Peer
75 Tin Hall
St. Louis, Missouri 67890

Dear Ms. Peer:

I hardly share your belief that effective communication is one of the biggest problems of business today. I am convinced that a great deal of effectiveness is lost in the simple mechanics of dictation. Perhaps a good communications training program would have some value in your organization. Mr. Pit of the Excell Company has developed an excellent dictation training course. If you call him at 444-8810, he will be happy to give you some suggestions. I am looking forward to seeing how you approach this problem in your company.

Sincerely,

Jack Fiden

Jack Fiden

Figure 4–9 Illustration of How Errors Are Made

5. The first row of the table contains these numbers: (dictate numbers). The second row contains these numbers: (dictate numbers). The third row contains these numbers: (dictate numbers), and so on.

Many business writers find it helpful to dictate draft copy that will be revised. Most transcriptionists would rather type from a recording than decipher an illegibly written draft. Reading and correcting each message that you dictate is important. You, not the transcriptionist, are responsible for final copy.

Proper use of the specialized dictation system within an office, together with the dictator's skill in speaking clearly and giving understandable instructions to the transcriptionist, contribute immeasurably to the efficiency of the word processing system—and to the effectiveness of the writer.

CHAPTER SUMMARY

In planning to write, you must first determine your purpose and then consider your reader. You must also determine appropriate content.

Once you have planned your writing, your next step to organize your material by outlining the topics. You then determine the appropriate order or sequence of topics.

The next step is the drafting process. During the actual writing, you need to be concerned about sentence and paragraph construction, as well as beginning and ending paragraphs and body composition.

Once the drafting is completed, you must edit your work. A number of suggestions are presented in this chapter that will enable you to edit more effectively. Once the final draft is prepared, proofreading is critical.

The development of a good dictation skill will also help you save considerable origination time and enable you to originate work at times when a secretary is unavailable to take your dictation.

REVIEW QUESTIONS

1. In considering the reader of the message you are preparing to write, what factors should you take into consideration?
2. How can you increase your reader's receptivity to your message?
3. Why is the careful outlining of your message prior to actual writing important?
4. To help determine the appropriate order of the topics you plan to discuss in your message, what questions should you ask yourself?
5. What is the most emphatic position of a complex sentence? A compound-complex sentence?
6. Why is variety in sentence construction important?
7. When is a dangling modifier most likely to occur?
8. How can you attain sentence brevity?
9. What is an expletive?
10. For what is the subjunctive mood especially useful?
11. What are the two prominent locations of topic sentences in paragraphs?
12. How can you increase the coherency of paragraphs?

13. Identify several ways to improve the effectiveness of the beginning paragraph of a letter.
14. Identify several ways to improve the effectiveness of the ending paragraph of a letter.
15. In editing your work, against what broad areas should you evaluate your work?
16. How are marginal notes used in the dictation process?

APPLICATION PROBLEMS

1. Assume you are about to write a letter requesting information about a new electronic stereo system you recently saw advertised. In the letter to the manufacturer of the system (Model No. K-80), you ask for answers about the following: the wattage of the speakers, the size of the speakers, the type of stylus (needle) the turntable is equipped with, whether or not the system is equipped with a tape deck, and cost of the system. Prepare an outline of the material you plan to include in your letter.

2. For each of the sentences/paragraphs that follow, identify the major flaw and then rewrite the material eliminating the flaw. No sentence/paragraph contains more than one major flaw. All but three flaws found in the following list are found in the sentences/paragraphs:

1. Lacks unity
2. Contains subjunctive mood
3. Lacks variety
4. Contains incorrect use of modifier
5. Contains faulty sequence of ideas
6. Lacks brevity
7. Lacks coherence
8. Includes faulty emphasis
9. Contains negative tone
10. Lacks parallelism
11. Contains expletive
12. Contains passive voice
13. Contains unclear topic sentence

a. Smelling of alcohol, the policeman arrested the driver.

b. Two prerequisites to good health, eating right and exercising, are important as early as age 3.

c. We cannot send you the new policy until you surrender your old policy.

d. There are three things you should remember when writing a business letter: consider your reader, determine your purpose, and determine the appropriate content to include.

e. You should first consider your reader when writing a business letter. Then you should determine the purpose of your letter. Then you should determine the appropriate content to include.

f. Apply the correct rules of grammar and punctuation after making sure you have spelled correctly each word in your letter will enable you to prepare more effective written communication.

g. The report was to have been prepared by him.

h. I plan to sit for the CPA exam in June, and my campus activities are outlined on the attached data sheet.

i. In order to be as successful as you can during your lifetime, you should remember that it is always important to work hard and it is also important to have clearcut, well-defined goals.

j. An effective business letter has a clear-cut purpose. Keep the reader in mind.

3. Revise the following material to include a variety of sentence structures:

> James Vickers is president of Vickers, Inc. W. A. Jones is vice-president in charge of investments. I. A. Evans is vice-president in charge of systems. T. V. Pickens heads purchasing. J. M. Stewart runs the legal department. Their investment portfolio totals more than ten million dollars. A new computerized system has contributed to a streamlined operation. The purchasing department has been divided into five divisions under Pickens' leadership. Stewart's skill in negotiation has been beneficial in the company's efforts to buy out some of their suppliers.

4. Revise the following opening paragraph of a letter that was prepared to acknowledge the shipment of the customer's order:

> Your order of October 3 is appreciated. It will be sent tomorrow. I am sure you will find that the Christmas ornaments you ordered will sell quickly in the upcoming Christmas season.

5. Revise the following closing paragraph of a letter that was prepared to inform a credit applicant that her application for credit is being denied:

> We regret that we cannot open a credit account for you at this time.

6. Compose a paragraph to accompany the following topic sentence that is to be used as its first sentence:

> Our Model 80, which is a new product in our television line, has become an instant success.

7. Compose a paragraph to accompany the following topic sentence that is to be used as its last sentence:

> Now you can see why we are so excited about our new Model 80 television set.

8. Using the proofreader's marks found in Figure 4–5, correct the following sentences:

a. The Annual management confernce of ABC, Inc., being scheduled for December and you hotel is being considered for the cite.

b. We are planning to use your the conference facilities.

c. The confernce is tentatively scheduled for Dec. 10–14.

d. Do think you that your facilities will accomodate 1200 participants?

e. There is a banquet scheduled for the evening of December 12.

f. Your well known catering service has been highly recommended to us by others who have attended conferences at your facility.

g. I will appreciate your responding by July 1.

9. The following topics are to be included in a paper about word processing. Prepare a topical outline, paying particular attention to the proper sequencing of the topics. Edit the wording of the topics.

The personnel component of word processing
The administrative support concept
The equipment component of word processing
Word processing defined
The cost reduction advantage of word processing
The procedures component of word processing
Text-editing equipment
Early developments in word processing
The faster-turnaround advantage of word processing
The centralized structure of word processing
Dictation/recording equipment
The better-quality-of-work advantage of word processing
The integrated structure of word processing
Historical development of word processing
Word processing: A description
Copier equipment
The greater-productivity advantage of word processing
The special-purpose structure of word processing
The increased-efficiency advantage of word processing
The decentralized structure of word processing
Current developments in word processing

10. Use a tape recorder to record your dictation of the letter shown in Figure 4–9. As you dictate the letter, provide the necessary directions to the transcriber so that the letter, when transcribed, will be identical to the "dictated" version of the letter in Figure 4–9.

Chapter 5

Direct-Request Letters

LEARNING OBJECTIVES

After studying this chapter, you should be able to

1. Identify the suggested plan used in writing each of the direct-request letters presented in this chapter.
2. Explain how the opening that is appropriate for a direct-inquiry letter may differ from the opening of an indirect-inquiry letter.
3. Identify the qualities of effective claim letters.
4. Identify the situations for which the different types of credit-request letters are written.
5. Identify several ways to improve the effectiveness of letters requesting favors.
6. Prepare effective letters of the type discussed in this chapter.

A variety of situations result in the need to write direct-request letters. For example, if you are interested in obtaining information about a product from a manufacturer or information about a job applicant from a former employer, you will prepare a direct inquiry. In addition to direct inquiries, other types of direct-request letters are: indirect inquiries, claims, orders, invitations, reservations, requests for credit, and favors.

How do direct-request and persuasive letters differ from one another?

Direct-request letters are among the most common types of letters written in the business world. While direct-request letters make requests of their recipients, they differ markedly from persuasive letters (sales, collection, and special request) that also make requests. The primary difference between direct-request and persuasive letters is the amount of motivationally oriented material that must be included to get the recipient to comply with the request. Recipients will be more willing to comply with the requests in direct-request letters than with the requests in persuasive letters. Therefore, the inclusion of motivationally oriented material designed to obtain compliance with a request is not as important in a direct-request letter as in a persuasive letter.

DIRECT-INQUIRY LETTERS

In this section, the preparation of two types of direct-inquiry letters is discussed: those that request information about products or services and those that request information about people.

Requesting Information About Products or Services

Organizations that receive letters of inquiry about their products or services find their responses to these letters can be an effective sales technique. Direct-inquiry letters are welcomed in most organizations because of their impact on generating sales. Large organizations often employ individuals whose major job responsibility involves preparing responses to inquiry letters.

What is your goal in preparing direct-inquiry letters?

Your goal in preparing direct-inquiry letters is to make responding as easy as possible for the recipient. For the reasons identified above, you need not be particularly concerned about motivating the recipient to respond. Rather, your main concern is to present your inquiry with as much clarity as possible so the recipient will be able to respond completely and accurately without having to prepare additional correspondence.

You are generally advised to begin a direct-inquiry letter with the request rather than with explanatory material. Placing the request after the explanatory material results in a slow-start opening, as the following example illustrates.

Change: I am thinking of purchasing a new letter-quality printer for my ABC personal computer system. This printer would primarily be used when I am using the computer as a word processor. I use the Electronic Word Processing software package. Will all of the F–10–80 printer functions be operational when using my computer system and word processing software?

To: Will all of the functions of the F–10–80 letter-quality printer be operational when using the Electronic Word Processing software on an ABC personal computer system?

Notice how much faster the revised version gets to the main purpose of the letter. The first version lacks conciseness and tells the reader something he/she can easily infer: The printer will be used primarily when the system is being used as a word processor.

The first of the following two paragraphs also has a slow-start beginning. You will notice that the second version is much faster because it avoids telling the reader something he/she can easily infer.

Change: My wife, son, and I are planning to travel to Yellowstone Park this summer. While in that area we want to do several things, including half-day hiking trips, horseback riding, and trout fishing. Could you please send me information about the hiking trails in the vicinity of Jackson Hole, as well as information about the dude ranches and the location of trout streams open to the public?

To: Could you please send me information about the following facilities in the vicinity of Jackson Hole: trails for half-day hiking trips, dude ranches, and trout streams open to the public.

Occasionally when you are requesting information about a product or service, you may have several specific questions to ask. The most important question is usually asked first, and the less important questions follow. If you are asking a number of questions, you may want to consider putting the questions in an enumerated list.

Which question should be asked first in direct-inquiry letters?

Could you please send me information that answers the following questions about the S–R electronic typewriter:

1. Can the typewriter be used as a computer printer?
2. If so, does it require a serial or parallel interface?
3. What is the typewriter's memory capacity?
4. What is the printing speed of the typewriter?
5. Can a fabric ribbon be used on the device?

After the request is presented in the opening of the direct-inquiry letter, explanatory material is then included. Explanatory material may include the reason for the request or information that the recipient will find useful in preparing the response. For example, assume you received the following letter.

Where is explanatory material included in direct-inquiry letters?

Could you please send me information about the activities available to families visiting the Jackson Hole area.

I would appreciate your sending this information as soon as possible as we are planning a trip to Yellowstone Park this summer.

When responding to this letter, the writer will either have to make several basic assumptions, which may or may not be correct, or will have to send a letter seeking clarification about several things. For example, if children are involved, what are their ages? Does the family prefer out-of-door or indoor activities? Does the family prefer strenuous or more sedentary-type activities? Is the family interested in nighttime as well as daytime activities? Including a few more details in the letter presented above would have simplified the task of preparing a helpful response.

The following paragraph illustrates an effective explanation section of a direct-inquiry letter.

> The TAC computer system I am thinking of purchasing comes with several software packages, including the Word Write word processing package. While I have the need for a word processing system, I also have the need for a typewriter for some of the work I do. Purchasing an electronic typewriter that can also be used as a computer printer will enable me to save several hundred dollars.

What type of closing should be used in direct-inquiry letters?

The last section of the direct-inquiry letter is the closing, which should be action-oriented. Suggesting the action you wish the reader to take is likely to produce better results than the familiar ''I will appreciate your assistance'' closing. Making it easy for the recipient to respond, when appropriate, is also advised. You may also want to consider providing the date by which you wish to have the reply to your request. Notice the difference between these two closings.

> Change: I will appreciate your sending me the requested information.
> To: A quick reply to my questions will enable me to decide if the S–R electronic typewriter will meet my needs. Your answers to my questions, which can be sent to me on the pre-addressed card I'm enclosing, will be appreciated.

What is the suggested plan for direct-inquiry letters?

The suggested plan for a direct-inquiry letter includes the following elements:

1. An opening that contains the primary request and secondary requests;
2. An explanation that includes the reasons for the requests or provides additional helpful background information;
3. A closing that suggests the action you wish the recipient to take, that makes action easy to take (if appropriate), and that expresses appreciation for assistance.

Figure 5–1 illustrates an ineffective letter that requests information about a database software program. The letter in Figure 5–2 is an improved version of the letter. Notice how much more specific the request is in Figure 5–2.

Figure 5–1 Ineffective Letter Requesting Information About a Product

I am interested in learning more about your database software program. Please send me any information you may have.	A slow-start opening that fails to make specific identification of desired information.
I plan to use the database software to maintain a variety of different types of records.	A section that contains a weak explanation about why the information is desired.
Thank you for sending this information to me.	A closing that "thanks in advance."

```
Could you please send me information that will
answer the following questions about your D-B
database software program:

1. Will the program operate on a DECCA 8000
   Computer?

2. Is this software program interactive?

3. How many fields can be created for each
   record?

4. Does this software package come with a teach
   disk?

5. Do you provide a toll-free number for user
   support?

I plan to use a database program to maintain the
following types of employee records:  name, Social
Security number, present job title, years with the
company, years in present position, number of
years of formal education, and present salary.

A quick response to my request will enable me to
decide soon which database program best meets my
needs.  Your answering these questions, in
addition to your providing any other information
that might be helpful, will be greatly
appreciated.
```

A fast-start opening that lists questions for which answers are desired.

A section that contains explanatory material.

A courteous, action-oriented closing.

Figure 5–2 Effective Letter Requesting Information About a Product

Requesting Information About a Person

Beginning a direct-inquiry letter with the request seems a little abrupt in some instances, especially when requesting information about a person. For example, when a person is being considered as a job applicant, the potential employer often requests information about the applicant's work performance from one or more previous employers. To begin the letter with the first of the following two paragraphs is abrupt, while the revised version is more effective.

What type of opening is appropriate when requesting information about a person?

Change: Does William Duff work well with others? Is his work always well done? Does he get his work done on time? In his application for a job as assistant personnel manager, he listed your name as a reference.

To: Mr. William Duff, who has listed your name as a reference, is being considered for the position of assistant personnel manager. I will appreciate your providing answers to the following questions:

1. How well does he work with others?
2. How effective are his oral and written communication skills?
3. How would you rate the quality of his work in comparison with your other employees?
4. How well does he meet deadlines?
5. How would you rate his enthusiasm and initiative?
6. Why did he leave your company?

The wording of the questions in a direct-inquiry letter will determine how much information you are likely to receive in the answer. If you desire more than a yes or no answer, structure the questions in such a way that more than a yes or no answer will be provided. For example, a yes or no answer is probably all that would have been provided had the first question in the example above been stated: "Does he work well with others?"

In selecting questions to pose in letters requesting information about the work performance of former employees, the writer has to make certain that the questions are bonafide. This means that only those questions relating to one's work performance can be asked. Unless the writer can prove that a question has job relevance, it should not be asked. Asking irrelevant questions may have legal repercussions.

What should be included in the explanatory section of letters that request information about a job applicant?

The explanation section of a letter requesting information about a job applicant can include a discussion of pertinent job requirements. By providing the recipient with this information, he/she will be in a better position to judge whether or not the applicant is qualified. Notice how the following two paragraphs differ in the amount of detail presented about job requirements.

Change: A customer service representative performs a variety of duties including the following: interacting with customers and other employees.

To: Among the duties performed by a customer service representative are the following: (1) answering questions asked by customers, (2) referring customers to others who can answer their questions, (3) keeping detailed records about the nature of the service provided, (4) keeping abreast of new developments that are likely to stimulate customers' questions, and (5) interacting with other employees.

What should be included in the closing of letters in which information about a person is requested?

The second of the following two paragraphs illustrates the benefits of using an action-oriented closing with a suggested reply date when requesting information about a person. You may also wish to affirm your intention to treat confidentially any information you receive.

Change: Your assistance will be greatly appreciated.

To: The answers you give us to the above questions will be helpful in assessing the suitability of Ms. Rickardo for the position of customer service representative. Having this input by June 15 will help us keep on our schedule for filling this position. Any information you can provide us about Ms. Rickardo, which we will keep confidential, will be greatly appreciated.

What is the suggested plan for letters that request information about a person?

The suggested plan for a letter in which information about a job applicant is requested includes the following elements:

1. An opening that mentions the name of the person who has given the reader's name as a reference;
2. A list of the questions that you would like to have answered;

3. A brief discussion of the common duties of the job for which the applicant has applied;
4. A courteous, action-oriented closing.

While Figure 5–3 illustrates a poorly prepared letter of inquiry about a person's work performance, Figure 5–4 is an effective revision. Specific answers are likely to be obtained for the specific questions asked in Figure 5–4.

Figure 5–3 Ineffective Letter Requesting Information About a Person

We have a vacancy on our staff for a sales representative. John Jack, a former employee of yours, has applied for this position and has used your name as a reference.	An opening that fails to contain the request for information.
Would you please provide me with information that will be helpful in deciding whether or not to hire Mr. Jack?	A section that contains a delayed request for imprecisely identified information.
I shall appreciate your assistance.	A closing that lacks action orientation.

Figure 5–4 Effective Letter Requesting Information About a Person

Mr. John Jack, a former employee of yours, has listed your name as a reference on his application for a sales representative position in our company. Your providing me with answers to the following questions will enable me to better assess his suitability for employment:	An opening that contains background information and the primary request.
1. How well does Mr. Jack work with others? 2. How well developed are Mr. Jack's oral and written communication skills? 3. How well developed are Mr. Jack's leadership skills? 4. In comparison with other employees of yours, how would you rate Mr. Jack's performance? 5. Why did Mr. Jack leave your company? 6. If you had an opportunity to do so, would you re-employ Mr. Jack? Why?	A section that identifies the desired information.
Among the duties commonly performed by our sales representatives are the following: serving our present clients, acquiring new clients, and preparing a variety of reports.	A section that contains a discussion of the duties to be performed by the job holder.
The information you provide, which will be held in strict confidence, will enable us to better assess Mr. Jack's qualifications for a sales representative position. Because we hope to fill this position by August 1, we will appreciate receiving your input within the next two weeks.	An action-oriented closing that mentions the confidential handling of information.

Direct-inquiry letters are also used to request information about credit applicants. While credit reports provided by credit bureaus are often used to obtain pertinent information about credit applicants, information can also be obtained from credit references.

What should be included in the opening of letters that request information about a credit applicant?

A fast-start opening that requests answers to questions and also mentions that the recipient of the letter was listed as a reference on the applicant's credit application is suggested. Notice the difference in the pace of the following two paragraphs.

Change: We have received Jack Chun's application for a charge account. He listed your name as a credit reference on his credit application. Would you please respond to the following questions?

To: Would you please respond to the following questions about Jack Chun who listed your name as a credit reference on his application for credit?

In soliciting information from credit references, questions similar to those shown below are asked. In some cases, the questions are printed on a separate form; in other cases, the questions are incorporated into the letter.

1. How long has this individual had a credit account with your company?
   ____
2. What is the credit limit this individual has been extended?
   ____
3. What is the highest amount of credit this individual has ever had?
   ____
4. Has this individual ever been delinquent in paying his/her credit account? Yes ______; No ______ (If no, go to No. 5) How many times? ______ What is the average length of time this individual's credit account has been delinquent? ______________
5. What is today's balance of this individual's account? ______________

What is the suggested plan for letters that request information about credit applicants?

The suggested plan for a direct-inquiry letter of this type includes the following elements:

1. An opening which mentions the applicant's name and that the recipient of the letter was listed as a credit reference on the applicant's application;
2. A list of the questions that you would like to have answered;
3. A statement that assures the information will be held in confidence;
4. An action-oriented closing that expresses appreciation to the credit reference.

An example of a letter requesting credit information from a credit reference is illustrated in Figure 5–5. Notice that specific questions are asked.

Your answering the following questions about the credit worthiness of Sally Brown, who has listed your name as a reference, will help us assess her suitability for a Skinner's charge account.

An opening that mentions the credit applicant's name and that makes a request for information about the applicant.

1. What is the credit limit you have extended to Ms. Brown?

2. How long has Ms. Brown had a credit account with your company?

3. What is the maximum amount of credit that you have ever extended to Ms. Brown?

4. How many times in the last three years has Ms. Brown been delinquent in paying her account?

5. What is the current amount of credit Ms. Brown has been extended?

A section that presents questions designed to facilitate the reader's ease in responding.

You have our assurance that this information will be treated as confidential.

A section that contains a statement which assures the confidential handling of information.

Your sending answers to these questions within the next 10 days will be appreciated. If we can ever reciprocate, please let us know.

An action-oriented closing that offers to return the favor.

Figure 5–5 Effective Letter in Which Credit Information is Requested

INDIRECT-INQUIRY LETTERS

For what are indirect-inquiry letters used?

The indirect-inquiry letter is used to request general information rather than answers to specific questions. In some instances a direct-inquiry letter is prepared because of questions that arise in the reader's mind after reading the general information he/she had earlier requested. In other instances, the general information answers any questions the reader may have.

The primary difference between the indirect- and direct-inquiry letter is the specificity of the request. If you have one or more specific questions, you will want to use the direct-inquiry letter. But if you simply desire general information, an indirect-inquiry letter will suffice.

Except for the request, the other sections of both types of letters are generally quite similar. In some instances, the nature of the request may cause you to provide more details in the explanatory section of a direct-inquiry letter than in the same section of an indirect-inquiry letter. The closing of some direct-inquiry letters may also be more detailed than the closing of indirect-inquiry letters.

How do the openings of direct- and indirect-inquiry letters differ?

The opening of an indirect-inquiry letter can be less specific than the opening of a direct-inquiry letter. You are cautioned to avoid preparing such a general opening for an indirect-inquiry letter that the recipient will have difficulty responding. The first of the following two paragraphs illustrates the opening of an indirect-inquiry letter that is too general to be of much help to the recipient. The revised version is more specific—and therefore will be more helpful to the individual who has to prepare the response.

Change:	Do you have packets available to individuals visiting your city? If so, please send me one.
To:	Would you please send me information about points of interest and scheduled events for families visiting in the Detroit area.

The first opening fails to make clear that the activities should be family oriented. Although the recipient of the letter can probably surmise that the desired information is to pertain to "things to see and do," the revised version removes all doubts about what type of information is desired. Both openings get to the point quickly; however, the later opening will be more helpful to the individual preparing the response.

How do the explanatory sections of direct- and indirect-inquiry letters differ?

The explanatory sections of direct- and indirect-inquiry letters may not vary much from one another. The paragraph that follows illustrates an appropriate explanatory section for an indirect-inquiry letter. You will notice that the writer decided to include several pertinent details.

> My wife and two sons (ages 14 and 12) plan to accompany me to Detroit for a convention that I am attending June 14–18. While I am attending daytime meetings, they want to do as much sight-seeing in the Detroit area as possible. Because they will not have access to a car, they will have to depend on public transportation to get around.

Had the details not been provided in the above paragraph, the individual making the request may have received a quantity of information that would not have been useful. By including these details, the recipient has a better idea of what information is appropriate to send to the person making the request.

What is the suggested plan for indirect-inquiry letters?

The suggested plan for an indirect-inquiry letter includes the following elements:

1. An opening that contains the requests;
2. An explanation which includes the reasons for the request or that provides additional background information that will be helpful in complying with the request;
3. A courteous, action-oriented closing.

The weaknesses in the indirect-inquiry letter shown in Figure 5–6 have been eliminated in the improved version shown in Figure 5–7. Notice the helpful details that have been included in Figure 5–7.

CLAIM LETTERS

Customer claims and requests for adjustments can be expected in today's high-volume business operations. In business, as in other human activities, errors occur. Regardless of how much effort a business puts into error-free operations, some errors will occur. The manner in which an organization deals with the claims it receives will affect its reputation.

When you have a legitimate complaint about a product or service, you should make it known to the manufacturer or supplier. Organizations espe-

I am interested in obtaining information about the Delta office copier I recently saw advertised in an office publication.	An opening that contains the request for imprecisely identified information about an imprecisely identified product.
Until now, my office could not justify the purchase of a copier. Rental was more feasible. Now, it appears that we may be able to justify purchasing a copier.	A section that contains a weak explanation of the reason for the request.
I will appreciate your assistance.	A weak closing that lacks action orientation.

Figure 5–6 Ineffective Indirect-Inquiry Letter

Would you please send me the illustrated promotional packet that was mentioned in a Delta Max office copier ad I recently saw?	An opening that contains a request for specific information about a specific product.
I am interested in investigating the feasibility of purchasing a copier for use in an office in which 350-500 copies are made per month. The copier will also need to be capable of reducing and enlarging material.	A section that presents a discussion of important background information.
Your sending the requested materials soon will be appreciated as I plan to make a purchasing decision within the next few weeks.	An action-oriented closing.

Figure 5–7 Effective Indirect-Inquiry Letter

cially welcome receiving claim letters when the nature of a complaint is likely to produce legitimate complaints from other customers. Remedying the situation giving rise to a complaint before it becomes a monstrous problem for the organization is a highly desirable business practice.

Bases for Claims

Most routine claims involving minor sums of money are usually easily adjusted. While some claims arise because products are actually defective, a greater number of claims arise because merchandise fails to meet expected quality standards. Although the seller may or may not be at fault for the defective product, the disappointed buyer naturally directs the claim to the company from which the item was purchased. Responsible business firms usually take immediate steps to settle claims and make adjustments.

What are the bases for claims about service?

Claims against service connected with purchases are far more common than against the products themselves. The following list summarizes the bases for claims about service:

1. Merchandise not received
2. Part of the merchandise not received
3. Wrong merchandise received
4. Substituted merchandise not wanted

5. Damaged merchandise received
6. Merchandise received too late
7. Merchandise sent to wrong address
8. Error made in prices of merchandise
9. Error made in discount
10. Error made in statement
11. Charge included for goods returned
12. Statement received for bill already paid
13. Employee incompetence or rudeness

Qualities of Effective Claim Letters

What qualities do effective claim letters possess?

Before you begin the process of preparing a claim letter, you will want to be familiar with the following qualities of effective claim letters:

1. An effective claim letter does not threaten.
2. An effective claim letter presents all the facts pertinent to the situation.
3. The writer of an effective claim letter does not take his/her anger out on the recipient—who most likely had nothing to do with the writer's dissatisfaction with the product or service.
4. An effective claim letter, by containing you-attitude material, will help the recipient realize the advantage of making an adjustment.
5. An effective claim letter makes a definite request, such as one of the following:
   a. Replacement of the product or service
   b. Partial or full refund on the purchase price of the product or service
   c. Replacement shipment which contains the merchandise that was ordered
   d. Repair of the defective product
   e. Cancellation of an order or a portion of the order
   f. Correction of an error in billing, such as overcharging for merchandise, tax, and shipping
   g. Clarification of a procedure

Structure of Effective Claim Letters

Carefully planned claim letters encourage the recipient to take a specific action that will benefit the writer. To ensure such action, your first concern must be to state clearly the nature of the claim. You should refer to your order number, date of the order, and any other specific reference material that is available. Exactly what happened? Just how has the firm failed to provide the goods or services that you expected? Precisely which merchandise was omitted from the order, and how did the original order read? All statements should be specific.

What is the primary purpose of claim letters?

Throughout the letter, you should remember that the primary purpose of a claim letter is to stimulate action that will rectify an error and compensate for a loss. The chances of your receiving a satisfactory adjustment will be enhanced if you avoid antagonizing the reader. You should also avoid making disparaging remarks about the quality of products or services you received.

The opening paragraph in a claim letter should mention the nature of the claim. Notice the difference between the two opening paragraphs that follow. In the first paragraph, the inclusion of disparaging remarks about product quality delays the request. The revised version is much more direct.

What should be included in the opening of claim letters?

> Change: Had I known on October 5 what I know now about the quality (or lack thereof) of your blank cassette tapes, I would not have purchased a box of 12 tapes. In fact, I would not have purchased even one tape.
>
> To: On October 5 I purchased from your company a box of 12 blank cassette tapes that I am returning in exchange for a cash refund of $45.48.

Once the request has been made in the opening, explanatory material should be presented as precisely and directly as possible in an impersonal and courteous manner. Notice the tonal differences between the following two paragraphs.

What are the characteristics of the explanatory materials included in claim letters?

> Change: Tapes of the quality of those I purchased should never be allowed on the market. The subtle sounds in the music I want to record cannot be detected on play back. In addition, I noticed distracting interference on play-back that I do not get when using higher-quality tapes. Perhaps this tape would be suitable for use on a child's recorder—but never for a professional musician.
>
> To: I record all of my professional appearances for use in the piano classes I teach at Oakdale College. Because my students learn much from these recorded tapes, recording clarity is essential. The three tapes I used did not produce the clarity I desire, especially in the play-back of the subtle sounds. The tape also contains distracting background noise that cannot be erased or recorded over.

The inclusion of you-attitude material in a claim letter is suggested when such material is appropriate for the situation. Inappropriate you-attitude material often weakens a claim letter more than its absence does. To include material similar to that found in the first of the following two paragraphs will obviously reduce the effectiveness of a claim letter.

> Change: I believe we all benefit by having the shortcomings of our products or services pointed out. By overcoming these shortcomings, we can improve our relationships with our customers or clients.
>
> To: Perhaps you will want to test the remaining nine unopened tapes to see if they are like the three that were used. I did not erase the material recorded on the three tapes so you can also hear the distracting background noise.

The closing of effective claim letters should be action oriented and leave no doubt in the recipient's mind of the action you want him/her to take. The first of the following two closings is ineffective because it is not action oriented and it is overused, worn-out, and sterile. The action-oriented nature of the revised closing is much more effective.

What type of closing is appropriate for claim letters?

Change: Your prompt attention to this matter will be greatly appreciated.
To: Because I have already replaced these tapes with others, I will appreciate your quickly refunding the purchase price of the 12 tapes being returned.

What is the suggested plan for claim letters?

The suggested plan for a claim letter includes the following elements:

1. A request for the desired adjustment;
2. An explanation that provides important details about the need for an adjustment;
3. A section containing you-attitude material (if appropriate);
4. A courteous, action-oriented closing that mentions the desired adjustment.

The claim letter illustrated in Figure 5–8 is not likely to enhance the relationship between the writer and the recipient. The weaknesses inherent in Figure 5–8 have been removed from the revised version found in Figure 5–9. Notice the you-attitude material in the third paragraph of Figure 5–9.

ORDER LETTERS

Normally, order blanks or purchase orders are used when ordering merchandise by mail. However, when neither order blanks nor purchase orders are available, you can prepare an order letter, which is considered by many to be the easiest type of letter to write. Because the recipient of your letter is in business to sell merchandise, getting his/her compliance with your request is not a concern. A much more significant concern is communicating clearly and thoroughly pertinent information about the merchandise you desire.

Figure 5–8 Ineffective Claim Letter

Let's see if you can stand behind your service better than the quality of products you manufacture. The third time the Transparency Maker was used that we purchased from you last month, it malfunctioned and has malfunctioned four more times since then. Obviously, we received a lemon that I am returning to you--along with a request that it be exchanged for a new machine.	A curt opening that contains a delayed request for the adjustment.
A machine as undependable as this one does not have much going for it. We simply cannot afford to keep such an undependable machine. It seems as if the machine was typically inoperable at the times when it was most needed.	A section that contains a weak discussion about why the adjustment is desired; lacks you-attitude material.
I will appreciate your prompt attention to the replacement of the Transparency Maker that is being returned.	A weak closing.

The Transparency Maker we purchased from you on December 12 is being returned, and we are requesting that it be replaced with a new Maker.	An opening that presents the desired adjustment.
On five occasions during the month that we have had the Maker, it was inoperable at critical times. Because we bought the machine primarily to make transparencies on very short notice, several of our executives were severely inconvenienced when they were unable to make transparencies for use during their presentations. When the Maker is inoperable, we either have to use an outside service or do without the desired transparencies.	A section that provides important details about the need for the adjustment.
The concern your company has for its customers convinces me that you will want us to own a Maker worthy of its excellent reputation.	A section that incorporates you-attitude material.
I will appreciate your replacing the Maker soon so we can provide a fast and efficient transparency-making service for our executives.	A courteous, action-oriented closing.

Figure 5–9 Effective Claim Letter

Order letters are comprised of three distinct content components: pertinent information about the items being ordered; directions for shipping the merchandise, including desired receipt date (if appropriate) and the desired shipping location (if different from your address); and the method of payment. The two common payment methods used are sending payment with the order or charging the order to an existing charge account. Some individuals also request the opening of a charge account in their name at the time the order is placed.

What content components are order letters comprised of?

Depending on the merchandise being ordered, the following information may need to be included about each item: quantity, catalog number, name of item, model number, color, size, pattern, finish, grade, weight, unit price, and extension (unit price multiplied by quantity). The omission of any of these details may result in the need for the recipient to clarify this information before the order can be filled—or the recipient may try to anticipate your preference, which may or may not meet with your approval.

What is the suggested plan for order letters?

The suggested plan for an order letter includes the following elements:

1. An opening which mentions your request: ''Please ship by parcel post the following items'':;
2. A section detailing the pertinent information about the items being ordered;
3. A section which outlines the method of payment;
4. A courteous closing that is action oriented.

The order letter found in Figure 5–10 omits several important details that could result in the need for clarification before the order can be filled. Figure 5–11 presents an effective order letter.

I am ordering the following items from your catalog I recently received: 1 crew neck sweater, 2 pairs of argyle men's socks, and 1 all-weather hat.	An opening that fails to include needed information about items being ordered.
Please charge these items to my MasterCard (Account No. 564-4444-554B) and send them to the address shown at the top of this letter.	A closing void of action-oriented material.

Figure 5–10 Ineffective Order Letter

Please ship by UPT the following items:

A fast-start opening that contains important information about items being ordered.

QUAN-TITY	CAT. NO.	DESCRIP-TION	SIZE	PRICE	UNIT TOTAL
1	55-89-3	Sweater	M	28.99	28.99
2 pr.	55-87-2	Socks	M	4.99	9.98
1	55-76-3	Hat	7	12.99	12.99
					$51.96

Please charge these items to my MasterCard (account number 564-4444-554B) that has an expiration date of 9/90.

A section that outlines details about merchandise payment.

Because the sweater is to be given as a gift, your filling the order promptly so that it will be received by July 10 will be appreciated.

An action-oriented, courteous closing.

Figure 5–11 Effective Order Letter

Letters of invitation include speaking invitations as well as informal and formal social invitations. While these letters may not pertain to business as often as other types of letters discussed in this chapter, individuals in the business world need to be knowledgeable about the various types of invitation letters.

Speaking Invitations

When writing a letter inviting someone to make a presentation, the inclusion of vital information about the event will help prevent inconvenience or misunderstanding. For example, failure to specify the exact time that the presentation is to be made may inconvenience the speaker. Even worse is the possibility that the speaker will have to decline the invitation he/she previously accepted because of a misunderstanding about the time of the presentation.

What details should be included in letters of invitation?

Important details to include in the letter of invitation are: the name of the group before which the presentation will be made; a few characteristics about the group to help the speaker tailor his/her remarks to the audience; the desired length of the presentation; the topic of the presentation; the date, the time, and the location. Any transportation and/or lodging arrangements that will be made for out-of-town speakers should also be mentioned in the letter as well as the amount of the honorarium if one is being given.

As with other direct-request letters, a fast-start opening that extends the invitation in the opening paragraph is desirable. The request is delayed in the first of the following two paragraphs, while the revised version contains a fast-start opening.

What type of opening is appropriate for speaking-invitation letters?

Change: The annual meeting of the Administrative Management Society chapters in Pennsylvania, Ohio, and West Virginia is being held in Pittsburgh on October 8–10. This meeting will be held at the downtown Holiday Inn.

To: The committee planning the annual meeting of the Administrative Management Society chapters in Pennsylvania, Ohio, and West Virginia cordially invites you to be a guest speaker at one of the sessions on the afternoon of October 10. Because you were recommended by several persons as an outstanding speaker, we especially hope that you will be able to accept this invitation.

After the opening, the next section contains details about the presentation. As much detail as possible should be presented, especially when inviting busy people to make a presentation. Failure to include this information may result in the need for the speaker to prepare a letter asking for additional information before being able to determine if he/she is available.

Notice how much essential information is missing from the first of the following paragraphs, while the revised version contains the essential information.

Change: The individuals who will be attending this meeting typically are involved with the administrative management function within their respective organizations. While some are more involved with the office function, others are more involved with the financial function. Would you be available to make an hour-long presentation during this meeting?

To: The individuals who typically attend this meeting have varied backgrounds, with the following job titles being the most common: office manager, comptroller, personnel manager, and executive vice president. While the decision about the topic of your presentation is yours to make, we suggest that it pertain to the functions performed by individuals with these job titles.

Sessions from 1–2 and from 3–4 are still available. We would like for you to choose the most convenient time. If you are unavailable at either of these times on October 10, we could schedule your presentation at another time during the afternoon of October 8 or any time during the day on the 9th. All sessions will be held in the downtown Holiday Inn in Pittsburgh.

As a token of our appreciation for your taking time to make a presentation at this meeting, we will pay you an honorarium of $150. We also cordially invite you to be our guest at the closing banquet which begins at 6:30 on the evening of October 10.

What type of closing is appropriate for speaking-invitation letters?

An action-oriented closing is appropriate for a speaking-invitation letter. This means that you will identify the action you wish the recipient to take, which is to let you know of his/her decision. You may also wish to indicate the date by which you would like a response.

While the first of the following two paragraphs lacks action-oriented material, the revised version is an appropriate closing.

Change:	I look forward to hearing from you.
To:	The program planning committee hopes you will be able to accept this invitation. Could you please inform me of your decision by July 16.

What is the suggested plan for speaking-invitation letters?

The suggested plan for speaking-invitation letters includes the following elements:

1. An opening in which the speaking invitation is extended, in addition to mentioning the date and location of the invitation;
2. A discussion of the characteristics of the audience that will be helpful to the speaker in gearing his/her presentation to the participants;
3. An invitation to the speaker to select his/her presentation time, if appropriate;
4. A discussion of the accommodation arrangements that will be made for the speaker, if appropriate;
5. A courteous, action-oriented closing.

The letter illustrated in Figure 5–12 lacks several of the important elements of speaking-invitation letters. By comparing Figure 5–13 with Figure 5–12, you will notice that these weaknesses have been eliminated in the revised letter.

Figure 5–12 Ineffective Speaking-Invitation Letter

Are you available to speak to a group of credit managers on August 10? If so, please let me know as soon as possible.	An opening that lacks important details about the event.
I am responsible for finding two speakers for our annual credit managers' association meeting that will be held here in Omaha August 10 and 11. So far, I have contacted six people to speak--and only one has accepted my invitation. I hope you will also be able to accept this invitation.	A section that presents a discussion of the event; written with an I-viewpoint.
Because our organization operates on a shoe-string budget, we are only able to pay you an honorarium of $200. We would like for you to be our guest at the luncheon on August 10.	A section that presents a discussion written with a negative tone.
Please let me know as soon as you can whether or not you will be able to accept this invitation.	A weak closing.

As program chairperson of the summer conference of the Credit Manager's Association of Nebraska, I cordially invite you to speak on time management at one of our morning sessions on August 10. The conference will be held at the Hilton Inn in Omaha.	An opening that contains the invitation and that presents important details about the event.
A time management presentation similar to the one you made at the Administrative Management Conference last year would be well received by many of our members. I have implemented a number of the time-saving suggestions you made during that presentation. Your suggestions have helped me eliminate many of the time-management concerns that our members frequently discuss.	A section that contains you-attitude material.
Our members who attend these conferences are typically credit managers in medium to large-size companies. Most also supervise a staff of one to three employees.	A section that contains a discussion of the characteristics of the audience.
If you are able to make a presentation at our conference, please select whichever of the following session times best fits into your schedule on the morning of August 10: 8:45-9:45, 10-11, or 11:15-12:15.	A section that invites the reader to select the time of the presentation.
As a token of our appreciation for your making a presentation, we will pay you an honorarium of $200. We also cordially invite you to be our guest at the luncheon which begins at 12:30 on the 10th.	A discussion of the reimbursement to be offered.
Because the conference planning committee wishes to have the program finalized fairly soon, could you please let me know your decision by May 1?	An action-oriented closing.

Figure 5–13 Effective Speaking-Invitation Letter

Social-Invitation Letters

Most social invitation letters are considered informal. When more formality is needed, a formal invitation, either printed or handwritten, should be considered. A printed formal invitation is illustrated in Figure 5–14.

When preparing social-invitation letters, you must include the event; the date, time, and location of the event; and the directions for responding, if appropriate. Any other information that might be of interest to the recipient should also be included.

The suggested plan for a social-invitation letter includes the following elements:

What is the suggested plan for social-invitation letters?

1. A fast-start opening that contains the invitation;
2. A discussion of the important details that pertain to the invitation;
3. A discussion of any other information of interest;
4. A courteous, action-oriented closing which mentions what you wish the recipient to do, including any deadline date.

Figure 5–15 illustrates an effective social-invitation letter.

Mr. Henry A. Albion
requests the pleasure of your company
at a dinner
in honor of

Governor Harold Exxon

on Friday, the twenty-first of April
at seven o'clock
in the Blue Room
Sheraton-Hilton
Dallas

R.S.V.P
498-3857

Black Tie

Figure 5–14 Printed Formal Invitation

Please join us at a luncheon on May 10 to celebrate Mr. John Brown's tenth year as president of Jundall Corporation. This important event, which begins at 12:30, will be held at the Cornwall Restaurant on Ridley Road in Des Moines.

A fast-start opening that presents the invitation and that contains important information about the event to which the reader is being invited.

In addition to Jundall's executive staff, a few of the Corporation's long-time clients are also being invited. If you wish, you will have an opportunity to join others in making a public tribute to recognize Mr. Brown's significant accomplishments during his career at Jundall.

A section that presents a discussion of other important information.

Please let me know by May 1 if you will be able to attend the celebration and if you wish to deliver a tribute.

An action-oriented closing.

Figure 5–15 Effective Social-Invitation Letter

RESERVATION LETTERS

Most reservations for hotel/motel accommodations are now made either though travel agencies or the toll-free reservation number of the hotel/motel. Use of the toll-free numbers is especially prevalent when making reservations at hotels and motels belonging to a chain.

When you are attending a convention, room reservations are generally made on a form provided by the hotel/motel. The same information that appears on the reservation form should be included in a reservation letter, such as the following:

1. The type of room needed (single, double, suite);
2. Number of persons to occupy the room;
3. Arrival and departure dates;
4. Arrival and departure times;
5. Mention of a deposit or late-arrival guarantee (if appropriate);
6. Request for a written confirmation.

Putting this information into a letter will be easier if you follow the following suggested letter plan:

What is the suggested plan for reservation letters?

1. A fast-start opening which identifies the type of room desired and the days needed;
2. A section which mentions arrival and departure times as well as information about a deposit or late-arrival guarantee;
3. A courteous, action-oriented closing which mentions your desire for a confirmation, if appropriate.

Figure 5–16 illustrates a reservations letter. Notice that all of the important elements are included.

LETTERS PERTAINING TO THE REQUEST FOR CREDIT

Generally, requests for credit and requests for credit information about an individual are transmitted on forms that have been designed specifically to obtain needed information. However, when appropriate forms are not available, letters are an effective substitute.

The types of letters pertaining to the request for credit covered in this section are:

1. Routine request for credit
2. Request for credit accompanying an order
3. Routine request for additional information from a credit applicant

A fourth type of letter pertaining to the request for credit—requesting information from credit references—was discussed earlier in this chapter. (An example of such a letter is presented in Figure 5–5.)

Credit bureaus, which are found in all parts of the country, significantly decrease the investigative work that precedes the granting of credit to a customer. The first time a person applies for credit, information about his/her background will be collected and stored in the computer of a credit bureau.

The type of information collected by the credit bureau typically includes the individual's name, current address, age, marital status, bill-paying characteristics, bank references, employment history, divorces, number of dependents, bankruptcy activity, tax liens, and court actions. The information stored

What types of information about individuals do credit bureaus collect?

Figure 5–16 Effective Reservation Letter

I will appreciate your reserving for my family a room with two double beds for the nights of September 20 and 21. The reservations are for my wife and me and our two sons (ages 6 and 4).	A fast-start opening that identifies the desired accommodation.
We will be arriving before 6 p.m. on the 20th and departing early on the 22nd.	A section that discusses the arrival and departure dates.
So that we can finalize our itinerary, would you please send me within 10 days a written confirmation of our reservation?	An action-oriented closing.

in the computer is periodically updated, which enables businesses to obtain up-to-date information when making credit decisions.

The vast majority of local credit bureaus belong to the Associated Credit Bureaus, Inc., which has files on most residents of the United States. Because the bureau is nationwide, a business in Los Angeles can instantly obtain information about an individual whose file is in New York City. To use the services of the Associated Credit Bureaus, Inc., businesses purchase a yearly membership in the Bureau and pay an activity fee each time the services of the bureau are used. The function of most bureaus is not to rate or assess credit potential, but rather to supply important information to a business whose credit department will decide whether credit should be extended to an applicant.

Routine Requests for Credit

When using a letter to request credit, you may send the letter without placing an order. In other cases, the letter requesting credit is combined with an order. Using a letter to request credit without an order is discussed in this section, while a letter combining the request for credit with an order is discussed in the next section.

What type of opening is appropriate for credit-request letters?

A fast-paced opening is desirable when preparing letters requesting credit. Notice the difference between the pace of the two openings in the following paragraphs:

Change: My family and I recently moved to San Antonio from Miami, where we resided during the last 15 years. The reason for the move was to take advantage of a promotional opportunity within Drummond Corporation, which has been my employer for more than 20 years.

To: Will you please open a charge account for my wife and me in the names of

Mary B. Brown
David S. Brown
1819 Darvin Avenue
San Antonio, TX 58764

What type of information should be included in the middle sections of credit request letters?

After the opening you will want to include relevant information to help the recipient make a decision about your credit worthiness. Included in this section is information about the length of time in your present location, length of time in former location, names and addresses of credit references, place of employment, job title, and annual income. In addition, you may want to provide the name of the bank where you have a checking account, as well as the name of your former bank if you have lived in the new location only a short time. The following paragraph illustrates how this section of the routine request for credit letter might be prepared:

We moved here last month from our former residence at 2839 Virginia Street in Miami, Florida, where we had lived for 15 years. The reason for the move was a promotional transfer by my employer of 20 years, the Drummond Corporation. My new job title is Branch Manager for which I am paid $43,500 annually.

Our checking account (No. 33–456–867) is at the San Antonio National Bank. We formerly banked at the First National Bank of Miami. While living in Miami, we had charge accounts at the following stores:

Dillinger's
12 Main Street
Miami, FL 02912

Deloy Department Store
22 Main Street
Miami, Fl 02912

J. Markums
18 Broadway Ave.
Miami, FL 02912

An appropriate closing will offer to provide any additional information that may be needed to make a decision about the credit application. To illustrate, consider the following closing:

What type of closing is appropriate for credit-request letters?

Please let me know if I can provide you with any additional information that will be helpful in making a credit decision.

The suggested plan for a credit-request letter includes the following elements:

What is the suggested plan for credit-request letters?

1. An opening in which a request for credit is made;
2. A section in which relevant information is provided that will help the reader detemine the applicant's credit worthiness;
3. A courteous, action-oriented closing.

The letter shown in Figure 5–17 is virtually ineffective as a routine request for credit. The letter in Figure 5–18 is an improved version.

Combined Request for Credit and Order Letter

When preparing a combined request for credit and order letter, you will include the essential elements of both order letters and letters requesting credit.

What is the suggested plan for combined credit-request and order letters?

Figure 5–17 Ineffective Credit-Request Letter

My wife and I are interested in opening a charge account at Dillmans Department Store. Would you please open an account for us?	A slow-start opening.
We lived in San Diego from 1975 until just recently when we moved here. We had charge accounts at the following stores in San Diego: Drake Department Store, J. L. Jackson Department Store, and Knapps.	A section that presents a limited amount of background information.
Because we enjoy the convenience of charge-account shopping, will you please open an account for us as soon as possible?	An action-oriented closing.

Please open a charge account for my wife, Ellen S. Brown, and me, John D. Brown.	A fast-start opening that presents the request.
I was recently transferred here by my employer, the Dickson Manufacturing Company, after I accepted the plant manager's position in the new Dickson facility that just opened. Prior to our moving here, I worked at the Dickson Plant in San Diego for ten years. Our address for the last five years that we lived in San Diego was 4539 Acron Avenue, San Diego, CA 87382.	A section that provides important details that will be helpful in making a credit decision.
You will find the following information helpful in assessing our credit worthiness: Annual income: $72,000; Present bank: Austin National Bank (Account No. 334-3567); Former bank: San Diego National Bank (Account No. 43338-2398); Present monthly mortgage: $650; Average monthly revolving charge-account balance: $235. In addition, while living in San Diego, we had charge accounts at the following stores: Drake Department Store 1 Main Street San Diego, CA 87380 Knapps 520 South Main San Diego, CA 87380 J. L. Jackson Department Store Crossroads Mall San Diego, CA 87389	A section that provides additional important details.
Please let me know if you need any additional information in making a credit decision.	A courteous, action-oriented closing.

Figure 5–18 Effective Credit-Request Letter

The suggested plan for a combined credit-request and order letter includes the following elements:

1. A fast-start opening that makes reference to an order as well as to the desire to have the order filled on credit basis;
2. A clear identification of items being ordered;
3. Essential information that will enable the recipient to make a decision about your credit worthiness;
4. A courteous, action-oriented closing.

An example of a combined credit-request and order letter is illustrated in Figure 5–19. Notice that all of the important elements are included.

Letter Requesting Additional Information from a Credit Applicant

Occasionally, companies find that additional information about the applicant is needed before making a credit decision. Because this type of letter is not a routine request for more information, the letter has to be written in a low-key, unoffensive manner. Requests for additional information are generally made after the applicant has returned a completed application to the company.

Will you please open a charge account for Bill's Hardware and Paint Store and then ship on credit the following items?	A fast-start opening that mentions the order and the desire to open a credit account.
(order table below)	A section that clearly identifies the items being ordered.

QUANTITY	CAT. NO.	DESCRIPTION	UNIT PRICE	TOTAL
4	189873	Power Saws	49.98	199.92
3	278171	Power Sanders	51.89	155.67
				$355.59

Because I anticipate ordering from you several times each month, being able to purchase merchandise on credit would add to the convenience of my operations. Letters of credit and other information helpful in your making a credit decision are obtainable from my bank, The First National Bank, 3451 South Street, Oklahoma City, OK 76488. Should you need additional information for use in evaluating my credit background, please contact me.	A section that provides essential information used in determining credit worthiness.
I will appreciate receiving the power tools by September 27 as I am planning a "Fall-Fixit Sale" that will begin on September 30.	A courteous, action-oriented closing.

Figure 5–19 Effective Combined Credit-Request and Order Letter

To begin this type of letter with the direct request is generally considered too blunt. A preferred beginning is to express gratitude or appreciation to the individual for submitting an application for a charge account. Notice the difference between the following two openings.

What type of opening is appropriate for letters in which additional credit information is requested?

Charge: Would you please send us an up-to-date list of your outstanding charge account balances. The data we received with your application were several months old.

To: We appreciate your interest in opening a charge account at Ballingers' of Oklahoma City.

The opening is followed with an identification of the desired information. Your goal in discussing the request is to avoid hurting the recipient's feelings or making him/her feel guilty or threatened. The first of the following two paragraphs could hurt the recipient's feelings, while the information in the revised version is presented much more tactfully.

Change: We restrict our accounts to those whose liabilities do not exceed a certain percentage of their assets. We are sure you can appreciate the restricting of our charge accounts to those who are worthy of credit. To do otherwise would obviously result in our having to increase the cost of our merchandise in order to cover the losses incurred by extending credit to individuals who are not worthy of credit.

To: Seeing an up-to-date list of your liabilities will enable us to obtain an accurate measure of the ratio between your asssets and liabilities.

Granting credit to individuals whose ratios are within a specified range benefits all of our customers because we are able to maintain our merchandise prices at a level lower than we would otherwise be able to do.

What is the purpose of resale material in letters in which additional credit information is requested?

The inclusion of resale material, which is wording designed to bolster the confidence of the applicant in the company, can be especially effective in combined credit request and order letters. You should always take advantage of an opportunity to include resale material in the letters you write. The following paragraph illustrates the effective use of resale material.

Ballinger's of Oklahoma City has just received word that it has been chosen to receive the "Yorktowne Distributor of the Year Award." This prestigious award is given annually to the distributor of Yorktowne products with the largest annual percentage increase in sales. The significant increase in sales that our company has experienced is attributed to our customers' growing awareness of the quality of Yorktowne products.

What type of closing is appropriate for letters in which additional credit information is requested?

The appropriate closing for a letter in which additional information is requested is action oriented. The closing tells precisely what will take place upon receipt of the requested information. A suggested date for submitting the requested information may help you obtain the requested information more quickly than when no date is mentioned. Compare the differences between these two closings.

Change: We look forward to hearing from you.
To: If you can send us the requested information by July 28, we should be able to make a credit decision by August 15. Please let me know if you would like for us to delay shipping your recent order until after your credit application has been processed or whether you prefer to send a check for $198.43 so that we can send your order immediately.

What is the suggested plan for letters in which additional credit information is requested?

The suggested plan for a letter requesting additional credit information includes the following elements:

1. An opening that expresses appreciation for the applicant's interest in a credit account, as well as appreciation for the order he/she placed, if appropriate;
2. An identification, stated in an interpersonal, courteous way, of the type of information needed;
3. Inclusion of resale material to bolster the recipient's confidence in the writer's company;
4. A courteous, action-oriented closing.

Figure 5–20 illustrates an effective letter requesting additional credit information.

Your interest in opening a charge account at Sampson Hardware Supply Company and your recent order are appreciated.

An opening that expresses appreciation for the applicant's interest in opening a credit account and that expresses appreciation for the order.

For us to continue processing your credit application, a list of your present creditors and the amounts owed is needed. This same information is requested from all of our credit applicants.

A section that presents an impersonal request for additional information.

You will be pleased to learn that we were just selected as the exclusive national distributor of the popular Kearney power tool line. If you decide to stock these tools in your store, your customers will enjoy the convenience of shopping locally rather than having to order from Kearney. We will send you the stock information on the Kearney line when it becomes available.

A section that presents resale material.

Just as soon as we receive the requested information, we will continue with the processing of your application. If you would like to receive your order before your charge account is opened, please send us a check for $355.59. Your order will then be sent within 24 hours.

A courteous, action-oriented closing.

Figure 5–20 Effective Letter in Which Additional Credit Information is Requested

LETTERS REQUESTING FAVORS

Business executives are often required to ask others for favors, not only in carrying out necessary executive action, but also in personal activities. When a favor is requested, the writer has a special reason for expressing his/her ideas tactfully and courteously as well as persuasively. The benefits to the reader will usually be less tangible than when an inquiry about products or services may lead to a sale.

The individual requesting a favor should first ask himself/herself two questions: (1) Have I sufficient reason for making this request? (2) Am I asking a favor of a person reasonably expected to be willing to grant the favor?

One of the best ways to obtain a special favor is to prepare a carefully worded letter. The letter should have a positive tone, be courteous, and show appreciation for the recipient's granting of the favor. However, the recipient should not be thanked in advance of his/her granting the favor.

What type of opening is appropriate for favor-request letters?

A letter requesting a favor should begin with a fast-start opening. The following two paragraphs illustrate the difference between a fast-start and a slow-start opening:

Change: The students in the data processing class I teach at State University are always interested in seeing state-of-the-art computer installations. The article in last week's *Business Record* about your installation was very interesting to my class. Would you be able to provide my students with a tour of your new computer installation?

To: Would you be able to give a tour of your new computer installation to a group of 15 eager-to-learn students in my data processing class at State University? We became aware of your state-of-the-art installation through the article in last week's Business Record.

Once the nature of the favor has been stated, additional pertinent information about the favor should be provided. This information will help the recipient become more aware of your desire to have the favor granted. This material should be followed by an explanation of why the favor is important to you and others. The following paragraph illustrates an effective request.

> All of the students in this class are seniors in the data processing program at State University. Nearly half of them have work experience in data processing. These students would be especially appreciative of having an opportunity to see a state-of-the-art installation. Seeing such an installation will contribute significantly to their understanding of the vital nature of the data processing function in an insurance company.

What type of closing is appropriate for favor-request letters?

The closing of a letter requesting a favor should be action-oriented and express appreciation for the possibility that the recipient may be able to grant the favor. While the first of the following two paragraphs expresses appreciation, it is not action oriented.

> Change: Any assistance you can provide will be greatly appreciated.
> To: I will call you next week to learn of your decision about the possibility of a tour. My students would be greatly appreciative of an opportunity like this to enrich their educational backgrounds.

What is the suggested plan for favor-request letters?

The suggested plan for a favor-request letter includes the following elements:

1. A fast-start opening that identifies the nature of the favor request;
2. A presentation of additional information that will help the recipient become aware of the writer's interest in having the favor granted;
3. A courteous, action-oriented closing.

While the letter in Figure 5–21 is not likely to motivate its recipient to grant the favor, the letter in Figure 5–22 probably will.

Figure 5–21 Ineffective Favor-Request Letter

A friend of my recently told me about the excellent presentation you made to a class of his several years ago. Would you be willing to make a similar presentation in my class?	An opening that presents the request but that is quite deficient in the information that is provided.
Having speakers come into high school classes is an excellent way to bridge the gap between the real and educational world. We often find that speakers are able to "tell it like it is" because of their vast, rich experiences.	A section that presents additional information.
Please let me know at your convenience if you might be available to speak to my accounting class.	A section that lacks action-oriented material.

```
Are you available within the next two months to
make a presentation on the topic of accounting
careers before my accounting class?  Because the
class meets from 1:00 to 1:50, a presentation
lasting thirty minutes with a twenty-minute
question-answer period would be ideal.
```

A fast-start opening that presents vital information about the request.

```
John Davidson recently told me about the excellent
presentation you made on accounting careers before
one of his classes several years ago.  He
indicated that several of his students chose an
accounting career after hearing your presentation.
Several of my students are considering an
accounting career--and your presentation would be
helpful as they make their decisions.
```

A section that provides additional information about the request.

```
Your helping enrich the educational experiences of
my students would be greatly appreciated.  I will
call you February 10 for your decision.
```

A courteous, action-oriented closing.

Figure 5–22 Effective Favor-Request Letter

CHAPTER SUMMARY

A variety of direct-request letters are used in the business world. Some make a direct request for information about products, services, or people. Others are classified as indirect inquiry.

Claim letters, order letters, letters of invitation, reservation letters, letters requesting credit, and letters requesting favors are other types of direct-request letters.

Regardless of the type of letter you are preparing, you will want to ensure that you include the essential elements for that type of letter and that your writing techniques are appropriate.

REVIEW QUESTIONS

1. What are the two basic types of direct-inquiry letters?
2. What should be included in the opening of a direct-inquiry letter?
3. What should be included in the closing of a direct-inquiry letter?
4. How does the opening of a direct-inquiry letter requesting information about a product or service differ from the opening of a direct-inquiry letter requesting information about a person?
5. How does a direct-inquiry letter differ from an indirect-inquiry letter?
6. Identify several qualities of effective claim letters.
7. What is the primary purpose of the claim letter?
8. In a claim letter, what material should follow the discussion of the nature of the claim?
9. What is the nature of the you-attitude material that is appropriate in a claim letter?
10. What are the content components of order letters?
11. What are the important details to include in social-invitation letters?

12. What material should be included in the opening of a letter that requests credit?
13. What is included in the effective closing of a letter requesting a favor?

APPLICATION PROBLEMS

1. Prepare a written critique of the following letter, evaluating grammar usage, punctuation, conformity with the suggested plan, and conformity with the writing essentials discussed in Chapters 3 and 4.

> It was certainly embarrassing to give my niece an electric knife that I purchased in your store which did not run. I had your store deliver the knife to my niece (Ms. Mary Brown, 43 Maple Street, Lincoln) so I did not try it before I gave it to her. One has the right to assume that when you pay the prices that you folks charge that the merchandise should not have problems. I probably could have purchased an identical knife that worked from M-Mart—and for much less. Please deliver a new knife (Sunray, Model 23, $29.95) to my niece as soon as conveniently possible. She will give you the first one at that time. Let me tell you this—I will think twice before I shop in your store again.

2. Rewrite the letter in application problem 1, making sure that the weaknesses you identified in your critique have been eliminated. Make any assumptions you need to make and supply any missing details.

3. Using the proofreader's marks shown in Figure 4–5, edit the following letter:

> Will you please tell me more about the building cite I recently saw advertised in the April 10 issue of the *Dallas Hearld*. I am looking for a faclity has that around 2500 square ft. of wearhouse space and around 1000 square feet of office space. Right off hand it appears that this faclity may meet me needs good. Could you please send to me a list of the specifcations it offeres.
>
> If it appears that the faclity may meet my needs I will want to inspect it soon. Due to the fact that our lease is about to expire on our present faclity, please respond without a lengthy delay.

4. You just learned that the job you have had for the first three weeks of the summer is being eliminated because of a business-slowdown that is affecting the company for which you work. You need summer work badly because you are putting yourself through college. You will be unable to afford your senior year unless you find another job immediately—or unless you receive a scholarship. Prepare a letter to send to the Director of Financial Aids at your college/university that inquires about the possibility of your obtaining a scholarship. You also want to know how you go about applying for a scholarship, assuming one may be available. Because most scholarship recipients have to meet specified criteria, you need to include the following information in your letter: major, grade-point average, and career objective.

5. Assume that you (vice-president of sales in the Mellon Electronics Company, 2890 South Street, Omaha, NE 68408) are considering hiring Mary Carneigy as your secretary. On her application blank, she listed John Smothers,

director of personnel at Smithson Corporation, 2876 North Street, Des Moines, IA 56745 as a reference. Prepare a letter to send to Mr. Smothers in which you solicit information about the following: the quality of Ms. Carneigy's work, her ability to work under pressure, her ability to handle "crises" situations, her level of initiative, and her skills in oral and written communication. You expect your secretary to be able to function with a minimum of direction, to have excellent secretarial skills, to compose effective letters and reports, and to handle adverse situations effectively. The job has to be filled three weeks from today, which is September 21, when your present secretary leaves.

6. You are the chairperson of a search committee responsible for finding a new head of the Business Department at Northern College, located at Miami, KS 45434. The deadline for receiving applications has now passed, and your committee plans to develop a form letter that can be used to solicit information from the individuals listed as references by the applicants. The following were listed as important criteria on the job vacancy notice: scholarly promise, leadership potential, effective administrative skills, effective teaching skills, and knowledgeable about the budgeting process. Prepare a draft of the form letter that will be sent to each individual listed as a reference on the application materials of the top five candidates.

7. You, the owner of the Parisian Gift Shoppe, 38 Main Mall Street, Atlanta, GA 23417, just took receipt of a shipment from the Hallwood Distributing Company, 5732 Baker Avenue, Charlotte, NC 21211. One reason you decided to place this order with Hallwood (your first) is because of its policy of shipping within 72 hours of the receipt of the order. Although the shipment date was within 3 days (you placed a phone order on September 21, and the postage on the package showed a September 23 mailing date), the shipment did not arrive until October 14. You were counting on having the merchandise available for your Fall-Fest, which ended on October 12. Obviously, Hallwood cannot be held accountable for the slowness of the U.S. Postal Service, but it can be held accountable for the fact that you received someone else's order. None of the 23 wood carvings, which cost $423, that you ordered were received. Instead, you received an assortment of 24 pewter figurines that you cannot use because you no longer carry pewter items. Write a letter asking for a cancellation of your order for the wood carvings and for a full refund of the $423 that you charged to your Value-Line charge account, which you have already paid. Indicate that the shipment of pewter is being returned COD by UPS.

8. You are the owner of the Happy Traveler Motel (Box 2334, Reno, NV 48434). From time to time, you have guests who remove a towel or washcloth from their room. The cleaning attendant just reported that the four bath towels, four hand towels, four washcloths, and four pillows are missing from room B–4. A quick calculation reveals a total loss of $134.93. Room B–4 was occupied last night by two young couples (Mr. and Ms. Ken Jones, 1221 Grant Street, Apt. 213, Boulder, CO 80394 and Mr. and Mrs. Jack Green, 1221 Grant Street, Apt. 214, Boulder CO 80394). You had to call them two times last night after their neighbors complained about the noise they were making in their room. Write a letter to each couple, requesting that the items either be returned or be paid for. Indicate that unless you have action within two weeks, you will report this situation to the law.

9. You recently ran across the catalog of Wisconsin Cheese Distribution Company (1819 Liberty Avenue, Milwaukee, WI 65989) in your doctor's waiting room. You found in the catalog the perfect Christmas gift for two of your uncles: an assorted cheese/sausage box. Because you did not want to take the catalog with you, you wrote down the vital information so that you can order these items by letter. You would like to have Gift No. 345, the Party Pak, which costs $23.95, sent to Mr. James Skinner, Box 298, Martin, NE 68756 and Gift No. 549, the President's Choice, which also costs $23.95, sent to Mr. John Skinner, 2398 Canyon Road, Rapid City, SD 45874. You are enclosing with the letter a check for $52.40, the amount of the two items, plus $4.50 for postage and handling. Remind Wisconsin Cheese that these gifts are to be received by your uncles on or before December 24 and that the gift card is to read, "Merry Christmas from (your name)."

10. You were recently looking at the catalog of Builder's Supply Company, Towne Square, Salem, MA 01229. As the owner of Pete's Hardware, 13 Main Street, Pella, IA 58575, you are always interested in finding sources for some of the hardware used by those residents in your community who are remodeling old farm houses. Specifically, you are interested in expanding your line of brass hinges, door knobs, and strike plates, in addition to period light fixtures. Builder's Supply Company carries a complete line of the brass hardware and period light fixtures that you have so many requests for. Because the catalog you were looking at did not have an order blank, you have to prepare a letter in which the following items are ordered:

8 pair of brass hinges (No. 1343) at $7.49 for each pair
6 pair of brass hinges (No. 1279) at $5.49 for each pair
6 brass door assemblies (No. 1894) at $15.49 each
4 brass door assemblies (No. 1984) at $21.49 each
5 antique brass light fixtures (No.2181) at $34.98 each

Send along a check for the amount of your purchase. Shipping is free, and no sales tax is applicable.

11. You are the convention chairperson for the Tri-State Business Educators Association.One of your responsibilities is to find speakers for the 12 sessions that will be held during the two-day convention that begins on May 14. The convention will be held at the Riverside Inn (12 Riverside Drive, Akron, OH 45765). A committee member has suggested that you contact Ms. Mary Maxum (8758 Greenwood Street, Apt. 23, Columbus, OH 45874) as a possible speaker for the information systems session that is to be held from 10–11 a.m. on May 14. This individual heard Ms. Maxum speak at a conference last year and found her to be very informative—as well as entertaining. While your association cannot pay its convention speakers an honorarium, it does pay transportation (22 cents a mile) as well as provide lodging and meals. Speakers are also invited as the association's guests at the closing banquet that begins at 6 p.m. on May 15. Because the convention is only five months away, you would like to have a response from Ms. Maxum relatively soon.

12. You, your spouse, and two children (ages 7 and 5) plan to travel to the Colorado Rockies during the two weeks that you are on vacation (August 2–16). You want to spend four nights (August 6–9) at the Day's Rest Inn on Highway 16 in Estes Park, CO 80773. Your brother and his family stayed at the Inn last summer and gave it a good recommendation. Write a letter in which you request a room that has two double beds on the backside of the motel. You decide to include a preaddressed post-card in your letter for use by the motel owner to confirm your reservations and inform you of the nightly rate.

13. You are interested in opening a charge account at the new Jackson's Department Store that just opened in the Cedar View Mall in Laramie, Wyoming. When you called Jackson's Credit Department recently, the credit representative suggested you send a letter that provides the following information: Number of years at present residence—6; job title/employer—associate professor, University of Wyoming; annual income—$38,000; and the name of your bank—First National Bank of Laramie. Prepare a letter requesting the opening of a charge account.

14. You are the credit representative for Jackson's Department Store in Laramie, Wyoming. You recently received a letter from William S. Brooks (2314 Harvard Avenue, Laramie, WY 78643) in which he requested the opening of a charge account. While he provided several pieces of information in his letter (number of years at present residence; job title/employer; annual income; and the name of his bank), he failed to include a list of the charge accounts he presently has. Nor did he provide the amount he presently owes (mortgage, loans, revolving charge accounts, etc.) Before you can open a charge account in his name, you must have this additional information—which all credit applicants are required to provide.

15. You are the new owner of Grant's Gift Box (No. 23, Southland Mall, Detroit, MI 48863). The individual from whom you purchased the store highly recommended Johnston Importer's Inc. (Box 229, Nashua, NH 10901) as an excellent source of your brassware. Prepare a letter in which you ask that the following items be charged to the charge account that you are also requesting be opened in your name:

12 brass boxes (Stock No. 23423), $18.74 each
10 pairs of brass candlestick holders (Stock No. 21221), $21.87 per pair
3 brass baskets (Stock No. 12231), $37.19 each

Orders exceeding $100 are shipped free and no sales tax is charged. Information about your financial background and credit history is available from Michigan Federal Bank, 2312 Grant Blvd., Detroit, MI 48834.

16. You have been invited to Boston for a home-office interview for an accounting position at Lemack, Selling, and Deman. You know nothing about Boston other than it has terrific seafood restaurants! Your father suggests that you contact one of his college friends (William S. Drake, 3443 Grambling Boulevard, Newton, MA 23821) to see if he might be able to show you around the Boston area. Mr. Drake retired from the military three years ago. While

you have never met him personally, you feel as if you are somewhat acquainted from the Christmas messages his family sent your family throughout the years. Write the letter to Mr. Drake, asking if he might have time to show you around Boston the morning of April 9 or the afternoon of April 10. You plan to arrive the evening of April 8 and you have hotel reservations at the Downtown Hospitality Inn. Your flight leaves Logan Airport at 5:30 p.m. on the 10th.

Chapter 6

Good-News Letters

LEARNING OBJECTIVES

After studying this chapter, you should be able to
1. Discuss the characteristics of good-news letters.
2. Identify the suggested plan used in preparing letters that reply to inquiries and respond to credit requests.
3. Discuss the factors that are considered in determining one's credit worthiness.
4. Identify ways to improve the effectiveness of letters that grant adjustments and order-acknowledgement letters.
5. Identify ways that will improve the effectiveness of letters that grant favors.
6. Identify the suggested plan used in preparing letters of congratulation and letters accepting invitations.
7. Prepare effective letters of the type discussed in this chapter.

Many situations in the business world require the preparation of good-news letters. When well written, these letters help organizations improve their relationships with their customers and clients. Writers of good-news messages wisely take advantage of every opportunity to capitalize on the positive elements of the situations about which they write.

The types of good-news letters covered in this chapter are:

1. Letters replying to inquiries
2. Letters extending credit
3. Letters granting adjustments
4. Letters acknowledging orders
5. Letters granting favors
6. Letters of congratulation
7. Letters that convey the acceptance of an invitation

What characteristics do good-news letters possess?

Good-news letters can be identified by the following characteristics:

1. *Begin with the good news or main idea.* One of the best ways to put the reader in a positive frame of mind is to present the good news first. When the letter you are writing is a reply to a letter you received, putting the good news or main idea in the opening paragraph is especially desirable.

2. *Use a fast-start opening.* The nature of each letter presented in this chapter enables you to use a fast-start opening in which you will avoid presenting obvious information. For example, telling the reader that you have received his/her letter is not a fast-start beginning. You obviously have received his/her letter—or you would not be replying.

3. *Provide explanatory details or information of primary and secondary importance.* In the majority of the letters presented in this chapter, you will have an opportunity to provide more information than just the good news. The letter will be incomplete if it is missing the details or information of primary importance. Although the message may be complete without including the material of secondary importance, you should consider its inclusion if the material will be helpful or of interest to the reader. Types of material of secondary importance that fit nicely into several of the good-news letters covered in this chapter are resale, sales-promotion, and reader-benefit material.

4. *Incorporate a you-viewpoint.* Because the letters included in this chapter contain good news for the reader, the material must be written from a you-viewpoint. The letters will have a much stronger psychological impact when the material focuses on the reader rather than on the writer. Minimizing the use of *I*, *we*, and *our* will help you achieve a you-viewpoint.

5. *Incorporate an appropriate closing.* A variety of closings are appropriate for the letters discussed in this chapter. In each type of letter, a courteous, friendly closing is important. In some letters, this is accomplished by offering to provide additional help if and when desired. In other letters, the closing will express the hope of anticipated future business.

LETTERS REPLYING TO INQUIRIES

Letters of reply to inquiries provide information about products, services, and persons, or answer an indirect inquiry. Each of these letter types possesses the general characteristics presented above, in addition to specific characteristics that are discussed in this section.

Letters That Provide Information About Products or Services

A favorable reply to a letter of inquiry about a product or service must be both accurate and comprehensive. Not only must you be certain about the correctness of your response, but also you must be certain you answered all the questions in the inquiry. You should also consider providing any additional information that will help the reader become more familiar with the product or service that led to the initial correspondence.

What characteristics do favorable-reply letters possess?

The response to a letter of inquiry should be sent as soon as possible. To delay the response you may send a signal that you consider the inquiry to be unimportant—or that you do not put a top priority on responding. Certain circumstances may prevent a timely reply, such as when you do not have readily available answers to the questions in the inquiry, your schedule does not permit a fast reply, or you have been out of town. If a response cannot be sent within a reasonable time, a short note that mentions the delay and the anticipated response date should be sent. The following is such an acknowledgement.

> The information you requested about our new line of desk-top computers will be sent next week after our systems staff prepares calculations on some technical data that will provide the answers to your questions.
>
> We appreciate your interest in this new line of computers.

Occasionally, you may not be able to answer all the questions asked in an inquiry letter or provide all the requested information. Ignoring these requests may be interpreted by the reader as an oversight on your part. The recipient may then waste time and effort preparing a second inquiry letter. Deal with these situations in as positive a manner as possible. If requested information will become available in the future, inform the reader in your letter. For example, the following is an effective response to a question that cannot be answered at this time.

> Information about the number of new employees that Dionnette Corporation plans to hire during 1987 will be available June 1. If you still desire this information at that time, please write or telephone me after June 1.

A letter responding to an inquiry about a product or service should have a fast-start opening. In preparing such an opening, you will want to present the main idea—probably the answer to the primary question asked in the inquiry letter—as early as possible. Notice the difference in the pace of the following two opening paragraphs.

What type of opening is appropriate for favorable-reply letters?

> Change: Thank you for your recent letter in which you inquired about our new desk-top computer.
>
> To: Yes, the memory of the H–D 3000 in our new desk-top computer line can be expanded to 512K by inserting two H–D 3987 boards. A service contract that you also inquired about is available for an annual charge of $125.

The opening is followed by the presentation of additional details or information of interest to the reader. This section is also used to present answers to questions of secondary importance. The reader's perception of your helpfulness will be affected by this section.

In the first of the following paragraphs, the writer provides a minimum amount of information. The writer of the revised version will be perceived to be much more helpful.

> Change: The installation of the memory boards is an easy process. Any of our trained service technicians can install these boards in a few minutes.
>
> To: The factory-trained service technicians who work for the H–D computer dealer in your area, the J. H. Johnson Computer Company, are able to install these memory boards in approximately 30 minutes. The cost of each board is $135. We estimate that the memory of the H–D 3000 computer can be upgraded to 512K for less than $300.

What is the nature of the resale material in favorable-reply letters?

Letters that respond to inquiries about a product or service are appropriate for the inclusion of resale or sales-promotion material. Resale material is used to help convince the writer that he/she has made (or will make) a wise decision in purchasing the product or service of interest. Sales-promotion material, on the other hand, is designed to promote a product or service in which the reader may be interested. The purpose of the sales-promotion material is not to put pressure on the reader, but rather to make him/her aware of another product or service he/she might find useful.

The following letter, responding to an inquiry about the H–D 3000 desktop computer, effectively uses resale material.

> During the six months that the H–D 3000 has been on the market, it has received rave reviews in several computer magazines. After you read the four reviews that I'm enclosing with this letter, I think you will agree that the well-designed keyboard, the high resolution of the screen, and the upgradable nature of its memory make the H–D 3000 a superior product. Add to these features our exclusive three-year warranty and you can easily understand why the H–D 3000 is receiving such positive reviews.

What type of closing is appropriate for favorable-reply letters?

The closing appropriate for a letter responding to an inquiry about a product or service should be friendly and courteous. You may want to express appreciation for the inquiry or offer to answer any other questions the reader may have. When appropriate, you may also want to suggest the action you would like for the reader to take.

The weaknesses inherent in the first of the following closing paragraphs have been removed from the revised version.

> Change: Thank you for your interest in the H–D 3000.
>
> To: We appreciate having the opportunity to answer your questions. Should you have any other questions, please write me. Or if you would like to see a demonstration of the H–D 3000, please visit our dealer in your area, the J. H. Johnson Computer Company.

The suggested plan for a letter that responds to an inquiry about a product or service includes the following elements:

What is the suggested plan for favorable-reply letters?

1. A fast-start opening that provides an answer to the primary question or which mentions that the requested information is being sent;
2. The inclusion of answers to questions and/or a presentation of details or information of secondary importance;
3. The inclusion of resale, sales-promotion, or reader-benefit material;
4. A friendly, courteous closing that, when appropriate, suggests the action you would like for the reader to take.

The letter illustrated in Figure 6–1 lacks a number of the elements of effective letters that respond to inquiries about products or services. The letter presented in Figure 6–2 is a much-improved version of the same letter. The inclusion of resale material in Figure 6–2 has a desirable impact.

Letters Responding to an Inquiry About A Person

Two situations necessitate the preparation of letters responding to an inquiry about a person. These situations occur when you are asked to provide information about (1) a person for whom you serve as a reference (such as a former or current employee) and (2) a person's credit worthiness. When you are able to provide either favorable or neutral information about individuals in either of these situations, you will find the information contained in this section helpful.

In addition to the general characteristics presented earlier in this chapter, letters that respond to an inquiry about a person possess a number of other characteristics. The information in this section pertains specifically to writing letters in response to an inquiry about a job applicant's work performance. The same material can be easily adapted for a response to an inquiry about a credit applicant's credit worthiness.

A fast-start opening in a letter that responds to an inquiry about a person is accomplished by referring to the individual's name and the nature of the relationship between the person and you, in addition to expressing apprecia-

What type of opening is appropriate for letters replying favorably about a person?

Figure 6–1 Ineffective Response to Inquiry

We have received your recent letter in which you inquired about the Model 87 printing calculator. Thank you for your inquiry.	A slow-start opening that presents obvious information.
The Model 87 can be used either as a printing calculator or as a display calculator. You also asked about whether it will operate on batteries as well as on 120-volt current. The calculator can be operated on either batteries or on 120-volt current.	A section that contains brief, almost-incomplete answers.
Please let me know if you have any other questions about our calculator.	A closing that lacks friendliness.

Yes, the Model 87 Omni printing calculator you recently inquired about can be used either as a printing calculator or as a display calculator. The calculator's dual power source will enable you to operate the machine either on batteries or on 120-volt current.	A fast-start opening that gives immediate answers to questions.
Another feature of the Model 87 that you may find especially useful is its triple memory, which enables you to hold three different amounts simultaneously in memory. This triple-memory feature is especially attractive to engineers.	A section that contains additional information designed to help create reader's interest in the product.
The Model 87 calculator performs more functions than any other comparably priced calculator. A review of this machine which recently appeared in the Office Equipment News indicated that the Model 87 has the best repair record among competing calculators and that it is the easiest calculator to learn to operate. These two advantages are undoubtedly responsible for the increasing popularity of the Model 87.	A section that contains resale material designed to entice the customer to purchase the product.
I appreciate your inquiry about the Model 87. If you would like to see a demonstration, please visit the Omaha Office Equipment Company, the Omni dealer in your area.	A courteous, action-oriented closing.

Figure 6–2 Effective Response to Inquiry

tion (if appropriate) for being able to provide the information. Notice the difference between the slow-start of the first of the following two paragraphs and the fast-start of the revised opening.

Change: I have received your letter of June 22 in which you inquired about Ms. Mary Smith who has applied for a secretarial position in your organization.

To: In response to your inquiry, I am glad to convey to you my satisfaction with Ms. Mary Smith's work performance during the two years that she was my secretary.

The section that follows the opening is used to answer the specific and general questions that were asked in the inquiry letter. You should also consider including any additional information that will be useful to the reader. The information—both solicited and unsolicited—must be honest. In addition to answering any questions contained in the inquiry letter, the inclusion of information about your impression of the person's ability to perform the duties of the job for which he/she is applying is also highly desirable.

What are evaluative statements?

Your response will also be more helpful to the reader if you can provide evaluative statements about the person's performance. This provision can be effectively done by making a comparison between the person's performance and the performance of others with similar duties. Specific information in your response will be more helpful to the reader than general information.

If you have negative information to present, you should make sure that it is pertinent to the situation. Unless these negative aspects are likely to affect the person's ability to perform his/her job well, you may want to consider omitting this information. Some experienced writers, when preparing such letters, invite a phone call from the reader at which time these negative aspects are mentioned.

The following paragraphs illustrate how the suggestions presented above can be effectively incorporated into a response to an inquiry about a person's work performance.

> The following are answers to your questions:
>
> 1. Yes, Ms. Smith is a self-starter. Rarely did I have to give her directions for carrying out her job duties.
> 2. Yes, Ms. Smith's work is meticulously done. I recall only one instance in which she had to retype work because of the manner in which the first typed draft was prepared.
> 3. Yes, Ms. Smith is a dedicated worker. On several occasions, she cheerfully worked after hours and on weekends when I asked her to.
> 4. Yes, Ms. Smith works well with others. She is pleasant to be around, has empathy for others, and is very helpful.
>
> Other information you may find helpful in evaluating Ms. Smith's suitability for employment includes the following:
>
> 1. Of all the secretaries I've had, Ms. Smith is the most eager to learn and to develop professionally. These are important attributes of a secretary to a vice president.
> 2. The level of Ms. Smith's secretarial skills, her understanding of business operations, and her personality will enable her to handle in a very competent way the work in a vice president's office.
> 3. I assume that much of the work you do as a vice president is confidential. I am not aware that Ms. Smith ever breached the confidential nature of any work she did for me.
> 4. Ms. Smith is able to defuse effectively, both in person and on the phone, many situations that have the potential of becoming problematic.

The ending of the letter responding to an inquiry about a person should include a statement summarizing your overall opinion about the applicant's suitability for the job for which he/she is applying. The statement should be presented with sincerity; otherwise, the reader may question your honesty.

What should be included in the closing of letters responding to inquiries about people?

The first of the following two paragraphs illustrates a general closing that detracts from the effectiveness of a letter. The revised version conveys a much different impression of the writer's feelings about the applicant.

> Change: I am glad to have had this opportunity to convey to you my impression about Ms. Smith.
>
> To: Ms. Smith, whom I found to be an exceptional secretary, is being referred to you with my top recommendation. If she is given the opportunity to work for you, I am sure you will readily concur with my evaluation of her work performance.

What is the suggested plan for favorable-reply letters?

The suggested plan for a letter responding to an inquiry about a person includes the following elements:

1. A fast-start opening that mentions (a) the person's name, (b) the nature of the relationship between you and the person, and (c) appreciation for being able to provide the requested information;
2. A section that answers specific and general questions asked in the inquiry letter, as well as any additional information that will be helpful to the reader;
3. A closing that provides an overall evaluation of your impression of tne person's suitability for the position for which he/she has applied.

The letter illustrated in Figure 6–3 does not follow several of the suggestions presented in this section. You will notice that these weaknesses have been eliminated in the letter presented in Figure 6–4. The additional details that are presented in the revised letter will be greatly appreciated by the reader.

Letters Responding to Indirect Inquiries

What type of opening is appropriate for letters responding to inquiries?

A number of the characteristics found in letters responding to direct inquiries are also found in letters responding to indirect inquiries. These characteristics are a fast-start opening, the presentation of material of primary importance first, followed by the presentation of material of secondary importance, and a friendly, courteous closing.

In preparing a fast-start opening, the presentation of obvious information is avoided. Notice the difference between the following two openings.

Change: Enclosed is the information you recently requested.
To: The list, which is enclosed, of the things to see and do in Detroit will enable you to preplan your trip. We are glad to send this information to you.

Figure 6–3 Ineffective Letter Responding to an Inquiry About a Job Applicant

Your letter in which you inquired about the suitability of Mr. John Diaz for a financial analyst position arrived recently. Mr. Diaz worked here from 1982-1985. His last position was assistant financial analyst.	A slow-start opening that presents obvious information.
Mr. Diaz is a bright, hard-working individual. He is cooperative, gets along well with others, and has a take-charge attitude. We were all very pleased with his performance.	A section that presents information about the applicant which will most likely diminish his chances of being offered a job.
I am glad to have this opportunity to recommend Mr. Diaz to you.	A weak closing.

Mr. John Diaz, about whom you recently inquired, was highly regarded when he worked for us from 1984 to 1987. I am glad to recommend him to you as a financial analyst, a position he is well qualified for.	A fast-start opening that contains the essential elements of the beginning for this type of letter.
Those of us who supervised Mr. Diaz found him to be a bright, hard-working individual. He was most cooperative, always got along well with others, and had a take-charge attitude. In addition, Mr. Diaz has an excellent aptitude for working with numbers. When compared with his co-workers, he consistently placed in the top 10 percent.	A section that provides a discussion which answers the questions that were asked by the person making the inquiry.
Mr. Diaz could always be counted on when needed, which was an especially fine attribute of his that I always appreciated. On several occasions, his performance was clearly beyond what was reasonably expected. Coupling this attribute with his philosophy that an employee never stops learning contributed to his considerable success while he worked here.	A section that provides a discussion of additional information of interest to the reader.
The respect I have for Mr. Diaz enables me to give him a top recommendation. If he is given the opportunity to work for you, I am confident that you too will soon feel the same way about him.	A closing that provides an overall evaluation of the applicant's suitability for employment.

Figure 6–4 Effective Letter Responding to an Inquiry About a Job Applicant

The nature of the situation for which you are preparing the response will determine whether you include resale, sales-promotion, or reader-benefit material. For example, when the letter you are preparing is a response to an inquiry about a product or service, the inclusion of resale or sales-promotion material is appropriate. On the other hand, when you are preparing a letter in response to an indirect inquiry, the inclusion of reader-benefit material is more appropriate. To illustrate, the following reader-benefit material is appropriate for inclusion in a letter responding to an inquiry about things to see and do in Detroit.

> You will find June to be a perfect month to visit Detroit. The warm days and delightfully mild nights will add to your family's sight-seeing pleasure.
>
> Among the attractions found especially interesting by families who have children the ages of yours are Greenfield Village, the Henry Ford Museum, and the Metropolitan Zoo. For the more culturally minded families, the Detroit Art Museum and Cranbrook Academy for the Arts are especially interesting. The Renaissance Center complex along the riverfront is another interesting attraction. The locations of these attractions, which are easily accessible by bus or taxi, are identified on the enclosed map.
>
> We are sure you will be eager to return for another visit once you spend a few days in Detroit.

The closing appropriate for a response to an indirect-inquiry letter is courteous, friendly, and offers to provide assistance when needed. Consider the differences between the following two closings.

Change:	I hope you will find the enclosed material helpful.
To:	Please let us know if we can provide any other information that will be helpful as you plan your trip to our city. Best wishes for a truly memorable, enjoyable experience.

What is the suggested plan for letters that respond to indirect inquiries?

The suggested plan for a letter responding to an indirect inquiry contains the following elements:

1. A fast-start opening that mentions your compliance with the initial inquiry/request—but that avoids presenting obvious information;
2. A section that includes additional information that might be helpful to the reader, including—when appropriate—resale, sales-promotion, or reader-benefit material;
3. A friendly, courteous closing that expresses your willingness to provide future assistance.

The letter presented in Figure 6–5 illustrates an effective letter of response to an indirect inquiry. The inclusion of resale material should have a positive impact on the reader.

Figure 6–5 Effective Response to an Indirect-Inquiry Letter

The Ergonomic Series in our clustered workcenter line about which you recently inquired is now our top-selling workcenter group. The full-color illustrated brochure that is enclosed shows the various design configurations available in the Ergonomic Series.

A fast-start opening that mentions the writer's compliance with the request.

Among the special features of the Ergonomic Series that you will find attractive are the following:

A section that contains resale material designed to help convince the reader of the wisdom of purchasing the product he/she inquired about.

*Power cords and communications cables are housed in a central core that keeps wires out of the way, yet makes them readily accessible.

*Panels are available in the following heights: 48, 60, 68, and 72 inches.

*The 24 fabric panel coverings are not only decorative, but also they have a high sound-absorbent rating.

*Task/ambient lighting panels are available that effectively illuminate the areas of each workcenter needing the greatest amount of light.

*Our patented hinge system facilitates changing the configuration of the workcenters in minimum time and with maximum ease.

After reading the brochure, please contact me if you have any questions about the Ergonomic Series. The Campbell Office Furniture Company in your area has a workcenter cluster on display, which will enable you to see firsthand the distinctive features of the Ergonomic Series.

A courteous closing that expresses the writer's desire to be of further service if desired.

Extending credit to customers is a complex process that often requires an extensive investigation into the backgrounds of the applicants. The investigation will center around the three C's of credit—capital, capacity, and character.

LETTERS RESPONDING TO CREDIT REQUESTS

What are the three C's of credit?

1. *Capital,* which refers to a person's assets, includes such things as cash, stocks, property, and real estate. This factor is given extensive consideration because if the customer fails to pay, his/her capital may be obtained through legal action in order to settle the account.
2. *Capacity,* which refers to the ability to pay, includes the amount of the individual's income, the amount of other debts, the health of the individual, and the nature of the individual's livelihood.
3. *Character,* which refers to a person's honesty and integrity, is important because a trustworthy person usually has a sincere desire to meet financial obligations, thus avoiding either interest charges or a poor credit reputation.

A common practice of most business enterprises is to extend credit to eligible customers. Because charge customers are likely to purchase at a faster rate, selling on credit is often used to increase sales volume. Businesses also use credit to increase their net profit by levying finance charges on their credit transactions.

Although advantageous in certain instances, the extension of credit is somewhat disadvantageous in others. For example, selling to customers on a credit basis requires businesses to install credit departments. The extension and refusal of credit add significantly to the amount of paperwork that must be processed. Much of this paperwork involves the use of the various types of credit letters presented in this text.

The types of credit accounts commonly used in the business world include the following:

What types of credit accounts are commonly used in the business world?

1. *Regular credit account*—this type of credit account is also known as a 30-day charge account. If the amount of the account is paid in full within the specified period (usually up to 30 days), no interest is charged. A variation of this account is the revolving charge account, which requires partial payment within a certain period while interest accrues on the unpaid balance.
2. *Ninety-day-same-as-cash-account*—this type of account requires three equal payments. If the account is paid in full within 90 days, no interest is charged. On accounts in which the balance is not paid in full by the due date, interest is generally charged from the date of purchase. This type of account is often used for the purchase of major home appliances or furniture.
3. *Long-term installment account*—this type of account generally is interest-bearing and may run as long as 60 months on major purchases. Long-term installment accounts are often used for the purchase of automobiles.

Letters commonly associated with the extension of credit are used to:

1. Solicit prospective credit customers
2. Submit a request for credit

3. Request information about credit applicants
4. Request additional information from credit applicants
5. Extend credit to credit applicants
6. Deny credit to credit applicants
7. Make a credit counteroffer

The letters listed above that have an inquiry or disappointing-news nature are discussed in other chapters of this text. For example, Chapter 5 provides information about letters that submit a request for credit, request information about credit applicants, and request additional information from credit applicants. Chapter 7 provides information about denying credit to credit applicants and making a credit counteroffer. This chapter discusses how to write letters to solicit prospective credit customers and extend credit to credit applicants.

Soliciting Prospective Credit Customers

Letters designed to solicit prospective credit customers are basically promotional letters. These letters must also be persuasive because their purpose is to entice prospective customers to open a charge account.

Letters designed to solicit prospective credit customers are well suited for the inclusion of sales-promotion, resale, and/or reader-benefit material. Including sales-promotion material will make the prospective credit customer aware of certain products or services offered by the company or an upcoming sale. Reader-benefit material, on the other hand, is designed to inform a recipient of the advantages of being able to charge purchases to a credit account. The inclusion of resale material is aimed at reselling the customer on a product or service he/she recently purchased.

What type of opening is appropriate for letters designed to solicit credit customers?

The opening of a letter designed to solicit credit customers will probably determine whether the letter gets read. The opening has to do four things: (1) attract the recipient's attention; (2) entice the recipient to read the entire letter; (3) stimulate the recipient to want to complete an application blank, and (4) ensure the reader's completion of the blank. The opening—more than any other section of this type of letter—is likely to determine whether or not your letter fulfills its purpose.

After the opening has attracted the reader's attention, he/she should be invited to open a charge account. To begin directly with the invitation may discourage some individuals from continuing to read. In the two paragraphs that follow, notice how much more inviting the second paragraph is.

Change: We want to take this opportunity to extend to you an invitation to open a charge account at Sniders'.

To: Sniders' has had a long-standing tradition of serving its customers' needs. In fact, concern for our customers has helped Sniders' become one of the leading furniture stores in the Greater Houston area. To help us better serve you—one of our preferred customers—we invite you to complete the attached application for credit.

A discussion of the advantages resulting from the use of credit follows the opening. The reader-benefit material included in this section has to be presented in a convincing manner. To cite weak advantages will not entice the reader to complete the application blank. The first of the following two paragraphs is weak, while the reader-benefit material in the revised version is more convincing.

What is included in the middle section of letters soliciting credit customers?

Change: By charging a purchase, you will have an opportunity to enjoy the use of the merchandise without having to wait until you can pay for it with cash.

To: Our customers who have a Sniders' charge account enjoy the following special benefits:

1. They receive notice of special sales before they are announced to the general public.
2. They are able to shop by telephone simply by charging their purchases to their charge accounts.
3. They are able to defer the full payment of their account balance. They simply pay the minimum amount, and a small interest charge is added to the amount of the unpaid balance.

Should you decide to use sales-promotion material in the letter designed to solicit credit customers, you should include it as the next section. This material can inform the customer about a product in which he/she may be interested, a new line of merchandise that the company has just added, a distinctive award the company has just received, or an upcoming sale. Resale material, if included, will also be included after the discussion of the advantages of having a charge account.

The following paragraph illustrates effective use of sales-promotion material.

Sniders' was just selected as the exclusive dealer of Markline furniture in the Greater Houston area. The dealers of this top-quality furniture line are carefully selected by Markline Corporation. The loyalty of long-term customers like you enabled us to be chosen as the Markline dealer in the Greater Houston area—and for that we are indeed grateful.

All of the material presented in the letter up to this point has been aimed at convincing the customer of two things: that he/she will wisely continue to do business with your company and that opening a charge account is in his/her best interest. Now is the time to review the action you wish the prospective customer to take—that is to complete the attached application blank. The following paragraph illustrates how this material can be effectively presented.

Within a few days after we receive your completed application blank, a Sniders' charge account will be opened in your name. Because you have been pre-qualified for a charge account, only a minimum amount of information is needed on the form. After you have entered the requested information on the form, simply sign your name on the appropriate line and drop your application in the mail.

What type of closing is appropriate for letters designed to solicit credit customers?

The closing of a letter soliciting credit customers should make the prospective customer feel appreciated. Notice the difference between these two closings.

Change: We are here to serve you. Please help us serve you better by opening a charge account.
To: We appreciate the many opportunities that we have had to serve you in the past and look forward to being able to serve you even better in the future.

What is the suggested plan for letters designed to solicit credit customers?

The suggested plan for a letter designed to solicit prospective credit customers includes the following elements:

1. A goodwill opening that causes the individual to want to read the letter;
2. A section that identifies for the customer the advantages of using credit;
3. A section that contains sales-promotion or resale material;
4. A discussion of the action you wish the prospective customer to take;
5. A courteous, friendly closing designed to make the prospective customer feel appreciated.

An ineffective letter written to solicit prospective credit customers is illustrated in Figure 6–6. An effective revision of the same letter is presented in Figure 6–7. The revised letter is sure to entice more customers to complete the credit application than the letter in Figure 6–6.

Letters Extending Credit to Applicants

Of all the letters associated with credit, those notifying customers of the opening of a charge in their name are perhaps the easiest to prepare. Because you

Figure 6–6 Ineffective Letter Soliciting Prospective Credit Customers

If you are like most of our customers who have a Continental charge card, you soon learn that it is one of your most valued possessions.	An opening that implies the reader is like many other people.
We are inviting you to complete the attached charge-card application so that you also can discover how valuable a Continental card is.	A delayed invitation to complete the application blank.
In addition to having all the advantages of being able to charge your purchases at Continental, you will also receive notices of our special sales before they are announced to the general public. Thus, you will have first pick of sale items.	A section containing a weak discussion of the benefits of having a charge account.
We suggest that you enhance the convenience of your shopping at Continental by opening a charge account. We look forward to receiving your application.	A weak closing that lacks you-attitude.

Since the time that the Continental Department Store was founded nearly fifty years ago, serving our customers has been paramount. So that we can serve you even better, we invite you to complete the attached application for credit.

An upbeat opening that will entice the recipient to read the entire letter and an invitation to complete the application blank.

As a Continental credit customer, you will enjoy several benefits, including the following:

A thorough discussion of the advantages of using credit.

1. You will be able to shop over the telephone--and your purchases can be simply charged to your account. Purchases of $25.00 and over are delivered free.

2. You will be able to take advantage of our sale prices two days before our spring and fall semi-annual sales are announced to the public.

3. You can defer paying in full your monthly account balance by paying a minimum amount of $10 or 10 percent of the balance, whichever is more. Unpaid balances are subject to a 1.5 percent monthly (18 percent APR) interest charge.

Continental just joined a buying group that several other large department stores belong to. Our customers benefit in two primary ways: they have a wider selection of merchandise from which to choose, and the savings resulting from volume buying enables us to reduce the price of our merchandise.

A section that contains sales-promotion material which is designed to help convince the customer to complete the application.

You are among a select group of our customers who have been pre-qualified for a Continental charge account. A few days after we receive your application, a Continental credit card will be sent to you. Simply put the signed application in the mail.

A section that contains a discussion of the action desired of the reader.

We look forward to the pleasure of continuing to serve you in the future as we have in the past.

A courteous, forward-looking closing.

Figure 6–7 Effective Letter Soliciting Prospective Credit Customers

are able to grant the applicant's request, the need to incorporate persuasive material or to minimize the impact of negative information—two concerns of various other types of credit letters—are unimportant.

Letters extending credit serve a threefold purpose: They inform the applicant that credit has been granted; they outline the credit policies of the company as a means of preventing future misunderstandings; and they serve as a sales-promotion device. Another purpose, when a combined order and request for credit is received, is to explain that the customer's order has been (or is about to be) shipped.

What are the purposes of letters that extend credit to applicants?

A letter that extends credit to a customer begins with the good news first. When a request for credit is not accompanied by an order, the letter should open by notifying the applicant that an account has been opened in his/her name. When the credit application is accompanied by an order, the customer may be more interested in learning about the status of his/her order than the credit account. Therefore, this type of letter should begin with the pertinent

What should be included in the openings of letters that extend credit?

information about the order. The opening will be followed by mentioning that the order has been charged to the customer's new account.

In a letter that extends credit to a customer, providing the good news first will give you a fast-start opening. Should you, however, begin with obvious information, the fast-start quality of your opening will be destroyed. To illustrate, notice the difference between these two openings.

Change: We have received your application for credit and have processed the information. We are glad to report that we can open a charge account in your name.

To: Welcome to Smyths' as a new charge customer. Your credit card, which is enclosed with this letter, will enable you to charge your purchases at all 29 Smyths' stores throughout the country. You may begin using the card just as soon as you sign your name on the backside of the card.

While the first opening contains wording that sounds as though the account was grudgingly opened, the revised opening is much more courteous, friendly, and helpful.

When a credit application accompanies an order, an appropriate opening that mentions the status of the order can be followed by a statement that mentions the newly established credit account.

Your order for six sets of the popular Linwood art prints was shipped via UPS this morning and should arrive within four days. The amount of the order ($397.43) was charged to your newly opened account.

What should be included in the middle section of letters that extend credit?

Following the opening, you may want to consider discussing the basis for extending credit, especially if the basis is exceptionally favorable. For example, if the applicant's credit references gave him/her especially high ratings, you may want to mention this fact because of its positive psychological impact on the applicant. Other favorable information you may want to consider including in the "basis for the extention of credit" section are the customer's prompt bill-paying habits and favorable ratio between assets and liabilities.

This section should outline the rules and terms governing the use of the charge account. Because the various types of accounts differ, special care should be taken to make sure the customer is fully informed of the rules and terms governing his/her account. Vital information to be covered is the closing date of the statement, finance charges, the date by which payment must be received to avoid further finance charges, annual membership charge, and whom to contact if (1) a billing error occurs, (2) a card is lost or stolen, or (3) an address needs to be changed. In addition to discussing the important rules or terms of the account in the letter, an increasing number of companies provide the credit customer with a separate document that thoroughly explains the provisions of the credit account.

Subtle differences exist between the various types of accounts. Finance charges on some accounts begin with the date of merchandise purchase; on other accounts, finance charges accrue only on unpaid balances. On still other accounts, discounts are given if the balance is paid within a specified length of time. For example, a 2/10, net 30 arrangement gives the customer a 2 percent discount if the balance is paid within 10 days; if the account is not paid within 10 days, the full amount is due in 30 days. A misunderstanding may arise if the customer is not made aware of when the 10-day period begins. Does it begin with the date of invoice, with the date of shipment, or with the date of merchandise receipt?

The following paragraphs illustrate a poorly written example of this section of a letter that extends credit to a credit applicant and a revised version of the same material.

> Change: Important information about your account is summarized on the enclosed sheet.
>
> To: You will be happy to learn that each of your credit references informed us about how pleased they are with your prompt bill-paying habits. I am sure we will be just as satisfied.
>
> Important information about your charge account is summarized on the enclosed sheet entitled "Rules Governing a Retail Credit Agreement." I want to call your special attention to the following: the closing date of your account is the first day of each month. No finance charges will be assessed if we receive your payment by the 25th day of the month. Finance charges of 1.5 percent (18 percent APR) are calculated on the unpaid balance of your account and will be added to your next month's statement.

What is the purpose of resale and sales promotion material included in letters that extend credit?

The inclusion of resale and/or sales-promotion material in letters granting credit to customers is recommended. If an order accompanied the credit application, resale material can be used to further convince the customer that the merchandise he/she ordered was a wise selection. Resale material can also be used to sell the customer on doing business with your company.

Sales-promotion material, on the other hand, is used to inform the customer of an upcoming sale, new merchandise just received, a new line of merchandise being sold by the company, or other merchandise related to the type that the customer just ordered.

The following paragraphs illustrate the use of resale and sales-promotion material in letters extending credit to customers.

> The art prints you ordered are among our best sellers this summer. The colors in the prints coordinate well with the new pastel colors that are currently popular in home and office interiors.
>
> You will be interested to learn that we have just received permission from Clare Weymouth, another popular still-life artist, to put together a portfolio of her work that will also coordinate well with today's popular pastel interior colors. This portfolio is sure to be just as popular as the sets of Linwood prints you recently ordered. As a credit customer, you will soon receive information about the Weymouth portfolio.

What type of closing is appropriate for letters that extend credit?

In the closing of a letter that extends credit to a customer, anticipation of a pleasant relationship should be expressed. This can be accomplished by mentioning the ability to serve the customer in a courteous, prompt manner; inviting the customer to a sale available only to charge account customers; making a personal offer to be of assistance whenever desired; or expressing a "satisfaction-guaranteed" policy.

Notice the difference between these two closings.

Change:	We appreciate your business and your interest in opening a charge account.
To:	We look forward to a long, pleasant association with you. You can always count on prompt, courteous service when ordering from us since we guarantee your satisfaction with our merchandise and service.

What is the suggested plan for letters that extend credit?

The suggested plan for a letter granting credit to customers includes the following elements:

1. A fast-start opening in which the customer quickly learns the good news: that his/her order is being shipped and/or that credit is being extended;
2. A section in which the most important rules and terms governing the account are discussed. Optional material to include in this section is a discussion of the basis for the extension of credit. (Note: If the latter material is included, it should be presented before the discussion of important rules/terms.);
3. A section that includes resale material or, when appropriate, sales-promotion material;
4. A courteous closing that focuses on the future.

The letter in Figure 6–8 is an ineffective letter that grants credit to customers. The letter in Figure 6–9 is an improved version. Notice the helpful nature of the material in the revised letter.

LETTERS GRANTING ADJUSTMENTS

Defects, errors, and misunderstandings occur regardless of how much a company tries to prevent them. A courteous, persuasive adjustment letter explains circumstances that might negatively affect company goodwill.

The content of adjustment letters depends upon several factors. Is the request to be granted? Is the company, the customer, or a third party at fault? In some cases, the cause of the difficulty may be unknown. The content of the adjustment letter will depend on these considerations and the company's policy toward adjustments.

Astute business people are continually reminded of the perishable nature of goodwill as no asset is more important to company success. To build and maintain customer goodwill, companies encourage employees involved in adjustment to become skilled in handling every type of adjustment with the greatest possible speed, courtesy, and tact.

Writers of business correspondence should recognize that good customer relations established through satisfactory products and services can evaporate

Your application for credit has been received and processed. An account has been opened in your name.	A slow-start opening that presents obvious information before the good news.
The closing date of your account is the 13th day of each month. Shortly after that, you will receive a statement listing current charges. To avoid an interest charge of 1.5 percent on the unpaid balance, payment must be received by the fifth day of the following month.	A section that contains an overly brief explanation of the important rules governing the charge account.
Other important information about your account is summarized on the enclosed sheet.	A section that makes reference to the rules sheet.
We appreciate your interest in opening a charge account at Drummonds.	A weak closing.

Figure 6–8 Ineffective Credit-Granting Letter

Your new Drummonds charge card is on its way. You may begin using the card just as soon as you sign your name on its backside.	An opening that presents the good news first, along with directions for the use of the card.
We always appreciate opening charge accounts for customers like you who receive especially favorable ratings. Each reference listed on your application mentioned your prompt bill-paying habits.	A section that explains the basis for the extension of credit.
The closing date of your account is the 13th day of each month. A few days later, you will receive a statement of current charges. No finance charges will be assessed if your payment is received by the fifth day of the following month. Should you wish to extend your payment period, all you need do is pay the minimum charge that appears on the monthly statement. A finance charge of 1.5 percent (18 percent APR) of the unpaid balance will be added to your statement the following month. Other information about your account is provided on the enclosed sheet entitled "Rules Governing a Retail Credit Agreement."	A section that outlines the important rules governing the use of the card and account.
Our new fall merchandise is arriving daily. We plan an "early-bird" sale on selected merchandise early next month. As a charge customer, you will receive advance notice of this sale before it is announced to the public.	A section that contains sales-promotion material designed to interest the customer in the merchandise.
Drummonds guarantees your satisfaction with its merchandise and service. You can always count on friendly, courteous service at each of our locations.	A courteous, forward-looking closing.

Figure 6–9 Effective Credit-Granting Letter

instantly if a single adjustment letter is negative or offensive to the reader. A positive company image has to be projected in every letter.

Good customer relations can be protected through well-planned adjustment correspondence based on the you-viewpoint. The central idea in the you-approach is *courtesy*. Customer-centered courtesy is a key point in developing a company's positive image. Every adjustment letter should be reviewed to make sure that the following points have been adequately considered.

1. Has a climate of goodwill been established between the company and the claimant?
2. Have words been chosen carefully to build goodwill?
3. Has the customer been encouraged to deal with the company again?

Why should letters that grant adjustments focus on the you-viewpoint?

By focusing on the you-viewpoint, the adjuster can sooth the irritant and retain good relations. In most cases, the actual message will matter less than the manner in which the message is presented. Just what the claim actually is depends upon the circumstances of the particular situation and the honesty of the individual. Even when the customer is wrong, focusing on the you-viewpoint means that he/she is given first consideration.

When adjustment policies are based on the idea of providing service and satisfaction, every claim can present an opportunity for good customer relations. For this reason, most companies, whenever possible, avoid disagreements with customers. The assumption is made that the customer is correct in his/her statements, honest in his/her intentions, and reasonable in making requests. Therefore, only one course of action may be appropriate—and that is to grant the customer's request.

Although most companies believe they can expand business by operating on the principle of absolute customer satisfaction, other companies adopt a modified point of view. In these companies, the following attitude prevails: "When the customer is right, give him full credit; when the company is right, sell the customer on the company's point of view."

Many companies do more than simply welcome claims—they invite them. Signs in stores, restaurants, hotels, motels, and other establishments invite comments on service or reports of any discourteous treatment by employees. Manufacturers enclose slips asking purchasers to report any defects in materials or workmanship. Some companies send letters at regular intervals inviting frank reaction to their services.

Three types of letters are commonly associated with the adjustment process:

1. A letter granting the adjustment
2. A letter denying the adjustment
3. A letter granting a partial adjustment

In this chapter the letter that grants the adjustment is discussed. The other two types of letters are discussed in Chapter 7 because they contain disappointing news. Should more information be needed from the claimant before an adjustment decision can be made, a direct-request letter similar to the one presented in Chapter 5 can be prepared.

In writing a letter granting an adjustment, the use of a begrudging tone should be avoided. The letter should not convey the impression that the granting of the adjustment is a questionable action. The reader needs to be given the courtesy he/she deserves when the adjustment is favorable to him/her.

Even if the customer receives a favorable adjustment, goodwill is damaged when the adjustment is made reluctantly. The use of words that have a negative connotation should also be avoided.

A letter that grants an adjustment should begin with the good news. To open with a statement similar to the one presented in the first of the following two paragraphs is a slow-start opening.

What type of opening is appropriate for letters that grant adjustments?

Change: We have received your letter of June 22 in which you requested a replacement of the inoperable electric mixer that was in an order we shipped you on June 15.

To: An electric mixer to replace the inoperable mixer you received in a recent order is on its way. Your request for a replacement mixer was certainly appropriate.

The next section of a positive adjustment letter involves an explanation of the cause of the problem. When your company is at fault, a frank admission is appropriate. You should avoid making excuses for the problem—as well as avoid making a promise that the problem will never occur again. Such promises will surely require a future retraction! While the explanation section is important, it need not be a lengthy one. An apology is also appropriate. Notice the difference between the tone of the following two paragraphs.

What is included in the middle section of positive-adjustment letters?

Change: It is hard for us to believe that our quality-control measures did not detect the problem with the mixer you received. Of one thing you can be sure: it will not happen again.

To: While our quality-control program is 99.5 percent effective—the highest achievement record in the industry—a few defective products slip by undetected. Our goal is to achieve a 100-percent detection record. We apologize for any inconvenience the inoperable mixer may have caused you.

The next section of a letter that grants an adjustment can contain resale and/or sales-promotion material. If you believe that the customer is discouraged with the product that caused him/her to prepare a claim letter or is upset with your company, resale material may be more appropriate than sales-promotion material. On the other hand, if discouragement does not appear to be setting in, then sales-promotion material may be more appropriate. The greater the number of frequently replaced products sold by your company that the customer may be interested in, the more appropriate is the inclusion of sales-promotion material. For example, clothing fits into the frequently replaced category, while carpeting, tools, and major home appliances fit into the infrequent category. Although companies that sell clothing, for example, may benefit by including sales-promotion material in their adjustment letters, companies that sell such merchandise as carpeting, tools, and major home appliances are likely to benefit more by including resale material in their adjustment letters.

The first of the following two paragraphs uses resale material designed to rebuild the customer's confidence in an electric mixer, while the second paragraph contains sales-promotion material about an upcoming sale.

> The first time you use your new electric mixer, you will readily discover how easy it is to use. The variable-speed control enables you to select the precise mixing speed for the ingredients you are mixing. The sure-grip handle comfortably fits hands of all sizes. And the powerful motor will not be slowed by hard-to-mix ingredients. We are sure your mixer will become an indispensible appliance in your kitchen the first time it is used.
>
> The brochure that is enclosed with your replacement mixer lists the merchandise that will be on sale until July 15. The prices of our mid-summer sale merchandise are as much as 50 percent lower than their regular prices. To order any of these items, just use the convenient order blank. Your order will be filled within 24 hours of its receipt.

What type of closing is appropriate for adjustment letters?

The closing of the adjustment letter gives you another opportunity to rebuild any goodwill that may have been lost. To be avoided in the closing is material that will remind the reader of the problem situation. Because you have already apologized, do not apologize again. Rather, focus on the positive by (1) mentioning the satisfaction the reader will derive from the item that has been replaced, (2) extending an invitation to take advantage of an upcoming sale, (3) mentioning your desire to serve the customer in the future, and so forth.

The tone of the following two closing paragraphs is distinctly different. The tone of the first lacks friendliness and cordiality, while the revised closing conveys the impression that the writer is concerned about the reader.

> Change: We regret that the first electric mixer you received was inoperable.
>
> To: Many excellent buys are available during our in-progress mid-summer sale. An order can be conveniently placed by calling us on our toll-free number (1–800–234–2345) or by using the order-blank attached to the sale brochure.

What is the suggested plan for adjustment letters?

The suggested plan for an adjustment letter includes the following elements:

1. An opening in which the good news is presented first;
2. A section in which the cause of the problem is discussed;
3. A section that contains resale and/or sales-promotion material;
4. A friendly, cordial closing.

Figure 6–10 illustrates an ineffective letter in which an adjustment was granted. An improved version of the same letter is presented in Figure 6–11. The resale material in Figure 6–11 is designed to rebuild the customer's confidence in the product.

Your letter of April 10 in which you requested a replacement of your GT clock-radio has been received. We are sorry you are having problems with this appliance.	A slow-start opening that presents obvious information.
You will be glad to learn that a new clock-radio is on its way to you. It should arrive within 10 days.	A delayed presentation of the good news.
An examination of the radio you returned to us revealed several manufacturing defects that were not found by our quality-control inspectors. Although defects do not often go unnoticed by our inspectors, they were not found in the radio you purchased.	A section that contains an overly negative explanation of the cause of the defect.
We are sorry for any inconvenience you may have been caused by our carelessness.	A redundant apology that ends on a negative note.

Figure 6–10 Ineffective Letter in Which an Adjustment is Granted

A new GT clock-radio was sent to you by UPT this morning. The $5 certificate that is enclosed can be applied toward the purchase of your next GT appliance.	An opening that presents the good news first.
The goal of our quality-inspection program is to achieve a 100 percent error-detection record. While we are almost there, a few defective products slip by--and yours was one of those.	A section that explains the cause of the problem; a negative discussion handled in a positive way.
The GT clock-radio like the one you recently purchased has become our top-selling appliance. Its unique features, especially the programmable station selector, are responsible for its popularity. This feature will enable you to go to sleep at night listening to one radio station and wake up in the morning listening to another station--without your having to change the station selector.	A section that presents resale material designed to rebuild the customer's confidence in the product.
We appreciate your giving us an opportunity to live up to our motto: "Absolute Satisfaction Guaranteed."	A courteous closing.

Figure 6–11 Effective Letter in Which an Adjustment is Granted

In some instances, a favorable adjustment is made even when the customer is at fault. Perhaps the claimant is a customer of long standing, and as an accommodation, his/her claim is granted. Suppose that a customer failed to follow the directions for using a product, which created the problem situation. As an example, the high temperature at which an all-cotton garment was washed and/or dried caused the garment to shrink. The claimant, assuming that the manufacturer was liable for the shrinkage, wrote a claim letter asking for a replacement garment. The writer, in preparing the favorable adjustment, may appropriately decide to include a section that informs the reader how to prevent a recurrence of the situation. The following illustrates an appropriate "education" section of such a letter.

> All-cotton garments tend to shrink when washed in hot water or dried in clothes dryers set at a high temperature setting. Laundering instructions are found on the label sewn into the collar of our cotton shirts. These instructions indicate that the shirts are to be washed in warm water and either line-dried or dried on a warm-temperature setting in a dryer.

An example of a well-written adjustment letter that outlines the proper use of a product is illustrated in Figure 6–12.

LETTERS ACKNOWLEDGING ORDERS

The reasons for acknowledging an order are to inform the customer that his/her order has been received and that it has been shipped (or it will be shipped), to express appreciation to the customer for his/her order, and to build goodwill.

While some companies acknowledge first orders from new customers, other companies acknowledge all orders exceeding a certain dollar amount. The information presented in this section pertains to the acknowledgement of a first order—and can easily be adapted when acknowledging an order other than the first one.

What type of opening is appropriate for order-acknowledgement letters?

A letter that acknowledges an order should begin with a fast-start opening which provides the best news first. The reader will be more interested in learning about the status of his/her order than receiving a "thank you." Although including a note of thanks in the opening is appropriate, information about the status of the order should be presented first. The following example illustrates the differences between slow-start and fast-start openings.

Figure 6–12 Effective Adjustment Letter that Contains Directions on Product Use

Within the next few days, you will receive a new lamp globe to replace the damaged one you recently sent us.	An opening that presents the good news first.
An analysis of the globe revealed that the damage resulted from excessive heat build-up, which occurs when a bulb larger than 60 watts is used in the lamp. A label attached to the lamp socket indicates that the maximum bulb size to be used in the lamp is 60 watts.	A section that contains "education" material designed to help the customer avoid the same situation in the future.
We just added a "touch-n-glow" line of table lamps. To turn these attractive lamps on or off, you simply touch any part of the metal base. The shades for these lamps are available in a variety of fabrics and shapes. The brochure that is enclosed illustrates the various types of bases and shades that are available.	A section that contains sales-promotion material designed to spark the reader's interest in other products.
We are pleased to have you as a customer.	A courteous closing.

Change: Thank you for your recent order for three pairs of slacks.
To: The three pairs of slacks you recently ordered from us were sent to you this morning by UPS, and they should arrive in three days. Your order and the check for $139.45 are appreciated.

What type of information is appropriate for inclusion in the middle section of order-acknowledgement letters?

The inclusion of resale and/or sales-promotion material is also appropriate in letters that acknowledge orders. To decide whether to include resale material or sales-promotion material, apply the rule that was presented in the section on letters granting an adjustment. For frequently replaced merchandise, the inclusion of sales-promotion material may be the better choice. But for infrequently replaced merchandise, the inclusion of resale material may be preferred.

The following paragraph illustrates the use of sales-promotion material.

You will be interested to learn that all of our summer stock goes on sale next week. Prices on this stock will be reduced between 30 and 50 percent, enabling you to purchase at greatly reduced prices much of next summer's clothing. A summer-sale catalog, along with an order blank, is enclosed with your shipment. Orders, most of which are filled within 24 hours of their receipt, can be charged as we honor all major credit cards.

In letters that acknowledge orders, you should, whenever possible, include material that reflects your desire to serve the customer. This material can take many forms, such as mentioning your practice of shipping within 24 hours of order receipt, your satisfaction-guaranteed policy, your honoring major credit cards, and so on. In some instances, service-attitude material is included as a separate section. In other cases, it is incorporated into other sections, as the paragraph above illustrates.

What type of closing is appropriate for the closing of order-acknowledgement letters?

The closing of an order-acknowledgement letter should be forward-looking. The material can mention your interest in serving the reader or your willingness to answer any questions the reader may have about your products.

The first of the following two closing paragraphs is weak, while the revised version is much more effective.

Change: We appreciate your business.
To: We appreciate having you as a new customer. You can always count on fast, courteous service when ordering from the Emmery Company.

What is the suggested plan for letters that acknowledge orders?

The suggested plan for an order-acknowledgement letter includes the following elements:

1. A fast-start opening that mentions the status of the order and that thanks the customer for his/her business;
2. A section that contains resale or sales-promotion material, whichever is appropriate, and that also incorporates service-attitude material;
3. A forward-looking closing.

Your book order that was shipped this morning should arrive in 3-5 days. We appreciate having your business.	A fast-start opening that presents good news first and that expresses appreciation for the customer's business.
We have just become a distributor of books published by Smith-Holly Publishers. As a new distributor, we are able to offer for a limited time a 10 percent discount on the wholesale price. A current list of Smith-Holly titles and the discounted prices is enclosed. You will notice that many of the year's best-selling books are Smith-Holly titles. An order blank is attached to the list.	A section that contains sales-promotion material designed to promote a new line of merchandise.
Our recently expanded warehouse facilities enable us to process most orders within 24 hours of their receipt. We also provide a rush-delivery service that will enable you to receive a shipment the day following the receipt of the order.	A section that contains service-attitude material designed to enhance the customer's desire to purchase from your company.
You can always count on efficient, courteous service when ordering from the Masters Book Distributing Company.	A forward-looking closing.

Figure 6–13 Effective Order-Acknowledgement Letter

The letter in Figure 6–13 illustrates a well-written order-acknowledgement letter. Notice how sales-promotion material is incorporated into the letter.

Rather than writing a letter to acknowledge an order, some companies use a form message that is often printed on a post card. The variable information is inserted either by hand or by a printer device. The following illustrates a message that mentions the shipment of the order (or the pending shipment of the order):

> Your order was shipped this morning (or will be shipped on) ______________________ by United Parcel Service. Normal delivery time for an order shipped this distance is ______ days.
>
> We sincerely appreciate your business.
>
> Very truly yours,
> JOHNSON PLASTICS COMPANY
> Mary Brown, Order Correspondent

LETTERS THAT GRANT FAVORS

Writing a letter to grant a favor should be one of the easiest letters to write. However, the intent of many favor-granting messages is diluted by wording that omits the spirit of willingness or that implies a grudging consent.

The opening paragraph of a letter that grants a favor should be cheerful and cordial. The granting of the request, which is what the reader is most interested in, is mentioned first. Beginning with any other information is likely to result in a slow-start opening. The following illustrates an effective beginning for such a letter.

What type of opening is appropriate for letters that grant favors?

> Yes, I look forward to showing your students our beautiful new facility. A tour of our building will enable them to see the latest in interior office design.

When a favor is granted with a limitation or a restriction, that information should be included in the letter. For example, consider the following as an appropriate discussion of a limitation.

> So that we can complete the tour before the employees leave at 4:30, it should begin no later than 3:00. Should you prefer to begin the tour earlier in the afternoon, that will be possible as my schedule is open all afternoon on May 23.

The granting of a favor with a limitation or a restriction often necessitates some action on the part of the reader. The following paragraph effectively outlines the requested action.

> Will you please call me at 453–3456 when you decide on the time you would like the tour to begin. We can finalize any other details at that time.

The closing of the letter that grants a favor should be cordial and courteous, as well as action oriented, if appropriate. If the reader of the letter is being asked to do something, reference to that action can be mentioned in the closing.

What type of closing is appropriate for letters that grant favors?

> I look forward to hearing from you—and also to showing your students our new facility.

The suggested plan for a letter that grants a favor includes the following elements:

What is the suggested plan for letters that grant favors?

1. A cordial, courteous opening that mentions the granting of the favor;
2. A discussion of restrictions or limitations that pertain to the granting of the favor;
3. A discussion, if appropriate, of any action the reader is to take in accepting the favor;
4. A cordial, courteous closing that is action oriented when appropriate.

An example of a well-written letter that grants a favor is presented in Figure 6–14.

I will be delighted to show your nephew around Des Moines when he is here on October 10. We are happy to show our city off to others every chance we get.	A cordial opening that mentions the granting of the favor.
Please have Rob call me at home (443-5643) on the evening of the 9th so we can arrange a time and place to meet. If he is available over the noon hour, perhaps we can arrange to have lunch together.	A section that contains a discussion of the action which the person receiving the favor is to take.
I appreciate having an opportunity to meet your nephew--and will do everything I can to make sure he gets a proper introduction to Des Moines.	A cordial, courteous closing.

Figure 6–14 Efficient Letter in Which a Favor is Granted

When a person receives a favor, the grantor should receive an immediate "thank you." The thanks can be extended over the phone, in person, or in a letter. The suggested plan for a letter of thanks includes the following elements:

1. An opening that expresses appreciation to or that thanks the grantor for the granting of the favor;
2. A discussion of how the granting of the favor will be beneficial;
3. An offer to be of similar help, if appropriate;
4. A friendly, courteous closing.

Figure 6–15 illustrates a letter of thanks for the granting of a favor. The sincerity of the message gives the letter a genuine tone.

LETTERS OF CONGRATULATION

An excellent—although often overlooked—way to recognize the achievement or accomplishment of an acquaintance is to send a letter of congratulations. These letters are one of the best ways for an individual and/or a company to build effective relations with others. Letters of congratulation would be one of the most common types of letters written in the business world if these letters were prepared as frequently as they should be.

Some business firms maintain a regular newspaper clipping service to identify the persons for whom these letters are appropriate. When a special event concerning a client or associate is reported in the paper, for example, the article is clipped and enclosed with the congratulatory message.

Some of the occasions or events for which congratulatory letters are prepared are: a job promotion, an election to an office, an achievement in a special interest or hobby, the receipt of an award, a birthday, a retirement, and so forth.

What qualities should letters of congratulation possess?

One of the indispensable qualities of letters of congratulation is sincerity. Trite, stilted phrases indicate a lack of sincerity and destroy the goodwill that

Both Rob and I appreciate your being available to show him around Des Moines on October 10. He will call you the evening of the 9th.	An opening that expresses appreciation to the reader for granting the favor.
Your showing him around Des Moines should enable him to decide if he wants to accept his company's offer to relocate there. Because he does not know any one who lives in Des Moines, he is having difficulty obtaining the information needed to make a relocation decision.	A section that presents a discussion of how the granting of the favor will benefit the person receiving the favor.
If I can ever return the favor, please let me know. Rob is also anxious to return the favor whenever he can.	A statement of an offer to reciprocate.
I appreciate your helping Rob.	A courteous closing.

Figure 6–15 Effective Thank You Letter for the Granting of a Favor

congratulatory letters should create. In addition, the achievement or accomplishment should be acknowledged with enthusiasm and friendliness. To be avoided is the conveyance of a patronizing attitude.

The suggested plan for a congratulatory letter includes the following elements:

What is the suggested plan for letters of congratulation?

1. An opening that congratulates the reader for his/her accomplishment or achievement;
2. A section that expresses your understanding of the importance of the accomplishment or achievement;
3. A courteous closing that extends best wishes for continued success.

An example of a well-written congratulatory letter is shown in Figure 6–16.

Figure 6–16 Effective Letter of Congratulations

Congratulations on your being recognized as Austin's Young Business Leader of the Year. You are certainly a deserving first recipient of this award.	An opening that congratulates the reader on the accomplishment.
The countless hours you have spent trying to improve the business climate of Austin finally "paid off" when it was recently recognized as one of the state's most desirable business communities. You can be proud of the fact that you gave your time and effort for the good of the community--and not for any personal gain.	A section that presents a discussion of your impression of the importance of the reader's accomplishment.
You have my best wishes for the continued success and happiness that you certainly deserve.	A courteous closing that extends best wishes.

LETTERS ACCEPTING INVITATIONS

A letter in which a social-business invitation or an invitation to an event is accepted should convey appreciation and enthusiasm and should be sent as soon as possible after receiving the invitation. Although these letters may be fairly brief, certain essential elements must be included.

In accepting an invitation to an event, the acceptance should be conveyed in the opening. Also incorporated into the acceptance are the important details about the event: date, time, and place. These details are wisely included (1) to verify the accuracy of these details in case an error has been made, and (2) to provide a record of the details in case the invitation becomes misplaced. The letter ends with a courteous closing that expresses appreciation for the invitation.

What is the suggested plan for letters in which social-business invitations are accepted?

The suggested plan for a letter of acceptance for a social-business invitation includes the following elements:

1. An opening in which the invitation is cordially and enthusiastically accepted;
2. A review of the important details about the event;
3. A courteous closing that expresses appreciation for the invitation.

The letter in Figure 6–17 illustrates a well-written letter accepting an invitation to a social-business event. Notice how the important details about the event have been incorporated into the letter.

After the event has taken place, good etiquette may require your sending a thank-you message to the individual(s) who hosted the event. The beginning of such a message should include a cordial expression of thanks. The highlights of the event are discussed next, followed by a cordial expression of appreciation in the closing.

What is the suggested plan for thank-you letters?

The suggested plan for a letter of thanks for an event includes the following elements:

1. An opening that contains a cordial, sincere thanks;
2. A discussion of the highlights of the event;
3. A courteous, cordial closing.

Figure 6–17 Effective Letter in Which a Social-Business Invitation is Accepted

Mrs. Brown and I enthusiastically accept your invitation to the retirement dinner for Mr. Robinson. This event will be a fine tribute to Jack whose accomplishments as executive vice president of Willoby Corporation are extensive.	An opening that mentions the enthusiastic acceptance of the invitation.
Because the retirement dinner is to be a surprise to Jack, we will say nothing to him about it before that evening.	A section that reviews the important details of the event.
Mrs. Brown and I appreciate your inviting us to this important event. We look forward to seeing you at The Embers Restaurant at 6 p.m. on October 20.	A closing that expresses appreciation and that reviews other important details.

Mrs. Brown and I sincerely thank you for inviting us to Mr. Robinson's retirement dinner. We were especially pleased to be able to join others in paying tribute to a hard-working, dedicated employee of the Willoby Corporation.	An opening that expresses cordial thanks for the event.
We were quite impressed with Jack's impromptu after-dinner remarks. The graciousness with which he delivered those remarks was impressive. As always, he gave others all the credit for his success.	A section that contains a discussion of the event's highlights.
We appreciate your giving us the opportunity to help honor Jack.	A cordial closing.

Figure 6–18 Effective Letter Expressing Appreciation for a Social-Business Invitation

Figure 6–18 illustrates a well-written letter that expresses appreciation for the invitation.

Occasionally you may receive a letter inviting you to speak before a group. In a letter accepting such an invitation, you should state your acceptance in the opening paragraph. Such important details as date, time, and place should also be mentioned as a means of confirming their accuracy. When invited to speak before a group, you may be given the opportunity to select the subject and/or topic of your presentation. The subject and/or topic of your choice should be included in your letter of acceptance.

The suggested plan for a letter that accepts a speaking invitation includes the following elements.

What is the suggested plan for letters that convey the acceptance of speaking invitations?

1. An enthusiastic opening that mentions the acceptance of the invitation;
2. A confirmation of the important details, including the subject or topic of your presentation, if appropriate;
3. A courteous closing.

The letter shown in Figure 6–19 illustrates an effectively written letter in which a speaking invitation is accepted.

Figure 6–19 Effective Letter Conveying the Acceptance of a Speaking Invitation

Yes, I am available to speak at the May meeting of the Personnel Administrators Association--and I enthusiastically accept your invitation to talk about new legislation affecting personnel management.	An opening that enthusiastically conveys the acceptance.
My schedule will enable me to join your group for the dinner that begins at 6 on the 18th. I will arrive at The Continental a few minutes before 6.	A section that provides a discussion confirming important details about the event.
Thanks for inviting me to speak to your group.	A courteous closing.

CHAPTER SUMMARY

Some of the good-news letters that you will have an opportunity to write in the business world are letters replying to inquiries about products, services, and people; letters responding to credit requests; letters granting adjustments and acknowledging orders; letters granting favors; letters offering congratulations; and letters accepting invitations.

Good-news letters should begin with the good news or main idea, use a fast-start opening, provide explanatory details or information of primary and secondary importance, incorporate a you-viewpoint, and incorporate an appropriate closing.

In deciding whether or not to grant credit to applicants, the factors of capital, capacity, and character are considered. These are known as the 3 C's of credit. The types of credit accounts commonly found are regular credit accounts, 90-day-same-as-cash accounts, and long-term installment accounts.

Although the suggested plans used in preparing good-news letters do have common elements, you need to be aware of the differences among the plans used in preparing the various types of letters.

REVIEW QUESTIONS

1. Identify the characteristics of good-news letters.
2. What type of opening should be used when writing a response to an inquiry about a product?
3. When is the inclusion of resale material in a response to an inquiry about a product advisable? The inclusion of sales-promotion material?
4. How does the opening of a response to an inquiry about a product differ from the opening of a response to an inquiry about a person?
5. What are the three C's of credit?
6. What types of credit accounts are typically used in the business world?
7. What should the opening of a letter that solicits credit customers accomplish?
8. What purposes are accomplished by the letter that extends credit to customers?
9. In a letter that extends credit, how does the use of resale material differ from the use of sales-promotion material?
10. What information should be included in the opening of a letter that grants an adjustment?
11. What determines if you should use resale or sales-promotion material in a letter that grants an adjustment?
12. What information should be included in the opening of a letter that acknowledges an order?
13. What are the elements of the plan for a letter that grants a favor?

APPLICATION PROBLEMS

1. Prepare a written critique of the following letter, evaluating grammar usage, punctuation, conformity with the suggested plan, and conformity with the writing essentials discussed in Chapters 3 and 4.

It is with a great deal of pleasure that I notify you that you have been qualified for one of our prestigious charge accounts. Not everyone qualifies, but then I'm sure I don't have to tell you that.

I hope you enjoy using the card often, just make sure you pay your account in a timely manner. We don't want to have to send the sheriff after you—but then we are sure you will pay as you don't want to have the sheriff coming after you any worse that we want to have to send him after you.

You have our best wishes and congratulations on being the proud owner of a Ellington's charge account.

2. Rewrite the letter in application problem 1, making sure that the weaknesses you identified in your critique have been eliminated. Make any assumptions you need to make and supply any details that may be missing.

3. Prepare a written critique of the following letter, evaluating grammar usage, punctuation, conformity with the suggested plan, and conformity with the writing essentials discussed in Chapters 3 and 4.

Thank you for your recent letter of October 3 in which you inquired about our fantastic car polish. We are glad to have an opportunity to respond to you.

The polish, although really a wax, is as easy to apply and remove as a liquid polish is. Therefore, you don't have to have the muscles of a champion weight lifter to use our product. One coat of wax is guaranteed to give your car a bright sheen for a whole year—just imagine, a whole year. Although I am not going to name names, but I am sure our competitors can't make that claim. Just think one time a year is all you need to keep your car looking as shiny as it did in the showroom, can you believe it?

Our dealer in your area will be glad to demonstrate how good our product is.

4. Rewrite the letter in application problem 3, making sure that the weaknesses you identified in your critique have been eliminated. Make any assumptions you need to make and supply any details that are missing.

5. Using the proofreader's marks shown in Figure 4–5, edit the following letter:

We are glad to be able to send you a new "n" volume to your *World Encyclopedia* set. Unfortunately, some of the pages were inserted upside down at the bindery—and we were unaware until you returned this volume to us.

The new volume is being mailed this morning by UPS. It should arrive at your destination within a week. Please do not let this situation tarnish your image of our company as we are the nation's leading publisher of encyclopedia's.

Enclosed is a copy of our sales booklet, please use the handy order blank to order any items you may want.

6. You are the customer service representative for the Arco Products Company, which is located at 19 Pine Avenue, Chicago, IL 67544. Your company is one of the nation's largest manufacturers of electronic entertainment equipment, such as video cassette recorders, televisions, stereos, tape recorders, and so forth. Your company is widely recognized for the superior workmanship in the products it manufactures. Because of its reputation, Arco has many customers who wouldn't have any equipment but Arco equipment. You recently had a letter from a potential customer (Charles Smith, 1212 Hornblower Avenue, Sacramento, CA 98944) who asked several questions about the Arco B–8910 video cassette recorder. Mr. Smith wanted to know the length of the programming period on the VCR and the number of programs that can be recorded during that period (4 programs in 14 days), how many heads the B–8910 has (4), and who is the closest Arco dealer to Sacramento (Walt's TV and Appliances, 1232 Jackson Boulevard, San Jose, CA 18234). You also decided to mention that the B–8910 has stereo audio. Arco's nationwide Mid-Summer Sale begins in two weeks. During this time, all dealers will be reducing the price of their entire Arco line by 30 percent. Prepare a response to Charles Smith's inquiry.

7. You are the manager of franchising for The Chicken House, which has franchise operations throughout the United States. The franchise operations are located at 8764 Deerfield Road, San Antonio, TX 57564. You recently received a letter from Mr. Bill Harper, 231 Buffalo Road, Pueblo, CO 48344 who asked for answers to several questions about The Chicken House's franchises. Answers to his questions are found in the parentheses: amount of cash needed for startup ($50,000), how much can be borrowed from the company ($25,000), interest rate on borrowed money (8 percent), nature of training provided by The Chicken House (owners/managers receive a three-week intensive training program), extent of help in making market analyses (extensive), and the monthly royalty fee (2 percent). A recent article in *Changing World,* an investment magazine, identified The Chicken House as one of the most desirable franchises available today. Franchise owners typically receive an 8–10 percent return on their investment, which is also one of the most attractive return rates provided in the franchise industry today. Prepare a letter to Bill Harper.

8. You are a public relations assistant for the Mass Central Insurance Company, which is located at 345 Beacon Street in Boston, MA 09821. Your company just developed a new term insurance policy that promises to become a leader in a short time. The Progressive Term Policy will be advertised in all the national magazines in two weeks. Accompanying the ad is a coupon that interested parties can send back to Mass Central to request more information. A letter is to accompany the packet of information that the interested parties will receive. You are responsible for preparing the "form" letter that will be included with the packet. Because high-speed word processing equipment is available, the letters are to be personalized with the recipient's name. You decide to mention several of the policy highlights in the letter: provides a greater amount of coverage per dollar of premium than the three leading term policies; after 20 years, the term policy can be converted to a paid-up whole-policy equal to 20 percent of the value of the initial term policy; insured has a choice of level premiums or level amount of coverage; and Mass Central has a well-trained, large field staff ready to serve insured's needs. Prepare the letter.

9. You are an assistant professor of business communications at Southwest State College in Tempe, AZ 98745. Mary Greenlee, one of the best students you had in your written communications class last semester, has used with permission your name as a reference in applying for a job in the customer service department of the Tempe Gas Company, which is located at 2900 Valley Drive, Tempe, AZ 98755. Ms. Ruth Beatty, manager of the customer service department, has asked for you to provide her with answers to the following questions regarding Ms. Greenlee and her background: 1. How effective are her oral and written communication skills?—excellent; has an excellent foundation in business writing. 2. How well does she work with others?—very well; on an in-class group project, she emerged as the leader of her group. 3. Is she motivated?—yes, very much so; often did more than what was reasonably expected. 4. Does she possess a good grasp of business fundamentals?—yes, is a business administration major. In addition, you feel she has excellent leadership potential as she is currently serving as president of the Business Management Club. Prepare the letter to respond to Ms. Beatty's request for information about Ms. Greenlee whom you are glad to give a top recommendation.

10. You are the credit manager for Handley's Department Store, which is located in the East Mall in Ponca City, TX 54478. One of your responsibilities is to prepare letters that are designed to solicit credit customers. Several months have now passed since you sent out the last letter so you decide to prepare another letter that will be mailed out around September 15—just before customers begin to think about the upcoming Christmas season. You know from experience that a number of the customers who have responded to your letters in the past have not been aware of the advantages of purchasing on credit until receiving your letters. Therefore, you have found the inclusion of this material in your letters to be quite useful. Among the specific advantages you like to promote are these: advanced notice of sales before the sales are announced to the public, being able to purchase merchandise without having to pay cash at the time of the purchase, occasional special discount offered to credit customers, and convenience of being able to shop without needing checks or large amounts of cash. You also know that charge customers, on the average, spend about 10 percent more per purchase than do cash customers, which is certainly financially advantageous to the store. Because the individuals on the list to receive your letter have already been pre-qualified, all they have to do is sign the credit application form you are enclosing with the letter. You feel the potential customer may also be pleased to learn that Handley's just joined an exclusive buying group that will not only double the number of merchandise lines now sold in the store, but also will result in lower prices of merchandise because of the volume buying. Prepare the letter.

11. You are being considered for a job in the credit department of the Grant Oil Company, which is located at 1823 Hammlett Road, Dallas, TX 65686. One of the duties of this job is the preparation of correspondence dealing with credit. As part of the selection process, you were asked to prepare a sample letter for use by Grant in soliciting prospective credit customers. The individual who asked you to prepare the letter suggested that you outline for the recipient the various advantages of purchasing on credit, including the following: being able to delay paying for the purchase, not having to carry large amounts of cash with you, and being able to use the card nationwide. He also suggested you might want to mention the latest *Consumer News* rated Grants' steel-belted tires as the "best tire buy in the country." These tires give their owner the greatest number of miles per dollar of cost of any tire currently on the market. Prepare the letter that is designed to solicit new credit customers.

12. You, as credit manager for Handley's Department Store (see application problem 5), are also responsible for preparing letters that extend credit to customers. In response to the letter you recently sent to solicit prospective credit customers, you received a signed application from Ms. Mary Jane O'Donnell, 345 University Drive, Ponca City, TX 54478. She is a senior at Ponca City College and will be graduating in three months. Experience has taught you that individuals who are about to be graduated or who have recently graduated from college are often excellent credit customers because they have higher-than-usual purchasing needs, they do not attempt to save as much as their counterparts, and their salaries enable them to pay their accounts on time. Prepare a letter extending credit to Ms. O'Donnell. Her credit limit is $300. Remind her that an enclosure entitled "Rules Governing the Use of Your Handley's Charge Account" accompanies the letter. Among the important rules you decide to mention in the letter are: 1) the interest rate on unpaid balances is 1.5 percent per month (18 percent APR); 2) a minimum charge of 10 percent or $10, whichever is greater, is to be paid each month the account shows activity; 3) the closing date of the account is the 28th day of each month; and 4) to be properly credited, payments on account have to be received within 25 days after the account's closing date. You might also want to mention that your Santa's Helper Sale will run from November 19–24, and the prices on many items in the store will be reduced by 20–25 percent.

13. You work in the adjustments department of the Arnold Manufacturing Company, which is located at 6876 Outer Belt Drive, St. Louis, MO 63723. The company manufacturers a variety of lawn and garden power tools. While Arnold's tools are sold in hardware and garden stores throughout the Midwest, it has customers throughout the continental United States who purchase by mail order. You recently had returned an electric hedge clipper that John Abrahamson (18 Lake Lane, Utica, NY 10189) purchased by mail order on June 2. The curt note attached to the clipper explained that the tool did not work when it was received. He is asking that you send him another clipper to replace this one. An examination of the clipper revealed that one of the internal electrical wires was not properly soldered, which prevented a suitable contact. While your company has quality-control measures that are to find such flaws, this one slipped by undetected. Grant Mr. Abrahamson's request that you replace the original clipper with another one that works properly. The replacement clipper was shipped this morning by UPS. Mention in the letter that Arnold is now carrying a rubber hose line. These hoses are guaranteed for seven years; they are available in a variety of colors, lengths, and diameters; and a new quick-coupler device is attached to each hose end that eliminates the threaded couplers. Quick-couplers with threaded ends are also available which facilitate attachment of hoses with conventional ends.

14. You are the head of the auditing unit at Jackson Electric Company, 1123 Industrial Drive, Omaha, NE 68443. You just received a letter from a college friend of yours (Nick Cormun, 18 Seaside Road, Boston, MA 18713) who asked if you would be able to spend a few hours with his younger brother Greg when he is in Omaha on June 18 and 19. Greg is an accounting major at Boston University and cannot decide what area of accounting he wants to go into. He has an interview at one of the banks in Omaha on the 18th and 19th. Nick suggested that the evening of the 19th might be good as Greg doesn't leave Omaha until the next morning. You are excited to meet Nick's brother, to tell him about a career in auditing, and to show him around Omaha just in case he gets the job in the bank. You would like for Greg to call you when he arrives (office phone: 484–0874; home phone: 854–4848) so you can make final arrangements. Suggest to Nick that Greg be a dinner guest in your home the evening of the 19th.

15. You are a student in Professor John Smith's written communications class at Eastern State College, Champion, IL 68543. You were just reading the school's paper, *The Advocate,* and noticed in an article that summarized the school's board of regents' actions that Professor Smith was just promoted from assistant to associate professor. You were especially glad to read this information because you have found his class to be one of the best—if not the best—that you have ever taken. He makes learning about writing exciting, he has helped you master writing fundamentals, he motivates his students to be the best that they can be, and he shows a considerable amount of concern for their welfare. Write a letter congratulating Professor Smith on his well-deserved promotion.

16. You are currently a director on the board of the North Platte Chamber of Commerce. One of your specific duties on the board is to represent the Chamber at a variety of social/business functions. You just received a letter from Ms. Sally Thomas, North Platte High School, North Platte, NE 58533 asking you to provide a short welcome at the banquet that follows a state-wide teachers' meeting. Your spouse has also been invited to attend the banquet. As a former teacher, you especially appreciate the opportunity to provide a short welcome at the banquet that will begin at 6:15 p.m. on April 12 in the White Horse Hotel. Both you and your spouse appreciate the dinner invitation that you can accept. Prepare a letter in which you accept this invitation.

Chapter 7

Disappointing-News Letters

LEARNING OBJECTIVES

After studying this chapter, you should be able to

1. Discuss ways to improve the effectiveness of disappointing-news letters.
2. Discuss the "do nature" suggestions when preparing disappointing-news letters.
3. Discuss the "don't nature" suggestions when preparing disappointing-news letters.
4. Identify the elements of the suggested plan used in preparing the various types of disappointing-news letters.
5. Prepare effective letters of the type discussed in this chapter.

A variety of situations arise in the business world that require the preparation of letters in which disappointing news is conveyed. Your goal in writing these letters is to state the refusal in an unoffensive way to avoid alienating your reader.

Because the potential exists for disappointing recipients of negative-news letters, special care should be exercised in planning and preparing these messages. The impact of each word you use has to be carefully weighed. The location of the negative information in each letter also has to be carefully considered. To place the refusal too early in the letter may destroy some of the goodwill that letter writers try to capture in their messages.

The types of disappointing-news letters discussed in this chapter are:

1. Negative answers to inquiries
2. Negative response to adjustment requests
3. Negative response to credit requests
4. Problem-order messages
5. Declining of invitations
6. Declining of favor requests

ORGANIZING DISAPPOINTING-NEWS LETTERS

Where is the refusal statement presented in direct- and indirect-plan letters?

Two options are available to you when organizing disappointing-news messages: the indirect organizational plan and the direct organizational plan. The location of the statement of refusal in the letter determines which plan is used. The indirect plan delays the refusal statement until after the facts have been presented and the reasons for the refusal have been discussed. The direct plan, on the other hand, presents the statement of refusal at the beginning of the letter. Of the two options, the indirect plan is generally preferred.

The following outlines show the difference between the indirect and direct options.

Indirect Option	*Direct Option*
1. Begin with a neutral or buffered beginning	1. State the refusal
2. Review the facts and analyze the reasons for refusal	2. Review the facts and analyze the reasons for the refusal
3. State the refusal (and make counteroffer if appropriate)	3. Make counteroffer (if appropriate)
4. Courteous closing	4. Courteous closing

A review of the indirect-plan letter in Figure 7–1a and the direct-plan letter in Figure 7–1b reveals noticeable differences. Although the letters contain essentially the same information, the order of the information varies considerably. The buffered opening of the indirect letter will most likely maintain goodwill more effectively than the opening of the direct letter that some readers will find quite abrupt and harsh.

SUGGESTIONS FOR IMPROVING THE EFFECTIVENESS OF DISAPPOINTING-NEWS LETTERS

Much of the negative tone in disappointing-news letters can be eliminated if you exercise care when selecting words in preparing the opening, in writing the refusal, and in making the counteroffer, if one is appropriate. The following discussion outlines how the various sections of disappointing-news letters can be effectively developed.

Neutral or Buffered Opening

The purpose of the neutral or buffered opening is to diffuse as much as possible the situation about which the letter is being written. Stating the refusal in the opening sentence, a characteristic of the direct plan, is likely to cause the reader

As a long-term financial contributor to several organizations that help the community's less-fortunate children, we are very supportive of the activities of the Providence House Society. We were delighted to read the recently published newspaper article about the successful lives that several of your former dependent children are now enjoying as adults.

Our property insurance carrier prohibits the use of our parking lot and adjacent lawn for non-company events. When we called our agent about purchasing a one-day liability insurance policy so you could hold your annual spring outing on our premises, we found that the special insurance had to be purchased for a minimum of 30 days. Because the cost of this special insurance is prohibitive, we are suggesting the use of the facilities at Palmer Park. You can purchase through the city's Parks and Recreation Department one-day liability insurance coverage for special events held at this park.

We would like to donate to Providence House Society an amount equal to the cost of this one-day special insurance coverage should you decide to have your outing at Palmer Park. As soon as you know how much the cost of the coverage will be, please let me know so that we can send you a check.

Best wishes for a successful spring outing.

Figure 7–1a Disappointing-News Letter Using Indirect Plan

to become even more angry or upset. In developing the neutral or buffered opening, you will find the following suggestions helpful.

1. Avoid the use of irrelevant material.
2. Avoid the use of information that might cause the reader to assume that his/her request is being granted.
3. Do not apologize unless you are at fault.
4. Keep the buffered opening an appropriate length. One that is too short may seem abrupt, while one that is too long is likely to arouse the reader's suspicion.
5. Consider the buffer to be a transitional section that paves the way for outlining the reasons that the request cannot be granted.
6. Avoid the use of a slow-start opening that contains such an obvious statement as "We have received your letter of March 2 in which you requested an adjustment on your account."

The types of material suitable for inclusion in the opening of disappointing-news letters are a discussion of the material in previous communication on which you and the reader agree; material that expresses your desire to be cooperative; material which assures the reader that his/her situation has been given full consideration; material that relays any favorable information that

The cost of the special insurance is prohibitive that would be needed for Providence House Society to hold its annual spring outing on our premises. Because our property insurance prohibits the use of our parking lot and adjacent lawn for non-company events, we contacted our insurance agent about purchasing a special liability policy. We learned that the special insurance had to be purchased for a minimum of 30 days.

As we are a long-time financial contributor to organizations that help the community's less-fortunate children, we want to make sure your annual spring outing is a success. Therefore, we suggest you use the facilities at Palmer Park. The city's Parks and Recreation Department sells one-day liability insurance coverage for special events held at the park.

We would like to donate to Providence House Society an amount equal to the cost of this one-day special insurance coverage should you decide to have your outing at Palmer Park. As soon as you know how much the cost of the coverage will be, please contact me so that we can send you a check.

We were delighted to read the recently published article about the successful lives that several of your former dependent children are now enjoying as adults. Success stories like these are certainly heart-warming. We hope Providence House Society continues to enjoy the same rate of success in the future.

Figure 7–1b Disappointing-News Letter Using Direct Plan

may be appropriate for the situation; and material that shows empathy for the reader's dilemma.

Review of the Facts and Analysis of the Reasons for the Refusal

Why should the facts be reviewed and the reasons for the refusal be analyzed?

The purpose of this section is to review the facts and analyze the situation in such a way that the reader will understand your refusal. The more convinced the reader is that you made the correct decision under the circumstances, the more likely the reader's goodwill can be kept. In the indirect plan, the reasons for the refusal are stated before the actual refusal. If the facts are carefully outlined, the reader may have already concluded that the refusal is warranted before actually reading the refusal.

In this section of the disappointing-news letter, you should present the facts of the situation in a clearcut, straight-forward manner. The reasons should be presented as convincingly as possible, and those reasons that benefit the reader should be emphasized. Any reason you incorporate that has reader benefit is more powerful than a reason that lacks reader benefit.

In addition, you should avoid making accusations in offering the reasons. To tell the reader that "Your steam iron malfunctioned because you failed to use only distilled water in it, as the directions indicated," is accusatory. A much-improved version of the same sentence would be: "The directions that came with your steam iron indicated that only distilled water—and not tap water—is to be used in your appliance."

In some cases, the reasons for the refusal may have both favorable and unfavorable elements. Psychologically, discussing the favorable elements before the unfavorable ones is preferable. To illustrate, suppose a credit applicant is being denied credit because of an unfavorable assets-liabilities ratio, although all of the applicant's credit references reported on-time bill-paying experiences with this individual. In this case, the bill-paying habits should be discussed before the unfavorable assets-liabilities ratio. In addition, presenting general reasons before specific reasons may be less offensive to the reader.

Stating the Refusal

How should the refusal be stated?

The more clearly you discussed the facts in the previous section, the less likely the reader will have ill feelings toward you when reading the refusal statement. In fact, in some instances, you may be able to imply the refusal rather than specifically expressing it. However, if the chance exists for a misunderstanding of the implied refusal, you will wisely use a more explicit statement.

When appropriate, the statement of refusal should be interwoven with the positive counterproposal. This section can be used to emphasize what you can do for the reader rather than what you cannot do. For example, suppose you are unable to extend credit in the amount requested but can extend credit for a lesser amount. Focusing attention on what you can do will likely maintain the reader's goodwill.

What is the purpose of resale material in the refusal statement?

Integrating resale material with the statement of refusal can also help soften the statement of refusal. Some disappointing messages appropriately contain material designed to resell the reader on the services, products, or practices of the organization for which you work. If the situation is appropriate for the use of resale material, you should consider its inclusion.

Where should the statement of refusal be placed?

The actual statement of refusal should be placed in the least emphasized position in the paragraph. Because the beginning and ending of paragraphs tend to carry more emphasis than the middle, consideration should be given to including the statement in the middle. The use of negative phrases, such as "we must refuse . . . ," "we are unable to grant . . . ," should also be avoided.

Courteous Closing

What characteristics should the closings of refusal letters possess?

A courteous closing should help reduce any negative feelings the reader has after reading your refusal. Consequently, the closing should have a positive rather than a negative tone. Care needs to be exercised in writing a closing that sounds sincere because the reader is likely to react negatively to an insincere closing.

Some of the ways that a courteous closing can be developed are by:

1. Explaining what further action the reader is to take (such as providing additional documentation, completing a form, and so forth) and the date by which the action is to be taken.

2. Reviewing why the reader's continued patronage or potential patronage will be appreciated.
3. Offering to be of help in the future (if appropriate).
4. Expressing good wishes (if appropriate).

Suggestions for enhancing the effectiveness of disappointing-news messages are presented below. Each suggestion is followed by one or more sentences that illustrate its use.

DO'S AND DON'TS TO FOLLOW IN PREPARING DISAPPOINTING-NEWS MESSAGES

What suggestions do you have for improving the effectiveness of disappointing-news letters?

Suggestions of a Do-Nature

1. Use a neutral or buffered opening that produces agreement rather than disagreement.

> When you purchase a Garden Wise lawn mower, you have every right to expect that it will be of the quality commonly associated with the Garden Wise name.
>
> The items you recently ordered from us have been selling very well.

2. Discuss the facts and analyze the situation in sufficient detail, which will help convince the reader of your honesty and sincerity.

> We consider a number of factors when reviewing applications for credit. Included are such factors as length of time at one residence, length of time of current employment, income, assets, bill-paying record, and amount of current financial obligations.

3. Consider using an implicit refusal rather than an explicit refusal.

> The warranty that came with your Mix-Rite electric mixer is in effect for the first year of ownership, beginning with the date of purchase. Our records show your mixer was purchased more than two years ago.

4. Capitalize on what you can do for the reader rather than what you cannot do.

> We are offering you a 2 percent discount on all cash purchases for the next six months.
>
> During the second year of ownership of your Compex computer, our warranty covers the cost of labor when making repairs if you purchase the parts from us. We are currently offering a 5 percent discount on the list price of all Compex parts.

5. Use resale material whenever appropriate.

> Of the various hardware lines we sell, our Brown & Dickson line is by far our best selling.
>
> Our nursery stock is found in more than half of the yards in Stillwell.

6. Use sales-promotion material whenever appropriate.

> You will be glad to know that we just received authorization to distribute the Stockton Sportswear line. To help introduce this new line to our customers, we are offering a 3 percent introductory discount on all Stockton merchandise ordered on or before July 1.

7. Offer suggestions to prevent a recurrence of the problem situation.

> To keep your Trim-Lite lawn and garden trimmer operating at peak performance in the future, we suggest that you use only Trim-Lite oil in the oil-gas mixture.

8. Make a counteroffer or counterproposal, if appropriate.

> We believe it will be in your immediate best interest for us to set your credit limit at $500 rather than the $700 you requested.

9. Make reader action easy, if appropriate.

> If you would like for us to substitute Ace nails in the same quantity and size for the out-of-stock Beckett nails that you ordered, please call me on our toll-free line (1–800–123–4567). The Ace nails can be shipped just as soon as we hear from you.

Suggestions of a Don't-Nature

What should you avoid doing in preparing disappointing-news letters?

1. Avoid the use of negative words or phrases.

> We regret that we cannot exchange your recently purchased X-213 radio for the R-174 radio, as you requested.

2. Avoid the use of an accusatory tone.

> Your new power rake malfunctioned because you failed to assemble it properly.

3. Avoid placing the statement of refusal in a position of emphasis.

> For the reasons outlined in the above paragraph, we are sure you will understand why we cannot honor your request for a full refund on the formal dress you recently purchased from us.

4. Avoid using company policy as the reason for justifying the refusal.

> Our company has a policy that prohibits the use of our facilities for anything other than official company business.

5. Avoid making suppositions that are not likely to occur.

> Now that you have heard our side of the story, we are certain that you will agree with our decision.

6. Avoid apologizing for the action you are taking.

> We are sorry that we cannot grant your request.

7. Avoid a slow-start opening.

> We have received your letter of January 2.

8. Avoid a meaningless closing.

> Thanks for getting in touch with us.

9. Avoid suggesting that problems may arise again in the future.

> Should you feel, after we repair and return your Recordex VCR, that it is not giving you the quality of service that you have the right to expect, please contact me.

10. Avoid phony or insincere empathy.

> We know just how upset you were when the heating coil in your coffee maker burned out in the middle of your dinner party.

TYPES OF DISAPPOINTING-NEWS LETTERS

Different types of disappointing-news letters are used in the business world. Although in most cases the indirect organizational plan is preferred, the direct plan is often used in situations that have already generated several disappointing-news letters from the writer to the reader. The writer now believes a more forceful, blunt opening in the direct-plan letter should be used, hoping that this letter will finally convince the reader this his/her request cannot be granted.

Negative Answers to Inquiries

The most common disappointing-news letters in the business world are negative answers to inquiries. Because the situations in this category rarely generate more than one letter, the indirect plan is used in the overwhelming majority of cases.

The situations necessitating negative replies to inquiries vary widely. In some instances, the writer has to respond negatively because of company policy (as in the case of a high school business class which requests a tour of a plant that does not open its premises to the public). In other instances, the physical inability of the writer to comply with the request necessitates a negative response (as in the case of a letter writer who had a prior commitment on the day that she was invited to deliver a keynote address at a realtors' state convention). In still other instances, the wise discretion of the writer results in a negative response (as in the case of a local non-profit group that asked to borrow from the writer's company several small vans for use in moving the group to its new location, but the company has no insurance on its vehicles except for official company use).

What type of opening is appropriate for negative responses to inquiry letters?

A neutral or buffered opening is appropriate for a negative answer to an inquiry because it will help neutralize the situation. Notice the difference between the slow-start nature of the first opening and the fast-start nature of the revision.

Change: We have received your letter of January 13 in which you inquired about the availability of the city's swimming pool for private use.

To: The gymnastics summer sports clinic you are planning is certain to be as well attended and received as the clinics you have coordinated in the past.

What should be included in the middle section of negative responses to inquiry letters?

The section that follows the opening provides a review of the facts and analyzes the reasons necessitating the refusal. This section should be written in a straight-forward, convincing manner. Once the facts have been presented, the refusal can be stated. For a psychological advantage, you should try to interweave the refusal into a counterproposal when the inclusion of a counterproposal is appropriate. Notice how effectively the revised paragraph reviews the facts and interweaves the refusal into a counterproposal.

Change: We regret that the city swimming pool can no longer be rented for private use. A policy prohibiting the rental of the city swimming pool for private use has now been in effect for six months.

To:	When the city commissioners negotiated a new liability insurance contract for various city functions/facilities last year, a provision was included that prohibited the renting of several city facilities, including the swimming pool, for private use. By taking this action, the city commission was able to save nearly $15,000 on its annual insurance premiums. While the city pool is no longer available for private use, the swimming pool at the YMCA can be rented for private use. You may contact the YMCA executive director, Jim Bellows, to discuss the rental of the Y pool.

The closing paragraph of a negative answer to an inquiry can include several types of material, including an expression of good wishes. Notice the difference between the following two paragraphs.

What type of closing is appropriate for negative responses to inquiry letters?

Change:	We were glad to learn of your interest in renting the city pool. We regret that we cannot accommodate your request.
To:	Your interest in helping our youth develop their gymnastics skills is commendable. Best wishes for another successful summer clinic.

The suggested plan for a negative answer to an inquiry includes the following elements:

What is the suggested plan for negative responses to inquiry letters?

1. A neutral or buffered opening;
2. A review of the facts and an analysis of the reasons necessitating the refusal;
3. A statement of refusal (and counteroffer, if appropriate);
4. A courteous closing with action orientation, if appropriate.

The letter in Figure 7–2 does not incorporate a number of the suggestions that have been made in this chapter for improving the effectiveness of disappointing-news messages, and it fails to follow the suggested letter plan. Letters like these have a negative impact on goodwill.

Figure 7–3 illustrates a rewritten version of the letter in Figure 7–2. Notice how much more effectively the buffered opening in Figure 7–3 maintains the

Figure 7–2 Ineffective Negative Response to an Inquiry

As of January 1, 1988, our company has had a policy that prohibits the touring of our facilities by the public.	An opening that contains negative news and that uses "policy" as an excuse.
We regret we had to implement such a policy. However, the disruptive and sometimes destructive nature of the public forced us to implement this policy that prevents our conducting tours, including those requested on a special basis, throughout our premises.	A section that presents a "harsh" explanation of the reason for the negative response.
We hope you understand our decision to implement this new policy.	A closing that lacks you-attitude.

The automobile industry project that your high school business class is undertaking sounds interesting. The various project activities the class is undertaking will add considerably to students' understanding of this vital industry.	An opening designed to help buffer the negative news presented later.
Since the first of the year, our plant has been closed to public tours. Because our tour guides have been reassigned to other positions in the company, even special requests for tours have to be declined. As an alternative to plant tours, our Public Relations Department recently put together a VCR tape that illustrates the various steps involved in manufacturing an automobile. The use of this tape is free of charge. The Public Relations Department also has a variety of brochures and pamphlets that you may wish to share with your students.	A section that reviews the reasons necessitating the refusal, in addition to presenting a counteroffer.
If you are interested in showing our tape to your class, please contact Ms. Brown at 624-5200 to arrange a showing time that will conveniently fit into your schedule. If you wish, Ms. Brown can send you multiple copies of the brochures and pamphlets.	A section that outlines the action to be taken if the counteroffer is accepted.
We in the automobile industry are especially appreciative of teachers who help increase student awareness about this important sector of the economy.	A courteous closing that contains you-attitude material.

Figure 7–3 Effective Negative Response to an Inquiry

reader's goodwill. By the time the reader has read through the material in the second paragraph, a subtle refusal—one made by implication rather than stated explicitly—is all that is needed. The counteroffer that the writer is able to make helps soften the disappointing material in the letter. Informing the reader how to take advantage of the counteroffer is also helpful, and the courteous closing expresses appreciation to the reader.

Negative Response to Adjustment Requests

Letters requiring a negative response to an adjustment request are among the more challenging of the disappointing-news messages to compose. You will typically write these letters when you are responding to an adjustment request or a complaint. While having to respond negatively, you must keep the reader's goodwill in mind if you hope to maintain the customer/client relationship with the reader. Because the reader most likely has a financial investment in the goods or services for which the adjustment is requested, the reader will have difficulty accepting a negative response to his/her request. This makes writing such letters even more challenging.

Why do adjustment-refusal letters need to be prepared?

Two common situations for which a negative response to an adjustment request is prepared are (1) the reader's failure to use a product according to the directions and (2) his/her misuse of the product. Customer complaints about account balances and services also generate correspondence. Companies vary widely in how they respond to these claims or complaints. Some will always give the reader the benefit of the doubt while others will not when the reader is clearly at fault. The material in this section pertains to those situations in which the reader is at fault and the writer is not willing to make the requested adjustment.

Because the reader could be leery of the quality of the products or services offered by the company for whom you work, incorporating resale material into negative adjustment letters is often wise. This material is designed to resell the reader on the company as well as its products and/or services. In some cases, sales-promotion material about other products in which the reader may be interested is also included in negative adjustment letters. When the problem situation arises out of the reader's misuse of a product or his/her failure to follow directions, constructive suggestions designed to prevent future misuse may be helpful.

The opening of a negative response to an adjustment request should contain neutral, buffered material. You should avoid an opening that delivers the bad news first, as the first of the following two paragraphs illustrates.

What type of opening is appropriate for adjustment-refusal letters?

Change: Because of negligence on your part, we cannot replace the Deloit chain saw that you recently purchased from us.

To: The Deloit chain saw, because of superior workmanship, is designed to give you many years of satisfied service when it is used according to the manufacturer's instructions.

Notice how the revised version incorporates resale material as it presents information with which reader will agree.

Before the refusal is stated or implied, a discussion of the reasons and an analysis of facts necessitating the refusal should be presented. The more effectively this section is presented, the more convinced the reader will be of the correctness of your decision. In addition, the reader will probably have an inclination that his/her request is being refused even before it is mentioned in the letter. Notice how much more effectively the revised version presents this important section of the refusal letter. The actual refusal is implied rather than explicitly stated.

What material should be included in the middle section of adjustment-refusal letters?

Change: The instruction manual that accompanied your chain saw clearly states on page 4 that "An oil-gas mixture (one 8 oz. can of Deloit 2-cycle oil to two gallons of gasoline) must be used." Failure to operate the engine on a proper oil-gas mixture will ruin the engine since no other lubricant is used. Because your negligence ruined the engine—and because the warranty is made void by operator misuse—we are not obligated to replace your saw as you requested in your recent letter.

To: One of the advantages of the Deloit chain saw, when compared with other chain saws, is its 2-cycle engine that operates on an oil-gas mixture. The lubricating oil is mixed with the gas (one 8 oz. can of Deloit 2-cycle oil to two gallons of gasoline), which eliminates your having to check the oil each time you use the saw or your periodically having to drain and replace the oil. The inspection of your saw engine revealed that the saw has been operated on gasoline that contained an insufficient amount of the 2-cycle engine oil, which voids the manufacturer's warranty that came with your saw.

The next section of the refused-adjustment letter can include resale material, sales-promotion material, or, if appropriate, constructive suggestions. The following is an example of resale material—designed to rebuild the reader's confidence—that might be included in a refused-adjustment letter.

> If you wish, your engine can be rebuilt at the Deloit Service Center. The normal charge for rebuilding our saw engines is $68.50, which includes parts and labor. A six-month warranty is given on our rebuilt engines. Repair time typically takes three weeks. For your convenience, we are enclosing with the saw—which is being returned to you by UPS—a mailing label on which the address of the Deloit Service Center is printed.

An appropriate closing for the refused-adjustment letter will thank the reader for his/her business. To be avoided is mentioning the nature of the problem, as the first of the following two paragraphs does.

> Change: We regret that you have experienced problems with your Deloit chain saw.
> To: We appreciate having you as a customer.

What is the suggested plan for adjustment-refusal letters?

The suggested plan for a letter refusing the adjustment request includes the following elements:

1. A neutral or buffered beginning;
2. A discussion of reasons and analysis of facts necessitating the refusal;
3. A statement of refusal;
4. Resale material, sales-promotion material, or constructive suggestions (if appropriate);
5. A courteous closing with action orientation, if appropriate.

Figure 7–4 illustrates a letter refusing an adjustment request that will be offensive to the reader. Not only is the letter inconsistent with the suggested

Figure 7–4 Ineffective Refused-Adjustment Letter

You are incorrect in assuming that we are obligated to repair your camera at no cost to you because it is still under warranty. You will see, if you read your warranty, that "Camex is not responsible for repair work on cameras resulting from misuse or damage." Your camera has obviously been dropped, which damaged the automatic winding mechanism.	A rude opening that contains the refusal, as well as several "put downs" in the explanation.
We will be happy to repair your camera for an estimated cost of $85.23 for parts and labor. While the actual repair cost could be less, it will not exceed the estimated cost.	A section that contains weak resale material designed to rebuild the customer's confidence in the product.
Let us know of your decision.	A discourteous closing.

letter plan, but also it is accusatory and attacks the reader. Such letters are certain to do irreparable damage to the writer-reader relationship.

The letter illustrated in Figure 7–5 is an improved version of the letter in Figure 7–4. The suggested letter plan has been followed, and the tone of the letter is considerably more appropriate. Although the adjustment has been refused, the reader is much more likely to agree with the writer's decision than will an individual who receives a letter similar to the one shown in Figure 7–4. The improved letter focuses on what the writer can do rather than on what he/she cannot do, and it contains resale material.

When is partial adjustment to an adjustment request appropriate?

Partial adjustments are sometimes appropriate for certain situations. For example, perhaps the individual requesting the adjustment is an excellent cus-

Figure 7–5 Effective Refused-Adjustment Letter

We agree with the statement in your recent letter that you feel you are entitled to many years of good service from the Camex camera you recently purchased from us. The quality of your Camex is unrivaled in today's market.	An opening that contains buffered material on which the reader and writer will agree.
When we received your camera, one of our service technicians examined it to determine why the film is catching in the automatic advancing mechanism. His examination revealed a broken pin and several bent or sprung parts in the mechanism, preventing the film from automatically feeding through the camera. The technician also found several scratches on the camera case that appear to have been caused when your camera was dropped on a hard, rough surface, such as a concrete floor.	A section that contains a thorough explanation of the reasons necessitating the refusal.
The limited warranty that came with your camera covers for a three-year period the cost of repair (parts and labor) resulting from defective materials or poor quality workmanship. The warranty also mentions several exclusions that make it void, one of which is damage resulting from the camera's being dropped. The warranty exclusions enabled you and thousands of our other customers to purchase the highest-quality camera equipment on the market today at the lowest possible cost.	A section that continues an explanation of the reasons why the request cannot be granted, followed by an implied refusal.
I asked the service technician who examined your camera to estimate the repair cost. His estimate is $85.23 for parts and labor. While the actual cost could be less, it will not be greater than the estimate. Our skilled service technicians can repair your camera so that it will again provide you with the photography quality you appreciate and the satisfaction to which you have become accustomed. The repair work should be completed in less than two weeks after we receive your authorization. Camex, the only camera manufacturer to do so, will guarantee the repair work with a two-year warranty that covers parts and labor.	A section that contains resale-material that will help rebuild the customer's confidence in the product and in the writer's company.
Please use the enclosed card to let me know if you want us to repair your camera or to return it to you in its present condition.	A courteous closing that mentions the action the reader is to take if he/she accepts the offer.

tomer with whom the company has enjoyed a long-time relationship. In these situations, maintaining the continued relationship with the reader is more important than the cost the company will incur in making the partial adjustment. Or, in some instances, a shared responsibility for the problem situation makes offering a partial adjustment desirable.

You have two alternatives available for organizing the content of a partial-adjustment letter. One alternative is to use the same suggested plan shown above for refusing adjustments, with one modification. Instead of stating the refusal (either implicitly or explicitly), the partial adjustment is clearly and thoroughly explained in a non-grudging manner. Because the partial adjustment is less than what the reader requested, your offer has to be presented in a convincing manner. The most appropriate closing for such letters is a discussion of the action you wish the reader to take if he/she decides to accept the partial adjustment.

What is the suggested plan for partial-adjustment letters?

The suggested plan for the partial adjustment letter discussed above includes the following elements:

1. A neutral or buffered opening;
2. A review of reasons or analysis of facts;
3. A discussion of the partial adjustment being offered;
4. Resale or sales-promotion material, or helpful suggestions (if appropriate);
5. A courteous closing with action orientation, if appropriate.

Figure 7–6 illustrates a letter using this organization plan.

The other alternative for organizing partial-adjustment letters is to discuss the adjustment in the opening. This alternative works better in some situations than the first alternative. Because the reader is receiving good news—although less than what he/she originally requested—the second alternative may restore goodwill more quickly than adjustment letters in which the discussion of the partial adjustment is delayed.

The suggested plan for a partial-adjustment letter that opens with a discussion of the offer includes the following elements:

1. A discussion of the partial adjustment being offered;
2. A review of reasons or analysis of facts;
3. Resale or sales-promotion material or helpful suggestions (if appropriate);
4. A courteous closing with action orientation, if appropriate.

A letter illustrating this organizational plan is presented in Figure 7–7.

Negative Response to Credit Requests

What is the desired goal in preparing credit-refusal letters?

When a business receives a credit application from an individual whose background and/or financial status are assessed to be substandard, a credit-refusal letter must be prepared. The desired goal is to present the information in a tactful way so the individual will remain a cash customer. Untactful letters could cause the individual to take his/her business elsewhere.

When you purchased the five silver-leaf maple trees from Green Thumb Nursery last spring, you had every right to assume that in a few years they would provide ample shade as well as enhance the attractiveness of your yard. Your continued patronage the last five years indicates that you have been pleased with our stock and service.	A neutral opening that contains information that the reader will agree with.
The soil samples we analyzed from the area of your yard where the trees were planted revealed high levels of salt. Although some trees can tolerate excessive levels of salt in the soil, silver-leaf maples cannot. The guarantee we offer on our trees expired three months before you reported to us the condition of your trees. By that time, they had suffered irreparable harm. Had we known about this soil condition before planting these trees, we would have recommended either another variety of tree or another location in your yard more suitable for silver-leaf maples.	A section that reviews the analysis of the situation, along with the implied refusal.
Silver-leaf maples of the size that you purchased from us last year are now on sale for $49.99 each (regular price is $64.99). We will be happy to plant for free as many as five of these maples (a $75 value) if you purchase replacement trees from us.	A section that presents a discussion of the partial adjustment being offered.
We would also like to do a free analysis of the soil in the various areas of your yard where you would consider having the replacement trees planted. Since other salt-sensitive trees you have purchased from us have done well, we assume the salt content in the soil is lower in some areas of your yard than in other areas.	A section that contains resale material designed to rebuild the customer's confidence in the company.
We encourage you to make your decision about our offer soon while large supplies of stock are still available. Now is also a good time to think about purchasing your bedding plants while our "Spring Dreams Sale" is in progress.	A section that contains sales-promotion material.
If you decide to accept our offer, please contact me. I will be happy to help you personally select top-quality replacement trees.	A courteous, action-oriented closing.

Figure 7–6 Effective Partial-Adjustment Letter with Buffered Opening

In some instances, the credit application is submitted along with a merchandise order. In other instances, credit is applied for before the applicant sends his/her order. When the application and order are submitted simultaneously, the credit-refusal letter can serve another purpose by acknowledging receipt of the individual's order.

In preparing credit-refusal letters, a total refusal is not always warranted. For example, suppose that although the applicant's current income is not sufficient to extend credit in the amount of the accompanying order, the applicant's current income is sufficient for a lesser amount of credit. Letters in which the applicant's request can be partially met are sometimes easier to prepare than those in which the request has to be totally denied.

An appropriate strategy in preparing some credit-refusal letters is to explain to the applicant what he/she must do in order to qualify for credit in the

The coupon that accompanies this letter entitles you to free planting of five silver-leaf maple trees (a coupon verifying this $75 value is attached) if you purchase your replacement trees from Green Thumb Nursery. Silver-leaf maples of the size that you purchased from us last year are now on sale for $49.99 each (regular price is $64.99). Your continued patronage the last five years indicates that you have been pleased with our stock and service.	An opening that discusses the partial adjustment; the refusal is implied.
The soil samples we analyzed from the area of your yard where the trees were planted revealed a high concentration of salt. Although some trees can tolerate excessive levels of salt in the soil, silver-leaf maples cannot. The guarantee we offer on our trees expired three months before you reported their condition to us. By that time, they had suffered irreparable harm. Had we known about this condition before planting these trees, we would have recommended either another variety or another location in your yard more suitable for silver-leaf maples.	A section that contains a review of the analysis of the situation.
So that we can plant your replacement trees in a suitable location, we would like to do a free analysis of the soil in the various areas where you would consider having the new trees planted. We know your yard has areas suitable for silver-leaf maples because a variety of other salt-sensitive trees that you have purchased from us are thriving.	A section that contains resale material designed to rebuild the reader's confidence in the company.
We encourage you to make your decision about our offer soon while large supplies of stock are still available. Now is also a good time to think about purchasing your bedding plants while our "Spring Dreams Sale" is in progress.	A section that contains sales-promotion material.
If you decide to accept our offer, please contact me. I will be happy to help you personally select top-quality replacement trees.	A courteous, action-oriented closing.

Figure 7–7 Effective Partial-Adjustment Letter with Adjustment Discussed in Opening

future. When the credit application must be denied because of an unacceptable ratio between the applicant's assets and liabilities, the writer may want to tell the applicant that another application will be welcomed when the assets-liabilities ratio meets the required standard.

Another important ingredient to consider including in credit-refusal letters is resale material. Carefully prepared resale material often convinces the reader that the merchandise he/she ordered is more suitable than the merchandise offered by another business and that it will be in his/her best interest to pay cash for the merchandise that was ordered. And readers often interpret the inclusion of resale material as evidence of the writer's desire to be helpful. Some writers effectively use resale material to compliment the reader's good judgment in selecting the merchandise and/or doing business with the vendor.

A neutral or buffered opening is needed when writing a credit-refusal letter. To be avoided is a slow-start opening in which the receipt of the reader's credit application is acknowledged, as the first of the following two paragraphs illustrates.

What type of opening is appropriate for credit-refusal letters?

> Change: We have received your application for a Brown's charge account.
> To: Your expressing confidence in us by applying for a Brown's charge account is sincerely appreciated.

After the opening, a section that explains the situation should be followed by the refusal. Depending on how well the situation is explained, you may be able to imply the refusal rather than explicitly state the refusal. The first of the following two paragraphs is bound to alienate the reader, while the revised version shows more sensitivity toward his/her feelings.

> Change: We are unable to open a charge account for you because you have too many debts in relation to your income. We have found that our charge customers whose monthly revolving charge account payments exceed 15 percent of their take-home pay often experience financial difficulties. Because your revolving charge account payments currently consume 22 percent of your take-home pay, we feel your assuming any more debt at this time is not advisable.
> To: One of the reasons Brown's has been able to sell merchandise at competitive prices for the last 50 years is that our operating costs are among the lowest of the country's major department stores. One way that we've been able to reduce operating costs is to open charge accounts for applicants whose monthly revolving charge account payments are less than 15 percent of their take-home pay. An analysis of the financial data you provided us reveals that your current monthly revolving charge account payments are 22 percent of your take-home pay. To assume any more debt at this time may result in your financially overextending yourself, a situation that I am sure you will want to avoid.

The revised paragraph implies rather than explicitly states that the credit application is being denied.

In some cases, you may want to make a counteroffer, such as extending a reduced line of credit, offering a cash discount on merchandise purchases, or suggesting that the applicant purchase on a cash basis until he/she may qualify for a charge account. The following paragraph provides an effective presentation of a cash-discount counteroffer.

> I am enclosing a cash discount coupon that will entitle you to a 10 percent discount on merchandise purchases up to $200. This coupon can be used at all of our stores, and the discount can be applied toward the purchase of several smaller items or one large item.

Resale or sales-promotion material can be effectively included in credit-refusal letters.

> Our annual summer sale begins July 5. You will find numerous items reduced from 25 to 50 percent. Because this sale will not be announced to the general public until July 7, you will have first pick of many items on which you can save up to 60 percent on the marked price with the use of your cash discount coupon.

What type of closing is appropriate for credit-refusal letters?

The courteous closing can be used to remind the reader that you will appreciate receiving another credit application in the future. The reader may find it helpful if you mention the conditions necessary to qualify for an application, as the second of the following two paragraphs illustrates.

> Change: Thank you for your interest in opening a Brown's charge account
> To: When your monthly charge account payments are reduced to approximately 15 percent of your take-home pay, we encourage you to submit another credit application. In the meantime, please take advantage of the many excellent values for which Brown's is well known.

What is the suggested plan for credit-refusal letters?

The suggested plan for a credit-refusal letter includes the following elements:

1. A neutral or buffered opening;
2. An explanation and tactful refusal to grant credit;
3. A counteroffer (if appropriate);
4. Resale or sales-promotion material (if appropriate);
5. A courteous closing with action orientation, if appropriate.

The letter illustrated in Figure 7–8 is certain to cause the credit applicant to take his/her business elsewhere, even when purchasing on a cash basis. An examination of the letter reveals that a number of the suggestions for writing effective credit-refusal letters have been ignored.

Figure 7–9 illustrates a much-improved version of the letter in Figure 7–8. The improved letter is consistent with the effective letter-writing principles that have been presented in this chapter and follows the suggested letter plan. The sales-promotion and reader-benefit material will be helpful in convincing the reader to maintain a relationship with the writer's company—even on a cash basis.

Problem-Order Letters

A variety of situations periodically make impossible the filling of customers' orders by merchandisers. In some instances, the situation creating the problem is the customer's fault. In other instances, the problem can be traced to the merchandiser. Regardless of who is at fault, the situation can be defused somewhat if the merchandiser sends a letter to the customer acknowledging the delay. These letters can also be effectively used to request additional informa-

Your order dated October 10, along with your application for credit, have been received. In addition, we have received references from those individuals you listed on your application.	A slow-start opening that contains obvious information.
It is not possible for us to grant you credit at this time. An examination of your assets to liabilities ratio reveals a substandard level. We require a 2:1 ratio; yours is 1.5 to 1. Therefore, we feel that it would be unwise for us to grant you credit. We have to be extremely careful in these days of declining profit to avoid the risk of incurring bad debts.	A section in which the refusal is stated at the beginning of the paragraph; negative wording used throughout.
We hope you will understand our decision and send to us a check for $598.32, the amount of your order, in the enclosed envelope. That will enable us to send you your order without additional delay. We encourage you to continue purchasing on a cash basis until your assets-liabilities ratio reaches the 2:1 level.	A section that presents a discussion of the desired action but that lacks you-viewpoint.
We hope to hear from you as soon as possible.	A closing that lacks you-viewpoint.

Figure 7–8 Ineffective Credit-Refusal Letter

tion from the customer. For example, perhaps the customer failed to state his/her choice of fabric color on the order form; and before the order can be filled, color choice is needed.

Specific situations that require the preparation of problem-order letters include the following:

What type of situations require the preparation of problem-order letters?

1. Incomplete orders
2. Orders requesting out-of-stock items that can be backordered
3. Orders requesting out-of-stock items that cannot be backordered
4. Orders requesting out-of-stock items that cannot be backordered, but the writer has substitute items to suggest

Some merchandisers prefer to use forms to convey the news about the problem order. While the use of forms is much faster than preparing letters, forms are considered cold and impersonal. Merchandisers who value their customers' business will wisely take the time and effort to prepare a personal letter.

Well-prepared problem-order letters will help you maintain a good working relationship with your reader. An effective way to accomplish this goal is to emphasize what you can do rather than what you cannot do. To illustrate, when an order cannot be totally filled because some items have to be backordered, begin with the positive information, i.e., the items that can be shipped immediately. When items are backordered, provide as much information about the situation as possible: how soon you expect to be able to ship the merchandise to the customer and the company's policy on backorders (some companies automatically send the backordered items unless the customer cancels the request, while other companies immediately cancel the request and

The children's clothing you ordered from us recently indicates to us that you have excellent taste in selecting spring merchandise for your store. Several items you chose are among our best sellers this season.	An opening that compliments the reader.
You can take pride in the fact that the references you listed on your credit application gave you good marks in each of the areas about which we requested information. This speaks favorably for a children's clothing store that has been in business for a relatively short time. It also speaks favorably about your management practices.	A section that presents additional compliments.
For us to be able to offer our merchandise at competitive prices, our credit customers are expected to have a 2:1 assets-liabilities ratio. We calculated your assets-liabilities ratio to be 1.5:1. Our experience shows that by our maintaining the 2:1 ratio requirement enables us to minimize our risks and subsequently to offer our merchandise at the lowest possible price. As a result of this practice, we are able to help our customers increase their profit margin because they are able to purchase their merchandise at a lower price.	A section that explains the situation, and an implied refusal is made.
We are encouraging you, because of your assets-liabilities ratio, to purchase on a cash basis for the time being. To help you improve your ratio as quickly as possible, we are offering you a 5 percent discount on all cash orders for the next six months, including the order we recently received.	A section that discusses the desired action and a counteroffer.
We have just added the Smart-Look line of children's clothing. Sales indicate that this line promises to be one of our most popular. You can see by examining the enclosed brochure that this line provides excellent values because of the smart look and moderate prices.	A section that contains sales-promotion material.
When your assets-liabilities ratio becomes 2:1, please complete another credit application. In the meantime, we can fill your present order if you send a check for $568.40 ($598.32 less the 5 percent discount) in the enclosed envelope. We are anxious to help supply your stock needs.	A courteous, action-oriented closing.

Figure 7–9 Effective Credit-Refusal Letter with a Counteroffer

require that the customer reorder the backordered items). Even when the customer is at fault—failing to state color choice, for example—avoid a negative or accusatory tone.

The use of resale material can be quite effective in preparing problem-order letters, such as when writing a letter about an incomplete order or a letter to inform the reader that some or all of the items on the order have been backordered. Effective resale material will help convince the reader that the wait for the order will be worthwhile. The promotion of merchandise similar to what the reader ordered can also be included quite effectively in some problem-order letters.

The opening of a letter responding to a problem order can either improve or worsen the situation. Your goal, of course, will be to improve the situation as much as possible. Conveying positive rather than negative information is crucial. Notice the negative impact that the first of the following two sentences is likely to have.

What is the goal of the opening of problem-order letters?

Change:	We regret that we cannot ship your order in its entirety at this time.
To:	The printer ribbons you recently ordered were shipped this morning by UPS and should reach you by the end of the week. These ribbons are guaranteed to print 40 percent longer than original Beta printer ribbons.

The revised paragraph shows much more concern for the customer than does the original, and although the letter conveys disappointing news, the opening contains positive information that will help defuse the negative situation.

The next section of the problem-order letter should explain the reasons for the delay. An honest explanation will be appreciated by the reader. The following paragraph illustrates how this section of the letter may be worded.

What is included in the middle section of problem-order letters?

> The popularity of our R–10 floppy disks that you ordered has occasionally resulted in their selling faster than our supply can be replenished. The manufacturer of these disks is about to open a new plant, which will result in the doubling of our monthly allotment. As soon as the plant reaches full production, we anticipate having a continuous supply of these disks.

Sometimes you will be in a position to suggest a course of action that may be helpful to the customer. For example, if a viable substitute is available for a backordered item, you might want to suggest the alternative. Or, if the customer needs to tell you whether or not he/she wishes to have the out-of-stock items placed on back order, this is an appropriate section in which to discuss alternatives. The first of the following two paragraphs is devoid of an attitude that shows concern for the customer.

Change:	Please let me know as soon as possible if you want us to send the out-of-stock floppy disks you ordered when they become available—or if you want us to cancel this portion of your order.
To:	As a substitute for the R–10 disks that are currently out of stock, I suggest you try our R–8 disks that we can ship immediately. While the R–8 disks cost $1.79 less per box than the R–10 disks ($11.97 rather than $13.76), the quality of both types of disks is comparable. If you decide to order the R–8 disks, we will refund $17.90, the difference between the cost of 100 R–8 and R–10 disks. Please call me on our toll-free line (1–800–567–1897) if you wish to order the R–8 disks. If we do not hear from you, we will send the R–10 disks once they become available.

What type of closing is appropriate for problem-order letters?

The closing in a problem-order letter must be sincere and courteous. The first of the following two paragraphs lacks sincerity.

Change:	We look forward to having the pleasure of your business in the future.
To:	To express our appreciation for your confidence in our products and service, a coupon is enclosed that will entitle you to a $5 discount on your next order.

What is the suggested plan for problem-order letters?

The suggested plan for a problem order letter includes the following elements:

1. A buffered beginning that expresses thanks for the order, mentions which items are being shipped now, or contains resale material;
2. An explanation of the reasons for the delayed shipment;
3. Suggested course of action that contains reader-benefit material (action you wish the reader to take, such as selecting an alternate item or accepting or rejecting the new shipping date for backordered items);
4. A courteous closing with action orientation.

The letter in Figure 7–10 is not likely to make the reader feel that the backordered items are worth waiting for. The absence of resale material adds to the cold, impersonal tone in this letter. The letter also emphasizes the negative rather than the positive.

The letter in Figure 7–11 is consistent with the plan presented for developing problem-order letters, and it emphasizes what the writer can do rather than what he/she cannot do. The resale material will help convince the reader that purchasing the suggested substitute items would be a wise decision.

Declining of Invitations

From time to time, invitations must be declined. The reasons necessitating regrets are varied, ranging from a potential conflict of interest to a lack of time. Regardless of the reason for the refusal, the letter of decline must be tactful and courteous. Whether or not you are likely to receive a future invitation from

Figure 7–10 Ineffective Problem-Order Letter

Unfortunately, we cannot at the present time ship all of the items you recently ordered from us.	An opening that immediately presents the rejection.
The twenty R-78 rakes that you requested are on backorder. At this time, we do not know exactly when they will be shipped. As soon as they come in, we will send all of your merchandise to you.	A section that presents a weak discussion of the facts and that lacks resale material.
Please give us an opportunity to serve you again.	A weak closing.

The hoes and shovels you recently ordered from us are on their way and should reach you by the end of the week. We appreciate having the opportunity to once again supply you with these top-quality gardening tools.	A buffered opening that expresses appreciation for the order.
The employees of the manufacturer of the R-78 rakes you ordered have been on strike now for a month. Because the manufacturer's inventory of these rakes is depleted, wholesalers like us around the country have also experienced a depletion of their stock of these rakes. The popularity of the R-78 rakes will keep them in short supply for a time after the manufacturer's employees go back to work.	A section that explains the reasons for the delayed shipment.
Because the spring planting season is just around the corner, having an adequate supply of rakes on hand in your hardware store is critical. Until the R-78 rake again becomes readily available, you may be interested in stocking the Garden-Rite 2304 rake which is even of higher quality than the R-78. Garden-Rite uses a steel alloy in its rakes that is twice as strong as the steel used in the R-78. This new alloy makes the teeth on the Garden-Rite rake much less susceptible to breakage. Mud is also much less likely to cling to this new alloy.	A section that contains resale material.
If you would like for us to send twenty Garden-Rite 2304 rakes, please let me know. We can have them on their way to you the same day we hear from you. Otherwise, we will backorder the R-78 rakes and send them to you just as soon as we receive them.	A section that discusses the suggested course of action, along with reader-benefit material.
We were pleased to learn from our sale representative how well your new store in Peoria is doing. We wish you continued success.	A courteous closing.

Figure 7–11 Effective Problem-Order Letter

the reader is an irrelevant consideration when preparing letters declining an invitation.

The need to emphasize the positive rather than the negative is just as important in letters of decline as in other types of disappointing-news letters. If you would welcome a future invitation—for example, to speak at a convention—your interest can be mentioned in the letter. Care needs to be taken in the expression of desired future invitations to avoid a begging, insincere tone.

Depending on the circumstances, you may be able to suggest an acceptable alternative. For example, suppose you have been asked to speak on a specific day at a convention. Although the presentation time originally suggested is not acceptable because of prior commitments, you are available to speak at another time during the convention. If suggesting an alternative time seems appropriate, consider doing so.

The tone of the opening in your letter will convey the extent of your interest in the invitation you received. Tactful wording is needed. The following two paragraphs will produce quite different impressions on the reader.

Change:	I am unable to accept your invitation to speak at the May meeting of the Claremore Civic Club.
To:	The Claremore Civic Club is doing many things to make our community a better place in which to live—thanks to you and its other dedicated, interested members. My son thoroughly enjoys playing on the new equipment your group recently purchased and installed at Johnson Park.

An honest explanation of the reasons for your decline will convey the sincerity of your action. The first of the following two paragraphs conveys insincerity.

Change:	I will be out of town on the day of your May meeting.
To:	On the day of your May meeting, my family and I will be in Florida enjoying a long-awaited ten-day vacation. If I were going to be in town on that day, I would be honored to speak to your group.

The sincerity of your interest in accepting the invitation can be enhanced by suggesting an alternative course of action, as the following paragraph illustrates.

> At the moment, my schedule is open on the days of your June, July, and August meetings, should you be looking for a speaker for any of those meetings.

What type of closing is appropriate for letters in which an invitation is declined?

The tone of the closing will also convey the sincerity of your interest. The first of the following two paragraphs is severely lacking in sincerity, while the second paragraph is a much-improved version.

Change:	Best wishes for finding another speaker for your May meeting.
To:	The impact of the Claremore Civic Club on our community is commendable. Please convey my appreciation to the club members for all of their hard work.

What is the suggested plan for letters in which invitations are declined?

The suggested plan for a letter declining an invitation includes the following elements:

1. An expression of appreciation for the invitation;
2. An explanation of facts;
3. A suggestion of alternative course(s) of action, if appropriate;
4. A courteous closing with action orientation, if appropriate.

The tone of the letter in Figure 7–12 is insincere and will cause its recipient to conclude that the reasons for the decline are not genuine. When this happens, the reader will get the impression that the writer simply was not interested in accepting the invitation.

I have another commitment during the time that you recently asked me to speak at your convention. Unfortunately, I will be unable to speak at your convention since I shall not be able to get out of the other commitment.	A discourteous opening that contains the refusal.
Thank you for thinking of me in your search for convention speakers who have expertise in microcomputer applications.	A discourteous closing that lacks the you-viewpoint.

Figure 7–12 Ineffective Letter Declining an Invitation

On the other hand, the letter in Figure 7–13 is sincere and genuine and will probably convince the recipient that the writer, if given another opportunity to do so, will be happy to accept the invitation. Therefore, the letter in Figure 7–13 is much more likely to produce a better relationship between the writer and the reader than is the letter in Figure 7–12.

Declining of Requests for Favors

From time to time, individuals have to prepare letters declining requests for favors. Situations for which these letters have to be prepared would include requests to use company facilities, to borrow company equipment, to delay a credit payment, and to change contract requirements. These situations are all business related. Individual requests of a non-business nature may also have to be declined from time to time.

Figure 7–13 Effective Letter Declining an Invitation

Thank you for inviting me to speak at the upcoming convention of the Computer Management Association. I've always found Boston to be an excellent site for conventions.	A courteous opening in which appreciation for the invitation is expressed.
Our consulting firm recently began offering public seminars in various cities throughout the country. I am scheduled to offer a three-day seminar in Los Angeles during the same three days of your convention. Otherwise, I would be happy to speak at your convention.	A section that contains an explanation of the facts that necessitate the decline of the invitation.
One of my colleagues who also has expertise in microcomputer applications is available during the time that you asked me to speak. Her presentation skills are excellent, and I am certain that she could contribute significantly to the success of your convention.	A section that presents an alternative course of action.
If you are interested in contacting my colleague about the possibility of her speaking at your convention, please send me a note or call me at (407) 345-1234.	A courteous, action-oriented closing.
Best wishes for a successful convention.	A cordial expression of good wishes.

When you decline a request for a favor—regardless of how absurd you feel the favor request is—a courteous opening is essential. Notice the lack of courtesy in the first of the following two openings.

> Change: Your request to use our facilities for the organizational meeting of a personnel management association has to be denied.
>
> To: I'm glad you are spearheading what several business people have talked about for some time: the founding of a local chapter of Personnel Administrators Association. The potential for such a chapter here is tremendous.

The next section of a letter in which a favor is denied should explain the reasons for the refusal and present an implied refusal. The following illustrates how this section can be effectively presented.

> Our community room is normally available for such uses as you requested. However, because of the extensive remodeling project underway at Smith-Jackson, our new community room will not be available until September 15.

In some instances, you will find the inclusion of reader-benefit material or the suggestion of a counterproposal appropriate. Notice how effectively the the counterproposal is mentioned in the following paragraph.

> The new community room will be available to non-profit groups, such as the Personnel Administrators Association, on an on-going basis. The facility will be furnished with tables and chairs and will accommodate up to 100 persons. Our new community room can be reserved up to a year in advance of the event's being scheduled.

The closing of the letter in which a requested favor is declined must be courteous; and if appropriate, it should be action oriented.

> Please call me at your convenience if the PAA executive board decides to hold its meetings in our new community room.

What is the suggested plan for letters in which requests for favors are declined?

The principles of negative-news letters identified throughout this chapter are also pertinent for letters in which requests for favors are declined. The suggested plan for a letter refusing a favor includes the following elements:

1. A buffered opening;
2. An explanation of reasons that the favor will have to be declined;
3. An implied refusal;
4. Reader-benefit material and/or counterproposal (if appropriate);
5. A courteous closing with action orientation (if appropriate).

If we made a financial contribution to each charitable organization that solicited us, we would soon become financially burdened. As you can appreciate during these economically tough times, we are fortunate some months when we just break even. What little we have left over after our expenses are paid is now being used to retire early some of our debt.	A discourteous opening that lacks tact in discussing the reasons necessitating the refusal.
When conditions improve and our company becomes more profitable, we will consider requests such as yours.	A closing that lacks you-viewpoint.

Figure 7–14 Ineffective Letter Declining a Favor Request

Figure 7–14 contains a letter declining a request by a charitable organization for a financial contribution. The tone of the letter is cold and impersonal, and the recipient of the letter will feel she erred in requesting a contribution.

Figure 7–15, on the other hand, is a warm, personal letter that shows support for the charitable organization's activities, even though the request for a financial contribution in declined.

Figure 7–15 Effective Letter Declining a Favor Request

The residents of Merrimac appreciate the fine work of the Christmas Connection on behalf of the community's less fortunate residents. The Christmas Connection has a long tradition of making Christmas available to those who would not otherwise be able to enjoy the Christmas Season.	A courteous opening that expresses appreciation.
For each of the last ten years, the Arjay Corporation has provided financial support to a number of the community's charitable and non-profit organizations by making a significant contribution to Worthy Cause. The Board of Directors of Arjay decided that because the company may not always be able to make a financial contribution each time it received a request from a charitable or non-profit group, the fairest way to help such groups is to make contributions to Worthy Cause. Because Christmas Connection receives funds from Worthy Cause, a portion of our recent contribution will be coming your way.	A section that explains the reasons why the favor request must be refused.
Because we want to do everything we can to assure the success of your flea market on November 15, we have asked each of our employees to donate items that can be sold at this event. We will collect these items here and deliver them to you in time for the flea market. The proceeds from the sale of the items our employees donate can certainly be put to good use during the Christmas Season. If you need volunteers to help with the flea market, please let me know and I will "spread the word" throughout our company.	A section that outlines a counter proposal that is designed to help rebuild any ill will resulting from declining the favor request.
You can take great pride in the accomplishments of the Christmas Connection during the years you have served as its executive director. Our community is indeed fortunate to have you among its residents.	A courteous closing that contains you-viewpoint.

CHAPTER SUMMARY

The types of disappointing-news letters that are presented in this chapter are: negative answers to inquiries, negative responses to adjustment requests, negative responses to credit requests, problem-order letters, declining of invitations, and declining of requests for favors.

Two options are available for organizing disappointing-news letters: the indirect plan and the direct plan. When the indirect plan is used, the refusal is delayed until after the facts have been presented and the reasons for the refusal have been discussed. The direct plan presents the refusal at the beginning of the letter.

To improve the effectiveness of disappointing-news letters, you should use a neutral or buffered opening and make sure the facts are properly reviewed. In addition, you need to be concerned about analyzing the reasons for the refusal as well as your statement of the refusal. The closing can also contribute to the effectiveness of your letter.

Suggestions of a ''do nature'' that will help you write more effective letters are: consider an implicit rather than an explicit refusal, focus on what you can do rather than on what you cannot do, use resale material, and make reader action easy, if appropriate. Some ''don't nature'' suggestions are to avoid using an accusatory tone, placing the statement of refusal in a position of emphasis, and apologizing for the action you are taking.

REVIEW QUESTIONS

1. What two options are available when organizing disappointing-news messages?
2. In developing an effective neutral or buffered opening in a disappointing-news letter, what suggestions can you offer?
3. Where should the statement of refusal be found in a disappointing-news letter?
4. In developing an effective closing in a disappointing-news letter, what suggestions can you offer?
5. Identify several suggestions of a ''do-nature'' when preparing disappointing-news messages.
6. Identify several suggestions of a ''don't-nature'' when preparing disappointing-news messages.
7. What type of opening is appropriate for a negative response to an inquiry letter?
8. What situations are typically responsible for the writer's inability to grant an adjustment request?
9. What type of material can you include in a refused-adjustment letter that is aimed at rebuilding the customer's confidence?
10. Under what circumstances might you make a partial adjustment?
11. What types of counteroffers might be presented in credit-refusal letters?
12. At what point in a letter that declines a request for a favor is the refusal included?

APPLICATION PROBLEMS

1. Prepare a written critique of the following letter, evaluating grammar usage, punctuation, conformity with the suggested plan, and conformity with the writing essentials covered in Chapters 3 and 4.

> It is with great disappointment that I inform you that we are unable to open a charge account in your name, as you requested. The reason being that you simply have too many outstanding bills at this point in time.
>
> If at some point in time in the future you are able to reduce your debt-load, we encourage you to apply again for a charge account. Those of our customers who have these accounts tell us how great it is.
>
> As I mentioned before, I am truly sorry that I cannot accommodate your request—but perhaps we can in the future. You have my personnel best wishes for success.

2. Rewrite the letter in application problem 1, making sure that the weaknesses you identified in your critique have been eliminated. Make any needed assumptions, and supply any details that may be missing.

3. Prepare a written critique of the following letter, evaluating grammar usage, punctuation, conformity with the suggested plan, and conformity with the writing essentials discussed in Chapters 3 and 4.

> Maybe now that we are refusing to fill your recent order on a credit basis until we receive payment on your passed-due account, you will see that we meant business when we sent you the three previous requests that you pay us $558.84, the amount of your charge account that has been delinquent now for at least three months. Some of the charges on this account are from a year ago.
>
> We should think that you are concerned about having a good credit reputation. For the life of ourselfs, we cannot phantom why you would want your credit reputation to go down the tubes like this. Is it because you simply don't care—or are you just plain mad at us because we did not take back the merchandise bought from us that time that you later decided you didn't want? If it is the later, let me remind you that that is a very poor way to do business. Let us have your payment soon so we can send the items you recently ordered.

4. Rewrite the letter in application problem 3, making sure that the weaknesses you identified in your critique have been eliminated. Make any needed assumptions, and supply any details that are missing.

5. You work in the customer service department of Halley Publishing Company, which is located at 349 Smithfield Road, Lyme, CT 10922. One of the books your company recently published, *Writing Powerful Letters and Reports*, is receiving a considerable amount of attention—which pleases you very much. Early sales reports from the sales staff indicate that the book is tentatively being adopted for use in business writing classes at nearly 100 colleges and universities this fall. Halley's policy is to provide free of cost the teacher's manuals that accompany its textbooks only after the company has received a firm commitment that a given text will be used at a given college/university. Without a firm commitment, the company charges $5 for each teacher's manual. You just received a letter from Dr. Donna Jacobson, Professor

of Business Communications, Ridley College, Ridley, NJ 07845 in which she requested a copy of the manual. An examination of your records indicates that a firm commitment has not been received from Ridley College as yet; therefore, you will need the payment in hand before you can send the manual. Indicate that should this text be adopted at Ridley in the future, you will be happy to refund the $5 charge for the teacher's manual. Write the letter in which you deny her request. Keep in mind that the tone of your letter may determine whether or not *Writing Powerful Letters and Reports* is adopted at Ridley College in the future.

6. You are in charge of scheduling the community room that your employer (First State Bank, 6844 Grant Boulevard, Tulsa, OK 74874) makes available on a first-come, first-served basis to service/civic groups in the community. Because the room is provided free of charge, you ask those who use it to leave it in the same condition as they find it. Six weeks ago, the Tulsa City Group, which sponsors many youth/children projects/activities throughout the community, failed to leave the room in a clean condition. Litter was strewn about the floor, the tables and chairs were scattered about the room, and used refreshment cups were left on the tables. When you mentioned this situation to the bank's executive vice-president, he emphatically stated that the Tulsa City Group was forever barred from using the community room facilities again. You just received a letter from the vice president of the Tulsa City Group (Mark Browning, 38 Courrier Court, Tulsa, OK 74877) inquiring into the possibility of the group's reserving the room for its June meeting. Write a letter to Mr. Browning in which you deny his request.

7. You are the manager of the Fashion Palace, one of the most popular ladies' clothing stores in Springfield, MO 58575. The store, which is located at 12 Main Street, just celebrated its 50th anniversary with a store-wide sale. The sale items were offered on a final-sale basis. The no-returns policy enabled you to reduce the price of sale merchandise an additional 10 percent over its normal sale price. To make sure that all customers who purchased final-sale merchandise were aware of the no-return policy, a large notice mentioning the final-sales condition was attached to the sale rack. The sales slip was also stamped "Final Sale—No Returns." In this morning's mail, you received a package from Mrs. Gladys Day, 387 Freeman Road, Joplin, MO 58986. The package contained a "final-sale" dress she bought during the anniversary sale and a note asking that you take the dress back and refund the $94.95 plus sales tax that she paid for it. She said in the note that after she got home, she didn't like the dress as well as she thought she did. She hopes "you understand." Although Mrs. Day shops in your store frequently, she is considered by the sales staff to be "rude, demanding, and nasty." In fact, several of the experienced sales people refuse to wait on her. Write her a letter explaining that the dress is being returned to her by UPS and that she is not entitled to a refund because she bought the dress on a final-sale basis. Consider suggesting that if the fit of the dress is what bothers her, your alterations department could make alterations. (Her large size does make her hard to fit). The store values her business enough that you do not want to alienate her.

8. You are the claims manager of the Gateway Furniture Company, which is located at 34 Valley View, White Water, MN 58543. Mr. and Mrs.

Kenneth Johnson, 4543 South Street, Highland Park, IL 60074, recently purchased a wooden serving tray on which a picture was laminated. A sticker attached to the tray clearly stated the following: "Do not put hot pans or dishes on this tray. Do not submerge tray in water." The delicate finish that gives the picture a three-dimensional image somewhat restricts its use. You just received the tray Mr. and Mrs. Johnson purchased and a note in which they requested a full refund of $39.95 plus sales tax because the picture "has not been mounted properly, which causes bubbles to appear under the picture." Each tray was carefully inspected before it was put on the floor. Therefore, you know the tray was not like that when the Johnsons purchased it. A close examination of the picture reveals that a hot dish or pan has been placed on the tray, which caused the bubbles under the picture. While you cannot afford to replace the tray, suggest that they contact the tray manufacturer (Superior Products Company, 384 Dell Road, Raleigh, NC 23484) to see if the tray can be fixed. Indicate in the letter you prepare that the tray is being returned by parcel post.

9. You are the credit manager for Jameson's Auto Supply Company, which is located at 454 Western Avenue, Little Rock, AK 68754. You recently received a credit application from Mr. John Atterly, the owner of John's Auto Parts located at 5686 Dukat Road, Memphis, TN 58543. On his application, he indicated that he has been in business now for 7 years. He listed The First National Bank of Memphis as his bank reference. In checking with the bank, you learn that he has been in business for 3 years, that he is often slow in making payments on his loans, and that he has a loan with an outstanding balance of $10,898. The bank also mentioned that the store's sales have almost tripled in each of the 3 years it has been open. What really bothers you as credit manager is Mr. Atterly's dishonest response with regard to the number of years he reported that he has been in business. In completing the form, he signed his name certifying that the information he provided was accurate, when, in fact, it was not. Write a letter in which you deny Mr. Atterly's request for credit. You do want his business—but on a cash basis. Offer Mr. Atterly a 5 percent cash discount on his next order in any amount up to $700.

10. You are the credit manager for John Hart Company (9865 Wilson Avenue, Detroit, MI 48856), a distributor of exercise equipment. You recently received a credit application from the Be-Strong Exercise Room (6574 Grant Avenue, Mt. Pleasant, MI 48865) owned by Jack and Bill Smith, who are brothers. The application indicated that the business opened two months ago. You received favorable reports about the two owners from their credit references—but quite a different story was given in the Mt. Pleasant Credit Bureau report you received. You learned from the report that Jack declared bankruptcy last year after his home construction company began experiencing financial problems. His liabilities were $103,453.24; assets were valued at $9,045. You also learned that Bill Smith served three years in a Michigan prison (from January 1975 to December 1977) after he was convicted of the armed robbery of a convenience store. Your analysis of the data supplied by the Smiths on their application for credit reveals an unbalanced assets-liabilities ratio. By increasing their assets by $10,000 or by decreasing their liabilities by the same amount, the ratio would come closer to meeting your expectations. While you would welcome filling orders from the Be-Strong Exercise Room on a cash basis, you cannot open a credit account. To entice them to order from you on a cash basis, send along two $20 cash discount coupons that can be applied toward the cost of two different orders that exceed $150. Write an appropriate letter.

11. You are the manager of the Sanger Sewing Shoppe, which is located at 4585 Duncan Drive, Wichita Falls, TX 68674. One of your present credit customers, Mrs. Jane Quigley, 5847 Washington Boulevard, Plano, TX 68675, has sent you a letter requesting that her present $200 credit limit be increased to $400 so that she can purchase a new sewing machine that will enable her to sew clothing for others. Since her husband no longer has steady work, the Quigley family has been having trouble making ends meet. The Quigleys have three small children, which makes it all but impossible for Mrs. Quigley to work out of the home. She claims that if she had the new machine, she could take care of her family as well as sew. Making a few more dollars would help them pay some of their past-due accounts. In fact, Mrs. Quigley currently owes you $150. In the last year, she has never paid more than $15 a month on the account—and some months she can afford to pay only $5. In three years' time, she has only missed making four monthly payments. The garments that you have seen sewn by Mrs. Quigley were poorly done—which leads you to believe that she has very little chance of getting paid for her sewing jobs. Write a letter in which you deny Mrs. Quigley's request that her credit limit be increased. By the way, several of your customers who sew professionally use the same type of machine that Mrs. Quigley purchased from you four years ago.

12. You are the manager of the order department at Metalcraft Lawn Furniture Company, 4564 Greenwood Avenue, Deerfield, IL 60015. Until recently, your company was strictly a mail-order operation. Four months ago, you began selling through dealers. Now, if a dealer is located in an area from which a mail order was received, your policy is to decline the order and refer the customer to your local dealer. You recently received an order for a wrought-iron patio set (glass-top table and 4 chairs) from Mr. Grant Parker, 12 Summit Circle, Branson, MO 54484. Your dealer in Branson is Ozark Lawn and Garden Center, 2834 Main Street. Write a letter in which you decline Mr. Parker's order, send along a manufacturer's rebate coupon worth $20, and explain that the patio set he ordered has become your best-selling item. Remind him also that the set now comes in two additional colors: slate gray and midnight blue.

13. You work in the order department of Smith Toy Distributors, Inc., which is located at 4433 Canal Street, Indianapolis, IN 48454. The toy stores where you sell are now beginning to order their Christmas stock. You recently received an order from the Toy Box, 4542 Harvard Avenue, Tulsa, OK 74504. The Toy Box has been one of your best customers over the 15 years that your distributing company has been in existence. Among the items ordered by the Toy Box is the Co-Co Monster, which has become one of the hottest new toys throughout the country this fall. Unfortunately, your stock of the Co-Co Monster has been depleted, and the manufacturer tells you that it may be December 1 before your order can be filled. Therefore, you are unable to fill any orders for the Co-Co Monster until at least December 1. Write a letter that acknowledges the shipment of the other items on the Toy Box order and ask Mrs. Jane Carpenter, the owner/manager, if she wishes to have the order for the Co-Co Monster canceled or placed on backorder status. Indicate that if she chooses the latter, you will express ship (at your expense) the Co-Co Monsters to her when they become available.

14. You work in the order department of Townley Tool Company, which is located at 4543 Connecticut Street, Albany, NY 14430. You just received an order from A–B–C Hardware, Main Street, Adoka, IA 78685 for five socket sets (Stock No. 58574). You dropped this particular item several months ago when you began carrying another socket set (Stock No. 58665) that contained 10 more sockets (for a total of 44 sockets). The wholesale cost of the No. 58665 set is only $2.14 more (total of $14.12) than the cost of the No. 58574 set. Write a letter to A–B–C's manager, Mr. Jack Price, explaining that you no longer sell the set he ordered. Ask if he would like to have you send him 10 sets of the No. 58665 set. If so, you will bill him for the $21.40 cost difference.

15. You are well known as a speaker on a variety of management topics. In addition to your full-time job as executive assistant to the president of A–1 Insurance Company (900 East Street, Decatur, IL 61005), you give, on the average, three or four of these presentations a month. Most requests come from professional associations that have evening dinner meetings. You just received an invitation to talk on time management—the topic you receive the most requests to speak about—from the vice-president (Mr. Tom Bennett, 1893 Niles Road, Bloomington, IL 64334) of the Bloomington (IL) Chapter of Professional Engineers. The letter of invitation indicated that this group meets the first and third Tuesdays of each month—and you were invited to speak the first Tuesday in May. In looking at your calendar, you notice that your son's high school graduation ceremony is that evening. Your schedule, however, is clear for the evening of the third Tuesday should a speaker be needed for the meeting. Write Mr. Bennett a letter in which you decline his invitation.

16. You, the president of Allied Building Materials, Inc., 7868 Rand Road, Wheeling, IL 60984, just received a letter from Mr. Mark Lee, 1873 Greenbelt Drive, Des Plains, IL 60985, asking permission to use your park-like grounds for a picnic the Wheeling Rotary Club hosts each year for the children in the Wheeling Children's Home. The grounds on which your building is located attract a considerable amount of attention, which means that you get many requests similar to this one. Allied decided several years ago when it received its first request that it would not make these grounds available for public use. The lake on the grounds could provide a liability situation for which the company does not have insurance protection. Write Mr. Lee a letter in which you decline his request. Suggest the use of the Wheeling City Park for the picnic.

Chapter 8

Persuasive Letters

LEARNING OBJECTIVES

After studying this chapter, you should be able to

1. Discuss the elements of the persuasion strategy.
2. Discuss the suggestions for preparing effective sales letters.
3. Identify the characteristics of collection letters.
4. Discuss the types of appeals in the collection series.
5. Discuss the differences between the stages of the collection series.
6. Prepare effective letters of the type discussed in this chapter.

Why is persuasion incorporated into persuasive letters?

A different approach is taken in preparing persuasive letters because the nature of the situation necessitating a persuasive letter may not generate sufficient desire on the part of the reader to comply with your request. Therefore, persuasion is incorporated as a means of obtaining compliance. Persuasive letters should include information that will entice the reader to want to comply with the request.

In writing persuasive letters, you need to be aware of potential barriers that may prevent the reader from complying with your request. The major barriers are:

1. Reader's lack of interest
2. Reader's lack of need
3. Reader's dissatisfaction with products or services

Getting the reader to comply with your request will be doubly difficult if any of the barriers are present, but by anticipating these barriers you will be able to take the necessary action to minimize their impact.

The two types of persuasive letters discussed in this chapter are sales and collection letters. Although these two types of persuasive letters play different roles in the business world, they share one ultimate objective—to get the reader to comply with the request.

THE PERSUASION STRATEGY

Persuasive letters primarily use the indirect approach because the direct approach may be a deterrent to success. The four steps discussed in the following sections should help you prepare effective oral and written messages that will influence the choice and action of others.

Attracting Favorable Attention

How is favorable attention attracted in persuasive letters?

Attracting favorable attention is accomplished with a carefully designed theme that has reader or listener benefit. The main purpose of this step is to maintain attention and interest. Your first sentence should create desire as well as gain attention. For example, you should sell the sizzle—not just the steak. You should sell homecoming—not just the mum; you should sell the technique—not just the product.

Notice how the first of the following two paragraphs does little to attract the reader's attention.

Change: Wouldn't you like to help keep America beautiful? You can do your share with a small monthly donation to "Cleaning up the American Highways." I know you agree with me that this is an important and worthy project, and I am pleased to welcome you aboard.

To: "America the Beautiful" is one thing you and I can enjoy and preserve for our children and grandchildren. The diversity, the unspoiled beauty, and the freedom—yes, the freedom to enjoy all this beauty—is a basic American right and privilege.

The American highway is rapidly becoming a convenience junkyard for America's mobile society, and I need your help in preserving the beauty of our highways for our children and grandchildren. "Cleaning up the American Highway" is a select non-profit volunteer organization dedicated to maintaining the beauty of America's highways. For a small donation of $15 a month, you can do your part in maintaining "America the Beautiful."

You can gain attention by beginning your message with a question or statement that encourages the reader's continued reading because he/she wants to know "What's in this for me?" You should try to highlight an idea that is close to the reader's needs, interest, curiosity, or excitement. Like the other letters you have learned to write, the first paragraph of the persuasive message is critical because it must transcend the obvious meaning of the words while addressing hidden appeals.

Many techniques have proven to be successful in gaining the attention of an intended audience. Some of them are the following:

1. Using a famous quote
2. Outlining a bargain
3. Asking a question
4. Describing an outstanding feature
5. Making a shocking statement
6. Announcing a gift
7. Asking a question and outlining an outstanding feature
8. Using a famous proverb
9. Using a news announcement

Examples of opening sentences using the techniques designed to capture the reader's attention are now presented.

1. Famous quote: Home is where the heart is, and coming home is the best part of the day.
2. Bargain: Earn while you learn on your own personal computer!
3. Question: Could you use an extra hour a day?
4. Outstanding feature: Take a look at this proven best seller—and with a customary 14 percent markup, you can increase your profit.
5. Shocking statement: Twenty-five percent of America's high school age students drop out before finishing.
6. Gift: Here's a gift for the new mother.
7. Question/feature: Would you like to own your own business and have employees who pay you for the privilege of working?
8. Proverb: A stitch in time saves nine.
9. News announcement: According to recent governmental reports, the financial protection of Americans is 36 percent below the family-need level.

Creating Interest

How can interest be created in persuasive messages?

After attracting the attention of the reader, the persuasive letter should follow with a lead-in that captures the emotion of the reader. Start by telling what the product or service is, what it will do, and describe it clearly and specifically. This is normally accomplished by being positive, giving clear definitions of the product or service, and identifying special features.

While product information is important to persuasive messages, a sales appeal must be psychological in nature. This is accomplished by explaining or describing the product or service in terms of emotional benefit to the reader. Chinaware, for example, is basically plates, but to a host or hostess, it represents much more. Described psychologically, chinaware

1. Provides memorable meals
2. Has beautiful patterns that tell guests they are important
3. Provides for total color coordination
4. Has unique shaping for better balance

5. Treats your table to a new look
6. Sets the mood for relaxed dining

A 100-watt stereo rack system provides music and flexibility for the real music lover. Described psychologically, it

1. Provides completely integrated music
2. Has electronic synthesized quartz-lock tuning
3. Has sound adjustment through a 5-band graphic equalizer
4. Has a noise-reduction system for taping clarity
5. Has eight AM and FM memory presets for fingertip selection ease
6. Has soft touch controls for positive operation

Creating interest is often accomplished by clear and precise descriptions of the tangible or physical characteristics as well as the intangible or value aspects of the product or service. Physical descriptions include such points as construction, beauty, performance, and functions. Value descriptions include more emotional aspects, such as comfort, entertainment, recognition, health, and security. Reader interest can be increased by stressing one or more of the following advantages:

Appreciation and approval by others	Popularity
Beauty	Prestige
Comfort	Pride
Distinction	Profit
Efficiency	Recognition
Enjoyment	Respect
Entertainment	Safety and security
Health	Savings
Money	Self-preservation
Peace of Mind	Solution to a problem
Pleasure	Success

While the first of the following two paragraphs fails to create reader interest, the second paragraph is designed to be captivating.

Change: A year's subscription to *The Modern Home* costs just a few cents each day. Yet, you will find it difficult to put a price on much of the information you find in each issue.

To: You can almost smell the aroma of the food pictured in the foods section of each issue of *The Modern Home*. The fragrance of the flowers shown in the gardening section of each issue almost becomes reality. And the descriptions of the vacation spots presented in the traveling section of each issue are so vivid that you will have to pinch yourself to realize that you are not really there. For only pennies a day, you can receive a magazine containing much information that you will find almost priceless.

Establishing Reader Desire and Conviction

How are reader desire and conviction established in persuasive messages?

Successful sales letters are carefully planned to draw on the obvious and sometimes the not-so-obvious elements of motivation. Many hidden forces, such as fear, frustration, and human desire, can be used effectively to convince people to purchase a product or service.

Psychological emphasis is more successful when it attracts the true desire of the reader. What a person says he/she wants may not be what he/she actually desires. For instance, the majority of people will appear to be conservative, rational, and open-minded about products and services, but experienced writers of sales letters have learned they can successfully reach people by selling

1. Style, attractiveness, and neat appearance rather than just clothing
2. Feelings, ideals, respect, happiness, and comfort rather than items or products
3. Knowledge rather than books
4. Round holes rather than drill bits
5. The economy and pleasure of making personal items rather than tools
6. Comfort rather than air conditioners
7. Cleanliness rather than soap
8. Beauty and hope rather than cosmetics

Facts and information provide a base for such objective descriptors as height, weight, width, shape, size, watts, texture, and other product qualities and specifications. Ideas stress the more important intangible psychological appeals, such as sensation, satisfaction, and pleasure.

To attract attention, develop interest, and establish desire and conviction, you may use many different combinations and approaches, including 1) facts, figures, and information; 2) detail about construction, design, or quality control; 3) product quality and reliability as tested and verified by independent laboratories or specific manufacturers; 4) testimonials; and 5) samples, trials, and free demonstrations.

The first of the following two paragraphs is weak in reader conviction, while the revised version is much more effective.

Change: Your personal integrity and self-preservation need not be challenged by other people. With just a few low-cost lessons, you can be the successful, confident person you have always dreamed of being.

To: Remember: no one can intimidate you without your permission. You can develop and control a new self-concept simply and easily with the Delta Home Study Course.

Explaining What Should Be Done

The reader should not have to work at determining what action he/she must take. Rather, the action should be stated clearly and concisely. An action closing should accomplish two things: First, it should ask for action in a confident, unassuming manner. Second, it should remind the reader of the benefit he/she may expect and the approximate timing of the action.

Not only should you emphasize the action, but also you should make it easy to understand and accomplish. You should encourage the reader to act now or within a stated time frame. You should close with a reader-benefit statement that very often will incorporate the same information included in the opening paragraph.

Eliciting appropriate action may be accomplished in several ways. The action-getting methods illustrated in the following sentences have proven to be successful.

Stimulating action through persuasive offers

1. Send no money. . .
2. Examine for ten days on approval. . .
3. This offer is good until November 26. . .
4. The price will be increased by $20 after July 4. . .
5. Enjoy a special 15 percent discount if full payment accompanies your order. . .
6. We will refund your money if you are not satisfied. . .

Action is the overall intent of persuasive letters, and specific wording achieved through precise planning ensures the intended results. Emphasis on simple action is more important than simply emphasizing action.

Emphasizing simple action

1. Send your order on the enclosed easy-order blank. . .
2. A postage-free envelope is enclosed for your convenience. . .
3. You may pay by check, money order, or through our deferred-payment plan. . .
4. Our toll-free number is. . .

Action orientation can also be accomplished by suggesting an immediate response.

Suggesting immediate response

1. Mail the enclosed card today. . .
2. Mark the easy-order blank and send it today. . .
3. You can receive your free copy by returning the enclosed card today. . .

The importance of action orientation is illustrated in the second of the following two sentences.

Change:	The whole process of adequate hospitalization protection can be yours by filling out and returning the enclosed medical questionnaire.
To:	Call our toll-free number today to indicate your desire to receive three months of free hospitalization and medical coverage at no additional cost.

THE SALES LETTER

In actual volume, many organizations prepare more sales letters than any other type of letter presented in this text. These letters, which are often mass produced, are competing with the sales letters of other organizations for the reader's attention. The persuasion strategy presented in the previous section will help you prepare successful sales letters.

What is the suggested plan for sales letters?

The suggested plan for a sales letter includes the following elements:

1. An opening that attracts the reader's attention;
2. A section that captures the reader's interest in the product or service you are selling;
3. A section designed to establish desire and conviction on the part of the reader;
4. A courteous, action-oriented closing.

The letter in Figure 8–1 shows an ineffective sales letter. You will notice that the four essential elements of effective persuasive letters (attracting favorable attention, creating interest, establishing desire, and explaining what should be done by the reader) are either lacking or are weak. The letter in Figure 8–2 covers the same information but corrects the obvious weakness of the letter in Figure 8–1.

Sales letters are much easier to write when you have a top-quality product or service to promote. Avoid conveying an overconfident tone, which can have a negative effect on the impact of your letter. You should also avoid using statements that suggest a basic lack of confidence in the product or service, such as: "I hope you will agree. . ."; or "If you agree. . ."; or "I am quite sure you will agree. . ."; or "Many of our customers agree. . . ." Statements such as these tend to lead the reader into a feeling that the letter conveys doubts about the product, service, or overall quality. Similar doubts are, in turn, generated in the minds of the readers.

Figure 8–3 illustrates a sales letter from the Ortho-Vent Division of the Stuart McGuire Company. Notice how the writer gets the attention of the

Figure 8–1 Ineffective Sales Letter

Please allow me a few minutes of your most valuable time to explain the buy of a lifetime.	A weak opening.
Wouldn't you like to borrow without having to fill out all those complex financial forms normally required by a bank? Our quick-credit personal application card will provide you with $3,000, and your payments will be delayed for six months.	A section that fails to create interest.
If you are interested in our offer, please call us using the following toll-free number: 1-800-243-6781. For additional information, just return the enclosed card.	A closing that lacks emphasis or action.

You're one of several hundred carefully selected Electronics customers who have been pre-approved for a special credit opportunity.	An effective opening that creates interest.
Only a small percentage of Americans are financially responsible enough to meet the stringent selection criteria for a pre-approved Electronics credit card--and you are one of the few with exceptional credit worthiness.	A section that uses an effective interest-building approach.
Your preapproved credit authorization certificate is enclosed. Simply take the certificate to your local authorized Electronics dealer, and you can take your new Electronics equipment home with you the same day. A charge account agreement form is also enclosed.	A section that stimulates action.
As an Electronics charge customer, you will not only be able to charge your purchases, but also you will get advance notices of our sales. During two sales each year, our charge account customers are able to take advantage of our sale prices the day before the sale is announced to the public.	A section that outlines the advantages of being a charge customer, which also helps create interest.
Your Electronics charge account, which has a credit limit of $3,000, will arrive at your home just a few days after you sign and return the enclosed agreement form. Because this offer expires on December 31, act today to open your account. You will be glad you did.	A closing that outlines the action to be taken.

Figure 8–2 Effective Sales Letter

reader by providing a 100-percent-satisfaction guarantee. Next, examine how interest is generated by emphasizing the savings, the overall quality construction of the shoe, and the ease of wearability. Desire and conviction are established through detailed information about construction with the Ortho products. The only seemingly weak point of this commercial sales letter is the lack of a clear explanation of how to take advantage of the guarantee outlined in the letter.

The sales letter in Figure 8–4 contains "seasonal" persuasion that not only incorporates all of the previously discussed aspects of a successful persuasive letter, but also satisfies the element of timing.

Figure 8–5 illustrates a persuasive letter designed to create action through emphasis on health and self-preservation.

Persuasive letters are important if a business is to compete and succeed. Although the customer is always considered to be right, persuasive letters are designed to influence a person's attitude, choice, and hopefully his/her action.

After your persuasive letter is written, the last step involves a final check to see if the message is clear, concise, and logical. Each paragraph should be analyzed to determine if information and ideas are well founded and the flow from idea to idea and paragraph to paragraph is logical. The final check also ensures that your letter is grammatically correct.

The ORTHO-VENT DIVISION Inc.

The Stuart McGuire Co.
115 Brand Rd. Salem, Va. 24156 703-389-8121

1163H

Our policy is simple:

You must be 100% satisfied.

Dear Friend,

I was in a local shoe store the other night -- comparing prices as usual.

As I gloated over the price of "their" wingtip (now up to $69.95 -- "ours" is still just $43!) a guy walked up to the counter and plunked down a beautiful pair of ankle-high dress boots.

"I just can't wear these things," he said to the clerk. "I thought they'd limber up, but I've had them three days and they're still stiff. And the tops are about to rub my ankles raw!"

The clerk had a ready answer: "I'm sorry, sir, but I can't take them back. You've worn them. It's store policy."

"Store policy." Two magic words that retailers use when they want to make customers disappear.

"But they're not comfortable," the customer said.

"I'd like to help you, but there's really nothing we can do," said the clerk. Comfort obviously wasn't part of their "store policy."

But it is part of OURS...

★ WE GUARANTEE EXTRA COMFORT IN EVERY SHOE -- especially this season's style-right dress boots.

Who says boots must be stiffer, more confining than ordinary shoes? Spring-Step Construction makes our boots as flexible and lightweight as your favorite oxfords. Select upper leathers and linings insure extra softness in the shaft. And we do special things with tops to prevent chafing at the ankles!

And what shoe store lets you WEAR-TEST their shoes...?

★ **WE GUARANTEE PERFECT FIT, COMPLETE SATISFACTION -- by letting you wear-test every shoe you buy for 30 days.**

The moment you walk out of a store wearing a pair of shoes, you're stuck. Even if they don't feel so good the next day. We let you be SURE the shoes are right -- by wearing them a full 30 days.

★ **WE GUARANTEE YOUR MONEY BACK** -- including return postage -- with no questions asked.

Even if that guy had talked the clerk into taking the boots back, **HE WOULDN'T HAVE GOTTEN HIS MONEY BACK.** After he left, I checked. Like many stores, that one only gave exchanges or merchandise credits, NOT refunds. Once they've got your cash, that's it. It's "store policy." But it's not fair. If you're dissatisfied in any way, we'll refund your money immediately. You don't have to threaten the store manager or fill out endless papers.

We guarantee comfort. We guarantee satisfaction. Or your money back. That's OUR "store policy." Has been for 75 years. And we're not about to change it now. We guarantee.

Sincerely,

Jerry Blankenship

P.S. -- **I'm a shameless football fan. And for years I've been looking for the perfect shoe to wear to games. I finally found it -- our new STORM BOOT on page 5. It's dressy enough to make me look like a V.I.P. -- and the soft acrylic fleece keeps my feet warm as toast. A little rain or snow is no problem -- because the sole is specially designed for extra traction on slippery surfaces. And that's just one item from our exciting new Fall lineup!**

Figure 8–3 Commercial Sales Letter

Who really thinks much about furnaces in the summertime?	An opening that gains attention by asking a precise question.
National Heat-Pump, Inc. does, and we recommend that you give some thought to your heating system while the weather is still warm--and before the first freezing temperatures arrive.	A section that contains information designed to create interest.
Furnaces are built to last; but even the best, most efficient systems need regular pre-season check-ups. Pipes, pressure gauges, combustion chambers, controls, switches, thermostats, and gas or oil lines need to be checked periodically to ensure safe, economical heating.	A section that creates desire and conviction.
Our pre-season heating system service is more economical and efficient when we are not on the run with emergency service requests brought on by the season's first cold snap. Knowing your heating system is ready for the winter months will also give you peace of mind because you can be certain that your furnance is in good operating condition. You will be able to avoid the inconvenience and cost of obtaining emergency service.	A section that creates desire and conviction.
Don't put off having your furnace checked. Call us now at 661-6666 to make an appointment. At your convenience, we will send to your home a qualified heating system specialist.	A closing that explains the action to be taken.

Figure 8–4 Effective Sales Letter Based on Time Persuasion

COLLECTION LETTERS

Collection letters are also considered persuasive because the inclusion of motivationally oriented material is designed to get the reader to comply with your request. Because the reader may not be readily able nor willing to comply with your request, you have to take extra measures to assure compliance. To write a simple direct-request letter asking for payment most likely will not be successful because these letters do not contain the motivationally oriented material characteristic of persuasive letters.

In writing a collection letter, you need to attract the reader's attention, you need to get him/her interested in complying with your request, and you need to explain what action you wish him/her to take. You will notice that this pattern parallels the one used in preparing sales letters.

Collection letters are prepared when a creditor fails to meet one or more payment deadlines. While a collection letter most likely will not be prepared immediately after the creditor misses the first payment deadline, most companies do use collection letters after the second or third deadline is missed. Although as many as 15 to 25 percent of all transactions are not paid on time, all but 5 percent are eventually paid.

Credit procedures require the screening of applicants, although screening applicants too closely will probably cause the company to lose a certain number of sales. Some potential customers who are denied credit will take their business elsewhere. Most companies extend credit to good-risk customers who will always pay, although perhaps not on time. The credit policies in the majority of

Of the top ten risk factors leading to cardiovascular disease, seven are directly related to diet.	An opening designed to attract favorable attention.
Consider these startling statistics: Recent estimates suggest that 29 million Americans suffer from cardiovascular disease. The United States Department of Agriculture estimates that proper diet might reduce cardiovascular disease mortality by 25 percent. An average American male has a 33 percent chance of developing some form of heart disease before age 60.	A section that creates interest.
An optimum health program involves five essentials: 1. Building superior cells. 2. Improving body chemistry. 3. Improving body immunity. 4. Aiding digestion and assimilation. 5. Reducing toxins in the body.	A section that creates desire and conviction.
With today's typical American diet, these five essentials are absolutely necessary for an optimum health program. Health Care will outline for you a complete health restoration and maintenance program. We guarantee that our program will enable you to look and feel better and healthier--or we will refund your money.	A section that creates desire and conviction.
Don't wait another minute; return the enclosed card. At your convenience, an experienced Health Care representative will tell you about our program on a no-risk, no-obligation basis.	A closing that outlines the desired action.

Figure 8–5 Effective Sales Letter About Health

companies prohibit the extension of credit to customers known to be poor risks, even though these customers also may eventually pay. Because the vast majority of customers who are subjected to collection procedures eventually pay, most collection correspondence is written with this assumption in mind.

Requiring customers to pay promptly is necessary for two reasons. First, working capital in the form of accounts receivable is not available for the company's use until it is converted into cash. Excessive levels of accounts receivable can create cash flow problems for the company. Second, customers who have past-due accounts with a company are likely to take their business elsewhere. When this happens, the company is missing potential sales. By attempting to get customers to pay before their accounts become past due, the company may benefit from their continued patronage.

What is the goal of collection letters?

The goal of collection letters is to keep the customer's goodwill while securing the money owed the company. Lack of concern about the customers' goodwill will probably cause the customers to trade elsewhere, making the collection process that much more difficult.

Collection letters should make extensive use of psychology, which will persuade the customer to want to pay the past-due account. An example of an ineffective approach is insinuating that the slow-paying nature of the customer makes him/her a poor credit risk. A more effective approach is to imply that the company is sure the customer intends to pay but just hasn't done so yet. When used effectively, the latter approach will probably cause the customer to decide to pay.

Characteristics of Collection Letters

What characteristics should collection letters possess?

Well-designed collection letters possess several distinct characteristics. For example, the first letters in the series, which are generally low-key, suggest that perhaps the customer has forgotten to pay. If the first letters are not successful, a stronger approach is used, ultimately threatening the customer with legal action. But to make a threat of legal action too early will generally cause the customer to take his/her business elsewhere.

Another characteristic of collection letters is the use of the circumstances of the situation to determine the proper wording of the letter. For example, a collection letter that is sent to a customer of good standing for twenty years will be worded quite differently from a collection letter sent to a customer who is continually late in paying.

Timing is also important in preparing a collection series. Prompt-paying customers will receive letters less frequently than slow-paying customers. The time span between letters in the collection series will be longer during the first letters in the series and shorter during the last letters in the series. The time differential gives the customer the benefit of the doubt.

In writing collection letters, the use of wording that does not alienate the customer is crucial. The company also wants to avoid losing the customer after the account has been paid.

Collection letters should contain resale material designed to convince customers that they made the proper decision in dealing with the company. Effectively used, resale material will help induce the customer to pay as well as to continue to do business with the company.

Use of Appeals in the Collection Series

Another characteristic of the collection series is the use of one or more appeals in writing the message. Because of the importance of these appeals in writing effective letters, each is discussed in detail.

Appeal to fair play

What message is contained in the fair-play appeal?

The fair-play appeal essentially says to the customer: "We've been fair with you by providing the quality of product and service that you have the right to receive, and now you need to be fair with us by paying your account in full." The wording in this type of appeal may remind the customer that the charge account or sales contract states that in return for providing goods and services, the company has the right to expect the customer to pay promptly. In other words, you may imply: "Now that we've done our fair share, please be fair with us by doing your share." When this appeal is used, the message also tells the reader that you are confident that he/she wants to play fairly.

The following example illustrates the use of the fair-play appeal in a collection letter.

> The special instructions in your order indicated that the glassware was needed by March 31, so we sent the order to you by air express—at our expense.
>
> We believe that we have been fair with you, and we are certain that you intend to be equally fair with us. Will you, therefore, please send us your check for the amount due?

Appeal to good credit reputation

What message is contained in the appeal to good credit reputation?

A collection letter that appeals to the reader's good credit reputation concentrates on the company's desire that the reader maintain a good credit rating. The appeal to a good credit reputation is most effective for the first letter in a collection series. Because the majority of credit customers do not want to be classified as a poor credit risk, most will feel compelled to pay their accounts. For those few credit customers who care very little about their credit ratings, this appeal will probably be no more effective than most other appeals. An effective appeal to a customer to maintain a good credit reputation is illustrated below.

> We remember very well the favorable comments made by several of your credit references when you applied for credit. Because of this good credit reputation, we do not want you to lose it. Is the past-due status of your account an oversight?
>
> So that we will be able to recommend you some day as a credit customer, please protect your credit reputation by sending us your check for $389.04.

Appeal to pride

What message is contained in the pride appeal?

Another appeal commonly used in collection letters is to pride, which involves asking the reader to act in ways that he/she can be proud of—in this case, paying the past-due account. The message may tell the customer that the company has always been proud of him/her because of the manner in which credit transactions with the company have been handled. The hope is that the customer will decide to pay so that others can continue to be proud of his or her bill-paying practices.

> During the six years that you have had a charge account with us, we have been very proud of the way in which you have met your financial obligations. We are sure that you, too, take a great amount of pride in keeping your account balance paid up.
>
> We are confident that you will want to pay the balance of your past-due account very soon, which will enable you to continue to take pride in your good credit reputation.

Appeal to fear of legal action

When all other appeals have failed to entice the customer to pay, the company may include a statement of intended action in the final collection letter. In most cases, the realization that such an action may be taken will cause the customer to decide to pay the company. This appeal is appropriate only as a last resort. To use the appeal early in the collection process will undoubtedly cause irreparable damage to the reader-writer relationship.

What message is contained in the legal-action appeal?

An appeal to fear of legal action against a customer is presented in the following illustration.

> We believe that we have given you ample time to pay your account or at least to explain to us why you have chosen not to pay. Now we are forced to take more drastic action.
>
> Unless we have your full payment by August 1, we will turn your account over to our collection agency. At the same time, we will inform the Allied Credit Bureau of your unwillingness to pay your account.
>
> To avoid the inconvenience of a poor credit reputation, will you please pay your account in full by August 1? Doing so will enable you to protect your credit reputation.

The Collection Series

Most collection series consist of several stages, and the message contained in each successive stage becomes more insistent that the reader pay the past-due balance. The amount of time that is allowed to pass between each stage of the series is determined by the credit reputation of the customer. Less time is allowed to pass during the later stages than during the earlier stages.

The stages in the collection series may be modified to meet the needs of the situation. In some instances, perhaps two letters in the same stage are mailed to the customer. If evidence warrants the elimination of one or more stages, the series may be compressed. The various stages in the collection series include the following:

What stages are found in the collection series?

1. Duplicate statement
2. Reminder letter
3. Inquiry letter
4. Request letter
5. Ultimatum letter

Each stage in the collection series is discussed in detail in the following section.

Duplicate statement

Circumstances normally warrant the sending of a duplicate statement to the customer whose account is delinquent. In many cases, a rubber stamp is used to imprint the duplicate statement with one of the following: ''Please remit today,'' ''Second request,'' ''Past due,'' or ''Just to remind you.'' Gummed stickers with these phrases imprinted may be attached to the statement to remind the customer of the past-due balance of the account.

If the company has had difficulty previously in collecting money from a particular customer, the duplicate-statement stage may be bypassed. If the customer has been late in the past, the use of this stage probably will not produce results either.

Reminder letter

If the duplicate-statement stage of the collection series is not successful, the next stage is to send the customer a reminder letter. At this point, the assumption is still made that the customer has forgotten to pay. Therefore, the intent of this letter is to remind the customer about the past-due account. Many companies use reminder letters to promote sales, in addition to reminding the customer of the past-due account.

What should the opening of reminder letters do?

The opening of a reminder letter either courteously asks for payment of the past-due balance or presents neutral material. If several reminder letters are sent to a customer before an inquiry letter is sent, the first of the reminder letters is likely to open with neutral material while the later ones are likely to open with a suggestion that the customer pay.

Notice the difference in the tone of the following two reminder-letter openings.

Change:	Don't you think the past-due status of your charge account has existed long enough? We do. Therefore, we will appreciate your paying us as soon as possible.
To:	As the owner of a profitable business, you are well aware of the benefit of a good credit reputation. That is why we are sure you have just overlooked paying the $187.54 balance on your charge account that is now two months past due.

In some cases, the reminder is included in a separate paragraph; in other instances, it is incorporated into the opening paragraph, as the example above illustrates.

Regardless of the location of the reminder section, you will have to guard against alienating the reader. If the customer is alienated, collection will become even more difficult. The first of the following two paragraphs is an ineffective reminder. Notice the much-improved tone of the second paragraph.

Change:	I am sure you are aware that your account has a past-due balance of $238.83. The duplicate statement that we sent you last month should have been a sufficient reminder to settle your account.
To:	Won't you please take a minute to write a check for $238.83, the past-due balance of your account? We are certain you have just overlooked sending us your check.

The next section of the reminder letter can include sales-promotion material and/or resale material. The first of the following two paragraphs contains sales-promotion material while the second contains resale material.

What should be included in the middle section of reminder letters?

> Our two-week Summer Breezes Sale begins June 4 when many items will be reduced as much as 10 to 30 percent. You will find many excellent values during this sale.
>
> The Browning food processor you charged on your account two months ago has likely become an indispensible appliance in your kitchen by now. The manufacturer just introduced several new attachments that will make your processor even more versatile. Stop by our housewares section to see a demonstration of these new items.

The appropriate closing for a reminder letter is courteous and action oriented. The first of the following two closings lacks an action orientation.

What type of closing is appropriate for reminder letters?

> Change: We appreciate your business.
>
> To: A stamped, preaddressed envelope is enclosed for your convenience in mailing us your check today. Or, if you plan to shop in Ballards within the next few days, just bring your check by the credit department. We will be glad to stamp your statement "Paid in Full."

The suggested plan for a reminder letter includes the following elements:

What is the suggested plan for reminder letters?

1. A courteous opening;
2. A reminder that the customer's account is past due;
3. A section that includes resale and/or sales-promotion material;
4. A courteous, action-oriented closing.

Figure 8–6 illustrates an ineffective reminder letter. Notice how much better the letter in Figure 8–7 meets the requirements of effective reminder letters.

Figure 8–6 Ineffective Reminder Letter

If you were like the majority of our other customers, you would never have allowed your Grayson's charge account to become past-due.	An opening that lacks courtesy.
You have now owed us $342.87 since June 10, the day on which payment was to have been received for the merchandise we sold you on account on May 2. In case you have forgotten, the past-due status of your account is costing you money because 1.5 percent interest per month is being charged on the unpaid balance. As of July 11, the interest charge is $5.14, making the current balance of the account $348.01.	A discourteous section that explains the facts.
Get a check to us as soon as possible so that you can avoid further interest charges.	A discourteous, action-oriented closing.

Because I know you are familiar with the benefits of a good credit record, the past-due status of your Grayson's charge account must be an oversight on your part.	A courteous opening.
Please take just a minute to write us a check for $348.01, the current balance of your account. Since June 10, the day by which payment of $342.87 was to have been received, your account has accumulated $5.14 in interest charges. To avoid additional charges, please send us a check for the current balance of the account.	A section that reminds the customer that his/her account is past due.
We are sure the Collingwood metal art frames you purchased from us are popular with your customers. The corner clamp patented by Collingwood makes these metal frames easy to assemble.	A section that contains resale material.
Please send us a check today in the stamped, preaddressed envelope that is enclosed.	A courteous, action-oriented closing.

Figure 8–7 Effective Reminder Letter

Inquiry letter

When the duplicate statement and the reminder letter are not successful in getting the customer to pay the balance of the past-due account, an inquiry letter may be successful in enticing payment. At this point, you will no longer assume that the customer has forgotten to pay. Rather, you will make the assumption that the customer has either become dissatisfied with the products or service or that he/she has experienced a personal catastrophe and is unable to pay at this time.

The ultimate goal of the inquiry letter is to entice the customer to pay. However, you may have to settle for an intermediate goal of just getting a response that explains why he/she has not paid. If the customer has experienced a catastrophe, a deferred-payment schedule can perhaps be arranged whereby the customer will pay an agreed-upon amount each month.

What type of opening is appropriate for inquiry letters?

An effective way to begin the inquiry letter is to use a buffered opening containing material with which the reader will agree. Notice the difference between the following two openings.

Change:	Why haven't you paid the $129.58 that you have now owed us for three months? We are running out of patience.
To:	As the owner of a business, you are aware of the need for customers to pay their accounts on time. You appreciate your customers who pay their accounts on time, just as we appreciate our customers who pay on time.

What should be included in the middle section of inquiry letters?

Following the opening, a review of the facts should be presented. In this section, you should identify the length of time the account has been past due as well as the balance of the account. You may also include in this section an inquiry about the reason the account is past due. Notice the difference between the following two paragraphs.

> Change: On June 10, we credited your account for $124.34, the amount of the fishing gear that you ordered from us. Interest charges of $5.24 have now accrued on that account. We are sure that all of this gear has sold, so what seems to be the problem?
>
> To: Since June 10 when we shipped your order of fishing gear and credited your account for $124.34, interest charges of $5.24 have accrued, giving your account a past-due balance of $129.58. Because you have always paid your account on time, thus avoiding interest charges, we are concerned that perhaps some unforeseen circumstances have arisen that are preventing your usual prompt payment. If this is the situation, please let us know immediately so we can arrange an alternative payment plan.

Notice the pride appeal that has been included in the revised paragraph. This appeal subtly tells the customer that he/she can take pride in the fact that interest charges have been avoided in the past—and future interest charges can be avoided by paying the account.

Resale and/or sales-promotion material can be effectively included in the inquiry letter. An example of resale material is shown in the following paragraph.

> Many of our customers have been telling us this summer that they are unable to keep a sufficient supply of our fishing gear on stock to meet customer demand. We are sure that you also have found our fishing gear to be popular among your customers.

Following this section of the inquiry letter, a discussion of the action you wish the reader to take should be included. Even though you may have requested payment or an explanation earlier in the letter, this section can be used to reinforce your desire to receive payment. The following paragraph outlines this important section.

> We will appreciate your sending us a check for $129.58 today. If you are unable to pay the balance of your account now, please let us know why. Perhaps a deferred-payment schedule can be arranged.

The closing of the inquiry letter, which should be courteous, should also be action oriented. When appropriate, an appeal can also be included.

> We will be glad to keep your account among our "preferred-status customers" if you will send us your check today or explain the reason for the past-due balance of the account.

What is the suggested plan for inquiry letters?

The suggested plan for an inquiry letter includes the following elements:

1. An opening that contains buffered material;
2. A review of the facts of the situation and an inquiry about the reasons for the past-due status of the account, incorporating an appeal if appropriate;
3. A section that contains resale and/or sales-promotion material;
4. A discussion of the action desired by the company;
5. A courteous, action-oriented closing that incorporates an appeal, if appropriate.

The letter in Figure 8–8 illustrates an ineffective inquiry letter, while the letter in Figure 8–9 presents an effective revision.

Request letter

If the earlier collection attempts have not been successful, the request letter in the collection series is prepared. The purpose of this letter is to make a strong request that the reader pay the balance of his/her account. At this point, you can no longer assume that the reader is not paying his/her account because of an oversight or because of dissatisfaction with the company. Rather, the assumption is made that the customer is being somewhat troublesome and that a little more force needs to be exerted.

The appeals discussed previously can be used to good advantage in this stage of the collection process. In some instances, one appeal is more appropriate than others. You should make sure that the appeal used in the letter is appropriate for the individual and the circumstances surrounding the situation.

What type of opening is appropriate for request letters?

The request letter opens with a presentation of the facts. Although the letter should not be discourteous, some of the courtesy expressed in the opening of the earlier letters in the series is omitted from the opening of the request

Figure 8–8 Ineffective Inquiry Letter

Your inattention to our previous correspondence about your past-due account is particularly annoying.	A discourteous opening.
The deadline for paying for the merchandise you purchased from us on May 2 was three months ago. Each month that you allow this account to remain unpaid, you are being charged 1.5 percent. The original charge of $342.87 has now accumulated $10.36 in interest charges. Your account today has an outstanding balance of $353.23. We are unable to allow this inattention to go on much longer.	A section that explains the facts.
We will give you until August 20 to send us a check for $353.23.	A threatening closing.

We know you value prompt-paying customers just as much as we do. We also know that you become concerned, just as we do, when a long-time, valued customer allows an account to remain unpaid.	A buffered opening.
We are concerned that a purchase of $342.87 which we credited to your account on May 2 has not yet been paid for. Interest charges of $10.36 have now accumulated, giving your account a current balance of $353.23. Because you have always taken pride in paying your account on time, we are wondering if an extenuating circumstance prevents your paying this account. If so, please let us know immediately. We will try to work with you in arranging an alternative payment plan. Otherwise, we will appreciate your paying us as soon as possible.	A section that reviews the facts and inquires about the reason for the past-due status of the account.
Have you yet had an opportunity to examine our sale catalog that we recently sent you? This sale, which lasts until Labor Day, offers many items reduced by as much as 50 percent.	A section that contains sales-promotion material.
To help you protect your credit record, we will appreciate your sending us a check for $353.23 or an explanation why you are unable to pay at this time.	A section that discusses the action desired by the company.
If we hear from you soon, we will be able to protect the "preferred-customer" status of your account that entitles you to privileges you will not want to be without.	A courteous closing that contains a credit-reputation appeal.

Figure 8–9 Effective Inquiry Letter

letter. While the opening should be to the point, it should not be rude as is the first of the following two paragraphs.

Change: Customers like you are difficult to understand. We have given you every opportunity to protect your credit rating by paying the $459.94 you owe us, but apparently you really don't care much about your rating. We insist that you pay us immediately.

To: If you pay the $459.94 that you have owed us now for three months, you can avoid losing the good credit reputation that you have enjoyed for so long. As the owner of a business, you are well aware of the necessity of maintaining a good credit record.

After the opening, an appropriate appeal can be included. The following paragraph illustrates the use of the pride appeal.

What should be included in the middle section of request letters?

For the four years that you have been a credit customer of ours, we have been very pleased with your payment record. I am sure you are just as proud of your preferred-customer status—and that you put a high priority on keeping that status.

Following the appeal, you discuss the action you wish the reader to take. In some instances, two alternatives are available: either payment of the past-due account or an explanation for his/her lack of payment. Ideally, the first alternative will be the one the reader chooses. If not, getting an explanation will enable you to make other payment arrangements. Notice the difference in the tone of the following two paragraphs.

> Change: You decide which of the following two alternatives you want to choose: paying your account in full or explaining why you haven't made a payment in three months. If you fail to do either, our last-resort alternative will be exercised the next time we have to write to you requesting payment.
>
> To: Your lack of response to our correspondence now leaves us with two alternatives: to request immediate payment of your account balance or to explain why you have not paid your account in full. If unforeseen circumstances are responsible, please let us know so that we can help you make alternative payment arrangements. Doing so will enable you to reduce your financial obligations while protecting your credit reputation.

The inclusion of resale material and/or sales-promotion material in a request collection letter is appropriate. The following paragraph is an example of sales-promotion material.

> We have just become the midwest distributor of Grant's paints, which are well known throughout the country for their durability and application ease. If you would like to carry this product line in your paint store, please let us know.

What type of closing is appropriate for request letters?

The closing of the request letter should be courteous, strong, and action oriented. The following paragraph possessess these criteria.

> Please take advantage of this opportunity to protect your good credit rating. We must have your check or an explanation by June 10.

What is the suggested plan for request letters?

The suggested plan for a request collection letter includes the following elements:

1. An opening that presents the facts;
2. A section that includes the appropriate appeal;
3. A request for action (either payment or an explanation);
4. A section that contains resale or sales-promotion material;
5. A courteous, action-oriented closing.

The letter presented in Figure 8–10 is an ineffective request letter. Notice that the revised version presented in Figure 8–11 contains the information needed for an effective request letter.

We simply cannot figure out why you would allow your credit reputation to almost dissolve right before your eyes. When the reputation is gone, it is very difficult to get back.	A discourteous opening.
You now have two alternatives: to continue to allow your account to remain past due, which will virtually destroy your credit reputation with us; or to pay us $358.52, the amount you owe us, immediately. Should the latter not be possible, the least you can do is to explain this situation to us.	A section that discourteously presents the facts.
You simply cannot afford to continue to ignore our requests for payment. Let us hear from you by the end of the week.	A discourteous closing.

Figure 8–10 Ineffective Request Letter

Paying the $358.52 that you currently owe us will enable you to avoid losing your good credit reputation. As a merchandiser, you certainly are aware of the benefits enjoyed by those who have a good credit reputation.	An opening that presents the facts.
We are sure that you value your preferred-customer status because you have always paid your account on time. Please take the necessary steps so you can continue to maintain the preferred status of your account.	A section that presents the credit-reputation appeal.
To avoid losing your preferred-customer status, we will need your payment of $358.52 by August 20. If you are unable to pay your account in full by that date, please send a partial payment now, and we will make arrangements with you to pay the remainder on a deferred basis. Acceptance of either of the alternatives I've suggested will enable you to maintain your account status.	A section that presents a request for action.
Collingwood Art Frames just expanded its metal product line to include bronze-finish frames. Because you have been so successful selling Collingwood frames in other finishes, I am sure you will want to carry this new line as well. The bronze frames are illustrated in the brochure I've enclosed.	A section that contains sales-promotion material.
We will maintain your account status if we receive by August 20 your payment or partial payment and explanation.	A courteous, action-oriented closing.

Figure 8–11 Effective Request Letter

Ultimatum letter

The last letter in the collection series is the ultimatum letter. This letter is used when the other letters have not produced satisfactory results. The basic characteristic of this letter is a statement that legal action will be initiated unless prompt payment is received. Once the threat of legal action is made, it should be carried out immediately if the customer again fails to meet the payment deadline. Although the ultimatum letter should be polite, it must stress the urgency of the situation.

What type of opening is appropriate for ultimatum letters?

The content of the ultimatum letter should convey to the reader that he/she must pay now or be prepared to face the consequences—which should also be clearly outlined in the letter. Among the consequences most companies use are the courts, a collection agency, or an attorney.

The opening of the ultimatum letter once again reviews the facts for the reader. Because he/she is well aware of the situation, the opening can be quite brief.

> Five months ago when you asked us to charge to your account an order amounting to $434.23, we readily agreed to do so because you had always paid us on time. We are giving you one more opportunity to pay the amount you owe.

What should be included in the middle section of ultimatum letters?

Following the opening, the legal-action appeal can be incorporated. Notice how the following paragraph incorporates this appeal.

> To avoid the inconvenience of a damaged credit reputation as well as the inconvenience of having to go to court, please send us a check for $434.23 by July 1.

To remove any doubt in the reader's mind as to your course of action, a statement of ultimatum should be included after the legal-action appeal. While the ultimatum in the first of the following two paragraphs is not clear, the second paragraph is.

> Change: Your continued lack of response to our request for payment will cause us to take drastic action. Please help us avoid having to do so.
>
> To: If we do not have your check for full payment of your account by July 1, our attorney will immediately begin the legal process of collecting the amount. A report classifying you as a non-paying customer will also be filed with your local credit bureau. Both of these actions will have a serious impact on your credit reputation.

What type of closing is appropriate for ultimatum letters?

The closing of the ultimatum letter should be courteous, as well as firm and action oriented. Notice the difference between the following two closings.

> Change: Let us hear from you immediately.
>
> To: While we do not want to take steps that will damage your credit record, your continued lack of response to our payment requests will force us to do so. A pre-addressed envelope is enclosed for your convenience in sending us your check today.

The suggested plan for an ultimatum letter includes the following elements:

What is the suggested plan for ultimatum letters?

1. A review of the facts;
2. A section that includes the legal-action appeal;
3. A statement of ultimatum;
4. A courteous close.

Figure 8–12 presents an ineffective ultimatum letter. A revision of this letter is presented in Figure 8–13.

Figure 8–12 Ineffective Ultimatum Letter

You have now backed us into a wall. If we do not have your check for $363.89 by September 10, we will turn your account over to our collection agency and also notify the Metropolitan Credit Bureau of your defaulting on this account.	A threatening, discourteous opening.
We have been very reasonable with you. We can wait no longer.	A section that mentions an ultimatum but that fails to mention what it is.
This is the last time you will hear from us requesting payment on this account. Should you fail to pay by September 10, our collection agency will be in touch.	A discourteous closing.

Figure 8–13 Effective Ultimatum Letter

On May 2 we shipped you on credit an order amounting to $342.87. A few days after that, we sent you your monthly statement indicating that the balance of your order was due on or before June 10. Since that original statement, we have sent you four letters asking for payment or an explanation. None of our letters brought a response from you.	An opening that reviews the facts.
Because we cannot afford to let customers carry past-due balances on their accounts, we are asking you one last time to pay by September 10 the balance of your account, which is now $368.89. Failure to pay in full by that time will force us to turn your account over to our collection agency. The Metropolitan Credit Bureau will also be notified of this situation.	A section that presents the legal-action appeal.
Please send us your check for $368.89 by September 10 so we can avoid undertaking legal action to collect the amount you owe us.	A section that presents the ultimatum.
I am sure you can see why we can no longer allow this inactivity on your part to continue, just as you most likely are not able to allow your customers to carry outstanding balances on their accounts. A stamped, preaddressed envelope is enclosed for your convenience in sending us your check today.	A courteous closing.

THE USE OF FORM LETTERS IN THE COLLECTION SERIES

The use of form letters in the collection series is widespread. Letters that have been found to be particularly successful in the past usually comprise the bulk of a company's standard collection messages.

The current widespread use of text-editing equipment (see Chapter 18) simplifies the personalizing of form messages. Although standard form paragraphs are used, the equipment can be programmed to stop at each point where variable information (such as the name, amount owed, length of time owed) is to be inserted. As a rule, personalized letters not only create a better impression, but also are more effective than mass-produced letters.

Many organizations have a number of standard paragraphs that can be used to construct collection letters. For example, ten different opening paragraphs may exist for the request letter. Perhaps fifteen different paragraphs are available for the various appeals. To construct a collection letter, the most appropriate opening paragraph is used, the most appropriate appeal paragraph is used, and so on. Because each paragraph has an identification number, the collection manager gives the typist the paragraph numbers that are to comprise the letter. If each paragraph is stored in text-editing equipment, the appropriate numbers are used to recall the desired paragraphs that are printed automatically.

CHAPTER SUMMARY

Persuasive letters include sales letters and collection letters. The goal of these letters is to get the reader to comply with your request. Both types of letters use persuasion strategy to attract favorable attention, create interest, establish reader desire and conviction, and clearly state what should be done.

Effective collection letters possess several characteristics, including the use of appeals. The types of appeals used in the collection series are appeal to fair play, appeal to good credit reputation, appeal to pride, and appeal to fear of legal action.

The collection series is comprised of the following stages: duplicate statement, reminder letter, inquiry letter, request letter, and ultimatum letter. The content of the letter is dependent upon the stage. Every collection letter, regardless of the stage in the series, should be written with the assumption that the customer will eventually pay.

REVIEW QUESTIONS

1. What steps should be taken to develop an effective persuasive letter?
2. What techniques are available to capture the reader's attention in the opening of an effective persuasive message?
3. What type of material should be included in the last section of the persuasive message?
4. What are the characteristics of collection letters?
5. What types of appeals are used in preparing collection letters?
6. What are the stages in the typical collection series?
7. What appeal is most appropriate for use in the ultimatum letter?
8. Explain the use of word processing in preparing collection letters.

APPLICATION PROBLEMS

1. Prepare a written critique of the following ultimatum letter, evaluating grammar usage, punctuation, conformity with the suggested plan, and conformity with the writing essentials discussed in Chapters 3 and 4.

> In case you think you have gotten by without paying the $349.87 you now owe us, please think again. We demand your payment before January 10, otherwise we will turn your account over to our attorneys' for collection. Letting your account be delinquent for four months is unfortunate. Had we known what kind of credit risk you were we sure would not have granted you credit. You can be sure that we shall think twice before we allow you to purchase on credit again. Consider this as our final letter about this matter.

2. Using the proofreader's marks shown in Figure 4–5, edit the following letter.

> One of our goals is to make certain our customers are totaly satisfied with our service. Only when our customers' are satisfied can we be satisfied.
>
> Perhaps you are not aware that the payment for the materials you ordered from us on July 17 for $357.54 is now 2 months past due. We will appreciate your sending us a check for that amount today.
>
> We have just added a new line of womens' clothing and new stock is arriving at our store daily. We are sure you will find these garments not only attractive in styling, but also in quality.
>
> The next time you are in our store why not have lunch in the new Gardenia Room. The food is superb and the service impeccable. The new facility is designed to make our customer's shopping trips not only convient but also pleasurable.
>
> A stamped addressed envelop is enclosed for your convience in sending your check today.

3. Assume that you are the collection manager for Grant Manufacturing Company, 10 Airway Blvd., Lincoln, NE 68509. Grant manufactures a variety of equipment used by dentists. One of your customers, Dr. John Kramer, 80 Blaine Drive, Boise, ID 48493, purchased $10,000 of equipment from you two months ago. Dr. Kramer paid $2,000 down and the rest was to be paid in monthly installments of $1,000. He appears to have stopped making the monthly payments after his first one. The reminder letter you sent him brought no response. The information you collected about Dr. Kramer to assess his credit suitability reveals that he graduated near the top of his dental-school class, that he is married and the father of three children, and that he has assets worth nearly $400,000. He has a good credit record. Consider the adequacy of each of the following sentences/paragraphs for this letter. Critique each on the basis of punctuation and grammar usage, as well as on letter-writing mechanics. Rewrite each sentence/paragraph to make it conform with effective writing principles.

a. (opening section) Your purchase of Grant equipment was a wise one.

b. (opening section) As you can imagine Dr. Kramer it is quite difficult to operate a business properly when you have numerous accounts receivable.

c. (opening section) As a owner of a business, you can see our concern in your past-due account. If you are not satisfied with our services, please let us know.

d. (opening section) After reviewing your credit record with us, we've found that this months payment has not yet been received.

e. (opening section) One of Grants primary goals is customer satisfaction. We try to do this by selling the best equipment for less; a task that we can accomplish by holding down our overhead expenses.

f. (middle section) Presently we have collected $3,000 of the $10,000 account you have with us. The $1,000 monthly check was received in August, however, not is September. We would appreciate the prompt payment of the September and October installments.

g. (middle section) Two months ago you purchased $10,000 of dental equipment. At the time of purchase, you made a down payment of $2,000. Since that time, you have paid one of the eight monthly installments of $1,000. We have sent you a reminder letter, but still have received no payment.

h. (middle section) I have enclosed our catalog with all our latest equipment along with an order card. I hope you will consider purchasing more merchandise through our mailed-order program which includes a 10 percent discount for charge customers.

i. (middle section) The dentistry equipment that you have purchased is the highest-quality merchandise on the market. The reputation of Grant equipment is known all over the world.

j. (middle section) The equipment you purchased two months ago had a cost of $10,000. You paid $2,000 down, and you were to pay the rest in $1,000 monthly installments. We have not received a payment from you since your first monthly payment. I am sure that what ever the reason we can work something out that will suit both of us.

k. (closing section) We hope to hear from you soon.

l. (closing section) We know you will make your payment soon so you can remain on our preferred-customer list.

m. (closing section) We appreciate your prompt action, and if we can be of any more assistance let us know.

n. (closing section) Thank you for doing business with Grant Manufacturing Company.

o. (closing section) You prompt attention will be appreciated.

4. Assume that you just graduated from college and that you have accepted a position in the High School Relations Department of Grant College. Your major responsibility is to recruit freshman students. The college is primarily an undergraduate institution with strong programs in business, liberal arts, and science. Last year, 8,600 students attended Grant College, which is located in Des Moines, Iowa. Grant College uses the trimester rather than the semester plan. An advantage of the trimester plan is that students can complete more credits each year than they can in a college using semesters. The end result is that they can complete a bachelor's degree in less than the traditional four years. The first trimester begins the last week in August and ends the Friday before Christmas each year. Second trimester begins the first available school day after January 1. The third trimester begins on the Monday following the

15-week second trimester and continues for 15 weeks. The trimester system involves one-hour classes rather than the usual 50 minutes in the semester system. Actual total time in class is the same for both systems, but the semester requires 16 weeks of classes.

Prepare a persuasive message that will encourage high school seniors to attend Grant College next fall. Some of the points you should try to weave into your persuasive message are the following:

1. A trimester system will allow graduation in two and two-thirds years if students take 15 credit hours per trimester.
2. A trimester system allows those who prefer attending two terms a year to get into the job market earlier in the summer than those who attend a semester-system college.
3. Having more time to work during the summer helps students earn more money for their college expenses.
4. Summer school is available for those who wish to take two trimesters and a summer session.
5. Students on a three-term trimester plan can take six hours for the full term and another nine hours during the nine-week summer session, which totals 15 credits for the trimester.

As you prepare your message, remember that many schools are recruiting these same students and that your job is to present the most important information in the most acceptable manner.

5. Select a magazine or newspaper ad that includes a picture of a product. Now, draft a sales letter designed for a cross-section of the population in a metropolitan area of your choice. Utilize the basic principles for effective persuasive messages. Be sure to attach the picture of the product you selected when you submit your assignment to your instructor.

6. Write a sales letter about a new product called the ''Night Byte Light.'' The letter is to be sent to regional discount stores in your area. This invention operates with a battery (not included) and attaches to the end of a fishing pole. The line passes through the gadget. When a fish bites, the light blinks. Suggested retail price is $9.95 and wholesale price to the stores is $4.50. This is a new, untested product. However, your company, ''The Fish Fad Farm,'' boasts several new big sellers during the past eight years, including the easy hook hanger and the scrappy sea bait, both of which were million-dollar sellers for the ''The Fish Fad Farm.'' These two products were also highly profitable items for the stores that contracted to sell them.

7. Compose four attention-getting and interest-building first paragraphs of persuasive messages that utilize the following: outlining a bargain; applying a famous quote; asking a question; and outlining an outstanding feature. Your purpose is to gain attention and to build interest in a special vacation offer to sunny Bermuda. The cost is $1900 per person for 10 days, which includes all transporation, meals, tips, and admission to a minimum number of events of interest.

8. The Picture Perfect Studio, for which you work, specializes in modern settings for family pictures taken with a quality-satisfaction guarantee. Several family options are available, but the main emphasis of this particular sales campaign is on annual family pictures with individual poses for each member of the family and a special Mom and Pop pose taken absolutely free. The charge for the five-year service is only $275. The total cost represents a $125 savings over the five-year period. In addition to the price benefits, the additional advantages include the unique selection of poses from at least four different proofs from each individual and group setting. Another advantage lies in the notification process because the company will notify each family well in advance of its next appointment opportunity. This notification process will remove the burden of having to remember appointment-anniversary dates.

Use your creative imagination in selecting and developing a persuasive appeal that will influence families to utilize this opportunity to protect the precious memories of family maturation and growth. For the $275, each family will receive one 8 × 10 color group portrait, one 5 × 7 color portrait of each family member, and ten billfold-size pictures of any one of the poses. Additional pictures, of course, can be purchased at a special wholesale price.

Two other studios in your area are also planning a special family portrait plan at similar cost. Your job is to gain the attention, create the interest, establish desire and conviction, and explain clearly what the prospective customer must do to take part in this excellent family memory-building opportunity.

9. Select a product from a catalog of your choice and prepare a sales letter to be mailed to a cross section of the general population designed to enhance sales in the particular product you select. In addition to following the steps for persuasive message-preparation, describe the product psychologically. Many companies and brand names compete for a share of the same market, and your responsibility is to gain a marketing edge in a competitive area by mentioning the emotional benefits of the product. Be sure to attach a copy of the catalog page showing the product you selected.

10. You are the collection manager for the Davidson Lumber Company. Four months ago, Mr. Jack Green, 8132 Fairmont Drive, Albuquerque, NM 68987, charged $239.18 worth of building supplies to his charge account that was opened just the month before. His first payment was due on February 10, which he missed. Today is April 10. Mr. Green has missed each of the payment deadlines. He has not responded to any of your correspondence asking that he pay. You now decide to write an ultimatum letter in which you indicate that his account will be turned over to the Albuquerque Collection Agency if you do not receive a check for $248.10 (principal plus interest) by April 20.

11. You are the collection manager for Allgren's, a department store in Denver, Colorado. One of the store's preferred charge customers, Ms. Mary Greenlee, 123 United Street, Denver, CO 87434, purchased an on-sale 19-inch color television set four months ago. Until she made this purchase, Ms. Greenlee regularly used her charge account and always paid her account on time. The last time she used the acount was to charge the television set. While you know that she had to have the television set worked on twice the first month of its use, you do not know why her account has had a past-due balance of $478.48 since June 4 (today is September 1). Ms. Greenlee purchased the television set on a 120-days-same-as cash plan. Therefore, no interest is charged on the purchase until October 4, at which time the account will be charged 1.5 percent per month (beginning with the first month) if the account is still past due. Write her a letter (this will be the third one) asking that she pay immediately. Explain that if she fails to pay the balance by October 4, an interest charge of $29.64 will be charged to the account, plus an additional 1.5 percent per month for each month thereafter.

Part IV—The Essentials of Communication About Employment

Chapter 9

The Resume

LEARNING OBJECTIVES

After studying this chapter, you should be able to

1. Discuss the preliminary activities that one must undertake before writing the resume.
2. Discuss the different styles of resumes.
3. Identify the content sections typically found in resumes.
4. Discuss what factors should be considered when determining an appropriate order for various sections found in a resume.
5. Discuss the guidelines that will be helpful in preparing effective resumes.
6. Prepare an effective resume.

The resume and the letter of application, which typically accompany one another, determine whether a job applicant creates a favorable impression on a potential employer. During the preliminary screening process, many applicants are eliminated from further consideration because their resume and letter of application do not create as favorable an impression as the materials of other applicants.

The resume, which is discussed in detail in this chapter, and the letter of application, which is discussed in Chapter 10, are two of the final activities in the job-seeking process. Before the applicant is able to prepare the resume and the letter of application, several preliminary activities need to be completed.

PRELIMINARY ACTIVITIES

The applicant should consider undertaking the following preliminary activities: an analysis of one's self, an analysis of the job market, and an analysis of the company or companies to which he/she is sending applications.

What preliminary job-application activities should one undertake?

Analyzing One's Self

Before you can determine whether you meet the requirements of the job(s) for which you are applying, you need to analyze your qualifications. A self-analysis will help you better understand yourself and enable you to prepare more effective job application materials. It typically consists of identifying your strengths and weaknesses. Self-analysis will also enable you to identify which of your qualifications are especially well matched with the requirements of the jobs.

What questions should you ask yourself when undertaking a self-analysis?

In the process of analyzing yourself, you should answer three different questions: Who am I? What are my aspirations? What are my qualifications?

Who am I?

To help you fully understand yourself, you should begin with an analysis of your family background. Consider the extent of parental or guardian influence on your aspirations, beliefs, ideals, and values.

In addition to examining your family background, examine your relationships with others. In many instances we come to a better understanding of ourselves by assessing how others view or react to us and to our beliefs. In addition, assess your leadership potential and your ability to work with others. You may also wish to evaluate your personal and professional accomplishments.

Assess your philosophy of life and your attitude toward work. Try to determine the amount of satisfaction you will derive from the kinds of tasks that comprise the jobs for which you are applying.

What are my aspirations?

Another important aspect of the analysis is your aspirations. Most individuals, when applying for a job, have fairly definite ideas about their career goals. While most college graduates typically apply for the types of jobs for which their college studies have prepared them, some seek jobs totally unrelated to their college major. You may also need to determine which of the following types of work may be more satisfying: general or specific work, physical or mental work, structured or unstructured work, or creative or routine work. In determining your aspirations, you will undoubtedly want to consider the challenges inherent in the jobs for which you are applying as well as the potential for career progression.

What are my qualifications?

Why do you need to analyze your qualifications?

An especially important aspect of your self-analysis is determining if your qualifications match the job requirements. Several experiences in your background, such as education, work experience, and leadership potential, will probably help qualify you for the position you desire.

Although your high school preparation may be only remotely related to the position in which you are interested, some employers like to have information about your high school experiences outlined on the resume. For each position, an applicant should decide whether to include information about his/her high school preparation. Your college experiences are most likely specifically related to the position for which you are applying and therefore should be thoroughly detailed on the resume.

Another aspect of your life that may be an important job qualification is your work experience. Although some work experience may not be related to the jobs for which you are applying, most potential employers appreciate being apprised of the nature of your work experience. For example, working as a cafeteria bus person while in high school may have nothing to do with the job you are seeking, but it does indicate to those who are evaluating your background that you have initiative and are willing to work.

Leadership potential may also be a qualification for the job for which you are applying. For example, high school and/or college activities are often indicative of your desire to be involved. If you held leadership positions in various organizations, some potential employers may interpret this as evidence of leadership potential. Extracurricular activities may also be indicative of your ability to assume responsibility.

Analyzing the Job Market

Some job applicants, especially those who are not familiar with the job market or the requirements of certain jobs, find it necessary to analyze the job market thoroughly before applying for a particular job. Several resources are available to assist you in your assessment.

Assessing the job market

A wealth of information awaits you in your analysis of the job market. The following sources may be useful in assessing job opportunities in general or specific areas:

Accountants Index
Guide to American Business Directories
Insurance Year Book
Kelley's Directory of Merchants, Manufacturers, and Shippers of the World
Oil and Petroleum Yearbook
Polk's Bank Directory
Standard and Poor's Register of Corporations, Directors, and Executives
McKittrick Directory of Advertisers
Moody's Manual of Investments, American and Foreign
Standard and Poor's Facts and Forecasts
Standard and Poor's Corporation Records
Survey of Current Business

Thomas' Register of American Manufacturers
Rand McNally's Banker's Directory
Reader's Guide to Periodical Literature
Dun and Bradstreet's Reference Book of Corporate Managements
U.S. Census of Manufactures
U.S. Government Organization Manual
The Wall Street Journal

In some instances, job opportunities may be discussed in these references. In other instances, the references will provide you with listings of other sources to which you may refer. Classified advertisements in local and regional newspapers may also be helpful.

Determining job requirements

After you have assessed the job market and identified the types of jobs in which you are most interested, the next step is to determine job requirements. In some instances, you may be familiar with these requirements, while in other instances, you may need to study or analyze the requirements.

What sources are helpful in determining job requirements?

One of the best sources to use when determining job requirements is the *Dictionary of Occupational Titles,* a publication of the U.S. Employment Service. The dictionary contains descriptions of more than 20,000 job titles and alternate titles. After reading the types of duties that normally comprise the jobs in which you are interested, you can easily determine their specific requirements. Two other helpful sources are the *Occupational Outlook Handbook* and the *College Placement Annual.*

When undertaking an analysis of an occupational field, being able to answer the questions found in Figure 9–1 will be helpful. The answers can be obtained from a variety of sources.

After assessing the job market and determining the job requirements, the next step is to analyze the company or companies to which you are applying.

Figure 9–1 Questions to be Asked When Undertaking an Occupational Analysis

1. What is the history of the occupation?
2. How does the occupation fit into society in general?
3. How many workers are employed in the occupation and what are the growth trends?
4. What common duties comprise the job?
5. What qualifications are job holders expected to have?
6. What is the nature of the education and experience requirements?
7. Is the position generally considered to be at job-entry level?
8. How much time is required for one to become fully qualified?
9. What is the nature of the career path?
10. What occupations are related to this one?
11. What is the average beginning salary? anticipated salary trends?
12. What fringe benefits are common?
13. What is the nature of the employment conditions?
14. What section of the country has the greatest number of positions available at this time?
15. What are the advantages and disadvantages of this occupation?
16. Is the occupation likely to become obsolete during my lifetime?
17. Does technology affect this occupation now; is it likely to in the future?

Analyzing the Company to Which You Are Applying

An analysis of each company is important for the following reasons: (1) it will help you decide whether you want to work for the company you are considering; (2) it will help you determine whether you are qualified for the job; and (3) it will provide you with information that will be helpful during an interview.

Why should you analyze the companies to which you are applying?

Many sources of information about companies are readily available. The following are some of the most common.

Company annual reports

A considerable amount of information about companies is contained in their annual reports. Besides financial information, annual reports also contain information about company officers, local, branch, or regional offices, the products manufactured (or services provided) by the company, and perhaps an organization chart. Possible career-progression tracks may be identified by examining an organization chart.

Annual reports can be obtained in a variety of ways. Most college and university libraries have the annual reports of the nation's larger companies. In addition, the placement offices of many colleges and universities also have up-to-date annual reports for the companies that interview on their campuses. You can also obtain an annual report by writing directly to the companies in which you are interested.

Local offices or companies that sell the company's products

In many instances, companies have local offices in numerous cities throughout the country. Because the company's products and/or services are likely to be available locally, you may be able to obtain information from a local office or from a local company. Employees of these local offices or companies are generally quite willing to discuss the company in which you are interested as well as its products or services.

Individuals who are familiar with the selected company

In some instances, you may also be able to talk with someone in your area who is familiar with the company of interest to you. Even if you are unable to learn much from a local individual about the company to which you are applying, you may be able to obtain from these persons a wealth of valuable information about your chosen field.

Individuals affiliated with college and university placement offices

Individuals affiliated with college and university placement offices can often provide information about the company in which you are seeking employment. Although placement officials are often able to provide useful information, more complete or detailed information may be obtainable from some of the other sources of information.

Financial manuals

Moody's Manual and *Poor's Register* are two financial manuals that can be used to obtain information about a company. The types of information found in these manuals are the names of company officers, locations of home and branch offices, products lists, and financial information. A number of industries also have specialized manuals that are useful for obtaining background information about a company.

Journal and newspaper articles

Journal and newspaper articles sometimes contain information about a company. *The Wall Street Journal* is probably the most helpful newspaper for obtaining corporate information. *The Wall Street Journal Index* can help you locate specific articles of interest to you in the *Journal*. The *Business Periodicals Index,* which is updated several times each year, is also helpful for locating journal articles about specific companies.

Once you have analyzed yourself, the job market, and the company or companies to which you are applying, your next activity is to consolidate your information and prepare a personal-position analysis, an example of which appears in Figure 9–2. You should include the following information: the requirements of the position, your educational preparation for the position, and relevant work experiences that have prepared you for the position. The personal-position analysis may also contain a section that identifies other experiences that help qualify you for the position.

THE RESUME

What is the function of resumes?

The resume, also known as a data sheet, a vita, or a personal qualifications profile, presents information about your background. The resume, which supports the letter of application, is prepared before the letter is written. Essentially, the resume is your autobiography. Because it presents your entire back-

Figure 9–2 Personal-position Analysis

1. Position Requirements:
   a. Ability to prepare sales forecasts
   b. Ability to supervise field salespeople
   c. Ability to prepare budgets
   d. Ability to conduct market research projects
   e. Ability to analyze information about competitors
2. Education:
   a. Completed courses in sales management, marketing, and marketing research
   b. Completed courses in human relations, management, and accounting
3. Work Experience:
   a. Have worked for marketing research firm for two summers
   b. Have worked as a salesman during vacations for three years
   c. Have worked as a bookkeeper for one summer
4. Other Factors:
   a. Have held leadership positions (president, vice-president, and treasurer) in three different organizations
   b. Was selected as the Marketing Student of the Year at Community College
   c. Like to work with people
   d. Can relocate anywhere in the country

ground, the information in the letter of application that accompanies your resume can be condensed.

Types of Resumes

Two types of resumes are found: general and specific. While general resumes are appropriate for any number of different jobs for which you are applying, specific resumes are appropriate for only one job in a particular company.

What two types of resumes are used?

The type of resume you are preparing will influence your wording of certain parts of the document, including the heading, the career goals section, and the experience section. The following example illustrates the differences between the headings found on the two types of resumes.

<u>General</u>

Resume
MARY ANDERSON

<u>Specific</u>

Mary Anderson
Applicant for Sales Representative Position
with
ARNOLD-PIERCY CORPORATION
January 10, 1987

Some individuals believe that a specific resume is more advantageous than a general resume in securing a particular job. The personalization of the resume with the title of the position for which you are applying as well as the company name indicates that the resume was prepared specifically for a particular job in a particular company.

Individuals who have ready access to text-editing or word processing equipment may find the specific resume the better of the two alternatives. The information that will vary from resume to resume (heading and career goals sections, primarily) can be easily changed to include the pertinent information for each company to which you are applying. Individuals who do not have ready access to such equipment may find that they need to prepare a printed (offset or xerography) general resume that is appropriate for a number of jobs in a number of companies.

In addition to the heading, specific and general resumes differ from one another in the career goals and work experience sections. Specific differences between the two sections will be pointed out in the following discussion.

Content of the Resume

Although the content sections of resumes are fairly standard, some flexibility does exist in selecting which sections to include. Perhaps the best guide to use in determining appropriate content is to weigh the potential impact of the inclusion of certain information on the reader. If a specific bit of information will, in your estimation, help you sell your qualifications to the reader, you would be wise to include that information. The following sections are typically included in a resume:

1. Heading
2. Career goals or objectives

3. Education
4. Experience
5. Miscellaneous
6. Personal information
7. References

Each of these sections is discussed below.

Heading

Headings on a resume can range from one with only the applicant's name to a heading that includes the applicant's name, temporary address, permanent address, telephone number, the title of the position being applied for, and the name of the company to which the resume is being sent. In addition to considering the type of resume (general or specific) being prepared, the applicant should use his/her judgment in deciding what other information to include in the heading. Some applicants may prefer to present their address(es) and telephone number(s) in the personal information section rather than in the heading.

Several examples of effective headings are shown below.

a) RESUME

Anthony B. Roberts

Address (until May 15, 1987)	Address (after May 15, 1987)
135 Liberty Court Omaha, NE 67501 (204) 377-8673	1987 Deerfield Road Wahoo, NE 67234 (204) 675-9812

b) RESUME

Susan Henry's Qualifications

as a buyer for

JOHNSON'S DEPARTMENT STORE

c) QUALIFICATIONS OF SUSAN HENRY AS

BUYER FOR JOHNSON'S DEPARTMENT STORE

Address: 4567 Dryden Street, Ely, NV 89111 Phone: (309) 367-2304

d) MARY D. BROWN

145 Franklin Drive
Bowling Green, KY 45890
Phone (214) 564-3356

Career goals or objectives

The specificity with which the goals section is prepared is greatly determined by the type of resume you are preparing. If you are preparing a general resume, this section will by necessity be more general than if you are preparing a specific data sheet. Preparing a resume for a specific job in a specific company will enable you to state your goals so they clearly reflect the requirements of the job in which you are interested. When you are preparing a specific resume, you can mention the name of the company in your goals statement (see example No. 4 below).

What are the characteristics of an effective career goals section on a resume?

The career goals section is designed to present the reader with additional information about your goals or objectives. Therefore, this section must be prepared with as much clarity of thought and specificity as possible. Avoiding general statements that portray you as a jack-of-all trades is wise.

If you believe that your chances of being offered a job would be improved by providing both a short-range and a long-range goal, do so. If you are willing to relocate and/or to travel, you may also provide this information in the goals section.

The following are examples of career goals.

1. My short-range goal is to sell small business computers. My long-range goal is to become a marketing executive in a company that manufactures computer equipment.
2. Responsible position as a computer programmer. Willing to travel.
3. A staff accounting position in a leading public accounting firm. Ultimate goal is to become a partner in leading public accounting firm.
4. A women's fashion buyer for a progressive department store, such as Bullock's. Eventual goal is to become the manager of the Marketing Department in such a store.
5. To obtain a responsible entry-level job as a word processing operator and eventually to become the manager of a word processing center.

Education

For most college graduates seeking their first job, their education better qualifies them for employment than does their work experience. If this is true in your case, you should present information on the resume about your education before you present information about your work experience. On the other hand, if your work experience is more important—and it is likely to be after you have five to ten years of experience in your field—then that section should be presented first.

Why do most college students present their education information before their work experience information?

The information in the education section is generally presented in reverse chronological order, which means that the most recent education experience is listed first. Your least recent educational experience, such as high school, will be presented last. Eventually, you may decide not to list your high school experience.

The following information should be included in the education section.

What type of information about education is presented on resumes?

1. Colleges/universities attended, including location and dates
2. Major area studied

3. Degree(s) awarded or to be awarded
4. Relevant courses completed, including support courses
5. Grade point average, if it is in your favor

Several examples showing the presentation of educational information on the resume follow. You will notice three specific formats: (a) by date, (b) by skills attained, and (c) by college/university.

a) 1983–1987: University of Michigan, Ann Arbor. Accounting Major. Bachelor of Science in Accounting degree to be awarded on May 10, 1987.

Accounting Courses	Support Courses
Principles of Accounting	Money and Banking
Intermediate Accounting	Finance
Cost Accounting	Written Communications
Tax Accounting	Investments
Advanced Accounting	Small Business Computers
Accounting Systems	Systems Analysis
Auditing	

Grade-point average: In major, 3.78/4.00; overall, 3.75

1979–1983: General Brown High School, Dunlap, Michigan, College Preparatory Program. Graduated in top 10 percent of class.

b)

University of Michigan, Ann Arbor—1983–1987
Major: Accounting
Degree: Bachelor of Science in Accounting
GPA in Major: 3.78/4.00

Accounting Skills Principles of Accounting, Intermediate Accounting, Cost Accounting, Tax Accounting, Advanced Accounting, Accounting Systems, Auditing

Business Skills Management, Marketing, Business Law, Business Policy, Personnel Management

Communication Skills Written Communication, Technical Writing, Speech and Oral Communication

Quantitative Skills Calculus, Quantitative Methods, Statistics, Finance, Production and Operations Management

General Brown High School, Dunlap Michigan—1979–1983
College Preparatory Program
Graduated in top 10 percent of class

c) University of Michigan, Ann Arbor; 1985–1987
Major: Accounting
Degree: Bachelor of Science in Accounting
GPA in Major: 3.79/4.00

Accounting Courses: Principles of Accounting, Intermediate Accounting, Cost Accounting, Tax Accounting, Advanced Accounting, Accounting Systems, Auditing

Support Courses: Money and Banking, Finance, Investments, Written Communications, Small Business Computers, Systems Analysis

McComb Community College, Bixby,Michigan, 1983–1985
Major: Accounting
Degree: Associate of Arts in Business
GPA: 3.89/4.00

General Brown High School, Dunlap, Michigan, 1979–1983
College Preparatory Program
Graduated in top 10 percent of class.

Work experience

The order in which you present information about your educational background and work experience is determined by which of the two areas best qualifies you for the position in which you are interested. While your educational background most likely will be more important for your first full-time job as a college graduate, experience is likely to be more important after you have worked a few years.

Do not underestimate the value of your part-time work experience during your school years. While these jobs may have little if anything to do with the type of job you are seeking upon graduation, part-time jobs can teach valuable lessons in becoming a responsible employee, in dealing with the public, in showing the proper attitude toward work, in learning to work with others, and so forth. Most employers like to be made aware of your part-time jobs, regardless of how remotely related or unrelated to the type of job you are presently seeking.

Some employers give preference to applicants who have used their part-time jobs to pay for substantial portions of their college education. Listing your part-time work experience enables prospective employers to evaluate you better when using experience as a selection criterion.

The information you present about your work experience should include:

What information about work experience is presented on resumes?

1. The job, including its title and responsibilities
2. The month and year that you began and ended each job
3. The name of the employer
4. The significant accomplishments of the job
5. The reason you left the job (optional)

The information in the work experience section and the education section of the resume should be arranged in the same order. Because the reverse chronological order is preferred, your present or most recent job should be listed first.

The use of action verbs in presenting the material in the work experience section is recommended. Examples of action verbs are *worked, performed, handled, maintained,* and *developed.*

What formats are available for presenting information on resumes?

Several formats exist for presenting your work experience information on the resume. You may list it (a) by date, (b) by job title, (c) by functional skills attained, and (d) by employer name. Using the functional-skills format is especially appropriate when you have had several years of work experience after graduating from college.

If you choose to use the date format for presenting educational information, you may also want to use the date format for presenting work experience information. Likewise, if you use the skills-attained format for presenting educational information, you may want to use the parallel format when presenting information about your work experience. Using the college/university name format in the education section parallels using the employer name in the work experience section.

The four formats for presenting work experience information on the resume are presented below by date, by job title, by functional skills attained, and by employer name.

a) September 1985 to present — Davidson's Furniture Store, Darby, Michigan
Worked part time during school year as a bookkeeper and full time during the summers. Performed computerized bookkeeping operations. Developed several of the computer bookkeeping programs that are used. Occasionally served as store manager during absence of store owner.

June 1985 to September 1985 — Fuller Construction Company, Dunlap, Michigan
Worked full time as a construction laborer on a road construction project. Frequently drove a dump truck and occasionally operated an asphalt roller.

September 1984 to June 1985 — Men's Dormitory, Algoma College, Darby, Michigan
Worked part time as a front-desk receptionist and as a cashier in the snack bar. Took messages, answered questions, gave directions, counted snack bar cash receipts, and prepared deposit slips.

b) Bookkeeper, Davidson's Furniture Store, Darby, Michigan, September 1985 to present (part-time during school year and full time during summers). Performed computerized bookkeeping operations. Developed several computer bookkeeping programs that are used. Occasionally served as store manager during absence of store owner.

Construction laborer, Fuller Construction Company, Dunlap, Michigan, June 1985 to September 1985. Worked full time as a construction laborer on a road construction project. Frequently drove a dump truck and occasionally operated an asphalt roller. Quit job to return to college.

Receptionist and Snack Bar Cashier, Men's Dormitory, Algoma College, Darby, Michigan, September 1984 to June 1985. Worked part time as front-desk rceptionist and as cashier in the snack bar. Took messages, answered questions, gave directions, counted snack bar receipts, and prepared deposit slips. Quit job to take full-time summer job.

c)

Have developed effective management skills	As production manager (1973–1977) and later as vice-president (1977 to present) of Arjay Corporation, Cincinnati, I have had many varied management experiences. As vice-president, I am responsible for five operating units. During my vice-presidency, these five units have reduced their operating costs by 43 percent and have increased their productivity by 15 percent.
Have excellent record in program development and implementation	During my vice-presidency, I have developed several programs designed to increase employee job satisfaction that have been very well received. Several companies have patterned their programs after the ones I developed. Programs include quality circles, team building, MBO, and job enrichment.
Have excellent communication skills	Communications was my minor in college. Since that time, I have won several public speaking awards in Toastmasters. Have also had several articles published in professional management journals.
Have excellent analytical skills	A significant part of my job as vice-president involves analyzing data and making decisions on the basis of my analysis. Am frequently consulted by president for analysis and interpretation of data with which he works.

d) R–K Engineers, Inc., Cleveland, Ohio

Draftsperson, June 1984 to present
Duties: Work part time preparing engineering drawings to show location of utilities in new residential subdivisions, as well as preparing drawings for street construction in new areas.

Engineering Aide, September 1983 to June 1984
Duties: Worked part time performing a variety of tasks, including data calculations, some basic drafting, and lettering on engineering drawings.

Intern, September 1982 to September 1983

Duties: Worked part time during senior year of high school performing a variety of tasks, including running errands, maintaining library, filing materials, and duplicating engineering drawings

Parisian Restaurant, Cleveland, Ohio

Bus person, September 1981 to September 1982

Duties: Worked part time clearing tables, setting tables, preparing table set-up for banquets, and cleaning floors in eating area

Miscellaneous

What type of information is presented in the miscellaneous section of resumes?

Many different types of information can be included in the miscellaneous section. If you are about to graduate from college or are a recent college graduate, you may want to present information about your college activities, including honors, awards, club memberships, positions held in these clubs, special interests, hobbies, and travel experiences. If you graduated from college several years ago, you may want to include information about your present organizational memberships and leadership positions held rather than about your college activities. Even though you received honors and awards a number of years ago, you may include information about them in your resume. Your high school activities most likely will not be outlined on the resume.

The two most common formats for presenting miscellaneous information are (a) by date and (b) by title. Each format is presented as well as a display of how you might present information about special interests and hobbies.

(a) College Activities

1985–1987	Member, Accounting Club. Held the following positions: treasurer, 1985–86; president, 1986–1987
1983–1987	Member, Phi Beta Lambda, National Business Fraternity. vice-president, 1984–1985; president, 1985–1986
1983–1985	Residence Hall Council, Undergraduate Dormitory. floor representative, 1983–1984; secretary, 1984–1985

Honors

1983–1987	Dean's List, Algoma College
1987	Chosen as the Accounting Student of the Year, Algoma College
1986	Elected to Beta Gamma Sigma, National Business Scholastic Honorary

Special Interests

Reading, working with disadvantaged children, skiing, listening to music, and photography.

(b) College Activities

Accounting Club, Algoma College, 1985–1987

Treasurer, 1985–1986
President, 1986–1987

Phi Beta Lambda (National Business Fraternity), Algoma College, 1983–1987

Vice-President, 1984–1985
President, 1985–1986

Residence Hall Council, Undergraduate Dormitory, Algoma College, 1983–1985

Floor Representative, 1983–1984
Secretary, 1984–1985

Honors

Dean's List, Algoma College, 1983–1987
Chosen as the Accounting Student of the Year, Algoma College, 1987
Elected to Beta Gamma Sigma (National Business Scholastic Honorary) Algoma College, 1986

Special Interests

Reading, working with disadvantaged children, skiing, listening to music, photography

Personal information

What information is presented in the personal section of resumes?

The purpose of the personal information section is to provide additional information about yourself. The amount of information you include is dependent upon how much information you present in the heading. Some of the items you will want to consider are your telephone number and address (unless they are presented in the heading) and date of availability. Including information about physical characteristics, family background (information about spouse and children), and location is optional.

Much of the information you present in this section cannot be legally requested by a potential employer. However, once you are on the job, your employer can ask for some of the information. If you feel that the information may better your chances for employment (although legally most of it cannot), then you can consider including it. If you believe the information will have either a negative or neutral impact, you should reconsider the wisdom of its inclusion.

Including a picture of yourself in the resume is *not* recommended. If you do decide to include a photograph, it should be attached to the resume with a paper clip so that it can be easily removed should the recipient wish to do so. A few years ago, many individuals had their photographs printed on the resume, a practice now considered unadvisable and not recommended. Many employers today believe that removing the photograph eliminates the possibility of their being accused of using the photograph in a discriminatory manner. However, this belief may not be upheld in a court of law.

The following examples show how you might arrange the personal information on a resume.

<u>Personal Information</u>

Local Address (Until June 8)	Permanent Address (After June 8)
233 Conrad Hall	17 Market Street
Algoma College	Apartment 12
Darby, MI 48875	Dunlap, MI 48894
Phone (212) 377–7797	Phone (312) 873–9835

Available for employment after June 8

Birthdate: June 17, 1965	Health: Excellent
Birthplace: Darby, Michigan	Height: 6 feet
Marital Status: Married, 1 child	Weight: 180 pounds

References

How much emphasis is put on information supplied by references?

An increasing number of employers are not placing as much emphasis on references as they did in the past. The prime reason is the awareness that you will probably use only individuals who will give you a favorable recommendation, which tends to diminish its validity. Although references are not as important as they used to be, they nevertheless should be made available.

In identifying the references on the resume, the full name, title, address, telephone number, and the nature of the relationship between you and each reference should be listed. Before you use an individual as a reference, you need to obtain his/her permission. Individuals you will likely use as references are your professors, employers, and other business people.

A growing number of individuals, rather than listing their references on the resume, indicate that credentials are available upon request. Most college students put their credentials on file in the placement office at their college or university. If your credentials are on file in the placement office, you might place a statement similar to the following in the references section of the resume: ''Credentials are on file in the Placement Office of Algoma University and are available upon request.'' Making credentials available only to interested employers is more economical than sending a set to each employer to whom you are sending a resume and letter of application.

Some individuals, rather than putting their credentials on file in a placement office, have individual letters of recommendation prepared by their references. Making these letters available to only interested employers is especially appreciated by these individuals.

If you decide to list your references on the resume, the following is an acceptable format.

Dr. James Smith Associate Professor Algoma College Darby, MI 48875 (212) 587–9834 (College Advisor)	Mr. Hal Dickens Attorney at Law 123 Main Street Darby, MI 48875 (212) 879–7893 (Former Employer)	Dr. David Jones Professor Algoma College Darby, MI 48875 (212) 879–7892 (Accounting Professor)

GUIDELINES FOR PREPARING RESUMES

What guidelines can you suggest to aid in the preparation of resumes?

When preparing your resume, you may find the following guidelines helpful.

1. If you are preparing a quantity of resumes, select a duplicating process that produces excellent copies. Good quality bond paper, either white or off-white, should be used. You should not use carbons in preparing resumes, nor should you use a spirit or mimeograph duplication process. Preparing copies by offset, copier, or word processing is recommended.
2. Try to keep your resume to one page, if possible. However, if your resume is two pages in length, you should put an appropriate heading at the top of the second page, such as the following:

   Data Sheet for Mary Smith, Page 2

   If the two pages becomes separated, the recipient can easily determine which pages go together.

3. Your resume must be free of errors. A resume that contains errors reflects adversely on the applicant.
4. Use capitalization, underlining, boldface, and indentation to emphasize certain words or phrases.
5. You should avoid the use of special design techniques, such as borders or other types of graphic features.
6. Your resume and letter of application should be prepared on the same quality of paper.
7. Have your resume typeset if possible for a more attractive appearance than typewritten resumes. In addition, more information can be presented in less space when using typesetting.
8. You should use a format that has eye appeal.

Sample resumes are shown in Figures 9–3 and 9–4.

CHAPTER SUMMARY

Before you prepare a resume, you need to undertake several preliminary activities, including analysis of yourself, the job market, and the company or companies to which you are applying. The more thorough you are in undertaking the preliminary activities, the easier you will find the resume-preparation process.

Two types of resumes are found: general and specific. General resumes are appropriate for any job for which you are applying, while a specific resume is appropriate for only one particular job.

JOHN D. SMITH
123 Grover Street
Batting, Ohio 61312
(212) 387-8844

Career Goal: My career goal is to work as an accountant; and as soon as I have three years of experience, I plan to sit for the CPA Examination. Eventually, I would like to become a partner in a large CPA firm.

Education:

1986-1990 STATE UNIVERSITY, BATTING, OHIO. Major: Accounting. Was awarded a Bachelor of Science in Business Administration (with high honors) degree on June 1, 1990.

Have completed 36 hours of accounting courses and 24 additional hours of business/economics courses. Major grade-point average: 3.80/4.00. Overall grade-point average: 3.76/4.00

1982-1986 PORT ARTHUR (OHIO) HIGH SCHOOL. Program: College Preparatory.

Work Experience

June 1988 to June 1990 KEN'S AUTO SALES, BATTING, OHIO. Worked part time during school year, full time during summers as a bookkeeper and cashier. Maintained accounts receivable and accounts payable ledgers, operated cash register. During the last year, I supervised another part-time bookkeeper.

June 1987 to June 1988 STATE UNIVERISTY HEALTH CENTER, BATTING, OHIO. Worked part time as an orderly. Duties included helping patients in and out of bed, walking patients, transporting patients to and from the laboratory.

June 1986 to June 1987 PORT ARTHUR HOSPITAL, PORT ARTHUR, OHIO. Worked full time as an orderly, performing typical orderly duties.

Personal Information Birthdate: June 30, 1968; Birthplace: Port Arthur, Ohio; Married, 1 child; 6 feet, 175 pounds; Excellent health.

Special Interests Jogging, skiing, swimming, reading, and photography

Figure 9–3 Resume

MARY HALL'S

Qualifications for Marketing Researcher

in Poncey's Corporation

Career Objective

To work as a marketing researcher for Poncey's Corporation. Ultimate goal is to become director of marketing research.

Education

DAVENPORT UNIVERSITY, SMITHFIELD, MICHIGAN
Major: Marketing
Minor: Psychology
Degree: Bachelor of Science in Marketing (May 10, 1990)
Grade point average: 3.78/4.00

Research Skills	Statistics, Marketing Research, Quantitative Analysis, Business Calculus, Consumer Behavior, Advanced Marketing Research, Operations Management
Business Skills	Management, Personnel Management, Logistics, Accounting, Marketing Management, Promotional Strategy, Sales Management, International Marketing, Distribution
Communication Skills	Written Communication, Report Writing, Technical Writing, Speech and Oral Communication, Sales Promotions

SMITHFIELD COMMUNITY COLLEGE, SMITHFIELD, MICHIGAN
Major: Business
Degree: Associate of Arts degree (June 1, 1988)
Grade point average: 3.90/4.00

Work Experience

Have developed effective marketing research skills	As a part-time employee of Thomas Marketing Research Corporation (September 1988 to present), I have been involved in many research projects. During the last year, I have been the manager of several of these projects. My duties on these projects included all phases of marketing research. I have received special commendations from clients on the quality of three of these projects.
Have developed effective managerial skills	As manager of a number of marketing research projects for Thomas during the last year, I have been totally responsible for all phases of several of these projects. This has given me an opportunity to work closely with others. I have received high ratings from those with whom I've worked on these projects.

Figure 9–4 Resume Presented in a Functional Format

Resume for Mary Hall, Page 2

Have developed effective communication skills	As a marketing researcher, I have had considerable experience in writing reports and orally presenting research results. I received the 1988 marketing research project award for a course project I developed.
Have developed effective analytical skills	Much of my time spent during the last year has been helping others analyze the data collected for other research projects. This experience has broadened my analytical skills considerably.

College Activities

Marketing Club, Member 1988-1990. Was vice-president in 1989 and president in 1990.

Beta Gamma Sigma, Member 1989-1990. Membership limited to top 10 percent of graduating class.

Alpha Kappa Psi, Member, 1988-1990. Was elected vice-president for 1989-1990.

Special Interests

Boating, water skiing, stamp collecting, reading, traveling, swimming, playing chess.

Personal Information

Address: (until May 15) 1318 Adams Street, Apt. 318, Smithfield, MI 48187
(518) 323-8794

(after May 15) 398 East Ave., Baltimore, MD 09847
(204) 345-8732

Birthdate: June 10, 1969
Height: 5 feet
Health: Excellent

Marital Status: Single
Weight: 110 pounds

Available for employment after May 16.

References

Credentials, which are on file at Placement Office at Davenport University, are available upon request.

Figure 9–4 (cont.)

The sections found in most resumes include the heading, career goals or objectives section, education section, work experience section, miscellaneous section, personal information section, and references. The order of the sections may vary, depending on the length of your work experience.

When preparing resumes, you should be aware of what is acceptable and what is not acceptable. For example, although resumes can be printed, they should not be duplicated using a mimeograph or spirit-duplication process. You will want to make sure they resemble an original copy as much as possible.

REVIEW QUESTIONS

1. In getting ready to apply for a job, why should you do a self-analysis? How do you analyze yourself?
2. How does one analyze the job market in getting ready to apply for a job?
3. Why should you analyze the company to which you are applying? How do you analyze the company?
4. What is the purpose of a personal-position analysis?
5. What two types of resumes are found, and how do they differ?
6. What are the basic content sections found in resumes?
7. What suggestions can you offer that will be helpful in writing an effective career goals section of a resume?
8. What types of information about your educational background should be presented on your resume?
9. Why might your educational background be presented before your experience background on a resume?
10. What is unique about the functional format some people use to present work-experience information on their resume?
11. What types of information are commonly included in the "miscellaneous" section on the resume?
12. Offer several useful suggestions for preparing resumes.

APPLICATION PROBLEMS

1. Using the information presented in this chapter, undertake a thorough self-analysis. Be honest with yourself as you make the self-analysis. Once completed, did you learn anything about yourself that you were not already aware of?

2. Using the information presented in this chapter, undertake a thorough analysis of the job market of interest to you. What did you learn about the job market that you did not already know?

3. Using the information presented in this chapter, undertake a thorough analysis of the company (or one of the companies) in which you would like to work after graduating from college. After completing the analysis, did your level of excitement about working for the company change? If so, how?

4. Using the guidelines presented in this chapter, prepare a personal-position analysis.

5. Using the example resume headings illustrated in this chapter, prepare three different headings for your own resume. Which one do you like best?

6. Prepare a career goals section for your resume.

7. Assume you have now been out of college for ten years and that the career goals section of the resume you prepared ten years ago parallels exactly what you have done so far in your career. You now decide to seek a higher-level job than the one you presently have. Prepare the career goals section for the resume you plan to use in seeking a new job in another company.

8. Using two of the following three formats—date, skills attained, and college/university—prepare the education section of your resume.

9. Using two of the following three formats—date, job title, and employer name—prepare the work-experience section of your resume.

10. For the career goals section of a resume that you prepared in application problem 6, use the functional format to prepare the work-experience section of your new resume. Assume that you have had a variety of good work experiences during the ten years following your graduation from college and that you have developed a number of important job skills.

11. Using either of the following two formats—date, title—prepare the miscellaneous section of your resume.

12. Prepare a resume using the format you most prefer. Make sure your resume follows the guidelines shown in this chapter.

Chapter 10

Letters About Employment

LEARNING OBJECTIVES

After studying this chapter, you should be able to

1. Discuss the qualities of well-written letters of application.
2. Discuss the items that should appear in the opening, middle, and closing sections of the letter of application.
3. Identify the suggested plan used in preparing interview follow-up letters, letters of acceptance, letters of refusal, and letters of resignation.
4. Prepare effective letters of the type discussed in this chapter.

Several letters are used in the process of seeking employment. In addition to the letter of application, the interview follow-up letter, the letter of acceptance, the letter of refusal, and the letter of resignation may be used. Information that will be helpful in preparing each of these types of letters is presented in this chapter.

In most cases, the letter of application is the first letter you will write when you are seeking employment. Your suitability for employment in a specific company may be judged by the quality of the letter you prepare.

LETTER OF APPLICATION

What is the purpose of letters of application?

Once you have prepared your resume and you have identified the position you plan to apply for, your next step is to prepare a letter of application. The basic purpose of this letter is to inform the reader of your desire for the position and to request an interview. A secondary purpose of the letter of application is to provide the reader with information that reveals your qualifications for the position you are seeking.

In the letter of application, you must sell the reader on the extent of your qualifications for the position in which you are interested. To sell yourself, focus on what you can do for the prospective employer and why you feel you are well qualified for the position. Because your resume and letter of application will compete with resumes and letters from other applicants, the better you sell the prospective employer on your qualifications, the better are your chances of being granted an interview.

What types of letters of application are used?

Three different types of application letters are used. An unsolicited application is used when an individual sends a letter to a company without knowing whether or not an opening actually exists. The blind-ad letter of application is sent to a post office box number or to a newspaper box number without knowing the identity of the company in which the opening exists. The solicited application is used when the individual writing the letter knows of an opening in the company to which the letter is being sent.

When a resume accompanies the letter of application, the letter need not be as thorough as when the letter is sent by itself. The letter, therefore, becomes a supplement to—rather than a substitute for—the resume. A common practice is to include in the letter of application some of the important information that is found in the resume—especially the information that highlights your qualifications for the job for which you are applying. You should consider your letter of application as an interpretation or elaboration of the information presented on your resume—and not simply a repetition of that information.

Qualities of Well-Written Letters of Application

What qualities should letters of application possess?

One of the most important qualities of any effective business letter, and especially the letter of application, is the use of the "you-attitude." Although the letter of application is about you, it should be written with the reader's needs in mind.

The following example illustrates the difference between "you-attitude" and the more selfish-sounding "I-attitude."

Change:	I wish to be considered an applicant for the position of sales representative.
To:	My college training and personal qualities will enable me to be the "enthusiastic, hard-working sales representative" you advertised for in Monday's *State News*.

The latter sentence is more effective because it provides a reason for the interviewer to hire the applicant.

Another illustration of the difference between "you attitude" and "I-attitude" is found in the following two sentences.

Change:	In June, I was graduated from Marshall College, where I was an accounting major.
To:	Because I have the qualifications for the auditing position you listed in your letter recently sent to the State College Placement Office, I am confident I could perform well in your company as an auditor.

How long should letters of application be?

The length of letters of application is another important quality. Although a two-page resume is permissible, the letter of application should be limited to one page. If your first draft is longer than one page, the letter should be revised.

Being able to address the letter of application to a person rather than to a title is preferred. For example, to address a letter to the "Personnel Manager" does not create as favorable an impression as addressing the letter to "Mr. John Ching." If you do not know the name of the person to whom you are sending the letter, taking the time and effort to learn the person's name may be well worthwhile.

Several means exist for obtaining the name of the person to whom the letter of application is being sent. The *College Placement Annual,* which you can probably find in your college's placement office, identifies the name and title of the person responsible for college-level recruiting in many companies. *Moody's Manual* may also provide you with the name of the person to whom the letter should be sent. In some cases, you may have to call the company to obtain the name of the person.

Well-written letters of application should be neat and free of errors. While you may send a photocopied or a printed version of your resume, the letter of application should always be an original. The letter of application also creates a better impression when it is typed on the same kind of paper as that on which the resume appears. The letter should be error-free because you may be automatically eliminated from consideration for employment in some companies when errors are found in your application materials.

Another goal is to convey the impression that you are confident of your ability to do a good job for the company. Somewhere between being overconfident and underconfident is a happy medium—a confidence that should be conveyed to the reader. Letters that create the impression of your being overconfident may convey the impression that you are a braggart or an egotist—traits viewed negatively by recruiters.

What is the nature of the reader-benefit material included in letters of application?

The inclusion of reader-benefit material that explains what you can do for the reader is another quality of well-written letters of application. Your education and training and/or personal traits are usually the qualifications that will enable you to be hired for the job you want. A major weakness of many letters of application is the writer's failure to convert factual information to reader-benefit material.

The most important information should be presented at the beginning of your letter. This principle also applies to the resume. Therefore, if you believe that your education better qualifies you for a position than your work experience, you may find it advantageous to present information about your educational preparation before work experience information.

Finally, do not pattern your letter of application too closely after the sample letters you study. If you and others pattern your letters after the same sample, a prospective employer may receive several similar letters. If this happens, your chances of being granted an interview may diminish.

Letter Plan

What is the suggested plan for letters of application?

A letter of application, like most other types of letters, should follow a suggested plan, which includes the following elements:

1. An opening with reader-benefit material that will make the reader want to read the letter and the resume;
2. A middle section that outlines your qualifications for the job;
3. A closing section requesting an interview.

Opening section

What information is included in the opening section of letters of application?

The opening of your letter of application will probably "make or break" the letter. Your goal is to entice the reader to want to read the entire letter—and respond favorably to the request for an interview.

The type of opening varies from one letter to another. For example, you may wish to include in the opening the name of the person making the referral, or you may decide to provide information about how your qualifications fit the requirements of the position. Another type of opening includes a discussion of news worthy information about the company—or information about one of its significant accomplishments. Regardless of the type of opening you use, the title of the position for which you are applying should also be included in the opening paragraph.

What information should be included in the opening section of solicited letters of application?

When preparing solicited applications, you should consider mentioning in the opening paragraph the means by which you found out about the vacancy: either the name of the individual who informed you of the vacancy or the publication in which the vacancy was listed. Doing so might create more interest in the letter, especially if the individual named in the opening and the reader know one another. For example, perhaps the director of the placement office at your school told you about an opening in a certain company. If the individual to whom you are sending the letter and the director of the placement office know each other, the reader will probably be motivated to read your letter. Some readers will assume that you are a well-qualified applicant if a credible person suggested that you apply for the position.

The first of the following three examples is weak. The second example mentions the name of the person making the referral, while the third example mentions the name of the publication. The effective examples are written from a "you-viewpoint" and mention the position for which the writer is applying.

Change:	Please consider me an applicant for the position that I recently learned was available in your company.
To:	Ms. Lea Dunham, Director of Placement Services at State University, told me about an opening for an auditor in your accounting department. Because my college training and work experience qualify me for such a position, please consider me an applicant.
To:	Your ad in the June 21 issue of *Community News* for an ambitious, hard-working sales representative lists requirements similar to my qualifications. With my degree in marketing and four years of sales experience, I am confident of my ability to be the type of employee you wish to hire. I would like to be considered as an applicant for this position.

Another type of opening you may wish to consider using is one that mentions several of your most important qualifications for the position. In using this approach, make sure that you write with a "you-viewpoint" rather than an "I-viewpoint," a principle violated by the first of the following three paragraphs.

Change:	I would like to have the opportunity to put my educational and work experience qualifications to use as an employee in your company. Please consider my application for an open position in your company.
To:	Several years of retail work experience in a women's clothing shop, a degree in fashion merchandising, and an appreciation for hard work would enable me to perform well as the sportswear buyer you are seeking. I would like to be considered for this position.
To:	An ability to communicate well both orally and in writing, a degree in business administration with a concentration in information processing, and a summer internship in the data processing department of a petroleum company are the qualifications I have that closely match the requirements of the systems analyst position open in your company. I would like to be considered for this position.

You may also be able to attract the reader's attention by beginning your letter with an opening that mentions a significant accomplishment of the company or a news worthy event. Compare the effectiveness of the first and second paragraphs.

Change:	The article about your company that I recently read certainly convinced me that your company would be an excellent place for me to begin my career. Please consider me an applicant for an opening in your company.
To:	The recent article about Baylor Steel Company which appeared in the *Houston Gazette* convinces me that the foresight of your managers will allow the company's expansion plans to succeed at a time when other steel companies are scaling back their operations. Please consider me an applicant for a transportation coordinator position should your expansion plans create such an opening.

What information should be included in the opening section of unsolicited letters of application?

When preparing an unsolicited letter of application, beginning the letter with a listing of your qualifications provides an effective opening. The following opening of an unsolicited letter outlines the writer's qualifications for a particular job.

> If you have an opening for a sportswear buyer who has several years of retail work experience, a degree in fashion merchandising, and an appreciation for hard work, I would like to be considered as an applicant for this position.

Middle section

What information is included in the middle section of letters of application?

The middle section of your letter will be the longest as it is designed to present your qualifications for the job. Your goal in writing this section is to convince the reader that you are qualified for the job. In developing the middle section, you have considerable freedom in deciding which of the following elements to include.

1. Your understanding of the requirements of the position (if this is a solicited letter)
2. Your educational preparation that helps qualify you for the position
3. Your work experience that helps qualify you for the position
4. Any special qualifications you may have that others may not have
5. Personal information, such as your grade-point average, the percent of college expenses that you have earned, the college activities you have participated in, honors and awards you have received, and evidence of your ability to work with others.

Because of the one-page limitation on letters of application, you will need to focus on what you consider to be the most important information. You will need to emphasize the key ideas that show what you can do for the potential employer.

Should you provide in your letter of application a lengthy discussion of the requirements of the job for which you are applying?

When reviewing the requirements for the position, you need not provide a lengthy discussion because the reader is aware of the job requirements. Your goal is to convince the reader that you have studied the position sufficiently to know that your qualifications match the requirements of the position.

In the following examples, notice the difference between the first paragraph in which the job requirements are discussed and the revised paragraphs.

> Change: I understand you are looking for a hard-working, ambitious employee.
>
> To: My understanding is that you are looking for a research coordinator who has an analytical background, who is familiar with statistical applications, and who writes well.
>
> To: My background matches the following requirements you have identified for the vacant sales representative position: leadership ability, knowledge of business fundamentals, and previous experience in sales.

When you are preparing a solicited letter, you will need to show how your qualifications match the requirements listed in the vacancy notice. Most vacancy notices list educational and experience requirements or other requirements such as the ability to work well with people, a positive attitude toward travel, and effective communication skills. When preparing an unsolicited letter, you will have to use your own judgment in deciding which of your qualifications to highlight.

If you are about to graduate from college or are a recent college graduate, your educational preparation is likely your most important qualification for the job. On the other hand, if you have several years of relevant work experience, then your experience could be the more important qualification. The more important of these two qualifications should be discussed first.

What determines if you present educational or experience qualifications first in letters of application?

In writing the educational background section of your letter of application, you should show that you have a broad background in your primary area of study (such as business), as well as depth in your major (such as accounting). In addition, you should consider showing how your educational background has prepared you for the job you seek. If appropriate, you could also show how certain electives you took helped prepare you for the job for which you are applying.

The first of the following three paragraphs does not effectively present the writer's educational qualifications for the job for which he is applying. Notice how much more thoroughly educational qualifications are presented in the revised paragraph.

Change: The training I received as a business major in college will enable me to perform well as an employee in your company.

To: As a marketing major at the University of Colorado, I studied the broad functional areas of business, as well as completed 12 marketing courses and a number of elective courses that will be helpful to me as a sales representative. In the advanced selling course, my sales presentation enabled me to win the R. D. Bell Outstanding Sales Presentation Award. Courses in marketing research, technical writing, and business communication were beneficial in my learning how to write effective marketing reports.

In presenting information about your work experience in the letter of application, you should avoid calling undue attention to a lack of work experience. Employers realize that college students may not have had an opportunity to work in a job closely related to the jobs for which they are applying. The jobs you have held—regardless of whether they are full-time or part-time jobs or they are related to the job you are seeking—have strengthened your qualifications. Most likely, each of your jobs has given you something of a positive nature that you can take with you to the job you are seeking.

Should you call attention to a lack of work experience in a letter of application?

As you present information about your work experience background, show how your previous experience will be helpful in the job for which you are applying and how it has taught you to be a responsible, hard-working employee who can work with others.

Notice how ineffectively the first of the following two paragraphs presents information about the writer's work experience—and how much more effective the revised paragraph is.

Change: Many aspects of my previous work experience would be useful should I be given an opportunity to work in your company.

To: For each of the last three summers, I have worked as an intern in a Big 8 CPA firm. This experience has given me an opportunity to apply much of the textbook knowledge I have acquired. My job this past summer in the accounting systems unit enabled me to acquire a considerable amount of experience in computerized accounting. For the last half of the summer, I was allowed the privilege of making client visitations by myself. My ability to handle responsibilities and to work well with others—two important lessons my work experience has taught me—would be valuable as a junior accountant in your firm.

If you believe that you have any special qualities for the position for which you are applying, discussing them may be to your advantage. For example, assume that the company to which you are applying is expanding internationally and that you can fluently speak one or more foreign languages. Or perhaps the company is opening a branch office in the northeast section of the country near where you grew up.

The following paragraph illustrates how you might present information about a special quality you have.

An article about your company that appeared recently in *Today's News* indicated that a branch is about to be opened in Paris. Having lived in France for two years, I am able to speak French fluently—and I have a strong desire to once again live in France.

The final part of the middle section of your letter of application may be used to outline personal information that will enable the reader to better assess your qualifications for the position. In writing this section, write from a "you-viewpoint" rather than an "I-viewpoint."

The following paragraphs illustrate how a variety of different types of personal information might be presented in the letter of application.

My ability to work well with others has been developed in a variety of ways, including the following: working as a student volunteer in a local senior citizens' home, serving as vice president and president of my sorority, and having a part-time cashier's job in a local department store.

My part-time and full-time jobs enabled me to earn approximately 80 percent of my educational expenses. Scholarship money was used to cover the remainder of my expenses. Although the necessity of my working did not allow me to become as involved in college activities as I would have liked, I did hold leadership positions in Alpha Kappa Psi, a national professional business organization, and in the Management Club. My experiences in these organizations would be invaluable as a management trainee.

Of the eight semesters that I have attended State University, I was on the Dean's list for six. My grade-point average of 3.45 (4.00 scale) will enable me to graduate with honors. During my sophomore and junior years, I was presented certificates for having the highest grade-point average among the management majors.

In developing the middle section of your letter of application, be sure to provide all the information requested in the vacancy notice. If the notice to which you are responding asks you to identify the salary you expect to receive, provide the requested information. Some people believe you should state the dollar amount; others suggest you include a statement similar to: "I would expect to receive a salary that is commensurate with the requirements of the position and with my qualifications." If you identify a specific dollar amount, try to avoid over- or under-pricing yourself.

The middle section of your letter will generally comprise two to four paragraphs. In developing this section, concern for paragraph unity is important, but you should also guard against including too many short paragraphs that will detract from the appearance of your letter.

How many paragraphs does the middle section of letters of application normally comprise?

Somewhere in the letter—and perhaps in the middle section—you should make reference to an enclosed resume if one is being enclosed. As the reader will be aware that a resume is being enclosed, the statement "A resume is enclosed" is obvious. A more appropriate reference might be: "My work experience, which is outlined on the enclosed resume, has taught me a number of things about working with others."

Closing section

Asking for an interview in the last paragraph of your letter makes the closing action oriented. Guard against being too abrupt by simply asking for an interview. Your request will seem less abrupt if you include other material, such as an offer to provide additional information, if desired, or the dates that you might be available for an interview. Notice how the inclusion of additional material in the revised paragraphs removes the abruptness of the first paragraph.

What information should be included in the closing section of letters of application?

Change: May I have an interview at your convenience?

To: Although this letter and the resume that is attached outline my qualifications, I would appreciate having a personal interview with you. You can reach me at 764–1234 between 10 a.m. and 1 p.m. each week day to let me know a time that is convenient for you to talk with me about the auditing position.

To: After you have studied my resume, please call or write to let me know a time that would be convenient for you to discuss the sales representative position with me. Should you need additional information, please let me know.

Figure 10–1 illustrates a well-written solicited letter of application and Figure 10–2 illustrates an unsolicited letter. Notice the difference between the openings of the two letters.

Your company's accounting vacancy notice that recently appeared in the Denver Gazette listed two primary job requirements that match my qualifications: A bachelor's degree in accounting and one year of successful accounting experience. Please consider me as an applicant for this accounting position.	An opening containing reader-benefit material that mentions how the writer learned of the vacancy and that mentions the job requirements.
My educational preparation and work experience have enabled me to acquire several other important qualifications, including the following: The ability to communicate effectively in writing as well as orally, to work well with others, and to accept responsibility. In addition, I have learned how to manage my time well.	A section that presents the writer's job qualifications.
As an accounting major at the University of Texas, I completed 36 hours of accounting, in addition to related courses in computer systems, computerized accounting systems, systems analysis, and management information systems. The accounting courses I have completed are listed on the enclosed resume. I was selected by the accounting faculty at the University of Texas to receive the John Cole Distinguished Senior Accounting Student award. My 3.89 overall grade-point average enabled me to be graduated with high honors.	A section that presents a discussion of the writer's educational preparation, including honors and grade point average.
Since graduating last spring, I have been employed as a junior accountant at the Cromwell Accounting Group where I have received two promotions since beginning work. Other experience includes working as an intern in a Big 8 accounting firm during my junior and senior years. My work experience and educational preparation recently enabled me to pass all five parts of the Texas CPA exam.	A section that presents a discussion of the writer's work experience.
During this past year, I have been actively involved in several professional and civic organizations. Leadership positions currently held include serving as vice-president of the Boulder CPA Association and secretary-treasurer of the Boulder Optimists Club.	A section that presents a discussion of the writer's leadership activities.
After you have reviewed my resume, please notify me of a time that would be convenient for you to talk with me about the accounting position. If you need additional information, please let me know.	A closing that presents a request for an interview and an offer to provide additional desired information.

Figure 10–1 Effective Solicited Letter of Application

What is the suggested content of application-inquiry letters?

If you have not received a response to your letter of application within three to four weeks, you should perhaps consider sending an inquiry about the status of the application. In this type of letter you should

1. Mention that a letter of application had been sent earlier;
2. Identify the title of the job in which you are interested;
3. Reaffirm your interest in the job;
4. Identify any new qualifications you may have since the letter of application was sent;
5. Offer to send any additional information that may be desired.

An article that recently appeared in the Chicago Post convinces me that your company will be one of the leaders in the electronics industry during this decade. If your company will need additional sales representatives to accommodate expanded business operations, please consider me an applicant for such a position.	An opening containing reader-benefit material that mentions the basis for the writer's desire to work for the company.
For the last three years, I have worked as a sales representative for the Harmson Company here in Chicago. In each of the last two years, I have received the company's award for having the highest annual dollar sales volume. In addition, I have received several letters of commendation from Mr. Jack Raymer, Harmson's president, in recognition of my sales performance.	A section that presents a discussion of the writer's work experience and job-related awards received.
Illinois State College awarded me the bachelor's degree in marketing in 1988. I completed 32 hours of coursework in marketing and 18 hours in a communications minor. As a senior, I won the Sales and Marketing Student Association's Sales Presentation of the Year award. Other details about my educational preparation are outlined on the resume that is enclosed.	A section that presents a discussion of the writer's educational preparation.
Integrating the knowledge from both the marketing and communications areas of study with my work experience gives me the following important job qualifications: how to make effective sales presentations, how to prepare effective oral and written reports, and how to conduct market analyses.	A section that presents a discussion of the writer's job qualifications.
I would like to discuss with you my qualifications for a sales representative position in your company. Please let me know a time that is convenient for you to talk with me.	A closing that presents a request for an inteview.

Figure 10–2 Effective Unsolicited Letter of Application

An ineffective inquiry letter is illustrated in Figure 10–3. A revised version appears in Figure 10–4.

Figure 10–3 Ineffective Letter That Inquires About the Status of an Application

Three months should be ample time for you to decide whether or not my qualifications match the requirements of the auditing position I applied for.	A curt opening that puts the reader down.
As I explained to you in the application, I am very much interested in working as an auditor in your company.	A weak reaffirmation of why the writer wishes to work for the company.
Please let me hear from you as soon as possible about the status of my application.	A weak closing that lacks the you-viewpoint.

On March 1 I sent you a letter of application and a resume for the auditor's vacancy that was advertised in the February 25 issue of the <u>Daily Moines Chronicle</u>. I am inquiring whether you received these materials.	An opening that provides a discussion of the background details and that inquires if the application materials were received.
Because my qualifications match the requirements listed for the auditor's position, I am confident of my ability to perform well as an auditor. I was recently notified of my passing the Iowa CPA exam, which should enhance my qualifications for an auditing position.	A section that reaffirms the writer's interest in the job and that mentions recent additional job qualifications.
Please let me know if you would like any additional information for use in assessing my qualifications for the auditing position.	A closing that offers to provide additional material that may be needed.

Figure 10–4 Effective Letter That Inquires About the Status of an Application

OTHER TYPES OF EMPLOYMENT-RELATED LETTERS

In addition to the letter of application, several other employment-related letters are commonly used. Among these letters are interview follow-up letters, letters of acceptance, letters of refusal, and letters of resignation. Each of these letters is discussed in the following sections.

Interview Follow-Up Letter

What is the purpose of interview follow-up letters?

The purpose of the interview follow-up letter is to thank the interviewer for spending time with you. The letter should be sent within a week's time after the interview—in less time, if possible.

What should be included in the opening section of interview follow-up letters?

An effective way to begin the letter is with a fast-start opening that thanks the reader for spending time with you. In some cases, you will have been asked to return a completed application form. Mentioning its inclusion in the opening is recommended. To be avoided is an opening in which obvious information is provided, as in the first of the following paragraphs.

> Change: I interviewed you last week for the position of systems analyst.
> To: Thank you for talking with me last week about the systems analyst opening. The more I hear about the position, the more convinced I am that it is just the type of job that greatly interests me.

What information should be included in the middle section of interview follow-up letters?

Several types of information can be included in the section that follows the opening. You can provide new material that may be helpful to the interviewer in his/her assessing your qualifications, clarify any mistaken notion you feel the interviewer may have gotten from your responses during the interview, discuss how you feel about the job or the firm now that you have had the interview, or express gratitude to the interviewer for special insight that you may have gained from him/her.

Sample paragraphs appropriate for the middle section of the interview follow-up letter are presented in the following revised paragraphs.

Change:	I was favorably impressed with everything I learned during the interview.
To:	During the interview, you stressed the need for all employees in your company to have well-developed writing skills. Upon my return home from the interview, I was delighted to learn that a paper I wrote in a marketing class has been selected for publication in the *Marketing Review,* the official journal of the student division of the American Marketing Association. One of the factors that determines the suitability of an article for publication in this journal is quality of writing. I am confident that my writing skills developed through my work experience and educational background would meet the requirements of the job.
Change:	The information you gave me during the interview was helpful.
To:	The additional insight I gained during the interview further convinced me that I should begin my professional career as a sales representative. If given the opportunity to work for Dixon Corporation, I am confident my educational and experience background would enable me to be the enthusiastic, progressive, and innovative sales representative you want to hire.

What information should be included in the closing of interview follow-up letters?

Several types of material can be included in the closing of the interview follow-up letter, including an offer to send additional information that may be needed, a statement of thanks for the interview (if not already expressed earlier in the letter), a statement which expresses confidence that your qualifications meet the job requirements, or a statement which mentions that you are looking forward to hearing from the reader. Notice the difference between the first of the following paragraphs and its revised versions.

Change:	I appreciate your spending time with me.
To:	Should you need any additional information that will help you assess my qualifications for the accounting position, please let me know. You can depend on me to be a hard-working, dedicated employee.
To:	Because my educational background and work experience meet the requirements of the job, I am confident of my ability to be the caliber of employee you are seeking. Please let me know your decision.

What is the suggested plan for interview follow-up letters?

The suggested plan for an interview follow-up letter includes these elements:

1. A fast-start opening in which the interviewer is thanked;
2. A section in which one or more of the following is presented: new material that may be helpful to the interviewer, material that might clarify any mistaken notion the interviewer received from your answers during the interview, material that discusses your present feelings about the firm and/or the job, or material that thanks the interviewer for his/her assistance;
3. A courteous closing in which one or more of the following is presented: an offer to send additional material, a statement of appreciation (or thanks

I am one of the students at Northeast College who interviewed you last week while you were on our campus. I hope your visit here was enjoyable.	An opening that contains obvious information.
You certainly gave me an excellent insight into the career opportunities at Dartmouth Company. Now, more than ever, I would like to have the opportunity to work for your company.	A section that presents a weak presentation of how the interview was helpful.
I do appreciate your spending the extra few minutes with me.	A weak closing that fails to convey the writer's interest in the job.

Figure 10–5 Ineffective Interview Follow-Up Letter

Thank you for telling me about your company's management training program last week when you visited Northeast College. I am convinced that it is exactly the type of program in which I would like to begin my professional career.	An opening that thanks the reader for the interview and that reaffirms the writer's interest in the job.
I especially appreciated your explaining in detail the types of experiences management trainees have during their participation in the training program. Because I want to explore several managerial areas before making a final career choice, this feature of your program is especially attractive.	A section that presents a discussion of the part of the interview that the writer found especially helpful.
If you would find any additional information helpful in assessing my qualifications, please let me know. I am confident of my ability to perform well as a management trainee.	A closing that offers to provide additional information and that mentions the writer's confidence in his/her ability to perform well.

Figure 10–6 Effective Interview Follow-Up Letter

if not included in the opening), a statement that expresses confidence in your ability to perform well, or a statement that expresses your desire to hear from the interviewer.

Figure 10–5 illustrates an ineffective interview follow-up letter; Figure 10–6 illustrates its revised version.

Letter of Acceptance

How soon should a letter of acceptance be sent?

You will know your hard work has paid off when you receive a job offer that you want to accept. The letter of acceptance should be sent fairly soon after the receipt of the offer—perhaps within a week.

The opening of the letter should mention your appreciation for the offer and that you are accepting. Notice the difference between the tone of the first paragraph and the revised version.

Change: I accept your offer to join your staff as a production assistant.
To: I am glad to accept the production assistant's job at a salary of $1800 a month.

In the next paragraph, you should outline why you feel you will enjoy working for this company. The first of the following paragraphs lacks sincerity.

Change: I was very impressed by the quality of the working life your company provides its employees.
To: Ever since I made an in-depth study of Armco Company for an assignment in a finance class two years ago, I have wanted to work for Armco. Undertaking this project convinced me that Armco is at the leading edge of the electronics industry. The information I heard during my recent interviews further convinced me that Armco has a bright future.

You should also include a statement that confirms your plans for beginning work, as the following paragraph illustrates.

Of the two alternative dates you gave me for beginning work, the first date, July 1, is entirely acceptable to me. I will report to Mr. Johnson's office at 8 a.m.

The ending of your letter of acceptance should communicate your enthusiasm and appreciation for the opportunity to work for the company whose offer you are accepting. The first of the following paragraphs fails to convey enthusiasm or excitement about beginning the job.

Change: My plans are to report for work at 8 a.m. on July 1.
To: I am enthusiastic about working for Armco Corporation and am appreciative of having the opportunity to join its staff.

The suggested plan for a letter of acceptance should include these elements:

What is the suggested plan for letters of acceptance?

1. An expression of appreciation for the offer and a statement that you are accepting the offer. (Mentioning the job title and the monthly salary is recommended.);
2. A statement that suggests why you believe you will enjoy working for the company;
3. A statement that outlines your plans for beginning work;
4. A courteous closing in which you convey your enthusiasm.

An example of a letter of acceptance is illustrated in Figure 10–7.

```
I gladly accept your offer of $2000 a month as a
production assistant in your Toledo plant.

The management style used at Jimanez Corporation
is especially attractive to me.  I sincerely
believe that most employees not only want to be
able to provide more input into their jobs, but
also that their input can be a significant
contributor to organizational success.  The
extensive use of participative management
throughout Jimanez Corporation undoubtedly
contributes considerably to its success.

The starting date of May 12 is acceptable to me.
I will report to Mr. Thompson's office at 8 a.m.

I appreciate having the opportunity to work for
Jimanez Corporation and am enthusiastic about
beginning my career as a production assistant.
```

An opening in which the enthusiastic acceptance of the job offer is conveyed.

A section that presents a discussion about why the writer is pleased to be able to work for the company.

A section that discusses the writer's plans for beginning work.

A closing that conveys enthusiasm.

Figure 10–7 Effective Letter Conveying the Acceptance of a Job Offer

Letter of Refusal

Although the letter of refusal is basically a negative letter, you should avoid including anything in the letter that may cause the reader to develop a negative reaction toward you. Although you may not be interested in working for this particular company at the present time, you may be in the future. As a general rule, you will want to make the reasons for declining the job as impersonal as possible. Furthermore, you will want to avoid hurting the reader's feelings.

What information should be included in the opening of letters of refusal?

The opening of the letter of refusal should express appreciation for having been offered a job. The first of the following examples is blunt, while the revised version is much more courteous.

Change: Because I have accepted a job in another company, I am not interested in your offer.
To: Thank you for offering me an auditor's position in your Accounting Department.

What information should be included in the middle section of letters of refusal?

After the opening, you should include an impersonal, brief explanation of your reasons for declining the offer. Notice the difference between the tone of the following two paragraphs.

Change: The company in which I accepted a job offer has more to offer its new, young employees than any other company I interviewed.
To: At the time of the interview, I explained why a staff accounting position was my first job choice. Dartwell Corporation of Memphis has offered me a staff accounting position that I have accepted.

The closing of a letter of refusal should provide a courteous expression of appreciation.

What information should be included in the closing of letters of refusal?

> Your taking time to talk with me about career opportunities in your company is greatly appreciated.

The suggested plan for a letter in which a job offer is declined includes these elements:

What is the suggested plan for letters of refusal?

1. A courteous opening in which you express appreciation for having been offered a job;
2. An impersonal—but brief—explanation of the reasons for your declining the offer;
3. A courteous closing.

An example of a letter of refusal is illustrated in Figure 10–8.

Figure 10–8 Effective Letter of Refusal

Thanks for offering me a position in your Public Relations Department.	An opening in which the writer expresses appreciation for the offer.
During one of my interviews, I indicated that my preference, if given the opportunity, would be to work in Atlanta. I will have that opportunity as Reston Paper Company has offered me a position that I've accepted.	A section that presents an impersonal discussion of why the writer is not accepting the offer.
Your interest in and concern for me as an applicant for a job in your company was especially gratifying.	A cordial closing.

Letter of Resignation

Even if a person has negative feelings about a job, the expression of those feelings is inappropriate in a letter of resignation. The writer has nothing to gain from doing so—and perhaps has much to lose. For example, the person is likely to remember the negative feelings the former employee expressed in resignation when asked to recommend the employee for another job. This, in turn, could result in a less positive recommendation for the former employee.

Most people believe that the exit interview is the appropriate time for an employee to express the negative feelings about the job from which he/she is resigning. Increasing numbers of companies are encouraging employees to participate in exit interviews when they terminate their employment. The purpose of these interviews is to seek the employee's suggestions about ways the company might improve its operations.

What information is included in the opening of letters of resignation?

In the opening of the letter of resignation, begin with a courteous statement that mentions your intent to resign from the position you hold and the reason for the resignation. The first of the following paragraphs lacks several important elements.

> Change: I hereby resign from my present position, effective July 31.
> To: Because I have accepted another job that will enable me to take advantage of new job skills recently acquired through the completion of the master's degree course work, I have decided to resign from my present job, effective July 31.

What information is included in the middle section of letters of resignation?

The next section of the letter of resignation includes a discussion of the elements of your present job that have been especially rewarding or enjoyable. By examining the following paragraph, you can see how one individual worded this section of a letter of resignation.

> The five years that I have worked for Bagnell Company have been most enjoyable. Especially rewarding were the opportunities I had to orient and train new employees. In fact, I found working with new employees so enjoyable that I chose training and development as the major thrust of my master's degree.

What information is included in the closing section of letters of resignation?

The closing of the letter of resignation should contain a sincere statement of appreciation. The first of the following paragraphs lacks sincerity.

> Change: Thanks for all that you have done for me.
> To: Mr. Jones, you are largely responsible for the satisfying and fulfilling experience I have had here. I will always be grateful to you for encouraging me to be creative and innovative in my job.

What is the suggested plan for letters of resignation?

The suggested plan for a letter of resignation contains the following elements:

1. A courteous opening in which you state your intent to resign from your present position and the reason for the resignation;
2. An identification of the aspects of your position that you have enjoyed or benefited from;
3. A courteous closing.

Figure 10–9 illustrates a letter of resignation.

CHAPTER SUMMARY

Before you can prepare an effective letter of application, you need to be aware of the qualities of well-written application letters and the content typically included in the opening, middle, and closing sections.

Other types of letters used in the employment process are interview follow-up letters, letters of acceptance, letters of refusal, and letters of resignation.

Because I have accepted another job that will enable me to become extensively involved in computer systems, I wish to resign from my present job, effective June 30.	An opening that mentions the writer's intention to resign.
On several occasions I have mentioned to you my desire to become more involved with computer systems because that is my area of greatest interest. The various positions I've held here have given me the necessary background to become more involved in computer systems. Your letting me expand my job duties was also beneficial as I was able to become more knowledgeable about this area.	A section that presents an impersonal discussion of the reasons for the resignation.
Ms. Brown, I will always be appreciative for all that you've done for me while I've worked here.	A closing that expresses appreciation for having had the opportunity to work for the present employer.

Figure 10–9 Effective Letter of Resignation

Each type of letter has a rather standard plan that you will find helpful when you have an opportunity to write these letters.

Your ability to prepare effective employment-related letters is a skill you will find helpful each time you look for another job during your career.

REVIEW QUESTIONS

1. How do the three different types of letters of application differ from one another?
2. Identify the qualities of effective letters of application.
3. What is the purpose of the opening section of a letter of application?
4. What different types of content can be included in the opening of a letter of application?
5. What elements might be included in the middle section of your letter of application?
6. In writing the work-experience section of your letter of application, what should you try to show?
7. What is the purpose of the closing section of your letter of application?
8. What constitutes an effective opening in an interview follow-up letter?
9. What types of material can be included in the closing of an interview follow-up letter?
10. What are the elements of an effective job acceptance letter?
11. What are the elements of an effective job resignation letter?

APPLICATION PROBLEMS

1. Critique the following letter of application on the basis of grammar usage, punctuation, conformity with essential elements of a letter of application, and conformity with the writing essentials presented in Chapters 3 and 4.

I may be just the hard working, dedicated sales representative you recently advertised for. If being judged the marketing major most likely to succeed—which I was—means anything, then I am certain I could be the successful employee you are looking for, please give me a chance to prove my worth you.

During the three years I have attended State College, I have always made the deans list. In fact, because of my above average intelligence, I have been able to handle an accelerated academic load which will enable me to graduate in three and one-half years.

Because I was so busy with various campus activities and studying, I did not have time for a part-time job. But then I really didn't need to work as my parents are financially able to put me through college. In the summers, I chose to travel rather than work, and got to spend three summers in Europe.

Heres hoping you will give me the opportunity to prove my worth to you by inviting me to come for an interview.

2. Critique the following letter of application on the basis of grammar usage, punctuation, conformity with essential elements of a letter of application, and conformity with the writing essentials presented in Chapters 3 and 4.

The high distinction recently bestowed upon your company, which was recognized as having this great nation's most popular automobile, was very impressive to me. I have always wanted to work for an industry leader, and that is why I am corresponding with you now to see if you might have the need for someone who is dedicated to becoming an efficient, effective manager.

I had the good fortune of having the necessary qualifications of being accepted into State University upon graduating from high school. As a business major, my educational preparation was stimulated by several individuals who have made a permanent impact on me. You will find their names listed as references on the complete and thorough resume that is attached to this letter.

My commitment to working in the business field was enhanced by having several worthwhile part time and full time jobs. These jobs gave me an excellent arena in which to apply the substance of my classwork to a real-world environment. I am glad to say that the concepts my teachers have expounded during the four years of my schooling have considerable merit.

I would consider it a distinct honor to be invited to your company for an interview. May I have the considerable pleasure of meeting you personally so that I can tell you more about the nature of my background? You can be sure that I shall make myself available at any point in time that you are free for such an occasion.

3. Critique the following letter on the basis of grammar usage, punctuation, conformity with essential elements of a letter of application, and conformity with the writing essentials in Chapters 3 and 4.

I sure did enjoy the time I spend with you last Tuesday when you chatted with me about the opening in your company. I must say that of all the interviews I have had so far, you done a better job of explaining to me the requirements of the job you are looking to fill. So many times interviewers are not all that familiar with the job duties and that leaves me with lots of questions.

If only I can have an opportunity to work for your company, I can prove to the higher-ups that I am a worthy employee. If I didn't believe that I wouldn't be applying for a job.

I told you that I would let you know what kind of perfume I was wearing at the interview. As I told you, I borrowed if from my roomate and didn't pay any attention to what it was. It was "Scandia". I am sure your wife would greatly appreciate a bottle.

Please let me hear from you soon as I have to make a decision before to much longer.

4. You will be graduating from college at the end of this semester and are now beginning to look for full-time employment. Prepare a letter of application for a job opening that you learned about from your major advisor. He/she just informed you about the vacancy. He/she feels that you are especially well qualified for the job. By the way, your advisor knows Mr. Jack Harmeson, the individual to whom you are to send your letter of application.

5. You will be graduating from college at the end of this semester. Because you want to live in Denver after graduating (the college you attend is four states away), you do not have many leads on many actual openings. You decide to send several letters inquiring into the possibility of openings in several companies in which you would like to work. Prepare a letter in which you present your qualifications in addition to inquiring about the possibility of an opening.

6. You have applied for several jobs in a variety of companies. So far your efforts have resulted in your being interviewed for positions in two companies. One of the jobs for which you have interviewed really appeals to you. Write the interviewer a follow-up letter in which you mention that you were especially intrigued by the management by objectives philosophy used by the company as well as intrigued by the flexible benefits package the company offers its employees. Convey your impression that you are well qualified for the position.

7. You have just received a job offer from the company that you were so impressed with in application problem 6. You received an attractive offer for the job you really want. Write a letter of acceptance and confirm your intention of beginning work at 8 a.m. on May 10, two days after your college graduation. Convey your enthusiasm for being given the opportunity to work for this company.

8. You have just received a job offer from the company that you thought you were so impressed with in application problem 6. Now that you have had an opportunity to learn more about the job and the company during the home-office interview, you have decided to accept another offer from a company that you believe better meets your needs. Specifically, you want to work for an international company, with the expectation that you may eventually get to work abroad. The company that you were originally so impressed with is not an international company—and the more you learned about international companies, the greater was your desire to work in one.

9. You have now worked for three years in the company whose job offer you accepted after graduating from college. You had hoped during that time

to get an overseas assignment. So far, this hope has not materialized and the prospects of it materializing in the near future are rather bleak. You recently had a job offer from another international company—and this job will immediately take you to its Paris office. You have decided to accept the job offer. Write a letter in which you state your intention to resign from your present job 60 days from today. Explain your reasons for accepting the new job. During the time you have worked for your present employer, you have been especially pleased with the assistance you have gotten from several people, including your immediate supervisor—the person to whom the letter of resignation is being sent. You appreciate your supervisor's continual encouragement, her giving you a chance to try new things (some of which worked and others that didn't), and her letting you assume new tasks only when she was certain that you were ready.

Chapter 11

Communicating Through Interviews

LEARNING OBJECTIVES

After studying this chapter, you should be able to
1. Identify the types of interviews commonly used in the business world.
2. Discuss the purpose of the different types of interviews used in the business world.
3. Discuss the differences among the types of questions used in interviews.
4. Identify several ways that you can increase the effectiveness of the employment interview.
5. Participate in an effective employment interview.

Executives and managers spend a large portion of their communicating time interviewing and being interviewed. Effective interviewing is a skill most interviewers and interviewees develop through practice. The information in this chapter is aimed at providing you with the fundamentals of interviewing. Once you are familiar with this material, practice in interviewing will facilitate the development of effective interviewing skills.

Discussed in this chapter are the different types of interviews found in the business world and the types of questions commonly used in interviews. Because you will be involved with interviews as part of the job-hunting process, the major portion of this chapter is devoted to employment interviews.

TYPES OF INTERVIEWS

Some of the types of interviews found in the business world are employment interviews, performance appraisal interviews, disciplinary interviews, persuasive interviews, and exit interviews. Each has specific uses.

What types of interviews are found in the business world?

Employment Interviews

What two types of employment interviews are used?

The employment interview is often the most important aspect of the job-seeking process. Two types are used: the initial interview, which is generally a screening interview, and the office interview in which only the finalists for the job participate. While the purpose of the initial interview is to determine if the applicant possesses the minimum qualifications for the job, the office interview is aimed at assessing the applicant's poise, enthusiasm, interests, and so forth. The employment interview is covered in detail in the last section of this chapter.

Performance Appraisal Interviews

What is the purpose of the performance appraisal interview?

The purpose of the performance appraisal interview is to give the employee feedback about the quality of his/her work performance. Such interviews are generally scheduled on a regular basis—perhaps every six months while the employee is on probation and once a year thereafter. During the interview, the rater—normally the supervisor—should emphasize the ratee's strengths and minimize his/her weaknesses. Because most employees are aware of their weaknesses, an extensive discussion is counterproductive. Disciplinary action should be avoided during performance appraisal interviews. This is an appropriate activity of the disciplinary interview for an employee whose performance is substandard.

An important part of performance appraisal interviews is the joint rater-ratee determination of ways or strategies for the ratee to overcome his/her weaknesses. Discussing this information will be much more useful to the ratee than a lengthy discussion of his/her weaknesses. Ratees are generally quite concerned about the quality of the performance appraisal interviews because of the belief that their salary increases and promotions may be affected negatively by a poor-quality interview.

Disciplinary Interviews

What is the purpose of the disciplinary interview?

This type of interview is conducted when an employee's actions result in the need for him/her to be disciplined. Therefore, disciplinary interviews are conducted on an as-needed basis. The purpose of the interview, which is often conducted by the employee's supervisor, is to help the employee eliminate the behavior or actions that necessitated the disciplinary action. Depending on the nature of the situation, the interviewer should perhaps consider obtaining legal counsel before conducting a disciplinary interview, especially if the situation may cause the interviewee to take legal action against the interviewer or the company.

Persuasive Interviews

The purpose of the persuasive interview is to persuade someone to take a specific action. The interviewer generally follows the strategy of outlining the desired action and providing a rationale for the action. This step is followed by giving the employee an opportunity to react, which may be followed by the interviewer's providing additional persuasive information. The types of situations for which persuasive interviews are used range from the simple (asking someone to represent you at a meeting) to the complex (convincing the interviewee to take on expanded job duties).

Exit Interviews

What is the purpose of the exit interview?

An exit interview is conducted when an employee terminates employment. The interview should be conducted by someone other than the employee's immediate supervisor on one of the last days the employee is on the job. In many cases, the interview is conducted by an employee who works in the personnel department.

The exit interview is designed to obtain feedback that will help the organization implement changes for overall improvement of its operating effectiveness. For example, suppose a number of employees are leaving because of low pay. Unless this information is made available to the appropriate individuals, the organization will continue to have a high attrition rate, especially among its most valued employees. If the organization has the financial resources to increase employees' salaries, doing so will likely reduce attrition.

Those who conduct exit interviews have to become skilled in "reading between the lines." In some cases, employees will try to disguise their true feelings, especially negative feelings. When a discrepancy occurs between what employees verbalize and what their nonverbal cues communicate, the latter are generally the more accurate.

TYPES OF QUESTIONS USED IN INTERVIEWS

During an interview, the questions asked can be open questions, closed questions, loaded questions, neutral questions, probing questions, leading questions, and mirror questions. Each is used to accomplish a specific purpose.

Open Questions

What are open questions?

Open questions are designed to give the interviewee leeway in responding. They are typically quite broad and generally require a fairly lengthy answer. When asking open questions, the interviewer provides the topic or subject on which he/she wishes the interviewee to expound.

One of the prime advantages of open questions is that they are considered by the interviewee to be nonthreatening because of their general nature. Another advantage is that they are typically easy for the interviewee to answer and give the interviewee an opportunity to do most of the talking, which enables the interviewer to observe.

Disadvantages of open questions are their time-consuming nature, as well as the difficulty of quantifying answers, which may create problems when trying to compare applicants' answers.

Examples of open questions are:

1. Tell me about your childhood.
2. Why do you want to work for our company?
3. What is your philosophy of life?

Closed Questions

What are closed questions?

When compared to open questions, closed questions are much more restrictive. The answers to closed questions will be much more brief, sometimes requiring only a few words to answer.

The advantages of closed questions, when compared with open questions, are: They consume less time, the answers are easier to quantify, and they are easier for inexperienced interviewers to use.

Disadvantages of closed questions, again compared with open questions, are their tendency to provide limited information and to diminish the interviewer's ability to evaluate certain elements of the interviewee's communication skills.

Examples of closed questions are:

1. Which course in your major did you like best?
2. Do you feel you have well-developed leadership skills?
3. Have you enjoyed your college experience?

Loaded Questions

What are loaded questions?

Loaded questions provide the direction of the interviewee's response. Their nature makes them unsuitable for use in certain types of interviews because of their tendency to put the interviewee under pressure and to create a stressful situation. As you will see from the following examples, a loaded question will often require the interviewee to justify his/her attitude, belief, or action.

1. Why is your grade point average so low?
2. Why haven't you participated in more extracurricular activities?
3. What do you like least about your present job?

Leading Questions

What are leading questions?

Leading questions are designed to guide the interviewee in a specific direction—but not to the degree that loaded questions do. Many interviewers use leading questions to verify the accuracy of information the interviewee has provided. When improperly used, leading questions may bias the interviewee's responses. Examples of leading questions are:

1. You do have a car, don't you?
2. You have enjoyed college, haven't you?
3. You do have a good relationship with your present supervisor, don't you?

Neutral Questions

What are neutral questions?

Neutral questions differ from leading or loaded questions in that they do not attempt to direct or guide the interviewee's responses. Because neutral questions are pressure-free, they do not create as stressful a situation for the interviewee as some loaded or leading questions might. Examples of neutral questions are:

1. How do you feel about management by objectives?
2. How do you feel about participating in a six-month training program?
3. Why did you choose to minor in ___________?

Probing Questions

A probing question is an unplanned question that arises because of something the interviewee has said. Generally, these questions are used by the interviewer to seek clarification or additional information about an earlier response. Examples of probing questions are:

What are probing questions?

1. Why do you believe your education has not been put to good use in your present job?
2. Why do you think that the future is bright for mechanical engineers?
3. Why do you want to leave a job that you really like?

Mirror Questions

Mirror questions, used to solicit additional information from the interviewee, mirror the interviewee's previous response. A portion of the interviewee's previous answer is incorporated into the question.

What are mirror questions?

Interviewee's response:	I really like my present supervisor because he continually challenges me.
Interviewer's question:	Challenges you?

THE EMPLOYMENT INTERVIEW

Before you actually participate in an employment interview, you most likely will have prepared a resume and a letter of application. While both of these documents play a vital role, the employment interview will actually determine whether or not you are offered the job.

Interviews should not be viewed as a stressful experience dominated by the interviewer. Because of your research and planning efforts and your self-assurance, the interview process should produce a meaningful dialogue between you and the interviewer.

Preparing for the Employment Interview

The employment interview is actually a discovery process whereby both the interviewer and the interviewee attempt to gain additional information about one another. The interviewee is interested in learning more about the company and the job, while the interviewer wants to learn more about the interviewee's background. While you have already provided the interviewer with some information about your background, he/she will be interested in learning more about you. And even though you have conducted an investigation into the company, you are interested in learning more about it and the job for which you are being interviewed.

What should you do to prepare for the employment interview?

You will probably be asked to complete an application blank. Most companies use blanks similar in form and style, although some may include specific questions common to a particular field or specialty. A few of the most important items of information found on blanks are the following:

1. The names, addresses, titles, and phone numbers of individuals who can attest to your ability and accomplishments. These are the persons you list as references.
2. Your Social Security Number.
3. Your employment experience, including the names and addresses of your current and previous supervisors.
4. Your educational preparation, including college/university attended, dates attended, major, and degree awarded.
5. A list of your special skills and qualifications.

Once the interview date has been set, you should begin preparing for the interview. Your preparation should include undertaking appropriate research to strengthen your personal credibility and enhance your self-assurance. Taking the initiative to learn about the company you are interviewing will help you avoid asking elementary questions and will enable you to demonstrate personal interest in and enthusiasm for the organization and the job. The information you collect during the personal-position analysis (see Chapter 9) will be helpful in your preparation.

Some sources of information that you will find helpful are the company's annual report, *Dun and Bradstreet's Million Dollar Directory, Moody's Manual,* and *Poor's Register.*

Becoming familiar with the following types of information will be helpful in preparing for the interview.

1. Names of chief officers
2. The products manufactured (or chief type of business)
3. Annual gross revenues
4. Significant recent accomplishments of the company
5. Significant recent problems experienced by the company
6. Projected outlook for the company

By being familiar with this information and incorporating it into your answers and/or questions, you will be able to distinguish yourself as an applicant who is well prepared for the interview. For example, asking, "Considering last year's gross revenue of $850 million, what are the company's plans to expand into other areas or products?" is more impressive than asking how large the company is in terms of gross revenue.

Getting Ready

Several suggestions are offered to help you get ready for the interview.

1. Write down the date, time, place of the interview, and the interviewer's name. Because many interviews are arranged over the telephone, this step will help you avoid forgetting vital information.

2. Review your resume. Try to determine which parts may need further clarification or which areas of information on your resume are likely to generate questions. Determine which additional information you should be prepared to provide.

3. Formulate answers to questions you are likely to be asked about your goals, achievements, activities, and so forth.

4. Become as familiar with the company and the position as you can. Be prepared to ask questions to obtain desired relevant information about the position and/or the company.

5. Try to find out information about the interviewer's background, including his/her job title and the authority he/she has for hiring.

6. Become familiar with nonverbal cues that can enhance your interviewing performance—good eye contact with the interviewer and a poised, relaxed (but not too relaxed) image.

During the Interview

The interviewer will begin to evaluate you the moment you meet face to face. Eye contact is necessary, but a firm handshake, self-assurance, and assertiveness are equally important. Because interviewers are trained to evaluate what you say as well as how you say it, the interviewer is likely to have formed an initial impression of your employment acceptability within the first few minutes of the interview.

During the interview, you will need to be a good listener. Like writing and speaking, listening—which is an important communication skill—can be improved with practice. The following suggestions will be helpful in developing a better listening skill.

1. Concentrate on listening. Increase your listening awareness by becoming alert to all the sounds around you. Do not tune people out, but practice on voices and sounds to increase your awareness.
2. Listen eagerly and with an open mind.
3. Pay attention. Concentrate on what the interviewer is saying. Do not let your mind wander. Failure to pay attention may result in your asking a question that the interviewer has already answered.
4. Listen for the most important ideas. Be sure you comprehend the information provided by the interviewer. Ask questions for clarification.
5. Look at the interviewer. Maintaining eye contact with the interviewer conveys the impression that you are interested and confident.

The main part of the interview begins when the interviewer starts to discuss the organization and the job or asks questions about your background and experience. While you most likely will be invited to ask questions whenever they arise, you may be requested to delay asking them until the end of the interview.

What questions should you ask during the interview?

Among the questions you will want to ask the interviewer—unless, of course, the interviewer volunteers the information—are the following:

1. What does the job actually entail? (This question is aimed at becoming familiar with job duties, the immediate supervisor, etc.)

2. Where does the job fit into the organizational structure? (This question will help you become familiar with normal promotional channels.)
3. Does the position require extensive travel?
4. Does the company have an in-house training program?
5. What is the nature of performance reviews?
6. How often are transfers likely to be made? Does the employee usually have input into the relocation decision?
7. What is the normal time between promotions?

If your qualifications are somewhat less than those listed in the job vacancy notice, you should consider trying to convince the interviewer—if you have an opportunity to do so—that these limiting qualifications will not be all that detrimental. Examples of limiting qualifications are a low grade point average, limited participation in outside activities, and limited work experience. Accentuating the positive while responding to—but not hiding—the negative is a wise course of action.

You will often be asked a series of open-ended questions, such as why you chose the major you did or what your present and future career goals are. These questions are designed to determine how well your qualifications match the stated requirements of the position for which you are applying. Even though anticipating every possible question is impossible, you will find it advantageous to prepare answers to questions that have become rather standard. Among these questions are the following:

1. Tell me about yourself.
2. For what position are you applying?
3. What are your long-term goals? Where do you hope to be in ten years?
4. Why do you feel that you will be successful in this job?
5. What leadership positions or roles have you held?
6. How do you spend your spare time?
7. What have been your most satisfying and least satisfying experiences?
8. What are your strongest and weakest personal qualities?
9. Give me some examples that support your stated interest in ______.
10. Why did you select this company as one to interview?
11. Which college courses did you like best? Why?
12. What did you learn or gain from your part-time and summer job experiences?
13. Which geographic location do you prefer? Why?
14. Would you prefer on-the-job training or a formal training program?
15. What can you do for us now? What can we do for you?
16. Why did you choose your major?
17. Why are your grades so low?
18. Tell me about your extracurricular activities and interests.

19. Why did you quit your last job?
20. Why did you select the __________ major?
21. How have you handled a major problem or crisis?
22. What do you know about our company?
23. Are you willing to relocate?
24. What are your plans for graduate study?

Naturally, the list of possible questions the interviewer might ask is virtually limitless. However, preparing some mental answers to questions you think you might be asked is strongly recommended.

Interviewing is a two-way process. The interviewer will be evaluating your suitability for employment in his/her company, and you will be trying to determine if you want to work for the company. A well-planned, effective interview will allow both parties to accomplish their interview objectives.

Making a Good Impression During the Interview

What can you do to make a good impression during the interview?

Throughout your lifetime, you will have many opportunities to create a good impression. During an employment interview, you will try to create a good impression by presenting yourself as the most desirable person for the job. The interviewer, on the other hand, is looking for the applicant who possesses the specific attributes or capabilities considered important for job success. Unfortunately, no formula exists that guarantees success, but paying attention to the areas listed below will help you avoid common pitfalls encountered during interviews.

1. Appropriate dress is important for a good first impression. Be sure you are neat and clean. You need not worry about the cost of the outfit you are wearing. Rather, concentrate on simple, tasteful, and comfortable business attire. Do not wear gaudy clothing or flashy jewelry. The image you project can greatly influence your career destiny. Because first impressions are formed within 30 minutes, you should have a professional look.

Changing from casual attire to business attire can be uncomfortable. Before the actual interview, you will wisely give a new wardrobe a test run. Finding out before the day of the interview that a shirt collar is too tight or that a belt is the wrong color will help decrease pre-interview stress.

Interviewers are keenly aware of two rather visible symbols of potential success—a commanding presence and an instinctive ability to act and react in an appropriate manner. These two symbols reflect how you will see yourself, which, in turn, affects how others perceive you. Remember: interviewers are more favorably inclined toward the well-qualified candidate who looks the part.

2. Be on time. Arriving a few minutes early is far better than arriving just on time or even a few minutes late. Interviewers know that lateness is a habit that can be quite costly in terms of achievement and job-related success.

3. Be confident and courteous. Sit when asked, shake hands when prompted, avoid smoking (even if offered a cigarette), and concentrate on the

interview process. Make sure you pronounce the interviewer's name correctly during the interview. Sit in a relaxed position, but do not sprawl out or place your feet on another chair or table. Demonstrate a reasonable sense of humor, but do not participate in jokes or funny stories.

4. Keep eye contact with the interviewer. Concentrate on the question you are being asked. Listen carefully and wait until the interviewer has finished asking the question before you begin answering.

5. Provide thoughtful, direct, and honest answers. Think—really think—before answering any of the questions.

6. Avoid asking questions about salary. When you are considered a serious candidate for the position, the interviewer will bring up the topic of salary. If you are asked the salary you expect to receive, providing a salary range is appropriate.

Visiting the Office

What is the purpose of the office/plant interview?

Following a campus interview, you may be invited to visit the company's office or plant. This is a second opportunity for you to sell your skills and qualifications and will help you make the interviewer aware of your potential worth to the company.

During the office visit, anticipation is important; but mental, emotional, and professional flexibility are even more important. For example, you may or may not be met at the airport. Representatives of the company may take you out for meals, or you may have to fend for yourself. A company may schedule your flight and make your hotel reservations but allow you to find your way around—just to see if you can still arrive on time for your first appointment.

The company visitation usually consumes at least one whole day and may even include some employment testing. You should be prepared for a variety of tests that are aimed at assessing your aptitude and your decision-making ability. Some companies use a paper-and-pencil-type test, while others assess your ability through simulated on-the-job situations.

Company interviews may also be used to provide an indication of your poise, stamina, enthusiasm, and knowledge. During the day, you can expect to have interviews with a variety of people in many different positions, such as supervisors, managers, prospective departmental peer-group members, and informal conversations during lunch and breaks.

Larger companies often have personnel departments that employ individuals who are professionally trained in the interview process. You, as a prospective employee, must assume your fair share of the responsibility for establishing the rapport needed for a productive interview session. To do so, you should be as natural, confident, and relaxed as possible.

What do interviewers evaluate during office/plant interviews?

During the interview, the interviewer will be observing and evaluating. Specific questions the interviewer will be asking him/herself are:

1. How mentally alert and responsive is the applicant? Competition for top jobs is very keen. Factors such as eye contact, real or manufactured interest, and responding to questions in the correct and expected manner will be some of the ways an applicant's alertness and responsiveness will be assessed.

2. Is the applicant able to draw proper inferences and conclusions? Open-ended questions and even elusive political inquiries will often be used to determine the applicant's judgmental ability.

3. Does the applicant demonstrate a degree of intellectual depth when communicating, or is his/her thinking ability shallow and lacking in depth?

4. Has the candidate used, up to this point, good judgment and common sense regarding career/life planning? While common sense is difficult to identify, the following factors might prove relevant: evidence of physical energy, reaction to pressure, resistance to or acceptance of change, sense of humor, appearance and grooming, breadth of interests, creativity, and financial stability.

5. What is the applicant's capacity for problem solving? Ability to see the big picture and to apply a textbook type of learning to actual business situations are key focal points for identifying the ability to solve problems.

6. How well does the applicant respond to stress and pressure? Application of ability and skill in difficult and pressure-filled situations is a common denominator of success. Many interview situations are designed to place the applicant in controlled stress situations in order to view his/her reactions and to measure his/her ability to handle stress.

7. Can the applicant succeed in the position for which he/she is being interviewed? Does the applicant possess the technical skill, personal traits, and the ability to succeed?

8. Will the applicant succeed in this position? Does the applicant have the personal and intrinsic motivation to succeed? Are interests and objectives consistent with organizational goals?

9. Can the applicant be trusted? Personal integrity, honesty in dealing with people, and moral and ethical standards are often evaluated by assessing the applicant's candor in answering questions, spontaneity, consistency in responses, and the willingness to discuss shortcomings.

10. Is the applicant professionally and socially mature? Self-confidence is important to job success. Applicants are evaluated in relation to their willingness to take risks, their ability to accept shortcomings and leadership potential, and their promise as indicated by a willingness to make decisions.

Following Up

One of the simplest—yet commonly ignored—rules of successful interviewing is acknowledging a company's time and interest. Successful people make it their business to thank others for favors, whether big or small. During the entire job search, you should always acknowledge and thank the people who assisted in the interview process.

A timely and well-written interview follow-up letter (see Chapter 10) can enhance the overall success of the interview process. Even if your interest in a particular company begins to wane after the interview, common courtesy requires a letter of thanks.

During the interview process, a personal job search record will help you remember the people and the companies that have extended interview courtesies to you. A sample job search record is shown in Figure 11–1.

What is the personal job search progress record used for?

JOB SEARCH RECORD

	CONTACT METHOD					EMPLOYER RESPONSE				FOLLLOW-UP METHOD			EMPLOYMENT OFFER		COMMENTS
Employer Contacted Person, Title Address, Phone	Date	Campus Interview	Letter	Resume	Phone Call	Date	Letter	Phone Call	Date of Interview	Date	Letter	Phone Call	Starting Date	Salary	

Figure 11–1 Job Search Record

After you accept a job offer, you will also distinguish yourself as a courteous person if you notify those companies where your application is still viable that you are no longer available. Information about a letter appropriate for this use is discussed in Chapter 10.

CHAPTER SUMMARY

A variety of different types of interviews are used in the business world: employment interviews, performance appraisal interviews, disciplinary interviews, persuasive interviews, and exit interviews. Each has a specific purpose and function.

Interviewers use a number of different types of questions during the questioning phase of an interview. Those most often used are open, closed, loaded, leading, neutral, probing, and mirror questions. Because some types are particularly helpful in obtaining certain kinds of information from the interviewee, the interviewer should know the specific uses of the different types of questions.

Before you participate in an employment interview, you should prepare adequately for the event. By being aware of the qualities interviewers look for in job applicants, you will be able to do your best.

REVIEW QUESTIONS

1. What is the purpose of the performance appraisal interview?
2. What is the purpose of the exit interview?
3. Prepare a list of suggestions you should follow in preparing for an interview.
4. Of what value are such publications as *Dun and Bradstreet's Million Dollar Directory, Moody's Manual,* and *Poor's Register* in getting ready for an interview?
5. What suggestions can you offer that will enable you to become a better listener during an interview?
6. How can you make a good initial impression during an interview?
7. What is the purpose of the office visit?
8. What are some of the things the interviewer will be evaluating during an interview?
9. What two types of letters are commonly associated with the interview follow-up process?

APPLICATION PROBLEMS

1. Assume you are preparing for an on-campus interview. Prepare a list of your goals, your strengths, and your experience. Include evidence of specifics that demonstrate your character and ability.

2. In preparing for the on-campus interview (application problem no. 1), make a list of the questions you would like to ask the interviewer.

3. Select three companies for which you would like to work. Using the information sources at your disposal, compile information about each company that will be helpful in an interview.

4. Assume you have scheduled an on-campus interview. Study your resume and prepare a list of ten questions that you think the interviewer is likely to ask.

5. Obtain a copy of a friend's resume and conduct a mock interview. Give your friend a copy of your resume and ask him/her to conduct a mock interview. After the interview, discuss the ways that each of you could improve your interview performance.

6. Using the library resources available to you, prepare a three-page report on "Improving Interviewing Effectiveness." Address the report from the interviewer's perspective.

7. Using the library resources available to you, prepare a three-page report on "Improving Interviewing Effectiveness." Address the report from the job applicant's perspective.

8. Using the library resources available to you, prepare a one-page report on "Improving the Reliability of Information Provided by Persons Listed as Job References." Write the report from the employer's perspective.

9. Using the library resources available to you, prepare a two-page report on "Interviewer Assessment of the Job Applicant's Ability." Include in your report a discussion of the techniques that might be used in the assessment process.

Part V—The Essentials of Business Reports

Chapter 12

Preparing Informal Reports

LEARNING OBJECTIVES

After studying this chapter, you should be able to

1. Discuss the differences among the classifications of business reports.
2. Discuss the differences among the types of informal reports presented in this chapter.
3. Discuss the purpose of each type of informal report presented in this chapter.
4. Discuss the uses of each type of informal report presented in this chapter.
5. Prepare effective informal reports of the type discussed in this chapter.

The reports used in today's business world present information in a factual, objective, and orderly manner. The information contained in these reports is often used by managers to facilitate their decision-making and problem-solving efforts. The effectiveness of their decisions can be greatly affected by the sufficiency and accuracy of the information presented in the reports they use.

THE IMPORTANCE OF REPORTS

The pace of today's business operations seldom allows managers sufficient time to gather all the information they need to make important decisions or to solve problems. In many instances, a subordinate is assigned the task of gathering or collecting the information to be used by managers, and he/she will often present this information in a report.

What is the most important function of reports?

The most important function of reports is to provide information for use in managerial decision making and problem solving. Another important function is to provide a permanent record of information, a feature that is unavailable when information is conveyed orally. Written reports are becoming more important because of the growing need in an increasing number of organizations to provide information permanency.

What are the secondary functions of reports?

In addition to providing information for others, reports serve other useful functions. They are often used to outline processes or procedures that individuals are expected to follow. A third function of reports is to create goodwill for the organization.

Reports serve an important function not only within the organization but outside the organization as well. For example, reports that are used to present information to stockholders and other interested parties can also create goodwill for the organization.

In addition to the functions discussed above, reports are used in organizations in many other ways. In some instances, reports may be used to evaluate the competency of the writer in certain areas. The information contained in reports can also be used as a springboard to create or generate additional ideas for solving problems. Furthermore, reports are used by some managers to fill technological or information voids in their backgrounds.

CLASSIFICATIONS OF BUSINESS REPORTS

Business reports can be classified in several different ways. The most popular scheme involves classifying reports by their level of formality. Therefore, reports are often classified as either *informal* or *formal*.

How are reports classified?

How do informal reports differ from formal reports?

Informal reports are typically written and presented in a less structured manner than formal reports. The types of informal reports discussed in this chapter are: memorandum reports, letter reports, short reports, justification reports, periodic reports, progress reports, staff reports, feasibility reports, and audit reports.

Formal reports, which are discussed in Chapters 13 and 14, tend to be more analytical than informal reports, although some informal reports—especially short reports—may also be analytical. When compared with informal reports, formal reports generally have a more "dressed-up" appearance, are often longer, and are typically written in a more formal style.

While formal reports are decreasing in popularity in the business world, informal reports are increasing in popularity. The types of informal reports used by organizations vary considerably, with some organizations using most or all of the various types of informal reports, while others use only one or two types.

INFORMAL REPORTS

Discussed in this section are the different types of informal reports. Each type of report is illustrated to enhance the reader's understanding of its similarities and differences.

What are the categories of informal reports?

Informal reports can be categorized by their format and content. The format category includes memorandum, letter, and short reports, while the content category is comprised of justification, periodic, progress, staff, feasibility, and audit reports.

Memorandum Reports

Although the memorandum report is primarily an internal report, it may also be used externally. Memorandum reports are considered to be informal because of their format, not necessarily because of their content. The memorandum format can be used to present information contained in justification, periodic, progress, and staff reports.

For what are memorandum reports commonly used?

Memorandum reports are commonly used for routine matters. Therefore, they can be used for initiating action, responding to a request, following up telephone conversations and numerous other purposes. They may be sent upward, downward, or laterally within the organization.

The format of memorandum reports is fairly standard. If printed memorandum forms are not available, the following headings can be typed on a sheet of paper:

TO:
FROM:
DATE:
SUBJECT:

If the writer's signature is important, the memorandum can be signed or initialed beside the writer's name in the heading or below the message. The typist's initials should be typed on the left margin below the message. A report presented in the memorandum format is shown in Figure 12–1.

Letter Reports

How do letter and memorandum reports differ from one another?

One of the basic differences between memorandum reports and letter reports is their destination. Memorandum reports are generally used internally, while letter reports are often transmitted outside the organization. Letter reports are useful for presenting limited amounts of information. They are usually one to four pages in length and use a regular letter format.

The structure of letter reports varies widely as the circumstances determine which parts to include. The opening sentence may refer to the authorization, the date of the authorization, and the name of the individual who made the authorization. Such an opening sentence follows.

As you requested on December 14, I am submitting the following report on the 1988 capital expenditures of the Rockland branch office.

In many instances, letter reports are sent to individuals as a response to a request they made. In such cases, the following opening sentence may be appropriate.

Attached is the report on the feasibility of expanding health care facilities of General Hospital that you wrote us about on July 17.

INTEROFFICE MEMORANDUM

August 14, 1990

TO: Jack Hatchell, President

FROM: John Doe, Office Manager

SUBJECT: Records Management Conference

A summary of the Records Management Conference I attended in Detroit on August 10 is included in this report.

Summary of Sessions Attended

The following summarizes each of the sessions I attended:

1. Filing Equipment: This session was designed to acquaint the participants with the latest filing equipment. Much of the equipment on display was automatic.

2. Computer Output Microfilm: This session was designed to familiarize the participants with the computer output microfilm concept and its various applications.

3. Records Retrieval: The purpose of this session was to acquaint the participants with the various factors that need to be considered in developing a records retention schedule.

4. Records Transfer: In this session, the participants learned about new developments in transferring records from active status to inactive status.

Recommendations

On the basis of my attending the conference, I am making the following recommendations:

1. That we investigate the possibility of purchasing lateral filing equipment.

2. That we evaluate the validity of our records retention schedule and revise as needed.

I appreciate having had the opportunity of attending this most informative conference. If you have any questions regarding the sessions I attended or the recommendations I have made, I would be glad to talk with you about them.

sd

Figure 12–1 Memorandum Report

Some letter reports are unsolicited. The following opening sentence is appropriate for an unsolicited report.

> Because you are vitally concerned with hospital facilities, you might be interested in the enclosed report that is concerned with the feasibility of expanding the health care facilities of General Hospital.

The second section of the letter report is the report body, which may include: (1) a presentation of findings about the situation being studied; (2) an analysis of the situation being studied; (3) information of general interest to the report reader.

What is included in the second section of letter reports?

To add credibility to the report, some writers include information pertaining to the depth of the study, the individuals consulted, and the nature of the materials read in preparing the report.

Many reports present only information because the situation does not require analysis or recommendations. But if recommendations and suggestions based on the findings or data are appropriate, they should be included. If the report reader is likely to consider the recommendations section the most important part of the report, it can be presented before the findings section. This pattern will immediately give the reader the information of greatest concern or interest.

The last section of the letter report—the closing—often contains an offer to be of further assistance. The offer indicates a willingness to be cooperative or helpful, which is desirable in building goodwill.

The appropriate writing style for letter reports is often determined by the writer-reader relationship. Although an informal writing style is typically used, the relationship may make the formal writing style more appropriate. For example, while the use of personal pronouns (I, you, we) are appropriate for an informally written report, they are not appropriate for more formally written reports.

Any acceptable letter style can be used for presenting the report to the reader. If the report is lengthy, the use of side and paragraph headings is appropriate, as is the enumeration of material, which makes the report easier to read. To further aid the reader, graphic illustrations and tabular information may be included in the letter report. Information on preparing graphic aids is included in Chapter 14.

An example of a letter report is presented in Figure 12–2.

Short Reports

Reports that are too long to be presented in memorandum- or letter-report format but which need not be presented in formal-report format can be presented as a short report. Short reports are not as long as formal reports; do not contain a synopsis, letter of transmittal, table of contents, letter of authorization, appendix, or bibliography; and are usually written in a less formal style.

How do short reports and formal reports differ from one another?

The short report is appropriate for a variety of research, investigative, or survey problems. In most instances, the report will deal with only one topic,

RICHARDSON, INC.

1200 Main Street (201) 456-5845 Grant, NY 01232

November 12, 1989

Mr. Henry Jackson
General Manager
Richardson, Inc.
1200 Main Street
Grant, NY 01232

Dear Mr. Jackson:

Here is the report you requested on June 15 concerning the nature of the physical improvements made at the branch office.

Physical Improvements to General Office Area

The general office area has been completely renovated. New tile has been installed in the general office area, and the carpet in the managers' and supervisors' offices is new. A new fluorescent lighting system has been installed, which adds greatly to the overall appearance of the office area. Heating and cooling ducts are integrated into the lighting fixtures.
New furniture was purchased for some employees and work areas. Because the new furniture is streamlined and the old furniture has traditional styling, the two styles are not coordinated.

Suggestions for Additional Improvements

As a response to your request for suggestions to improve the branch office facilities, the following recommendations are being made:

1. Purchase more of the new streamlined furniture.

2. Renovate the restroom facilities.

I think we are making substantial progress toward improving the appearance of the facilities here at the branch office. If you need any additional information, please let me know.

Sincerely,

Darlene James

Darlene James
Administrative Assistant
op

Figure 12–2 Letter Report

which limits the scope of most short reports. Formal reports, on the contrary, sometimes contain information about more than one topic.

Two plans are used to present the information in short reports: the *direct,* or deductive plan, or the *indirect*, or inductive plan. When the direct plan is used, a short summary, the conclusions, and the recommendations are presented first. The facts, ideas, or findings follow. When the indirect plan is used, the facts, ideas, and findings are presented before the conclusions and recommendations. The direct plan is used more often because it attracts the immediate interest of the reader. Busy executives often prefer the use of the direct plan because the most important information is presented at the beginning of the report. The indirect plan is used in reports prepared for general readership.

How does the direct plan differ from the indirect plan?

In many formal reports, supporting data, including diagrams, illustrations, and tables, are included as appendices; in short reports, such supporting data are usually included in the body. Any supporting data that are included should be discussed.

The following suggestions will be helpful in writing a short report.

What suggestions will help you write more effective short reports?

1. State at the beginning the purpose or objectives of the report.
2. Avoid making broad generalizations that cannot be substantiated by the data.
3. Write the report in a style appropriate for the reader-writer relationship.
4. Make sure the conclusions and recommendations are based on the data or findings.
5. Write the report in a concise, direct style.
6. Use side headings and enumerations when and where appropriate as a means of aiding the reader.

The format mechanics that are appropriate for the formal report are also appropriate for the short report. These mechanics are discussed in detail in Chapter 14.

A short report is presented in Figure 12–3.

Justification Reports

The justification report is prepared by the report writer to justify a recommendation, a course of action, or a decision. In most instances, the justification report is not authorized or commissioned. Instead, the report writer initiates the writing of the report.

For what are justification reports used?

The justification report follows a direct or deductive plan, which means that the recommendation and conclusions are presented before the facts and findings. This plan is used because the most important section of justification reports typically is the recommendation.

The suggested plan for a justification report includes the following elements:

What is the suggested plan for presenting justification reports?

1. *Statement of purpose and recommendation:* The purpose for writing the report and the ensuing recommendation should be presented as concisely as possible.

SUBCOMMITTEE REPORT ON CURRICULUM REVIEW

The Subcommittee on Curriculum Review was organized on August 10, 1989, by Dean Jon Fritchie and was given a three-part assignment: (1) to review the required business core in the College of Business Administration, (2) to report the findings of the faculty, and (3) to make recommendations the Subcommittee considered appropriate.

Summary of Findings

The Subcommittee on Curriculum Review found the business core required of all majors in the College of Business Administration to be realistic for the most part, although the Subcommittee believes that several recommendations are appropriate for consideration at this time.

Conclusions

The Subcommittee arrived at the following conclusions about the required business core in the College of Business Administration:

1. Although the business core is realistic for the most part, certain modifications are appropriate.
2. Most colleges and universities are attempting to provide more flexibility within their required business cores. Any revisions in the core within the College of Business Administration should be made to provide more flexibility.
3. The suggested revisions can be made without affecting the integrity of the business core.
4. The suggested revisions will be received favorably by the majority of the faculty in the college.
5. The revisions can be made without affecting the accreditation of the various programs in the college.

Recommendations

The Subcommittee was asked to make appropriate recommendations. On the basis of its investigation, the Subcommittee submits the following:

1. Accounting III (the first course in a two-course sequence of Intermediate Accounting) should be an elective, except when required for a specific program, such as accounting.
2. Business Writing should be a required course.
3. An additional three-credit economics course should be required in addition to the already required eight credits of economics.
4. The content of Business Law I, II, and III should be condensed into two business law courses to be identified as Business Law I and II.
5. For all majors, Introduction to Business should be an elective rather than a required course.
6. Business Statistics I, II, and III should be reduced to a two-course sequence to be identified as Business Statistics I and II.
7. A course in Computer Science should be required of all majors in the College of Business Administration.

Figure 12–3 Short Report

2

Findings of the Investigation

The findings of this study were obtained through extensive investigation procedures. The sources of information used in the investigation process were:

1. Reports from various accreditation agencies.

2. Catalogs from colleges and universities generally recognized as having reputable programs.

3. Information and opinions from various faculty members.

4. Published magazine articles.

The findings of the investigation are presented in the same order as the recommendations are presented. Only the significant findings pertaining to specific recommendations are included in this report.

Accounting. The majority of colleges and universities whose programs were examined now require a two-course sequence in principles of accounting. Of

business law requirement from three courses to two courses. (To conserve space, the remainder of this report is not presented.)

am

Figure 12–3 (cont.)

Because of the increasing difficulties with Brand X typewriters, I recommend that they be replaced with Brand Y typewriters.

2. *Outcome of the recommendation, if adopted:* A brief statement outlining the expected outcomes of adopting the recommendation should be included. The expected outcomes should be in the form of cash savings, increased productivity, better service, and so forth.

3. *Suggested plan for implementing the recommendation:* Although this section is optional, its inclusion is essential in some justification reports. Before a decision is made about whether or not to implement the recommendation, the individual or individuals responsible for making the decision should be made aware of the suggested implementation procedures.

4. *Discussion of recommendation and/or advantages and disadvantages:* In order for the reader to make an objective decision regarding the recommendation, he or she may need more information. This section is designed to provide that information. Depending upon the nature of the recommendation, a detailed discussion may be needed. If the recommendation involves an easily understood situation or a situation the reader is familiar with, a listing of advantages and disadvantages of implementing the recommendation will be sufficient. In some instances, a thorough discussion of the recommendation as well as its advantages and disadvantages is appropriate.

5. *Statement of conclusions:* The last section outlines the writer's conclusions regarding the implementation of the recommendation. To be useful, the conclusions must be valid, supportable, and concisely written.

The justification report can be presented to the reader in one of three formats: the memorandum report, the letter report, or the short report. Because the justification report is generally an internal report that is transmitted from one employee to another, the memorandum format is often used.

The justification report is easier to read if headings are used to identify each section. If the memorandum format is used, the subject line should accurately identify the nature of the recommendation that is being made. If the letter format is chosen, a subject line that identifies the nature of the recommendation should also be provided. When using the short report format, the title of the report should appear on the title page and on the first page of the report.

A justification report is presented in Figure 12–4.

Periodic Reports

For what are periodic reports used?

Another type of report designed for a specific purpose is the periodic report, which is prepared to present information on a regular basis, perhaps weekly, monthly, quarterly, semiannually, or annually. Its basic purpose is to provide a written record of past or present situations or events. Some of the more familiar periodic reports are annual reports, stockholder reports, bank statements, balance sheets, and budgets.

Periodic reports are often prepared by subordinates for use by their superiors. For example, a department manager may ask each of his or her supervisors to prepare a monthly cost breakdown of anticipated expenditures. The department manager may then synthesize the information in each of the reports into one departmental report to be transmitted to a higher managerial level.

Periodic reports can be prepared in narrative format, in tabular format, or on a form. Presenting quantitative information in a table or on a form often facilitates the reader's comprehension of the material.

The memorandum, letter, and short report formats are also appropriate for presenting periodic reports to the reader. A subject line or title that accurately reflects the report's content should be used.

Although most periodic reports do not include suggestions or recommendations for a particular course of action, some report writers believe that the inclusion of such information is desirable. The nature of the writer-reader relationship should guide the writer's decision as to the inclusion of this information.

An example of a periodic report is presented in Figure 12–5.

Progress Reports

For what are progress reports used?

Used to keep the reader informed about the status of a project, progress reports are prepared on an occasional basis, usually when substantial progress on a project needs to be reported. Therefore, while periodic reports are prepared on a regular basis, progress reports are prepared on an irregular basis. The distinction between periodic and progress reports is becoming less clear as an increas-

INTEROFFICE MEMORANDUM

DATE: July 15, 1989

TO: William Buck, Office Manager

FROM: Sally Brown, Office Services Supervisor

SUBJECT: Need for Automatic Collator

The following information outlines the need for the purchase of an automatic collator:

Statement of Purpose and Recommendation

Because of the increasing employee time consumed by manually collating documents, the possibility of purchasing an automatic collator should be investigated.

Outcome of Recommendation

By using an automatic collator, a considerable amount of employee time could be saved. The result would be higher employee productivity and greater efficiency because employees could utilize their time to perform more worthwhile work.

Suggested Plan for Implementing Recommendation

An examination of the automatic collators manufactured by several different companies is recommended. Because of the different features found on the various devices, some collators would be more suitable than others.

Advantages and Disadvantages

The use of an automatic collator would result in the following advantages: (1) employees would not have to perform the rather menial task of collating; (2) employee time could be better utilized by performing other tasks; (3) employee morale would improve if employees do not have to collate manually; and (4) greater accuracy of collated documents could be expected.

The only disadvantage seen in purchasing an automatic collator is the purchase cost, which is estimated to be approximately $800.

Conclusions

Among the conclusions are the following:

1. An automatic collator can be justified on the basis of the number of sheets that have to be collated.

Figure 12–4 Justification Report

INTEROFFICE MEMORANDUM

August 10, 1989

TO: Richard Dawson, Executive Vice-President

FROM: Mark Sanchez, Manager, Credit Department

SUBJECT: Expenditures for the Credit Department During July, 1989

The expenditures you asked me to calculate for the Credit Department for July, 1989, follow:

	Beginning Balance	Ending Balance	Expense
Salaries	$96,000	$87,000	$9,000
Supplies	9,000	8,200	800
Telephone (Long Distance)	300	230	70
Printing	250	220	30
Equipment Rental	480	440	40

dm

Figure 12–5 Periodic Report

ing number of organizations are interchanging the uses of these two types of reports. Progress reports are useful for keeping top-level decision makers informed in the event that crucial decisions have to be made about a certain phase or element of a project.

The content of a progress report is determined by the familiarity of the report reader with the project. If the reader is fairly well informed, less detail will probably be needed. Readers who have limited familiarity or who are unfamiliar with a project will need considerably more background information. Although a progress report that is one of a series should briefly review the progress of the project up to the point when the last report was written, it should concentrate on progress since the last report.

What is the suggested plan for progress reports?

The suggested plan for a progress report includes the following elements:

1. *Introduction:* This section includes a discussion of the purpose of the project, individuals involved (if needed), and projected completion dates.

2. *Summary of progress already reported:* The detail required in this section depends to a large extent on the reader's familiarity with the project. Essentially, this section provides a synopsis of the preceding progress reports.

3. *Detailed summary of progress since last reporting:* This information is designed to give the reader an accurate picture of progress since the last report. This section is often considered as the most important one for a reader who is familiar with the project.

4. *Nature of exceptional progress:* This part, which is optional, can be used to report any work that is ahead of or behind schedule. Depending on the circumstances, the individuals responsible for making decisions about the project may find this section quite useful.

5. *Summary of work yet to be completed:* To give the reader a clear picture of what remains to be done on the project, a short summary is useful. Individual progress reports that comprise a series should be put in the same format for the reader each time one is prepared. Each of the three informal report formats (memorandum, letter, and short report) is suitable for presenting progress reports. The writer-reader relationship and the degree of formality should determine which format to use. The same headings and categories should also be used each time a progress report is prepared.

Figure 12–6 presents a progress report.

Staff Reports

The staff report, which is generally presented in the memorandum format, is often prepared upon request rather than on the initiative of the report writer. Staff reports can be used for a variety of purposes. Because they are frequently prepared after a particular problem has been solved, their format generally follows a problem-solving sequence.

Although the plan used in preparing staff reports is flexible, the following sections are appropriate for inclusion:

What is the suggested plan for preparing staff reports?

1. *Overview:* Provides a brief view of what is to follow. For some readers this is essential for putting the problem into proper perspective.
2. *Purpose:* Outlines the nature of the problem being studied and identifies the primary objectives of the study. The scope of the study should be identified, not only to provide assistance for the reader, but also to help the writer more clearly delineate the problem being studied.
3. *Discussion of facts:* Identifies the important facts for the reader and discusses the facts. In a statistical study, this section will be comprised primarily of the data and a discussion of them. In an informational report, this section will deal with the important facts surrounding the problem being studied.
4. *Conclusions:* Provides a list of conclusions based on the analysis of data or facts. The conclusions must be supportable by the available data or facts.
5. *Recommendations:* Provides a list of recommended courses of action. The recommendations must be realistic and consistent with the analysis of facts and data. Because the competence of report writers is often judged by this

INTEROFFICE MEMORANDUM

July 17, 1989

TO: David Smith, Vice-President

FROM: Dick Johnson, Assistant Vice-President

SUBJECT: Status Report on the Development of a Training Program

The following outlines the status of the development of the training program I have been working on for several months.

Introduction

The purpose of this research project is to determine the need for a training program in XYZ Corporation. The project, which is being undertaken by Beth Smith and me, is to be completed by January 1, 1990.

Summary of Progress Already Completed

The progress that has been reported up to this point includes the following:

1. Determination of objectives of the project.

2. Definition of parameters of the project.

3. Development of an appropriate research instrument (questionnaires and interviews).

Detailed Summary of Progress

Since the last progress report was prepared, the following have been completed:

1. Obtained approval of the questionnaire and interview record.

2. Pilot tested the questionnaire and interview record.

3. Determined method for selecting the respondents.

4. Selected the respondents.

Nature of Exceptional Progress

The project is six days behind schedule because of a strike at Johnson Printing, the company we have contracted with to print the questionnaires. The strike ended July 14, and we expect printed questionnaires this week.

Summary of Work Yet to be Completed

The following work remains to be done: distribution of questionnaires, completion of interviews, analysis of data, and preparation of the final report.

rt

Figure 12–6 Progress Report

section, the writer has to be especially careful in preparing the recommendations.

The staff report can be made more effective if the writer considers the reader's background and need for the report. In many cases, the manager will assign a subordinate the task of writing the report. A subordinate who is familiar with the reader is generally aware of the type of information the reader will need in order to assess the problem being studied or to make a decision concerning the problem.

An example of the staff report appears in Figure 12–7.

Feasibility Reports

What is the purpose of feasibility reports?

The primary purpose of these reports is to provide information about the feasibility of undertaking a particular course of action. Feasibility reports have a two-fold function: to provide information about whether the course of action is feasible, and if so, to present information about various alternatives for undertaking the course of action. In some instances, the course of action is designed to solve a problem; in other instances, the course of action is designed to improve a situation that is not necessarily problematic at the moment.

The credibility of the writers of feasibility reports is critical, especially when the reports are prepared by outsiders, such as consultants. Because the success of feasibility reports is directly related to the credibility of their writers, determining the credibility of employees who write these reports is less of a concern than when feasibility reports are prepared by outsiders.

What is the suggested plan for presenting feasibility reports?

Some of the sections that may be included in feasibility studies are the following:

1. *Identification of the nature of the situation (and a statement of the problem, if appropriate).* This section must be written with as much objectivity and clarity of thought as the writer can provide. When the writer allows his/her biases to contaminate the information in this section, much of the usefulness of the report is lost.

2. *Identification of the important characteristics that the writer feels should be met in improving the situation (or solving the problem).* When the important characteristics are identified and discussed, the reader can more easily assess the appropriateness of the various alternatives that are presented for improving the situation or solving the problem. In addition, the reader can determine whether or not the suggested alternatives are feasible in light of these characteristics.

3. *Identification and comparison of the various alternatives for improving the situation (or solving the problem).* This section provides a discussion of the various alternative solutions, in light of the characteristics presented in the second section. In addition, the alternatives are compared with one another in terms of their relative advantages and disadvantages.

4. *Identification of the recommended alternative.* Of the various alternatives presented in the third section, the one that appears to be most advantageous is the one that is usually recommended in this section. It is likely to be the one that has the greatest number of relative advantages and fewest relative disadvantages.

INTEROFFICE MEMORANDUM

October 17, 1990

TO: David Jones, President

FROM: Dan Brown, Vice-President

SUBJECT: Investigation of the Word Processing Center

Overview

A report on my investigation of the word processing center, which you requested on May 16, follows. This report includes a discussion of the facts of the investigation, conclusions, and recommendations.

Purpose

This study was undertaken because of apparent inefficient procedures being utilized in the word processing center. The result is skyrocketing costs for producing work, as well as poor production rates.

The primary objectives of this study were:

1. To identify the reasons for increasing costs.
2. To determine why the production rates in the word processing center have been decreasing.
3. To determine why the employees in the word processing center are not happy with their jobs.

The scope of this study is limited to the word processing center. Other office areas or procedures were not included in the investigation.

Discussion of Facts

One objective of this investigation was to determine why the costs of producing work are increasing so rapidly. The investigation revealed that the cost of supplies has increased by 32 percent during the last two years. Although we have no control over the increase, the employees in the word processing center might become more waste-conscious as a means of reducing the costs of supplies.

The cost of equipment maintenance has also increased because of rising costs as well as increased equipment malfunctions. One automatic typewriter in the word processing center that is only two years old has had a much higher breakdown record than any of the other typewriters.

Figure 12–7 Staff Report

2

We have also had an increase in employee salaries, which, of course, adds to the cost of the center's operations.

Another objective of this investigation was to determine why the production rates of the word processing center have been decreasing. The investigation revealed than an increasing number of the managers are using the word processing center for preparing more technical and statistical information than has been prepared in the past. Because of frequent changes in this material, which results in the retyping of much of the material, the production rate of the center has, understandably, decreased.

Production rates have also decreased because the word processing center has had difficulty hiring trained employees. The production rate cannot be optimized while new employees are being trained.

In addition, because of low morale among the employees in the word processing center, some of their work is of such poor quality that it has to be redone. This is one of the major reasons that the production rate in the word processing center is lower than it should be.

Conclusions

The following conclusions are based on the results of the investigation:

1. Definite problems exist within the word processing center. Some of these problems can be easily remedied whereas others are quite complex.

2. The word processing center concept is worthwhile; but as it exists in our organization, the center should be modified to become more efficient.

3. Because of the complexity of some of the problems in the word processing center, outside professional help is needed to solve the problems.

Recommendations

The following recommendations are offered:

1. That the structure of the word processing center be modified as quickly as possible.

2. That because of the magnitude of the job and expertise needed, outside consultants be hired.

dp

Figure 12–7 (cont.)

The feasibility study should enable the reader to answer several questions, such as:

1. Is this situation in need of improvement (or does this problem warrant a solution)?
2. Can this situation be improved (or this problem be solved)?
3. What alternatives are available for improving the situation (or solving the problem)?
4. What are the advantages and disadvantages of each of the identified alternatives?
5. What alternative appears to have the greatest amount of potential for improving the situation (or solving the problem)?

Each of the informal report formats discussed in an earlier part of this chapter can be used to present the feasibility report. The formal report format discussed in Chapter 13 should be used if a higher degree of formality is needed. The writer should use whichever format is most appropriate for the situation.

Figure 12–8 presents a feasibility report.

Audit Reports

For what are audit reports used?

Audit reports are used to provide information about an investigation into some phase of organizational operations. Perhaps the most familiar type of audit report is the one prepared annually by an accountant that provides information about the organization's financial condition. In addition to financial audit reports, other areas that may be investigated and reported upon are affirmative action, complex or extensive projects, quality of newly hired personnel, salary plans, and fringe benefits.

In some cases, audit reports will be prepared by employees. In other cases, such as financial audits, they must be prepared by outsiders. The two factors that will determine whether they are prepared by insiders or outsiders are: (1) legal requirements governing the preparer, and (2) level of expertise needed by the preparer. If none of the employees has the expertise needed to undertake the audit and prepare the report, an outsider most likely will need to be hired.

What is the suggested plan for presenting audit reports?

The sections that should be included in an audit report are:

1. *Introductory section* that contains a variety of information, including the need for the study, relevant background factors that pertain to the area being studied, and an overview of the review process.
2. *Body section* that presents the data that are gathered and subsequently evaluates the collected data.
3. *Closing section* that presents the conclusions based on the data that are collected and provides recommendations.

An example of an audit report is included in Figure 12–9.

INTEROFFICE MEMORANDUM

October 12, 1989

TO: Jack Adamson, Executive Vice-President

FROM: Darlene Jensen, Office Services Supervisor

SUBJECT: Installation of a New Word Processing System

On several occasions, we have discussed the desirability of installing a new word processing system to replace the six-year-old stand-alone word processing system we currently use. At the time the stand-alone system was installed, the equipment was state of the art.

In installing a new word processing system, the following identify the important characteristics that should be used in judging its desirability:

a. The system should be expandable. One of the concerns that I have had for several years is that we can no longer obtain equipment identical to our present stand-alone equipment. Since we have the need for additional workstations, a different brand of equipment will have to be purchased, which will destroy system compatibility if we continue to use the present stand-alone system.

b. The equipment should be integrated. An efficient word processing system is integrated, which means that various pieces of office equipment--such as desk-top computers, microcomputers, and terminals--are capable of being electronically attached to one another. Thus, each word processing station can also function in other ways--to prepare graphics, to maintain spreadsheets, etc.

c. The system should be capable of performing all word processing functions currently found. To purchase a system that cannot perform all functions is tantamount to purchasing a system that is several years old.

Among the alternatives available for installing a new word processing system are the following:

a. Replace the old stand-alone system with a new stand-alone system. While stand-alone systems can be expandable, they cannot be integrated. Stand-alone systems are capable of performing all word processing functions.

b. Replace the old stand-alone system with a new integrated system. These systems are expandable, they can be integrated with other devices, and they are capable of performing all word processing functions.

The recommended alternative is the installation of an integrated system since it possesses the essential characteristics that a new system should possess. The primary disadvantages of the integrated system are their cost and the installation time. Training time on both systems should be approximately equal.

Figure 12–8 Feasibility Report

INTEROFFICE MEMORANDUM

January 12, 1990

TO: David Wellman, Vice-President for Corporate Affairs

FROM: Sam Snead, Director of Personnel

SUBJECT: Fringe Benefits Program at Americo Company

Several weeks ago you asked that I provide you with some information about our fringe benefits program. Specifically, you wanted to know what percent of our total payroll is paid out for fringe benefits so you can determine the relative cost of our fringe benefits program.

After undertaking a fairly laborious search of the information related to this topic, I discovered that last year (the most recent year for which data are presently available), companies on the average spent 37.6 percent of their total payroll costs for the company-provided fringe benefits. This percentage is expected to increase by approximately 8 percent for this year. Last year, we spent 37.2 percent of our payroll costs on fringe benefits. The following statistics are available for the years 1984-1989:

Year	National Average	Our Average
1989	37.2	37.1
1988	37.1	37.0
1987	36.8	36.9
1986	36.3	36.5
1985	36.0	36.1
1984	35.8	35.7

I was unable to find separate statistics for the various categories (banking, wholesale, manufacturing, etc.). The composite information presented above was made available by the Colorado Clearing House. I have complete faith in the accuracy of the information that has been provided.

The information presented above provides rather conclusive evidence that our expenditures for fringe benefits are neither too high nor too low. Therefore, I recommend that we make no changes. In some years we are somewhat above the national average, while in other years we are a little below the national average. As long as we continue to pay out in fringe benefits an amount that approximates the national average over the long run, I recommend that we make no changes. On the other hand, if our average ever becomes significantly more or less than the national average, then I would recommend that we implement the necessary changes to assure the consistency of our fringe-benefit expenditures average with the national average.

jk

Figure 12–9 Audit Report

CHAPTER SUMMARY

Business reports are used extensively by managers as they carry out their assigned duties. They are used to support their decision-making and problem-solving efforts as well as to outline processes or procedures that individuals are expected to follow. Reports can also create good will for the organization.

Business reports are often classified as either informal or formal. Both classifications are distinctly different. Informal reports are now used more commonly than formal reports.

Many different informal reports are used, including memorandum, letter, short, justification, periodic, progress, staff, feasibility, and audit. Each has specific purposes and uses of which you should be aware.

REVIEW QUESTIONS

1. Identify the important functions of reports used in the business world.
2. What types of informal reports are frequently used in the business world?
3. Why are memorandum reports considered to be informal?
4. What is the typical destination of a memorandum report? A letter report?
5. How do short reports and formal reports differ?
6. How does the direct plan differ from the indirect plan in presenting information in a short report?
7. What is the primary purpose of justification reports?
8. For what is a periodic report typically used?
9. For what is a progress report typically used?
10. What content sections are often found in staff reports?
11. For what is a feasibility report typically used?
12. For what is an audit report typically used?

APPLICATION PROBLEMS

1. You work in the office services department of Browning Corporation, a manufacturer of fishing gear. You are responsible each month for preparing a memo for your supervisor (Mr. Jack Green, manager of office services) in which you present the number of copies run through each of the company's copy machines. The following is that information: Copy machine No. 1 (Executive Suite), 4,890 copies; Copy machine No. 2 (Computer Room), 5,987; Copy machine No. 3 (Word Processing Center), 8,804; Copy machine No. 4 (Duplicating Room), 12,874; Copy machine No. 5 (Mail Room), 2,876. Prepare the memo report in which you clearly present this information to Mr. Green.

2. You are the manager of training in the Browning Corporation. You recently got permission from your boss, Ms. Susan Findley, executive vice-president, to survey Browning's employees to determine the topics they wish to have covered during the next year's Noon Seminar Series. These noon seminars have been offered now for four years—and each year they have become more popular. The seminars last for one hour—12–1—and the employees eat their lunch during the presentation. The speakers are to allow a 20-minute question-answer period at the end of their presentation. The seminars are scheduled for the first Wednesday of each month. Of the 310 questionnaires you distributed, 278 were returned. This high return rate reflects positively on the employees'

enthusiasm for the seminars. The 12 topics on the list that received the greatest number of first-place votes include the following: Wills and trusts, 98; Creative financing of mortgages, 89; Home security, 84; Improving your personality, 80; Time management, 78; Planning for retirement, 71; Investing wisely, 65; Rights of the consumer, 60; Planning the ideal vacation, 58; Getting in shape by exercising, 55; Home computers, 50; CPR, 45. Prepare a memo report to send to Ms. Findley in which this information is presented. You might also indicate that you just calculated the average attendance of last year's seminars. On the average, 97.3 persons attended each seminar. The seminar with the greatest attendance was concerned with the stock market (143 in attendance), and the seminar with the smallest attendance was the one that pertained to pet care (78).

3. You, the manager of office support in Dickinson Corporation, which is located at 8447 Middle Belt Road, Wichita, KS 54419, recently received a letter from Dr. John Harlow, professor of office management, Midwest State University, Topeka, KS 54432. Dr. Harlow indicated that he is undertaking an informal research study to determine the number of desk-top computers found on employees' desks in Dickinson, the brands of equipment found, and the different applications these computers are used for. Dr. Harlow also indicated that after he receives this information from Dickinson and several other companies, he may prepare a formal research study that will be sent to a far larger number of people. Prepare a letter in which you provide Dr. Harlow with the following information: Of the 459 white-collar employees who presently work for Dickinson, 289 now have computers on their desks. The various brands of equipment found, in rank order, are the following: IBC, AT & S; Oranges, Ebsom, Zenia, and Tampa. The applications these computers are used for include: word processing, desk management, file management, spread sheet, data base, and graphics preparation. Indicate that the company plans to purchase an additional 25–30 desk-top computers each year until all employees who can justify the use of a computer have access to a computer on their desk. Also indicate that the company is looking at standardizing computer purchases because eventually they may need to be capable of interacting with one another should the company move towards office automation. Prepare a letter report in which you provide this information.

4. You are president of the college chapter of the American Marketing Society. You recently received a letter from the national president, Wade Thurston, 4543 Midville Road, Midville, OH 48455, in which he requested information about various aspects of last year's chapter activities. He wanted to know the topics of the monthly meetings, the speaker's name, and the number of members and nonmembers who attended. He also wanted to know what kinds of fund-raising projects your chapter sponsored, as well as the amount of money each netted. Finally, he wanted to know what types of member recruitment activities the chapter held. The following summarizes the information he requested: September—The Proctor-Smith Story, John Bennett, 48 members/5 nonmembers; October—Successful Marketing Surveys, Theresa Blackstown, 50/10; November—Creative Selling, Tim Riley, 45/7; December—A Marketing Career in Federal Department Stores, 45/3; January—How to Sell Yourself in the Employment Interview, Don Smith, 56/12; February—Field trip through Brown Advertising Agency, 31/14; March—A Career in Marketing Research, Janet Cole, 51/5; April—Spring Banquet, 54/20; May—Success: How is it Measured? Jack Green, 56/5. Three fund-raising projects were held: Used-book sale, netted $367.44; college calendars, $183.23; stadium cushions, $311.22. To recruit new members, the following activities were held: a get-acquainted social and a picnic. Prepare a letter report in which you provide the information Mr. Wade Thurston requested.

5. You are the assistant manager of Watson Men's Dormitory on the Southwest State College campus. The dormitory council requested several weeks ago that a questionnaire be developed to assess the residents' satisfaction with a variety of factors, including room/dormitory maintenance, food service, dormitory activities, and overall quality of life. The following summarizes the data which were collected from the 150 questionnaires that were returned (200 were distributed).

a. How satisfied are you with the quality of the maintenance in the rooms and throughout the dormitory as a whole?

Room: Very satisfied—32; Quite satisfied—38; Satisfied—50;
Somewhat dissatisfied—20; Very dissatisfied—10

If you answered "somewhat dissatisifed" or "very dissatisfied," please identify your reasons: Rooms need to be painted more often—15; Hallways are often dirty—10; Hallways need to be painted—5

Dormitory: Very satisfied—25; Quite satisfied—50; Satisfied—40;
Somewhat dissatisfied—20; Very dissatisfied—15

If you answered "somewhat dissatisfied" or "very dissatisfied," please identify your reasons: Lobby area is often strewn with trash—10; Laundry room is often cluttered with trash and unclaimed clothing—15; Study rooms are often cluttered with cups, candy wrappers, etc.—10

b. How satisfied are you with the quality of the food service?

Very satisfied—24; Quite satisfied—36; Satisfied—48;
Quite dissatisfied—32; Dissatisfied—10

If you answered "somewhat dissatisfied" or "very dissatisfied," please identify your reasons: Lack of variety in menu—23; Taste of food—10; Noise in dining room—5; Food lacks eye appeal—4

c. What suggestions do you have for improving the quality of the food service: Offer greater variety in menus—58; Offer greater number of choices at evening meal—48; Have a greater number of special or theme dinners—32; Let students work with food service in planning menus—12

d. How satisfied are you with the quality of dormitory activities?

Very satisfied—47; Quite satisfied—53; Satisfied—30;
Quite dissatisfied—10; Very dissatisfied—10

If you answered "somewhat dissatisfied" or "very dissatisfied," please identify your reasons: Not enough organized sports programs—8; Not enough social activities—7; Not enough cultural activities—5

e. How would rate the overall quality of life in Watson?

Very adequate—55; Quite adequate—65; Adequate— 20;
Somewhat inadequate—10; Very inadequate—0

If you answered "somewhat inadequate" or "very inadequate," please list your ideas for improving the quality of life: Need a "24-hour-a-day quiet floor" for the serious students—6; Need a snack bar—4

Prepare a short report in which you discuss these findings. Submit the report to your boss, Calvin Key, the manager of Watson Dormitory.

6. You have been asked by the director of the Cultural Arts Program of Midwest College to collect a variety of data that she and her advisory committee can use as input in planning next year's cultural activities. The reason Ms. Laura Smith, the director of the CAP, desires this information is that she noticed the number of students attending these programs has diminished over the last few years. Therefore, she is concerned that perhaps events programmed in the last few years have not met their needs. The following summarizes the information you collected from 100 students whom you interviewed about their CAP experiences last year:

a. Year in School: Senior—22; Junior—25; Sophomore—28; Freshman—25

b. Major: Undeclared—15; Business—18; Arts and Letters—22; Physical Science—18; Education—17; Agriculture—10

c. Of the Cultural Arts Programs held last year, how many did you attend? None—27; 1—28; 2—15; 3—11; 4—10; 5—9

d. Did you have a CAP season ticket last year? Yes—34; No—66

If you answered "yes," what caused you to want to purchase a season ticket? Breadth of programs—10; quality of programs—8; interest in any cultural event—8; interest in becoming more "worldly" through attending cultural events—8

If you answered "no," what caused you to not want to purchase a season ticket? CAP events conflicted with work/class schedule—27; Not interested in majority of CAP events—23; Cannot afford price of CAP season ticket—10; Have other extenuating commitments—6

e. What would you like to see included in CAP programming that was not included during the last year? Scheduling of more pop-music groups—29; Scheduling of more rock-music groups—25; Scheduling of more operatic groups/individuals—21; Scheduling of more ballet groups—18; Have no complaints about programming—7

f. How do you feel about the pricing of the CAP events? Too costly—43; Moderately costly—23; Priced fairly—18; The CAP is a bargain—16

g. Would you be willing to pay more for CAP if the quality of programming improved as a result? Yes—34; No—66

Prepare for Ms. Laura Smith a short report that contains the data presented above.

7. You work for Allied Distribution Corporation, a company that is vitally concerned about the welfare of its employees. On numerous occasions, suggestions made by employees have been implemented by management. Because management is receptive to receiving suggestions, you decided to prepare a report for Ms. Grayson Hunter, executive vice-president, in which you outline the desirability of a flexible benefits package, sometimes called a ''cafeteria approach'' to fringe benefits. When a flexible benefits plan is used, each employee is given a specified dollar allocation that can be used to purchase the type of fringe benefits that best meets individual needs. This plan is especially attractive to employees whose spouse also has a good benefits package. To illustrate, assume that all members of a family have medical insurance coverage paid for by the employer of the one of the family members. Therefore, an Allied employee who also has medical insurance coverage provided as a fringe benefit may wish to allocate the dollars for medical insurance coverage to another fringe benefit, such as increased life insurance. As a result, employees whose spouse has fringe benefits provided by another employer do not end up with duplicate benefits that may not provide them with the best use of their fringe benefits investment. The companies that offer fringe benefits typically hire the services of a consulting firm to develop the program. Once the plan is in effect, employees should be given several weeks in which to make their decisions about the benefits in which to enroll. After employees enroll in certain benefits, they should be able to make changes on a regular basis—perhaps every six months. Before any final decisions are made about which benefits to offer, the employees should be surveyed to determine which benefits they would like to have available. An advisory committee made up of various categories of employees should be involved in the development process. Among the advantages of the flexible benefits package are the following: employees can tailor their fringe benefits package to meet their individual needs; employees can allocate their fringe benefit dollars where the most good will be accomplished; the actual cost of fringe benefits may decrease over time because employees are able to choose the benefits they most want, eliminating those that are not desired. Present the justification report in memo format.

8. You work for the Zee-Mart Corporation. You, along with several of your co-workers, belong to the local Administrative Management Club. At a recent meeting you heard the guest speaker, Mr. John Grantham, explain in detail the quality-circle concept. You and those you work with who attended the meeting believe that the quality-circle concept has enough merit to suggest the development of such a program at Zee-Mart. Accordingly, you decide to prepare a report that will be sent to Mr. Adam Whiteburg, the company's president, in which you recommend the development of the program. The quality-circle concept, which has enjoyed enormous success in Japanese companies, functions through the voluntary participation of employees in various work units. The members of the various quality-circle groups meet on a regular basis for the purpose of devising ways to overcome problems they experience in their jobs. In some cases, outsiders are brought in to help solve the problem. The supervisor normally serves as the leader of the quality-circle group. The program begins functioning by training supervisors to become leaders of their groups. Then the groups are formed and begin operating. The meetings are held during the work day. One hour per week might be allocated for the quality-circle group meetings. Because the suggestions for overcoming or solving the problems brought before the various groups come from the employees themselves, the suggestions are often very workable and are typically readily accepted by the employees. In companies that begin such programs, Mr. Whiteburg suggested that an employee be given the responsibility for organizing and developing the concept. He also recommended the appointment of a committee responsible for providing advice to the person who is organizing and developing the concept. Too, he mentioned that the typical quality-circle program is very cost effective because the savings resulting from solving work-related problems exceed the expense incurred by giving employees company time for their meetings. Present the justification report in memo format.

9. You are the assistant to Ms. Janet Miller, vice-president for production at Grant Computer Company, a manufacturer of components used in desk-top computers. Ms. Miller is quite involved in a number of professional associations. She serves as treasurer of the local chapter of Administrative Marketing Society. One of her responsibilities as treasurer is to present an updated budget at each of the monthly meetings of the Society's executive board. She has asked you to prepare an updated budget for the June board meeting. The figures presented below were prepared for May's budget presentation:

	Monthly Expenditure	*Year-to-Date*	*Balance*
Membership	$63.54	$129.69	$298.88
Publicity	14.98	87.87	112.89
New-Member Orientation	23.85	23.85	76.75
Newsletter	9.88	45.87	87.12
Postage	4.88	18.82	64.10
Supplies	00.00	54.12	94.32
Board Meeting Expenses	43.89	129.09	420.80
Speaker Recognition	8.98	35.92	103.32
Spring Banquet	00.00	00.00	150.00

Prepare a report, using the memo format, in which Ms. Miller presents the current budget that incorporates the changes resulting from the following expenditures during this month: Membership, $34.23; Publicity, $12.87; New-Member Orientation, 00.00; Newsletter, $10.83; Postage, $1.87; Supplies, 00.00; Board Meeting Expenses, $39.43; Speaker Recognition, $8.98; Spring Banquet, $34.40. By the way, you need to remember that the "Year-to-Date" column does not include expenses for the current month; rather, it summarizes data from January through the last month.

10. You, as the administrative assistant for Ms. Janet Miller, (see application problem 9) also prepare the bank reconciliation that Ms. Miller presents to the executive board each month. The following represents last month's bank reconciliation:

Bank balance on this month's statement	$1810.87
Add deposits not credited	348.81
Sub Total	$2159.68
Less outstanding checks	20.41
No. 745—$7.78	
No. 747—$3.89	
No. 750—$8.74	
Balance of bank account and checkbook	$2139.27

This month ended with a bank balance of $1790.02, all deposits have been credited, and three checks are outstanding: No. 767—$8.98, No. 768—$4.88, and No. 770—$7.34. The checkbook shows a balance of $1768.82. Prepare the bank reconciliation report that Ms. Miller will present to the executive board.

11. You are director of personnel for the Rambo Insurance Company, which is located in Detroit. You have noticed that during the summer months—especially during July and August—many employees begin to slow down on their jobs around 3:30 to 4 each afternoon. Part of the slowdown can be attributed to having less work to do during these two months—and part, you surmise, can be attributed to the fact that employees are tired and are anxious to leave. You have also noticed that employee socializing has increased during the slack period. You have observed that the slow-down phenomenon has had a negative impact on the employees' attitudes. You are willing to present to the executive committee a plan in which one-fifth of the employees would get to leave at 4 p.m. each day. During a week's time, all employees would get off an hour early. You estimate that the cost of this would be $498.87 per week, a figure that is based on the average hourly salary for all employees in the company. Actually, the cost would be considerably less since most employees are likely to be less productive that last hour regardless of the amount of work they have to do. When you mentioned your desire to investigate the leave-early plan to Mr. Grant Becker, executive vice-president of Rambo, he suggested that you prepare a staff report in which your ideas are presented. He will take the report to the executive committee. Present the report in memo format.

12. You are an assistant to the vice president for corporate affairs of Blackburn Corporation, Mr. David Thoreau. You were asked by Mr. Thoreau several weeks ago to prepare a staff report for him that he could use to provide support for the need to develop a training program in Blackburn. Over the years, the installation of a training program has been discussed, but nothing has ever come of the discussions. Mr. Thoreau believes that the need for a training program has never been greater. While some informal training does take place in some of the individual work units, a formal program has never been developed. You believe that the best support you could obtain that would provide evidence of the need for a training program would be to survey the employees themselves. Accordingly, you conducted an informal survey that helped you gather a variety of information. The following outlines this information: while 74 percent of the employees favored having the benefit of a training program, 87 percent of the managers support the development of a training program. The managers claimed that their jobs would be made much easier if employees had access to an effective training program. The areas identified by employees as those in which they would appreciate more training include the following: effective communications, office automation, microcomputers, policies and procedures, and time management. The employees listed the following as reasons for desiring a training program: they would be able to perform more effectively, their production levels would increase, the quality of their performance evaluations would improve, their promotability to higher-level jobs would increase, and their job satisfaction would improve. The managers cited the following as reasons for installing a training program: the managers' jobs would be made much easier because they would not have to spend as much time helping subordinates, and the subordinates would become more productive. Prepare the staff report and present it in memo format.

13. You are the administrative assistant to Mr. John Davidson, executive vice-president of Smith-Harold Corporation, which is located in Memphis, Tennessee. Several employees have suggested to Mr. Davidson that the company install an in-house travel agency because of the number of employees who travel and because of the amount they travel. Accordingly, Mr. Davidson asked you to undertake the project. In collecting the data, you decided to contact several other companies that have an in-house travel agency. In each case you were told that in-house agencies are cost effective when the company spends $50,000 or more per year on travel. Last year's travel expenditures for Smith-Harold were $37,874. The expenses seem to be running about the same for this year. You were repeatedly told by the companies, that have in-house agencies, that cost effectiveness is critical. You were also told that unless the agency can be a full-service agency, employees will not use the services enough to justify installing such an agency. Those that offer limited services will not be used by employees because they appreciate the convenience of comprehensive one-stop service. In addition, you were told that the agency has to be capable of doing more for the employees than the community's agencies presently do. Unless these conditions can be met, the installation of an in-house agency is most likely not feasible financially. As you see it, the company has several alternatives: do nothing, deal exclusively with one of the full-service agencies, install a very limited in-house agency primarily for making plane reservations and use exclusively an outside agency for all other services, or install a full-service agency. Of the alternatives, the one that seems to be most feasible at this point is to deal exclusively with one outside agency. Prepare an appropriate feasibility report, using the memo format.

14. You are the personnel manager of Abbott Corporation. At several recent executive committee meetings, some of the vice-presidents have expressed concern about the apparent decline in the quality of employees the company has been hiring. This disturbs them very much as the company has always prided itself on the quality of its employees. Among the complaints heard about the newly hired employees are the following: employee skill levels are not as good as they used to be, employees' attitudes are not as positive as they used to be, employees' tardiness and absenteeism rates are on the increase, and employee turnover is up. The vice-presidents have asked you to prepare for them an audit report that they will use in making decisions about this situation. You decided to collect a variety of information before you began writing the report. Among your findings are the following: employee skill levels are decreasing throughout the nation (article that appeared in the August 12 issue of *The Wall Street News;* employees are not as loyal as they used to be, and this is reflected in their attitudes (article that appeared in July issue of *Psychology News*); across the country, employee absenteeism, tardiness, and turnover rates are higher now than they were as recently as three years ago (article that appeared in the *Houston Post*). After collecting this information, you conclude that the problem of concern to the vice-presidents is not unique to your company—that the problem exists nationwide. This evidence makes you feel a little better about the situation. Obviously, you would like to be the exception rather than the rule. You also conclude that the problem began about three years ago when your company first started feeling a financial pinch and it could no longer afford to pay the top-level salaries that it had in the past. You believe that the company is getting just about the type of employee that it is paying for. Prepare the audit report, and present it in memo format.

Chapter 13

Preparing Formal Reports: Prewriting Phase

LEARNING OBJECTIVES

After studying this chapter, you should be able to

1. Explain how the report problem is determined, how the reader is identified, and how the report topic is limited.
2. Develop effective preliminary outlines of a formal report.
3. Explain how you determine the appropriate method for collecting the information for a report.
4. Discuss the various primary and secondary research methods.
5. Explain how the data are categorized, tabulated, and interpreted.
6. Discuss why objectivity is needed in report writing.

A number of the activities involved in preparing a formal report must be completed before beginning the actual writing process. Exercising care in undertaking each activity of the prewriting phase will ease the completion of the writing phase.

The majority of the activities in the prewriting phase need to be completed in sequence. For example, before you can begin collecting data or gathering information for the report, the report problem and the report purpose should be determined.

What steps does the report writer normally complete when writing formal reports?

To prepare a formal report, a report writer normally needs to

1. Determine the report problem (and purpose, if appropriate)
2. Identify the reader(s)

3. Limit the topic of the report
4. Develop a preliminary outline of the report
5. Determine appropriate method—primary or secondary—of collecting data/information
6. Collect data/information
7. Classify and tabulate data/information (if appropriate)
8. Interpret the data/information
9. Write the report

The purpose of this chapter is to provide information about the prewriting phase of report preparation. Chapter 14 provides information about the writing phase and includes a discussion of the various parts that are included in a formal report. Also included in Chapter 14 is a discussion of the different types of graphic illustrations often included in formal reports.

When the report writer fails to exercise care in the prewriting phase, faulty interpretation of data can invalidate the research results discussed in the report. Furthermore, failure to identify correctly the intended readership of the report may result in the use of a writing style inappropriate for the report reader or the failure to include needed background information to assure reader understanding.

Several steps are required in the prewriting phase of a formal report. Depending on the complexity and length of the report, several of these steps can be completed rather quickly. The report writer should complete the steps in approximately the same sequence as they are presented in this chapter.

DETERMINING THE REPORT PROBLEM

The first step in the prewriting phase is to determine and analyze the report problem. If you receive authorization to prepare the report in either a memorandum or a letter, the person who makes the authorization often identifies the report problem. The *report problem* identifies the reason or reasons for the preparation of the report. The problem should be stated as specifically, clearly, and succinctly as possible.

What is the difference between the report problem and the purpose?

In some cases, you may choose to let the report problem stand alone, while in other cases, the problem is combined with the *report purpose*. The purpose identifies the benefits to be realized by solving the problem. Stated another way, the report problem provides the basis for the purpose.

What three formats are used to present the report problem and purpose?

The problem and purpose of the report can be presented in three different ways: in a statement, in a question, or in an infinitive phrase. In each of the following examples, the problem is presented in italics while the purpose is presented in boldface.

Statement

1. The *causes of low employee productivity will be examined* as a means of **increasing the profitability of ABC Corporation.**
2. The *feasibility of installing a word processing system will be investigated* as a means of **reducing operating costs of XYZ Corporation.**

Question

1. Will examining the *causes of low employee productivity* help ABC Corporation **increase its profitability?**
2. Will the *installation of a word processing system* help **reduce the operating costs of XYZ Corporation?**

Infinitive Phrase

1. To identify the *causes of low employee productivity* in order to **increase the profitability of ABC Corporation.**
2. To investigate the *feasibility of installing a word processing system* in order to **reduce the operating costs of XYZ Corporation.**

To illustrate the difference between the report problem and purpose, in the first example, low employee productivity (reason for preparing the report) is the problem, while the purpose involves determining ways to increase the firm's profitability (benefits to be realized by solving the problem). In the second example, investigating the feasibility of installing a word processing system is the problem (reason for preparing the report), while the purpose involves reducing operating costs (benefit to be realized).

Not all formal reports are designed to provide information for solving a problem. A different approach is sometimes used when the primary reason for preparing a report is simply to present information. Although the problem needs to be stated, the purpose does not have to be included in such reports. For example, assume that a report is to be prepared to present information about a new product. In this case, the problem of the report might be stated in the following way: "The reason for preparing this report is to present information about Product A."

You should guard against working with report problems that are not specifically or clearly worded. You will most likely have considerable difficulty providing recommendations for solving problems when the nature of the problem has not been made clear. If you receive authorization to prepare a report, but are unclear about the nature of the problem to be pursued, you are advised to prepare a more specific statement of the problem and then ask the person who originally authorized the report to approve the revised wording of the problem.

What suggestions are useful in formulating the report problem?

Some suggestions for helping you formulate the report problem are the following:

1. *Review and analyze all available information.* If the authorization is in writing, the written authorization should be reviewed and analyzed. If you receive an oral authorization, the problem may need to be discussed thoroughly with the individual who made the authorization.

2. *Conduct a preliminary investigation.* When a review and analysis of available information is not sufficient, you need to conduct a preliminary investigation prior to formulating the report problem. The preliminary investigation may consist of one or more of the following: research of secondary sources or library materials, investigation of pertinent organizational records, and/or dis-

cussion with individuals who are closely associated with the nature of the problem being studied.

3. *Obtain approval of the statement of problem.* If you are responsible for formulating the report problem, a considerable amount of time, effort, and money can be saved by asking the individual who authorized the preparation of the report to examine your statement. Ambiguities and omissions may be corrected before the actual research efforts get under way. If the report problem is clearly and specifically stated in the authorizing document, this should not be necessary.

What are the factors of the report problem?

After the report problem has been clearly worded, you should identify the *factors* that have a significant impact on the report problem. In reports that are primarily problem solving in nature, the factors are the causes of the problem. If the report is primarily informational, the factors are the areas to be investigated.

To illustrate the factors of a problem-solving report, consider again the following statement.

> The reason for preparing this report is to identify the causes of low employee productivity in order to increase the profitability of ABC Corporation.

The factors involved in this illustration are the causes of the problem, which may include poorly trained employees, low employee morale, inefficient work procedures, or lack of adequate equipment or materials.

Now consider the following statement.

> The feasibility of installing a word processing system will be investigated as a means of reducing operating costs of XYZ Corporation.

The factors involved in this situation may include the following areas that will be investigated: actual per-unit cost of document preparation using present procedures, anticipated per-unit cost of document preparation using word processing, acceptability of word processing to employees, impact of word processing on reducing turnaround-time of document preparation, and impact of word processing on the quality and efficiency of the document-preparation process.

In an informational report that is prepared to "present information about Product A," the following factors may be identified and investigated: specifications of the product, characteristics of the product, processes used in manufacturing the product, uses of the product, and servicing requirements of the product.

IDENTIFYING THE READER(S)

To prepare an effective formal report, you must identify the individual or individuals who will read the report. Failure to gear the report to the reader can significantly reduce the report's effectiveness. Although in most cases the reader will be the individual who authorized the preparation of the report, it may also be transmitted later to other individuals for their reading.

Why should you identify report readership during the prewriting phase?

The important reasons you should identify the readership during the prewriting phase are:

1. By knowing who will read the report, you can provide sufficient background information. Without knowing the report reader, you risk presenting either too much or too little background information.
2. To have its greatest impact, the report should be written in a style and at a level that takes into consideration the readers' capabilities. Writing at too high a level prevents the reader from fully understanding the content of the report, and too low a level results in uninteresting reading. Using jargon, technical language, or terms that the reader will not understand can also significantly reduce the report's effectiveness.
3. By knowing who the report reader will be, you are likely to be familiar with the uses of the information presented in the report. You should be able to provide the reader with information needed to make full use of the report.

LIMITING THE TOPIC OF THE REPORT

Another step in the prewriting phase of the preparation of a formal report involves the report topic. The factors of the problem discussed earlier in this chapter will be helpful in determining the boundaries of the report by specifying what will be included and what will not be included. Some people refer to this activity as determining the scope of the report.

How can you limit the report topics?

Report topics can be limited in several ways:

1. By functional area (marketing, sales, production)
2. By time (1950–1960, 1960–1970, 1970–1980)
3. By geographical region or area (South, Northwest, Central)
4. By product (chemicals, rubber, wood)
5. By problem (lack of communication, decreased production, increased costs)
6. By characteristics (size, specifications, uses)

In most cases, when the limits of the topic of the report are broad, coverage will be broad. On the other hand, when the topic is more narrow, coverage will be more detailed.

DEVELOPING A PRELIMINARY OUTLINE OF THE REPORT

The next activity in the prewriting phase of report preparation is developing a preliminary outline. Outline development can be simplified considerably when you consider each activity that has taken place up to this point: (1) defining the report problem and purpose, (2) determining the readership, and (3) setting the topic limits.

Without an outline, you may have the tendency to develop the report illogically, to ''wander'' in discussing the important facts, and to exclude important information while including irrelevant or unimportant information.

The preliminary outline is used to guide the information/data collection process. It will identify the topics you plan to investigate. Preliminary outlines are often developed using the topic format shown later in this section. After the information/data are collected, you may find making another outline, which is called the final outline, helpful. The final outline, by identifying the sequence of topics for the final report, is used as the "map" that will be followed in getting to your destination. Many writers prefer to use the discussion format, also presented later in this section, in developing the final outline. In some cases, the sentences that are used in developing the outline can be used as the topic sentences in the paragraphs contained in the report.

For what is the preliminary outline used?

Organizational Arrangements

The three organizational arrangements used in preparing reports are inductive, deductive, and chronological. Each arrangement is appropriately used under certain circumstances. To determine which arrangement to use, take into consideration the nature of the situation.

What three organizational arrangements are used in preparing formal reports, and how do they differ from one another?

When the inductive arrangement is used, the report moves from the known to the unknown or from the specific to the general. Introductory information is presented first, followed by the facts that have been obtained through research. Presentation of the facts is followed by the analysis of the facts. The unknown, which consists of the summary, conclusions, and recommendations, is then presented. Most formal reports utilize the inductive arrangement.

The deductive arrangement goes from the unknown to the known or from the general to the specific, which means that the summary, conclusions, and recommendations are presented first, followed by facts and analysis of the facts. The deductive arrangement is useful for readers who are concerned primarily about the summary, conclusions, and recommendations. Readers may use the facts and the analysis of facts only if more information is needed than is contained in the summary, conclusions, and recommendations.

The third arrangement for organizing the report puts the information in chronological order, which means that the facts and findings are presented in the order in which they happened or will happen in relation to time. Several different chronological sequences are available: past to present, present to past, and present to future.

Both the inductive and the deductive arrangements may be used within the chronological organizational plan. Summary, conclusions, and recommendations are at the beginning or end of the report, depending on whether the inductive or deductive plan is used, and the findings are arranged chronologically. The chronological arrangement is best suited for reports having historical or time significance.

Outline Notation

Outline development requires the use of some form of symbolic notation. The most common type of notation uses Roman and Arabic numerals as well as letters of the alphabet.

I. XXXXXXXXXX
    A. XXXXXXXXXX
    B. XXXXXXXXXX
        1. XXXXXXXXXX
            a. XXXXXXXXXX
            b. XXXXXXXXXX
                (1) XXXXXXXXXX
                (2) XXXXXXXXXX
                    (a) XXXXXXXXXX
                    (b) XXXXXXXXXX
        2. XXXXXXXXXX
II. XXXXXXXXXX

The second type of symbolic notation, which is increaasing in popularity, replaces Roman and Arabic numerals with numbers and decimals. Major sections of the report are identified with decimals.

1. First degree
    1.1 Second degree
    1.2 Second degree
        1.21. Third degree
        1.22. Third degree
            1.221. Fourth degree
            1.222. Fourth degree
                1.2221. Fifth degree
2. First degree (second major division)

The preliminary outline, after you have made any necessary adjustments based on your data/information findings, will greatly assist you in preparing the report's headings and subheadings. The information contained in the updated preliminary outline can also be useful when preparing the table of contents. Suggestions for preparing headings and table of contents are presented in Chapter 14.

Report writers must determine an appropriate division for the information presented in the body of the report; the discussion depends on the nature and intended use of the information. Types of divisions that can be used in breaking down the information are: chronological or time element, geographical area, important factors, characteristics, and quantity elements.

To illustrate, consider a formal report designed to present information about the potential customer of a new typewriter. The most appropriate division for breaking down the information would be by characteristics of the potential consumer—such as buying habits, household income levels, and educational attainment of heads of households. A faulty division would result if the information were divided by geographical location of potential consumers or by a time element, for example. Neither of the latter two divisions is logical in this situation.

Using characteristics of the potential consumer to break down the information might result in the following subdivisions:

Buying habits:

1. Utilization of the comparative shopping technique
2. Utilization of performance ratings of comparable products
3. Utilization of store sales, etc.

Income levels of households:

1. $8,000 or less per year
2. $8,001 to $10,000 per year
3. $10,001 to $12,000 per year, etc.

Educational attainment of heads of households:

1. 11 years of schooling
2. 12 years of schooling
3. 13 years of schooling, etc.

This example illustrates the use of parallelism in constructing an outline. The wording of each subdivision under each major division is parallel. An example of faulty parallelism would be to have "Taking advantage of store sales" as a subdivision under "Buying habits."

Wording

You have two options in selecting the wording of the divisions and subdivisions on the preliminary outline. These options include the topic format and the discussion format. Topic format uses one or two words to identify a division or subdivision. The discussion format, on the other hand, provides information about the division or subdivision. While the topic format is often used in preparing the preliminary outline prior to collecting the information/data, the discussion format is used in preparing the final outline after the information/data are collected. Both formats are shown below.

How do the two outline wording options differ from one another?

Topic:
I. Introduction
   A. Background
   B. Purpose
   C. Scope, etc.
II. Characteristics of the Potential Consumer
   A. Buying habits
   B. Income level of households
   C. Educational attainment of heads of households, etc.

Discussion: I. Introduction to the Report
A. Report authorized by Jack Adams in September 1989
B. Purpose of the report is to study potential consumers of Acron Typewriter III
C. Scope of the report is limited to the study of potential consumers of Acron Typewriter III
II. Characteristics of Potential Consumer are Varied
A. Buying habits of potential consumer are different from habits of consumers of competing products
B. Income levels of households of potential consumers are below national average of $14,267
C. Educational attainment of heads of households of potential consumer is less than 13 years

Although the discussion format tells a more complete story about the report than the topic format, its use requires the rewording of the headings and subheadings in the text of the report and in the table of contents. Many readers prefer the discussion format because it provides a good preview of what will be found in the report text.

Determining Appropriate Method of Collecting Information

What factors should be considered in determining the appropriate method for collecting information?

The ultimate value of a formal report is greatly dependent upon the appropriateness of the information that is presented. The various methods of collecting information are not equally suited for all situations. To determine the appropriate method for collecting the information, the report writer should consider:

1. The intended use of the report
2. The nature of the topic of the report
3. The availability of information
4. The financial and time constraints for completing the report
5. The ability of the report reader to understand the research methodology
6. The ability of the report writer to use the various methods of collecting information

How do primary and secondary research methods differ from one another?

Information-collection methods can be categorized as either primary or secondary research methods. Primary research methods consist of those used to collect data or information directly through such techniques as questionnaires, and interviews. Secondary research methods involve collecting information using printed sources of information, such as books or periodicals.

Primary Research Methods

Primary research methods you can use are company records, observation, questioning people, questionnaires, interviews, and experimentation. In most instances, the use of a primary research method will require the categorization, tabulation, and interpretation of data before the actual writing process begins. Each of these steps is discussed in subsequent sections of this chapter.

Use of company records

Company records are especially suited for collecting information for use in formal reports dealing with the various operations of an organization. In fact, you would probably be unable to obtain the needed information from any other source.

Use of company records frequently involves financial and statistical information, which can be easily misinterpreted unless extreme care is exercised. You should work closely with those employees who are familiar with financial and statistical information. If you are unfamiliar with the information but try to interpret and analyze it, misinterpretation may result. When company records are the major source of information for formal reports, their information frequently has to be adapted to fit the needs of the situation. For example, if the information is primarily financial in nature, additional calculations may have to be made before the data are appropriate for the situation.

Observation

For what situations is the observation technique especially suited?

Another method used to collect information involves observing a certain occurrence or occurrences and subsequently recording what is observed. The observation method is especially suited for situations in which the number of occurrences of a certain phenomenon is important for the report problem. In some instances, the only way to determine the number of occurrences is to observe and record them as they take place.

To illustrate a situation in which the observation method is appropriate, assume that a clothing manufacturer wishes to determine the popularity of six new spring colors. One way to assess the popularity is to determine the number of times each of the six colors is seen in a garment within a given time period. An assumption is made that the more frequently the color is seen, the more popular the color is. The researcher has to devise a method, perhaps a log, for recording the number of times a garment in each of the colors is seen being worn by a person.

Questioning people

Another method for collecting information involves questioning people. Because some research projects involve a large number of people, the inclusion of data provided by each person is not always feasible. In an election year, for example, media personnel frequently conduct surveys to determine which candidates are most likely to win the election. Because questioning all voters is not feasible, a portion—called a sample—of the voting population is used.

The theory of sampling is formulated on the assumption that if a sufficiently large number of items are randomly selected from the whole or total, the sample will possess the same characteristics as those which constitute the whole. In the illustration cited above, if a sufficiently large number of voters are selected randomly from the lot or universe of all qualified voters, the voting sample will have the same election preferences that the total voting population has. The researcher can therefore determine which candidates are likely to win by determining the preferences of the voters in the sample.

What is a random sample?

Sampling theory is based on the use of a random sample, which means that each person in the population has an equal chance of being selected. Assume that the population for a particular research project consists of all students enrolled in a particular university. If the total student population of the university is too large to include all the students in the project, a random sample should be used. For a sample to be random, each student at the university (which serves as the universe in this particular illustration) must have an equal chance of being selected for inclusion in the research project. A random sample does not exist unless the equality-of-participation condition is present.

Several techniques exist for randomly selecting the individuals to include in the survey. One of the most efficient, precise methods is to use a table of random numbers. Such tables and the directions for their use may be found in statistics books.

Questionnaire method

The questionnaire method, which is used to collect information anonymously from people, requires considerable care in the development of the data-collection instrument. Although the wording of the items may appear to be clear and precise to the individual who developed the questionnaire, respondents may have difficulty determining the intent of some of the questions.

What suggestions will help in developing effective questionnaires?

The following suggestions should be considered when developing a questionnaire.

1. *Construct an easy-to-complete questionnaire.* The easier the instrument is to complete, the greater is its chance of being completed. In addition, easy-to-complete questionnaires usually improve the accuracy with which individuals respond to the items. To make the questionnaire easy to complete, provide checklists rather than requiring respondents to make listings, use questions that require an objective rather than a subjective answer, and use words that are understood by the respondents.

2. *Avoid using questions that will prejudice the respondents' answers.* An example of this kind of question is; "Is red your favorite color?" Some respondents may be influenced to respond that red is their favorite color because it was mentioned in the question. The accuracy of the responses to the question could be improved by listing the color possibilities on the questionnaire and asking the respondents to place a check beside their favorite color.

3. *Avoid the use of words that mean different things to different people.* In a question that asks respondents if they frequently shop in the downtown area of a particular city, the meaning of the word "frequently" will be interpreted differently by different people. One respondent may consider twice a month to be frequent, whereas another interprets frequent to mean at least 12 times a month. This question could be improved by asking the respondents how often within a given period they shop downtown.

4. *Include instructions for completing the questionnaire, if instructions are needed.* When instructions are used, they should be placed as close as possible to the items to which they pertain.

5. *Construct the questionnaire so that the respondents' answers are easy to tabulate.* If essay-type questions are included on the questionnaire, the researcher should decide how the information in these answers will be tabulated. Without sufficient preplanning, the researcher may be unable to tabulate the answers, a situation that renders such questions useless. The arrangement of checklists in a vertical rather than a horizontal pattern enhances the ease with which answers are tabulated.

6. *Give the respondents a deadline for returning the completed questionnaire.* Because of human nature, many people will delay responding to a questionnaire. If a deadline is given, people are more apt to respond.

7. *Consider eye appeal and the format of the questionnaire.* A questionnaire presented in an appealing design and format is more apt to be completed than one which lacks eye appeal.

8. *Arrange the questions in a sequential pattern.* Related questions should be placed in close proximity to one another rather than interspersed throughout the questionnaire. Psychologically advantageous is the arrangement of questions in a general-to-specific sequence when possible. Also desirable is the placement of the easy-to-answer questions at the beginning of the questionnaire and the more difficult-to-answer questions at the end of the questionnaire.

9. *Avoid questions considered to be of a personal nature by the respondents.* Questionnaires frequently contain items concerned with the respondents' yearly incomes or ages. Some people are sensitive about reporting this personal information, and asking them to provide it will probably adversely affect their willingness to respond. Respondents are less likely to find the use of ranges for personal items to be offensive. To illustrate, the following technique can be used for asking respondents to identify their age.

18–24 ________; 25–31 ________; 32–38 ________; etc.

10. *Keep the number of questions to a minimum.* One of the most common reasons that individuals do not respond to a questionnaire is its length. If the questionnaire becomes too long, the researcher should consider omitting or consolidating questions.

11. *Avoid asking compound questions in a single questionnaire item.* Compound questions, which can result in two answers, are difficult for individuals to answer. Such an example follows.

Do you prefer a two-color or a four-color book? ________ Yes ________ No

Two basic categories of items are found on questionnaires: unstructured or open-ended items and structured or closed-ended items. The nature of the questions being asked will determine which category to use.

How do structured and unstructured questions differ from one another?

Unstructured questions are designed to elicit detailed responses from the respondents. For example, asking respondents to "identify the three most common causes of employee job dissatisfaction'' is likely to elicit a more detailed response than giving the respondent a list of causes and then having him/her rank the causes. Responses to unstructured questions are more difficult to categorize in the data-tabulation process than responses to structured questions.

What types of structured questions are found on questionnaires?

Some types of structured questions are multiple-choice, ranking, either-or, checklist, fill-in, and scaling.

Multiple-choice questions usually give the respondent three or more choices from which to choose a response. Because you cannot always identify all the possible choices, an ''other'' choice is often provided.

Which one of the following best describes your present position?
_______ A. Dean
_______ B. Department chairperson
_______ C. Professor
_______ D. Associate professor
_______ E. Assistant professor
_______ F. Other (please specify) ______________________________

The *ranking* technique is designed to give the respondent an opportunity to rank order a list of items in order of preference. This type of item is well suited to determining preferences.

Please rank order the following list of fringe benefits in your order of preference by placing a ''1'' beside the benefit you most prefer, a ''2'' beside your second preference, etc.:
_______ Retirement program
_______ Medical insurance
_______ Life insurance
_______ Paid vacations
_______ Dental insurance
_______ Disability insurance

Either-or questions give the respondent an opportunity to choose between two alternatives. In some instances, the adding of a third choice, such as ''Don't know,'' ''Am not sure,'' ''Undecided,'' etc., may be appropriate.

Do you believe that all managers should have a college degree?
_______ Yes _______ No _______ Am not sure

Checklists give the respondent an opportunity to check more than one choice. To make the categorizing and tabulating process as easy as possible, all potential alternatives should be listed among the checklist items. In addition, an ''other'' alternative is often included.

Please place a checkmark beside each of the following major household appliances that you presently own.

_______ Washer
_______ Dryer
_______ Range
_______ Refrigerator
_______ Trash compactor
_______ Dishwasher
_______ Freezer
_______ Television set
_______ Stereo
_______ Video cassette recorder
_______ Home computer
_______ Other (please specify) _______________________

Fill-in questions require short answers. These questions are useful when you cannot predetermine all possible alternatives that should be provided for a specific question. In addition, they can be used when the list of alternatives that would have to be provided is too long.

Please list the foreign countries in which you have traveled. _______________
____
____.

Scaling questions are used to obtain information about the intensity of the respondents' feelings about a particular topic or issue. Also called the Likert scale, a scaling question gives the respondent several choices, perhaps as many as five or seven, and he/she selects the choice that most clearly reflects his/her feelings.

All business majors should have a speaking fluency in a foreign language.

_______ 1. Strongly agree
_______ 2. Agree
_______ 3. Neutral
_______ 4. Disagree
_______ 5. Strongly disagree

Interview method

Another method used to collect information involves interviewing the persons to be included in a research study. The interview method is well suited for collecting detailed information. It lends itself well to asking unstructured or open-ended questions.

When the population contains a large number of individuals, a random sample may be required. Depending upon the nature of the situation, one or more interviewers may be used. Large research studies are especially likely to use multiple interviewers. Because a lack of consistency among interviewers may have an effect on the data collected, each interviewer must use the same interrogative procedures. To assure consistency, interviewer participation in a training program prior to conducting the interviews may be desirable. Field testing the questions for clarity and understandability before beginning the actual interview process is also advisable.

What is an interview guide?

Most interviewers use an interview guide that lists questions to be asked and provides space for the interviewee's answers. If the interviewee does not fully understand a question after it is read, the interviewer is able to clarify the intent of a question. This feature of the interview method results in a significant advantage over the use of the questionnaire method.

Experimentation

The final method used for collecting primary information that is discussed in this chapter is experimentation. This method is being used with ever-increasing frequency in the business world. Well-designed experimental research studies produce extremely accurate results.

What is involved in using the experimental method?

In simple terms, the experimental method involves measuring one or more variables of interest to the researcher. By measuring the variables, then subjecting the participants to the treatment, and again measuring the variables after the treatment, the researcher can determine the effect of the treatment on the variables.

The experimentation method typically uses either one group or two groups. In the one-group alternative, the researcher measures the variable of interest (pre-test), administers the treatment to the group, and then measures the variable of interest a second time (post-test). Assuming that the experimentation process has been tightly controlled by the researcher, any differences between the first and second measurements of the variable of interest can most likely be attributed to the treatment. However, the measurement differences can also possibly be attributed to a variety of extraneous factors, which, if present, will weaken the research results.

To illustrate the one-group experimentation method, assume that a researcher wishes to determine the impact of a ten-hour training program on workers' skill in operating a new piece of equipment. The researcher will first pre-test the level of skill (the variable) demonstrated by each worker in operating the equipment. The workers then participate in the training program (treatment). When the training program has been completed, the level of skill possessed by each worker is again measured, this time by means of the post-test. If the workers' skill levels increased and if the researcher can be sure that the increase is due to the training program alone, the amount that the workers increased their skill in operating the equipment can be used to assess the impact of the training program.

The two-group alternative is often used by the researcher to provide more credible research results than the one-group alternative may provide. The researcher uses two groups: the control group and the experimental group. The individuals in both groups must be essentially alike in terms of relevant background factors (sex, age, intelligence, years of employment, etc.). Greater credibility can be achieved if the individuals are randomly assigned to the respective groups.

The two-group research process begins by pre-testing the variable of interest among both groups. If the pre-test scores of both groups are similar, the researcher can be reasonably sure that the two groups are essentially the same. The experimental group is then subjected to the treatment, while the control group is not. The researcher then post-tests both groups on the variable of interest. Assuming that both groups were treated alike—except for the treatment—any differences between the post-test measurements of both groups can be attributed to the treatment.

To illustrate the two-group experimental research process, assume that the researcher wants to determine the impact of a new training program on the efficiency of employees' use of word processing equipment. After each employee is randomly assigned to either the control or experimental group, a pre-test measurement of employee efficiency in operating the equipment is administered to both groups. The experimental group is then subjected to the new training program (treatment). After the treatment has been completed, both groups are again evaluated in terms of their efficiency of equipment operation. Any differences in the post-test scores of the two groups can most likely be attributed to the training program, especially if the pre- and post-test scores of the control group did not change significantly.

Secondary Research Methods

The use of secondary information in formal reports should not be overlooked. If someone else has already prepared material related to the area or topic of interest to you, the use of secondary information is often quite expedient.

Sources of secondary information include the following:

What sources of secondary information are used?

Abstracts	Dictionaries
Almanacs	Directories
Annual reports	Documents
Articles (periodicals)	Encyclopedias
Biographies	Government publications
Books	Handbooks
Brochures	Manuals
Bulletins	Newsletters
Company correspondence	Pamphlets
Company reports	Yearbooks

Depending on the nature of the situation, you should, however, be cautioned about using material prepared by someone else without assessing the technical accuracy of the material. When using someone else's material, you must acknowledge that fact. If an abundance of secondary information is available, you will have to use discretion in determining which information should be used and which should be eliminated.

Information pertaining to specific topics can easily be found in most libraries. The card catalog contains listings of books, manuals, handbooks, and government publications that pertain to specific categorical topics. Several guides or indexes that contain listings of periodical articles are also available. The contents of these indexes are typically arranged alphabetically by topics. The listings of periodical articles pertaining to each topic are presented below each topic heading. The *Readers' Guide to Periodical Literature* is one such guide.

Most of the academic disciplines now have guides or indexes that list articles pertaining to specific topics within specialized disciplines. For example, the *Business Periodicals Index* lists titles of articles found in business-related periodicals. Because the various guides and indexes available commonly list the articles by topic, you will turn to the topic of interest. For example, if you wish to obtain a list of periodical articles pertaining to quality circles, simply look under the topic of ''Quality Circles.'' Under this heading, you will find a list of the articles pertaining to quality circles which have been published during a specific time period in the various periodicals that are indexed in the *Business Periodicals Index.* Some of the more widely circulated newspapers, such as *The Wall Street Journal* and the *New York Times*, also have topical indexes of articles printed in the respective papers.

GUIDES TO SOURCES OF SECONDARY RESEARCH

The following is a list of guides and indexes that report writers may find helpful.

Guides to Periodicals

Magazines for Libraries, R. R. Bowker, Co., New York

Standard Periodical Directory, Oxbridge, New York

Ulrich's International Periodicals Directory, R. R. Bowker, Co., New York

Union List of Serials in Libraries of the United States and Canada, H. W. Wilson Co., New York

New Serial Titles, Library of Congress, Washington, D.C.

Guides to Periodical Indexes

Accountants' Index and Supplements, American Institute of Certified Public Accountants, New York

Accounting Articles, Commerce Clearing House, Chicago

AMA 10 Year Index of AMA Publications, American Management Association, New York

Applied Science and Technology Index, H. W. Wilson Co., New York

Bibliographical Index, H. W. Wilson Co., New York

Business Education Index, Delta Pi Epsilon, Little Rock, Arkansas

Business Periodicals Index, H. W. Wilson Co., New York

Cumulative Index of the National Industrial Conference Board Publications, National Industrial Conference Board, New York

Engineering Index, Engineering Index Service, New York

Engineering Index Annual, American Society of Mechanical Engineers, New York

Funk and Scott Index of Corporations and Industries, Funk and Scott Publishing Co., Detroit

Index of Economic Journals, Richard D. Irwin, Inc., Homewood, Illinois

Management Index, Keith Business Library, Ottawa, Canada

Poole's Index to Periodical Literature, Houghton-Mifflin Co., Boston

Readers' Guide to Periodical Literature, H. W. Wilson Co., New York

Social Science and Humanities Index, H. W. Wilson Co., New York

Guides to Periodical Abstracts

Journal of Economic Literature, American Economic Association, Menasha, Wisconsin

Personnel Management Abstracts, Bureau of Industrial Relations, Ann Arbor, Michigan

Psychological Abstracts, American Psychological Association, Washington, D.C.

Sociological Abstracts, Sociological Abstracts, Inc., New York

Guides to Newspaper Indexes

Index of the Christian Science Monitor, H. M. Cropsey, Corvallis, Oregon

National Observer Index, Dow Jones and Company, New York

New York Times Index, New York Times Co., New York

The Wall Street Journal Index, Dow Jones and Company, New York

Guides to Books

Books in Print, R. R. Bowker, New York

Cumulative Book Index: A World List of Books in the English Language, H. W. Wilson Co., New York

National Union Catalog, Library of Congress, Washington, D.C.

Paperbound Books in Print, R. R. Bowker Co., New York

Publisher's Weekly, R. R. Bowker Co., New York

Subject Guide to Books in Print, R. R. Bowker Co., New York

An increasing number of libraries now have computerized data bases available. Sources of information pertaining to an enormous number of topics can be made available in a matter of minutes. Rather than your having to undertake a manual search for the needed sources of information, the computer can make the search.

What is a computerized data base?

When using a computerized data base, key words or phrases are entered into the computer. Before beginning the actual search, the report writer should examine the data base directory to determine the key word or phrase to be entered to obtain the desired information. Only key words or phrases found in the directory can be entered into the system. After the search is completed, the computer produces a printout of the text citations contained in the data base.

Data bases of interest to business report writers are the following:

ABI/INFORM
ACCOUNTANTS
DOW JONES NEWS RETRIEVAL
PREDICAST F & S INDEX
LABORDOC
MANAGEMENT CONTENTS
TRADE AND INDUSTRY INDEX

Vertical files that contain brochures, pamphlets, handouts, and reports on selected topics are also found in many libraries. The use of these files should not be overlooked when using secondary sources of information.

Note taking

How do bibliography and data set cards differ from one another?

When collecting secondary information, the report writer will have to use a systematic means of note taking. One efficient method involves preparing two sets of cards: the bibliography set and the data set. The bibliography set, which is prepared first, contains the bibliographic information for each source the researcher plans to use. After the bibliography set is prepared, the cards are then alphabetized and numbered sequentially. As shown in Figure 13–1, the number in the upper-right corner is the sequential number and indicates that this particular card is the fifth card in the bibliography set.

A second set of index cards—the data cards—contains the notes that the writer recorded when reading the various material sources. In the upper-right

Figure 13–1 Cards in Bibliography Set Used in Note Taking

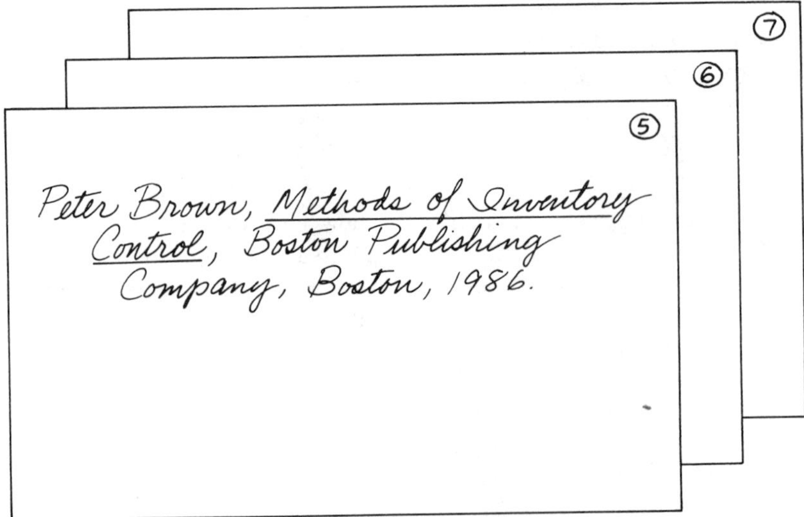

corner the researcher enters the sequential number from the appropriate bibliography card. The number 5 in the upper-right corner of a data card means that the notes on that card came from the fifth card in the bibliography set. When organizing the information prior to writing the report, the researcher will find that recording only one category of information on each data card is helpful. For example, instead of entering two categories of information, such as characteristics and advantages of LIFO, on the same card, two cards are prepared: one that contains the characteristics of LIFO and another that contains the advantages of LIFO. The page number(s) where the information is found is also entered on each data card. Page numbers are typically recorded immediately following the material that is entered on the card. This process is illustrated in Figure 13–2.

Each subdivision found in the preliminary outline of the report is now entered on separate sheets of paper. When the report writer finds information on a data card that pertains to a specific subdivision found in the report, that information is entered on the appropriate sheet, along with the sequence number and the page number references of each piece of information. A system

Figure 13–2 Cards in Data Set Used in Note Taking

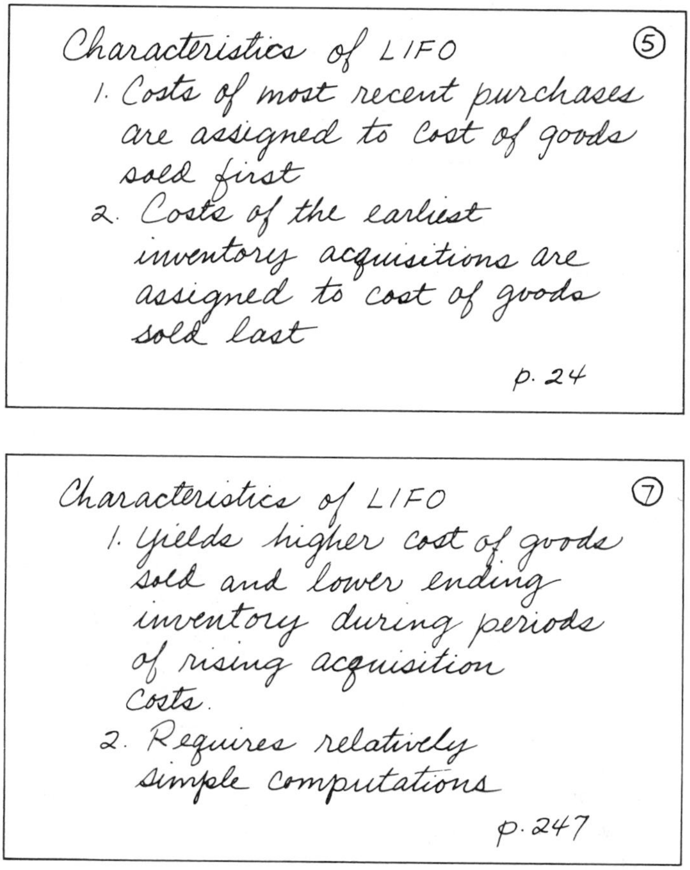

Characteristics of LIFO ⑤
1. Costs of most recent purchases are assigned to Cost of goods sold first
2. Costs of the earliest inventory acquisitions are assigned to cost of goods sold last
p. 24

Characteristics of LIFO ⑦
1. Yields higher cost of goods sold and lower ending inventory during periods of rising acquisition Costs.
2. Requires relatively simple computations
p. 247

V. Characteristics of LIFO
1. Costs of most recent purchases are assigned to cost of goods sold first
2. Costs of the earliest inventory acquisitions are assigned to cost of goods sold last
(5:24)
3. Yields higher cost of goods sold and lower ending inventory during periods of rising acquisition Costs
4. Requires relatively simple computation
(7:247)

Figure 13–3 Subdivision of Report Outline with Notes

frequently used puts the sequence number before a colon and the page number after, as the following shows: (5:239). As a shortcut, the writer can also attach the cards (by tape or staples) to the appropriate sheets. Figure 13–3 illustrates this process.

CATEGORIZING THE DATA

What is involved in categorizing data?

If the formal report contains primary data that must be tabulated before they are usable, you will have to determine appropriate categories for use in tabulating the data. To illustrate, assume that a questionnaire contains an item that asks respondents to list the number of books they have read during the past year. To give more meaning to the responses, you should consider developing categories.The categories in this example might be: 0–3 books; 4–6 books; 7–9 books; 10–12 books, etc. If you choose not to present the data in a category format, the number of respondents who have read no books, 1 book, 2 books, 3 books, etc. will all need to be listed.

Unless systematic categorization is used, questionnaire items having more than eight to ten possible responses may become very cumbersome when presented in the report. In many instances, the categories are determined at the time the questionnaire is developed. The same categories are then used in tabulating the data.

Unstructured items on the questionnaire are often more difficult to categorize than structured items. You will need to make sure that the categories into which you place individual responses are accurate. In some cases, you may find it necessary to "read between the lines" in determining the appropriate category for an individual's response.

When determining the categories, care should be taken to use those that give significant meaning to the data. Use of extremely broad or narrow categories is likely to obscure the true meaning of the data presented in the report.

TABULATING THE DATA

After the appropriate categories have been determined, the next step involves tabulating the data. When only a few questionnaires are included in the study, the tabulating process may be done manually by recording on a tally sheet the responses to each item in the questionnaire.

When many questionnaires need to be tabulated, a mechanical process may be especially desirable. One of the more common mechanical means involves coding each possible response for each item on the questionnaire. The coded response to each item is then entered on a medium (such as punched cards or optical scanning sheets) that is capable of being mechanically processed. The machine tabulates the number of responses to each category.

Once numerical data are tabulated, the mean, median, and mode can be calculated. The mean, which is the average of the numbers, is found by adding a series of numbers and dividing the total by the number of items found in the series. To illustrate, consider the following array of numbers: 10, 9, 7, 6, 6, 5, 4. The mean is 6.71 (47/7). The median is the number found in the middle of a series (6, in this instance) that is arranged in either ascending or descending order. The mode is the number that occurs most frequently (6, in this instance).

INTERPRETING INFORMATION

Why does information have to be interpreted?

The last step in the prewriting phase of the preparation of a formal report is the interpretation of the information. During this step, you give meaning to the data. The mere presentation of facts and data does nothing to help the reader benefit from the report. But once the facts and data have been given meaning, you are likely to benefit substantially from their inclusion. To illustrate, assume that a report writer states that the sales volume of a certain product increased $10,759 over last year's sales. This statement lacks meaning. Unless you know the percentage amount of increase or the base sales figure, this statement is virtually useless.

What types of interpretation errors are made?

You can also misinterpret information, causing the reader to draw inappropriate conclusions. Some of the more common types of interpretation errors include the following:

1. *Supporting the contrary because of lack of evidence.* An interpretation error occurs when the report writer believes that the lack of evidence can be used to support a contrary conclusion. To illustrate, assume the report writer wished to prove that employee absenteeism tends to be higher on clear days than on cloudy days. The evidence did not support this claim. The report writer would be making a false interpretation error by stating that because insufficient

evidence existed to support the original claim (absenteeism is higher on clear days), the opposite must be true (absenteeism is lower on clear days).

2. *Drawing conclusions on an insufficient amount of information.* Many inexperienced report writers are guilty of interpretation errors that result from drawing conclusions based on inadequate information. The greater the amount of evidence available to the report writer, the more certain the writer can be in drawing accurate conclusions on the basis of the evidence. This error in interpretation occurs because report writers fail to remember that conclusions cannot always be logically drawn from the evidence. To draw such conclusions reflects adversely on the work of the report writer.

3. *Exaggerating information.* The report writer can render information useless by exaggerating the quantitative value of the information. Another way that information can be distorted is to misrepresent the significance of the information. By emphasizing insignificant information, the report reader is led to believe that the information is much more significant than it really is.

4. *Using unreliable data or information.* A report that includes unreliable data or information is also useless. If the report writer collects primary data and if the statistical procedures are valid, the chances are fairly good that the data are reliable. When the report writer uses someone else's data or information, the writer should make certain that the data are reliable. This can be done by assessing the appropriateness of the statistical procedures. In some instances, second-hand information can be validated by comparing it with another person's research efforts.

5. *Using faulty cause-effect relationships.* Another interpretation error of some significance is a faulty cause-effect relationship, which means that the effect of a certain cause is unrealistic. An example of a faulty cause-effect relationship is that cloudy skies cause rain. This is faulty because rain is caused by certain atmospheric conditions that are present when skies are cloudy—not by the cloudy skies themselves.

6. *Allowing personal feelings to influence the interpretation process.* Some writers have difficulty keeping their personal feelings from surfacing in written reports. Especially inappropriate is letting personal feelings influence the interpretation of data. Not only is the interpretation of data distorted, but also the influence of personal feelings could result in making an incorrect decision. The best way to prevent this type of interpretation error is to use only information that is supportable.

7. *Comparing data that are not comparable.* Report writers who compare noncomparable data are likely to make serious errors in interpretation. For example, to compare the purchasing power of the average family today with the purchasing power twenty years ago will result in the comparison of data that are not comparable unless a base value of the dollar is used. Because the value of today's dollar is considerably less than it was 20 years ago, a valid comparison cannot be made unless today's dollar and the dollar of 20 years ago are put on a comparable base.

Once the interpretations have been made, the report writer should point out the relationships, consistencies, inconsistencies, similarities, and differences in the information and data presented in the report. This gives meaning to the information and data in the report.

At this point, the writer may draw conclusions and make recommendations. Remember that conclusions must be supportable by the evidence presented in the report. The recommendations outline the writer's ideas for action, based on the evidence presented in the report.

NEED FOR OBJECTIVITY IN REPORT WRITING

Just as errors in the interpretation of data can diminish the usefulness and effectiveness of formal reports, so can a lack of objectivity. An objective report contains material that is free of the report writer's prejudices and biases.

Report writers diminish the effectiveness of their writing by allowing their prejudices or biases to influence either the interpretation of data or the presentation of information. In addition, a lack of objectivity in report preparation often results in a lack of content believability. Even though the writer's biases or prejudices may be very subtle, experienced report writers can readily detect their presence.

What situations inject bias or prejudice into the report-writing process?

The report writer can inject bias or prejudice into a report by

1. Presenting information or data in a distorted manner
2. Presenting information or data findings not as they actually occurred but as he/she wished them to occur
3. Withholding information that should be included in the report
4. Presenting information or data as though they are supportable by evidence when in fact they are not
5. Presenting information or data primarily to accommodate his/her prejudices
6. Using a sensational writing style to alter the importance or meaning of the report contents

CHAPTER SUMMARY

Before you can begin writing a formal report, several preliminary steps must be completed, including a determination of the report problem. In addition, you will need to identify the reader(s) of the report, as well as the scope of the topic. The next step involves developing a preliminary outline of the report.

Another important aspect of report preparation is determining the appropriate method of collecting information. Primary research can be gathered through company records, observation, questioning people, questionnaires, interviews, and experimentation. An alternative is using secondary research.

After the data are collected, categorizing, tabulating, and interpreting them are important. When you begin to write, you should be aware of the ways you can improve your objectivity. Maintaining objectivity is critical to the success of your report.

REVIEW QUESTIONS

1. How does the report problem differ from the report purpose?
2. In what formats can the report problem and purpose be presented?

3. What suggestions can you offer that will be helpful to the writer of a report problem?
4. Why should the writer of the report identify the reader before beginning the writing process?
5. In what ways can report topics be limited?
6. How does the inductive arrangement differ from the deductive arrangement of the material in a formal report?
7. How does the topic format differ from the discussion format in the wording of report outlines?
8. What factors need to be considered in determining the most appropriate method for collecting information for use in writing a formal report?
9. What types of primary research methods are available to the report writer?
10. What suggestions can you offer that will be helpful in developing a questionnaire?
11. How is a computerized data base helpful to report writers?
12. Why does primary data have to be categorized?
13. What is the purpose of data interpretation?
14. What are the interpretation errors that a report writer should guard against?

APPLICATION PROBLEMS

1. Prepare a report problem and purpose for each of the following situations:

a. A study that compares the effectiveness of merit salary increases versus across-the-board salary increases. The individual who authorized the study was interested in determining the impact that each had on employee motivation.

b. A study that determines the nature of employees' communication strengths and weaknesses. Information will be helpful in designing a training program to help employees overcome their weaknesses.

c. A study that determines the impact of work standards on increasing employee productivity. Information will be helpful in determining need for implementing a work measurement/work standards program.

d. A study that compares the advantages and disadvantages of FIFO (first in, first out) and LIFO (last in, first out) inventory control methods. Input will be used to help determine if XYZ Company should change from using the LIFO to the FIFO method.

e. A study that determines the effectiveness of storing records in microrecord format. Information will be used to determine the need for installing a micrographics program.

2. Critique the following report problems and purposes and then rewrite each:

a. The purpose of this report is to compare the relative effectiveness of an in-house letter-writing seminar in helping employees overcome their writing problems.

b. The purpose of this report is to assess the impact of MBO on employees' attitudes in order to help improve the motivation of employees in ABC Corporation.

c. The purpose of this report is to evaluate the desirability of installing a profit-sharing plan as a means of motivating employees to increase their efficiency.

3. For each of the situations in application problem 1, identify the factors of the problem.

4. For each of the situations in application problem 1, identify the report limits.

5. Select one of the situations in application problem 1 and prepare a tentative outline, using the inductive arrangement. Then revise the outline, using the deductive arrangement.

6. Using the topic captions, prepare an outline for application problem 1 in Chapter 14.

7. Using discussion captions, prepare an outline for application problem 2 in Chapter 14.

8. Develop a questionnaire that is designed to collect data about students' attitudes toward a required English proficiency examination that they must pass before they can graduate from Northern College. Include at least one question in each of the following formats: multiple-choice, ranking, either-or, checklist, fill-in, and scaling.

9. Prepare an interview form that will be used when interviewing students to learn their preferences for the "ideal" spring-break vacation. This information is desired by a travel agent who will use your findings in developing a variety of spring-break packages.

10. You have been hired by a representative of a fast-food franchise chain to develop an interview form that will be used to assess the eating-out habits of the students at your college. The information will ultimately be used to assess the need for another fast-food restaurant near the campus. Develop the interview form.

11. You have been hired by a local grocery store to develop a questionnaire that will be sent to a selected sample of community residents. The purpose of the questionnaire is to determine which television programs that are broadcast on the local television station (Channel 6, KSTV) are viewed on a regular basis by the questionnaire recipients. The store plans to have its commercials run during the most widely viewed programs between 7 p.m. and 10 p.m. on Tuesday and Thursday evenings. (Make up the titles of the programs.)

12. Using the data presented in application problem 2 of Chapter 14, prepare the questionnaire that might have been used to collect those data.

13. Using the data presented in application problem 3 of Chapter 14, prepare the questionnaire that might have been used to collect those data.

14. Using the information presented in application problem 4 of Chapter 14, prepare the form on which the data might have been tabulated.

Chapter 14

Preparing Formal Reports: Writing Phase

LEARNING OBJECTIVES

After studying this chapter, you should be able to

1. Discuss the purpose of each of the preliminary parts of a formal report.
2. Discuss the appropriate content for a letter of authorization and letter of transmittal.
3. Discuss the purpose of the introduction section of a formal report.
4. Discuss the differences among the summary, conclusions, and recommendations sections of a formal report.
5. Prepare an effective formal report of the type discussed in this chapter.

Formal reports serve an important information-dissemination function. For example, a formal report may be used to disseminate the findings of a comprehensive study of the marketing potential of a new product. Although one or more of the informal reports discussed in Chapter 12 could also have been used to distribute the findings of this comprehensive study, a formal report would be more appropriate and effective. In addition, the information presented in formal reports is often used as input for managerial decision making.

How are formal and informal reports different from one another?

Formal reports can be distinguished from informal reports in the following ways:

1. Formal reports are generally longer.
2. Formal reports follow a rather conventional, standardized format.

3. Formal reports are likely to make significantly greater use of graphic illustrations in the presentation of information.
4. The writing style used in preparing formal reports is likely to be more formal.

The information presented in formal reports may be primary information, secondary information, or a combination of both. Primary information refers to data or information most often collected through questionnaires or interviews. Secondary information is collected from books, periodicals, reports, and other types of documents. When using secondary information in a report, its source(s) must be identified.

PARTS OF THE FORMAL REPORT

What parts are included in formal reports?

One of the distinctive characteristics of formal reports is the rather standardized format used in presenting the information. As a report writer, you should be familiar with the need for and uses of the various parts that comprise a formal report.

Although most of the parts are required in a formal report, some are optional (*) and are incorporated only if a given situation calls for their use. The parts that may be included in a formal report are:

1. Preliminary parts
   a. Title fly*
   b. Title page
   c. Letter of authorization*
   d. Letter of transmittal*
   e. Table of contents
   f. List of illustrations*
   g. Abstract/synopsis
2. Body parts
   a. Introduction
   b. Text
3. Ending parts
   a. Summary*
   b. Conclusions
   c. Recommendations
4. Appended parts
   a. Appendices*
   b. Bibliography

In the list presented above, the parts marked with asterisks are optional and should be included when the situation makes their use desirable. The optional parts are typically used when the report is quite long or when a high degree of formality is needed.

A formal report is illustrated at the end of this chapter. The report illustrates each of the parts mentioned above as well as the proper mechanics of presentation.

Preliminary Parts

Of the four main sections of formal reports—preliminary, body, ending, and appended parts—you have greater flexibility in deciding which parts to include in the preliminary section than in making decisions about the other three sections.

Title fly

What information is included on the title fly?

The title fly page contains only the title of the report. Because the title page, which is discussed below, also contains the title of the report, some believe that the title fly is virtually useless. The report title is typed in capital letters and begins approximately 1 to 1 $\frac{1}{2}$ inches above the vertical center of the page.

If the title requires two or more lines, the appearance of the title fly page is improved by making the top line of the title the longest, with each successive line shorter than the previous line. The title, therefore, appears in a "V" arrangement. Although the title fly page is counted in numbering pages, the page number is usually not typed on this page.

Title page

What information is included on the title page?

Because most report writers choose to omit the title fly page, the title page is typically the first page of a formal report. Most title pages contain:

1. The title of the report
2. The name and title of the individual for whom the report is prepared
3. The name and title of the individual who prepared the report
4. The company, city, and state of the report writer
5. The date of presentation

Like the title on the title fly page, the title on the title page should be typed in capital letters. A "V" arrangement of the title is also the recommended format.

Even when a title fly page is used, a page number need not appear on the title page. However, the title page is considered in the page count of the preliminary pages. If a title fly page is used and you choose to number the title page, the Roman numeral ii is centered at the bottom of the page.

Letter of authorization

Another optional preliminary part of the formal report is the letter of authorization. Although the letter (or memorandum) of authorization is not prepared by the report writer, a discussion is included in this chapter to assist those who prepare such documents.

Many report assignments are made orally. Even though oral authorizations are as legitimate as written authorizations, you should guard against undertaking reports that are authorized orally, especially if the report assignment is considered to be somewhat controversial. You are advised to obtain a written authorization in case any aspect of the report assignment eventually needs to be verified. Written assignments are less likely to be disputed at a later date.

With a written authorization, important aspects of the report assignment are clearly and concisely recorded. The written authorization, which may appear in either letter or memorandum format, typically includes the following sections:

What information is included in the letter of authorization?

1. An authorization for you to begin preparation of the report;
2. The statement of problem (and purpose, if appropriate), the scope, and the limitations of the report;
3. A discussion of pertinent background information pertaining to the report topic;
4. A discussion of conditions for preparing the report, including the due date, budgetary allowances, and if appropriate, the amount of compensation you are to receive;
5. A courteous closing with an offer to be of assistance if needed.

Lowercase Roman numerals are used in putting page numbers on the letter of authorization. The page number is centered at the bottom of the page. If the letter is continued to a second page, the page number is also centered at the bottom of the second page.

Many managers now prefer that the letter of authorization be eliminated from all but the most formal of formal reports.

Letter of transmittal

Your last task in preparing a formal report involves composing the letter of transmittal for the formal transmission of the report to the reader. If the report is to be used internally, the transmittal message can be sent on a memo. If the report is transmitted outside the organization, a letter more appropriately conveys the transmittal message.

What is the purpose of the letter of transmittal?

The letter of transmittal should refer to the date on which the report was authorized as well as mention the topic of the report. You should also summarize the limitations, report contents or findings, conclusions, and recommendations. Most writers will express appreciation for having had the opportunity to write the report as well as offer to answer any questions the reader may have about the report contents.

If the letter of transmittal occupies only one page, the page number is typed in lowercase Roman numerals and is centered at the bottom of the page. If the letter continues to a second page, a Roman numeral page number is centered at the bottom of the second page. In some cases, you may prefer to attach the transmittal to the cover of the report. When this is done, no page numbers are necessary on the transmittal document.

Table of contents

The purpose of the table of contents is to give the reader an opportunity to scan the contents of the report without having to read the entire document. The table is comprised of the headings found within the report. The page number on which each heading is found is also included on the table of contents. Leaders (alternating periods and spaces) are used to fill the space between each heading and its page number.

The preliminary parts of the report that appear before the table of contents are typically not listed on the table. Because the reader would have already seen these pages, little need exists to list these pages on the table. The first preliminary part that is listed is the page immediately following the table of contents.

The major headings and subheadings should be included in the table. You will decide whether to include the third-degree headings. Just as the headings in the report should be written using parallel construction, so should the material in the table be presented in parallel form.

What format guidelines will help you prepare an effective table of contents?

Some guidelines to help you design a table of contents are:

1. Align Roman numerals and page numbers on the right.
2. Place the second line of a heading immediately beneath the first line. The second line should be single-spaced.
3. Use double spacing before and after second-degree headings (A, B, C, and D in the example presented below), but single-space third-degree headings (1 and 2 in the illustration) with double spacing before and after.
4. Fill the space with leaders, which are alternating periods and spaces, between the headings and the page numbers. The leaders should align vertically.
5. Align the preliminary parts and the appended parts, which are not part of the report body, flush with the left margin.

The following illustrates a portion of a properly designed table of contents.

Abstract iv

I. Introduction. 1

II. Background of the Report 2

  A. Purpose of the Report 2

  B. Objectives of the Report 2

    1. Short-range objectives 2
    2. Long-range objectives 3

  C. Research Methods 4

  D. Limitations 6

.

.

Appendix 39
Bibliography 43

List of illustrations

To help the reader rapidly locate the graphic aids included in the report, a list of illustrations is useful. The list identifies the number of each graphic aid, the title of the graphic aid, and the page number on which it appears. Leaders are also used to fill the space between the titles of the graphic aids and the pages on which they appear.

What information is included in the list of illustrations?

If the table of contents and the list of illustrations are both quite short, you have the option of presenting both the table and the list on the same page.

Some writers prefer to separate the tables from all other graphic aids. The appropriate heading for the page on which the tables are listed is "List of Tables." The other graphic aids are presented on a page identified as "List of Illustrations."

Abstract

The purpose of the abstract, which is prepared after the report is completed, is to present a condensed version of the report. The abstract, also known as a synopsis, should briefly summarize the introduction, findings, interpretation of the findings, and list the conclusions and recommendations.

What is the purpose of the abstract?

For many readers, the abstract provides most or all of the needed information. Therefore, readers may not have to read the entire report, especially if the abstract is accurate and thorough and the reader is able to obtain the required information from the abstract. A well-prepared abstract enables the reader to pass over certain sections of the report. In addition, it provides a preview of the report and gives the reader an opportunity to become familiar with the report material prior to beginning the reading process.

The abstract may be presented to the reader using either the deductive or the inductive organizational arrangement. When using the deductive arrangement, the conclusions and recommendations are presented first, followed by the other sections. The inductive arrangement presents the material in the abstract in the same order as it is presented in the report.

If the letter of transmittal includes a short summary of the report, the abstract need not be as detailed as when a letter of transmittal is not used. Although the length of the abstract is governed somewhat by the length of the report, you are generally advised to try to keep the abstract to a one-page single-spaced document.

If an abstract is included, the first page is numbered with a lowercase Roman numeral centered at the bottom of the page. The page numbers of successive preliminary pages also appear at the bottoms of pages.

Parts of the Report Body

The body parts of the formal report consist of the introductory sections and the text of the report. Several types of introductory sections are available for inclusion.

Introduction

The first part of the body, which is the introduction, serves a useful purpose. It provides the reader with a considerable amount of background information.

What information is included in the introduction?

Some readers use the introduction to assess the quality of the writer's research methods and procedures.

The items to be included in the introduction are determined by the formality and the perceived readership of the report. If the readership would benefit from the inclusion of a greater number of introductory items and if the report is to be quite formal, you should consider including most or all of the following introductory parts.

1. *Background of the report.* Although some repetition may occur between the letter of transmittal and the background of the report section, you may want to include both, especially in more formal reports. The background of the report section identifies the details of the authorization, including who authorized the report, how the authorization was made, and the date on which the authorization was made. This section may also include your name.

2. *Statement of problem.* Because some reports do not include a background section, the first section in the body of many reports is the statement of problem section. The statement identifies the reasons the report was prepared. In some cases, the purpose and the statement of problem are included in the same section and even in the same sentence. The purpose identifies for the reader the benefits to be realized by solving the problem that is being investigated, while the problem provides the basis for the purpose. In many instances, report problems involve an investigation designed to provide data or information for use in solving problems.

An example of an effective sentence that contains both the problem and the purpose would be: "This report was undertaken to identify the cause of the breakdown of communication between the home office and the branch offices of the XYZ Corporation, for the purpose of improving the firm's operating efficiency." Any secondary purposes of the report should also be identified in this report section. The primary and secondary purposes of the report will help the reader evaluate the benefits resulting from the undertaking of the report.

What is the function of the scope?

3. *Scope.* Another important section found in some formal reports is the scope. Unless the report scope is provided, the reader has no way of knowing what you considered to be appropriate topics or areas for investigation. By not including the scope, some readers may think that you inadvertently failed to cover some topics, which may raise questions about your report-writing ability. The scope clearly identifies those areas the report writer intended to include and those that were meant to be excluded.

4. *Methodology.* A discussion of the research methodology is often used to assist the reader in assessing the quality of the writer's research methods. Therefore, the research methodology should be discussed in sufficient detail for the reader to make this assessment.

When the report contains a considerable amount of primary information, you should explain how the information was obtained. If a statistical test was used on the data, you should identify which statistical test was used and the reasons that particular test was selected. If a questionnaire was used to collect the data, you should explain how it was developed and validated. You should also explain how the interview questions were developed and how the interviewees were chosen for the interview.

When secondary information is used, you should explain for the reader's benefit the location of the periodicals, reports, and other documents that were used in the report. A listing of the publications that were used in the report should be included in the bibliography, which appears at the end of the report. If only a few publications are used, they may be listed in the methodology section.

5. *Definitions.* Some reports contain words or terms that the reader either may not be familiar with or that are used in a context that is unfamiliar to the reader. The purpose of the definitions section is to provide a definition of these words or terms for the reader. Their inclusion will give the reader and writer a common frame of reference.

6. *Limitations.* The content of some reports is hampered by conditions over which you have no control. Such conditions are referred to as limitations and should be identified in the introduction section of the report. By discussing the limitations, the reader has greater assurance that you are not trying to cover up an apparent weakness in the report. Your credibility is not jeopardized because any conditions that may affect the report are identified for the reader.

What are limitations?

Some situations that may limit the report are an inadequate amount of time, an inadequate monetary allocation, an inadequate amount of available information, and a lack of cooperation on the part of certain individuals.

7. *Historical background of the report topic.* In some instances, the report being prepared is one of a continuing series of reports pertaining to a specific topic. In such cases, the historical background of prior research concerning the topic is useful to the report reader. By making the reader fully aware of previous work on the topic, he/she is aware of any continuing problems relating to the topic. In addition, the reader has a better understanding of any prior decisions that have been made.

8. *Report organization.* A discussion of the organization of the report is often contained in a formal report. The reader is familiarized with the parts that are included in the body of the report, which will enable him/her to understand more readily the report's content.

Text of the Report

The text of the report immediately follows the introductory sections and is the major portion of the report. Findings of the research efforts are presented in the text, together with an interpretation and analysis of the findings.

Writing style

You should be concerned with all the qualities that characterize good writing. The text of the report immediately follows the introductory section and is the strive to use only words that the reader will understand. To add variety to the writing style, different types of sentences should be used, including simple, compound, and complex sentences. Transitional words, phrases, and sentences should also be used.

How do deductively and inductively arranged paragraphs differ from one another?

You have the option of selecting either deductive or inductive development of paragraphs. Deductive development, which most report writers prefer to use, puts the topic sentence at the beginning of each paragraph. Therefore, the topic sentence essentially summarizes the content of the paragraph. When paragraphs are developed using the inductive arrangement, the summary sentence appears at the end of the paragraph.

The present verb tense is generally recommended as the tense most appropriate for use in business reports, except when referring to situations that are clearly in the past or future. In such cases, whichever tense—past or future—that is appropriate for the situation being discussed should be used. Continual shifts in tense are difficult for the reader to follow.

Headings

You also will be concerned with the use of headings in the report. Headings are similar to road signs—they tell readers what is ahead. Headings, which should be descriptive, yet concise, may be presented in three different degrees. The following illustrates each of the three degrees.

How do first, second, and third degree headings differ from one another in their format?

1. First degree: Centered and in capital letters

> THE CHARACTERISTICS OF PARTICIPATIVE MANAGEMENT

2. Second degree: On the left margin and underlined; first letter of each word capitalized

> Employee Advantages

3. Third degree: Indented same number of spaces as paragraphs, underlined, and followed with a period. Only the first word of the heading and proper nouns are capitalized.

> Improved relations. The use of participative management for improving relations among workers . . .

The proper spacing to use before and after headings is illustrated in the sample report found at the end of this chapter.

Graphic aids

The use of graphic aids in the body of the report helps the reader in interpreting and understanding the report. Because graphic illustrations are not complete in themselves, they need to be explained. The writer must guard against a lack of complete interpretation of the data contained in illustrations. The preparation of graphic illustrations is discussed in detail in another section of this chapter.

If the report contains secondary information, which means that material was quoted from texts, periodicals, reports, and other documents, the writer should identify the various sources of secondary information that he/she used. This involves the use of footnotes, which enable you to give credit to outside sources.

The following guidelines may be used in helping determine which material to footnote.

What guidelines should be considered to help determine what material should be footnoted?

1. Sentences, ideas, and thoughts that are solely those of the report writer need not be footnoted.
2. All material quoted verbatim must be footnoted.
3. Paraphrased material is footnoted unless the material is commonly considered to be general knowledge in a particular field and it cannot be attributed to a particular individual.
4. Even though material may be regarded as general knowledge in a particular field, such material needs to be footnoted if the material is being quoted verbatim.

Several different styles of footnoting exist. The traditional method, which is decreasing in popularity, places footnotes at the bottom of the page on which the quoted material appears. A superscript number is placed at the end of the material being quoted, and the same number is used to identify the footnote to which the quoted material pertains.

When the traditional footnote system is used, several different footnote styles are available. The following style is widely used for quoting material from texts.

[1]John D. Brown, *New Perspectives in Interviewing* (New York: Business Publishers, Inc., 1986), p. 10.

A different format is used for periodicals and newspaper articles. The following illustrate the proper footnote formats for periodicals and newspaper articles, respectively.

[1]Samuel White, "The Art of Interviewing," *Personnel Functions,* 14:34, September 1986.

[2]*Detroit Times,* January 16, 1986, sec. C, p. 2 col. 2.

Some report writers prefer to start footnote numbers with "1" on each page; others continue the numbers sequentially from one page to the next.

Although the use of *ibid., op. cit.,* and *loc. cit.* is losing vogue, report writers need to be familiar with their use. *Ibid.* is used when material from two different pages from the same source is quoted.

[1]John D. Brown, *New Perspectives in Interviewing* (New York: Business Publishers, Inc., 1986), p. 10.

[2]*Ibid.*, p. 12.

The second footnote refers to page 12 of Brown's book.

When at least one intervening footnote from a different source is found and when the material being quoted is from a different page than that of the original footnote, an *op. cit.* footnote is used.

[1]Jack Jones, "The Art of Persuasive Interviewing," *Journal of Practical Communication,* 10:15, January 1986.

[2]Mary Coswell, *Practical Personnel Management* (Denver: Readers Publishing Co., 1986), p. 72.

[3]Jones, *op. cit.*, p. 19.

Footnote 3 refers to page 19 of the document referred to in Footnote 1.

A *loc. cit.* footnote is used when material is quoted from the same page of a source two or more times regardless of whether or not intervening footnotes are found. Therefore, page numbers are not needed when using *loc. cit.* footnotes.

[10]David Samuels, "The Advantages of Functional Interviews," *Personnel Magazine,* 29:16, May 1986.

[11]Johnson, *op. cit.*, p. 14.

[12]Samuels, *loc. cit.*

[13]*Ibid.*, p. 14.

Footnote 12 refers to page 16 of the Samuel article previously quoted in Footnote 10. Footnote 13 also refers to Samuels' article, page 14.

Several variations to the traditional footnoting method are used. One method requires the use of a bibliography in which the citations are alphabetized and each bibliography entry is assigned an Arabic number that appears to the left of the entry.

4. Brown, John D. *New Perspectives in Interviewing.* New York: Business Publishers, Inc., 1986.

If material was quoted from page 87 of Brown's text, the footnote entry in the text would appear as:

". . . are the characteristics of the patterned interview" (4:87).

Another variation, also dependent upon a bibliography, is used by the American Psychological Association and other organizations. It uses the author's name, the year of publication, and the page of the document from which the material is being quoted. This method is increasing in popularity.

> ". . . identify the characteristics." (Brown, 1986, p. 87).

The year of publication is used to differentiate between bibliographical items. If the bibliography contains two documents by the same author or by two authors with the same last names, the year of the publication usually indicates, without further distinctions, which document is being quoted. The year also differentiates between two or more works authored by the same individual.

In some instances, discussion footnotes are used in formal reports. Rather than making reference to a document from which materials were quoted, you can use discussion footnotes to present a certain point you wish to make. For example, instead of including a discussion of the derivation of a certain word in a report, you may decide to discuss the derivation in a footnote at the bottom of the page on which the word is first used.

What is an endnote?

An ever-increasing number of writers prefer to use endnotes rather than footnotes. When material is quoted, a superscript number appears in the text at the end of the quotation. An endnote, which is typically presented in the traditional footnote format, is then placed on the endnotes page which appears at the end of the report. The endnotes are numbered sequentially, beginning with "1." The following is an example of the fourth endnote that appeared in a report.

> [4]David Johnson, "The Art of Interviewing," *Personnel Topics,* 23:18, May 1985.

The appropriate heading for the endnotes page(s) is simply "Endnotes" typed in all capitals.

Some writers now believe that the bibliography can be omitted when using endnotes. However, a bibliography should continue to be prepared for the more formal of formal reports.

Material that is quoted verbatim and that consumes three or more lines in a report is single spaced and indented five spaces from either margin. Quotation marks are not used to surround material set off in this manner. Material that is quoted verbatim but that consumes only one or two lines is not set off. In this case, quotation marks are used to enclose the quoted material. The citation number appears immediately after the final quotation mark.

Paraphrased material is never set off, nor are quotation marks used with paraphrased material. The citation number appears at the end of the paraphrased material.

Ending of the Report

The ending of a formal report typically consists of conclusions and recommendations. Depending upon the circumstances, a summary of the report findings may also be included. If an abstract is not included in the report, you may want to include a summary of the report findings. Even if an abstract is included, a summary of findings at the end of the report may also be used.

Summary

What is the purpose of the summary?

The purpose of the summary is to recap for the reader the major findings of the report. The most common practice for organizing the summary is to recap the findings pertaining to each of the report's major divisions. Presenting the summary in the same order as the material in the report enables the reader to locate more readily the information in the report to which the summary findings pertain. Such an arrangement is especially useful if you refer to the original discussion that pertains to a specific summary finding. In most instances, the findings are enumerated, which adds to the readability and understandability of the summary section.

Conclusions

What are conclusions?

You should remember to base the conclusions of the report on the facts and details discussed in the report. In other words, no information new to the report can be introduced in the conclusions section. Conclusions, which are essentially answers to the report problem, must be objective and free from contamination of your preconceived ideas or notions.

Some inexperienced report writers provide conclusions that are essentially summary findings. While findings pertain to the data or information presented in the report, conclusions go one step further and provide answers to the report problem. In a report that was prepared to identify a number of causes of poor employee productivity as a means of increasing XYZ Corporation's profitability, the following example illustrates the difference between a summary finding and a conclusion.

> Finding: The employees in XYZ Corporation were found to be producing at 80 percent of their capacity.
>
> Conclusion: Subjecting the employees of XYZ Corporation to a training program will help them become more productive.

The following sentence is an example of a finding incorrectly labeled as a conclusion.

> Employees of XYZ Corporation are not as productive as they used to be.

To facilitate the reading of the report, you are advised to number the conclusions and to present them in the same order as the findings from which they were drawn.

Recommendations

What are recommendations?

The recommendations section of a formal report, which is based on your opinions and thoughts, identifies the actions that you believe should be taken in light of your research. Generally, you will, where appropriate, make a recommendation for each of the conclusions. For example, in the report problem cited in the conclusions section, an appropriate recommendation might be:

> XYZ Corporation should investigate the feasibility of installing an employee training program designed to help employees improve their productivity.

Like the conclusions, the recommendations should be numbered, and they should be presented in the same order as the conclusions.

Appended Parts

The appended parts of the formal report, typically appendices and the bibliography, are the two final parts of the formal report.

Appendices

Materials that are appended to the report are usually supplementary or supportive in nature and, therefore, do not appropriately belong in the text of the report. You must make a decision about what to include in the text and what to include in the appendices. Examples of items frequently included as appendices are data-gathering instruments, such as questionnaires, data tables, diagrams, and illustrations, that are not necessary for understanding and interpreting the material contained in the text.

When you are in doubt about whether to include certain materials in the text or as an appended item, the material should probably be included in the appendices.

If only one item is to be included in this section of the report, the appropriate terminology is *appendix* rather than *appendices.*

Bibliography

In all but the shortest of formal reports, a bibliography should be included. In short formal reports, a bibliography is sometimes omitted if only a few secondary sources of information are used because the reader is able to grasp the sources that are used without having them listed in the bibliography.

The sources listed in the bibliography may be categorized according to the following breakdown:

What categories are used in presenting a bibliography?

1. Books
2. Periodicals
3. Newspapers
4. Reports
5. Unpublished materials
6. Miscellaneous

The bibliography entries are alphabetized under each of the categories. If only a few sources are used in preparing the report, categorizing the sources in the bibliography may not be needed.

A specific format is used for each bibliography category. The following are the appropriate styles for each category:

1. Books

Brown, John D. *New Perspectives in Interviewing.* New York: Business Publishers, Inc., 1986.

2. Periodicals

Samuels, David. ''The Advantages of Functional Interviews,'' *Personnel Magazine,* 29:16, May 1986.

3. Newspapers

Detroit Times, January 16, 1986.

4. Reports

Brown, David. ''How to Prepare Reports.'' East Lansing, Mich.: Michigan State University, 1986.

5. Unpublished Materials

Johnson, Mary. Personal Interview. January 10, 1986.

6. Miscellaneous

Administration Club, Michigan State University. *Constitution and By-Laws.* 1986.

Arabic numbers are used to number the bibliography. The page number is centered at the bottom of the first page of the bibliography but appears in the upper right corner of succeeding pages. Alternate methods of presenting bibliographic entries can be found in style and theses manuals and handbooks.

GRAPHIC PRESENTATION

Graphic presentation of material in a formal report helps the reader more quickly grasp the significance of the material. If properly developed and used, graphic aids are quite beneficial. Aids are not to be used as a primary means of presenting material, but rather to support or further explain the material presented in the written sections of the report. In numerous instances, a portion of the material will be presented to the reader in paragraph format, with the remainder presented in a graphic aid.

A new trend in graphics preparation is the use of computer technology. With the exception of the tables presented below, each of the aids in this chapter can be prepared almost effortlessly by use of a computer, the appropriate software, and a printer/plotter. Most plotters now available are capable of producing multiple-color aids. In addition, some plotters can produce color transparencies for use on overhead projectors.

When using a computer to prepare graphics, the following steps are typically performed.

What steps comprise the computerized graphics preparation process?

1. Enter into the computer the type of chart desired (pie, multiple bar, etc.).
2. Enter the title and subtitle of the chart.
3. Enter the identity of the various components.
4. Enter the type of design desired for each component (hatching, cross hatching, solid, open, etc.).
5. Enter the quantitative data for each of the components.
6. Enter the total magnitude of each of the components.
7. Enter the source notation.

Whether preparing graphic aids by hand or by computer, the reader should never be responsible for interpreting the material presented in the aids. The following list summarizes guidelines for using graphic aids in a report.

What steps encompass the use of graphic aids in formal reports?

1. Introduce the material to which the graphic aid pertains.
2. Refer the reader to the graphic aid. For example, "As Figure 12 illustrates. . . . "
3. Provide additional discussion and/or interpretation of the material presented in the graphic aid.
4. Place the graphic aid as close as possible to its discussion in the report.
5. In discussing the graphic aid, make reference to it. For example, "The demographic characteristics of the consumers included in this study are summarized in Table 2."
6. If possible, the discussion of the material contained in a graphic aid should appear before and after the presentation of the aid.
7. If the aid and its discussion appear on different pages, tell the reader where the aid can be found. For example, "The cost breakdowns are illustrated in Figure 4, which appears on page 23."
8. Tables are identified as tables (for example, Table 3); all other graphic aids are identified as figures or illustrations (for example, Figure 4 or Illustration 7).
9. If the graphic aid is not your creation but is obtained from another source, the source of the aid should be fully identified. For example: *The Working Man,* p. 74. The source notation appears directly below the graphic aid.

10. Color, shading, cross hatching, and variation in lines (solid, broken, etc.) are useful in preparing certain graphic aids.
11. Extreme care should be exercised in determining the appropriate wording of the title as well as the various other components of the graphic aid.
12. The size of the graphic aid should be determined by the importance and amount of data presented in the aid.

The sections that follow are designed to assist you in preparing the various types of graphic aids. Because the material illustrated in graphic aids can be easily distorted, you need to be especially concerned with the accuracy of the material being presented.

Tables

For what are tables typically used?

A table is a vertical (columnar) and horizontal (row) presentation of information. Tables are typically used to present numerical information, although they can be very effectively used to present alphabetic information as well. The arrangement of the information in tables readily facilitates comparison and analysis of the information that is presented.

The complexity of tables varies considerably. Whereas some tables contain only a small amount of information and are quite simple, others contain much more extensive amounts of information. The components of a rather simple table are identified in Figure 14–1. Only the simplest of information could be presented in this illustration. The information in each of the columns must be comparable or related. For example, the table is appropriate for presenting the population of the various states for two different decades. Each of the states should be listed in the left-hand column and their populations for the two decades (1961–1970 and 1971–1980) listed in the middle and right-hand columns, respectively.

More complex information may require the use of stubs and braced headings, as shown in Figure 14–2. Although a subtitle is used and the totals of each of the columns are given, they are not required in a table of this design. The stub heading relates to the information contained in each of the rows beneath the various columnar heads, and the braced heading identifies the nature of the material contained in the various columnar headings. For exam-

Figure 14–1 Simple Table

Table Number
Title of Table

Columnar Head	Columnar Head	Columnar Head
XXX	XXX	XXX
XXX	XXX	XXX
XXX	XXX	XXX

Table Number Title of Table Subtitle of Table			
	Braced Heading		
Stub Heading	Columnar Head	Columnar Head	Columnar Head
XXX	XXX	XXX	XXX
XXX	XXX	XXX	XXX
XXX	XXX	XXX	XXX
XXX	XXX	XXX	XXX
Totals	XXXX	XXXX	XXXX

Figure 14–2 Table with Stub and Braced Headings.

ple, if you wished to compare the population of each state over a period of several decades, an appropriate stub heading would be "States." An appropriate braced heading would be "Population by Decades," and the columnar heads could be "1951–1960," "1961–1970," and "1971–1980."

If numerous rows are to be included in a table, you should use either of the following two techniques: double space after every third row or insert a horizontal line between every third and fourth row. Each technique provides visual guidance for the reader.

Pie Charts

For what are pie charts especially suited?

Pie charts are especially useful for comparing the various parts that comprise a whole. For example, pie charts are frequently used to show the percentages of the component parts of a whole. Because readers sometimes have difficulty visualizing the size of each part, the magnitude of each component should be printed on the chart, as shown in Figure 14–3.

In constructing a pie chart, place at the twelve o'clock position the section that consumes the largest amount of space and work in a clockwise direction. The smallest section is placed to the left of the twelve o'clock position.

The use of shading helps the reader grasp the material being presented. The identity of the smaller components can be presented outside the wedge. When doing so, however, a line or arrow should be used to connect the identification and the wedge.

Bar Charts

For what are bar charts especially suited?

Another graphic aid useful for comparing the magnitude of numerical data is the bar chart. The bars on the bar chart may be placed on the chart in either a vertical or horizontal arrangement. Care has to be taken to provide sufficient space for labeling the identity of each bar. Grid lines are placed at 90-degree angles to the bars. Therefore, if the bars are horizontal, the grid lines are verti-

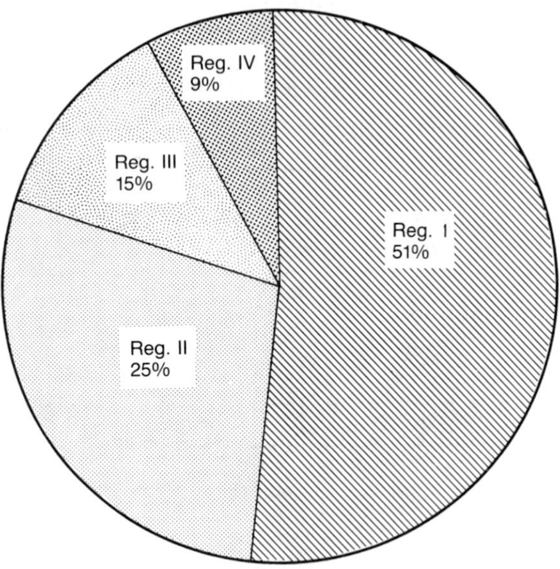

Figure 14–3 Pie Chart

cal. The value of each grid line should also appear on the chart. The primary purpose of grid lines is to help the reader visually determine the length of each bar. Although the reader may be able to approximate the magnitude of each bar by comparing its length with the grid lines, the magnitude of each bar should be identified on the chart. A bar chart is shown in Figure 14–4.

Several variations of the bar chart are discussed in the sections that follow.

Figure 14–4 Bar Chart

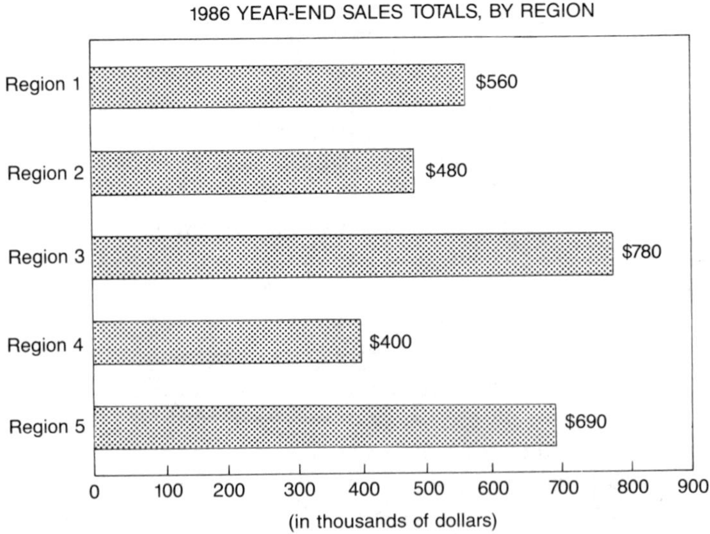

Multiple bar charts

The multiple bar chart is useful for comparing two or three variables in a series. For example, if you are interested in graphically illustrating the sales volume of hardware, painting supplies, and floor coverings in the five stores that comprise a particular chain, a multiple bar chart could be used. Rather than prepare a separate chart for each of the variables, a multiple bar chart could be prepared to illustrate all three variables for the five stores.

For what are multiple bar charts especially suited?

To help the reader visually grasp the material contained in the multiple bar chart, each variable should have its own design. Possibilities include open or blank design, crosshatching, angled lines, and the like. The design legend for each variable should be provided on the chart. Other suggestions for preparing multiple bar charts are: (1) limit the number of variables to a maximum of three; (2) use grid lines; and (3) identify the magnitude of each variable. Figure 14–5 presents a multiple bar chart.

Bilateral bar charts

When you wish to show positive and negative values for one variable, the bilateral bar chart is useful. To illustrate, the bilateral bar chart is useful for showing the positive or negative percentage changes in the population of five selected U.S. cities for the years 1977–1985.

For what are bilateral bar charts especially suited?

The bilateral bar chart differs from the other two bar charts discussed. It is used when the report writer wants to illustrate the percent of change from zero. The bilateral bar chart has two sections—positive and negative. As with the other bar charts, the use of grid lines is recommended. The exact amount

Figure 14–5 Multiple Bar Chart

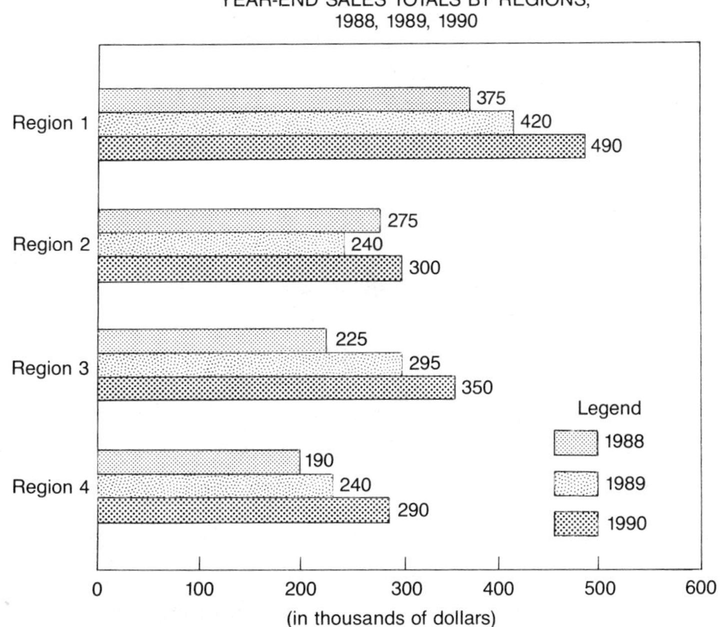

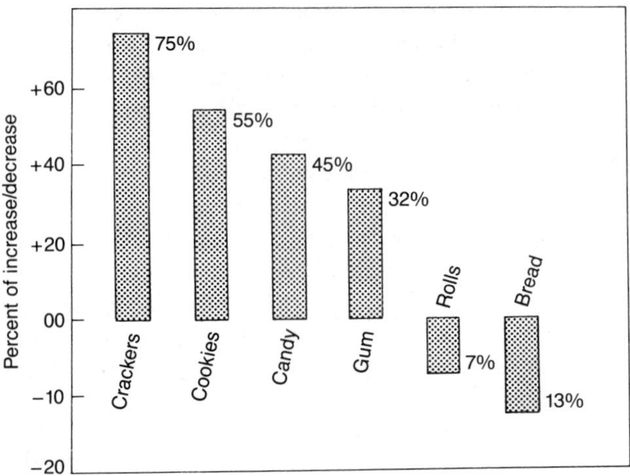

Figure 14–6 Bilateral Bar Chart

of change for each item should also be recorded on the chart. A bilateral bar chart is shown in Figure 14–6.

Divided Bar Charts

For what are divided bar charts especially suited?

Another variation of the bar chart is the divided bar chart. This variation is especially useful for illustrating the magnitude of each of the components of one variable. As an example, the divided bar chart is useful when you wish to illustrate the yearly number of books acquired in each of five academic disciplines by a university's library. The total number of books acquired in each of five years as well as the number acquired in each discipline could be determined from the chart.

Like the multiple bar chart, each component in the divided bar chart will have a different design legend. The use of grid lines is also recommended, as is the identification of the magnitude of each bar. A divided bar chart is shown in Figure 14–7.

Symbol Bar Charts

The final bar chart to be presented is the symbol bar chart. This chart is quite similar to the first bar chart discussed in this section, with the following exception: Instead of the usual bar construction, the bars are comprised of symbols appropriate for the situation. If a chart is used to illustrate the population of certain cities, the bars might be comprised of drawings that depict people. As is true of the other types of bar charts, using grid lines and identifying the magnitude of each bar is recommended. An example of a symbol bar chart is presented in Figure 14–8.

Line Charts

For what are line charts especially suited?

As a means of graphically illustrating data, line charts are especially suitable for showing changes in a continuous series of data during a given period. Line

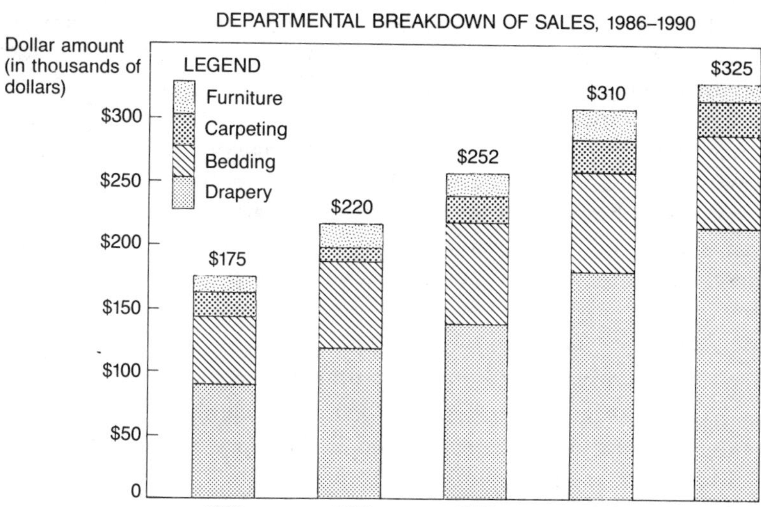

Figure 14–7 Divided Bar Chart

Figure 14–8 Symbol Bar Chart

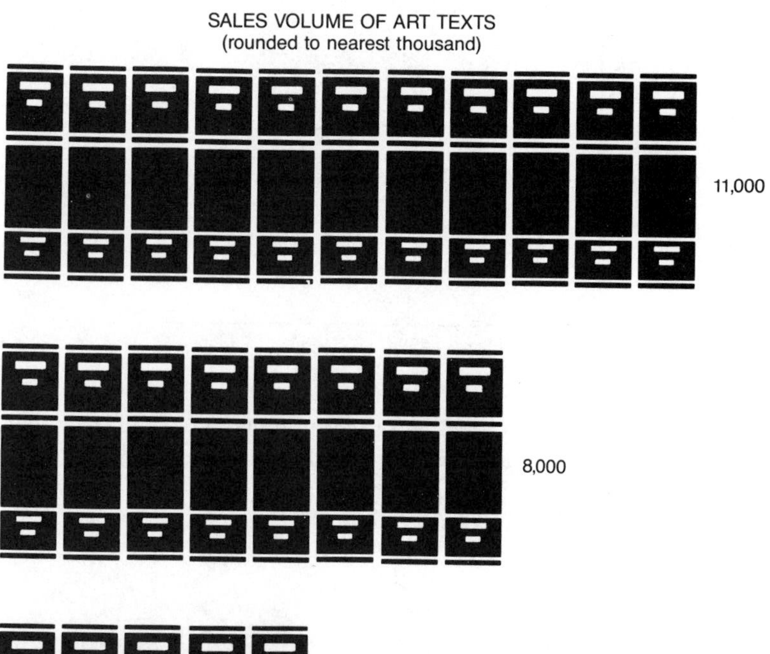

charts are the only graphic aids especially suited for illustrating changes in a continuous series discussed in this chapter. Such charts are appropriately used for illustrating changes in the stock market, sales volume, absenteeism, and production totals, for example.

When line charts are used to illustrate more than one variable, different line patterns are used for each variable. For example, a solid line may be used for one variable, a broken line for another, and a pattern of dots and dashes for a third. The legend for each variable must be clearly identified on the chart.

The following guidelines should be followed in preparing the charts.

1. Time should be plotted on the horizontal axis.
2. Quantity should be plotted on the vertical axis.
3. The magnitudes on the vertical and horizontal scale should be reasonably proportionate to one another. Although they may not be equal, they should be comparable to eliminate distortion.
4. The vertical axis must begin at zero, no matter how high the quantity values extend. If the values are quite high, the vertical axis can be broken, as the following chart illustrates.

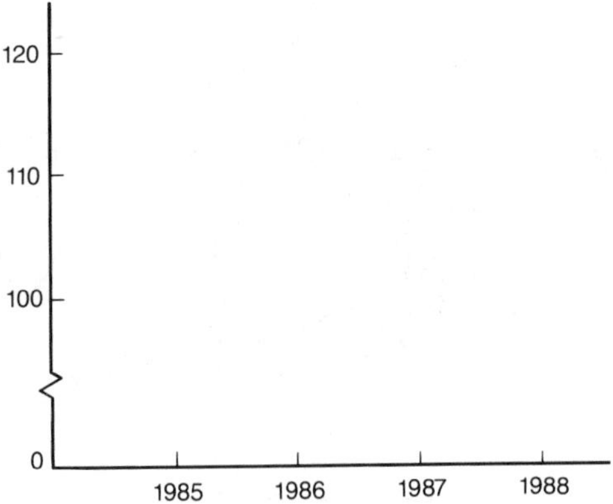

5. To facilitate the plotting of lines and the interpretation of the chart, both vertical and horizontal grids should be used.

A line chart is presented in Figure 14–9.

Belt Charts

For what are belt charts especially suited?

Belt charts, a variation of line charts, are used to illustrate the total values of a series as well as the various component values that comprise the total.

Belt charts are constructed by placing the largest component against the horizontal axis. The remaining components are placed on the chart, with the second largest component placed next and the smallest component placed last. A belt chart is presented in Figure 14–10.

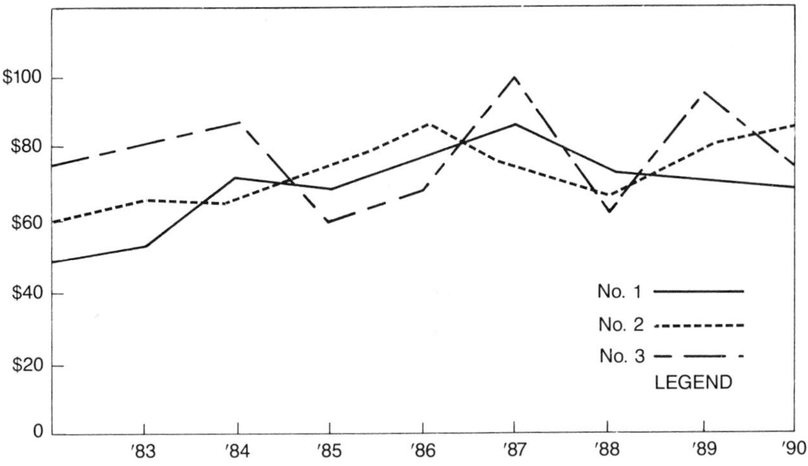

Figure 14–9 Line Chart

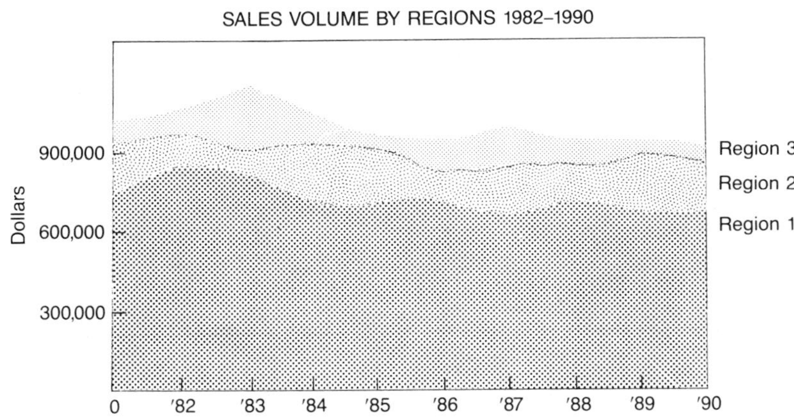

Figure 14–10 Belt Chart

Maps

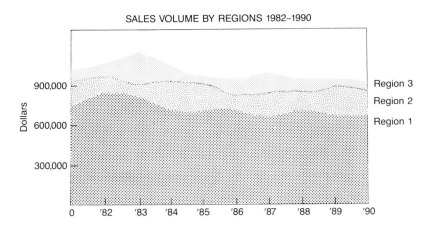

The final graphic aid to be discussed in this chapter is maps, which are especially useful when you wish to illustrate certain data characteristics of various areas or regions. Although maps are frequently used to illustrate quantitative data, they can also be used to illustrate nonquantitative data.

If needed, different designs should be used for each of the areas illustrated. Depending on the nature of the data being presented, a legend may be needed. A map is presented in Figure 14–11.

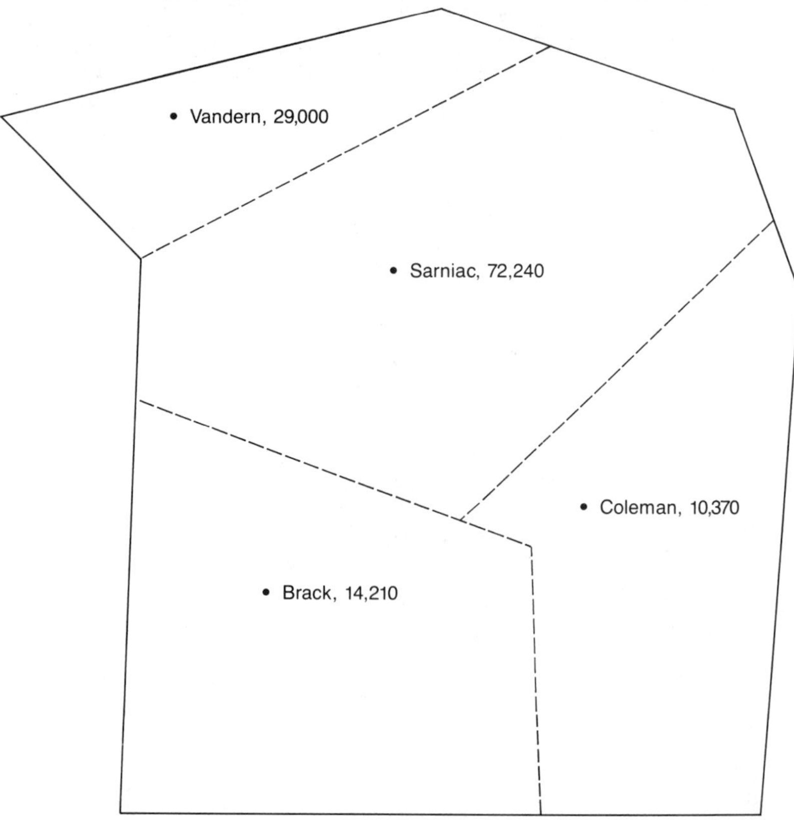

Figure 14–11 Map

FORMAT DIRECTIONS

Specific format directions for presenting left-bound formal reports are presented below.

Title fly:

Title begins on line 30
1 ½ inch left margin
1 inch right margin
Page number not needed

Title page:

2 inch top margin
1 inch bottom margin
1 ½ inch left margin
1 inch right margin
Page number not needed

Letter of authorization:

2 inch top margin
Minimum 2 inch bottom margin
1 $\frac{1}{2}$ inch left margin
1 $\frac{1}{2}$ inch right margin
Single space body
Use Roman numeral for page number and center $\frac{1}{2}$ inch from bottom

Letter of transmittal:

2 inch top margin
Minimum 2 inch bottom margin
1 $\frac{1}{2}$ inch left margin
1 $\frac{1}{2}$ inch right margin
Single space body
Use Roman numeral for page number and center $\frac{1}{2}$ inch from bottom

Table of contents:

2 inch top margin
1 inch bottom margin
1 $\frac{1}{2}$ inch left margin
1 inch right margin
Double space body
Use Roman numeral for page number and center $\frac{1}{2}$ inch from bottom

Abstract:

2 inch top margin
1 inch bottom margin
1 $\frac{1}{2}$ inch left margin
1 inch right margin
Single space body
Use Roman numeral for page number and center $\frac{1}{2}$ inch from bottom

First page of body:

2 inch top margin
1 inch bottom margin
1 $\frac{1}{2}$ inch left margin
1 inch right margin
Double space body
Page number not needed
Center first-degree headings; triple space before and after
Put second-degree headings on left margin; triple space before and double space after

Remaining pages of body:

1 inch top margin
1 inch bottom margin
1 $\frac{1}{2}$ inch left margin
1 inch right margin
Use Arabic number for page number and put in upper right corner, $\frac{1}{2}$ inch from top and 1 inch from right margin; triple space after
Center first-degree headings; triple space before and after

Bibliography:

2 inch top margin
1 inch bottom margin
1 $\frac{1}{2}$ inch left margin
1 inch right margin
Use Arabic number for page number and center at bottom of page, $\frac{1}{2}$ inch from bottom

SAMPLE REPORT

Figure 14–12, which presents parts of a formal report, identifies the proper mechanics to use in the various report parts.

CHAPTER SUMMARY

One of the distinguishing characteristics of formal reports is the number of parts or sections they contain. While some of the parts are optional, others are required.

The preliminary parts, some of which are optional, are the title fly, title page, letter of authorization, letter of transmittal, table of contents, list of illustrations, and abstract. Each part has a specific format that should be followed.

The actual body of the report is comprised of the introduction; the text of the report; and the report ending, which consists of the summary, conclusions, and recommendations. The appended parts are the appendices and the bibliography.

Several additional features, such as the proper use of headings, graphic aids, and documentation, will enhance the effectiveness of your report.

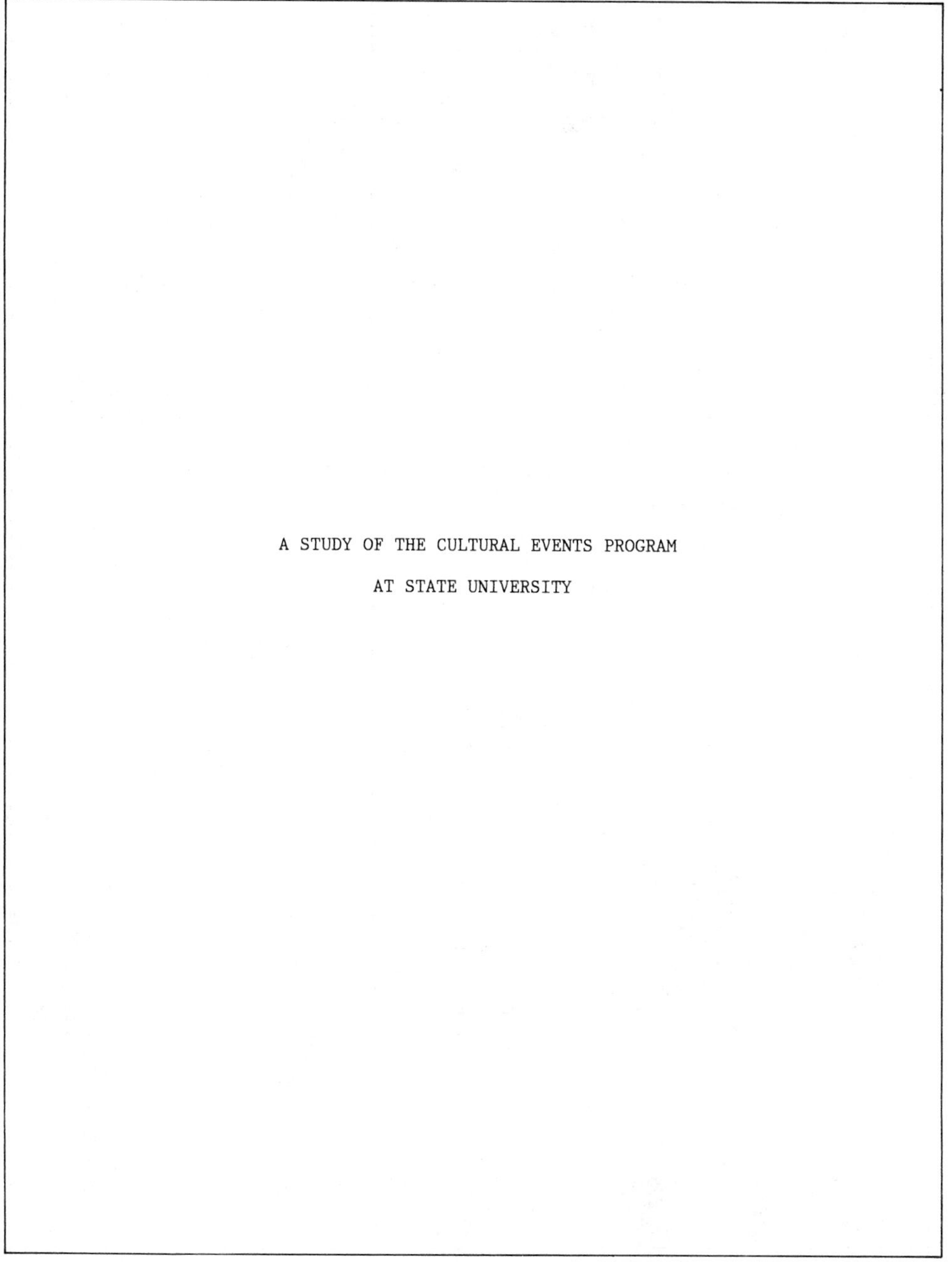

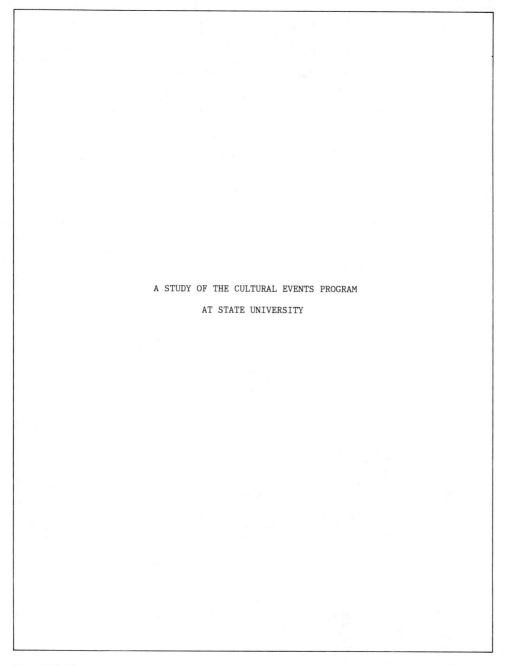

A STUDY OF THE CULTURAL EVENTS PROGRAM

AT STATE UNIVERSITY

Figure 14–12 Formal Report, Title Fly

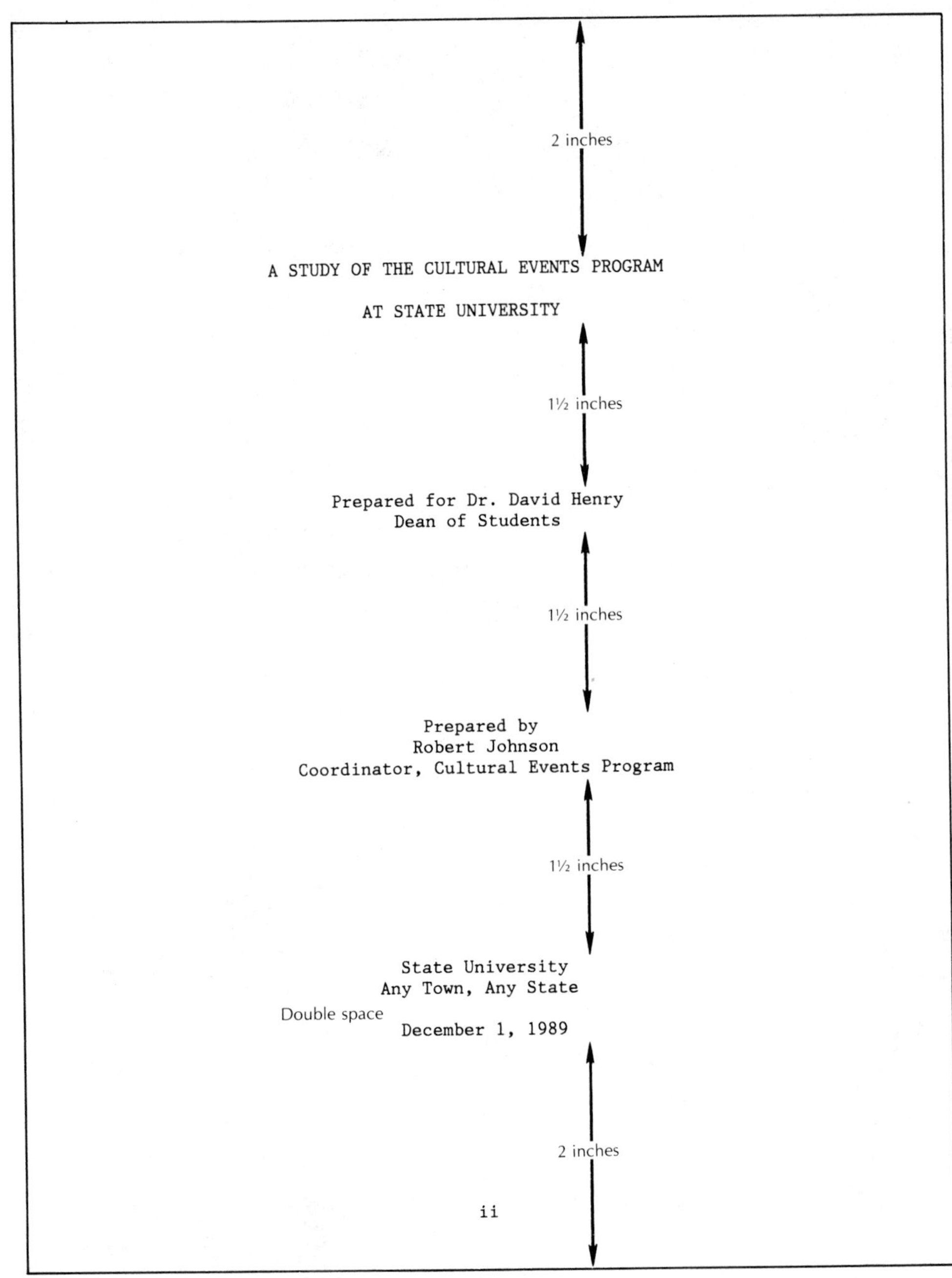

2 inches
A STUDY OF THE CULTURAL EVENTS PROGRAM
AT STATE UNIVERSITY
1½ inches
Prepared for Dr. David Henry
Dean of Students
1½ inches
Prepared by
Robert Johnson
Coordinator, Cultural Events Program
1½ inches
State University
Any Town, Any State
Double space
December 1, 1989
2 inches
ii

Figure 14–12 Title Page

STATE UNIVERSITY

Any Town, Any State 12345

September 19, 1989

Mr. Robert Johnson, Coordinator
Cultural Events Program
State University
Any Town, Any State 12345

Dear Bob:

At your earliest convenience, I would like you to undertake a study of the Cultural Events Program at State University. I can think of no one better qualified to undertake the study than you are because of your position as coordinator of the Cultural Events Program.

In your study, I would like for you to determine the students' needs and interests that should be considered in developing a new Cultural Events Program. Any residual benefits you can obtain from your study will also be greatly appreciated.

As you are well aware, a rather vocal student element has frequently criticized the Cultural Events Program at State University. I have been assured by President Wilson that if we have a good solid basis for further developing the program, he will do all he can to support its strengthening. Of course, the Board of Trustees has final approval of any recommendations we may propose.

I should like to have the report by December 1 if this is possible. I know you are busy; but before we can make any changes, we do need facts. My budget will cover the cost of any expenses incurred in the preparation of this report.

Please call on me if I can be of assistance.

Sincerely,

David Henry

David Henry
Dean of Students

jm

iii

Figure 14–12 Letter of Authorization

STATE UNIVERSITY

Any Town, Any State 12345

December 1, 1989

Dr. David Henry
Dean of Students
State University
Any Town, Any State 12345

Dear Dr. Henry:

The study of the Cultural Events Program at State University that you authorized me to undertake in your letter of September 18 is attached.

I'm confident of the validity of this study. As you will note, several instances are mentioned in the report which indicate that our random sample is truly a representative sample of the total student population of State University.

I have been contacted by three other colleges in the area, asking about the possibility of their using the questionnaire developed for this study. Similar studies are being undertaken in these colleges. I have given each of the colleges my permission to use the questionnaire that I developed for this study.

If you have any questions after you read the report, please call me.

Sincerely,

Robert Johnson

Robert Johnson, Coordinator
Cultural Events Program

ts

Attachment

iv

Figure 14–12 Letter of Transmittal

TABLE OF CONTENTS

Triple space

v

Figure 14–12 Table of Contents

LIST OF ILLUSTRATIONS

Triple space

Tables

Double space

Triple space

Figures

Double space

Figure 14–12 List of Illustrations

ABSTRACT

Triple space

Single space

The purpose of this study is to survey the students enrolled at State University, Fall Term, 1989, to determine their needs and interests for developing a new Cultural Events Program.

To determine the needs and interests of the students at State University, a questionnaire was developed. A randomly selected sample of 550 students received the questionnaire, and a 90 percent return (450 questionnaires) was achieved.

Of the respondents, 42.8 percent were male and 57.2 percent were female. Freshmen constituted 31 percent of the sample; sophomores, 26 percent; juniors, 23 percent; and seniors, 20 percent. The respondents' majors were as follows: liberal arts majors, 27 percent; social science majors, 24 percent; business majors, 18 percent; education majors, 16 percent; and science majors, 15 percent.

Fifty-three percent of the respondents work 20 or fewer hours per week. Eight percent work over 40 hours per week. Sixty percent of the hours are worked between 5 p.m. and 10 p.m. Monday through Thursday.

Forty percent of the respondents indicated that they were able to attend all the events they cared to attend. Another 40 percent were unable to attend the events because of work or study.

vii

Figure 14–12 Abstract

I. INTRODUCTION

Triple space

A. Background of the Report

Double space

Dr. David Henry, Dean of Students at State University, authorized the preparation of this study on September 18, 1989. Dr. Henry's letter of authorization instructed Mr. Robert Johnson, Coordinator of Cultural Events at State University, to begin work on the study at the earliest possible time.

Triple space

B. Purpose

Double space

As outlined in Dr. David Henry's letter of authorization, the purpose of this study was to survey the students enrolled at State University, Fall, Term, 1989, to determine their needs and interests for developing a new Cultural Events Program at State University. Among the secondary purposes are the following:

1. To determine the popularity of the current cultural activities provided by State University.

2. To determine the factors discouraging students from taking greater advantage of the Cultural Events Program.

3. To determine which categories of cultural activities the students would like to have offered in greater abundance.

C. Scope

The writer did not attempt to determine the names of groups, the titles of movies, etc., that the students would like to have available at State University. Since this represents information with a time-value element, the writer did not wish to include such information in this report.

Figure 14–12 Body

D. Methodology

The methodology of this report consisted of developing a questionnaire (See Appendix for a copy of the questionnaire) designed to obtain the necessary information. An article entitled, "The Necessity of Cultural Activities," in the September, 1988, issue of College Student Journal provided some background information (Jacobs, 1988).

After the questionnaire was developed, a randomly selected group of students at State University was used to validate the instrument. Once validated, the questionnaire was finalized and printed for distribution to a randomly selected group of students.

The Office of Institutional Research provided considerable assistance in determining the number of students to include in the survey, the names of students to include, and recommendations for follow-up, if necessary.

Of the 4,239 students enrolled at State University, the Office of Institutional Research determined that a randomly selected sample of 500 students would be sufficient. Of the 500 questionnaires distributed, 450 were completed, which represents a 90 percent return.

Once the data were compiled, percentages were computed. The information in this report is based on the percentage of student response to each item on the questionnaire.

E. Limitations

The quality of the information in this report is limited by the accuracy with which the students responded to the questionnaire. If they responded honestly, the content of the report is considered to be accurate.

Figure 14–12 Body (Cont.)

3

F. Historical Background

This report is essentially a follow-up of the 1982 report previously mentioned, although this report is more comprehensive. Both reports were undertaken to make the Cultural Events Program at State University more relevant to the needs of the students.

G. Report Organization

The organization of the sections that follow is the same as the organization of the items that are included on the questionnaire. The responses to each item are summarized, followed by a summary of the major findings of the report, conclusions, and recommendations.

The year-in-school percentage breakdown for the students responding to the questionnaire is as follows:

Freshman--31 percent
Sophomore--26 percent
Junior--23 percent
Senior--20 percent

These percentages correspond roughly to the percentage breakdown for the total school population.

C. Major in School

As shown in Figure 1, the greatest percentage of the respondents (27 percent) are liberal arts majors. Social science majors follow closely with 24 percent. Business (18 percent), education (16 percent), and science (15 percent) majors comprise the remainder of the students' areas of concentration.

Figure 14–12 Body (Cont.)

G. Number of Work Hours per Week

Of the respondents who work either part time or full time, a majority of 53 percent work 20 or fewer hours per week, as shown on Table 1. The largest percentage of those who work do so 16-20 hours per week. Eight percent of the respondents work over 40 hours per week.

Table 1

PERCENTAGE OF RESPONDENTS WHO WORK PART TIME OR FULL TIME

Number of Hours Worked	Percentage of Respondents
Fewer than 6	4
6-10	10
11-15	17
16-20	22
21-25	17
26-30	12
31-35	3
36-40	7
More than 40	8

H. Hours Worked After 5 P.M.

Because the majority of cultural events take place after 5 p.m., the report writer felt that determining the percent of hours worked between 5 p.m. and 10 p.m. was important. The results obtained by the questionnaire indicate that 60 percent of the hours are worked between 5 p.m. and 10 p.m., Monday through Thursday, 20 percent are worked between 5 p.m. and 10 p.m. on Friday, and five percent of the hours worked are between 5 p.m. and after 10 p.m. on any of these days.

Figure 14–12 Body (Cont.)

O. Reasons for Not Attending More Cultural Events

The last item on the questionnaire was included to determine the respondents' reasons for not attending more cultural events. Forty percent of the respondents indicated that they attended all the events they cared to attend, 25 percent indicated that their work schedules prevented them from attending more cultural events, and 15 percent indicated that the cultural events conflicted with their study schedules. Nineteen percent of the respondents indicated a lack of interest in the cultural events sponsored by the university. One percent identified "other" reasons for not attending more cultural events. The reason most frequently given was conflict with religious activities.

Triple space

III. SUMMARY, CONCLUSIONS, RECOMMENDATIONS

Triple space

This section provides a summary designed to recap the findings of the research efforts, conclusions based on the findings, and recommendations for improving the Cultural Events Program at State University.

A. Summary of Findings

Fifty-three percent of the respondents who work either part time or full time work 20 or more hours per week, while 18 percent work more than 30 hours per week.

While 15 percent of the hours worked by students are before 5 p.m. and after 10 p.m., Monday through Saturday, 85 percent are between the hours of

B. Conclusions

The following conclusions are based on the findings of the research efforts:

Figure 14–12 Body (Cont.)

1. A need for a new Cultural Events Program does not exist at the present time. Overall student satisfaction with the program is evidenced in part by (a) the number of favorable responses about certain aspects of the present program, and (b) the fact that the current program seems to meet the needs of most students. Only 19 percent of the respondents indicated a lack of interest in the present program.

2. The number of students who attend at least one cultural event each week attests to the popularity of the Cultural Events Program. Reasons cited for students' failure to take greater advantage of cultural activities included their work (25 percent) and study (15 percent).

Figure 14–12 Body (Cont.)

BIBLIOGRAPHY

Triple space

Jacobs, Ellory. "The Necessity of Cultural Activities," College Student Journal, 17:24-26, September, 1988.

(Author's Note: Although a bibliography is not normally prepared for one reference, this one is included for illustration purposes.)

11

Figure 14–12 Bibliography

12

Appendix

QUESTIONNAIRE

Cultural Events Program

1. Sex: Male____; Female____

2. Year in School: Freshman____; Sophomore____; Junior____; Senior____

3. Major in School: Science____; Social Sciences____; Business____; Liberal Arts____; Education____

4. Age: Less than 18:____; 18____; 19____; 20____; 21____; 22____; 23____; 24____; 25____; 26____; Over 26____

5. What percent of your educational expenses (board, room, tuition, books, supplies) do you personally pay for as opposed to someone else paying for these expenses?

   I pay for ____ percent of my educational expenses.

6. Do you work either part time or full time during the school year?

   Part time____; Full time____; Don't Work____

7. If you work during the school year, what is the average number of hours you work each week?

   Fewer than 6____; 6-10____; 11-15____; 16-20____; 21-25____; 26-30____; 31-35____; 36-40____; More than 40____

8. What percent of your work hours are between

   5 p.m.-10 p.m., Mon.-Thurs.: 0-25____; 26-50____; 51-75____; 76-100____
   5 p.m.-10 p.m., Fri.: 0-25____; 26-50____; 51-75____; 76-100____
   5 p.m.-10 p.m., Sat.: 0-25____; 26-50____; 51-75____; 76-100____

9. On the average, how many hours do you spend each week attending university-sponsored cultural events?

   0____; 1-2____; 3-4____; 5-6____; 7-8____; 9-10____; More than 10____

10. Rank the following in terms of the amount of time you spend each week attending the following university-sponsored cultural events. (1 = greatest amount of time; 8 = least amount of time).

    Movies____; Recitals____; Plays____; Concerts (instrumental)____; Operas____; Concerts (vocal)____; Ballet____; Concerts (instrumental and vocal)____

Figure 14–12 Appendix

11. Rank the following in terms of the amount of time you would like to spend each week attending, assuming that each is offered as many hours each week as you desire. (1 = greatest amount of time; 8 = least amount of time).

Movies____; Recitals____; Plays____; Concerts (instrumental)____;
Operas____; Concerts (vocal)____; Ballet____;
Concerts (instrumental and vocal)____

12. Which of the following statements do you most agree with?

____A portion of student tuition should be allocated for financing the cost of university-sponsored cultural events.
____Students who attend the cultural events should bear the costs incurred in sponsoring the events.

13. Would you like to have an opportunity to help determine which groups and/or cultural events appear at State University?

Yes____; No____

14. For what reason do you not attend more cultural events?

____I attend all that I wish to attend.
____I have a work conflict.
____I have a study conflict.
____The programs do not interest me.
____Other (please specify)________________________________

Figure 14–12 Appendix (Cont.)

REVIEW QUESTIONS

1. In what ways are formal and informal reports distinguished from one another?
2. What parts of the formal report are required? What parts are optional?
3. What is the purpose of the letter of transmittal?
4. What is included in the introduction of a formal report?
5. Which verb tense is generally recommended for writing business reports?
6. Explain the differences in the format of each of the different degrees of headings used in formal reports.
7. What material found in a business report has to be footnoted?
8. When is an *ibid.* footnote used? an *op. cit.* footnote? a *loc. cit.* footnote?
9. What are the characteristics of effective report conclusions?
10. What is the substance of the recommendations found in a formal report?
11. What are some of the important guidelines to consider when preparing graphics to include in a formal report?
12. For what types of data/information are pie charts especially suited?
13. For what types of data/information are bar charts especially suited?
14. For what types of data/information are multiple bar charts especially suited?
15. For what types of data/information are belt charts especially suited?

APPLICATION PROBLEMS

1. Prepare a formal report based on the data/information presented below. The data/information were collected by means of a questionnaire completed by 240 of the 300 individuals included in the study. The study was undertaken by First City Bank to assess customer satisfaction with its automatic tellers. The results of the study will be used in assessing the effectiveness of the teller-machine operations. Incorporate graphic aids in your report. Your instructor will tell you which parts he/she wants you to include.

a. What is your age? 16–25: 31; 26–35: 47; 36–45: 51; 46–55: 71; 56–65: 30; over 65: 10

b. What is your sex? Male: 145; Female: 95

c. On the average, how often do you use an automatic teller machine each week? 0 times: 34; 1 time: 45; 2 times: 56; 3 times: 58; 4 times: 33; 5 times: 10; 6 times: 4; more than 6 times: 0

d. Which teller machine do you use most often? 9th Street: 74; Bob's Grocery Store: 60; Drive-in Bank: 106

e. Which one of the following best explains the reason you use the teller machine most often at the location you identified in item d above? Convenient location: 156; Near where I work: 40; Near where I live: 20; Speed: 24

f. How would you rate your satisfaction with the use of teller machines? Very satisfied: 48; Quite satisfied: 74; Neither satisfied nor dissatisfied: 78; Quite dissatisfied: 30; Very dissatisifed: 10

g. If you marked "Quite dissatisfied" or "Very dissatisfied" in item f above, which of the following most accurately reflects the reason for your dissatisfaction? Machine sometimes malfunctions: 13; Machine is sometimes out of order when I have made a special trip to use it: 20; I miss having a person assist me: 4; Machine is not always able to take care of my banking needs: 3

h. How would you rate the ease with which the machines are operated? Very easy to use: 110; Quite easy to use: 91; Neither easy nor difficult to use: 20; Quite difficult to use: 14; Very difficult to use: 5

i. For what type of transaction do you most often use the teller? Withdrawing cash: 154; Depositing money to account: 45; Transferring money from one account to another: 31; Making an inquiry about bank balance: 10

j. Are you satisfied with the maximum daily amount of cash that you can withdraw from the machine? Yes: 198; No: 42

k. If you answered "No" in item j above, do you believe the maximum should be increased or decreased? For increasing: 34; For decreasing: 8

l. What percent of your total banking needs is the teller able to accommodate? 75 to 100 percent: 78; 50 to 75 percent: 124; 24 to 50 percent: 32; 0 to 25 percent: 6

m. In addition to the services the teller is capable of performing, list one additional service you would like for the teller to be able to perform: Use to make loan payments: 184; Use to make inquiry about current money-market rates: 20; Use to inquire if a check with a specified number has cleared the bank: 10; Use to inquire about amount of direct deposits to account: 26

n. Do you think First City Bank should install more tellers throughout the city? Yes: 210; No: 30

2. You are the assistant to the manager of East Side Shopping Center. Several weeks ago, you and the manager decided that a survey should be undertaken to determine the shoppers' level of satisfaction with the shopping center. The results will be used as input in assessing the effectiveness with which the Center is operated and managed. You were asked by the manager to prepare the questionnaire, to distribute it, and to prepare a report that summarized your findings. Incorporate graphic aids into your report. Your instructor will tell you which report parts to include in the report.

After the questionnaire was developed and piloted on a small sample of shoppers, you handed it out randomly to individuals who were shopping at East Side during the week of September 24. You handed out 80 questionnaires on each of the seven days of that week. Of the 560 that were given out, 400 were returned in the postage-paid envelope that was attached to the questionnaire.

The following summarizes the data/information you received:

a. Age: 12–18: 52; 19–25: 64; 26–32: 69; 33–39: 53; 40–46: 40; 47–53: 40; 54–60: 38; 61–67: 30; Over 67: 14

b. Yearly individual income: Under $10,000: 123; $10,000–$19,999: 130; $20,000–$29,999: 73; $30,000–$39,999: 34; $40,000 and over: 40

c. On the average, how many days per week do you shop at East Side Shopping Center: 0–1: 165; 2–3: 145; 4–5: 50; 6–7: 40

d. Which one of the following most clearly reflects the time of day you most often begin shopping at East Side: Between 9 a.m. and 12 noon: 87;

Between noon and 3 p.m.: 76; Between 3 p.m. and 6 p.m.: 176; Between 6 p.m. and 9 p.m.: 61

e. During which group of days do you most often shop: Monday through Friday: 189; Saturday and/or Sunday: 211

f. What percent of your total shopping is done at East Side: less than 50 percent: 137; 50–59 percent: 132; 60–69 percent: 65; 70–79 percent: 32; 80–89 percent: 24; 90–100 percent: 10

g. Of the various major shopping shopping areas in the Greater Ft. Johnson area, which one do you frequent most often: Downtown: 145; East Side Shopping Center: 179; West Side Shopping Center: 176

h. How satisfied are you with the cleanliness of the public areas of East Side Shopping Center (restrooms, corridors, entrances, etc): very satisfied: 159; quite satisfied: 116; neither satisfied nor dissatisfied: 101; quite dissatisfied: 20; very dissatisfied: 4

i. How satisfied are you with the attractiveness of the public areas of East Side Shopping Center (restrooms, corridors, entrances, etc.): very satisfied: 134; quite satisfied: 142; neither satisfied nor dissatisfied: 40; quite dissatisfied: 40; very dissatisfied: 44

j. How satisfied are you with the parking facilities at East Side Shopping Center: very satisfied: 189; quite satisfied: 134; neither satisfied nor dissatisifed: 23; quite dissatisfied: 24; very dissatisfied: 30

k. How satisfied are you with the hours that East Side Shopping Center is open: very satisfied: 329; quite satisfied: 20; neither satisfied nor dissatisfied: 15; quite dissatisfied: 10; very dissatisfied: 26

l. How satisfied are you with the eating establishments at East Side Shopping Center: very satisfied: 174; quite satisfied: 121; neither satisfied nor dissatisfied: 42; quite dissatisfied: 30; very dissatisfied: 33

m. How satisfied are you with the general merchandise stores at East Side Shopping Center: very satisfied: 192; quite satisfied: 102; neither satisfied nor dissatisfied: 33; quite dissatisfied: 43; very dissatisfied: 30

n. How satisfied are you with the specialty stores at East Side Shopping Center: very satisfied: 210; quite satisfied: 86; neither satisfied nor dissatisfied: 42; quite dissatisfied: 32; very dissatisfied: 30

o. How satisfied are you with the special events held at East Side Shopping Center: very satisfied: 152; quite satisfied: 240; neither satisfied nor dissatisfied: 8; quite dissatisfied: 0; very dissatisfied: 0

p. What other types of stores do you wish were located in East Side Shopping Center that are not presently found there: No other stores desired: 234; Computer equipment store: 40; Electronics store: 30; Home furnishings store: 34; Maternity clothing store: 62

q. Which one of the following factors most likely determines whether you shop at East Side Shopping Center or at another location: What I am wanting to purchase: 176; Time of day: 43; In-progress sales at stores in the Center: 123; Whether I am shopping alone or with family/friends: 34; Whether I am intent on purchasing or just looking: 24

Prepare the report.

3. You are the assistant to the manager of the Food Place, the cafeteria in the Student Union at Westmont University. From time to time, the students who eat their meals in the cafeteria are asked to complete a questionnaire that solicits their answers to a variety of questions. The information is used as input for making decisions about various aspects of the cafeteria's operations. The data below are the responses received from 100 of the 150 students who were randomly asked to complete the questionnaire. In preparing the formal report for the manager, incorporate graphic aids. Your instructor will tell you which report parts to include.

a. Year in school: Senior: 38; Junior: 33; Sophomore: 17; Freshman: 12

b. Sex: Male: 57; Female: 43

c. Major: Arts and Letters: 23; Business: 31; Engineering: 31; Physical Science: 15

d. On the average, how many meals do you eat each week in the Food Place: 0: 0; 1–3: 25; 4–6: 30; 7–9: 12; 10–12: 8; 13–15: 5; 16–18: 10; More than 18: 10

e. Which meal do you eat most often in the Food Place: Breakfast: 21; Lunch: 59; Dinner: 20

f. Overall, how satisfied are you with the Food Place: Very satisfied: 25; Quite satisfied: 43; Neither satisfied nor dissatisfied: 20; Quite dissatisfied: 10; Very dissatisfied: 2

g. How satisfied are you with the taste of the food served in the Food Place: Very satisfied: 35; Quite satisfied: 38; Neither satisfied nor dissatisfied: 20; Quite dissatisfied: 7; Very dissatisfied: 0

h. How satisfied are you with the appearance of the food served in the Food Place: Very satisfied: 32; Quite satisfied: 35; Neither satisfied nor dissatisfied: 17; Quite dissatisfied: 13; Very dissatisfied: 3

i. How satisfied are you with the variety of the food served in the Food Place: Very satisfied: 29; Quite satisfied: 32; Neither satisfied nor dissatisfied: 14; Quite dissatisfied: 17; Very dissatisfied: 8

j. How satisfied are you with the service you receive in the Food Place: Very satisfied: 36; Quite satisfied: 34; Neither satisfied nor dissatisfied: 20; Quite dissatisfied: 8; Very dissatisfied: 2

k. How satisfied are you with the atmosphere in the Food Place: Very satisfied: 18; Quite satisfied: 32; Neither satisfied nor dissatisfied: 30; Quite dissatisfied: 12; Very dissatisfied: 8

l. How satisfied are you with the cleanliness of the Food Place: Very satisfied: 52; Quite satisfied: 30; Neither satisfied nor dissatisfied: 10; Quite dissatisfied: 6; Very dissatisfied: 2

m. How do you feel about the price of the food available in the Food Place: Very expensive: 10; Moderately priced: 34; Neither expensive nor inexpensive: 40; Quite inexpensive: 8; Very inexpensive: 8

n. Which one of the following most clearly reflects your reason for eating meals at the Food Place: Convenient: 46; Quality of food: 34; Price of food: 10; Atmosphere: 2; My friends eat at the Food Place: 8

Prepare the formal report.

4. You, the executive vice-president of Willoby Corporation, have had several requests from department heads, supervisors, and employees, to investigate the need for establishing a company-wide training program. To help you determine the need for such a program, you decide to call a meeting of interested individuals to discuss the situation. At the end of the meeting, you distributed a questionnaire that the participants were to complete. Tabulated results of the questionnaire are presented below. You received a completed questionnaire from each of the 50 participants. You decide that a formal report should be prepared summarizing the questionnaire responses. The report is to be prepared for Mr. Grant Skinner, Willoby's president.

a. Sex: Male: 34; Female: 16

b. Department affiliation: Accounting: 5; Word Processing: 8; Production: 7; Executive Area: 12; Marketing: 3; Data Processing: 10; Maintenance: 5

c. Years with the company: 0–3 years: 18; 4–7 years: 12; 8–11 years: 4; 12 or more: 16

d. Which of the following best reflects your job: Administrative: 8; Manager: 6; Secretary: 10; Clerk: 12; Specialist: 2; Supervisor: 12

e. Which of the following best reflects how you became trained for your present position: Came into position trained: 22; Supervisor trained: 18; Self-trained: 10

f. What is your level of agreement with the following statement: "A training program is badly needed at Willoby Corporation." Strongly agree: 20; Agree: 14; Neutral: 5; Disagree: 3; Strongly disagree: 8

g. Which of the following best describes your reasons for wanting a training program at this time: Help me do better work in my present job: 20; Help my subordinates become better qualified: 20; Help me qualify for a job I would like to be promoted to: 7; No clearcut motive for wanting a training program: 3

h. Would you be interested in attending training sessions held after work hours: Yes: 24; Perhaps: 10; No: 16

i. Of the following areas, which one is the area in which you would most like to have a training session offered: Time management: 10; Effective communications: 13; Specific job skills: 15; Interpersonal relations: 5; Conflict resolution: 4; Organization of work: 3

j. If you believe you are qualified to provide a training session on a topic that others are interested in, would you be willing to volunteer your time to provide the session: Yes: 37; No: 13

Prepare the report.

5. You are a member of the local chapter of Personnel Management Association. Mr. Brian Gullett, president of the local chapter, has asked that you prepare a report which provides a profile of the members of your association. The vice president of the association, Ms. Margaret Cowles, developed the questionnaire. Before she finalized the questionnaire, she piloted it on several members of the association. After the questionnaire was validated, it was completed by 150 of the 170 members who attended the September 24 meeting. Include in your report the parts that your instructor asks you to include. Make use of graphic illustrations when appropriate.

a. Sex: Male: 80; Female: 70

b. Age: Less than 26: 10; 26–35: 15; 36–45: 45; 46–55: 55; 56–65: 25; Over 65: 0

c. Present salary: Less than $19,000: 0; $19,000–$21,999: 10; $22,000–$24,999: 12; $25,000–$27,999: 14; $28,000–$30,999: 14; $31,000–$33,999: 16; $34,000–$36,999: 18; $37,000–$39,999: 55; $40,000–$42,999: 7; $43,000 or more: 4

d. Highest educational degree attained: high school diploma: 5; bachelor's degree: 79; master's degree: 49; Doctoral degree: 17

e. Bachelor's degree major: Did not attend college: 5; Liberal arts: 5; Business: 82; Education: 32; Social Sciences: 21; Other: 5

f. Total number of years of work experience: 0–1 years: 2; 2–4 years: 8; 5–7 years: 15; 8–10 years: 43; 11–13 years: 37; 14–16 years: 12; 17–19 years: 14; 20–22 years: 13; 23–25 years: 4; 26–28 years: 2; 29 or more years: 0

g. Years with present employer: 0–2 years: 2; 3–4 years: 10; 5–6 years: 18; 7–8 years: 34; 9–10 years: 28; 11–12 years: 25; 13–14 years: 14; 15–16 years: 10; More than 16: 9

h. Before your present job, how many other jobs have you had within the company for which you presently work: 0: 24; 1: 49; 2: 47; 3: 23; 4 or more: 7

i. Present job title: personnel director (or manager): 94; Assistant personnel director (or manager): 23; Vice president: 12; Director of manpower planning: 8; Other: 13

j. Title of immediate supervisor: President: 57; Vice president: 49; Personnel director (or manager): 24; Other: 20

k. Number of employees in your company: 0–50: 10; 51–100: 12; 101–150: 16; 151–200: 39; 201–250: 35; 251–300: 10; over 300: 28

Prepare the report.

6. You are the administrative assistant to Mr. John Heathrow, vice-president for business and finance, Western Hills College. From time to time, Western Hills College purchases the stock of companies assured of providing a fair return to their investors. Before the college is able to purchase the stock, the investments committee has to give its approval. Mr. Heathrow likes to use a formal report to present to the committee vital information about the company under consideration. Mr. Heathrow recently ran across the balance sheet and income statement of a company that looks like a good investment possibility. Accordingly, you are responsible for preparing the report that will be used by the investment committee in its deliberations. Among the data the committee likes to look at are the following:

a. Current ratio: found by dividing the current assets by the current liabilities

b. Quick ratio (also known as the acid-test ratio): found by subtracting the inventories from the current assets and then dividing this result by the current liabilities

c. Inventory turnover: found by dividing the cost of goods sold by the inventory

d. Fixed assets turnover: found by dividing the sales by net fixed assets
e. Total sales turnover: found by dividing the sales by total assets
f. Debt ratio: found by dividing total liabilities by total assets

DICKINSON COMPANY
Comparative Balance Sheet
December 31, 1988 and 1989

	1989	*1988*
Assets		
Current Assets:		
Cash	$ 50,898	$ 45,988
Notes Receivable	40,982	37,994
Accounts Receivable	76,983	58,123
Inventories	419,089	401,234
Total Current Assets	587,952	543,339
Fixed Assets (Net)	564,984	497,908
Total Assets	$1,152,936	$1,041,247
Liabilities		
Current Liabilities:		
Notes Payable	$ 39,083	$ 31,089
Accounts Payable	143,091	101,876
Accrued Payables	45,089	47,981
Total Current Liabilities	227,263	180,946
Long-Term Liabilities	198,098	109,085
Total Liabilities	425,361	290,031
Capital		
Capital Stock	$ 706,575	$ 734,216
Retained Earnings	21,000	17,000
Total Capital	727,575	751,216
Total Liabilities and Capital	$1,152,936	$1,041,247

The investments committee also likes to have the following data available that are calculated from the information presented on the comparative income statement and the comparative balance sheet:

a. Gross profit margin: found by dividing gross profit by sales

b. Net profit margin: found by dividing the net profit before Federal income taxes by net sales

c. Return on investment: found by dividing net profits after taxes by total assets

DICKINSON COMPANY
Comparative Income Statement
for the Years Ended December 31, 1988 and 1989

	1989	*1988*
Net Sales	$ 809,081	$ 708,064
Cost of Goods Sold		
Inventories, January 1	$ 431,089	$ 412,098
Net Purchases	569,984	531,095
Cost of Goods Available	$1,001,073	$ 943,193
Less Inventories, December 31	403,763	410,048
Cost of Goods Sold	$ 597,310	$ 533,145
Gross Profit	$ 211,771	$ 174,919
Operating Expenses		
Selling Expenses	$ 49,901	$ 45,110
Administrative Expenses	59,181	65,010
Total Operating Expenses	$ 109,082	$ 110,120
Net Profit Before Federal Income Tax	$ 102,689	$ 64,799
Federal Income Tax	27,842	18,192
Net Profit After Federal Income Tax	74,847	$ 46,607

Incorporate appropriate graphic aids into your report. Your instructor will tell you which parts he/she wants included in the report. As another dimension to the problem, your instructor may ask you to undertake library research to determine the significance of the various ratios you are calculating so this information can be incorporated into your report.

7. Write a report on one of the topics listed below. Each topic is one for which a variety of secondary-source information is available, including textbooks and journal articles that you will find in the library. You may wish to interview appropriate individuals as a means of adding primary information to your report. To help you determine the appropriate content to include in your report, a variety of subtopics (identified as A, B, C, D, E, etc.) are listed for each topic. Your instructor may ask that you include others as well. Because the subtopics may not be listed in a logical sequence, make sure you determine an appropriate order before you begin preparing your report. After you have completed your library research, your instructor may ask that you present to him/her a tentative outline of the report's content.

1. Office automation—A, D, E, G, H, I, J
2. Employee motivation—B, C, H, I, Q
3. Flextime—D, E, G, H, I, J
4. Team building—C, D, E, G, H, I, J

5. Quality circles—D, E, F, G, H, I, J
6. Employee selection procedures—A, F, K, L, Q
7. Word processing—A, D, E, G, H, I
8. Evolution of management theory—M, N, C, T
9. Computer security—A, F, H, J, Q
10. Evolution of computers—M, N, S, T
11. Financial ratios—B, C, H, J, Q
12. Nonverbal communication—A, C, D, E
13. Product promotion—A, B, R, Q
14. Advertising channels—B, O, R, Q
15. Employee performance-appraisal techniques—B, C, D, E, H, I, L
16. Controlling office costs—B, C, D, E, H
17. Employee training techniques—A, B, K, Q, R
18. Oral communication—C, P, Q, R
19. Health maintenance organizations (HMO)—D, E, G, J, O
20. Effective employer-employee relations—A, B, C, H, J, Q
21. White-collar unions—D, E, H, I, O, P
22. Quality of work life (QWL)—A, C, D, E, H, I, R
23. Job enrichment—B, C, D, E, G, I, J
24. MBO—A, C, D, E, F, G, H, I, J
25. Salary incentive plans—A, C, D, E, H, I, J
26. Participative management—B, C, D, E, G, H, I, J
27. Employee compensation—A, B, F, J, L
28. New electronic office equipment—A, C, P, Q, R
29. Electronic mail—C, D, E, F, G, H, J
30. Telecommunications—A, C, D, E, G, H, J

A—Components of ______________
B—Techniques of ______________
C—Why ______________ is important
D—Advantages of ______________
E—Disadvantages ______________
F—Steps involved in ______________
G—What ______________ is
H—What ______________ do/does for the organization
I—What ______________ do/does for the employee
J—How ______________ works
K—Building quality into ______________
L—Forms used in ______________
M—Stages of development of ______________
N—Important individuals affecting development
O—Characteristics of ______________
P—Functions performed by ______________
Q—Benefits of ______________

R—Measuring effectiveness of ______________

S—New developments on the horizon

T—Lasting contributions of each stage of development

8. Using secondary-source information, write a report about the career field you plan to enter upon graduating from college. Include in your report information about topics such as the following: qualifications needed, opportunities available, salary, promotional opportunities, and future outlook. Your instructor may also suggest other topics that he/she would like you to include in your report as well as identify the report parts to be included. Incorporate appropriate statistics and graphic aids in your report.

Chapter 15

Administrative Communications: Proposals, Manuals, Instructions, Performance Evaluations, and Product Information

LEARNING OBJECTIVES

After studying this chapter, you should be able to

1. Discuss the differences among the types of proposals commonly used in the business world.
2. Identify the types of manuals commonly used in the business world and discuss how they are used.
3. Discuss the suggestions for writing effective proposals and manuals.
4. Discuss how instructions are effectively written.
5. Discuss the purpose of performance evaluation.
6. Discuss how product information is effectively written.

Administrative communications vitally affect the organization, both internally and externally. Although many other categories of administrative communications exist, this chapter deals with writing proposals, manuals, instructions, performance evaluations, and product information. Several other chapters in this text provide coverage of other types of communication, including letters and reports, written by administrators.

Proposals are prepared for unique situations, such as responding to a request for a proposal, soliciting funds, outlining benefits of a product or service, or outlining a proposed research project.

Manuals that are developed and used to acquaint employees with policies, procedures, and regulations of a company are categorized as policy, procedures, company, employee, functional, and desk manuals.

Well-written instructions facilitate the step-by-step completion of a task by employees and consumers. Examples of instructions are the manuals that accompany products.

Whenever an individual supervises another individual, the supervisor is generally responsible for evaluating the performance of his/her subordinates. The evaluation form used by most organizations requires the preparation of a written statement about the subordinate's performance. This section of the text is designed to help you learn how to write more effective performance evaluation statements.

Product information is often used internally to keep employees informed about new company products as well as the new products of competitors.

Although the information in the various administrative communications presented in this chapter differs substantially, the manuals are similar in one respect: the manner in which they are written. The writing found in administrative communications should follow all of the suggestions found in Chapters 3 and 4.

PROPOSALS

What is a proposal?

A proposal is a document that provides a plan for undertaking a proposed activity or suggests a specific course of action. The most common types of proposals are those that:

1. Respond to a request for a proposal (RFP)
2. Solicit funds to undertake a project
3. Outline for a prospective customer how a manufacturer's product or an organization's services can be used by the customer and the benefits that would result from such use
4. Outline a proposed research project

Proposals vary considerably in their content and organization. While some proposals are short and simple, others are fairly complex, consisting of hundreds of pages.

Because proposals are prepared for unique situations, no universal organizational plan exists. The proposal prepared in response to a RFP will likely be quite different from the proposal that solicits funds from a foundation to support a research project. The proposal that outlines the use and benefits of a manufacturer's products will be quite different from a proposal seeking authorization to undertake a research project.

What criteria are used in making evaluative comparisons of proposals?

All proposals must be persuasive in order to convince readers that your proposal will benefit them. As your proposal will often have to compete with others, you will find helpful the following criteria that are likely to be used by a reader in making an evaluative comparison.

1. What is the nature of the project presented in the proposal?
2. What benefits are likely to accrue from undertaking the project discussed in the proposal?
3. What steps/procedures does the writer propose for carrying out the project, and are these steps/procedures feasible?

4. How well qualified is the writer to carry out the project presented in the proposal?
5. What potential problems are likely to surface in carrying out the proposed project?
6. How long will the project take to complete?
7. How much will the project cost to complete?

Requests for proposals (RFPs) are common in various state and Federal government agencies. They are prepared frequently by government agencies that want to undertake a research project or develop a specific program. The RFP contains a description of the project an agency or company wants to undertake or the goods or services it needs. In addition, the RFP frequently provides an outline of the specific work to be done and lists detailed instructions on how the proposal is to be prepared. The more closely a proposal's content matches the information sought in the RFP, the better are its chances of being chosen. The writer should include any additional information in the proposal that might enhance its success.

Proposals That Solicit Funds

Proposals to solicit funds that enable a person to carry out a project or to conduct research differ from proposals that respond to RFPs. Proposals that respond to RFPs are concerned with an activity initiated by someone other than the proposal writer, whereas those that solicit funds are initiated by the writer.

The suggested plan for a proposal that solicits funds for undertaking a project includes the following elements:

What is the suggested plan for proposals that solicit funds?

1. Cover letter briefly outlining the nature of the proposal;
2. Statement of the problem of the project and a discussion of the situation to be remedied;
3. Objectives of the project;
4. Procedures to be used in carrying out the project;
5. Dissemination of the findings of the project (if appropriate);
6. Evaluation of the project (if appropriate);
7. Facilities and equipment needed to carry out the project;
8. Personnel involved in the project;
9. Budget requirements needed for carrying out the project.

Proposals That Outline Uses and Benefits of Products and Services

Manufacturing and service organizations use proposals to identify for prospective customers the uses and benefits of their products or services. For example, a small company in need of installing its first data processing system may solicit proposals from several computer vendors in which each vendor is asked to outline a proposed data processing system. By comparing each system as outlined in the proposal, the company then selects the one that best meets its needs.

What is the suggested content for proposals that outline uses of products/services?

When preparing a proposal for a prospective client, the following topical outline may be followed.

1. Cover letter with a brief outline of the nature of the proposal;
2. Background information about the organization whose products and/or services are being proposed;
3. Summary of analysis of the client's need for the proposed products and/or services;
4. Information about the products and/or services being proposed, including specifications, configurations, and costs;
5. Support services provided by the vendor (if appropriate);
6. Outline of vendor and customer responsibilities;
7. Implementation schedule (if appropriate);
8. Additional information or material that would strengthen the proposal.

Proposals That Seek Authorization to Undertake A Research Project

The content of research-oriented proposals is quite different from those already discussed. These proposals frequently are prepared by researchers to obtain approval for a specific project, such as the research project required by those working on certain college degrees.

What is the suggested content for proposals that seek authorization to undertake research projects?

The outline that follows is useful in preparing such proposals.

1. Statement of problem of proposed research project;
2. Objectives of proposed research project;
3. Hypotheses of proposed research project (if appropriate);
4. Work schedule, including dates for completing various phases of the project (if appropriate);
5. Outline of proposed research procedures, methodology, and design;
6. Procedures used to disseminate research findings (if appropriate);
7. Procedures used to evaluate the research project (if appropriate);
8. Additional information to support the worthiness of the project.

Figure 15–1 illustrates a proposal prepared for a prospective customer in which the installation of a word processing system is discussed. This is an edited version which eliminates much of the technical material that was included in the original proposal.

Proposal-Writing Suggestions

Some suggestions you will find helpful in writing a proposal are:

1. Clearly describe the work you expect to do.
2. Explain in your own terms the problem you intend to study or the project you intend to undertake.

Cover Letter

ARCOT CORPORATION

Rapid City, SD 57908 1231 Brownell Street (405) 343-8743

August 10, 1990

Mr. David Woloski, Vice President
Decco Company
117 East Main Street
Port Huron, SD 57901

Dear Mr. Woloski:

The proposal outlining Decco Company's use of Concept 5 text-editing equipment is attached. We appreciate your giving us an opportunity to explain how our equipment will meet your needs.

The proposal contains information about the nature of your text-editing equipment needs, as well as information about the equipment we are proposing. This proposal also contains information about the support services we provide our customers.

Concept 5 has just become the No. 1 selling equipment in the country. Our quality products and unmatched service record have enabled us to achieve this distinction.

If you have any questions after reading the proposal, please write or call me.

Sincerely,

Mary Linowitcz

Mary Linowitcz
Customer Support Representative

jd
Attachment

Figure 15–1 Proposal Outlining the Installation of a Word Processing System

PROPOSAL FOR DECCO COMPANY

This proposal, which is prepared specifically for Decco Company, recommends the installation of a word processing system that uses Concept 5 text-editing equipment.

Background Information

Arcot Corporation, the manufacturer of Concept 5 equipment, was founded in 1957. The company, which is located in London, New Jersey, has grown steadily since its founding. Arcot made the Fortune 500 list for the first time in 1972. Text-editing equipment now accounts for 74 percent of Arcot's sales. The corporation, which first started selling word processing equipment in 1970, also manufactures copiers and mail-processing equipment.

Ninety-two percent of Arcot's customers are "repeaters," which is the highest repeat-customer percentage for any company in the industry.

Analysis of Need

Various types of work-load data were collected in Decco Company from July 18 to 29. These data enabled Arcot to determine the types and quantities of typing/transcription tasks performed in Decco. This analysis resulted in the following conclusions:

1. That the installation of a word processing system in Decco is justifiable and cost worthy.

2. That on the basis of the work-load data, four Model 210 Concept 5 word processing units are needed.

3. That typing/transcription tasks can be performed more efficiently, at a lower cost, and with better quality than is possible with the present equipment.

Proposed Equipment

Arcot Corporation recommends that Decco Company install four Concept 5 (Model 210) text-editing typewriters. These devices have a one-page video display unit. The printer, which uses a daisy print wheel, is capable of printing 530 words per minute. The Model 210 uses floppy disks that have a 130-page storage capacity.

Optional features include a communicating component and several programmable packages, including records management and financial management.

The Model 210 sells for $8743, which includes the installation charge, a training manual, and a three-month free service warranty. This same device currently rents for $289 per month for a 12-month period.

Support Services Provided by Vendor

Thorough training manuals accompany each Concept 5 text-editing typewriter. These manuals, which are self-paced, take an average of 24-28 hours to complete.

Arcot has developed a program to train operators on the use of the equipment. This is a 24-hour program that costs $100 per trainee.

Figure 15–1 (Cont.)

2

Arcot has a no-charge consulting service for its customers. The purpose of this service is to help customers get the most from their Concept 5 equipment. This is an especially useful service for customers who change their systems from time to time.

Vendor and Customer Responsibilities

Concept 5 equipment carries a customer-satisfaction guarantee. In the event that a customer is not totally satisfied with the equipment after three months of use, Arcot will remove the equipment, with no financial obligation to the customer.

This proposal is concerned only with text-editing equipment. The customer is responsible for obtaining dictation/recording equipment and for providing the furniture on which the equipment is placed. The customer is also responsible for orienting and training the word originators on the use of the word processing system.

Arcot Corporation will supply Decco with a production control system and the training manuals once the decision has been made to use Concept 5 equipment.

Implementation Schedule

At the present time, a three-week backlog in filling orders exists. Arcot guarantees a three-week delivery date, excluding any extenuating circumstances. Operators can begin training once the equipment has been installed, which takes less than an hour.

Additional Information

The appendices contain brochures on the Model 210, as well as information from trade publications. Also included is a list of local customers whom you may contact regarding their use of Concept 5 equipment.

Figure 15–1 (Cont.)

3. Provide explicit details about the procedures, methods, equipment, materials, and personnel you plan to use.
4. Take the reader's needs and concerns into consideration as you develop the proposal.
5. Include all the parts needed for the type of proposal you are preparing.
6. Provide a cost-benefit analysis.
7. Show how your proposed solution is superior to that of others.
8. Make sure the proposal is well written.

MANUALS

Many organizations use a variety of manuals and handbooks or other written communications to acquaint employees with policies, procedures, and regulations. Well-developed manuals not only make employees' jobs much easier, but also they enable them to perform their duties faster and with greater efficiency.

Types of Manuals

What types of manuals are used in organizations?

Although the manuals found in organizations may be categorized in several ways, the ones most frequently found are policy manuals, procedures manuals, company manuals, employee manuals, functional manuals, and desk manuals. In some organizations, the information found in two or more manuals is consolidated in one special-purpose manual.

Policy manuals

What are policy manuals?

The policy manual provides rules and regulations pertaining to employees whether their responsibilities are focused within the organization or outside the organization.

Figure 15–2 illustrates the table of contents from a policy manual on effective communications that was developed for use by employees and volunteer personnel in a national organization. Some of the major topics included in the manual are ''Planning Your Public Relations Program,'' ''How to Facilitate Internal Communication,'' ''How to Facilitate External Communication,'' and ''Planning for Emergencies.'' Because some personnel may be unfamiliar with the program of the organization, the manual includes specific guidelines for each topic. For example, ''How to Facilitate External Communication'' includes guidelines for dealing with print and electronic media, using photographs to tell stories, planning good unit publicity, preparing exhibits and displays, and running a speakers' bureau.

Illustrated in Figure 15–3 is an example of a health center's managerial policy on parking.

Occasionally, a company needs to prepare a short policy statement to guide employees' actions when emergencies arise. The following is an example.

PRESS RESPONSE PROCEDURES

To prepare for possible emergencies, our organization must be capable of responding quickly to inquiries from the media. In an emergency, all calls from the media should be automatically transferred to the public relations department. Should an official statement be needed, the department representative should immediately call the president. If he/she is not available to make a statement, the call should be transferred to the executive vice-president. Every effort will be made to provide the media with answers in the shortest possible time.

Well-written policy manuals, as well as statements, save time. However, if strict adherence to all policies is expected, regardless of the individual circumstances of the situation, excessive organizational rigidity may result.

Procedures manuals

The procedures manual is used to help employees perform their various job duties. The content and format of procedures manuals vary from organization to organization. In preparing a procedures manual, the first consideration

TABLE OF CONTENTS

Figure 15–2 Excerpt from a Policy Manual. *Courtesy,* Boy Scouts of America.

E. PREPARING EXHIBITS AND DISPLAYS

F. RUNNING A SPEAKERS BUREAU

1. Considerations to Keep in Mind
2. Suggested Topics

G. PREPARING A SPEECH: GUIDELINES FOR SCOUT EXECUTIVES

1. The Outline
2. Message Organization
3. Introducing and Concluding Messages
4. Tips on Preparing Successful Speeches

H. A WORD ABOUT BILLBOARDS

IV. PLANNING FOR EMERGENCIES

A. CRISIS MANAGEMENT — WHY DO WE NEED IT?

1. Objectives to Keep in Mind

B. USING FOURTEEN STEPS TO HANDLE PUBLIC RELATIONS EMERGENCIES

C. ORGANIZING AN EMERGENCY PLAN

1. Know Your Objectives
2. Agree on Policies
3. Write a Concept of Operations
4. Agree on Terminology
5. Establish Organizational Responsibilities
6. Prepare a Notification List
7. Compile Other Lists and Forms

D. RESPONDING TO DIFFERENT TYPES OF EMERGENCIES

1. Coping with Natural Disasters
2. Reacting to Man-made Adversities

E. UNDERSTANDING LEGAL CONCERNS

1. Areas in which Problems May Arise
2. Ways to Avoid Legal Problems During Emergencies

F. ACTING ON MEDICAL EMERGENCIES

G. MAINTAINING GOOD COMMUNITY RELATIONS

H. DEALING WITH THE MEDIA DURING A CRISIS

1. Choose an Official Spokesperson
2. Make Statements That Are Fast, Fair, Frank and Factual
3. How to Release Statements
4. Handling Inquiries From Reporters and the Public
5. Defining What Is in the Public Domain
6. Controlling Rumors

I. EVALUATING YOUR CRISIS PLAN

Figure 15–2 (Cont.)

SAINT ELIZABETH COMMUNITY HEALTH CENTER

MANAGEMENT POLICY MANUAL

SUBJECT:	Parking	SUPERCEDES:	All Previous Parking Policies
CLASSIFICATION:	General Policies	RECOMMENDED BY:	
EFFECTIVE DATE:	January 1, 1987		
LAST REVIEW:	October 1, 1983	Director of Human Resources Date	
NEXT SCHEDULED REVIEW DATE:	January 1, 1990	APPROVED BY:	
		President Date	

PURPOSE: To insure adequate, safe and equitable parking arrangements for all Health Center patients, volunteers, visitors and employees.

POLICY:

1. All employees shall, within ten days of starting employment or trading automobiles, obtain and display an approved parking decal from the Health Center Security Department.

2. Employees issued red decals shall park within the white-lined parking area at the southermost end of the south (visitor) lot. Employees issued blue decals shall park in the north (employee) lots.

3. Use of the 3-11 lot will be restricted to those female employees leaving the Health Center after 9 P.M.

4. Volunteers shall park in the south (visitor) lot.

5. Health Center students shall be provided free off-street parking in the SRI lot (immediately north of the Health Center campus). Students leaving the Health Center before 2 p.m. shall be eligible to park in the evening shift employee area (3-11 lot) with an approved permit from the Security Department. Students leaving the Health Center after 9 p.m. shall park at the southermost end of the south (visitor) lot. Student vehicles parked in visitor lots, along the emergency drive or in employee areas without a permit will be subject to fine and/or towing.

6. Employees are encouraged to form carpools or use alternative transportation as a conservation measure.

7. Security personnel shall enforce this policy through spot checks and the issuance of violation slips to inappropriately parked employee vehicles. When records reveal a second violation, the offending employee's Manager/Head Nurse will be notified. Should infractions continue, security personnel will report the violation to subsequently higher levels of authority for disciplinary action.

8. Health Center students, volunteers and employees are encouraged to lock their automobiles and report any suspicious individuals in the parking areas to the Security Department.

Figure 15–3 Policy on Parking. *Courtesy*, St. Elizabeth Community Health Center, Lincoln, Nebraska.

should be its use. Some manuals will need much more detail than others, but regardless of the purpose of a manual, it should be written concisely so its users can complete a job by following the information presented in the manual. Figure 15–4 illustrates a portion of a reference manual written for use by student workers on a university campus.

Generally, a procedures manual contains a table of contents and an index. The effective date of the manual should be included, and additions or changes should also be dated to facilitate future reference. In a large manual, both section identification and page numbers are provided, as Figure 15–5 illustrates.

Figure 15–4 Procedures Manual Index. *Courtesy,* Kay Stevens, CPS.

INDEX

General Information

- Department Heads
- Time Keeping
- Absences
- Dress Code
- Confidentiality
- Visiting
- Phone Calls

Student Work-Study Employment Information

To Report Emergencies

- Ambulance
- Fire
- Police
- Bomb Threat
- Tornado
- Explosion
- Lightning
- Earthquake
- Radiation Accident

Effective Telephone Usage

- University Services
- Call Transfer
- Time Zones
- Area Codes

Parking and Traffic Regulations

Mailing Information and Instructions

- UNL Campus Mailing Regulations
- How to Address Envelopes
- Folding and Inserting Letters into Envelopes
- State Abbreviations
- Nebraska Zip Code Directory
- Bulk Mail Guide

Guidelines for Typing a Report

Bibliography

Holiday Schedule

TABLE OF CONTENTS

Figure 15–5 Procedures Manual Table of Contents. *Courtesy,* Brunswick Corporation, Lincoln, Nebraska, 1984.

A procedures manual should include standard procedures and identify the exceptions or special considerations. Sometimes the person responsible for each task or activity is identified in one column and the task or activity for which he/she is responsible is identified in another column, as Figure 15–6 illustrates.

Illustrations are also helpful to users of procedures manuals. For example, if you are explaining the use of certain forms, the inclusion of samples of these forms will be helpful to the users.

To eliminate errors and omissions, you should ask personnel who will be using the manual to read the final draft. The employee on the job can readily spot unclear or ambiguous statements.

Company manuals

What is the purpose of company manuals?

The company manual or organizational manual is designed to provide information about the company or the organization and the functions of departments or divisions. The manual, which is often used in the orientation of new employees, provides them with an overview of the organization, its history, and its services and/or products. Because the employee is not expected to complete a specific job by reading the manual, it usually does not include step-by-step procedures.

Figure 15–6 Procedures Manual

SUBJECT: Original dictation (letters, memos, reports)

Responsibility	Action
Originator	1. Identifies self by name and department. 2. Indicates type of communication (letter, memo, report). 3. Identifies number of copies needed. 4. Dictates material. 5. Gives copy distribution.
Supervisor	6. Removes belt and indexing slip from recorder and places in input file. Marks indexing slip with: Date and time of removal from recorder Recorder number
Word Processing Specialist	7. Removes belt from first folder of input file. 8. Prepares a job assignment card. 9. Transcribes material on continuous form paper using standard formats and recording instructions. 10. Proofreads recorded copy before playback. 11. Corrects any errors. 12. Logs playback production and sends completed copy to supervisor.
Supervisor	13. Reviews copy, inserts in routing envelope for distribution to originator.
Routing Clerk	14. Delivers to department.
Originator	15. Proofreads, signs, and prepares copy for outgoing mail or, 16. Edits and revises material and returns document to center where changes are made.

Employee manuals

The employee manual provides vital information about employment practices, employment policies, and other information of interest to the employee. Because of the numerous categories of information generally needed in the employee manual, the writer should pay particular attention to its organization.

What is the purpose of employee manuals?

Functional manuals

Functional manuals, which are more specialized than procedures manuals, may outline the procedures for one specialized area or function. A variety of these manuals are found in organizations. Examples are an organization's records management manual and accounting manual. The table of contents for an accounting manual is illustrated in Figure 15–7.

What is the purpose of functional manuals?

Desk manuals

The desk manual is typically prepared by its user. This manual contains all the information that will be helpful to an individual in carrying out the responsibilities of his/her job. Some users leave their desk manuals with their successors or make the manuals available to temporary employees as a means of helping them become readily acclimated to the job.

What is the purpose of desk manuals?

Figure 15–7 Functional Manual

TABLE OF CONTENTS

Specific items that might be included in a desk manual are:

1. A brief statement of overall scope, purpose, and duties of the job
2. A breakdown of the daily duties performed
3. A listing of the special duties performed—those that are performed at specific intervals, perhaps weekly, monthly, or annually
4. The forms commonly used in performing various job functions, including completed samples, as well as information on completing the forms, the number of copies typically prepared, from whom the forms are received, to whom the forms are sent, when they are sent, where the forms are kept, why used, etc.
5. A section listing special terminology
6. A key to your filing system—indexing; coding: how done and who does it; who has access to the files; when and how materials are actually filed; when and how the files are charged out
7. A list of who's who in the department, in the company, in related or allied companies, in supplier firms, in dealer firms, and in customer firms
8. A list of lines of authority—to whom are you responsible and for what, and to whom they are responsible, etc.
9. A correspondence section that includes samples of letter styles, the content of letters you commonly prepare, various stationeries used, etc.
10. A section that contains information about mail collection and delivery times, who answers what information, and who is to see what
11. A section about telephone use—including etiquette, taboos, long-distance charges, etc.
12. A section about company travel—including vouchers, the manner of computing mileage, expenses, etc.
13. A section about "fringe" duties—when performed and for whom
14. A section on "bottleneck" areas—being aware of potential bottlenecks will help you better deal with them when they arise
15. A section outlining company policies
16. A list of machines and equipment used on the job, including the telephone number of the repair service
17. A list of supplies you use in your job—including the names, addresses, and telephone numbers of suppliers
18. Miscellaneous information

Desk manuals are often developed and used by individuals who provide administrative support to others. Well-developed desk manuals become indispensable not only to the developer—but also to the developer's successor.

Writing Manuals

The responsibility for preparing manuals is frequently assigned to a committee, especially when the manuals contain technical information. Manuals prepared by committees tend to be more thorough and complete than those written by individuals, simply because several individuals are likely to have more material to include in a manual than one individual does.

After all the information to be included in a manual has been gathered, the information should be organized. You may wish to use the following guidelines in organizing the material.

What guidelines should you use for help in organizing the material in manuals?

1. *Use broad categories in organizing the information.* For example, all the information that pertains to one subject (policies, for example) should be grouped together, the information that pertains to another topic should be placed in another category, and so forth.

2. *Arrange the information in each category according to the most appropriate sequence.* In some instances, the most appropriate sequence for arranging the information is by order of importance. If no order of importance exists, the information can be arranged by some other sequence, such as alphabetically or chronologically.

3. *Organize the information in a way that will make it useful to the employees.* For example, several policies could be discussed in the same paragraph. However, because this organizational pattern may make it difficult for the employee to use the information, a more useful pattern is to discuss each policy in a separate paragraph.

The effectiveness of the manual can be enhanced or destroyed by the writing style. To improve the writing style found in manuals, keep in mind the following suggestions.

What suggestions can you offer that are designed to improve the quality of writing found in manuals?

1. The writing should be clear, concise, straightforward, and in a style that is easily understood by the manual readers.
2. The use of enumerated sentences should be considered wherever possible, especially in identifying or discussing steps or procedures.
3. The highlighting of important words, phrases, or sentences should be considered.
4. The definition of unfamiliar words used in the manual should be considered.

Thoughtful consideration of illustrations, size of pages, binding, use of different colors of paper, and the inclusion of a table of contents, index, and a coding system to facilitate page removal and additions will make the manual more attractive and readable.

As revisions of manuals become necessary because of changes in organizations, the individuals who prepared the original manuals may be assigned the task of revision. Employee participation and/or feedback is encouraged when revising existing manuals or when preparing new manuals.

INSTRUCTIONS

What is the purpose of instructions?

Instructions inform personnel how to follow a procedure or how to complete an assignment. Clear, concise, easy-to-follow instructions are helpful to employees as they perform their jobs.

Audience

The first step in preparing instructions is to assess how much knowledge the typical reader has of the area for which the instructions are being prepared. If a wide variance exists in the amount of knowledge the readers possess, you will wisely write the instructions to accommodate those whose knowledge is limited. Incomplete or unclear instructions that result in injury or damage may result in the filing of a liability claim against the organization.

Content

In determining the appropriate content for instructions, two preliminary steps must be completed before you begin the writing process. You need to determine exactly what you are preparing instructions for and become as knowledgeable as you can about the procedure, system, or equipment. Observing the procedure and talking with those who perform it are helpful.

What questions can you ask yourself that will help you write more effective instructions?

Once these two steps have been completed, answering the following questions will be helpful in determining what to include in the instructions you are writing.

1. What does the audience already know?
2. What should the audience know that it does not know?
3. What materials, equipment, tools, devices, or conditions are necessary in order to be successful in following the instructions?
4. What steps/procedures are involved in the process for which instructions are being prepared?
5. What is the appropriate order for these steps/procedures?
6. What is the average completion time for each step/procedure?
7. Can any of the steps/procedures be bypassed under certain circumstances?
8. Should the reader be made aware of any cautions or pitfalls to avoid in undertaking each step/procedure?
9. What should the reader be advised to do in the event of a problem?
10. What drawings or other visuals will help the reader better understand the instructions?

Once you have completed your first draft, you will find a pilot test helpful. This test is completed by having individuals who are unfamiliar with the procedure use the instructions to perform the procedure. Unclear or incomplete instructions should be noted so these weaknesses can be eliminated before the final draft is prepared. Each revised draft should also be piloted on another group of individuals who are unfamiliar with the procedure. The instructions should continue to be revised and piloted until their completeness and clarity are adequate.

Language

The language you use should be familiar to your reader(s). Words used in a unique way or that are likely to be unfamiliar to the reader should be clearly defined. The nature of your audience determines how many definitions you will need to provide.

In writing the instructions,

1. Use active rather than passive voice and write in the imperative mood.
2. Write as precisely and as concisely as possible. Tell the reader exactly what steps need to be completed, as the illustration in Figure 15–8 does.
3. Break instructions into short, simple steps. Reader understandability can be increased by using short, simple sentences. Each step should also be numbered to facilitate the referencing process.

Figure 15–8 Writing Instructions

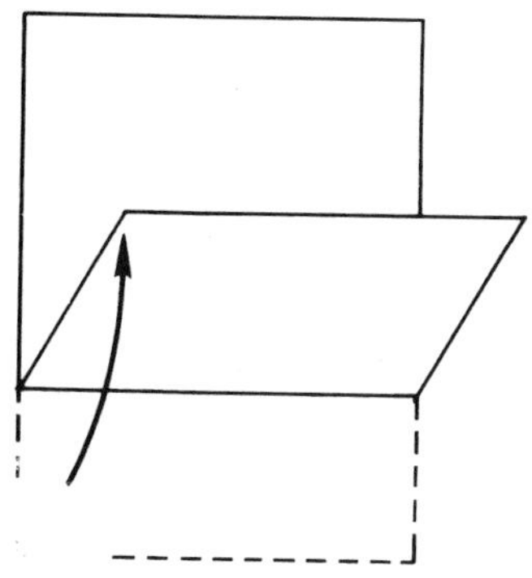

1. With paper flat on desk, fold bottom 1/3 up toward the top.

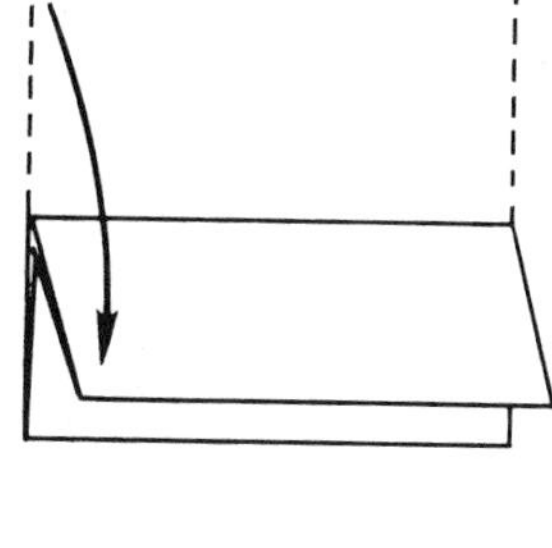

2. Fold the top 1/3 down to within 1/2 inch of your first fold.

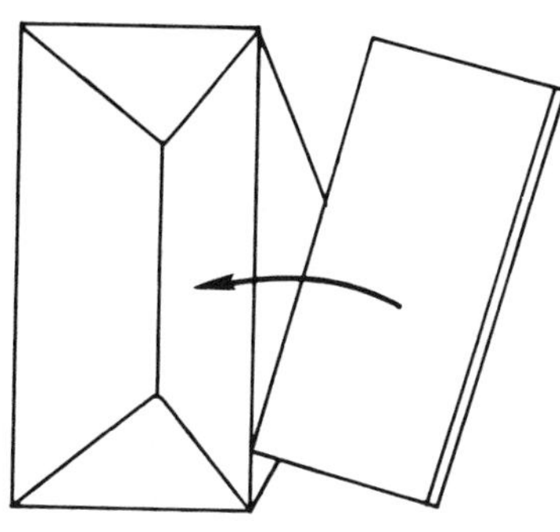

3. Insert the letter into the envelope with the open end at the top.

Visuals

What types of visuals are often included in instructions?

The inclusion of appropriate visuals in instructions is helpful. Visuals commonly used in instructions are photographs, maps, drawings, sketches, and diagrams. Visuals show relationships and steps, contribute to clear, concise instructions, and help the reader visualize the task. Placing visuals as close as possible to the text to which they refer—preferably immediately after the discussion—is suggested. Each visual should be labeled, and the identification number should be included at the appropriate location in the discussion. For example, when referring to Figure 14, you might reference it in the text by stating "(See Figure 14)." When using a drawing or a photograph, include only those parts or sections needed by readers to perform a particular action. You should also guard against including unnecessary visuals as they might interfere with the instructional process.

Instructions with a minimum number of steps that can be accomplished sequentially may be presented entirely through the use of visuals. However, when presenting technical information, including clearly written instructions that supplement the visual is recommended.

PERFORMANCE EVALUATION

What uses are made of the information obtained from performance appraisals?

Managers generally have the responsibility of evaluating the performance of their subordinates in order to identify employee strengths, weaknesses, and growth potential. The performance evaluations are used to provide input when making decisions about promotions, salary increases, training programs, employee transfer, and reduction in force.

Although most evaluation methods require a minimum of writing, the majority do require the preparation of a written statement regarding the employee's performance. Today evaluation methods rarely use only a checklist. Because the evaluation process is designed in part to help the employee improve his/her performance, the inclusion of effectively written statements on the evaluation form is helpful. Depending on the type of evaluation being used, the amount of writing may vary from a sentence or two (which is a characteristic of the rating-form technique) to many sentences (which is typical of the narrative evaluation technique).

Performance evaluation documentation has many uses. In addition to providing input when making decisions about promotions and salary increases, the documentation may also be used when making a just-cause termination of an employee. Should the employee challenge his/her termination in a court of law, the performance evaluation documentation will often be used to provide evidence that he/she was forewarned about the need to improve his/her performance. Because organizations are no longer able to terminate employees "at will" as they were able to do several years ago, performance evaluation documentation is used to build a case against the employee. The documentation can also be used in settling grievances filed against management by employees.

What guidelines can you offer that will help you write more effective appraisal statements?

When preparing written statements about employees' performance, the following guidelines will be useful.

1. Be as specific as possible. Generalities are not helpful.
2. Be honest. Should the performance evaluation documentation be used as evidence in a court of law and the employee received several undeserved favorable ratings, he/she has a good chance of winning.
3. Document with dates the write up of unfavorable performance.
4. Use concrete rather than abstract language.
5. Point out strengths as well as weaknesses.
6. Make sure the written comments are consistent with any checklist rating that may be included on the evaluation form.
7. Avoid the use of words that may mean different things to different people. Examples of such words are "somewhat," "nearly," "sometimes," and "almost always."

Should you ever be involved in a situation in which the unsatisfactory nature of an employee's work performance will likely result in his/her eventual dismissal, the use of legal counsel is advised. Abiding by the legal advice you receive will help you avoid violating the employee's due process.

Figure 15–9 illustrates an evaluation form that contains written comments about the employee's strengths, areas in need of improvement, and growth potential.

SUMMARY OF APPRAISAL

Staff Member Becky Brown Date of Review July 1, 1988

Position Title Coordinator Department Editorial

A. Narrative Evaluation

Write a summary of the employee's performance, highlighting those areas which best characterize him/her as an individual. Include key accomplishments, strengths, areas for improvement and plans for development, improvements expected and growth potential. If more space is needed, a separate sheet may be attached.

Becky has a great hunger to learn, to understand, and to apply her knowledge and insights to improving herself, her job, the journal, and the department. She is a self starter with the creative and organizational skills to develop and recommend improvements and the initiative and poise to see that they are implemented. Becky makes mistakes, but these most often occur when she has been willing to take a chance--an important aspect of development--and she rarely makes the same mistake twice. She has never shied away from taking responsibility for her actions and decisions. Becky reacts positively to my instructions and suggestions and is always careful to query me as appropriate and to inform me of her progress. She has excellent communication skills and is able to develop and maintain rapport with editors, authors, advertisers, and vendors. I have received very positive feedback from Editorial Board members, the ad representative, and the printer and typesetter that Becky responds to her questions and requests with confidence and competence, thereby instilling in them confidence in our organization.

Becky has worked hard to learn to manage her time and resources more effectively and to set priorities. She must continue to develop her time-management skills and must overcome her feelings of guilt about recruiting others to help with projects--guilt that stems from her concern that she is not able to accomplish everything singlehandedly. Becky tends to become impatient with others when they disagree with her, when they don't follow procedures, and when they don't meet deadlines/expectations, she is a perfectionist who expects perfection from others. She must learn to curb her impatience; to be assertive--but not aggressive--when dealing with coworkers; to give feedback in a positive, courteous, and timely way; and to accept the reality that change, even when badly needed, often (of necessity) takes time. I hope that Becky will make time in the coming year to get to know her coworkers outside the department and in this way come to understand their responsibilities, motivations, actions, and perspectives.

Becky is a professional of whom I may expect the highest quality of work in terms of accuracy, quantity, timeliness, and comprehensiveness. It is my pleasure to work with and to supervise her.

PLEASE COMPLETE THE REVERSE SIDE

The Summary of Appraisal (parts A & B) must be reviewed by those individuals indicated on the signature spaces before it is discussed with the employee.

Figure 15–9 Performance Appraisal. *Courtesy, American College of Emergency Physicians.*

PRODUCT INFORMATION

For what is product information used?

An increasing number of administrators are responsible for preparing information about products or services offered by their organization or by competitors. This information differs quite markedly from the product or service information prepared by the marketing or advertising department. Product or service information prepared by administrators is primarily designed to make others aware of the product or service, whereas the information written by the marketing or advertising department is designed to sell the product or service.

Administrators typically prepare product information for internal use, rarely for outsiders. They often incorporate product/service characteristics, specifications, and descriptions found in the advertising materials into the product-information write-up. However, the appeals found in the advertising materials are omitted.

What suggestions can you offer that will help you write more effective product information?

In writing product information, keep the following suggestions in mind.

1. Include only the most important information about the product or service.
2. Place the most important information about the product or service at the beginning of the message.
3. Make each word count. A shorter message with the most important information is preferable to a longer message that contains some unessential information.
4. Give your audience the information it will find most helpful. Unless your audience has an engineering background, avoid presenting technical specifications that are not likely to be understood by non-engineers, for example.
5. Provide the reader with as much information as he/she will need to determine if additional information about the product or service would be helpful.

Figure 15–10 provides an example of product information.

CHAPTER SUMMARY

Administrative communication is comprised of a number of different types of written materials, such as proposals, manuals, instructions, performance evaluations, and product information.

While some proposals solicit funds, others outline the uses and benefits of products and services. Some proposals are written to seek authorization to undertake a research project.

A number of different types of manuals are used in the business world: policy manuals, procedures manuals, company manuals, employee manuals, functional manuals, and desk manuals.

When writing instructions, you have to be concerned about your audience, the content of the instructions, and the language you use. Visuals will enhance the effectiveness of the instructions you write.

Utmost care must be exercised in writing performance evaluations as well as product information. Lack of care and good judgment may result in a serious legal situation.

Visit NBC's International Department

We understand your money needs in foreign lands.

Foreign Currency

NBC can exchange money from one currency to another. Our International Department keeps some foreign currency on hand. As a special service to travelers NBC will order foreign currencies as requested.

International Drafts

NBC can issue drafts in foreign currencies and U.S. dollars payable through foreign banks. A draft is a negotiable instrument generally requiring identification for negotiation.

International Wire Transfers

NBC can send wire transfers virtually anywhere in the world. These payments can be denominated in U.S. dollars and foreign currencies. As compared to a draft a wire transfer is not a negotiable instrument and remains in banking channels until executed.

Gold and Silver

The International Department can serve as an agent in the purchase and sale of gold and silver, coins, bars and certificates. Current quotes can be obtained by contacting the department. Some fees including sales tax apply to certain orders.

Traveler's Checks

In addition to the travelers' checks for U.S. dollars, which can be purchased at NBC's teller windows, NBC has travelers' checks in Canadian dollars, English pounds, German marks, French francs, Swiss francs and Japanese yen which are available in the International Department.

Ask about these other services from NBC's International Banking Department:

- Foreign Collections
- Export/Import Documentation and Negotiation
- Letters of Credit

Figure 15–10 Product Information. *Courtesy,* National Bank of Commerce, Lincoln, Nebraska.

REVIEW QUESTIONS

1. Identify common types of proposals.
2. What criteria are generally used to evaluate proposals?
3. What content should you include in proposals that solicit funds for a proposed project?
4. What content should you include in research-oriented proposals?
5. What purpose does a policy manual serve?
6. How does a procedures manual differ from a company manual? From an employee manual?
7. What questions may your audience ask as they read instructions?
8. In what ways are performance evaluations used?

APPLICATION PROBLEMS

1. You are a professor of business communication at a university in the midwest. You coordinate 16 sections of business communication classes that have a limited enrollment of 25 students in each class. You have conducted a study of 20 chief executives in a major metropolitan area to obtain their opinions about the need for skills in business writing at the college level. You have found that the major need as reported in this study is for a strong background in the basics—grammar, mechanics, punctuation, spelling, effective sentences and paragraphs, and organization. You wish to conduct a study in which eight classes devote half the semester to learning these basics through traditional teaching methodology. The other eight classes will devote half the semester to learning the basics through computerized instructions, using a software program, "Business Writing Basics." To conduct the study, you need 25 word processors for the classroom. Develop a proposal to send to a manufacturer of word processing equipment in which you request the 25 word processors for use in this study.

2. You are director of personnel in an organization that has 40,000 part-time representatives who sell cosmetics. Plans are underway for a computerized database in your firm. You wish to include personnel records in the database program. Write a memorandum to the vice-president in charge of organizational planning and development that details your needs, outlines your operational procedures, and includes anticipated benefits.

3. You are a chief executive of a young, fast-growing computer accessory manufacturing plant located in a metropolitan area where residents have become quite concerned about business and industrial growth. Prepare a policy statement relating to your organization's responsibility for the community's well-being.

4. Analyze a job that you recently performed (i.e., repairing an engine, conducting an interview, preparing data to present when obtaining a personal loan.) Prepare clear instructions appropriate for an individual you select to follow in completing the task.

5. Interview at least three personnel managers in business firms within your community. Determine the methods used for appraising employee performance, how employee strengths are identified, how areas for improvement of employee performance are identified and covered in appraisals, and the extent to which employee growth potential is monitored. Prepare a memorandum to your instructor which includes recommendations on employee appraisal that will be included in an employee manual.

6. You are administrative assistant to the vice-president in charge of operations for a large beef processing plant that employs approximately 1,200 people. Five other vice-presidents are in charge of finance, purchasing, sales, personnel, and processing. Types of communications include internal memoranda, external letters, reports, press releases, and media (TV and radio) releases. In addition, many forms are used in all divisions. The company has been considering the purchase of new word processing equipment, as the equipment now in use has become obsolete.

Contact the president of the Association of Information Systems Professionals chapter in your community to determine organizations within which one of the four organizational structures of word processing systems is located.

Interview the supervisor or manager of a system that is centralized, one that is decentralized, one that has a special-purpose structure, and one that has an integrated structure. Write a memorandum to the vice-president in charge of operations in which you compare the four structures based upon your interviews and observations. Recommend an organizational structure or structures to be implemented in your company.

7. You are editor of *MSP Flier,* a monthly newsletter distributed to sales representatives of Maximum Software Presentations. Prepare a release describing a new software program designed to assist writers. This package, ''Business Writer's Handbook,'' contains a review of principles of writing good-news messages, disappointing-news messages, and persuasive messages. Application problems enable the user to develop skill in applying these principles. Include appropriate descriptive factors in approximately 250 words to be released in the column, ''New Products.''

8. Your company has installed an electronic communication system which provides an electronic mailbox for each executive workstation. Prepare a user's guide which may be useful for an individual who is not familiar with the electronic mailbox feature.

9. Visit a vendor of electronic communication systems located in your community. Discuss the features of a specific executive workstation terminal. Prepare a description of the product, including cost and special features, which is appropriate for release in a ''New Products'' column of a monthly business publication.

Chapter 16

Professional Writing

LEARNING OBJECTIVES

After studying this chapter, you should be able to

1. Discuss the essentials of preparing news releases.
2. Discuss the essentials of preparing journal articles.
3. Discuss the types of materials broadcast by electronic communication media.
4. Prepare effective materials of the type discussed in this chapter.

In today's business, an increasing number of employees are concerned with some aspect of professional writing. While some of the material they write is printed in internal publications, most of the material is likely to be printed in an outside publication.

Professional writing, one of the widely used categories of business communications, uses the following channels to communicate with specific audiences: news releases, editorials, books, and articles. In this chapter, the writing of news releases, articles, and material for broadcast over electronic communication media are discussed.

NEWS RELEASES

Most large newspapers have a business editor who handles all business assignments. If this is not the case, the city editor or metropolitan editor generally assigns all stories and helps determine what material will be included in the paper. To establish a friendly relationship for more favorable news coverage, a visit to the appropriate editor could be helpful.

The news release is quite important when the objective is to reach a general audience through a published medium. The release is likely to create even more attention when it is accompanied by an appropriate photograph.

Subjects

The subject of the news release will probably be a new product, a new employee, a new company service, or an activity or organization in which the writer is interested. News releases, which are unsolicited, are sent to the appropriate editor in the hope that they will be used. Because editors are flooded with such material, only a small percentage is published. A news release, therefore, must be newsworthy in an editor's eyes and must contain news that will interest the readers of the publication.

What are news releases used for?

Editors judge a news release by the following criteria:

What criteria are used to judge the worthiness of news releases?

- Timeliness—is the event now?
- Proximity—is the event close to the reader's location, frame of reference, or field of activity?
- Importance—is the event significant to the reader?
- Policy—is the event consistent with the publication's editorial policy?

Ideally, every news item should answer the following questions:

1. *Who* did it?
2. *What* did he/she/they do?
3. *Where* did he/she/they do it?
4. *When* did he/she/they do it?
5. *Why* did he/she/they do it?
6. *How* did he/she/they do it?

Many news releases are concerned with the activity of an individual or a group of individuals, as Figure 16–1 illustrates.

A personal business release may be a short item from a company house organ that contains some interesting news about an employee. A longer column in a daily newspaper may include a photograph that publicizes the appointment or promotion of a business executive to a high-level position. Sometimes personal items about business people are grouped under a general heading that appears in one section of the newspaper, as shown in Figure 16–2.

An item emphasizing personal information should be brief, perhaps consisting of only one paragraph. The most important news, either the person's name or what has happened to the person, should appear first.

Another type of release may be termed the "human-interest" story, which, like the personal story, emphasizes the activities of an individual. It may not, however, deal directly with the business affairs of that individual. In a plant newspaper or house organ, stories of unusual experiences of employees, unusual hobbies, and many other topics lend themselves to subjects of reader interest for a news release.

Dr. John Grantham, chief horticulturist for Johnson Seed Company, is the 1988 recipient of the Outstanding Iowa Horticulture Award.

The award was presented at the 40th annual convention of the Iowa Nursery Association, held recently in Ames.

Grantham has been on Johnson's staff since 1971. He began his career at Johnson as a junior horticulturist. In addition to his duties at Johnson, he is an adjunct professor of horticulture at Iowa State.

Grantham, a native of St. Louis, has a B.S. degree from the University of Missouri and M.S. and Ph.D degrees from Iowa State.

He is active in Rotary International and Ames Area Lions. Grantham is a past member of the Ames Board of Education.

Figure 16–1 News Release About a Person

ILLINOIS NATIONAL BANK--Grant Barnes, formerly vice-president of Continental State Bank, Chicago, was named president of Illinois National Bank.

ABC TRANSPORTATION COMPANY--Sally Gray was named vice-president for planning and analysis at ABC Transportation Company, a Chicago-based subsidiary of Frontier Corporation, New York City.

CONTINENTAL BANKING CORP.--Ronald Jackson was named chief financial officer of this company's Home Products, Inc., subsidiary. He succeeds Marjorie Thayer who retired earlier this year. Jackson was previously controller of Smith-Grant Corporation.

Figure 16–2 Items About Business People

What are letters-to-the-editor releases used for?

A letter-to-the-editor release is another channel that enables the business executive to explain his/her viewpoint. Brief, concise letters have the best chance of being printed. The executive may compliment favorable articles. Or, when a printed article contains unfavorable information about an industry or organization or fails to explain adequately both sides of an issue, he/she may respond with a letter to the editor, as Figure 16–3 illustrates.

When considering news releases of different types, the small weekly or bi-weekly newspapers should not be overlooked. Although their readership is not as extensive as a metropolitan newspaper's, the editors of these publications

To the Residents of Greenwood:

This year's United Way Drive raised more money than ever before--thanks to all of the concerned residents of Greenwood. Not only did we meet our goal of raising $131,000, but also we surpassed the goal by $10,871, for a total contribution of $141,871!

The Greenwood United Way Board of Directors will be meeting shortly to determine how the monies will be distributed. Never before have so many worthy requests for United Way funds been received.

Several individuals are largely responsible for the success of this year's drive. The following division chairpersons challenged one another to see whose division could achieve the largest percentage increase over last year's contributions: Sadie Parcher, Division I; John Smith, Division II; Barbara Howell, Division III; and Mike Kendall, Division IV. While each division surpassed last year's contributions by at least 10 percent, Division III had the largest percentage increase of 29 percent.

Please help us make next year's drive twice as successful as this year's drive was! Thanks to all of you, it works!

Delores Brown, Chairperson
1988 Greenwood United Way Drive

Figure 16–3 Letter to the Editor

will often print news releases. They must fill space and, therefore, may accept stories of different lengths.

The public relations story generally attempts to create an attitude toward certain products, a business organization or industry, a contemplated legislative action, or some tendency of social pressure. Today, for example, such stories relating to financial institutions are appearing in response to public concerns about the safety of various types of banking facilities.

Mechanics

The typical news item consists of three parts: the *headline,* which is ordinarily supplied by the editor (if the paper is small) or a copy editor; the *lead;* and the *body.*

What are the three typical parts of news items?

The lead or opening paragraph should immediately tell the editor why the story is important. The journalistic rule, "who, what, when, where, why, and how," applies to the news release, and all of these items should be included near the beginning. Succeeding paragraphs elaborate on the lead by explaining statements and by supplying further details. A news item other than current events may present the material in another format, depending on its nature, length, or the writer's purpose.

The best way to learn how to write news items is to study the journalistic style of the publication or publications for which you expect to write. The length and nature of the material included in the document should be observed.

Like other writing skills, skill in writing news items comes only with practice. The best way to learn is to begin by writing brief and relatively unimportant items and then advance to writing more important material as your skill develops.

What suggestions can you offer to help improve the effectiveness of the news items you write?

The following list of suggestions, although not all-inclusive, will assist you in getting copy into the paper.

1. Typewrite the copy. Although various types of duplicated copies might be used, they have the disadvantage of reminding the editor that someone else has an exact copy of the same story.

2. Triple space the copy. Most newspapers use computers in the printing process and want first copy triple-spaced.

3. Leave blank at least a third of the top of the first page. This step provides space for the copy editor to write the heading and leaves room to make the necessary notations to the printers.

4. Use a left-hand margin of at least 1 $\frac{1}{2}$ inches and other margins of at least 1 inch. If the item is short, a full page may be given to it, and wider margins may be used, making the material more attractive to the reader's eye.

5. Write short sentences. Twenty words are maximum; no sentence should be longer without good reason.

6. Write short paragraphs. The narrowness of the newspaper column and the difficulty of reading type in unbroken masses make this suggestion mandatory.

7. Use adjectives sparingly. The best rule is: ''When in doubt about an adjective, leave it out.''

8. Double check to be sure that all names, particularly names of persons and of business organizations, are spelled correctly.

9. Make certain that all titles of persons are correct—both professional titles and business positions.

10. Recheck any numbers included in the release. In business writing, an error in reporting an amount or a number may be disastrous.

11. If you wish to quote a person, obtain his/her permission and be sure that what you quote is a fair representation of the original.

12. Submit clean, legible copy on a good grade of paper. Copy coming from outside the newspaper office competes for space with other copy of the same kind; other things being equal, the copy that is easiest to handle and easiest to read will be accepted.

As most newspapers follow the AP/UPI stylebook, it should be a part of every professional writer's library. Strunk and White's *The Elements of Style* is also helpful.

The executive who has learned the value of exchanging ideas often belongs to various professional business associations, attends business conferences and conventions, pays for assistance and consulting services, and subscribes to miscellaneous business and trade journals. In turn, the executive's prestige may be enhanced by contributing ideas for the benefit of others.

ARTICLES

Why do executives write business articles?

Sources of Publication

Thousands of books on many aspects of business are published every year. In addition, a large variety of periodicals and business journals, both of a general and specialized nature, provide excellent sources of publication for the business writer.

Nation's Business, Dun's Review, and *Business Week* are examples of publications directed toward general business readership. *Fortune* contains in-depth articles on domestic and international business history, growth, and corporate transactions.

Periodicals cover almost every subdivision of business, such as advertising and promotion, personnel, accounting, management, computer systems, and so forth. In addition, the journals of schools of business administration of various universities frequently carry articles of general interest, as well as heavily documented research-based articles that are addressed to specialists.

Other sources of business articles and information are newspapers with special business sections that contain articles of a general nature and house organs published by various business firms. Other weekly publications, such as *Time* and *Newsweek*, carry special sections on business; these and other leading publications have their own staff writers.

In addition to these primary sources, many periodicals that one might pick up at random contain items of interest in the area of business. The general public is interested in the ways of business, the lives of business people, and the systems and procedures that serve business and the consumer.

Many business articles, whether addressed to readers who are engaged in business or readers who are interested only as consumers of the products of business, are composed by a business executive or a staff member. As an employee in a business organization, you may be asked to write for your fellow employees, organizations, customers, or suppliers. From the standpoint of the company's image—as well as your own reputation—having an article published in a professional publication related to the business with which you are associated is a distinct advantage.

Preparation

Why must readership be considered when preparing to write a business article?

Before you begin to write a business article, you must determine its readership. Your audience will dictate, to a great extent, your emphasis and style. If the article is written for readers who want information—explanations of business procedures or interpretations of laws affecting the conduct of business, for example—the writing will be more formal than if the article is written for readers who will read an article only if it attracts their attention.

Content

An article usually has four parts—the title, the opening, the body, and the conclusion. Illustrations—drawings or photographs—may also be included. Within these broad limits, the ways in which the article may be presented differ widely among magazines and among writers. The subject matter itself also has an effect upon the way in which the article is written. The business article is often an answer to the question of "how" and "why," with much emphasis upon the significance of the material presented as it relates to the activities of a business unit or of an industry.

In any event, the article must have a title that will gain attention, first from the editor and then from the reader. As this attention is affected by the amount of time the reader has available to read books and periodicals, the title and the first paragraph are the most important parts of the article. To attract attention, the title might be designed to

1. Create a feeling of suspense or excitement
2. Be novel or unusual
3. Suggest an unusual comparison or contrast
4. Connect with a current news topic
5. Make a bold statement
6. Ask a question that will arouse the reader's curiosity

From the standpoint of mechanics, the title should be brief and contain at least one verb expressing action. Brevity attracts attention to a title, and action in the title implies that the article to follow will also possess action or movement. The writer may, of course, substitute a striking phrase with no verb in it.

Effective titles are attention getters, brief, and contain a verb or a phrase: "A Gut-Wrenching Year for Chipmakers," "Small Businesses: The 'Tails of Capitalism' are Wagging," "The Tax Bite, How Painful," "A Better Mousetrap," or "It Was a Good Final Quarter—or Was It?"

Style

Because magazine articles differ much more in style than newspapers, you will find it helpful to study the style of the publication in which the article will appear.

First, you should consider the average length of articles. Some magazines never carry articles of more than 500 or 1,000 words; others use articles several times that length.

Next, you should read articles that have appeared in at least half a dozen issues of the magazine for which the article is being written. Through this procedure, you can learn something about the language usage of the publication, the types of illustrations used, and other points of comparison. The more closely the article fits the requirements of a particular magazine market, the more likely it will be printed.

When you are ready to write, follow these steps: Outline your thoughts, write, and then edit. By outlining your thoughts, you will have direction when you begin writing. Once you start writing, keep going. Spelling and punctuation can be checked later. Do not worry about using just the right words. You can change them after your thoughts are put on paper.

What steps should you follow when you are ready to write a business article?

When your thoughts are on paper and you are ready to edit, follow these three steps: (1) Read your work in its entirety without making any changes. This step will give you a sense of the unity of the article; (2) On the second reading, make changes in wording, punctuation, and rearrangement of ideas; (3) Read the piece again with all changes to see how they fit into the overall pattern.

Be certain that your audience will understand the terms you use. In a technical atmosphere, such as computer technology, for example, avoid using jargon familiar only to people well acquainted with the subject. These terms have a special meaning in the computing field, but they may have other meanings to people outside the field, thus creating confusion. The use of technical jargon is wisely avoided unless you are certain that your readers understand these specialized terms.

Mechanics

The mechanical details of preparing news items apply also to the preparation of articles. The following additional guidelines should be helpful.

What guidelines should you follow in writing business articles?

1. Type the article on a grade of paper that will withstand handling.
2. Pay particular attention to the title; a good title is very important.
3. Be sure that the name and address of the writer appear in the upper left corner of the first page and at the bottom right corner of the last page.
4. Number the pages. A guideline—repeating the title if it is brief, or repeating the first few words of it if the title is long—may be used on each page after the first.
5. Type captions below illustrations or drawings.

Although the objectives may vary for articles that you may be requested to prepare, all must be persuasive attention-getters. Figure 16–4 provides an example of a business article.

ELECTRONIC COMMUNICATION MEDIA

Radio and television are being used more and more for public relations purposes. Undoubtedly, you will be increasingly concerned with developing writing techniques applicable to mass communication media. You should learn the requirements of these media and develop the techniques unique to them. A radio or TV news item, for example, must be pithy, to the point, and immediately understood by the listener. In preparing news releases for radio or television, you need to supply usable visuals along with the copy.

The news director and assignment editor generally handle inputs into radio/TV programs. Although the attitude of stations varies on the preferred

Talking Mailboxes

Had enough of telephone tag? Technology has a solution — voice mail

By Harry Whittelsey

Telecommunications analysts say that every business call placed has only a 33 percent chance of connecting with the intended party. This means that two out of every three calls made lead to a series of callbacks and messages. Such telephone volleying has added an estimated $4 billion annually to the cost of doing business. To combat this expensive, time-consuming telephone tag, computerized voice-message delivery systems are now on the market.

Voice message delivery enables you to complete all calls. Accessed via any touchtone telephone, your voice is digitized and stored on a computer disk. Memos can be stored in the voice mailbox, retrieved, added to, forwarded to another individual's mailbox or group of mailbox users or delivered to any telephone at any time. Programmable to dial any call at a specific time and deliver a message, the system will redial until the party answers. In addition, a user can request a certified message, where the receiver mailbox activates a signal indicating the time and date the message was transferred. Security codes protect access to confidential information. The system makes sure information reaches its destination.

Voice mail is applicable to many business situations. It can be used to send instantaneous memos to one person or to an entire staff. Official bulletins can be distributed 24 hours a day from anywhere in the world, transcending time zones. The system can store recorded dictation and transcribe it the next day — even if recorded away from the office.

IN ACTION

At Whit-Tel-Com, Inc., we tested voice mail's range and reliability in our offices before offering it to our customers. Installation was completed in a few hours with no disruption to office operations.

Lou Cila, vice president of sales at Whit-Tel-Com, Inc., attributes more expedient sales operations to the use of voice mail. "I am certain that it has made the difference in speeding negotiations and securing sales."

In addition to benefiting the sales organization, voice mail enables secretaries and switchboard operators to perform their tasks without getting caught in a flurry of technical engineering jargon and the anxiety of missed deadlines.

Voice mail can supply a caller with detailed instructions on use, can process telephone orders, relay callers to an operator and even serve as a message center for international companies.

Voice mail has proven a valuable tool for the dispatch of service technicians. Ron Spellman, vice president of operations at Whit-Tel-Com, Inc., says, "Voice mail has given us an added hour's productivity per day from each technician by streamlining the service call assignment process. Every afternoon, our dispatcher leaves the next day's service agenda in individual mailboxes. The technicians have programmed the system to call them in the evening, conveying the detailed customer status and preparing them for the following day."

Voice mail allows a caller to place a service request at any hour. As soon as the call is completed, the system automatically activates the beeper of the technician on standby. The technician retrieves the message from his or her mailbox, making a return call to the customer within minutes. Upon completion of repair, customer status can be transferred to hard copy for permanent records, tracking each job to ensure prompt service.

Easily adapted to existing telephone equipment, a small voice mail system carrying five users can expand service capabilities and boost productivity for 75 cents per day, per user. A mid-sized voice mail system, capable of handling 40 users at the low end of its range, would cost as little as 50 cents per day, per user. Increasing the number of users decreases the charge. A system serving 100 persons would cost about 27 cents per day, per user.

It is also possible to rent voice mailboxes on a monthly basis from voice mail service bureaus. Costs average $40 per month for each mailbox rented.

Regardless of the business or the message, voice mail is an economical means of ensuring that information is received on time, accurately and by the intended individual. Its range of practical uses is not limited by the system size or by the number of users. It can be one of the keys in providing operational efficiency and prompt customer response. □

Harry Whittelsey is president of Whit-Tel-Com, Inc., a management company for Executone in South Hauppauge, New York.

Figure 16–4 Business Article *From* Harry Whittelsey, "Talking Mailboxes," *Management World*, p. 34, February/March, 1987. Reprinted by permission.

method of contact, writing a letter that contains a proposal and a request for an appointment to discuss the idea is most acceptable.

The suggested plan for a sample program proposal includes the following elements:

Date:

Series Title (if applicable):

Program Title:

Producer (your name):

Station/Network:

Day/Time (day and time of broadcast):

Introduction

1. Describe briefly the basic *idea* and *purpose* of the program. Include information concerning the *unique* way in which your program will be presented.
2. Specifically *define* the *objectives* of your program. Relate those objectives to the manner in which your program will be presented. How do you plan to achieve your objectives?
3. Describe the size, composition, and nature of the program's intended audience.

The Program

1. Develop a "run-down" sheet, including the placement of segments within the program, the length of time of each segment, the running time of the program, and a brief description of the information to be included in each segment.
2. Develop a written opening and closing to the program.
3. Include production notes concerning special problems, gimmicks, or methods which you use in your program.

Specifics

1. Special audio facilities, personnel, or equipment you'll need.
2. Special problems which can be predicted at this point with suggestions as to probable solutions.
3. Which channels and what quantity of promotion will be required for you to reach the audience for which your program is intended?
4. Will the program sell? What is the intended market for the program? Who will be the sponsor? What is your budget?

In order to be licensed by the Federal Communications Commission, radio and television stations must operate in the "public interest, convenience, and necessity." This means that "public service time" is available to certain organizations. Station officials—public service directors, program directors, and public affairs directors—are available to help arrange public service time. The types of public service announcements are discussed below.

What types of public service announcements are broadcast over electronic communication media?

Public service announcements (PSAs)

Brief "advertising messages" describing events or activities can be mailed to the station, along with a cover letter that explains the purpose for the announcement. Such a message is illustrated in Figure 16–5.

Station editorials

These are short statements on community and national issues that reflect the station's point of view. The executive might suggest that the station support a specific current campaign.

Free speech messages

These are statements of opinion by community groups on matters of general public concern. The typed statement to the public service director should contain about 125 words and include the name, address, and the phone number of the writer.

Community calendars

Announcements of special events open to the public should be sent to the public service director. These announcements should arrive at least two weeks before the event.

Public affairs programs

These are interviews or discussion programs in which interesting or complex issues are explored in depth.

Before the business or community representative contacts the radio or TV station about the airing of a public service announcement, the objective of the message should be considered. This will determine the method, station, or program best suited to meet the needs of the announcement.

Figure 16–5 Public Service Announcement

Public Service Announcement - Community Hospital - 30 seconds

Do you know who to call if a member of your family suddenly becomes critically ill? Which hospital would you use if you were injured at work?

Emergency physicians at Community Hospital can help you answer those questions. On Tuesday, August 25, tours of the emergency department and fire department ambulances will be given throughout the day. Emergency physicians will be available to answer your questions about emergency care.

The action takes place on Tuesday, August 25, at Community Hospital, 111 Main. For more information, call 555-2611.

Some guidelines to assist you in preparing a public service announcement are:

1. List key facts about the activity.
2. Keep sentences short, simple, and conversational.
3. Repeat telephone numbers and dates.
4. Read copy aloud, timing it carefully. Usual reading times for radio are 10, 20, 30, and 60 seconds.
5. Submit final copy on plain white, standard-sized paper, typed double spaced.
6. Place one announcement per sheet.

Local radio and television stations often have various other programs (i.e., forums, panels, talk shows) which can serve as outlets for various types of business publicity and public relations. The person who wishes to use these media prepares material by following the guidelines described in this chapter.

CHAPTER SUMMARY

As a business employee, you are likely to have numerous opportunities to write professional communications, including news releases, articles, and material for broadcast on electronic media, such as radio and television. The success of your professional writing will be determined by how effectively you write.

When writing news releases, you will want to make sure they contain the five journalistic W's—who, what, where, when, why—and how. Your news release stands a better chance of being printed if you observe the guidelines suggested by the publisher, as well as the standardized guidelines.

When writing an article for publication in a journal or periodical, you must first determine the general readership. Articles that are not appropriate for the readership of the publication—regardless of how well written they are—stand little chance of being published. You should also conform to the guidelines suggested by the publisher.

A common type of material broadcast over electronic media is the public service announcement. Several different types are used. Guidelines are also available to those who prepare public service announcements.

REVIEW QUESTIONS

1. On what criteria do editors judge news?
2. Compare the human-interest story with the business personal release.
3. For what reasons might a business executive write a letter to the editor?
4. List several suggestions that will assist you in getting copy into the newspaper.
5. What steps does the writer take in preparing for an interview that is to be reported?
6. Outline steps in writing and in editing an article for publication.
7. Concerning mechanical details of preparing news items, what additional guidelines may be helpful in preparing articles?

8. Specify writing techniques applicable to a radio or TV news item.
9. List several types of radio and television programs which can serve as outlets for the various types of business publicity and public relations releases.

APPLICATION PROBLEMS

1. You have been assigned the responsibility of writing an article for a journal on retail selling. The article is to be on the personal shopping service which most large department stores offer today. This service operates by mail, by telephone, or through personal contact with the "shopping consultant." If, for example, a man wishes to buy a gift for his wife but can't think of a gift that would please her, he might write or telephone the shopping consultant for assistance in selecting a suitable gift. He would describe his wife's interests, taste, personality, and other factors that would be helpful in selecting a gift.

The man might want to buy something for himself with the assistance of a shopping consultant, thus saving time for himself as well as getting the consultant's professional advice about what he ought to wear to look his best.

The shopping consultant services operate variously in different organizations. Your task is to look into this service by inquiring how it operates in specific retail stores, after which you are to write an article that presents the advantages, disadvantages, and recommendations for shopping consultant services. You will need to determine what the title should be, what your style should be (and your decision will be reflected in sub-headings), what proportion of your article should be devoted to adverse criticism, what proportion to recommendations for improvement, etc. Your article should be approximately 1200 words long.

2. You have observed that a new restaurant which has opened in your community seems to be doing an expanding business. Patrons and prospective patrons were telephoning for reservations for luncheon or dinner after the restaurant had been open for only a few weeks. The interest in eating in this particular restaurant would not be because of a desire for novelty and change alone; it would mean that certain patrons had been pleased and had passed along the word to others.

Find out what pleases the public when they are dining out in your community, why they return to some restaurants and shun others. Writing generally, without reference to a particular restaurant or to a particular community, prepare a business article of 800 words on your findings. Give careful attention to the title of this article, the style, and the sectional headings.

3. C. A. Swanson was just promoted to president of Financial Associates, Inc., a huge corporation (assets of $3.5 billion), which operates the nation's largest consumer finance business. At age 35, Mr. Swanson is much younger than most chief executives, and he has less than five years' experience with the company. He studied economics at Stanford and earned a law degree from Harvard. He is well informed. He plans to bring out a credit card, lower rates, and build up the executive-loan business. Some of the firm's best customers are themselves bankers who want to borrow anonymously, he says. As director of communications, prepare a publicity release to appear in a column, "Business People in the News," in a leading business publication.

4. Assuming the same information in application problem 3, prepare an announcement for a local TV program, "Business in the News," which is scheduled daily at 12:15 to 12:20 p.m.

5. Oscar Koefoot is a recent retiree with 25 years of service at the Goodplant Tire & Rubber Company. He worked in heating, ventilating, and pipefitting. He now has time for his favorite hobby—playing a banjo. Oscar made his first banjo from the hide of a bobcat, drawn tautly around a bowl. (The bobcat had been making nightly raids on the family springhouse in the wooded mountains of western North Carolina fifty-seven years ago.) Forty years ago Oscar and his band, the Southern Mountaineers, were common visitors to such radio stations as WADC and WJW in Akron, Ohio, and WJAY in Cleveland. Two years ago he finished second in banjo competition in an annual contest in Quaker City, and his goal is to be first this year. Since his retirement, he has also cultivated several acres of land near his home on Madison Road. Prepare a human-interest story of approximately 400 words, based upon Oscar Koefoot's hobby, to appear in Goodplant's house organ, *The Arrowfoot Clan.*

6. Your firm is concerned with housing construction, and you are responsible for the column "Briefs" in your bi-weekly company bulletin. Gather items of interest from daily newspapers and periodicals printed within the week. Prepare five summaries of no more than 50 words each for the weekly column.

7. Written business communications is an area of interest to business executives as well as to students. Develop questions to be asked during an interview of an executive in your city. The interview may be based upon the subject, "The Need for Skills in Written Business Communications." Major topics to be discussed might include written communications relating to (1) applications for employment, (2) company training programs, (3) employee promotions, (4) results of poor communication, or (5) suggestions for curriculum development to meet current needs in business communications.

Conduct the interview and prepare a report to be released in the Sunday edition of your local newspaper.

8. Hometown, USA, has created a good place in which to live and work. It is a city shaped for people, indoors and out. Its population has a work ethic, a strong sense of self-responsibility, and a zealous dedication to education. Hometown, USA, boasts good government. Corporate executives devote an astonishing amount of their time and money to good works and civic affairs. The compact downtown area provides a cosmopolitan atmosphere—with fountains, sidewalk cafes, and tree-filled plazas. Architectural gems include a new insurance building, a new 42-story bank, and a recently completed Gateway Mall along eight blocks of the main shopping street. The mall enables pedestrians to move about in climate-controlled comfort regardless of weather conditions. A sunken garden, Peabody Plaza, opened last June. The plaza cost $2,224,000 to build. Cedar Creek Center mixes apartment dwellers, a shopping center, and a roof-top recreation center. Cultural institutions include The Hometown, USA, Institute of Arts, and the semicircular Golden Gate Theatre. The Children's Zoo, a first of its kind, is financed by donations. Surrounding area provides a great natural playground for sports in all seasons—bicycling, dogsled racing, sailing, skiing, ice fishing, swimming, and picnicking. As manager of the Chamber of Commerce, prepare a public relations story based on Hometown, USA. The article is not to exceed 1200 words. It will be released to *Travel and Work.*

9. Assuming the facts about Hometown, USA, presented in application problem 8, persuade Charles Bickens (traveling newsman for ''Progressive Cities in the U.S.,'' a TV program which appears each Sunday morning at 9 a.m.) that Hometown, USA, is worthy of his consideration. Prepare media material for a 5-minute release, following guidelines for program proposals.

Chapter 17

Pre- and Post-Meeting Communication

LEARNING OBJECTIVES

After studying this chapter, you should be able to

1. Discuss the preparation of a meeting agenda.
2. Discuss the procedures involved in making arrangements for a meeting.
3. Discuss the preparation of reports about informal meetings, formal meetings, conferences, and conference calls.
4. Discuss the preparation of minutes of a meeting.

Business executives often spend a considerable amount of time in meetings. Because of the need for various types of meetings at different levels of business organizations, government agencies, and professional organizations, everyone in the working world should be familiar with the procedures involved in conducting meetings. An understanding of parliamentary procedures is especially helpful. Every meeting should follow a systematic schedule, and an agenda should be prepared well in advance of the meeting.

The material in this chapter is concerned with pre- and post-meeting communication. Preparing agendas, making arrangements for the meeting, and preparing a variety of reports about meetings or conferences are covered in this chapter.

AGENDA

What uses are made of agendas?

An agenda is important, regardless of the type of meeting being held. The agenda—which should be available to the meeting participants before the meeting—will not only help them prepare for the meeting, but also will help the individual presiding over the meeting keep the discussions "on track." Meetings are sometimes not as productive as participants expect because of an ineffective agenda or because of the leader's failure to follow the agenda.

Order

What determines the order of items on agendas?

The order of the items on the agenda is typically determined by parliamentary procedures, especially in formal meetings. The items outlined below are often included on the agenda of formal meetings of organizations or associations. A number of the items are omitted in informal committee meetings.

1. Call (the meeting) to order
2. Roll call
3. Read and approve the minutes of the previous meeting
4. Treasurer's report (if appropriate)
5. Officer reports (if appropriate)
6. Committee reports (if appropriate)
   a. Standing committees
   b. Special committees
7. Unfinished business
8. New business
9. Appointments of committees (if appropriate)
10. Nominations of officers (if appropriate)
11. Elections (if appropriate)
12. Announcements
13. Adjournment

The agenda is often included in the announcement of the meeting. In some instances, the person who presides over the meeting may also solicit in the announcement other items to be included on the agenda. The final agenda can be distributed either in advance of the meeting or at the beginning of the meeting.

For formal meetings of professional organizations/associations or corporations, the by-laws often stipulate how the meeting will be called, how the agenda will be prepared and presented, and how the agenda is to be amended to include additional items.

In presenting the agenda to the participants, the same order of items and format should be regularly followed. To make changes each time an agenda is prepared will create unnecessary confusion.

ARRANGEMENTS FOR THE MEETING

The individual responsible for arranging a meeting notifies the personnel to be included, regardless of whether it is a regularly scheduled or a special meeting. The notice should specify the day, the date, the time, the place, and the purpose of the meeting.

Some notices may need to arrive about a week before the meeting; special and/or official meetings generally require at least two weeks' advance notice. Some organizations require thirty to fifty days' advance notification. The individual responsible for making the arrangements will want to make sure that all policies and procedures are followed in announcing the meeting.

For small groups, a notice of the meeting may be transmitted by a typewritten message, a phone message, or increasingly by a computer message. In the notice, the names of all committee members often will be listed, as Figure 17–1 illustrates.

For notices of regular meetings, a form may be printed, duplicated, or entered into the computer at the beginning of the year. Before each meeting, the date, program topic, or other related information is filled in to complete the form.

Some meetings or conferences are of such importance that the announcement is written on letterhead paper. If only a few persons are to receive the

Figure 17–1 Duplicated Notice of Meeting

MEMORANDUM

May 20, 1990

TO: Finance Committee Members (Bill Johnson, Rupert Klasek, Pat McMann, Jim Norveson, Jack Owens, Fred Zankow)

FROM: John Jackson, Chairperson; Finance Committee

SUBJECT: Financial Audit

The Finance Committee must recommend to the Executive Board the name of a firm to audit the books at the end of the fiscal year. Since the Board meeting is June 7, we need to make a decision at once.

Will it be possible for you to meet with the Committee for lunch at 12 noon on Thursday, May 26, at the Lincoln Inn? Please let me know.

jk

notice, individual letters with the name, address, and salutation may be sent. With larger listings, electronic typing equipment makes it possible to prepare individually typed letters with addresses and salutations filled in.

The current trend, however, even in an individual letter, is to omit the salutation as well as the complimentary close. Where the mailing is a large one or the notice is sales oriented (to encourage attendance at a national meeting, for example), the addressee's name in the salutation is appropriate. Figure 17–2 is an example of an individually typed notice for a large mailing.

Figure 17–3 presents a formal notice of an annual meeting of shareholders.

When preparing meeting announcements, you should incorporate the effective-writing suggestions presented in earlier chapters.

Other Considerations

In addition to the activities already discussed, what other considerations must the meeting organizer be concerned with?

The individual arranging a meeting is responsible for a number of other considerations, such as reserving a meeting room, organizing supplementary materials, and making arrangements for needed equipment.

Reserving meeting rooms

If a large meeting is being planned, obtaining a written confirmation of the meeting place, dates, and schedule of room reservations for program sessions is advisable. Should questions arise about the reservation, the written confirmation will help resolve any misunderstandings.

Supplementary materials

The person responsible for the meeting assembles files and other written materials necessary for the business of the meeting. All special written materials must be obtained before the meeting begins.

Materials to be handed out during the meeting should also be assembled before the meeting begins. In a meeting where business is transacted, each participant should be given a copy of these materials, including the agenda, minutes from the previous meeting, treasurer's report, budget report, committee reports, and other special reports. These materials should be placed in envelopes or folders and arranged in the order in which they will be considered during the meeting. Generally, these materials are in place at the participants' seats before the meeting begins.

Equipment

Many small business meetings, conferences, and sessions of large conventions are recorded. The person responsible for the meeting either makes the arrangements for the needed equipment or assigns the responsibility to someone else. Following the meeting, a transcript of the proceedings is typed verbatim or summarized from the recorded sessions.

The chairperson of the meeting is responsible for many other details, several of which involve written communications. Experience has shown that a written record of decisions and agreements is highly desirable, even if not necessary.

INTERNATIONAL ENGINEERS

1247 Holloway Street (402) 377-4982 Des Moines, IA 45483

September 4, 1990

Mr. Raymond Osborn, President
Lapco, Inc.
P. O. Box 81120
Lincoln, NE 68501

Dear Mr. Osborn:

Subject: International Engineers Convention

The International Engineers will be holding their convention in New York from October 29-31. You are cordially invited to attend this convention.

Registration forms, a tentative schedule of official meetings, and a tour-preference sheet are included for your use. Instructions for registration are included on the registration form. We have decided to let participants handle their own transportation and hotel accommodations.

We believe we have some outstanding speakers this year, as well as a fine all-around program. We look forward to seeing you in October.

Cordially yours,

Joseph Kreider

Joseph Kreider, President

gm

Enclosures

Figure 17–2 Individually Typed Notice for a Large Mailing

215 SOUTH CASCADE STREET **Otter Tail** POWER COMPANY FERGUS FALLS, MN 56537

March 16, 1987

To the Holders of Common Shares
of Otter Tail Power Company:

You are cordially invited to attend the Annual Meeting of Shareholders of Otter Tail Power Company, which will be held in the Meeting Rooms at the Holiday Inn, Fergus Falls, Minnesota, on April 13, 1987, at 10:00 a.m.. The formal Notice of Meeting and Proxy Statement, which appear on the following pages, provide information concerning matters to be considered at the meeting.

At this Annual Meeting the Board of Directors has nominated for reelection as Directors, Mr. Donald R. Koessel and Mr. Dennis R. Emmen. Mr. Robert S. Davis, formerly a Senior Vice President with the St. Paul Companies, Inc., will be retiring from the Board of Directors and will not stand for reelection. The Nominating Committee has identified a number of qualified candidates for the position vacated by Mr. Davis' retirement; however, the Board has not had sufficient opportunity to evaluate all candidates and select a nominee for this Annual Meeting. Consequently, the shareholders are asked to fix the number of Directors at eight for the next year. This will allow the Board sufficient time to identify and present a qualified nominee for election at the 1988 Annual Meeting of Shareholders.

In order to ensure that your shares may be represented at the meeting and to save the Company additional expense of solicitation, we urge that you promptly sign and return the enclosed Proxy card. If you attend the meeting, as we hope you will, you may revoke your Proxy by written notice given to an officer of the Company and vote in person.

A question slip is also enclosed with this Proxy Statement. If you have any questions about Otter Tail Power Company that you would like to have answered at the meeting or in writing, please return the question slip with your Proxy.

Sincerely,

John C. MacFarlane
President and Chief
Executive Officer

Figure 17–3 Notice of Annual Meeting of Shareholders. *Courtesy,* Otter Tail Power Company.

WRITING A REPORT ON A MEETING OR CONFERENCE

What suggestions can you offer that will help you improve the effectiveness of the report you write at the conclusion of a meeting?

Special reporting services are often employed by large convention and conference groups. However, if the business executive is responsible for seeing that the meetings are covered, the following suggestions will be helpful.

1. When the business of the meeting is prearranged, a skeleton report form may be prepared beforehand with spaces to be filled in as the business of the meeting is acted upon. Such a note-taking guide may be set up so that only checkmarks need to be filled in during the meeting. When resolutions are to be presented during the meeting, a record of the resolutions should be prepared before the meeting. In note taking, these resolutions need only to be referred to by number. For regularly scheduled committee, directors', and stockholders' meetings, special minutes' books may be desirable. These books are available through suppliers of corporate forms.

2. The notes taken of the meeting must be accurate and inclusive because the conference group will be dependent upon these notes for a reliable

permanent record of the proceedings. The individual taking notes must pay close attention, employ intelligent knowledge of the vocabulary of business, and possess the ability to listen as well as to record the discussion.

3. Verbatim reporting of everything said at the meeting is usually not necessary, but the individual responsible for the record should possess the ability to determine what remarks are to be preserved intact. For instance, the exact wording of a resolution, an amendment, a decision, or a conclusion may be important. The recorder is responsible for ensuring that records in such cases are entirely reliable. The record should contain an accurate account of the meeting as a whole and specific reference to formal motions, important statements and statistics, and often the names of persons presenting opinions or plans.

4. If the recorder misses something in the procedures, he/she should not hesitate to inquire at the first opportunity. By prearranged signal, the recorder may indicate to the meeting chairperson a desire to have a statement repeated or a motion restated.

5. In addition to taking notes during the meeting, the recorder will usually be responsible for the preservation of additional items, such as copies of reports that have been read or proposals that have been submitted. The recorder makes certain that such material is made available for inclusion in the completed meeting reports.

6. The recorder will usually be expected to follow through on a number of matters arising out of the conference. Suggestions and promises that have been made, plans that have been proposed, questions that have been asked all have to be attended to.

7. The form in which the conference report is to be set up may already have been standardized by the company; if so, sample copies will be available for the recorder to copy. Lacking a sample, the inexperienced report writer should generally follow the form of report writing described in an earlier chapter, although all parts may not be necessary.

8. In reporting conference sessions, the recorder writes in a straightforward, third-person "news report" (expositive or narrative) style. If verbatim reporting is not required, all important proceedings are summarized in detail and direct quotations are included wherever desirable.

Generally, no personal opinion of the conference reporter is included, and no second-person admonitions to the reader are inserted, except as quotations of remarks made by members of the meeting group. The recorder who is unsure of the preferred writing style for the reporting of any special meeting should discuss with the chairperson the type of reporting he/she wishes as a record of the proceedings.

Informal Meetings

Many meetings of business people are informal and may be called at any time to discuss a specific problem or to pool ideas. A departmental or unit chairperson may call a staff meeting, an executive may call a meeting of department heads, or personnel may assemble for a variety of purposes.

These informal meetings—which are often in the form of committee meetings or informal office conferences—may be regularly scheduled. For ex-

What is the nature of formal meetings?

ample, the executive committee within a business organization, a corporation, a professional organization, or a specialized unit may meet on a regularly scheduled basis.

Meetings of special committees charged with one specific responsibility, such as implementing a new regulation, studying the feasibility of initiating a new service, or making recommendations for standardizing mailing procedures throughout the company, may be called. Small informal meetings designed to formulate a policy plan may require the executive's participation.

Many of these informal meetings are discussions where ideas are shared, conclusions are drawn, and recommendations are made without the observance of rules of order. One of the participants may serve as recorder or note taker. From the notes taken at the meeting, an informal report is prepared, usually in paragraph form, to include major points of discussion. A copy of the report is sent to those attending as well as to others who need to be apprised of the report's content.

Figure 17–4 is a report illustrating the format for informal minutes of a mayor's committee.

Formal Meetings

What is a common type of formal meeting?

Every business executive finds that a large percentage of his/her time is spent in meetings, many of which are formal. Reports of meetings vary with the degree of formality required. Accurate minutes of stockholders', directors', and committee meetings are essential. Formal meetings are necessary when the business to be conducted is particularly important or when a large group is attending. Business executives should be familiar with the rules of parliamentary procedure that are followed at formal meetings.

In addition to the required minutes that outline the actions taken at formal meetings, a report for stockholders is prepared, based upon the annual stockholders' meeting. The first page of such a report is presented in Figure 17–5. This summary includes statistical information on voting at the meeting, election results, reports from officers, and questions/answers from the meeting. All such reports contain basic information of interest to stockholders, although the report format may vary considerably from corporation to corporation.

Conferences

What are conferences?

Business executives often participate in conferences and conventions. A conference, usually a discussion or consultation on a specific topic, may be a formal meeting or it may be a short, informal meeting. A convention, on the other hand, is a formal meeting—typically scheduled on an annual basis—of members of a professional group.

Figure 17–6 provides an example of a preconference communication for a large conference. The advance agenda for the meeting includes speakers, a sketch of the sessions, a registration form, and other information about the conference.

Conference reporting is generally a specialized function, and trained reporters may be on hand to record proceedings. If reporters are available, the person responsible for the conference is concerned only with the processing and distribution of the conference report. The procedure at some conferences is to

MAYOR'S BLUE RIBBON COMMITTEE
January 31, 1990

A meeting of the Mayor's Blue Ribbon Committee was held at 3:30 p.m., Friday, January 31, 1990, in the Mayor's Conference Room, Third Floor, City-County Building.

All members were present as follows: John Makan, Elda Hardesty, Gwen Alred, Leeta Olin, Dick Taylor, Polly Howett, Robert Heil, Robb Watson, Tom King, Jan Nowke, Barbara Houghton, Jan Munson, and Lloyd Binkley.

Chair Polly Howett opened the meeting and explained she had met the previous Friday with John Biltmore, David Holley, Ron Tackett, Dana Loper, Jack Vanston, and Allen Walker to prepare the agenda and discuss the format for the upcoming meeting.

Jack Vanston, Finance Director, discussed the merit increase budgeting procedure and briefly explained other features of the City's budgeting process.

Assistant Police Chief Allen Walker discussed the present merit pay system.

Committee members asked Mr. Vanston and Chief Walker questions related to their presentations.

Dana Loper explained the way the Commission of Industrial Relations (CIR) functions.

Ron Tackett distributed and explained data requested by the Committee regarding employee benefits, appraisal system training sessions, and employee turnover.

Polly Howett distributed an article on pay and promotion for performance from the publication Government Executive, that Mayor Ellison thought the Committee might find interesting.

Members agreed to review all information received and to be prepared to address the Mayor's charge to the Committee at the next meeting.

The meeting adjourned at 5:20 p.m.

City resource staff present: John Biltmore, Ron Tackett, Arlene Dudley, and Dana Loper.

____
Recorder

Figure 17–4 Informal Minutes

REPORT OF THE 1987 ANNUAL MEETING

MacFARLANE ADDRESSES SHAREHOLDERS

In 1986 your company continued to see challenge and opportunity in the changes taking place in our service territory. Adjustments were made so operations remain in context with the marketplace. The low-growth pattern established in 1980, after two decades of 7% annual growth, is still with us and is likely to remain for at least the rest of the decade.

We have responded in a number of ways including lower construction budgets and decreased numbers of personnel. The result has been cash generation allowing the retirement of higher-cost preferred stock and first mortgage bonds. The lower construction budgets are not only the result of decreased load growth, but are also due in large part to the innovation and productivity of our employees. We have obtained generating capacity from others in small increments to fit our need at a fraction of the cost of building base-load capacity. Substantial dollars have been saved by uprating transmission lines rather than building new. Load management has provided the opportunity to make better utilization of existing facilities.

Emphasis on productivity improvement continues. In the last National Association of Regulatory Utilities Commissioners report comparing the 112 largest investor-owned utilities of this nation, Otter Tail was No. 6. Not as good as the No. 1 of the previous year, but still excellent performance in an area where high performance is difficult to maintain year after year.

Rate stability has been given additional emphasis as our business becomes more competitive. As measured by the aforementioned report, we retained our No. 1 position in rate stability. That is, we have had the least percentage increase in rates of any major investor-owned utility in the nation in the last 12 years. That period, however, does not include the current Minnesota rate case.

There are some negatives expressed in the reports today because that's the way things are. But I want to leave you with this: Today Otter Tail Power Company is as sound financially as it has been at any time in its history. It has a low capital budget, about equaling depreciation. We do not see the need to begin any major construction projects during the remainder of the decade, and we'll operate on internally generated funds until we do. The generating plants, the transmission lines, and the distribution systems are adequate and well maintained. We do not have excess generating capacity, the company's other property is in good to excellent shape, and we are applying technology to the facilities to maximize their usefulness. The company has the confidence of its customers and a management team and an employee group trained and capable of meeting almost any challenge. From my perspective the company is in good shape and is well positioned to meet the future.

Figure 17–5 Report to Stockholders. *Courtesy,* Otter Tail Power Company.

have a different reporter at each session. Each speaker or program participant is asked to provide a copy of his or her presentation so that it can be included in the proceedings publication. The reporter then summarizes the discussion that follows the presentation, edits the material, and writes appropriate introductions, conclusions, and/or recommendations.

Generally, registrants at a conference receive a copy of the proceedings, and additional copies are made available for a charge. Figure 17–7, which presents excerpts from a conference, illustrates the formal type of conference reporting with which the business executive should be familiar.

Wednesday, May 27

8:30 a.m. - 11:30 a.m. **A**

RIDING THE WINDS OF CHANGE

F.G. "Buck" Rodgers

Individuals and organizations need to understand the internal and external forces that will be affecting them, such as a changing value system, productivity issues, advanced technologies, new management techniques and the need to be more customer oriented.

Mr. Rodgers, an instrumental figure in making IBM the success it is today, will emphasize that against these forces of change there must be pursuit of excellence through acts of personal leadership. He points out that the ability to ride the "winds of change" will yield such benefits as increased productivity and quality products and services.

F.G. "Buck" Rodgers was with the IBM Corporation for 34 years. For 10 years, he was vice president of marketing with responsibility for IBM's worldwide marketing activities. He took early retirement in 1984, but still serves the corporation as a consultant.

Renowned within company circles as a motivator, an articulator of ideas and a practitioner of excellence, Mr. Rodgers is equally well known as a public speaker. In the past five years, he has spoken to a wide variety of business, academic and civic groups.

1:30 p.m. - 5:00 p.m. **B**

Panel Discussion

TERRORISM AND CORPORATE SECURITY: THE IMPACT AND COST TO BUSINESS

Howard Miller, Patrick O'Malley, Pierre Jeanniot, Sir Robin Gillett, Meir Amit

Over the past decade, incidents of terrorist attacks have posed an alarming and escalating threat to businesses worldwide, particularly to executives traveling abroad. It has been estimated that over the past year, corporations have spent over $20 billion on security.

In this special panel presentation, executives representing major security-conscious business interests in five nations, along with representatives from the airline and security industries, will relate how terrorism has altered the conduct of business. Security measures that reduce the threat of exposure to terrorist acts will also be presented.

Howard Miller is treasurer of the 1988 U.S. Olympic Committee (Moderator).

Patrick O'Malley is chairman emeritus of Canteen Co. and chairman of the Chicago Convention and Visitors Bureau.

Pierre Jeanniot is president of Air Canada.

Sir Robin Gillett is an underwriting member of Lloyd's of London and former Lord Mayor of London.

Meir Amit is a retired general of the Israeli army and former head of Israel's security service (Mosad).

Other panelists will be announced.

1:30 p.m. - 3:00 p.m. **C1**
3:30 p.m. - 5:00 p.m. **C2**

THE ONE MINUTE MANAGER GETS FIT

Dr. Marjorie Blanchard

While many managers can claim success in their professional endeavors, some would be considered unquestionable failures at staying physically fit. These managers, who eat on the run and don't even allow for a minimum of exercise, find that their weight explodes and their breath grows shorter. For these people, success is really bad for their health.

In this session, Ms. Blanchard will discuss the phenomenon of the unhealthy achiever and will present a blueprint for making a commitment to fitness and well being and achieving a new, healthier style of living.

Marjorie Blanchard, chairperson and co-founder of Blanchard Training and Development, Inc., is a widely known and respected consultant, lecturer and trainer. A compelling speaker, Dr. Blanchard has been training men and women in industry, education and convention settings. She specializes in communication, leadership, health promotion, life planning and team building.

As a consultant, Dr. Blanchard's most recent clients include Holiday Inns, Inc., Lockheed, Johnson & Johnson, Beverly Hills Savings and Loan, and Kidder Peabody, Inc.

1:30 p.m. - 3:00 p.m. **D**

THE IMPORTANCE OF CREATIVITY

Edward L. Wax

Historically, the British have been admired for their wit and creativity in advertising. Now, the United States has caught the fever and is experiencing a creative renaissance.

In a provocative and humorous discussion, Mr. Wax will explain why this creative revolution is taking place. He will show how this revolution will help North American marketers capture their target audience. An entertaining reel of foreign and domestic commercials will be shown.

Edward L. Wax is president and chief executive officer of Saatchi & Saatchi Compton, Inc. Previously, he served as executive vice president of Compton International and director of Multinational Client Services, Europe.

1:30 p.m. - 3:00 p.m.* **E1**

EXCELLENCE THROUGH LEADERSHIP

John F. Regan

Today, you must lead or choose to follow. If you choose neither, then get the heck out of the way. As today's organizations undergo great changes, managers must be leaders as opposed to administrators. They need to be the motivational models to their associates. This highly interactive and fast-paced workshop will teach the skills managers need, if they want to be the leaders of successful systems, services and employees in the pursuit of corporate goals.

Figure 17–6 Pre-Conference Communication. *Courtesy,* Administrative Management Society, Willow Grove, PA.

Wednesday, May 27

John F. Regan has had 20 years of frontline work as a corporate manager of education and training for a *Fortune* 500 company. He has presented workshops on a wide range of topics to all levels of management, from the executive to the first-line supervisor. He speaks at national seminars and business conferences.

* *This session will also be held Thursday, May 28, 1:30 p.m. - 3:00 p.m.*

1:30 p.m. - 3:00 p.m.* **F1**

WORKERS OVER 50: OLD MYTHS, NEW REALITIES

Representative from AARP

Growing old just isn't what it used to be. This session will discuss the results of a study on attitudes toward older workers, conducted by Yankelovich, Skelly and White, Inc., for the American Association of Retired Persons (AARP).

Until recently, the status of older workers has been governed by certain widespread assumptions: the privileges of seniority, the desire among employees to retire as soon as possible, an unlimited pool of young labor and the scenario of long service with a single company.

You will learn how and why these assumptions are actually myths and, in reality, there is a growing need for older workers and the flexibility and skills they offer.

* *This session will also be held Thursday, May 28, 1:30 p.m. - 3:00 p.m.*

1:30 p.m. - 3:00 p.m. **G**

POSITIONING YOURSELF FOR ADVANCEMENT

Marilyn Moats Kennedy

Advancement doesn't come to those who wait, though it may to those who appear to be waiting while they strategize, maneuver and generally create their own opportunities. In this session, we'll look at four crucial issues.

1) Positioning. How can you bring yourself to the attention of people with the power to promote?

2) Marketing yourself internally. What are the most appropriate ways to create an "upward draft"?

3) Doing a skills inventory. What skills should you be emphasizing to maximize your potential in your present position?

4) When do you cut your losses? What are the signals that there are no promotional opportunities where you now are?

Marilyn Moats Kennedy is managing partner of Career Strategies, a counseling firm in Wilmette, Illinois. She has authored books and frequently spoken on career-related topics. Most recently, she has provided AMS with a line of career videos and publications, including the *Manager's CareerLetter*.

1:30 p.m. - 3:00 p.m. **H**

QUALITY PERFORMANCE THROUGH QUALITY PERFORMANCE REVIEWS

Carol-Ann Price, C.A.M.

Writing or receiving a performance review should be exciting and rewarding for both manager and employee. This nuts and bolts session uses group exercises and handouts to help participants walk away looking forward to writing or receiving that next performance review.

You will develop results-driven performance standards that will motivate your employees or yourself. Ms. Price will share a review format that is built around the job description, that quantitatively documents performance and that provides for the planning of development opportunities.

***Carol-Ann Price*, C.A.M.**, is business manager with College of Saint Mary in Omaha, Nebraska, AMS International Vice President-Membership, and has spoken on leadership, goal-setting and office automation.

Buckingham Fountain, Grant Park

1:30 p.m. - 4:30 p.m. **I**

CAPITAL BUDGETING

Dr. *Moustafa* H. *Abdelsamad*

Dealing with capital budgeting can be a real problem for many managers. This program is designed to help participants understand what capital budgeting means, how to evaluate capital expenditures, what to do with risk, how to interpret the results and what role quantitative information should play in capital budgeting decisions.

Participants will learn how to better defend their proposals and feel more comfortable dealing with financial managers. The program will also help those who are interested in taking the financial management section of the C.A.M. exam.

NOTE: Bring your calculator with you.

Dr. *Moustafa* H. *Abdelsamad* is an associate dean for graduate studies in business and professor of finance at Virginia Commonwealth University, Richmond, Virginia.

1:30 p.m. - 5:00 p.m.* **J1**

INTRODUCTION TO BI-POLAR

Marlene Arthur Pinkstaff

Are you a risker or a thinker? Do you know? Would you like to find out? Participants in this seminar will be introduced to the concept and philosophy of the Bi-Polar Theory of Core Strengths.

You will identify your pattern of strengths and learn to apply these concepts to yourself and to your situation. Participants will benefit from the seminar with a better understanding of themselves, a better understanding of others, the ability to creatively use their strengths and improved communications and relationships with others.

Marlene Arthur Pinkstaff is president, co-owner and consultant of Pinkstaff Consulting Associates, Inc., based in Tulsa, Oklahoma.

She is chairperson of the AMS International Conference Planning Committee, and served as president of the AMS Tulsa Chapter for 1985-86.

NOTE: Enrollment is limited and pre-registration is required for this seminar. You must register by April 1, 1987, and complete an Inventory of Strengths in advance. Materials will be mailed immediately upon receipt of registration and will include a deadline for return.

* *This session will also be held Thursday, May 28, 1:30 p.m. - 5:00 p.m.*

Figure 17–6 (Cont.)

Thursday, May 28

1:30 p.m. - 3:00 p.m. **T**

MAKE THAT DECISION NOW

Prof. Wally D. Borgen

Stop putting off all those decisions you have to make. Get a start on the right track by deciding to attend this session, where Ms. Borgen will show participants how to: recognize the stages of decision making; develop the managerial self-confidence needed to handle problems; recognize various decision-making styles; and successfully solve problems.

Wally D. Borgen is associate professor and chair of the Behavioral and Applied Sciences Division at Concordia College, Bronxville, New York. She has been a national speaker and lecturer since 1977.

A member of AMS since 1980, Ms. Borgen is an assistant area director for membership and chair of the International College Chapter Relations Committee.

1:30 p.m. - 3:00 p.m. **U**

WHO DOES THE SELLING?

Patrick O'Malley

Everyone is responsible for selling, from your receptionist to the chief executive officer. Every employee in your company is a salesperson. The problem is that training for customer contact has always been limited to the sales department.

In this session, you will learn how to alert everyone in your company to the importance of being a salesperson. Everyone interacts with customers, and everyone should be able to treat them with the same courtesy and respect that is expected from salespeople.

Patrick O'Malley is chairman emeritus of Canteen Co. and chairman of the Chicago Convention and Visitors Bureau.

1:30 p.m. - 3:00 p.m.* **M2**

TRAVEL AND ENTERTAINMENT MANAGEMENT

Christine Day

These days, arranging business travel is not simply a matter of an employee planning a meeting, boarding a plane and flying off for a stay in a distant city.

Today's companies, faced with tighter operating conditions and increased budget constraints, must keep a careful eye on business-related travel and entertainment expenses incurred by employees.

Ms. Day will show cost-conscious managers the methods of keeping travel and entertainment expenses in control. Her discussion will touch upon the four key findings of the 1986-87 *American Express Survey of Business Travel Management*, which reveals eight steps that companies identified as important in controlling travel and entertainment expenses.

Christine Day is the director of Business Travel Sales for the central region of American Express Travel Management Services, Chicago, Illinois.

* *This session will also be held Wednesday, May 27, 3:30 p.m. - 5:00 p.m.*

The Museum of Science and Industry

1:30 p.m. - 3:00 p.m.* **E2**

EXCELLENCE THROUGH LEADERSHIP

John F. Regan

Today, you must lead or choose to follow. If you choose neither, then get the heck out of the way. As today's organizations undergo great changes, managers must be leaders as opposed to administrators. They need to be the motivational models to their associates. This highly interactive and fast-paced workshop will teach the skills managers need, if they want to be the leaders of successful systems, services and employees in the pursuit of corporate goals.

John F. Regan has had 20 years of frontline work as a corporate manager of education and training for a *Fortune* 500 company. He has presented workshops on a wide range of topics to all levels of management, from the executive to the first-line supervisor.

* *This session will also be held Wednesday, May 27, 1:30 p.m. - 3:00 p.m.*

3:30 p.m. - 5:00 p.m.* **L2**

THE "BORN AGAIN" MANAGER — THE CASE FOR OUTPLACEMENT

Herbert C. Hamilton

For a manager, saying "You're fired" to someone is almost as tough as hearing it from a superior. The unpleasant task of firing someone has resulted in a growing number of management consultants specializing in outplacement services.

Mr. Hamilton will answer some of the questions managers ask about this relatively new service and will show participants how to better prepare for the day when they must say or hear "You're fired."

Herbert C. Hamilton is president of H.C. Hamilton & Associates, an executive search and outplacement firm that consults to corporations. He has worked as an executive search consultant and as a consultant to management in corporate outplacement since 1977.

* *This session will also be held Wednesday, May 27, 3:30 p.m. - 5:00 p.m.*

3:30 p.m. - 5:00 p.m. **V**

PEOPLE IN TRANSITION: UNDERSTANDING EFFECTS OF CHANGE

Elaine Reagan-Jones

Change is often threatening to people, and their reactions to change may inhibit their ability to perform.

Ms. Reagan-Jones shows how to dissect the change monsters so that you can become a change manager. You will learn ways to adapt to change and how to assist

Figure 17–6 (Cont.)

Thursday, May 28

others with this process. She will also explain how to interact with people in changing situations, gain insight to their problems and enhance your sensitivity to their problems.

Elaine Reagan-Jones is controller and corporate secretary for Pacific Electric Motor Company, Oakland, California. She leads numerous seminars on various aspects of administrative management.

Ms. Reagan-Jones has held many positions with AMS, including president of the Oakland-East Bay Chapter for two terms. She is currently international director-elect for Area 14.

3:30 p.m. - 5:00 p.m. **W**

IS ANYONE LISTENING?

Prof. Wally D. Borgen

Participants in this session will acquire an understanding of the communication process through the techniques of reflective listening, which is designed to help managers deal more successfully with associates and employees on a one-to-one basis. Participants will be shown when and when not to listen reflectively.

Wally D. Borgen is associate professor and chair of the Behavioral and Applied Sciences Division at Concordia College, Bronxville, New York. She has been a national speaker and lecturer since 1977.

A member of AMS since 1980, Ms. Borgen is an assistant area director for membership and chair of the International College Chapter Relations Committee.

3:30 p.m. - 5:00 p.m. **X**

WHAT EVERY MANAGER SHOULD KNOW ABOUT THE COMPANY'S OFFICES

Howard L. Ecker

Get an insight into the national office market for this year and beyond, and find out what you should know about relocating your company's offices, as one of the nation's most quoted real estate authorities shares his expertise.

Potentially good office deals for companies will be covered along with the important factors a manager should consider when relocating an office. Mr. Ecker will also explain how to recruit a relocation team.

Howard L. Ecker is president of Howard Ecker & Company, a real estate firm in Chicago, Illinois. He has represented companies for office relocations across the United States and Canada.

3:30 p.m. - 5:00 p.m. **Y**

ROUNDTABLE: EMPLOYMENT TRENDS IN THE '80s AND '90s

Ann Schmidt

The job market changes almost as quickly as the stock market. Many factors contribute to changing trends in employment needs.

Ms. Schmidt will discuss present demands in employment, how to plan for applicant shortages in specialized areas and how to plan for future needs. Her predictions for the 1990s will address what jobs will and will not be in demand and what industries and technologies will succeed and fail.

Ann Schmidt is president and CEO of Corporate Resources International, Ltd., headquartered in Wilmington, Delaware.

Ms. Schmidt, a member of AMS since 1975, is a past member of the AMS International Board of Directors and past president of the Delaware Chapter.

Friday, May 29

8:30 a.m. - 11:30 a.m. **Z**

A PERSPECTIVE ON BUSINESS

Maureen Reagan

Maureen Reagan has been active on a national and international level in women's issues. Drawing on her experiences, she will discuss the changing role of women in all levels of society. She will present an outline on how business and government will have to readjust to changes in the family and economic structure as women develop and pursue their own careers.

Maureen Reagan is special consultant to the chairman of the Republican National Committee for Women's Campaign Activities. She serves as a liaison between the committee and women legislators and women's organizations across the United States.

Founder and present chair of the recently created GOP Women's Political Action League (GOPAL), Ms. Reagan is furthering her efforts on behalf of Republican women candidates and office holders. In addition, she has been appointed the United States representative to the United Nation's Commission on the Status of Women by Secretary of State George Shultz.

Figure 17–6 (Cont.)

A PANEL DISCUSSION:
ARTIFICIAL INTELLIGENCE, EXPERT SYSTEMS,
AND FOURTH GENERATION LANGUAGES IN MIS

"4GLS AND THEIR IMPACT ON THE MIS PROFESSIONAL"
Jeretta A. Horn

"ARTIFICIAL INTELLIGENCE: AI LANGUAGES
OR EXPERT SYSTEMS SHELLS"
G. Daryl Nord

"NONPROCEDURAL LANGUAGES: PRODUCTIVITY TOOLS
THAT HAVE COME OF AGE"
Richard Aukerman

Oklahoma State University

ABSTRACT

This paper addresses the concepts of artificial intelligence, expert systems, natural languages, and fourth generation languages in MIS. The impact of this new generation of software on 3GLs and the MIS professional is also discussed.

Artificial intelligence concepts are introduced including a discussion and illustration of expert or "rule-based" systems and natural languages. Characteristics, features, and associated problems of 4GLs are presented along with a discussion of the impact of these languages on third generation languages, and more specifically COBOL. Finally, the impact of 4GLs, artificial intelligence, and expert systems on MIS is addressed.

INTRODUCTION

Since the development of the electronic computer, the method of communicating human needs into a language the computer understands has evolved through four distinct stages or generations: machine, assembler, high-level or third generation, and finally fourth generation or "nonprocedural" languages. Each generation of software technology has enabled more people with less technical skill to directly obtain results from the computer; thus lessening the gap between people and machines. As this gap decreases, software development and utilization continues including what some experts refer to as fifth generation software; artificial intelligence and expert systems. This paper will address issues related to artificial intelligence, expert systems, fourth generation languages, and the impact of 4GLs on the MIS professional.

ARTIFICIAL INTELLIGENCE

Artificial intelligence has been defined as the development of software that permits machines to emulate man's ability to reason and make decisions. There is general agreement that although this field is over 30 years old; it still remains rather difficult to define and is significantly underdeveloped

-1-

Figure 17–7 Proceedings

and implemented in practice. However, it is predicted that revenues from AI software, hardware, and services will reach $8 billion by 1993, with 50% of the computers sold containing logic components rather than traditional arithmetic components.

The potential of AI technology and applications is beginning to flourish now as it never has in the past. Computers with speed and memory capacities only dreamed of in the past coupled with "new" programming tools and languages have helped unleash some of the dynamics of artificial intelligence.

As stated by Firdman, (9) AI is a system that contains three basic capabilities: knowledge acquisition, goal-directed behavior, and skill acquisition. Briefly, knowledge acquisition implies that the system obtains new knowledge by communicating with the external world as well as interfacing with current internal knowledge. Internal knowledge is inferred from the system's knowledge base. The better the inference capabilities a system has, the more "intelligent" it is said to be. Secondly, AI implies that the system possesses goal-directed behavior; given a set of goal strategies and adequate knowledge specified goals should be attainable. Skill acquisition is the ability of the system to improve it's performance over time. This infers that the system improves in speed and becomes more discriminating when problem solving.

There are numerous applications of AI that assist in promoting efficiency in the technological and business fields. These include: vision, speech recognition, robotics, expert systems, and natural languages. This section of our paper will discuss two of these: expert systems and natural languages.

EXPERT SYSTEMS

An expert system is a computer program that, when presented with a series of facts, follows a set of rules and reaches conclusions similar to a human expert. Composed of a knowledge base (a database of facts and the rules for dealing with them), an inference engine (which applies this knowledge to act on the specific situation facts), and a user interface (a means by which a user can communicate with the expert system); expert systems are intended to help non-experts in the decision-making process. Each time the system is presented with a problem, the inference engine attempts to "fire" the appropriate rules in the knowledge base to arrive at a solution. If the expert system cannot arrive at a solution, additional information is requested from the user. Because this information can be added to the knowledge base, the expert system is said to "learn" from experience.

-2-

Figure 17–7 (Cont.)

those applications where they provide the desired functionality. (6)

Finally, the impact of this new generation of software will continue to bring new perspectives to the MIS professional. Many corporations will invest in training for the end user. With 4GLs, end users can learn to create programs, consisting of a few lines of code, that produce meaningful results. As end user's responsibilities increase, information is available more quickly, expansion and changes are more easily implemented, and the usefulness of the report no longer depends on how effectively the programmers and users communicated. As a result, MIS professionals are able (1) to concentrate on long-term development projects, program maintenance, and assist in training and support.

As artificial intelligence, expert systems, and fourth generation languages permeate the computer industry, the widespread use and appeal will continue. Constant change is inevitable and to survive, the MIS professional and end user must adapt to the ever changing rapid pace of advancing technology.

REFERENCES

1. Lerner, Nancy B., Irv Brownstein, and Wallace W. Smith. "Winds of Change: The Impact of Fourth-Generation Languages on Documentation." Computerworld, 1982, In Depth Section, pages 1-8.
2. Cobb, Richard H. "In Praise of 4GLs." Datamation, July 15, 1985, pages 90-95.
3. Morison, Robert. "4GLs vs. Cobol." Computerworld, August 12, 1985, In Depth Section, pages 15-20.
4. Christoff, Kurt A. "Building a Fourth Generation Environment." Datamation, September, 1985, pages 118-124.
5. "The 'Fourth Generation' Makes Its Mark." Dun's Business Month, July, 1985, pages 79-82.
6. Case, Albert F., Jr., and John H. Manley. "Fourth Generation Languages Offer Pros and Cons." Data Management, March, 1986, pages 10-11.
7. "Fourth Generation DBMS Delivers Speed, Efficiency to Large Info Center." Data Management, November, 1984, pages 34-35.
8. Carlyle, R. Emmett. "Can AI Save COBOL." Datamation, September 15, 1985, pages 42-43.
9. Fridman, Dr. Henry Eric. "Artificial Intelligence: Understanding the Basics." Design News, March 3, 1986, Vol. 42, pages 89-97.
10. Mason, R. "Artificial Intelligence." Fortune, June 10, 1985, Vol. III, pages 96-103.
11. Robinson, Gail M. "Artificial Intelligence: An Emerging Technology Whose Time Has Come." Design News, March 3, 1986, Vol. 42, pages 73-74.

-7-

Figure 17–7 (Cont.)

Conference Calls

Business executives often engage in conference calls involving several persons at different locations. Because the purpose of the call may be to obtain the opinions of participants or to discuss major decisions, a record of the discussion and/or action needs to be maintained.

The recorder should get the names, telephone numbers, and locations of the persons on the line. With the permission of those on the hook-up, the conversation may be recorded. From that recording, a summary of important points and the items that were discussed may be written. The format for the summary may be similar to that of informal minutes, including the date, the time of the call, who placed the call, names of the conferees, and a summary of the conference discussion. Copies of the summary are generally distributed to each person participating in the conference call.

Preparation of Minutes

Because of the importance of an accurate record of meetings, the person who assumes responsibility for taking minutes should prepare thoroughly for the assignment. The recorder should carefully read the minutes for content, format, and detail. Taking verbatim notes is usually not necessary, except for motions. Making a tape recording may be advisable, even though the minutes are later written in summary form.

What should be included in written minutes of meetings?

Minutes should contain a record of important discussions and actions taken at the meeting. Written minutes should contain the following:

1. Date, time, and place of the meeting
2. Type of meeting
3. Presiding officer
4. Officers and members present
5. Approval or correction of the minutes of the previous meeting
6. Reports of officers and committees
7. Action on unfinished business from a previous meeting
8. Transaction of new business, including motions and resolutions
9. Appointment of committees
10. Election of officers
11. Adjournment

Although minutes of informal meetings may include important discussions, minutes of formal meetings should contain only the action taken on any matter, in accordance with Robert's Rules of Order.

Motions

What should be included in the write-up of motions?

A record of all motions must include the following:

1. The name of the person making the motion
2. The exact wording of the motion

3. The name of the person seconding the motion, or, in informal minutes, the fact that the motion was seconded
4. The result of the voting

Reports of officers and committees

The treasurer's report is included in or attached to the minutes. Other reports may be summarized; usually written copies of various reports are distributed to the members after oral reports are made.

Rough draft of minutes

The first step in the preparation of minutes is to prepare a rough draft. The recorder should write the minutes immediately after the meeting while events and actions taken are still fresh in his/her mind. A draft of the minutes should be submitted for approval to the presiding officer as well as to those who made reports. If the minutes are unusually long or complicated, copies of the motions should be prepared for each member.

Minutes in final form

After the rough draft of the minutes has been approved or corrected by the member(s) whose approval is needed, a final draft is prepared. Standard paper for minutes' books is of a special type and can be obtained from stationers who specialize in corporate supplies. Any kind of durable paper may be used for minutes of informal meetings. Some larger corporations have strict regulations about the arrangement of minutes.

The final form of the minutes must be correct. Details of typing, arrangement, spacing, and general appearance of the minutes' book require special attention. The spelling of names should be verified.

The following guidelines will assist you in preparing the final form of minutes.

What suggestions can you offer that will help you improve the effectiveness of the minutes you prepare?

1. Capitalize and center the heading.
2. Include the type of meeting, day, date, and hour; the place; and the name of the presiding officer.
3. List the names of members present and those absent. (In the minutes of stockholders' meetings, the names of those represented by proxies and the amount of stock represented by each member or proxy are shown.)
4. Indent paragraphs 10 spaces.
5. Double space between each paragraph, and triple space between headings.
6. Indent resolutions fifteen spaces and type single spaced. The word *whereas* is typed in capital letters, followed by a comma; the first word after *whereas* begins with a capital letter.
7. Capitalize the words "Board of Directors" and the word "Corporation" when reference is made to the group for which the minutes are written. References to specific officers of the corporation may be in capital or lower case letters, but the capitalization should be consistent.

8. If captions are used, type them in capital letters in the margin.
9. Amounts of money mentioned in resolutions are written in legal form—in words followed by numbers. Amounts should be checked in the rough draft by both the person quoted and the presiding officer.
10. Leave a $1\frac{1}{2}$ inch outside margin.
11. Use the past tense.
12. Record motions (except the motion to adjourn) exactly as stated, giving the name of the person who made the motion. In formal minutes, motions should be underscored or typed in capital letters.
13. In formal minutes, state the fact that the meeting was properly called. The notice of the meeting can be included.
14. Number each page at the bottom, placing the number in the center of the page.

Correction of errors in minutes

How are errors in minutes corrected?

The minutes of a meeting are approved at the next meeting. If corrections to the minutes are to be made, this is done at the meeting. If the error can be corrected easily, a line may be drawn through the error and the correction written; if the error involves a revision of the minutes, the report of the corrections is included in the minutes of the current meeting.

Minutes' book

Because minutes are important documents, they are often kept indefinitely in a minutes' book. Although copies may be distributed to the members, the original copy of the minutes is maintained in the minutes' book. Corporation minutes are arranged in the following order in the book: (1) the organization meeting or minutes of the meeting of incorporation; (2) minutes of the stockholders' meetings; and (3) minutes of the directors' meetings.

Indexing of minutes

To facilitate finding material in minutes' books, a card index can be prepared that contains important business that has been acted upon. These index cards contain the subject matter and the page reference in the minutes' book on which specific information appears. The marginal captions used in preparing minutes will be helpful in preparing the index.

Figure 17–8 includes communications about an executive board meeting, including a notice to the members, the agenda, and the minutes.

CHAPTER SUMMARY

During your professional career you will probably have many opportunities to prepare pre- and post-meeting communications, such as announcements, agendas, and reports, including minutes.

Agendas tend to follow a rather universal format. Unless you have good reason to change the format, the standard order of items is recommended.

A considerable amount of communication is involved in making arrangements for meetings. While some of the communication is oral in nature, written communication is also used. Included are such materials as notices of meetings, communication regarding the reserving of meeting rooms, preparing

MEMORANDUM

May 20, 1990

TO: NMS Executive Board Members

FROM: John Beckett, Executive Secretary

SUBJECT: NMS Executive Board Meeting
Conrad-Halton Hotel, Chicago
June 19-20, 1990

The agenda is attached for the June 19-20 NMS Executive Board meeting in Chicago. The board meeting has been scheduled in the Blue Room to begin Thursday morning at 9 a.m.

If you have suggested additions to the agenda, please notify J. L. Brown, President, NMS. If you plan to present a report, will you please prepare a written report for the Executive Secretary, making duplicate copies for all members of the board. Please bring your copy of the February, 1990, Executive Board minutes that are attached.

We are looking forward to seeing each of you in Chicago. If for some reason you are unable to attend the meeting, will you please appoint your proxy and notify him or her of the time and place of the board meeting. Please return your postal reply card to the executive secretary.

Enclosures: Agenda--NMS Executive Board Meeting, June 19-20, 1990
Minutes--NMS Executive Board Meeting, February 18, 1990
Postal Reply Card

* * *

NATIONAL MANAGEMENT SOCIETY EXECUTIVE BOARD MEETING

Agenda
June 19-20, 1990

Blue Room
Conrad-Halton Hotel
Chicago

1.	Call to Order	J. L. Brown
2.	Roll Call	John Beckett
3.	Approval of Minutes of February, 1990, Meeting	John Beckett
4.	Report of the Executive Secretary	John Beckett
5.	Report of the Treasurer	Dennis Hall
6.	Report of the NMS President	J. L. Brown
7.	Report of the NMS President-elect	Marcia Owens
8.	Membership Report	Margaret Lenn
9.	NMS Journal Editor's Report	A. C. Albert

Figure 17–8 NMS Executive Board Notice to Members, Agenda, and Minutes

10. 1989 Convention Reports — J. O. O'Brien
11. Unfinished Business — Jack Proctor
12. New Business — Greg Bumpers
13. Adjournment

* * *

NATIONAL MANAGEMENT SOCIETY MINUTES OF THE EXECUTIVE BOARD MEETING

February 18, 1990

Call to Order

The regular meeting of the National Management Society Executive Board was held in the Blue Room, Conrad-Halton Hotel, Chicago, Illinois, February 18, 1990. President J. L. Brown called the meeting to order at 9 a.m.

Roll Call

Roll was called by the executive secretary, John Beckett, with the following officers and board members present:

Officers: J. L. Brown, president; Marcia Owens, president-elect; Elmo E. Sanksar, treasurer; John Beckett, executive secretary; and William Watson, immediate past president.

Regional Representatives: C. J. Bomberger, Southern Region; B. B. Whatley, Eastern Region; Gary Finch, North Central Region; H. B. Jackson, Midwest Region; and Jack Proctor, Western Region.

Ex-officio Members: A. K. Curley, representative to the ALA Executive Board; Victor Beckham, ALA president; Bill Hackley, NMS journal editor; and Margaret Lenners, membership chairperson.

Minutes

William Watson moved acceptance of the minutes of the June 18-19, 1989, meeting of the board be approved as distributed; C. J. Bomberger seconded the motion; motion passed.

Report of the Treasurer

Treasurer Dennis Hall presented the income and expense statement, cash recapitulation, and balance sheet, showing an excess of income over expenses of $2,429.15 for the period of June 17, 1989, to February 17, 1990; cash on hand, $5,764.98 (checkbook balance); and net worth, $10,525.75.

Figure 17–8 (Cont.)

Report of the NMS President

J. L. Brown, president, represented National Management Society at Southern Region Management Society Association convention, New Orleans, in November; North-Central Region Management Society, Cleveland, in December, and Western Region Management Society, Honolulu, in April.

Report of NMS President

Marcia Owens reported that NMS service Bulletin, the NMS Aid, will be distributed in October.

Membership Report

Margaret Lenners distributed copies of the membership report, which listed numbers as of February 10, 1989. A total of 31,285 active memberships and 1,068 associate memberships were reported.

NMS Journal Editor's Report

A. C. Albertson, NMS journal editor, reported that 36,022 copies of the journal were distributed at a cost of $3,962.42 for postage and $751.44 for supplies.

Report of 1989 Convention Committee

J. O. O'Brien, program co-chairman, distributed copies of the 1989 NMS convention program. He reported 5,120 preregistrations, 1488 for the opening banquet, 206 for the North-Central Region luncheon, 919 for the tours, and 386 for the closing brunch.

Unfinished Business

Because the NMS convention will be held in the Western Region in 1991, Jack Proctor moved that the Western Region Management Society convention not be held in 1991. Marcia Owens seconded; motion carried.

New Business

President Brown appointed A. K. Curley as chair of the Revision of the Constitution and By-Laws Committee. John Beckett and Gary Finch were appointed to the committee.

Meeting adjourned.

Respectfully submitted,

____________________ President

____________________ Executive Secretary

Figure 17–8 (Cont.)

supplementary materials, and so forth. Letters, such as those discussed earlier in this text, are also used frequently in the planning of meetings.

If you have to write a report on a meeting or a conference, you will find the suggestions presented in this chapter helpful. In addition, minutes are often prepared that summarize the deliberations of the group during the meeting. A knowledge of parliamentary procedure will be helpful in preparing minutes.

REVIEW QUESTIONS

1. What benefits are provided by meeting agendas?
2. What content is likely to be included in the agenda?
3. What types of supplementary materials are often used in meetings?
4. What suggestions can you offer that will be helpful to a person responsible for writing a report on a meeting or conference?
5. How do formal and informal meetings differ from one another?
6. What information should be included in minutes?
7. Identify several format suggestions appropriate for the preparation of minutes in final form.
8. Explain the procedures to be followed in correcting errors in minutes.

APPLICATION PROBLEMS

1. You are the the secretary of the International Management Systems Association. The executive board of that organization met Friday, August 10; and you took the following notes at that meeting:

Called to order—10 a.m.

Buckley, President—presided

No. present—15. Minutes of February meeting approved as presented.

Treas. report—present bal.—$12,642.81 (You have copy of report.)

Budget Com.—Anderson, Chairperson Acceptance moved and seconded. Discussion. Motion carried.

Membership Com.—Crain, Chr., presented proposal for limiting membership. (You have copy of proposal.) Acceptance moved and seconded. Discussion. Motion carried.

Nominating Com.—Frazier, Chr.

Pres.—Joliet, Charles

V. P.—Hansen, T.J.

Secretary—White, Edward

Treasurer—Stout, Elbert

Acceptance of report moved, seconded, and carried. Nominations closed by motion. Buckley announced election of officers to be held at next regular meeting in conformance with the constitution.

Holder, Chr. of World Representation Committee, announced next IMSA meeting is scheduled in Tokyo.

Buckley announced next executive board meeting, February 6.

Motion for adjournment carried—12:45 p.m.

Prepare the minutes in good form.

2. You are convention chairperson for the American Business Management Association. Members of this organization are concerned with the management of U.S. business firms. Members are involved with problems in taxes, financing, social changes, personnel training and development, federal regulations, product development, and many other factors unique to individual firms. The convention this year is to be held September 4–8 in Dallas, Texas. The theme of the program is "A Profile—The Effective Manager." Prepare a personalized notice to be mailed to each of the 10,000 plus members whose names and addresses are on the computer. (Details of the meeting will be mailed later.) The date of your letter is July 10.

3. You are secretary of the National Communication Association. This organization meets annually, at which time reports are presented, business is transacted, and officers are elected. This year the meeting is scheduled for the Conrad Hilton Hotel in Chicago, April 15 and 16, in the Rose Room. Other officers are J. A. Axton, president; Glenn Berry, president-elect; and John Elliston, treasurer. Chairpersons of standing committees are Allen Oaks, membership committee; Winston Bell, convention committee; and Amy Colton, nominating committee. Beth Ownberry is chairing a special committee to revise the constitution. The group will discuss the possibility of an organization publication on "Guide to Effective Written Communications." Also, a special report has been requested from liaision officer W. T. Israel on "Legislative Efforts." The organization must also consider whether or not to follow through with efforts to develop a research project on "Business Communications in Higher Education," a project that was discussed at the last meeting. Lee Bartos was to look into this possibility. Prepare an agenda and a cover letter directed to those persons who should be notified of the meeting.

4. You are plant manager of Mawahowi Cycles, Inc., a manufacturer of motorcycles. You are calling a special meeting of your personnel staff to consider the problem of absenteeism among workers in the plant. The following members of your staff are expected to attend: C. A. Stewart, personnel officer; Cleat Sasson, assistant personnel officer; Harold Robinson, supervisor, payroll; Allen Young, public relations; John Allen, assistant manager, plant. You are asked for the following reports from members of your staff: Absentee Record—July 1, 19— to June 30, 19— Harold Robinson; and causes of absences reported by employees—Cleat Sasson. Prepare a notice of the meeting that will be held in the Conference Room, next Wednesday at 3:30 p.m.

5. You are program chairperson for a meeting of Texas Apartment Owners Association that will be held in Houston, Texas, May 5 to 8. You are to invite Mr. John Billingsley, Director, East Coast Apartments, Inc., 3221 Ocean Drive, Atlantic City, NY 55603, to address the group. You want him to speak at the opening session, May 5, at 10 a.m. on the topic, "Tenant Contracts." The time allotted to his presentation will be thirty minutes. TAOS can pay the speaker $1,000 plus transportation costs and hotel accommodations. Prepare the invitation.

6. As chair of the conference committee, you have the responsibility for selecting three alternative sites for next year's conference of The Society of Physical Fitness Program Directors, which is to be held in San Francisco. Your alternatives will be presented for final selection to the executive board. You need information on the location of each hotel/motel, availability of rooms, meeting facilities, meals, and exhibit space. Prepare a letter of inquiry to leading hotels and motels in San Francisco. Addresses can be obtained from the *Hotel Redbook* that is available in your library.

7. As president of the Society for Advanced Management, you were responsible for a tri-university meeting of SAM chapters. Three invited speakers discussed "The Role of the Professional Manager." Mr. Edward Elliott, IAX Corporation, 311 Michigan Avenue, Chicago, IL 60123, discussed "Power and Control"; Mr. Henry Bailey, managing editor, *Omaha World Hearld,* Omaha, NE 69234, discussed "Today's Manager and Company Visibility"; and Tom Benson, president of Investors Pension, 313 Tenth Avenue, Minneapolis, MN 47467, spoke on "Legislation and Business Growth." Write an appropriate thank-you letter to each of the individuals.

8. Prepare minutes of a formal meeting of a club, student organization, or other organization of which you are a member.

9. You are the administrative assistant to Mr. William Yoe, president of Gamble Industries, a chemical company that imports, mixes, and packages chemicals. Mr. Yoe has asked you to set up a meeting of the vice-presidents to discuss a proposal to be developed about the feasibility of the company's manufacturing caustic soda. The meeting will be held in the Conference Room on the fifth floor of the Gamble Industries Building at 2 p.m. on Friday. Write the notice to be distributed to J. A. Winkle, vice-president for production; Tim Harris, vice-president for marketing; Alan Landon, vice-president for manufacturing; and Allen Wood, vice-president for administrative services.

10. Investigate three of the organizations within your city that conduct annual meetings of shareholders. Obtain a copy of a notice to shareholders that announces the meeting as well as the report to stockholders on action taken. Compare formats, type of information provided, and readability level.

Chapter 18

The Electronic Office and Business Communication

LEARNING OBJECTIVES

After studying this chapter, you should be able to

1. Discuss the purpose of each of the equipment components of a word processing system.
2. Discuss the functional capabilities of a word processing system.
3. Discuss how machine dictation is used in a word processing system.
4. Discuss the purpose of facsimile and electronic filing.
5. Discuss the functional capabilities of electronic workstations.

Much of the electronic equipment found in today's offices affects business communication by enhancing the efficiency of the communication process and by improving the quality of the communication. The advent of the computer microchip has made many technological advances in communication possible.

The components of the electronic office that affect business communication are word processing, telecommunications, facsimile, electronic filing, and electronic workstations. In this chapter, these components and their applications are discussed.

WORD PROCESSING

How is the availability of word processing affecting business employees?

While a number of the components of the electronic office have changed the way in which written and oral communication is expedited, none has had a greater impact than word processing. Originally, word processing most affected the secretary who transcribed the material originated by managers and executives. Now, the impact is being felt by all employees in all types of positions. As increasing numbers of employees have desk-top computers that are capable of performing word processing functions, those with good keyboarding skills are preparing their own written communications. These individuals use a simultaneous originating-keyboarding process to prepare their own written communications rather than have an office employee keyboard the material they dictate.

Word Processing Equipment

Equipment used in word processing possesses several capabilities. It has keyboarding capability, as well as editing capability, that can be used to make changes in draft copy. The equipment is also capable of electronically capturing and storing keyboarded material.

What types of equipment are used in word processing systems?

The types of equipment now commonly used to perform word processing operations include:

1. *Text-editing devices* (also called text editors and word processors). This equipment performs word processing operations but very few, if any, additional operations.

2. *Desk-top computers* (also called personal computers). This equipment is capable of performing a variety of functions, including word processing and data manipulation, such as that found on spreadsheets and data bases. Depending on the word processing software and the type of equipment, desk-top computers may not perform word processing operations as efficiently as dedicated text-editing devices. However, their multi-functional capability often makes desk-top computers at least as attractive as dedicated devices. Many different word processing software packages are now available.

3. *Desk-top terminals.* This equipment is generally interconnected to a computer mainframe or to a small business computer. Because the desk-top terminals most likely do not possess their own intelligence (they are, therefore, often called ''dumb'' terminals), this equipment is inoperable when the main system is inoperable. Depending on the type of equipment, desk-top terminals may perform word processing operations as efficiently as dedicated devices.

What steps comprise the word processing cycle?

The equipment used to perform word processing functions consists of several devices, including the keyboard, the screen, the printer, the processor, and the storage device. Each device plays a vital role in the following steps of the word processing cycle: inputting, processing, and outputting. Several of the devices may also be used in a fourth step of the word processing cycle—distributing—when documents are distributed electronically. The following list identifies which devices are used in the various steps.

Inputting—keyboard, screen, processor, storage device
Processing—keyboard, screen, processor, storage device
Outputting—keyboard, screen, processor, printer, storage device
Distributing—keyboard, screen, processor, storage device

Keyboard

The keyboard is used to enter information into the system, as well as to send various commands to the processor. The keyboard resembles a typewriter keyboard, although most keyboards found on equipment capable of performing word processing operations contain a variety of additional keys. These keys include command or function keys and the numeric keypad keys which are especially useful when a large volume of numbers must be keyboarded.

Screen

The screen is used to display the material being keyboarded into the system. Because most word processing equipment no longer displays the first draft of the material on paper, as the early word processing devices did, the screen provides the visual image of the keyboarded material. When you are composing a message on a word processing device, you will keep your eyes on the screen to determine if typographical errors have been made and to assess the quality of your writing. Errors are easily corrected and changes easily made by moving the cursor to the location of the error and then keyboarding the desired change. Several types of screens are found on the equipment, including full-page screens, half-page screens, two-color screens, and multi-color screens.

Printer

What two categories of printers are common?

The printer functions by providing a hard copy of your work. Two broad categories of printers are now found: impact and non-impact. On impact printers, a part of the printer depresses the ribbon against the paper, thus forming the character image. In word processing, two basic types of impact printers are found: (1) letter-quality printers that use a print wheel or thimble and most likely a film ribbon and (2) dot-matrix printers that depress pins against the ribbon that produces character images in the shape of dots. Most dot-matrix printers are now capable of near-letter-quality printing, achieved by printing the dots quite close together. Because dot-matrix printers use cloth ribbons rather than film ribbons, the characters are not as sharp nor distinct as the material prepared on letter-quality printers.

Nonimpact printers are almost soundless because none of the printer mechanisms come in contact with the paper. The two common types of nonimpact printers—both of which produce letter-quality work—are ink-jet printers and laser printers. Ink-jet printers use electrostatically charged ink that is attracted to the paper in the same configuration as the character being printed. Images are first electronically formed on the printing drum to which the paper is adhered. Characters are formed when tiny bursts of the charged ink are attracted to the paper in the same shape as the images on the drum. Laser printers are capable of preparing book-quality print. Using laser technology, these printers are capable of printing a page at a time.

Processor

What is the processor?

The processor is the computer. In dedicated text-editing devices and in desk-top computers, the processor is a microchip housed in equipment's central processing unit (CPU). When desk-top terminals are used, the processor is in the CPU of the computer to which the terminal is interconnected. The processor enables the equipment to perform a variety of word processing operations and provides memory capability.

What two types of memory are commonly used in word processing functions?

The two types of memory commonly found are read-only memory (ROM) and random-access memory (RAM). Each type of memory performs a vital function. ROM, the system's permanent internal memory, runs the entire system. It contains the instructions that enable the equipment to function on command. RAM is temporary and holds the material you are working on. It enables you to enter material into the system as well as make changes in the material. The size of the device's RAM determines how much data it will hold. When the limit is reached, data must be transferred to a storage device (such as a floppy disk) to make room for additional data. Material held only in RAM will be lost should a power loss occur.

Storage

What functions is word processing equipment capable of performing?

The storage device enables you to store keyboarded material for as long as you want. When you wish to store material permanently, you simply transfer the material from RAM to a storage medium, such as floppy disk. The most common disk sizes used are 8-inch, $5\frac{1}{4}$-inch, and $3\frac{1}{2}$-inch. Disks are made of a magnetic material, similar to that found on tape-recorder tape. The highest-density disks are now capable of storing 250 to 300 double-spaced typewritten pages on one side. While floppy disks are commonly used to provide permanent storage of keyboarded material, tapes and hard disks can also be used.

A disk drive is used to "read" the material from RAM onto the disk. When you need to access the material later, the disk is simply inserted into the disk drive so the material can be read back into RAM. Two of the primary reasons you may need to use the material later are that you may wish to keyboard editing changes in the material or you may wish to have another copy of the material printed.

Functional Capabilities of Word Processing Equipment

The equipment used in word processing operations is capable of performing the following functions:

Arithmetic function: The equipment is capable of addition, subtraction, multiplication, and division on numerical data.

Block move and insert: The equipment can move a block of material from one location and insert the material at another location.

Copy: The equipment can copy a block of material for insertion at different locations in the same document, thus eliminating the extra effort of having to rekeyboard the same material several times.

Dictionary: The equipment can store in coded form words or phrases used repetitively, which makes these words/phrases available for later retrieval and use. To retrieve a word, its coded version is keyboarded and the word is automatically inserted at the desired location.

Footnote placement: The equipment can automatically move footnotes from one page to another, which is necessary when the material to which a footnote refers is moved from one page to another.

Global search and replace: The equipment can automatically search a document for each occurrence of a word or phrase. Some equipment, upon command, will automatically replace a word or phrase with another word or phrase. Other equipment requires the manual keyboarding of the replacement word at each location.

Page numbering. The equipment can automatically number the pages. When the number of a page changes because material has been added or deleted, page numbers are automatically corrected.

Pagination: The equipment can automatically place the prescribed number of lines on a page. When the page is filled with the prescribed number of text lines, the next page is automatically begun.

Repagination: The equipment can repaginate with the prescribed amount of material on each page after material is added to or deleted from a document.

Right-hand justification: The equipment can automatically produce printed material that has an even right margin.

Spelling dictionary: The equipment can automatically compare the spelling of keyboarded words with the spelling of words contained in the system's dictionary. Words that are not comparable because they are misspelled, because they are a proper noun, or because they are not stored in the dictionary are highlighted on the screen, which facilitates proofreading.

Word wraparound: The equipment can automatically wrap a word keyboarded at the end of a line around to the beginning of the next line when the word is too long to fit on the previous line.

Other Equipment Used in Word Processing Systems

Dictation equipment and copiers are also used extensively in word processing systems. While the use of dictation equipment significantly affects those originating material, the copier equipment is used primarily by the office employees.

Why is handwriting as material input discouraged in word processing systems?

In most word processing systems, employees are strongly urged—if not required—to input their material into the system through the dictation process. In most instances, especially for routine correspondence, inputting handwritten material into the system is not allowed. In some instances, technical reports can be input in handwriting. Because the office employees can transcribe dictation faster than handwritten material and because the employees who originate material (with a little practice) can dictate material faster than they can handwrite material, the emphasis on dictation makes sense. When dictating, you should follow the recommended procedures presented in Chapter 4.

Dictation equipment

The accessibility of dictation equipment is critical to the success of word processing. Those who originate material dictate their work into equipment that simultaneously records their words. The stored dictation is then played back by an office employee during the keyboarding (transcribing) process.

The dictation devices used by the originators and the recording/playback devices used by the office employees are typically connected either by telephone lines or by direct lines. Some dictation systems use the telephones in the originators' offices, while other systems use special dictation microphones. A recorder unit is used to record the dictation on a magnetic medium, such as a tape, disk, or belt. A distinct advantage of the equipment that uses telephones is the ability to dictate material whenever and wherever the originator has access to a telephone. Therefore, material can be dictated 24 hours a day, regardless of the originator's location.

What types of dictation/recording equipment are used in word processing systems?

Some common types of dictation/recording equipment are desk-top devices, portable units, and central systems. The *desk-top devices,* which have been around since the late 1880s, record dictation on a tape, disk, or belt. The magnetic medium then has to be transported to the office employee who will keyboard the dictation. Several functions are found on the dictation equipment, including playback and erase.

Portable units are often used by originators who do extensive amounts of traveling. The magnetic medium on which the dictation is stored is mailed back to the office employee who will transcribe the material. These units are primarily used by employees when they are out of the office. They are not generally meant to be a substitute for either a desk-top device or a central recording system.

Central recording systems are generally the most convenient. The magnetic medium on which the dictation is recorded is housed near the office employee who will be transcribing the material. Therefore, the medium does not have to be transported to the office employee as is the case with the other types of dictation equipment that were discussed above. When the telephone is used in the dictation process, the keys on the telephone are used to give the dictation and recording units the needed commands or instructions. In addition to telephones, special dictation microphones can also be used to input material into central recording systems.

Copier equipment

In a word processing system, neither the originator nor the office employee who keyboards the originator's material will always know for sure which draft of the document is the final draft. To make carbon copies of each draft is not cost effective. Therefore, a copy (or copies) of the document are not prepared until after it has been released for distribution. At this point, preparing a carbon copy is impossible. The only other alternative is to make a photocopy of the document.

FACSIMILE

For what is facsimile equipment used?

Although facsimile technology is nearly as old as telephone technology, the facsimile process has not received much attention until fairly recently. Facsimile is used to transmit identical duplicates of documents from one location to another. The signals depicting the images on the documents are transmitted over telephone lines, and compatible units at the sending and receiving locations are required. To transmit a document—whether it is a form, a letter, a chart, a photograph, or a report—the document is placed on the facsimile device. The sender then calls the receiver who activates the facsimile unit at the receiving location. After the sender's and the receiver's telephone handsets are attached to their respective devices, the transmission process begins.

Some of the more advanced facsimile devices are capable of operating unattended and automatically dialing up to 50 telephone numbers prestored in the unit's memory. These devices also transmit a page of material in approximately 6 seconds. Where such equipment is available, it is often used later at night when long-distance toll charges are the lowest, especially if multiple-page documents are being transmitted to various receivers.

ELECTRONIC FILING

As the office-equipment technology develops, an increasing amount of communication is being stored electronically, which will reduce the amount of material stored on paper. When you want to review a stored document, you retrieve it electronically rather than retrieve it from the files used to store paper records.

What advantages result from the use of electronic filing?

Several advantages result from the use of electronic filing.

1. It provides faster access to information than conventional filing methods.
2. It conserves valuable floor space because less equipment is needed for filing paper.
3. It allows all authorized users to access stored information.
4. It reduces the possibility of misplacing records.
5. It makes information available after work hours and off the premises to those who have the necessary authorization to retrieve the information and the necessary equipment to display the information.

Generally, computer terminals are used to retrieve and display desired information that has been filed electronically. The keyboard on the terminal is used to enter the necessary retrieval codes into the system, and the information is displayed on the user's screen. Should a hard copy of the information be desired, the user can direct the printer to prepare the desired material.

What advantages result from the use of optical disks for the electronic filing of material?

While the material filed electronically can be stored on a magnetic medium, such as a tape or disk, it can also be filed on an optical disk, which resembles a long-playing phonograph record. The primary advantage of optical disks is their extremely dense storage capacity. For example, the entire contents of a set of encyclopedias can be stored on one disk. Optical-disk systems also provide extremely fast retrieval times. For example, an optical disk system can search 55,000 frames in 5 seconds to retrieve the one that is desired. When compared with magnetic systems, the optical disk system is disadvantageous in that records stored on an optical disk cannot be updated.

Two elements of electronic filing having special implications for business communication. These are computer-based message systems (CBMS) and data-base management systems (DBMS).

A computer-based message system provides electronic storage of all messages that originate within an organization. Traditionally, in the conventional paper-storage systems, several to dozens of copies of a message might be stored. With a computer-based message system, only one copy of the message is stored—electronically—regardless of the number of individuals in the organization who received the message.

Computer-based message systems have two components: the master file in which the ''original'' of each message is stored and the personal files of each employee. Because the master file contains the message, the personal files need contain only a citation that lists the name of the message originator and the recipient(s) of each message, the date and time the message was entered into the system, the subject of the message, and perhaps key words in the message.

The employee uses his/her computer terminal or desk-top computer to enter messages into the system as well as to retrieve messages from the system. The actual procedures used to input and output messages are explained in the applications section of this chapter.

While the computer-based message system is used primarily to support the transmission, storage, and retrieval of information contained in messages, a data-base management system is used to maintain a large volume of data that has significant value to an organization. These data are often used by employees as they write reports, prepare documentation, etc.

How do computer-based and data-based management systems differ from one another?

Like computer-based message systems, data-base management systems reduce the amount of duplicate material that has to be stored. Rather than storing several paper copies of the same material, one electronically stored copy is accessible to all authorized users.

Data bases require an extensive amount of cross-referencing. If an employee wishes to review all the stored information that pertains to a specific topic, he/she simply uses a desk-top computer or computer terminal to input the appropriate parameters into the system, and the desired material is quickly retrieved and displayed on his/her screen.

Data-base management systems typically contain two basic types of files: data files and data banks. The information likely to be stored in the data files includes customer names, addresses, account numbers, account status, stock inventory status, and payroll. The ability to update easily and quickly the information in the data files is essential.

Data banks, on the other hand, contain a variety of correspondence, reports, and other types of useful information originated both inside and outside the organization. This information rarely needs to be updated—but is referred to often by employees as they prepare additional written communication. The information in data banks is also used by managers to support their decision-making efforts.

ELECTRONIC WORKSTATIONS

What functions are electronic workstations capable of performing?

Perhaps the most unique device found in the electronic office is the electronic workstation. The backbone of these workstations is a microcomputer that is capable of performing a broad variety of functions, including data processing, word processing, communications, and personal support. Of all the devices discussed in this chapter, this device is the one most personally useful to executives and managers.

Electronic workstations make possible the integration of several discrete activities, including keyboarding, filing, mailing, messaging, scheduling, conferencing, video conferencing, telephoning, and calculating. Most electronic workstations, in order to perform all of these activities, have to be electronically interconnected to the organization's central computer system, which extends their capability and increases their power. The workstations are interconnected to the computer by means of a network.

A thorough discussion of how an executive or manager might use his/her electronic workstation is presented in the applications section of this chapter.

TELECOMMUNICATIONS

What does telecommunications involve?

Most employees, regardless of their job title, make extensive use of telecommunications in carrying out their job responsibilities. No longer does telecommunications primarily involve the use of the telephone.

Today, telecommunications involves the transmission of voice, data, and images over telephone lines, microwave systems, and earth-orbiting communication satellites. As the technology matures, fiber optics will also be used extensively in the communication process. In addition to the uses mentioned above, telecommunications is also used extensively in networks that provide the electronic link between various pieces of office equipment. These networks enable the interlinked devices to communicate with one another.

Telecommunications supports the following specialized communication functions: teleconferencing, videoconferencing, electronic document distribution, and electronic messaging. While the equipment that supports these functions is described below, the applications are discussed in the "applications of electronic workstations" section of this chapter.

What is teleconferencing?

Teleconferencing is used as an alternative to holding face-to-face conferences among an executive group whose members are remotely located. Rather than having executives travel to a specified location, a teleconference can be arranged whereby they remain in their respective locations but "teleconference" with one another via telephones. Teleconferencing allows the executives to communicate with one another by voice only.

What is videoconferencing?

Videoconferencing takes teleconferencing one step further and allows the conference participants to see one another's images as they communicate. In addition to their own images, images of charts, graphs, and data can also be transmitted to each of the conference sites. Television equipment is extensively used in videoconferencing: Television cameras are used to input the images into the system, a telecommunications link (wire or communications, satellite) is used to transmit the image to the various destination sites, and a television monitor is used to receive incoming images. Many companies have found that both teleconferencing and videoconferencing are cost-effective ways to hold executive conferences.

What is electronic document distribution?

Electronic document distribution (or electronic mail) is dependent on telecommunications to transmit material electronically from one location to another. In some cases, word processing equipment that has communicating capability is used to transmit a document from one location to another. In other instances, facsimile equipment, which was discussed earlier, is used to transmit the material. In still other instances, desk-top computers equipped with modems are used to transmit the material. In each of these instances, electronic codes that represent alphanumeric information are transmitted over a telecommunications link. The equipment at the sending location encodes the material into signals that can be electronically transmitted. At the destination, the receiving equipment (which must be compatible with the sending equipment) decodes these signals so the material can be reconfigured into a format humans are capable of reading.

What is electronic messaging?

Electronic messaging also makes extensive use of telecommunication technology. Two types of electronic messaging are found: written messages and voice messages. Desk-top computers and computer terminals are used to send the written messages; voice-recording equipment is used to transmit voice messages. The distinct advantage of electronic messaging is that the recipient can access his/her messages from anywhere he/she has access to a communicating desk-top computer or computer terminal and a telephone. Thus, these messages can be accessed from a location thousands of miles away—any time of day or night.

THE IMPACT OF FUTURE OFFICE EQUIPMENT ON BUSINESS COMMUNICATION

In the future, voice-response equipment is likely to be a common piece of equipment on virtually every executive's and manager's desk. To use this equipment, the employee will simply speak into a microphone similar to the type found on today's dictation equipment. The material spoken into the microphone will be simultaneously transformed into written words. Thus, to prepare a letter or report, you simply dictate the material and the equipment prepares a paper copy. While this technology exists today, the equipment that is available has a limited vocabulary. In the future this equipment will make extensive use of artificial intelligence and will possess an extensive vocabulary.

The implications this equipment has for business communicators is clear: They will need to master the art of dictating as well as master grammar and punctuation fundamentals. Because office support personnel may not be available to "clean up" the material, communicators will need to possess well-developed skills to enable them to prepare a "polished" product ready for distribution.

WORD PROCESSING APPLICATIONS

When you work in a company that has a word processing system, you most likely will find that the majority, if not all, of the material you originate will have to be dictated. Therefore, the sooner you develop good dictation skills, the more comfortable you will be with word processing.

As a conventional word originator, you will probably find that the availability of a word processing system changes little for you. One significant change, however, is that you will be able to originate material from wherever and whenever you have access to a telephone. This feature has distinct advantages for you. Another advantage of word processing that you will appreciate is the ability to edit the material you originate—perhaps several times—without having to rekeyboard each draft. The fact that the material is stored on a magnetic medium once it has been keyboarded facilitates editing. The word processing operator has only to keyboard the changes resulting from the editing process. Therefore, unchanged material does not need to be rekeyboarded each time. The end result is that you can edit your work several times, thus improving its quality, with a minimum of rekeyboarding.

As a non-conventional word originator, you will perhaps do a large part of your own keyboarding, assuming you have a computer or computer terminal on your desk. Several prerequisite skills are important: an interest in operating computer equipment, good keyboarding and composition skills, and good grammar- and punctuation-usage skills. In years to come, more and more word originators will assume greater responsibility for doing their own keyboarding.

APPLICATIONS OF FACSIMILE

Facsimile facilitates the immediate transmittal of letters, reports, forms, photographs, and so forth. Suppose the originator of a document wishes to have a document transmitted immediately. Also suppose the originator knows that the recipient of the document has access to a facsimile unit that is compatible with the sender's unit.

The document, after it has been released for distribution, is taken to the location of the facsimile unit. The appropriate telephone number at the receiving location is dialed, and the employee operating the sending unit tells the employee operating the receiving unit that a document is about to be transmitted. Both equipment operators attach their telephone handsets to their respective units, and the transmission process begins. In just a few minutes—perhaps less than five, depending on the length of the document and the location of the recipient in relation to the receiving facsimile unit—the document will be on his/her desk.

APPLICATIONS OF ELECTRONIC FILING

As organizations become more electronically oriented, the paper work generated within will be stored electronically rather than on paper. Just as soon as a document is released for distribution, the "electronic copy" of the document will be properly indexed and sent to the electronic archives if the originator wishes to have the document permanently stored. When this procedure becomes widespread, perhaps the paper copy of the document that is made in many of today's offices can be eliminated. To retrieve the document from the electronic files, the originator simply enters the appropriate commands and index code. The document can most likely be retrieved instantly.

When this level of electronic filing becomes common, organizations will also begin electronically filing externally originated paper documents; the document is processed through an optical character reader (OCR) that transforms written characters on paper into electronic codes stored on a magnetic medium. This information also now becomes part of the organization's data base. Optical character readers are capable of inputting approximately 10,000 words per minute—and with incredible accuracy.

When a person receives material in electronic format from outside the organization, this material can also easily be put into the electronic files. This is done simply by using one's desk-top computer or computer terminal to enter the appropriate codes into the system.

APPLICATIONS OF ELECTRONIC WORKSTATIONS

The multifunctional nature of electronic workstations enables them to perform a wide array of applications, including word processing, information storing and retrieving, graphics displaying, data processing, electronic mailing, electronic messaging, electronic filing, scheduling, maintaining a tickler file, voice messaging, video conferencing, and teleconferencing. The following discussion describes how this device is used to perform these applications.[1]

The first thing you will probably do upon arriving at work is to command the workstation to prepare a visual display of the items in your electronic "mailbox." The items in the mailbox originate from both inside and outside the organization. Each item listed on the display is identified by the name of the sender, time and date of receipt, subject, etc. To obtain a visual display of any of the items, you simply depress the appropriate keys on the workstation keyboard. Depending on the type of equipment, you may also be able to touch the specific item on the screen with an electronic pointer or pen, and the item will be displayed instantly. In addition to displaying the item on the screen, you can also have a paper copy of the item prepared.

If you wish to prepare an immediate response to the item just displayed on your screen, two options are available: You can dictate a reply that will be keyboarded by another person or you can compose a reply on your own workstation keyboard. After the response has been keyboarded using either of these two options, the material can be easily revised. Information electronically stored in the organization's central computer system can be readily retrieved for use in preparing graphic displays (charts or graphs) of information that you might wish to include in the response. In addition, the workstation is capable of processing any raw data that you may need in preparing the response.

Once you are satisfied with the content and wording of your response, the workstation can transmit it electronically to the recipient. However, in some cases, you may choose to send a paper copy of the response, which is prepared by the workstation. The workstation is also capable of electronically filing any of the items received in your electronic mailbox, as well as filing the material you originate. These incoming and outgoing items can be held temporarily in an electronic in-basket or stored permanently in the organization's centralized electronic storage system, commonly known as archives.

Before working with any other items in the electronic mailbox, you may decide to examine today's schedule of appointments and events. By using the appropriate keys on the keyboard or the electronic pointer, you can see today's schedule on the screen. A paper copy of the schedule can also be readily obtained by depressing the appropriate keys on the keyboard. When individuals wish to make an appointment with you, they simply access your electronic cal-

[1]The material in this section was adapted from Zane K. Quible, *Administrative Office Management: An Introduction*, 3rd ed., Reston Publishing Company, Inc., Reston, VA, 1984.

endar and select an available block of time. The same process is used when you wish to make appointments with individuals in the organization who also use an electronic calendar.

You may also wish to use your workstation to schedule meetings with a group of employees. This is easily done by accessing the electronic calendars of each individual in the group. The computer provides a list of times that each individual in the group is available and then automatically schedules the meeting on each employee's electronic calendar. The computer is also capable of reserving a room that will accommodate the group.

In addition, your workstation can be used to maintain your electronic tickler file. This feature helps you better manage your time by keeping track of work deadlines. The tickler file helps you monitor work-completion deadlines that you have given others. The items in the file can be maintained in a priority order, which will help you plan your work day. In addition, the tickler file keeps track of pending work as well as keeps track of various projects with which you are involved.

You may use your workstation to receive messages. To illustrate, after returning from lunch, you can obtain on the screen a visual display of your messages. Rather than using the telephone to respond to a message, you can keyboard a reply and then direct the computer to transmit the response to the appropriate individual. This process is especially advantageous when your time is limited, because preparing a keyboarded reply will be less time consuming than talking with the individual on the phone. The time-saving nature of this feature is responsible for the preference of some executives to use electronic messaging, even when telephone contact with these individuals is possible.

Your workstation can also be used for voice messaging, which is essentially a one-way telephone call in which your verbal message is recorded on the recipient's recording device. Voice messaging devices permit the simultaneous transmission of a message to a number of persons; they can also delay transmission of the message. When compared with two-way phone calls, voice messaging saves a considerable amount of executive time.

Conferencing is another function of the electronic workstation. Perhaps you need to obtain information from individuals in several branch offices located throughout the country. If the individuals are in their offices at the time you send the request, information can be obtained immediately. But if they are not, they can provide the information at their convenience after they return. Information of this type is transmitted back and forth through the telecommunications networks.

You may also be able to use your workstation to accomplish two other conferencing techniques. With teleconferencing, a conference call is placed to each individual in a group with whom you wish to converse. Each participant hears all of the conversation that takes place during the call. The other conferencing technique for which your workstation may be used has both visual and audio components. A built-in camera will enable the other person to see you when you are speaking and you will be able to see the others when they are speaking. This feature also permits the transmission of visual images of documents.

As electronic workstations become more common in the business world, they will revolutionize many of the ways in which workers communicate. Not only do these workstations promise to make your job easier—but also they will enable you to perform your work more efficiently and effectively.

CHAPTER SUMMARY

An increasing amount of the material originated by employees in today's business world is prepared by office personnel who use word processing equipment. Many advantages result from the use of word processing equipment.

Most word processors or devices used for word processing are comprised of a keyboard, a screen, a printer, a processor, and the storage unit. Each performs a unique function in word processing.

When contrasted with yesterday's word processing equipment, today's systems perform many more functions. As new equipment and/or software are developed, more functions will become available.

Other types of electronic equipment found in offices are facsimile, electronic filing, electronic work stations, and telecommunications. When combined into a total system, the automation of office operations becomes possible.

REVIEW QUESTIONS

1. What capabilities must equipment that is used for word processing possess?
2. What types of equipment are used to perform word processing operations?
3. What is the function of the processor found in word processing equipment?
4. What are the differences between RAM and ROM?
5. What is the function performed by the word-wraparound capability found on some word processing equipment?
6. Why are carbon copies no longer made in most word processing systems?
7. What is the purpose of facsimile?
8. How do computer-based message systems and data-base management systems differ from one another?
9. How do teleconferencing and videoconferencing differ?
10. Explain the function of the various electronic messaging systems.

APPLICATION PROBLEMS

1. Assume your supervisor has given you the responsibility of making a comparative analysis of three different brands of dedicated word processing systems (You are to determine which brands of equipment you will compare.) The analysis is to be presented in a staff report to your supervisor. You have several alternatives for collecting the information you will use in making the comparative analysis: visiting equipment dealers, obtaining brochures/specification sheets about each brand of equipment you are comparing, or using equipment-evaluation information found in articles in word processing journals. Your supervisor is especially interested in a comparative analysis of cost and functional capabilities of the three brands of equipment.

2. Assume your supervisor has given you the responsibility of making a comparative analysis of three different brands of desk-top computers that are capable of performing word processing functions. (You are to determine which brands of desk-top computers you will compare.) The analysis is to be presented in a staff report to your supervisor. You have several alternatives for collecting the information you will use in making the comparative analysis: visiting equipment dealers, obtaining brochures/specification sheets about each brand of equipment you are comparing, or using equipment-evaluation information found in articles in computer magazines and journals. Your supervisor is especially interested in a comparative analysis of equipment costs and the electronic characteristics (size of ROM, type of disk drive, etc.) of each computer system.

3. Assume your supervisor has given you the responsibility of making a comparative analysis of three different word processing software packages that are used on desk-top computers. (You are to determine which brands of software packages you will compare.) The analysis is to be presented in a staff report to your supervisor. You have several alternatives for collecting the information you will use in making the comparative analysis: visiting software package dealers, obtaining brochures/specification sheets about each software package you are comparing, or using software-evaluation information found in articles in computer/software magazines and journals. Your supervisor is especially interested in a comparative analysis of memory requirements, functional capabilities, user support, and cost of each package.

4. Assume your supervisor has given you the responsibility of making a comparative analysis of one particular dedicated word processing system and one desk-top computer capable of performing word processing functions. (You are to determine which brands of equipment you will compare.) The analysis is to be presented in a staff report to your supervisor. You have several alternatives for collecting the information you will use in making the comparative analysis: visiting equipment dealers, obtaining brochures/specification sheets about each type of equipment you are comparing, or using equipment-evaluation information found in word processing and computer magazines and journals. Your supervisor is especially interested in a comparative analysis of functional capabilities of each type of equipment, cost, ease in learning to use, and user support.

5. Assume you are to give a short oral presentation before a group to which you belong. You decide to talk about the future of the electronic office. Prepare a written copy of your presentation. The information you include in your report could be obtained from library research, interviewing equipment dealers, interviewing knowledgeable individuals, etc.

6. Assume your supervisor has asked you to prepare a staff report on the potential use of facsimile in the company for which you work. Develop an outline of the material you plan to include. Prepare the staff report.

7. Assume your supervisor has asked you to prepare a formal report on the use of the electronic workstation. The primary purpose of this report is to make him/her more knowledgeable about the concept. Prepare the report.

8. Make arrangements to interview three employees who operate word processing equipment and three originators whose work is prepared on word

processing equipment in a company that uses word processing. Inquire into their perceptions of the advantages and disadvantages of the use of word processing. Prepare a report for your instructor that presents the information you obtained from these six individuals.

9. Make arrangements (either at your college or at a local equipment vendor) to work on a desk-top computer that can be used as a word processor. Using the user's manual, try to become familiar with how several of the functions operate. Then prepare an informal report for your instructor that outlines your impression of the system, the ease with which you learned to operate the equipment, etc.

10. Attend an office equipment trade show in which several different types of equipment used to perform word processing operations are displayed. Talk with the company sales representatives about the various types of equipment being displayed. Ask for a demonstration of each type of equipment.

Chapter 19

Oral Communication

LEARNING OBJECTIVES

After studying this chapter, you should be able to

1. Identify the essentials of oral communication.
2. Discuss the advantages and disadvantages of speaking from a manuscript, from memorization, impromptu, and extemporaneously.
3. Discuss voice characteristics.
4. Explain how one should prepare for a stand-up speech.
5. Discuss the importance of listening.
6. Discuss the levels of listening.
7. Identify ways that you can improve your listening skills.

Oral communication is another important element of the communication process. An effective skill in oral communication is equally as important as a well-developed skill in written communication. While written communication skills will often take more time to perfect, oral communication will consume much more of your personal and professional time.

Speaking before a large audience is an opportunity that many people may not have a chance to experience. However, speaking before smaller groups is a common professional experience. You may be called on to present a report at a business meeting or to express your views at a local, regional, or national meeting. In a more personal perspective, you may be asked to express your feelings at a PTA, city council, or scout meeting.

ESSENTIALS OF ORAL COMMUNICATION

Simply stated, oral communication involves making your wants, needs, ideas, and feelings known to other people. Successful oral communication involves a simultaneous combination of several mental and physical processes. The most obvious aspect of oral communication is the actual presentation, which is the physical process. However, the mental and psychological parts of oral communication are equally as important as the actual oral presentation.

What are the uses of oral communication?

Oral communication is used to inform, to persuade, and to entertain. The informative speech presents facts, information, or general knowledge to an audience. The purpose of a persuasive speech is to change attitudes or thinking about a certain event, idea, or campaign. The entertainment speech is designed to provide fun and pleasure for the intended audience. Those who give entertainment speeches often use humor to get the audience to see whatever point they are trying to make.

A speech can have more than one of the three main purposes. For example, a persuasive speech usually provides information, and a speech designed to entertain will often be used to persuade. Even though a combination of purposes might exist, the overall major purpose will determine the most appropriate design and style.

PREPARING TO COMMUNICATE ORALLY

Whenever you talk, you are involved in both a unique event and in a unique moment. Your voice, behavior patterns, choice of words, ideas, and feelings are either openly exposed or cleverly disguised. Therefore, an important first step toward improved oral communication is taking personal inventory of your likes, dislikes, attitudes, and habits. Each time you talk, you reflect your true feelings, biases, and value systems—unless, of course, you carefully conceal your true inner feelings and attitudes.

What elements does effective oral communication comprise?

Effective oral communication requires attention to several important elements, regardless of whether the message is designed for formal, informal, or social conversations. The elements you have to consider are:

1. *The purpose.* Each conversation has a predominant and hopefully predetermined intention. Before you speak, take a couple of minutes to establish the primary purpose for the oral communication. For instance, is the intended conversation needed to gather or present information? To make the other person more aware of a certain situation or event? To create an environment for appropriate feedback? To change or acknowledge actions or attitudes? After these ideas and viewpoints are determined, they are transmitted through a sequence of words.

2. *The audience.* The nature and background of the intended audience need to be considered and assessed prior to designing the message. Formal style is imperative for success in a formal presentation, while informal style is most desirable for person-to-person and small, intimate group conversation. You will wisely assess your audience to prepare a presentation that fits the occupational, educational, and experience characteristics of the intended audience.

3. *The data.* Successful oral communication is somewhat like a game plan for a sports team. Accurate data must be both organized and meaningful. A message should attract the attention of the intended audience, hold its attention, build interest, and set the stage for appropriate and intended action.

Presentation can be enhanced and improved through a variety of audio-visual aids, demonstrations, comparisons, statistics, and testimonials.

4. *The message.* The actual message is, of course, the single most important aspect of oral communication. Your message should be timely, to the point, and consistent with the overall intent of the communication. Key concepts and ideas should receive primary consideration. Attention and interest-holding devices should be woven into the context of the presentation.

5. *The format.* A speech contains three parts: the introduction, the body, and the conclusion. You should prepare the outline for your speech around these three major parts. The outline is then used as a guide to ensure clarity, completeness, and conciseness. Adherence to the outline will ensure maximum coverage with minimal drifting from the major and/or minor points. Shorter speeches are often more difficult to plan than longer speeches because very little time is available for emphasis and expansion of points and ideas.

6. *The delivery.* The actual delivery of the speech is as important as the content. You may select your delivery style from four basic procedures or formats: (a) speaking from a manuscript; (b) memorization; (c) impromptu speaking; and (d) extemporaneous speaking. As you might expect, each of these formats has its own advantages and disadvantages. For each of your speeches, you will need to decide on the delivery method that best suits you, your topic, your audience, and the occasion.

What delivery styles are used in speech making?

Speaking from a Manuscript

When speaking from a manuscript, you must write out the entire speech and read it aloud to your audience. You have witnessed this type of delivery most often in campaign speeches, official governmental reports, and radio or television reports.

Advantages

The main advantage of the manuscript delivery method is that you are able to explain ideas in great detail with little fear of forgetting important points or issues. An additional advantage is that you know how long your presentation will take to deliver, which allows you to reserve time at the end to answer any questions the members of the audience may have. Fear of being misquoted is minimized because copies of the manuscript can be made available upon request to people in the audience as well as to others.

Another advantage of the manuscript method is being able to coordinate the use of visual aids. Appropriate notes or marks placed on special copies of the manuscript will make available to those assisting with the visual presentation part of your talk the necessary information to coordinate the visual aids with the content of the speech.

Disadvantages

Any communication procedure or process requires transmission skill. In the manuscript delivery method, the major disadvantage lies in the fact that most people do not read aloud very well. Therefore, reading from a prepared manuscript tends to be boring, stilted, and basically unnatural. While the manu-

What are the advantages and disadvantages of the manuscript delivery method?

script method appears to be the safest way to give a speech, most people find it one of the most difficult.

Specific problems related to the manuscript delivery method include the tendency to lose your place, the development of a monotone presentation voice, difficulty in maintaining eye contact with the audience, difficulty in changing tone and language to better meet the makeup of the audience, and getting so involved in reading that maintaining interest in the audience becomes secondary.

Speaking from Memorization

The memorization method requires writing the entire speech and then memorizing it word for word. You deliver the speech from memory without the use of a manuscript, an outline, or notes.

Advantages

The significant advantage of the memorization method of delivery is its impact on the audience. Speakers who appear to have complete control of information, process, and application generate a feeling of trust and admiration from their audiences.

Disadvantages

What advantages and disadvantages result from the memorization method?

Speech memorization has more disadvantages than advantages. You might leave out an important part of the speech, or even worse, forget where you are and what comes next. You might experience some stage-fright that causes memory to lapse, which may result in your being in front of an audience with nothing to say. Because you are concentrating on remembering, you may display a way of speaking that is unnatural or uncomfortable for the audience to perceive.

Perhaps the major disadvantage of the memorization method lies in the difficulty of adding to the content or adjusting the speech to the audience. Responding to questions about content without a manuscript or notes to refer to is an additional disadvantage.

Impromptu Method

The most common type of oral communication in terms of both frequency and in time is the impromptu speech, which is given without extensive preparation—sometimes without any preparation. Most people can only utilize impromptu speaking when they are knowledgeable or well informed about the subject matter.

Impromptu speaking is not aimless rambling. Examples of impromptu speaking include providing information or remarks about a business meeting you attended, speaking at a city council meeting, or other expressions of information and opinion based on fact and experience.

Advantages

A major advantage of the impromptu method of oral communication is that you are not tied to an outline or manuscript. This allows for easy and rapid adjustment to audience needs and wants.

Disadvantages

Because an impromptu speech is not carefully planned and organized ahead of time, it can appear disorganized and hard to follow. In addition, you may find that you talk extensively about an issue without ever getting to the point. Because the disadvantages seem to outweigh the advantages, few people select the impromptu method when asked to speak before a business or community meeting. When you accept an invitation to speak, you should have in mind ideas or information that you wish to share. And you will find it helpful to have ideas, pertinent facts, and figures to refer to during the talk.

What advantages and disadvantages result from the impromptu method?

Extemporaneous Method

The extemporaneous speech is the most common method of delivery. For this kind of delivery, you first gather facts, information, and ideas, and then you organize them in outline form. Your actual speech is delivered using the outline as a guide. In the extemporaneous method, you know what ideas you will include and the order of presentation, but you will not have prepared the exact words and sentences you intend to use.

Advantages

Several distinct advantages are available to the speaker who chooses the extemporaneous method. First, the delivery is spontaneous. Second, you can easily add or delete material and ideas from the outline without distorting the sequence or changing the entire manuscript. Sometimes the changes based on the general reactions of the audience will occur almost immediately. Another advantage is being able to maintain contact with the audience because you will not have to look to a manuscript for exact wording.

Extemporaneous speeches must be prepared just as carefully as those that are written or memorized. Organization involves establishing a purpose, gathering information, conducting research, and then preparing the outline.

For the vast majority of speaking opportunities, all of its advantages generally make the extemporaneous speech better than the manuscript, memorized, or impromptu methods.

Disadvantages

Like the manuscript method, one of the main disadvantages of the extemporaneous method is the tendency to stick so close to the outline that the reactions of the audience are ignored. Practice and rehearsal will help eliminate the seriousness of this disadvantage.

What advantages and disadvantages result from the extemporaneous method?

When choosing which one of these four delivery methods to use, you should consider what is best for the topic, the intended audience, the material, and certainly the style that is best for you.

Delivery Techniques

After you have prepared your speech, you should work to improve the actual delivery technique. Keep the following three suggestions in mind as you deliver your speech:

1. Be sure to look over the audience before you begin speaking.
2. Use an appropriate ice-breaker to ease the tension and capture the attention of the audience.
3. Deliver your speech in a natural and normal manner. Avoid using slang and incomplete sentences.

Delivery techniques include personal and interpersonal communication because your voice, actions, dress, and overall appearance add to or detract from the intended impact of the message.

Voice Characteristics

What voice characteristics do speakers have to be concerned with?

Your voice is a most important aspect of message presentation. Because your voice is the vehicle for carrying information and ideas to the intended audience, the quality of your presentation will be partially judged by the overall characteristics of your voice. Voice characteristics include volume, pitch, speed, excitement level, overall voice quality, and clarity of pronunciation.

Volume

Emphasis can be given to important ideas by speaking more loudly or softly. When different environments require adjustments, be sure to speak loudly enough for the audience to hear you. If you speak too softly, the audience has to listen too intently, which tends to breed some general hostility toward the topic and the speaker.

Pitch

What is pitch?

Pitch refers to the highness or lowness of the sound or tones transmitted by your voice. When you talk, the pitch is often automatically varied in accordance with the topic or issue being discussed. When excited, a person has a tendency to speak at a higher pitch than when more somber and serious topics are being discussed. For maximum results, your voice should sound natural and relaxed. Avoid a monotone or an overly dramatic voice. For most speeches, your pitch will vary more than it would in an ordinary conversation; for maximum results, the change should be planned and controlled.

Speed

Some people tend to talk fast and others talk more slowly. During a speech, you will find talking more slowly is helpful when bringing out important ideas. When presenting ideas that are not quite as important, a faster speed can be used. You should, however, never speak so fast that the audience cannot follow your presentation. If you have a time limit for your speech, design your talk to fit that time frame. Do not just go faster at the end of the time in order to present all the material, as doing so will have a significant negative effect on the audience.

Enthusiasm

Your voice will show your interest in the material you are presenting. Allowing your voice to be dry, boring, or flat tends to drain the audience of interest and enthusiasm for you and your topic. Your inability to speak with enthusiasm will diminish the impact of your message. A boring voice can make the most interesting material seem uninteresting, while a voice full of excitement can make complex subject matter appealing to an audience.

Quality

Voice quality is the general tone of your voice. This characteristic is what makes your voice distinct from other voices. Voice quality may be harsh, nasal, pleasant, neutral, or unpleasant. You should tape record your voice to determine predominant qualities and take steps to improve how you sound to other people. Make every effort to train your voice to be as pleasant as possible. You will find that audiences are generally more receptive to ideas if they are presented by a person with a pleasant voice.

Clarity of pronunciation

Proper pronunciation is essential for successful oral communication. If you mispronounce words, your audience will have doubts about your ability and your knowledge. Separating content from such delivery techniques as pronunciation is virtually not within the capabilities of an audience. An audience will evaluate the speaker's refinement and learning on the basis of his pronunciation.

Clear speech consists of sounds that blend smoothly into words that combine to form phrases. In a continuous flow of sounds, a speaker will stress some words more than others. For example, consider the following sentence: "I was going to attend the meeting; but because guests arrived at the cabin, I couldn't leave to get there on time." The words *was, to, but, at, the, I, to, get,* and *on,* are somewhat unimportant to the speaker's intent. They will probably not be emphasized by the speaker. At the same time, the speaker will place additional stress on *attend, meeting, because, guests, arrived, couldn't,* and *time.* A speaker says a group of words in the same manner as a word with several syllables. When saying the word *individuality,* for example, you place emphasis on *in, vid,* and *al,* while *di, u, i,* and *ty* will be spoken with very little emphasis.

Placing correct emphasis will change a vowel from its full sound to a slight "uh" sound. This sound will be similar to the ending sound in the word *quota,* the beginning sound in the word *amount,* or the middle sound in *usable.* Speech and phonetics researchers refer to this as the *schwa* vowel, which is frequently used in speaking. By using the schwa sound, a speaker can establish a speaking style that has rhythm and that enhances the probability of communicating successfully.

The schwa sound, however, is not a substitute for consonants. Some commonly heard examples of failure to pronunciate correctly include the following:

Git (Get) Spose (Suppose) Finely (Finally) Probly (Probably)
Count of (On account of) Intrest (Interest) Cuz (Because)

Making any of these pronunciation errors will affect clarity, although perhaps not seriously. But if the errors are frequent, the result will be blurred, inarticulate, and distractive speaking.

The Importance of Word Choice

The difference between a word and the best word is as significant as the difference between watching a steak being grilled and eating a steak. One taste can do more for vivid memory and meaningful description than many detailed observations. Words are given greater emphasis through facial expressions, movements, gestures, and posture. Personal traits have an effect on the message because they are portrayed by the speaker. Messages can be partially or completely blocked by a speaker's personality traits and habits.

What factors are considered in selecting words for use in a speech?

If you concentrate on choosing the most effective words, you will decrease the chance of misunderstanding and increase the chance of successful communication. Words should be selected to match the situation, background, and knowledge of the listener.

Communication occurs when the intent of the sender and the understanding of the receiver are in agreement. Miscommunication, on the other hand, occurs when a lack of understanding occurs. Assume for a moment that you are a freshman in college, listening to the following short talk by the president of the college.

> Welcome to your university. During your tenure here, you will discover many vital and fortuitous occasions for enhancing your academic provocation and accomplishment. The efficacy of valid intellectual pursuit is certainly indisputable. However, personal integrity will prove to be the culminating constituent relative to ultimate professional fulfillment. While past accomplishments may substantiate intellectual inclination, the past is virtually incompatible with permanence at the upper division level. We are gratified with your propinquity and anticipate with exhilaration an exquisite and propitious semester.

Each time you talk, someone with a different background may be listening. The preceding paragraph illustrates the importance of planning and preparing your message for the intended audience. Now look at a revised and more appropriate sequel to the previous message.

> Welcome to State University. During the next four years, you will learn and grow through many social and academic experiences. A college degree will prove to be of great value in the years to come. However, you will succeed in direct proportion to the time and effort you are willing to expend. Your ability as shown in your previous academic success is obvious. However, you will now be competing with students who, like you, were also top students; and the competition will challenge your academic ability and test your ability to endure. We are pleased you are here, and we wish you our best for an exciting and successful semester.

You and Your Audience

Always keep the intent of your message and the overall make-up of your audience in mind. A message that is misunderstood not only fails to communicate, but also may actually create problems because additional time and effort have to be expended to correct misconceptions and faulty information.

Your personal appearance will affect your relationship with your audience. Your appearance can prove to be as important to successful communication as your voice. A general rule is to dress for the occasion. Wear something that is unassuming and comfortable and that will not distract the audience. Be neat and clean and avoid wearing jewelry that will take away from your presentation.

Your mannerisms also affect your relationship with your audience. Mannerisms include how you use your body when you speak. Some mannerisms can be distracting and even annoying to the audience. However, when mannerisms are properly used, they add a great deal to the overall presentation. Some of the mannerisms you can control and use are eye contact, facial expressions, posture, movement, and gestures.

What mannerisms do you have to be concerned with in making speeches?

Eye contact is a speaker's contact with the audience. You should establish eye contact with as many people in the audience as possible. Good eye contact provides constant feedback and portrays interest, which is the first step toward gaining the interest and respect of the audience.

Facial expressions help make the information more interesting and believable. Allow your expressions to change with the seriousness of the information being presented. Pay attention to how you stand—do not appear stiff, but don't slouch or slump either. Your facial expressions and your posture should portray the image of a speaker who is alert, confident, and energetic.

Movement and gestures refer to the movement of the head, hands, or arms to emphasize feelings or ideas. For maximum effectiveness, a gesture must be properly timed. A movement that is too early or too late is often worse than no gesture at all. Using too many gestures can become annoying to the audience. Movements and gestures that are very noticeable interfere with the communication process. Some common movements that are annoying to an audience include putting your hands in and out of your pockets, folding your arms across your chest or behind your back, playing with coins, pencils, or paper clips, and moving your eyes from the floor to the ceiling.

PREPARATION FOR A STAND-UP SPEECH

Nearly everyone has heard a speaker who was so dynamic that the audience almost came under a spell. Top speakers can control the emotion and personal attitudes of the audience and will nearly always include varying degrees of showmanship. Although people may react momentarily to the emotion of the speaker, the carryover effect is often minimal.

The ultimate purpose of effective oral communication is to create an intended response in terms of comprehension, perception, attitudes, beliefs, and future actions. Public speaking requires the speaker to determine the response or combination of responses that will best accomplish his/her overall purpose.

Even though the major purpose of your speech may be to inform or to entertain, this does not mean that you should ignore the other purposes. You may need to inform to persuade or to entertain to inform. The primary purpose may create a need for additional approaches.

Supporting Material

What categories of supporting materials are used in speeches?

After the purpose of your speech is determined and the topic is finalized, you should collect supporting material, using the following categories as a guide:

1. Explanation of topic, information, ideas, etc.
2. Comparison of trends, contrasting trends, etc.
3. Illustration of information in easy-to-perceive charts, graphs, etc.
4. Specific examples that add meaning to information
5. Statistics that add to the intended message
6. Opinions and conclusions of others
7. Statement of similar ideas in different words

Preparing Your Outline

What steps should be followed in preparing an outline of a speech?

Your outline is a roadmap to successful speaking and should be developed gradually and systematically. After you select your topic, you should make an outline using the following steps:

1. State your specific purpose. (A formulation of what you wish to accomplish in your speech)
2. State the leading ideas in order:
   a. Number the ideas consecutively
   b. Use complete, simple sentences to express yourself accurately and logically
   c. Use one sentence or phrase for each idea
3. State subordinate ideas
   a. Indent subordinating ideas and number them consecutively
   b. Use one sentence for each idea
   c. Use similar sentence structure for stating each subordinate idea
4. Recheck the entire outline
   a. Does it represent good outline form?
   b. Does it adequately cover the subject?
   c. Does it accomplish what you intended?

Outlining not only ensures organization, but also it enables you to make time and idea adjustments as the need arises. Without a solid outline, the audience may believe you don't have anything to say.

Body of Your Speech

What factors do you have to be concerned with in developing the body of a speech?

Naturally, the main part of a speech is the body. Your introduction should lead into the speech, while the conclusions should take you out. In developing the speech, you need to be concerned about unity, coherence, and emphasis.

Your outline will ensure unity and will make your speech easier to understand and deliver. Each point should be carefully placed and properly emphasized. Perhaps a good guideline to follow in developing the body of the speech is to include three or four major points with some explanation or elaboration of each.

Coherence is continuity of ideas and information. The parts of an outline must be tied together. Providing coherence in your outline makes the speech easier to deliver and, more importantly, easier for the audience to follow.

In the body of your speech you should expand on your most important, most complicated and most pertinent ideas or points. As a speaker, you help your listeners by emphasizing your key ideas.

Concluding Your Speech

The conclusions should tie together important points, state resolutions, crystallize thoughts, and summarize the main ideas. Although conclusions should follow the logic of your presentation, they may be in the form of summarizing a final point or making reference to the introduction.

THE IMPORTANCE OF LISTENING

Listening is an essential and extremely important aspect of oral communication and is estimated to consume more time than any other aspect of the communication process. Each day provides many opportunities to practice the skill of listening. Lectures, oral assignments, committee meetings, conferences, discussions, radio and television programs, telephone calls, announcements, and sermons require listening.

Why are hearing and listening not synonymous?

However, hearing and listening are not synonymous. Hearing is the mental recognition of sound, whereas listening involves perception, association, and appropriate reaction. Listening is perceiving sounds from the speaker, attaching meaning to the words, and designing an appropriate response, which involves remembering what the speaker has said long enough to interpret what is meant. Listening involves grasping what the speaker means by seeing the ideas and information from his/her point of view.

Levels of Listening

What levels of listening are found?

Several different levels of listening are found, including active listening, protective listening, partial listening, and preferential listening.

Active listening

Effective listening requires an active interest in the speaker. Developing a sincere active interest in the speaker is not an easy task. We all have habits and attitudes that we reveal even when we think we have them hidden. Therefore, active listening involves a certain amount of personal risk. If we actively listen to a speaker, we risk the chance of being changed as we begin to see a subject, a viewpoint, or a vantage point not previously encountered. Active listening is not easy to acquire; improvements normally come slowly and, at times, with considerable difficulty.

Protective listening

Listeners may not listen to a speaker because they have learned to tune out certain kinds of stimuli. Words such as control, taxes, and evaluation may set off a whole series of negative thinking in the mind of the listener.

Effective listening is imperative for successful oral communication. As a speaker, you will be aware of and sensitive to the true interest of the audience.

If you detect half-hearted interest on the part of the listener, your observation will tend to have a negative impact on you and your response.

Listeners become speakers, and speakers become listeners and the sequence goes on. As a listener, you will sometimes hear negative and even hostile expressions aimed directly at you. While no one really likes to be subjected to hostile remarks, you have to control protective listening so verbal attacks are perceived without your having to defend or retaliate.

Partial listening

Listening must be a complete process where all the communicative stimuli transmitted by the speaker are acknowledged and evaluated. Responding to some of the stimuli while ignoring others will make a listener miss important facts and points that are needed for clarity and understanding.

A speaker's voice, mannerisms, grammar, and pitch will increase or decrease the listener's tendency for partial listening. As a listener and a prospective speaker, you should consciously control the urge for partial listening. This will help create an environment that produces greater understanding, and, in turn, more effective oral communication.

Preferential listening

Listening that is directly affected by a person's beliefs, interests, or emotions is preferential listening. Just as people may see what they expect to see, listeners may listen for what they want to hear. Personal background, experiences, habits, and family tradition will many times change or distort the speaker's intended meaning into what the listener really wants to hear. Miscommunication is usually the result of preferential listening.

Improving Your Listening Skills

Improved listening requires concentration on what a speaker is saying or implying. Poor listening can many times be traced to a listener's having too much time to think. An average rate for speaking is 125 words per minute, but a person normally thinks about four times that fast, which gives a listener about 400 words of thinking time a minute to spare. An untrained or careless listener will allow the mind to wander and become impatient even during important and interesting talks.

What suggestions can you offer that will be helpful in improving listening skills?

Listening improvement results from improved hearing, understanding, evaluation, and responsiveness. To improve listening, you must be ready to listen. Some suggestions for improved listening are

1. Do not continue talking to or responding to people around you.
2. Have the necessary material to record important points, facts, figures, or ideas.
3. Do not write everything down, as this may keep you from hearing important points or ideas.
4. Listen for a speaker's main ideas and concentrate on their meaning.
5. Listen for supportive ideas and place them, without personal prejudices or biases, in the proper relationship.

6. Be fair and objective as you consider facts and ideas.
7. Listen for all the facts before you begin to form your opinions.
8. Avoid forming an opinion or evaluation too quickly, which will hinder your ability to be logical or objective.
9. Take the time to listen, weigh, and consider.
10. Keep an open and positive mind as a means of welcoming new viewpoints rather than resisting them.
11. Improve understanding by increasing your available vocabulary.

CHAPTER SUMMARY

One of the most important skills you can have as a business employee is an effective oral communication skill. Many business employees spend a large part of each working day communicating orally. In the business world, most oral communication is designed to inform or persuade. A third type of oral communication is designed to entertain.

In the business world, your oral communication will likely involve speaking from a manuscript, from memorization, impromptu, and extemporaneously. As you speak, your listeners will evaluate your voice characteristics—volume, pitch, speed, enthusiasm, quality, and clarity of pronunciation.

The ability to listen effectively is a very important attribute of managerial success. The types of listening include active listening, protective listening, partial listening, and preferential listening.

REVIEW QUESTIONS

1. What are the uses of oral communication?
2. Why should you assess your audience when making an oral presentation?
3. What are the advantages and disadvantages of speaking from a manuscript? Extemporaneous speaking?
4. What voice characteristics affect one's oral presentation?
5. Provide a list of several suggestions that will be helpful to one in preparing a stand-up speech.
6. What is meant by active listening?
7. How does protective listening differ from partial listening?
8. Provide a list of several suggestions that will help someone trying to improve listening skills.

APPLICATION PROBLEMS

1. Select a news story from the front page of your city newspaper and convert it into a talk to be presented to a local civic group. Explain the process you used in developing your talk for the intended group. Show your outline, complete with line-item detail needed for a 20- to 25-minute talk.

2. Observe, record, and analyze listening habits of students in one of your classes. Explain the types of listening you observed and prepare an appropriate speech. The information is to be presented at a national meeting of the National Business Communication Society.

3. Develop an outline and appropriate plan for presenting a solution to one of the major concerns of the student body at your college/university. Some

suggested problem topics are the following: registration, parking, library, cafeteria, athletics, curricula, traffic on campus, drop policy, etc.

4. Assume you are the chairperson of the convention site selection committee for the American Federation of Communication Concepts. This is a national organization of people from business and education who have research, process, and application interests in the improvement and enhancement of business communication.

Your committee visited several cities, including Las Vegas, Los Angeles, San Diego, Denver, Houston, and New Orleans. Las Vegas was selected as the site for the next convention, and your task is to prepare a report to present at the next meeting of the AFCC Executive Board meeting in Washington, D.C.

Using your college/university library or other available sources, prepare an outline for an extemporaneous presentation. Your outline should include points that you and your committee members considered important to the selection of Las Vegas. Some of the points to consider are excellent room rates, reasonable food costs, easy access by all major airlines, complete accommodations for large and small groups, and the quality of shows and entertainment. Keep in mind that each of the other cities had some advantages but that Las Vegas was the one site that appeared to have the least number of disadvantages.

Your oral report must address some of the major concerns expressed by strong and influential members of the AFCC, such as the following: going to Las Vegas demonstrates to the general membership that the organization is more committed to play than to work; 65 percent of the membership comes from east of the Mississippi River, and, therefore, an east-coast site should be given higher priority. In addition, gambling may both distract and disrupt the concentration and overall worthiness of the entire convention.

In addition to preparing your outline, include at least three sketches of information or drawings you are going to use. These sketches or drawings are to emphasize the more important or significant points.

5. Prepare an appropriate script for a speaking-from-memorization oral presentation using the information contained in application problem 3 in Chapter 8. Prepare for your instructor's review a cassette tape of your reading the script.

6. Prepare an outline for a 15-minute extemporaneous speech about the text material contained in this chapter on oral communication. You will need to select the points that will best present the overall picture of effective oral communication because the entire chapter cannot be presented in fifteen minutes.

7. Prepare a speaking-from-a-manuscript report on the advantages and disadvantages of leasing versus buying electronic equipment for use in today's modern businessworld Gather the facts you consider to be most important and prepare your manuscript for a maximum five-minute presentation. You may be called upon to read your report in front of the class.

8. Using the sample report in Chapter 14, prepare an extemporaneous speech. The material you are to present in your speech is found in the sample report. Be prepared to deliver your report before the class.

9. Listening is an extremely important aspect of effective speech. Prepare a speech to be read from a manuscript on the topic of "The Elements and

Process of Improved Listening.'' Your manuscript should be designed for a five- to seven-minute presentation.

10. Prepare an outline for an extemporaneous speech to be given before the personnel manager and his/her assistants concerning your training and experience for a position in the company communications division of the personnel division of Acme Company. Please include line-item detail that will provide the necessary information for a successful job interview. The position involves both writing and editing company correspondence in the areas of persuasion, sales, credit, and collections. You might wish to review the chapters covering these topics as you determine which points to include. Remember, you are selling both your ability and your suitability for this prestigious and important company communications position.

Chapter 20

International Business Communication

LEARNING OBJECTIVES

After studying this chapter, you should be able to

1. Discuss the cultural differences that affect international business communication.
2. Discuss the differences between values important to Americans and those important to people of other cultures.
3. Discuss the nature of language barriers that affect international business communication.
4. Identify the types of nonverbal communication that affect international communication.
5. Discuss the steps you would undertake if you were preparing for an international assignment.

As more American businesses become multinational, their employees' understanding of international business communication becomes increasingly important. The internationalization of American business and the rapidly increasing number of foreign companies with plants on American soil have made the United States an important part of the global business community. Of the recent developments affecting American businesses, the trend toward internationalization is among the most significant.

Employees involved in international business must view their functional responsibilities from an international perspective. For example, if you are involved with the marketing of products in a foreign country, you will need an understanding of international marketing. Or, if you have foreign financial responsibilities in the company for which you work, you will need an understanding of international finance and economics.

Cutting across all functional areas of international business is international business communication. Therefore, regardless of the nature of your responsibilities in international business, you will need to be familiar with international business communication. An understanding of this vital communication area will provide you with one of the most important tools for carrying out your job functions.

Some day you may be fortunate to receive an international assignment. The odds are continually improving that you will have this opportunity. Your stay will be more enjoyable the sooner you are able to become emersed in the new culture in which you are living. An understanding of international business communication will help you become acclimated much more quickly.

This chapter covers three important components of international business communication: cultural differences affecting international business communication, nonverbal differences affecting international business communication, and preparation for an international assignment.

CULTURAL DIFFERENCES AFFECTING INTERNATIONAL BUSINESS COMMUNICATION

What is ethnocentricity?

Because each of us is the product of our cultural environment, we have the tendency to react ethnocentrically to individuals of other cultural environments. This means we use our cultural background as an interpretative guide in judging the actions, views, customs, or manners of others. If we react ethnocentrically, we may condemn the other person because his/her views do not coincide with ours. In this sense, an ethnocentric reaction is similar to a stereotyped reaction. Unfortunately, an ethnocentric reaction will cause us to misunderstand the intentions of individuals from other cultural backgrounds.

Just as our avoidance of ethnocentric reactions to foreigners is necessary, their avoidance of ethnocentric reactions to us is just as important. To illustrate, if Americans are viewed by foreigners as greedy, materialistic, imperialistic, capitalistic, and brash, the relationship will be impaired just as much as when we stereotype Japanese as procrastinators in decision making or Arabs as ''hagglers.''

The most effective way to avoid reacting ethnocentrically is to accept the fact that cultural differences do exist—and to become aware of the nature of these differences. For example, if you are aware that the Japanese decision-making process is slow because of the ''ringi'' procedure (the process of requiring the approval of many people in making decisions) which is common in that culture, you will more readily be able to accept their customarily slow decision-making process.

Topics discussed in this section include customs, values, language barriers, decision-making processes, status, and manners.

Customs

As business is increasingly transacted in social situations, we need to be aware of the customs found in other cultures.

In European countries, the exchanging of gifts is customary. However, in certain Far East cultures, such as Korea and Japan, gift giving—especially on the occasion of the first visit—may be interpreted as bribery. And while you may open a gift in front of the giver in an European country, doing so in Japan or Korea is considered a lack of good taste.

Some religions prohibit the intake or use of certain items. For example, Moslems avoid the use of tobacco, alcohol, and meat. And Arabs avoid using the left hand to remove food from a serving dish as that hand is considered to be unclean.

While providing a detailed discussion of the customs of peoples from other countries is beyond the scope of this text, you will want to learn the differences between our culture and foreign cultures when you travel or live abroad. An enlightened individual will never assume that everything which is acceptable in our culture is acceptable in other cultures.

Values

What values in other countries differ from American values?

The values subscribed to by Americans are quite different from many of the values held by individuals in foreign countries. Because our ''melting-pot'' culture has primarily an European influence, the most significant differences occur between us and people of cultures in the Middle and Far East.

The American culture still values the work ethic. Accordingly, we believe, for several reasons, in the necessity of hard work—because the harder we work, the more money we are likely to earn. And the more money we earn, the more comforts we can provide ourselves. But in some cultures, materialism is condemned. We also believe in the necessity of working as efficiently and with as few people as possible. However, in cultures in which unemployment is high, creating jobs is more highly valued than getting the task completed efficiently with as few employees as possible. This is especially true in countries like India and Pakistan.

In our culture, we value making as much progress as possible as fast as possible. Nothing is inherently wrong with moving tons of dirt or rocks in the building of a super highway. Nothing is wrong with daming a river that results in the flooding of thousands of acres of land. But in Eastern cultures, humans believe in the necessity of adjusting to the physical environment rather than changing the environment to accommodate the population.

Respect for authority and the avoidance of questioning the decisions made by higher-ups are seen much more often in other cultures than in ours. Nor is the democratic process that we cherish well understood by people in other cultures.

In the Japanese culture, employment tends to be for life and employers play a more important role in employees' lives. Japanese employers provide living accommodations for their employees, pay for weddings, etc. And until fairly recently in Japan, losing one's job was disgraceful. In fact, little could happen to an individual that would be more disgraceful.

While our culture is based on competition and free enterprise, competition in some Eastern cultures is viewed as being destructive. From the time we are fairly young, we see competition in the United States as a healthy aspect of our way of life.

Decision-Making Process

The process of making decisions varies widely from culture to culture. Some cultures use authoritarian processes in which decisions are imposed by a higher authority or council, such as in Russia, while in other cultures decisions emerge slowly because of the group consensus process, as in Japan. The amount of shared responsibility for decision making varies widely from culture to culture.

How do decision-making processes in other countries differ from American decision-making processes?

In organizations in the United States, the goal is to reach decisions as quickly and as efficiently as the circumstances allow. This same goal is found in most Western European cultures. But in Latin American countries, emphasis is put on minute details and lengthy discussions, and failure to do so arouses suspicion and results in offenders' being considered untrustworthy.

Language Barriers

One of the most significant cultural differences that affects international business communication is language. Even though an individual may be able to read, write, and understand a foreign language, significant language barriers can still exist. Fortunately for Americans, English is the most common foreign language used in business abroad. Rather than having to learn a foreign language, more commonly we have to learn how to use English in a way that will be readily understood by those for whom it is a second language.

Most Americans who work overseas for any length of time find it desirable to learn the language native to the country in which they are living. While learning the language may not be absolutely necessary for their job assignment, a basic mastery of the language will be necessary if they hope to integrate themselves into their new culture.

While some companies provide language classes for their employees before they go abroad, other companies reimburse their employees for expenses incurred in arranging their own language study. Berlitz is well known for its language study programs.

The vast majority of the business letters in international communication are written in English. In large organizations, letters received that are written in a language other than English are often translated by professional translators, unless, of course, the recipient is competent in the foreign language. Those written in English by someone for whom English is a second language are generally clear enough to create understanding, even though they might not meet our standards of good business letters.

The written communications that create the greatest number of problems are advertisements, warranties, and manuals that must be translated from English to another language. In some instances, a major portion of the message is lost in the translation—and sometimes with disastrous consequences. To illustrate, when Pepsi Cola was introduced to the Asian market, its slogan, "Come alive with Pepsi," was interpreted to mean that Pepsi brings relatives back from the grave!

Why does oral communication in international business present more problems than written communication?

Oral communication presents more problems in international business communication than does written communication, which can be attributed to two reasons. First, many individuals who learn a foreign language develop a greater reading/writing fluency than a speaking/listening fluency. Consequently, they have more difficulty understanding and being understood when communicating orally. Secondly, we tend to use more idioms in oral communication than we do in written communication. Idioms, which are expressions peculiar to a certain people, tend to be confusing to individuals for whom English is a second language. Just as foreigners have difficulty understanding English idioms, we have difficulty understanding idioms in other languages.

What suggestions can you offer that will help you eliminate either oral or written language barriers in international business?

Some suggestions that will help you eliminate either written or oral language barriers are the following:

1. Use specific, concrete terms rather than abstract words to express yourself.
2. Use short, precise words, sentences, and paragraphs.
3. Avoid the use of idioms, slang, or jargon. Examples of idioms include the following:
   ". . . eat a hot dog."
   ". . . so hungry I could eat a horse."
   ". . . runs for office."
   ". . . shot my idea down."
   ". . . visit the "john" or "head." (meaning restroom)
   ". . . pulling my leg." (meaning lack of seriousness)
   ". . . threw the book." (meaning convicted)
   ". . . got bumped upstairs." (meaning promoted)
   ". . . got fired."
4. Use pointing expressions such as "for example," "furthermore," and "in addition," as well as transitional expressions such as "however" and "therefore."
5. Avoid the use of abbreviations.

If your job responsibilities eventually require the preparation of letters sent to foreign countries, you should, as much as possible, gear your correspondence to the recipients' expectations. Generally, this will require your being more formal than you are when writing to Americans. And if you are writing to someone in Japan, remember that Japanese tend to be more apologetic and humble than Americans. The fast-start opening that you were earlier taught to use may be offensive to Japanese as they believe that one should begin a letter with a comment about the weather or the season. For example, during the growing season, a letter may begin with the following: "In this season of abundant greenery. . . . " This section may be followed with a comment about the reader's health. After the expression of other pleasantries, the main point of the letter is finally introduced.

Status

How does status in other cultures differ from status in the American culture?

Cultures vary in the ways that status is accorded to business employees. In the United States, status is accorded to employees by the nature of the furnishings in their offices. To illustrate, the offices of top-level executives tend to be carpeted with thicker carpet than the offices of lower-level executives. While top executives are generally given wooden furniture, lower-level executives are issued metal furniture. And the higher one's hierarchical level, the more privacy and seclusion he/she has. Status is also gained by the organization if it names after itself the building in which it is located. The address can add to or detract from the status of the organization.

In foreign cultures, status appears to be less important. In the Middle East, offices tend to be much smaller and more modest than their American counterparts. In France, privacy and seclusion are not important to top executives, as they are typically located in large open areas with their subordinates surrounding them. In England, the offices of the highest-ranking individuals in organizations are sometimes located below ground level, while in the United States, the highest status location for top executives is the top floor.

Manners

How do manners in other cultures differ from manners in the American culture?

Manners in different cultures vary in what is considered to be acceptable. Introductions and farewells are more formal in many foreign cultures than in the United States. Natives of a Far East culture often bow when being introduced to someone else. In saying farewell, these same individuals will also bow and back out of a room. Being able to sit patiently through a three-hour lunch in most European cultures is the sign of "knowing your manners."

In certain Middle East cultures—Saudia Arabia for one—respect for elders is especially important. A hush falls over a room when an elder enters a room filled with younger people.

Being familiar with the manners considered acceptable in foreign cultures will enable you to conduct business more comfortably. Continually having to be concerned about offending the person with whom you are dealing will not enable you to concentrate fully on the business at hand.

NONVERBAL DIFFERENCES AFFECTING INTERNATIONAL COMMUNICATION

Individuals who communicate in an international environment need to be aware of the nonverbal differences affecting the communication process. This is true for the following reasons: (1) When the verbal and nonverbal messages are not consistent with one another, miscommunication can occur, and (2) nonverbal cues do not have universal meaning. The communication process will obviously be affected if a nonverbal cue acceptable in our culture has a negative connotation in a foreign culture. Among the types of nonverbal differences covered in this chapter are posture, movement, gestures, space, paralanguage, eye contact, touching, and time.

Posture

Our nonverbal signals that communicate a relaxed situation (slouching in a chair, crossing one's legs, and arms away from the body) are interpreted as showing disrespect in other cultures. In Saudia Arabia, a visible shoe sole is offensive when one's legs are crossed. Natives of Far East cultures believe that an appearance of being relaxed in a conversation results in the loss of control over the situation.

Movement

Americans typically move about faster and more abruptly than natives of many foreign cultures. We typically have had more room around us, and we tend to make use of that room as we communicate. Natives of the Middle and Far East cultures prefer a communication situation where less movement is displayed.

Gestures

What differences exist between gestures used in the American culture and gestures used in foreign cultures?

Some gestures that we find acceptable are obscene and/or insulting in other cultures. In India, a wink is insulting. The "A-OK" gesture we use (making a circle with the thumb and index finger) is a sign of contempt in South American countries but depicts money in Japan. The "V" gesture (formed by raising the index and middle finger) shows disrespect in Europe. Our gesture for saying "no" (moving the head back and forth) is not understood by Japanese who move their right hand to signal "no." In Italy, "no" is signaled by waving a finger in the speaker's face. The gesture used by hitchhiking Americans is considered obscene in Italy.

Americans tend to observe facial expressions to interpret the real meaning of the message. Evidence shows that when a discrepancy occurs between the verbal and nonverbal message, the nonverbal message is typically considered more accurate. In the Japanese culture, the face remains rather impassive regardless of the nature of the conversation. Therefore, we should not misinterpret an emotionless facial expression when communicating with Japanese. We can also easily misinterpret the meaning of a Japanese smile. While we tend to interpret the smile as a sign of agreement, the Japanese smile can mean several things. It may be used to disguise the individual's true feelings, or it may be used to say, "I understand." But it might also be used to say, "I don't understand."

Space

What differences exist between how Americans view space and how people in other cultures view space?

Americans tend to value space more than people of other cultures. We are uncomfortable when business associates get too close. Generally, Americans prefer to converse with business associates from a distance of at least four feet. People in Mediterranean countries, southern European countries, the Middle East, and Latin America prefer less space. Natives of these cultures may interpret our wanting more space when we communicate as an indication that we prefer a cold, distant, or even an aloof relationship. The sex of those communicating also affects the amount of space customarily allowed in some countries. In South America, men are obligated to position themselves a distance of at least five feet when communicating with female business associates.

How individuals occupy space also varies from culture to culture. Chinese prefer to sit side by side when they communicate, whereas we prefer a face-to-face arrangement. Our desire to put office callers at ease by standing when they enter the room or by moving from behind the desk has no communications significance in other cultures.

Paralanguage

Paralanguage appears to have fewer differences among the various cultures than the other elements. Natives in all cultures tend to talk faster and louder when they are excited and communicate happiness by a higher-pitched voice. The most significant difference among cultures is in the meaning of a pause in conversation. While an American may pause because he/she is uncomfortable about the situation being discussed, the Middle Easterners use pauses for reflection.

Eye contact

Americans often depend on eye contact as a means of interpreting one's honesty, genuineness, and sincerity. A break in eye contact frequently accompanies an untruth or insincerity. In other cultures, such as in Japan, the lack of eye contact has no significance. But in some cultures, eye contact is rarely broken, which tends to make Americans uncomfortable. In Spain and Latin American countries, direct eye contact with strangers is avoided as a means of showing them respect.

What differences exist between the use of eye contact by Americans and eye contact used by people in other cultures?

Touching

Some cultures, especially in the Middle East, Latin America, and European countries along the Mediterranean, do considerably more touching than Americans. Frequent touching, hugging, and kissing are common in these cultures. Male friends often greet one another with hugs and kisses, and people of these regions tend to touch one another more during conversation than do Americans. But in other foreign cultures, such as in Thailand, people avoid touching one another in public.

Time

The way we use our time differs considerably from other cultures. Americans tend to be schedule oriented and regimented in their daily lives. We value timeliness and promptness and abhor being kept waiting for more than just a few minutes. In Latin American countries, natives see nothing wrong with being 45 to 60 minutes late for an appointment. And the caller will be given as much time as he/she desires, even if it causes the next caller's appointment to begin an hour late! In these countries, business transactions are prolonged as protracted discussions are customary. The end result is not as important as the discussions that lead up to the end result, a phenomenon that Americans sometimes find quite frustrating. Those in the Middle East will also find that business dealings often progress at a snail's pace.

While Americans tend to have a negative interpretation for a slow response to their correspondence, natives in other cultures have just the opposite interpretation. After all, the important events in life take much longer than the unimportant ones. Therefore, why not give these events ample time?

PREPARATION FOR AN INTERNATIONAL ASSIGNMENT

Upon receiving an international assignment, a certain amount of preparatory work on your part will be well worth your effort. The extent of your preparation will likely affect the amount of satisfaction you derive from the assignment, at least initially.

Ways in which you can become better prepared are to attain a basic mastery of the language, become aware of the communication differences between the American culture and the culture in which you will be living, and learn as much as you can about the country.

What suggestions can you offer that would be helpful to one preparing for an international assignment?

Attain Language Mastery

During the past decade or so, American students have taken less interest in the study of foreign languages. Now that more American companies are becoming multinational, interest in studying foreign languages is increasing. You should not turn down an international assignment simply because you do not know the language used in the assigned country. Even if you have studied a foreign language, especially French or German, the odds are quite good that it is not the language used where you will be assigned. Japanese and Spanish are the two foreign languages that seem to be the most frequently needed.

English has been and continues to be the universal business language. You most likely will not need a basic mastery of the foreign language as much for your job as you will find it helpful in non-job situations. If you hope to become socially involved, a basic mastery of the language native to that country is imperative.

To attain a basic mastery of a foreign language you can enroll in college/university language classes, or classes offered by a private company, or work with a tutor who will give you private language lessons. While some companies will pay for the cost of this training, others make the employees responsible.

Become Aware of Communication Differences

Information presented earlier in this chapter will help you become aware of the differences between your culture and the one in which you may be living, as well as the differences between the nonverbal cues you have grown accustomed to using and those used in your new culture. While a number of detailed differences are presented in this information, you will benefit from a more thorough, in-depth study. A variety of information from a number of sources will help you develop a more intensive understanding of these differences.

You may also find it not only helpful, but also desirable if you become aware of the differences in the way letters, reports, and other documents are written in the United States and in the country where you will be living. As a rule, American business correspondence is more personal, informal, and written with less flair than correspondence originating in a foreign country. Foreign correspondence, on the other hand, tends to be more courteous, and it contains more flattery. In addition to the differences in the writing style, you may also find some rather significant differences in the formats that are used.

Learn About the Country

The more you know about the country to which you are relocating, the less frustration you will experience. The kinds of information you will find helpful are those things you find helpful in living in the United States. You may also be able to talk with others who have worked in the country to which you are locating. They will be able to provide you with a wealth of helpful information.

Organizations and printed information you will find helpful are the following:

American Society for Training and Development
P. O. Box 5307
Madison, WI 53705

The Business Council for International Understanding
American University
Washington, DC 20016

Country Updates, published by Intercultural Press Inc.

The Cultural Environment of International Business, Vern Tepstra, Cincinnati: South-Western Publishing Co., 1978

Intercultural Communications, Inc.
P. O. Box 14358
University Station
Minneapolis, MN 55415

Intercultural Network, Inc.
906 N. Spring Avenue
LaGrange Park, IL 60525

Intercultural Press, Inc.
70 West Hubbard Street
Chicago, IL 60610

Living Abroad, Ingemar Tobiorn, Chichester: John Wiley & Sons, 1982

Managing Cultural Differences, Phillip R. Harris and Robert T. Moran, Houston: Gulf, 1979

Overseas Briefing Associates
210 East 36th Street
New York, NY 10016

The Society for Intercultural Education, Training, and Research
1414 22 Street NW, Suite 102
Washington, DC 20037

Survival Kit for Overseas Living, Robert L. Kohls, published by Intercultural Network, Inc., 1979

Training for the Cross-Cultural Mind, published by The Society for Intercultural Education, Training, and Research, 1980

Understanding Intercultural Communication, Larry A. Samovar, Richard E. Porter, and Nemi C. Jain, Belmont, CA: Wadsworth, 1972

CHAPTER SUMMARY

International business communication is becoming much more important as increasing numbers of employees have international assignments or work in a branch of a foreign company located in this country. Being knowledgeable about international business communication will not only enable you to be more successful in your job responsibilities, but also will help you experience more satisfaction when you live abroad.

An individual who is involved with international business must be aware of the differences between the culture he/she is familiar with and the culture in the country where he/she is living. Important cultural elements include customs, values, language barriers, decision-making processes, status, and manners.

Another important area for those involved with international business is nonverbal communication. Because nonverbal communication is not universal, the various elements do not have the same meaning in all cultures. The important elements of nonverbal communication are posture, movement, gestures, space, paralanguage, eye contact, touching, and time.

If you are ever fortunate enough to receive an international assignment, you should prepare yourself as well as possible, especially if you have sufficient time. The more prepared you are, the more you will enjoy the experience.

REVIEW QUESTIONS

1. Why is the study of international business communication becoming more important?
2. What is an ethnocentric reaction in international business communication?
3. What is the nature of the differences between values held by Americans and those held by natives of the Middle and Far East countries?
4. What is the nature of the decision-making process commonly used in Latin American countries?
5. What suggestions can you provide that will help you avoid written and oral language barriers in international communication?
6. What is the nature of the differences between the movements used by Americans and the natives of many foreign cultures?
7. Of what significance is the smile as a nonverbal gesture in Japanese culture?
8. What is the nature of the differences between eye contact used by Americans and natives of other countries in the communication process?
9. What is the nature of the differences between the way Americans and natives of other cultures use time?

APPLICATION PROBLEMS

1. You have just received an opportunity to move abroad to work in a branch office of the company for which you work. After you select the country, prepare a report in which you present the following:

a. A discussion of the stereotyped image of the natives of that country. (If you can find a native of that country, discuss with him/her your stereotyped image as a means of determining the accuracy of your perceptions. In your discussion, use as much discretion as you consider appropriate.)

b. A discussion of the stereotyped image you perceive the natives of that country have of Americans. How accurate is that image?

c. A discussion of the nature of the differences between your culture and the culture in the country you selected.

d. A discussion of the nature of the differences between the nonverbal communication commonly used in the United States and the nonverbal communication used in the country you selected.

2. Obtain from an international student a business letter that is written in his/her native language. Ask the student to translate the letter into English. Prepare a report in which you discuss the differences and similarities between the translated letter and a comparable letter prepared by an American writer for an American reader.

3. Now prepare a letter for the international student you worked with in application problem 2. Either you or your instructor will select the situation about which you are writing. Adapt the content, format, and writing style so it is appropriate for your international reader.

4. Select ten types of nonverbal gestures commonly used by Americans. In a conversation with two international students from two different countries, display these gestures and explain their meaning. Then determine if the gesture means the same thing to each of these students. If the gesture means something else, determine what it means. Then determine what gesture (if any) is used to communicate the comparable nonverbal message communicated by each of your gestures.

Appendix A

Grammar Usage

GRAMMAR RULES: 1. SUBJECT–VERB AGREEMENT

1.1. The subject of a sentence and its verb must agree in number and in person.

He is the new professor in the department. (Singular subject *he* and verb *is* agree in number)

They are planning to arrive at noon. (Plural subject *they* and verb *are* are both in the third person)

John and Mary are enrolled in the same class. (Plural subject *John* and *Mary* and verb *are* agree in number)

You are too kind to him. (Second-person subject *you* always takes a plural verb even though the subject *you* refers to one person)

1.2. Words that fall between the subject and verb are not considered when determining the correct number of the verb to use in a sentence.

One of the professor's books has been returned. [Singular subject *one* agrees with singular verb *has,* although a plural word (books) falls between the subject and verb]

The contents of the report are questionable. [Plural subject *contents* agrees with plural verb *are,* although a singular word (report) falls between the subject and verb]

1.3. Two singular subjects joined with *and* require a plural verb.

John and Bill are roommates in college. (Singular subjects *John, Bill* require a plural verb)

1.4. Two nouns referring to the same subject require a singular verb.

The secretary and treasurer (*meaning the same person*) is to sign the document. [Two nouns (secretary and treasurer) refer to the same subject and therefore require a singular verb]

1.5. *Each, everybody, anybody, either, every, neither, a, an,* and *another* are always singular and require the use of a singular verb even though the subject may consist of two or more singular words.

Neither he nor she is to attend the meeting. [Two singular subjects (he, she) require a singular verb (is) when preceded by *neither*]

He and she are to attend the meeting. [Two singular subjects (he, she) joined by *and* require a plural verb (are)]

1.6. A subject comprised of two plural words and connected by *either, or; neither, nor; not only, but also* requires a plural verb.

Either the presidents or the vice-presidents of the student organizations are to file the report. [Two plural words (presidents, vice-presidents) require a plural verb (are)]

1.7. If the subject in a sentence is comprised of both singular and plural words and the words are connected by *either, or; neither, nor; not only, but also,* the plural word should be placed nearer the verb, which should be in the plural form.

Neither Mary nor her coworkers are planning to leave the building at 5 p.m. [Singular word (Mary) followed by plural word (coworkers) requires plural verb (are)]

1.8. The number of the subject determines the number of the verb when phrases such as *including, as well as, in addition, together with,* intervene between the subject and verb.

Your report, including the appendices, is due on Friday. [Singular subject (report) followed by an intervening phrase that contains a plural word (appendices) still requires a singular verb (is)]

Mary, as well as her two sisters, plans to go home this weekend. [Singular subject (Mary) requires singular verb (plans), although a phrase containing a plural word (sisters) intervenes]

1.9. The number of the verb is determined by the number of the noun to which such words as *any, none, most, all* refer.

Do any of the students present have questions? [The word *any* refers to *students,* which is plural; therefore, a plural verb (do have) is required]

All of the class was here. [The word *all* refers to *class,* which is singular; therefore, a singular verb (was here) is required]

All of the class members were here. [The word *all* refers to *members;* therefore, a plural verb (were here) is required]

1.10. The verb agrees with the subject rather than the predicate complement.

His main worry at the moment is his grades. [Singular subject (worry) requires singular verb (is); grades is the predicate complement]

Their chief goal is to become good students. [Singular subject (goal) requires singular subject (is); *students* is the predicate complement]

1.11. To determine easily subject-verb agreement in an inverted sentence, rephrase the sentence in the normal order to ascertain the correct number of the verb to use.

Inverted: Together we will go to the movie.

Rephrased: We will go to the movie together. [Plural subject (we) and plural verb (go) agree]

Inverted: Of these facts we are sure.

Rephrased: We are sure of these facts. [Plural subject (we) and plural verb (are) agree]

2. VERBS

2.1. The mood of the verb is used to indicate the intent of the statement: a fact, a command, or a wish, for example.

2.1.1. *Indicative mood.* This is the mood used to express a fact or ask a question.

They will go home tomorrow. (fact)

When does he plan to leave? (question)

2.1.2. *Imperative mood.* This is the mood used to express a command or to make a request.

Do your assignment before you return to class. (command)

When you come to class, please be prepared. (request)

2.1.3. *Subjunctive mood.* This is the mood used to express a statement that is contrary to fact or to make a wish.

I wish I were going with you. (wish)

I wish it were summer. (contrary to fact, because it is fall)

2.1.3.1. When a verb in the present tense is used, the subjunctive form of the verb *to be* requires the use of *were.*

If I were angry, I would tell you.

2.1.3.2. When the auxiliary (helping) form of a verb is required in the subjunctive mood, *be* precedes the remainder of the verb.

She insisted that she be given a chance to redeem herself.

2.1.3.3. In a sentence that is contrary to fact (which requires the subjunctive mood) and that refers to past time, the correct verb is *had been*.

If they *had been* here yesterday, they would certainly have been proud of you.

2.2. Tense is the verb element that expresses time in relation to the action stated in the verb.

2.2.1. The three major tenses are present tense, past tense, and future tense. In addition, the three perfect tenses—present perfect, past perfect, and future perfect—are used to indicate a state of being or the state of a completed action. The progressive tenses—present progressive, past progressive, and future progressive—are used to indicate the state of progress on certain actions.

2.2.2. The principal parts of the verb—present, past, past participle, and present participle—are used to form the nine tenses mentioned in 2.2.1.

2.2.2.1. Regular verbs are those whose past and past participle forms are developed by adding a *d* or *ed* to the present form.

Present	*Past*	*Past Participle*	*Present Participle*
work	worked	worked	working
shave	shaved	shaved	shaving
paint	painted	painted	painting

2.2.2.2. Irregular verbs are those whose past and present participle forms cannot be developed by adding a *d* or *ed* to the present form.

Present	*Past*	*Past Participle*	*Present Participle*
do	did	done	doing
see	saw	seen	seeing
eat	ate	eaten	eating
drink	drank	drunk	drinking
write	wrote	written	writing
swim	swam	swum	swimming

2.2.2.2.1. An auxiliary verb (is, are; was, were; can, could; do, did; had, has; shall, should; will, would) must be used with a verb in the past participle form.

I *did* my part. (past tense)

I *have done* my part. (past participle)

2.2.3. *Present tense* is used (1) to express present time or (2) to make statements that are always true.

I am at home. (statement that expresses present time)

I eat everyday. (statement that is always true)

2.2.4. *Past tense* is used to express action that occurred in the past.

I worked yesterday. (past action)

I wrote a letter yesterday. (past action)

2.2.4.1. Using the past participle form of an irregular verb to express an action that should be stated in past tense is not possible.

I swum for an hour. (incorrect—swum is a past participle)

I swam for an hour. (correct—swam is in past tense)

I drunk my coffee. (incorrect—drunk is a past participle)

I drank my coffee. (correct—drank is in past tense)

I had drunk my coffee before they arrived. [correct because past participle *drunk* requires an auxiliary verb (had)]

2.2.5. *Future tense* is used to express time in the future. Future tense is formed by inserting *shall* or *will* before the present tense of the verb.

2.2.5.1. To express simple future tense in ordinary conversation, use *will* with all three persons.

I will go to town this afternoon.

You will be able to do well on that project.

They will be here shortly.

2.2.5.2. To express simple future time in formal conversation, use *shall* with the first person (I, we) and *will* with the second person (you) and with the third person (he, she, it, they).

I shall be delighted to read your report when it arrives. (first person)

You will be delighted to know that I received your report. (second person)

They will be in class until noon. (third person)

2.2.5.3. To express future determination, promise, or threat in ordinary conversation, use *will* with all three persons.

2.2.5.4. To express future determination, promise, or threat in formal conversation, use *will* with the first person and *shall* with the second or third person.

No matter what circumstances result, I will be there on Friday. (determination)

You shall return by dusk or be prepared to suffer the consequences. (threat)

We will overcome our barrier. (determination)

2.2.6. *Present perfect tense* is used to refer to action started in the past that is completed at any moment before the present. The present perfect tense is formed by placing *have* or *has* before the past participle form of the verb (done, seen, eaten, drunk, etc.).

I have completed my homework. (*have* plus the past participle form of *complete*)

I have drunk all the coffee that was in the cup.

2.2.7. *Past perfect tense* is used to refer to an action that was completed before another past action. This tense is formed by placing *had* before the past participle.

I had eaten my dinner before she arrived.

I had written the answers to the problem before I left.

2.2.8. *Future perfect tense* is used to refer to an action that will be completed before a specific time in the future. It is formed by adding the verb *shall have* or *will have* to the past participle.

We shall have completed the assignment by the time she arrives.

They will have completed the assignment by the time you arrive.

2.2.9. *Present progressive tense* is used to refer to an action that is still in progress. It is formed by adding the verb *am, is,* or *are* to the present participle form of the verb.

We are working as rapidly as we can. (present participle of *work,* which is *working,* is added to *are*)

I am doing the assignment now.

2.2.10. *Past progressive tense* is used to refer to an action that was in progress at some time in the past. It is formed by adding the verb *was* or *were* to the present participle form of the verb.

They were sleeping at the time the fire drill was conducted. (present participle of *sleep,* which is *sleeping,* is added to *were*)

2.2.11. *Future progressive tense* is used to refer to an action that will be in progress at some future time. It is formed by adding the verb *shall be* or *will be* to the present participle.

We shall be working on the assignment this weekend when you are in Washington. (present participle of *work,* which is *working,* is added to *shall*)

I will be sleeping when you arrive.

2.3. Voice of verbs is used to indicate whether the subject of the verb is (1) performing the action or (2) being acted upon.

2.3.1. If the subject is performing the action, a verb in the *active voice* is being used.

The student prepared the report. (subject, *student,* performed action, *prepared*)

The girl ate the dinner. (subject, *girl,* performed action, *ate*)

2.3.2. If the subject is being acted upon, a verb in the *passive voice* is used.

The report was prepared by the student. (subject, *report,* was acted upon, *prepared*)

The dinner was eaten by the girl. (subject, *dinner,* was acted upon, *eaten*)

2.3.3. The active voice is suited for straightforward, direct, concise writing of a personalized nature. Most business writing should utilize active voice.

2.3.4. The passive voice is suited for writing of an impersonal nature. It is particularly suited for removing a harsh, blunt tone from writing. Some writers prefer to use passive voice when making suggestions or recommendations as a means of removing a dictatorial tone.

I recommend that you take drastic action. (active)

It is recommended that you take drastic action. (passive)

2.3.5. Do not frequently shift back and forth from active voice to passive voice. To do so creates an awkward writing style that is difficult to read.

Poor: John wrote the report. (active)
The report was typed by Mary. (passive)
Sally proofread and duplicated the report. (active)
The various copies were distributed by Tom. (passive)

Improved: After John wrote the report, Mary typed it. (active)
Sally proofread and duplicated the report, and Tom distributed the various copies. (active)

3. PRONOUNS

3.1. A pronoun is used in place of a noun (*she* is used for *Mary, he* is used for *John, it* is used for *car*).

3.2. Pronouns have qualities of number, person, and gender.

3.2.1. Number refers to—

Singular (I, he, she)

Plural (we, they)

3.2.2. Person refers to—

First person (I)—person speaking

Second person (you)—person being spoken to

Third person (he, she, they, it)—persons or things spoken about

3.2.3. Gender refers to the sex of the pronoun.

Masculine—he

Feminine—she

Neuter—it

3.3. A pronoun must agree with its antecedent (the noun which is replaced by the pronoun) in number, person, and gender.

Jim said that he could do the assignment. [antecedent *he* agrees with *Jim* in number (singular), person (first), and gender (masculine)]

The members of the organization are to express their views. [antecedent *their* agrees with *members* in number (plural), person (third), and gender (neuter)]

The committee presented its report. [antecedent *it* agrees with *committee* in number (singular), person (third), and gender (neuter)]

3.4. When the antecedent consists of two nouns joined by *and,* a plural pronoun should be used.

May and Susan plan to take their makeup exams this afternoon. (*their* agrees with plural subject in number)

3.5. When the antecedent consists of two singular nouns joined by *or* or *nor*, a singular pronoun should be used.

Either Ted or Jim will have to give me his book. [*his* is required because two singular nouns (Ted, Jim) are joined by *or*]

3.6. When the antecedent consists of two plural nouns joined by *or* or *nor*, a plural pronoun should be used.

Either the Smiths or the Browns will have to use their car. [*their* is required because of two plural nouns (Smiths, Browns) joined by *or*]

3.7. When the antecedent refers to both males and females, a masculine pronoun should be used.

Everyone should take his seat. (even though females may be in the room, a masculine pronoun is required)

Everyone needs to turn in his grades. (even though female teachers may be present, a masculine pronoun is required)

Note: In the interest of specificity, saying, "Each teacher needs to turn in his or her grades," is permissible."

3.8. When any of the following indefinite pronouns are used, a third person singular pronoun should be used: *anyone, each, every, either, neither, no one, one, anybody, someone.* (*Note:* Use masculine pronouns if the gender cannot be determined.)

Anyone who has not already done so needs to turn in his report soon. (*his* agrees with *anyone*)

Every person who plans to go to the picnic is responsible for finding his own ride. (*his* agrees with *every person*)

Every woman who plans to attend the tea must make sure her name is on the reservation list. (*her* agrees with *every woman*)

3.9. When any of the following indefinite pronouns are used, a plural pronoun is required: *many, both, others, several.*

Many of the students have completed their assignments. (*their* agrees with *many*)

Both of them are ready to return their books. (*their* agrees with *both*)

3.10. The indefinite pronouns that follow may be either singular or plural, depending upon the noun to which they make reference: *any, more, most, none, all, some.*

Most of them are ready to turn in their projects. (*their* agrees with plural *most*)

Most of the report is completed, but it has not yet been typed. (*it* agrees with singular *most*)

3.11. Case refers to the form of pronouns that show their relation to other words in a sentence. Three cases of pronouns are found: subjective, objective, and possessive.

3.11.1. The following illustrates the three cases for the following pronouns: I, you, he, she, it, we, they, who.

Subjective: I you he she it we they who
Objective: me you him her it us them whom
Possessive: my your his her its our their whose

3.11.2. The *subjective case* is used as the subject of a verb or with a linking verb (form of the verb *to be*).

We did our homework. (*we* is used as a subject of the sentence)

It was I who called you earlier. (*was* is a linking verb and should be followed by a pronoun in the subjective case)

3.11.3. The *objective case* is used as an object of a verb, the object of a preposition, and the subject of an infinitive.

They had dinner for my brother and me last night. (object of verb)

Just between you and me, I don't like his decision. (object of preposition)

Professor Jones asked me to stay after class. (subject of an infinitive)

3.11.4. The *possessive case* is used to show possession and to modify a gerund, which is a verb form used as a noun and ends with an *-ing*.

This is my book. (possessive)

I appreciate your talking to him. (*your* modifies the gerund, *talking*)

3.12. In a clause in which the verb is omitted, the pronoun which precedes the omitted verb should be in the same case as if the verb were present.

She is taller than I. (This sentence is actually saying, ''She is taller than I am.'')

I have been here longer than they. (''. . . than they have.'')

3.13. Pronouns ending in *-self* (myself, yourself, himself, herself, themselves, etc.) are used (1) to refer the verb's action back to the subject or (2) to emphasize a noun or pronoun expressed earlier in the sentence.

They are putting themselves in a precarious position. [*themselves* refers the verb's action (putting) back to the subject *they*]

I will go myself. (*myself* emphasizes *I*)

3.14. *Who* and *whoever* are pronouns in the subjective case. They can be used whenever another pronoun in the subjective case (I, you, she, he, etc.) can be substituted in the sentence for *who* or *whoever.* For example, in the sentence, "Who is there?" *he* could be substituted for *who.* (See 3.15 for the use of whom or whomever.)

Who is there? (he is there)

Who went with you? (he went with you)

It is John who I think will go. (he will go)

Whoever succeeds is fortunate. (he succeeds)

3.15. *Whom* and *whomever* are pronouns in the objective case. They can be used whenever another pronoun in the objective case (me, him, her, us, them, etc.) can be substituted in the sentence for *whom* or *whomever.* For example, in the sentence, "Whom am I to go with?," *him* could be substituted for *whom* (I am to go with him).

The manager to whom I was referred was Ms. Johnson. (I was referred to her)

Whom do you plan to support? (they plan to support him)

He should hire whoever has the best score on the test. (she has the best score, not her has the best score)

3.16. The use of the relative pronouns, *who, which,* and *that* should be guided by the following:

3.16.1. *Who* is used when referring to individual persons.

John is the student who received the highest grade on the exam.

3.16.2. *That* is used when referring to a type or class.

John is the type of person that works well with others.

3.16.3. *Which* is used to introduce nonessential clauses that pertain to objects, animals, or places.

John's paper, which was handed in late, was very poor. ("which was handed in late" is a nonessential clause)

3.16.4. *That* is used to introduce essential clauses that pertain to objects, animals, or places.

The road that I take to work is very rough. ("that I take to work" is an essential clause, and without it, the meaning of the sentence is changed)

4. ADJECTIVES

4.1. As modifiers of nouns or pronouns, adjectives are used to describe, to quantify, or to identify.

A small house—a description

A few pens—a quantity

The man with the red hair—an identity

4.1.1. Adjectives cannot be used to modify verbs, other adjectives, or adverbs. Adverbs are used for this purpose. (See Section 5.)

4.2. An adjective should be used in the following situations:

4.2.1. When the word that follows the verb refers to the subject of the sentence.

That picture is beautiful. (*beautiful* refers to picture, which is the subject of the sentence)

4.2.2. After a verb referring to one of the senses (sound, look, taste, smell, feel).

She feels bad. (not *badly,* which is an adverb)

John sounds poor. (not *poorly,* which is an adverb)

Dave looks neat. (not *neatly,* which is an adverb)

4.2.3. After a linking verb (form of *to be, become, seem, appear, grow*)

She seems to be well.

He grew tall.

She appears to be sick.

4.3. Adjectives show comparison in three degrees: positive, comparative, and superlative.

Positive	*Comparative*	*Superlative*
tall	taller	tallest
small	smaller	smallest
big	bigger	biggest
good	better	best
bad	worse	worst
productive	more productive	most productive
efficient	less efficient	least efficient

4.3.1. The *comparative* form is used when comparing two persons or two things.

She is prettier than her sister.

He is the more efficient of the two workers.

4.3.2. The *superlative* form is used when comparing three or more persons or things.

Of the three sisters, she is the prettiest.

He is the most efficient worker in the department.

5. ADVERBS

5.1. Adverbs, which modify verbs, adjectives, and other adverbs, describe how, when, where, or to what degree.

He ran quickly. (how)

She came early. (when)

John scored well on the test. (how much)

5.2. An adverb should be used when the word that follows the verb refers to the action of the verb.

He talks slowly. (not slow)

She works rapidly. (not rapid)

5.3. Although most adverbs end in *-ly,* an *ly* ending is not a definitive characteristic of all adverbs, because some adjectives also end in *ly.* Examples are costly, timely, matronly, lively, lovely, and friendly.

Her accident was costly. (*costly* modifies *accident,* which is the subject of the sentence and, therefore, *costly* must be an adjective)

John's advice was timely. (*timely* modifies *advice* and therefore is an adjective)

John's advice was very timely. (*very* is an adverb modifying the adjective *timely*)

5.4. Like adjectives, adverbs show comparison in three degrees: positive, comparative, and superlative.

Positive	*Comparative*	*Superlative*
well	better	best
soon	sooner	soonest
bright	brighter	brightest
often	more often	most often
hard	harder	hardest

He arrived sooner than she. (comparative)

The sun shone more brightly than it did yesterday. (comparative)

Of all the students in the class, he works the hardest. (superlative)

5.5. Although the adverb typically follows the verb it modifies, it may be placed before the verb. A guiding rule is to place the adverb where it clearly conveys the meaning that was intended. The following example illustrates the placing of the adverb in several different locations in the sentence.

Only I did the assignment.
I only did the assignment.
I did only the assignment.
I did the assignment only.

5.6. The word *real* should not be used when *very* is required.

She is real beautiful. (incorrect)
She is very beautiful. (correct)

6. CONJUNCTIONS

6.1. Conjunctions are used to connect verbs, phrases, or clauses to other parts of the sentence. In certain instances, conjunctions are used to show the relative importance of the ideas conveyed in the words, phrases, or clauses.

6.2. Conjunctions are used as coordinating conjunctions, subordinating conjunctions, or correlative conjunctions.

6.2.1. *Coordinating conjunctions* are used to convey a relationship of equal importance. They include *and, but, or, for, nor, yet,* and *so.*

Their book is here, but their workbook is missing.

6.2.2. *Subordinating conjunctions* are used to convey a relationship of unequal importance. They include *when, where, how, since, because, although.* A subordinate conjunction joins a subordinate clause and a principal clause.

I have to hurry because I am behind schedule.

6.2.3. *Correlative conjunctions* are used in pairs, with the first conjunction introducing and the second conjunction connecting the elements. They include *both, and; not only, but also; either, or; neither, nor.*

7. PREPOSITIONS

7.1. Prepositions are used to join a noun or pronoun to some other word in the sentence in order to show a relationship. Examples of prepositions are *by, for, in, to, of, before, at, up, with, from.*

7.2. Prepositional phrases, which consist of a preposition and its object, should be placed as closely as possible to the words they modify.

7.3. A sentence may end with a preposition if the writer wishes to emphasize the preposition.

What play is she appearing in? (*in* is emphasized)

In what play is she appearing? (emphasis is not on the preposition *in*)

7.4. *Like* and *as* have specific uses in sentences, and their uses are not interchangeable.

7.4.1. *Like* is a preposition and is followed by a noun or pronoun, not followed by a verb.

His father looks like his grandfather.

7.4.2. *As* is a conjunction and is used to join clauses or phrases containing verbs.

It looks as if it will snow. (correct)

It looks like it will snow. (incorrect)

Appendix B

Punctuation

PUNCTUATION RULES: A-CROP[1]: FIVE WHY'S FOR USING PUNCTUATION

A key to clearness in writing is expert punctuation. Five letters—A-CROP—outline the following simple, definite rules of punctuation.

This device gives rules of punctuation for *A*rbitrary usage, *C*oordination, *R*estriction, *O*mission, and *P*osition. Learning the ''whys'' for punctuation—learning to punctuate only when necessary for clarity or to comply with situations described in A-CROP—prepares students to handle all punctuation problems.

ARBITRARY USES

A1. Sometimes, punctuation marks are used arbitrarily. These uses frequently are affected by changes in style and change from one generation to another. The punctuation used in the address of a letter is an illustration.

COORDINATION

The term ''coordination'' is used here to describe those words, phrases, and clauses that exist in pairs or groups, each member of which is of the same importance or value or significance. Compound sentences, the compound predicate, or a series of adjectives or adverbs or of modifying clauses represent the most common constructions involving coordination.

[1]W. Arthur Allee, Mountain-Plains Business Education Association *Service Bulletin No. 16,* 1974.

The most common coordinate conjunctions are *and, but, or, nor, for.*

C1. A comma is ordinarily used to separate independent clauses that are joined by a coordinate conjunction.

The committee was willing to cooperate, but the school authorities were not.

C2. If no conjunction is used between the clauses of a compound sentence, the semicolon—not the comma—is used between them. Sometimes the sentences are made by using terminal punctuation.

The committee was willing to cooperate; the school authorities were not.

C3. A comma may be omitted before a coordinate conjunction if the elements of the compound sentence are short, if they are closely related, or if they have the same subject. The comma is usually needed before the conjunctions *but* and *for* to prevent confusion with the prepositions *but* and *for.*

The price is low and the quality is poor.

The price is high, but the quality is poor.

C4. When a sentence connector (*however, therefore, nevertheless, consequently*) connects two independent clauses, a semicolon precedes the connecting link and a comma follows it.

You mailed your report on January 11; therefore, you are not responsible for the delay.

C5. A two-member coordinate series of words, phrases, or clauses connected by a conjunction needs no punctuation.

Orange and black signs indicate the route to be followed. (two adjectives)

Your paper is one of the best and should be published. (two verbs)

Your paper is very good and it should be published. (two short independent clauses)

C6. Commas are used to separate a series of two or more coordinate adjectives that modify the same noun. If the word *and* can be used between the two adjectives, the comma is always necessary.

Mr. Jones had a long, hard struggle to reach the top.

C7. The coordination of a three-part series of words or phrases should be indicated by punctuation. Ordinarily, commas are sufficient, but when one member of the series contains commas, a semicolon should be used between members of the series.

Present usage advocates the use of the comma before the conjunction that precedes the last item in a series. Some writers, however, omit the final comma.

Washington, Lincoln, and Jefferson of Monticello were well-known presidents.

The typewriter, the pen, and the pencil are tools for writing letters.

The day is cold, the snow is falling, and the trains are late. (short independent clauses)

The day is cold; the snow is falling; and the mail, which is carried by train, is delayed. (the short sentences should be separated by semicolons because the nonrestrictive clause is set off by commas)

Red, gold, and yellow; lazy, hazy days; cool, invigorating weather—all these are features of our autumn months.

Mr. Jones from Houston, Texas; Mrs. Terry from Oakland, California; and Mr. Wright from Denver, Colorado, met the manager at the convention. (semicolons separate the members of the series because commas appear in the series)

C8. Use a comma after each word or group of words in a series when the conjunction has been omitted. Sometimes a dash is used in this position. When the abbreviation *etc.* closes the series, a comma should precede and follow the abbreviation. (Many writers today try to avoid the use of *etc.* entirely.) Do not use a comma before the ampersand (&) in a company name.

Red and blue, blue and gold, blue and pink are the suggested class colors.

Letters, packages, etc., should go here.

The manufacturer is Ames, Johnson & Company.

C9. When two or more words are used together to form a single descriptive term describing a noun, a hyphen is used between the two.

I like the fragrance of new-mown hay.

Up-to-date information is given in the book.

The information in this book is up to date. (the compound follows the word modified)

The newly organized company is well known. (*newly organized* would not be hyphenated because the word *newly* is an adverb modifying the adjective *organized. Well known* would not be hyphenated because the two words follow the noun *company.*)

The fresh-laid eggs were sold at higher prices.

Points to Remember

1. Modifiers that contain adverbs ending in *ly* as their first word are not hyphenated.

   A privately owned company

2. The hyphen is also omitted when the descriptive word follows the noun it modifies.

   The man is well known.

3. When a two-word proper noun is used as an adjective before a noun, the hyphen is not used.

   Supreme Court decision.

4. When one or both of the proper nouns before a noun consist of two words, the combined form is hyphenated.

   The New Orleans-San Francisco flight

C10. The members of a formal list or enumeration occurring at the end of a sentence may be separated from the sentence by a semicolon or colon. The semicolon is used before such introductory words as *namely* and *viz.* (*Note:* Some writers use a colon instead of a semicolon before these words.) The colon is not used after the verb *to be* unless the list is formally tabulated. Never place a colon between a verb and a compound object.

The primary colors are red, blue, and yellow.

The awards will be given to three members of the class; namely, Carl, Helen, and John.

The awards will be given to three members of the class, as follows:

John Jones
Carl Smith
Helen Jacobs

The requirements of a good secretary are:

a. Ability to take rapid dictation.
b. Ability to transcribe notes rapidly.
c. Ability to punctuate correctly.

RESTRICTION

The term *restriction* implies that one sentence element distinguishes between two objects or ideas of the same class or narrows the scope of possible meanings or defines or designates a specific object or idea.

A restrictive phrase or clause is needed to identify the word it modifies and is not set off by commas.

A nonrestrictive phrase or clause is not needed to identify the word it modifies and is set off by punctuation. The comma and the dash—never a semicolon or colon—are used to indicate nonrestrictive elements.

Restrictive

The senator who lives in Des Moines will speak tonight. (In this sentence, we are trying to distinguish between the senator living in Des Moines and those who do not live in Des Moines.)

Nonrestrictive

The senator, who lives in Washington, will speak tonight. (How many senators live in Washington? Does the clause restrict or limit or does it enlarge or add to the main thought? So many senators live in Washington that the clause cannot limit the meaning.)

R1. If the sentence element designates, points out, or narrows the scope of meaning of the major thought of the sentence, no punctuation is used. The element is restrictive. Adjective clauses introduced by the word *that* are always restrictive.

I myself will see that this job is completed. (myself is an intensive pronoun)

I will go myself. (myself is a reflexive pronoun)

My brother John is in the Army. (usually, writers do not set off one-word appositives or those appositives forming parts of proper names, such as *William the Conqueror*)

The man who came yesterday will leave today. (restrictive dependent clause; of several men, the one who came yesterday will leave today)

The year 1943 was a year in which the world was at war. (the figure *1943* designates a specific year)

R2. When a sentence element supplies an added idea, when the principal thought is completed without that element, punctuation is used at both ends of the element. Such elements are nonrestrictive. Clauses introduced by *which* are usually nonrestrictive.

The day is cold; the snow is falling; and the mail, which is carried by train, is delayed.

Mary, please type this letter quickly. (direct address)

You may go now, John. (direct address)

The shipper, Mr. Jones, claims damages. (apposition)

The man, who came yesterday, is leaving today. (nonrestrictive dependent clause; one man only, two thoughts about him equally descriptive)

Mr. Bradley, who is responsible for the project, will present his ideas to the staff. (phrases or clauses following proper nouns are always nonrestrictive; the proper noun needs nothing else to identify it)

We are, of course, inclined to question the truth of your statement.

(if words, such as *of course, however, therefore, consequently,* interrupt the main thought in the sentence, they are considered parenthetical and are usually set off by commas; however, some writers prefer to omit commas with parenthetical words in order to avoid overpunctuation, especially if the interruption to the flow of the sentence is slight)

Your report dated January 5, 1980, gives interesting information. (most writers agree that a comma must follow the year if the date precedes it)

The name of Pittsburg, Kansas, is spelled differently from that of Pittsburgh, Pennsylvania. (when the name of a city precedes the name of the state, a comma should follow the city and the state)

R3. When an explanatory emphasis is to be read into a nonrestrictive element, dashes instead of commas may be used.

The books—which were beautifully bound in leather—were destroyed by fire. (dependent nonrestrictive clause)

R4. Sometimes a nonrestrictive element contains commas within itself. If so, the dash can be used at the beginning and end of the element to show where the main thought is.

The demands of war—which are so imperative, so pervasive, and so rigorous—reveal both weaknesses and resourcefulness, of which fact the nation is now fully aware.

R5. When a nonrestrictive sentence element is totally unrelated to the thought, as in giving references to sources, parentheses are used instead of commas. Brackets are often used for this purpose in printed material, but the typist must use parentheses for such elements.

The court ruled that this case is subject to the Statute of Limitation in Texas (p. 66).

R6. Beginning participial phrases are always nonrestrictive.

Retracing his steps slowly, Jim looked carefully for the missing item.

OMISSION

. , ,
...
***
' '

When a single letter of a word or a whole word or phrase is left out, punctuation is used to indicate the omission.

O1. When letters are omitted from the end of a word, a period indicates the omission. (Abbreviation) Abbreviations are used very rarely in the best correspondence. The list of unquestioned abbreviations is as follows:

Mister	Mr.
Mistress	Mrs.
Junior (after a name only)	Jr.
Senior (after a name only)	Sr.
Saint (not street)	St.
Incorporated (after a name only)	Inc.
Limited (after a name only)	Ltd.
Number (only when a sequence of digits follows the word)	No.
Northeast (in an address only)	N.E.
Southeast (in an address only)	S.E.
Northwest (in an address only)	N.W.
Southwest (in an address only)	S.W.
Mount (in a proper name)	Mt.

O2. A letter or letters omitted from the body of a word are indicated by one apostrophe. (Contraction)

do not   don't

The apostrophe also marks omissions in numerals.

the class of '79

O3. An ellipsis of three *spaced* dots indicates words omitted from a quoted sentence; an ellipsis of four dots indicates an omission that includes a sentence ending.

Fourscore and seven years ago our fathers brought forth on this continent a new nation . . . dedicated to the proposition that all men are created equal. . . . We are met on a great battlefield of that war.

If one or more paragraphs are omitted, the omission is indicated by three asterisks typed on a line by themselves.

O4. When words necessary to a complete understanding of the thought are omitted, the omission is indicated by a comma.

The boys are smiling; the girls, laughing.

POSITION

Variations from the normal position in a sentence are indicated by commas. Normal English sentences progress in the following order:

Adjectives	noun	adverb	verb	adverb	adjective	object	adverb
(1)	(2)	(4)	(3)	(4)	(5)	(6)	(4)

The young man ran swiftly. (intransitive verb)
1 1 2 3 4

The young man ran down the lane swiftly. (intransitive verb)
1 1 2 3 4 5 6 4

The young man swiftly climbed the tall tree. (transitive verb)
1 1 2 4 3 5 5 6

The young man climbed the tall tree swiftly. (transitive verb)
1 1 2 3 5 5 6 4

P1. An adjective following the noun it describes should be enclosed by commas.

The woman, old and weathered, carried a huge basket on her bent shoulders.

John, satisfied, was uncomplaining.

P2. An adverbial element (word, phrase, or clause) placed at or near the beginning of the sentence is usually set off from the rest of the sentence; but for short elements, this usage is changing.

Quickly the runner regained his stride. (the adverb *quickly* is out of order; but because it is very short, no punctuation is used unless the meaning of the sentence demands it)

By quickly regaining his stride, the runner overtook his opponent.

When you go home, please close the laboratory windows.

If the class wishes, we shall meet only on Monday.

After he had spoken, Mr. Smith left on the train.

Adverbial clauses following the main clause in a sentence are usually restrictive and are not set off by commas. In some instances, however, clauses that add a reason or concession are clearly nonrestrictive. These nonrestrictive clauses usually begin with *because, as, since,* or *though.*

I gave him the book, although I doubt that he will use it. (nonrestrictive)

James went because he was invited. (restrictive)

P3. A beginning *ing* phrase used as an object of a preposition and a beginning infinitive phrase used as a modifier are always followed by commas.

In planning a parade, one must consider many details. (*ing* phrase used as an object of the preposition)

To obtain the best results from the item, follow the directions in the booklet. (beginning infinitive phrase used as an adverb)

P4. The use of a comma after the beginning prepositional phrases usually depends on the length of the phrase. Authorities usually agree that short prepositional phrases at the beginning of a sentence need no punctuation unless the sentence needs punctuation to avoid misreading.

In short books help to give a richer experience. (a comma *should* follow *short* to prevent misreading)

P5. When a given name is inverted (last name first), the inversion is indicated by a comma after the surname.

Normal Order	*Inverted Order*
Carl Thomas	Thomas, Carl
John Jones	Jones, John

P6. When the name of a state is written before the name of a city (inverted), a comma separates them.

Minnesota, Duluth

Appendix C

Letter Format

USE THE RIGHT PAPER

High-quality paper should be used for letterheads as well as for envelopes. To save money, purchase letterhead paper in a lighter weight for use as envelopes. Therefore, you may use a 20-pound or 24-pound bond paper for letterhead and a 16-pound paper for mailing envelopes. The use of good-quality paper is important. The typing stands out more clearly, and any corrections that you may have to make are neater and easier to make on good-quality paper. This is always an important consideration.

Most business letters are typed on $8\frac{1}{2}$- by 11-inch stationery, imprinted with the name of the company, the division, and the branch office. This is known as letterhead stationery.

If a letter is longer than one page, plain paper is used for the extra pages. This paper should be of the same size, color, and quality as the letterhead.

For writing memos within an organization, a smaller-sized letterhead is normally used. Such paper is commonly $8\frac{1}{2}$ by $5\frac{1}{2}$ inches or $5\frac{1}{2}$ by $8\frac{1}{2}$ inches but may be as large as $8\frac{1}{2}$ by 11 inches.

Special lightweight paper, such as onionskin or manifold-copy paper, is used for carbon copies.

LETTER STYLES

Four basic business letter styles are commonly used in business offices: full block, modified block with blocked paragraphs, modified block with indented paragraphs, and AMS Simplified.

Full Block (Figure C–1)

Each part of a full-block letter begins at the left margin. This letter style saves typing time and diminishes the opportunity for error. This letter style should not be used unless it compliments the letterhead.

Modified Block with Blocked Paragraphs (Figure C–2)

The modified block with blocked paragraphs letter style is more streamlined than the modified block with indented paragraphs. The modified block with blocked paragraphs style is gradually becoming the preferred business letter style. The date line begins at the center, as do the complimentary closing and originator's name and title.

Modified Block with Indented Paragraphs (Figure C–3)

The modified block with indented paragraphs letter style differs from the modified block with blocked paragraphs style in that the paragraphs are indented

Figure C–1 Full Block; Mixed Punctuation

ABC CORPORATION

111 Main Street (406) 422-2682 Johnson, IA 47631

January 30, 198-

4 spaces

Mr. John Grant
Arcom Office Products Company
1243 Main Street
Jefferson, MI 48832

Double space

Dear Mr. Grant:

Double space

Would you please send me the illustrated promotional packet that was mentioned in a Delta Max office copier ad I recently saw?

Double space

I am interested in investigating the feasibility of purchasing a copier for use in an office that makes between 350-500 copies per month. The copier will also need to be capable of reducing and enlarging material.

Your sending the requested materials soon will be appreciated as I plan to make a purchasing decision within the next few weeks.

Sincerely,

4 spaces

William Doe

William Doe
President

bl

ABC CORPORATION

111 Main Street Johnson, IA 47631

January 30, 198-

4 spaces

Mr. John Grant
Arcom Office Products Company
1243 Main Street
Jefferson, MI 48832

Double space

Dear Mr. Grant:

Double space

Would you please send me the illustrated promotional packet that was mentioned in a Delta Max office copier ad I recently saw?

Double space

I am interested in investigating the feasibility of purchasing a copier for use in an office that makes between 350-500 copies per month. The copier will also need to be capable of reducing and enlarging material.

Your sending the requested materials soon will be appreciated as I plan to make a purchasing decision within the next few weeks.

Sincerely,

4 spaces

William Doe
President

bl

Figure C–2 Modified Block with Blocked Paragraphs; Mixed Punctuation

5 spaces. The date line and closing lines begin at the same locations as they do with the modified block with blocked paragraphs letter style.

AMS Simplified Letter (Figure C–4)

A simplified letter style omits the salutation and closing and includes a subject line in capital letters. All lines begin on the left margin. The simplified letter is an interesting example of the movement toward simplifying letter formats. This style is supported by the Administrative Management Society but has not yet been widely accepted in the business world.

Interoffice Memorandum (Figure C–5)

The interoffice memorandum is used when one writes to another employee in the office. The inside address, salutation, and complimentary closing are omitted to save time and effort.

ABC CORPORATION

111 Main Street Johnson, IA 47631

January 30, 198-

4 spaces

Mr. John Grant
Arcom Office Products Company
1243 Main Street
Jefferson, MI 48832

Double space

Dear Mr. Grant

Double space

Would you please send me the illustrated promotional packet that was mentioned in a Delta Max office copier ad I recently saw?

Double space

I am interested in investigating the feasibility of purchasing a copier for use in an office that makes between 350-500 copies per month. The copier will also need to be capable of reducing and enlarging material.

Your sending the requested materials soon will be appreciated as I plan to make a purchasing decision within the next few weeks.

Double space

Sincerely

4 spaces

William Doe

William Doe
President

bl

Figure C–3 Modified Block with Indented Paragraphs; Open Punctuation

BUSINESS LETTER PUNCTUATION

Two types of punctuation, open and mixed, are used in letters presented in the full block, modified block with blocked paragraphs, and modified blocked with indented paragraphs letter styles.

Open Punctuation

Marks are omitted after the lines of the return address, salutation, and complimentary close, unless an abbreviation is used. In that case, the period is typed as part of the abbreviation. Figures C–3 and C–6 are presented with open punctuation.

Mixed Punctuation

This is the punctuation style commonly used in business. A colon is used after the salutation and a comma after the complimentary close. Figures C–1 and C–2 are presented with mixed punctuation. No other end-of-line punctuation is used in the opening and closing lines. However, any abbreviation that ends a line must be followed by a period.

ABC CORPORATION

111 Main Street (406) 422-2682 Johnson, IA 47631

January 30, 198-

4 spaces

Mr. John Grant
Arcom Office Products Company
1243 Main Street
Jefferson, MI 48832

Triple space

REQUEST FOR PROMOTIONAL PACKET

Triple space

Would you please send me the illustrated promotional packet that was mentioned in a Delta Max office copier ad I recently saw?

Double space

I am interested in investigating the feasibility of purchasing a copier for use in an office that makes between 350-500 copies per month. The copier will also need to be capable of reducing and enlarging material.

Your sending the requested materials soon will be appreciated as I plan to make a purchasing decision within the next few weeks.

4 spaces

William Doe

WILLIAM DOE - PRESIDENT

bl

Figure C–4 AMS Simplified

Although punctuation in other parts of the letter is no different, a colon after the salutation and a comma after the complimentary close may be used or omitted in the full block, modified block with block paragraphs, or modified block with indented paragraphs letter styles.

PARTS OF A BUSINESS LETTER

Business letters are comprised of the following parts: date line, mailing notation, inside address, salutation, subject line, body, complimentary close, signature line, reference initials, copy notation, and post script.

Date Line

When letterhead is used, type the date line $2\frac{1}{2}$ inches from the top edge of the sheet of paper. Some individuals prefer to locate the date line a double space below the last line of the letterhead. If plain paper is used, type the date line about 12 or 14 lines from the top of the paper.

The date line on letters typed in full block and AMS Simplified is typed on the left margin. The date line on modified block letters begins at the center.

INTEROFFICE MEMORANDUM

January 30, 198-

Double space
Double space
Triple space
Double space

TO: John Brown

FROM: Dick Smith

SUBJECT: January Sales Figures

The January sales figures you requested during our phone conversation this morning are attached.

Please let me know if you would like for me to provide you with additional information that would be helpful in your preparing your report.

bl

Attachment

Figure C–5 Interoffice Memorandum

Mailing Notation

If a letter is to be delivered by messenger or by registered, certified, or special-delivery mail, the appropriate notation is to be typed on the letterhead. The notation is typed on the left margin a double space below the date line.

Inside Address

The name and address of the person or company receiving the letter are identified in this section of the letter. It begins at the left margin of the letter and is single spaced. Four lines are left between the date line (or mailing notation) and the inside address.

Unless the inside address is unusually long, the addressee's title may be typed on the line with his/her name or on a separate line.

When the letter is addressed to an individual, a personal title such as Mr., Miss, Ms., or Mrs. must be used.

Salutation

The salutation is typed two lines below the last line of the inside address. A colon follows the salutation if you are using mixed punctuation (see Figure C–1). The colon is omitted when open punctuation is used (see Figure C–3). In addition,

1. The salutation must agree with the first line of the inside address.
2. Only the first word and all nouns in the salutation are capitalized.
3. If an "Attention" line is used, the salutation is typed on the second line after the attention line.

ABC CORPORATION

111 Main Street | (406) 422-2682 | Johnson, IA 47631

January 30, 198-

Mailing Notation — REGISTERED

4 spaces

Mr. Grant Green
Delvin Equipment Company
8907 South Street
Yukon, IA 58984

Dear Mr. Green

The Transparency Maker we purchased from you on December 21 is being returned, and we are requesting that it be replaced with a new Maker.

On five occasions during the month that we have had the Maker, it was inoperable at critical times. Because we bought the machine primarily to make transparencies on very short notice, several of our executives were severely inconvenienced when they were unable to make transparencies for use during their presentations. When the Maker is inoperable, we either have to use an outside service or do without the desired transparencies. You can see by examining the enclosed transparency that the machine is not working properly.

The concern your company has for its customers leads me to believe that you will want us to own a Maker worthy of its excellent reputation.

I will appreciate your replacing the Maker soon so that we can provide a fast and efficient transparency-making service for our executives.

Sincerely

Jason Brown

Jason Brown
Executive Vice-President

JB:cm
Enclosure — Enclosure
Copy notation — pc: William Doe

Post script — The Transparency Maker was shipped this morning via UPS.

Figure C–6 Business Letter Parts

4. The salutation is omitted when the AMS Simplified letter style is used. Following is a list of preferred salutations.

Singular	*Plural*
Dear Mr.	Ladies and Gentlemen
Dear Miss	
Dear Mrs.	
Dear Ms.	

Subject Line

The subject line, when used, may be typed on the second line (double space) below the salutation. When the paragraphs are blocked on the left margin, the subject line is also likely to be blocked. When paragraphs are indented, the subject line can be centered on the page.

The word ''subject'' may be typed with each letter capitalized or with only the first letter capitalized. It should be followed by a colon.

In the AMS Simplified letter, the subject line is started a triple space below the address and a triple space above the body. The word ''subject'' is omitted, and the subject line is typed in all capitals.

Body of the Letter

The body of a letter is started on the second line (double space) below the salutation. When a subject line has been used, it is started a double space below the salutation. Paragraph indentation is consistent with the letter style you are using.

Complimentary Close

The complimentary close is typed on the second line (double space) below the body of the letter. Only the first word of the complimentary closing is capitalized. A comma follows the complimentary close when mixed punctuation is being used (see Figure C–1) but is omitted with open punctuation (see Figure C–3).

In full-block letters, the complimentary close is typed at the left margin, while in modified block letters, it is begun at the center. The complimentary close is omitted in the simplified letter.

The Signature

Much variation appears in the style of the signature. The full signature includes the company's name, which is typewritten two spaces directly below the complimentary close. If the name is so long that it would overrun the right margin, the name is centered below the complimentary close. The name, the name and title, or only the title of the originator is typed three or four spaces below the company's name and flush with the complimentary close. If the signer has no formal title, the department affiliation may be indicated. The signer signs his or her name in the space between the lines. In many companies, the company name is omitted in the signature. The name on the letterhead is considered sufficient for purposes of identification and responsibility.

Reference Initials

Reference initials are used to identify the persons who dictated and typed the letter. They are usually typed at the left margin a double space below the typed name and title. However, in long letters, they may be typed on the same line with the official title. You may use only the typist's initials if you wish.

If an item is to be included in the envelope with the letter, indicate that fact by typing the word Enclosure at the left margin on the line below the reference initials. If more than one item is to be enclosed, use the word Enclosures and indicate the number of items.

Copy Notation

If the writer wishes the addressee to know that other people will be receiving a copy of the letter, type a "pc" (photocopy) or "xc" (xerox copy) notation at the left margin on the line below the enclosure notation (if used) or on the line below the reference initials. If several persons are to receive copies, the names should be listed according to the rank of the persons, or alphabetically, if the individuals are of equal rank.

If the addressee is not to be informed about another person's being sent a copy of the letter, type a "bpc" (blind photocopy) notation in the upper left corner of the copies only—never on the original.

Postscript

A postscript can be quite effective when it is used to express an idea that has been deliberately withheld from the body of the letter. A postscript may also be used to express an afterthought; this usage, however, may not be effective if it suggests that the body of the letter was badly organized.

Start the postscript on the second line below the copy notation (or whichever notation was last typed). If the paragraphs are indented, indent the first line of the postscript; otherwise, begin it at the left margin.

You may type PS, P.S., or begin with the first word of the postscript, omitting the PS.

Figure C–6 shows these letter parts.

Two-Page Letters

Use plain paper of the same quality as the letterhead (never a letterhead) for the second and each additional page of a long letter. Use the same left and right margins that you used on the first page.

On the seventh line from the top of the page, type a continuation-page heading consisting of the following: the name of the addressee, the page number, and the date. Either of the following styles is acceptable.

Mrs. C. P. Canady 2 March 1, 1987

or

Mrs. C. P. Canady
Page 2
March 1, 1987

Resume typing the message on the third line below the last line of the continuation-page heading.

Always type at least two lines of a paragraph at the top of a continuation page, and leave at least two lines of the paragraph at the bottom of the previous page. Do not divide a paragraph that contains three or fewer lines.

Never use a continuation page to type only the closing section of a business letter. (The complimentary closing should always be preceded by at least two lines of the message.)

Leave a bottom margin of at least 1 inch at the foot of each page of a letter (except the last page), and keep the bottom margin as uniform as possible on all pages except the last.

Addressing Envelopes

Always use single spacing and blocked style when addressing an envelope. Type the city, state, and ZIP code on one line. Leave one or two spaces between the state and the ZIP code. The U. S. Postal Service recommends that the information be typed in all capitals with no punctuation.

MR KEITH CARRADY
JOHNSON PRODUCTS DIVISION
1383 MAIN STREET
LITTLE ROCK AK 43312

When addressing a large (No. 10) envelope, begin the address on line 14 from the top and about 4 inches from the left edge. When using a small (No. 6) envelope or when addressing a postcard, begin the address on line 12 about 2 inches from the left edge.

If the return address is not imprinted on the envelope, type a return address in the upper left corner of the envelope. The return address should contain the following information arranged in three lines: (1) the name of the writer or company, (2) the street address, and (3) the city, state, and ZIP code. The following example illustrates the appropriate format for a return address.

Ms. Caroline Brown
1288 Liberty Avenue
Tempe, AZ 98744

Type an attention line or a notation, such as personal or confidential, below the return address. It should begin on line 9 or at least 2 lines below the return address. Begin each word with a capital letter and use underscoring.

If a special mailing procedure is used, type the appropriate notation, such as SPECIAL DELIVERY or REGISTERED, in capital letters in the upper right corner of the envelope, beginning on line 9. The notation should end about $\frac{1}{2}$ inch from the right margin.

Appendix D

Legal Aspects of Business Communication

Each person who composes messages must carefully guard against statements or facts that could generate unnecessary legal action. Statements that attack the reputation of another person may be very costly in time and money, even if they are true. Covering all the legal constraints which affect communication is not possible; but in the material that follows, you will be exposed to several of the legal risks and complications common to business communication. Comprehensive treatment is not possible in this appendix, and you should consult legal counsel to advise you on specific details about complicated situations. Remember: ignorance of the law is not an acceptable defense.

Paying attention to the risks that follow will help you avoid defamatory statements and should minimize expensive misunderstandings.

DEFAMATION

Every person has the right to be free from malicious gossip and unjustified attempts to undermine his or her reputation. Any breach of this right is referred to as defamation. When the defamation is spoken, it is slander; when it is written, it is libel.

Before legal action is encouraged, the statements must be (1) untrue, (2) communicated to another person, and (3) cause some personal injury, such as contempt, ridicule, or disrepute.

In a legal sense, any means of communicating a defamatory statement to a third party is considered a defamatory action. The third-party element is interesting because it emphasizes the point that statements made to someone's face are not defamatory. But repeating the statement to just one additional person could be considered as defamation.

Case point

Mr. Jones tells Mr. Smith that he considers him to be an incompetent architect. This is an opinion, and a successful legal action would be very rare.

However, Mr. Jones tells Mr. Strong the same thing, and now Mr. Smith may be legally justified and perhaps successful in challenging Mr. Jones's statement. Mr. Smith would have to prove personal injury, but that is often not difficult to do.

Libel vs. Slander

Libel (written defamation) is naturally more permanent than slander (spoken defamation) and also easier to prove, so the laws pertaining to libel are more severe than those about slander. Libelous statements may appear in all permanent-type communications, such as letters, memos, circulars, pictures, newspaper stories, and published articles. Even letters marked "personal" or telegrams may become grounds for libel if the receiving party can prove that you were aware of the possibility of the message's being intercepted.

If a third party receives information by eavesdropping or reading other people's mail, you would normally not be held liable unless you knew of such possibilities.

Defamatory Terms

Successful libel cases show that the following words may be considered libelous and might well be avoided or used with extreme caution:

bankrupt	forger	profiteer
communist	fraud	quack
corrupt	hypocrite	shyster
crook	incompetent	swindler
dishonest	inferior	thief
disreputable	insolvent	unchaste
drug addict	kickbacks	unworthy of credit
falsified	misappropriation	worthless

When composing letters about overdue accounts, you should write like a prudent person and not harass, oppress, or abuse a person unreasonably. Harassment could include abusive language, anonymous communication, and using the telephone in an abusive manner.

Defamation is considered to apply when the statements affect an essential characteristic of a person's work. For instance, saying that a teacher is addicted to a drug may be much more libelous than saying the same thing about a popular singer. As you write, remember that statements which chastise the ability of a person to do his or her job are defamatory.

If what you write is true, your defense in a libel suit is probably adequate. However, if no evidence of truth or good reason exists for your statements, you may have to pay large money damages.

Invasion of Privacy

A person's name, picture, or other identifying information may represent excellent material for sales and promotion letters. If material is used without permission, a person may have cause for legal action because his or her privacy has been invaded.

Fraud

The basis of fraud is false representation or concealment. However, fraud is not that cut and dried. For fraud to exist, the following circumstances must be present:

1. *False representation or deliberate concealment of a present or past fact must exist.* To constitute fraud, misrepresentation or concealment must be deliberate and be a definite action on the part of the accused party. Facts or material that fall into the area of opinions, judgments, or prediction of the future normally do not constitute fraud. You may honestly claim that something "is a bargain" or "is the best on the market" with little fear of your remarks being fradulent.
2. *Misrepresented or concealed facts must be material facts.* A fact is considered material if knowing the true or complete facts would have allowed the defrauded party to avoid entering into the agreement. Whether the fact is very important or only of minor importance is of little consequence. The action encouraged by the misrepresentation or concealment is the major point.
3. *The person who makes the false representation must know it to be false or make it recklessly without regard to its truth.* Fraud is clearly existent when a person deliberately makes a false statement, conceals a material fact, or intentionally acts in such a way as to mislead another person into an agreement or contract. Fraud also exists when a person makes a statement without determining its truth or falsity, especially if he or she happens to know the facts.

Example

McElroy, a registered firearms dealer, represented to Wetzel that a Winchester rifle was an authentic 1906 model previously owned by one person. McElroy had purchased the rifle at a southern gun show and wanted to sell it as soon as possible. To ensure the sale, he told Wetzel what he thought he wanted to hear. When Wetzel checked the serial number, he discovered the gun was sold in 1904 to the military. Wetzel was successful when he sought to have the sale set aside on grounds of fraud.

McElroy made statements concerning the rifle with reckless disregard of the truth. As a registered firearms dealer, McElroy is expected to know the facts, and his action was considered fraudulent.

4. *Misrepresentation must be made with the intention of influencing the other person to act on it.* For a statement to be fraudulent, the person making it must intend that the fact will be relied upon and acted upon.
5. *The misrepresentation or concealment must induce action and cause injury to the other party.* Fraud does not actually exist until the person who was intended to be misled actually is convinced and enters into the agreement or contract. Even then, the defrauded party must be able to prove injury, or no legal right or need to recover damages exists.

Fraud in communication can be avoided if you are to the point and honest. People who find themselves in court because of their statements should have previously weighed the chance of such an occcurrence or paid more attention to the actions that constitute fraud.

Warranties

A seller usually assumes certain obligations concerning the goods being sold. These obligations may involve the quality of the goods, clear title, or other information about the nature of the goods.

Express warranties center around an assurance of quality or promise of performance explicitly stated by the seller of goods. Implied warranties may consist of an obvious fact, such as conveying clear title to goods that were sold. It may also refer to quality and performance standards required by law. Express warranties are usually easier to prove in a legal action, but any warranty, express or implied, should be avoided if it cannot be substantiated.

If sellers simply exaggerated the merits of goods as part of a sales talk, it is referred to as puffing and does not constitute a warranty. These kinds of statements are considered personal opinions or value judgments, and buyers are not justified in relying on them. If, however, the buyer asks the seller's opinion as an expert, the seller's remarks as to quality are made part of the bargain and may be considered a warranty.

Some of the more obvious activities that involve legal problems are letters and printed matter concerning lotteries, obscene literature, extortion, and solicitation of illegal business.

Copyright laws must be honored when material is duplicated, and other legal constraints must be considered before preparing written messages.

Perhaps a good summary to the ''Legal Aspects of Communication'' is write, act, and promise as you would like to receive. In other words, always act like a prudent person.

Index